THE POETICS OF BIBLICAL NARRATIVE

Ideological Literature and the Drama of Reading

MEIR STERNBERG

INDIANA UNIVERSITY PRESS
BLOOMINGTON

First Midland Book Edition 1987

Indiana University Press
Bloomington

Library of Congress Cataloging in Publication Data

Sternberg, Meir
The poetics of biblical narrative

(Indiana Studies in Biblical Literature)
Includes bibliographical references.
1. Bible as literature. I. Title. II. Series
BS535.S725   1985   809'.93522   85-42752
cl. ISBN 0-253-34521-9
pa. ISBN 0-253-20453-4

6 7 8 99

To the memory of my beloved mother,
Esther Sternberg, née Friedmann

CONTENTS

PREFACE

Some of the book's theses and analyses have appeared in a long series of articles on the subject, and I am grateful for permission to use the material: "The King Through Ironic Eyes: The Narrator's Devices in the Story of David and Bathsheba and Two Excursuses on the Theory of the Narrative Text," *Hasifrut* 1 (1968) 263-92; "Caution, A Literary Text! Problems in the Poetics and Interpretation of Biblical Narrative," *Hasifrut* 2 (1970) 608-63; "Delicate Balance in the Story of the Rape of Dinah: Biblical Narrative and the Rhetoric of Narrative," *Hasifrut* 4 (1973) 193-231; "The Structure of Repetition in Biblical Narrative: Strategies of Informational Redundancy," *Hasifrut* 25 (1977) 109-50; "Between the Truth and the Whole Truth in Biblical Narrative: The Rendering of Inner Life by Telescoped Inside View and Interior Monologue," *Hasifrut* 29 (1979) 110-46; "Patterns of Similarity: Part and Whole In Biblical Composition," presented to the Eighth World Congress of Jewish Studies (1981); "Language, World, and Perspective in Biblical Art: Free Indirect Discourse and Modes of Covert Penetration," *Hasifrut* 32 (1983) 88-131; "The Bible's Art of Persuasion: Ideology, Rhetoric, and Poetics in Saul's Fall," *Hebrew Union College Annual* (1983) 45-82. The two earliest articles were written in collaboration with Menakhem Perry. As the notes will indicate, I have also freely transplanted ideas and examples from my various theoretical studies; or perhaps I should say retrieved, since the theories themselves often trace back to my exploration of biblical practice.

This being a rather long book, it is only fair to point out that the argument covers both less and more ground than may appear. Less, because it does not incorporate all the work I have done on the Bible since the sixties, not even all the published work. The emphasis here falls not just on narrative as distinct from other genres but on those narrative principles crucial to the marriage of ideology to reading that governs biblical poetics. Involving problems underrated or neglected in literary theory itself, the working and rules of this ideological art need systematic reconstruction. To keep the argument in focus, therefore, I reserve for separate treatment issues like the Bible's generic variety, its composition of units into books, or its modes of rendering speech and thought, discussed in some of the papers listed above.

xi

On the other hand, this volume covers more ground than its table of contents may suggest. For one thing, since narrative always works in opposition to other genres and biblical narrative even incorporates them into its prose, questions of generic variety often rise to the surface. Such glances at the meaningful opposition between prose narrative and poetry or parable bear, for instance, on speech situation, rhetorical strategy, transparence of discourse, making sense of discrepant or, on the contrary, parallel and apparently repetitive units. Within narrative itself, for another thing, my tracing of the Bible's rich and novel repertoire of forms is intentionally distributed (up to the end of chapter 12, where the whole picture emerges) in order to put it in its proper place. However impressive that repertoire, it still figures only as a means to an end, offering the biblical artist an assorted set of choices to be made and coordinated and varied according to higher principles. Contrary to what some recent attempts at "literary" analysis seem to assume, form has no value or meaning apart from communicative (historical, ideological, aesthetic) function. Nor has its typology as such. Accordingly, I have decided against isolating several of the Bible's protean forms that I am most concerned with in a variety of roles and contexts. To mention three that recur throughout: analogical structure; modes of naming or reference; types of quotation, including dialogue and free indirect style. Readers with special interest in such techniques may want to consult the Index (as well as the references to more continuous discussions given in the notes).

In emphasis and arrangement, more generally, this differs from the book that I might write, indeed from the drafts I did write, without the benefit of hindsight. For its thrust reflects the experience gained from the reception and fortunes of my published work on the Bible over the last fifteen years. Starting from the repercussions of the very first essay in the series ("The King Through Ironic Eyes," 1968), the need for a poetics offering a new language and sense of purpose has turned out even deeper, certainly more widespread, than one familiar with the unhappy state of the field might expect. Even the antagonism evoked, often to be silently revoked in time, would appear only differently revealing from the more common welcome and acceptance. By a process too recent and multiple to trace, but clearly gaining momentum, the situation has changed for the better since. Gaps, ambiguity, redundancy, exposition, temporal ordering, omniscient viewpoint, reading process, patterns of analogy, alternative forms of reference, indirect characterization and rhetoric: such concepts (among the most productive so far) show signs of generating a powerful discourse about the Bible, which traditional scholarship must come to terms with. I for one am now more convinced than ever that here lies the future of biblical studies as a whole. Yet time has also revealed some covert (perhaps not even conscious) variations within this evolving discourse, uniformly oriented though it seems to the text itself as object and to literary study as a discipline. Of course, the new approaches need no more speak with one voice than the old; but nor must terminological pass for conceptual unity, or reaction for reorientation. Ironically enough, it is on such matters that I have increasingly found it necessary to enlarge from one version of the book to another, with a view to sorting out the lines of inquiry as well as in pure self-defense against the good intentions of fellow inquirers in Israel and elsewhere. Hence the care taken, as early as the opening chapter, to spell out the business of biblical poetics, historical dimension included; to dissociate it from some assumptions about text and context recently made (and attributed to me) by the "literary approach"; and to suggest how far the relationship between literary theory and biblical analysis is from the one-way traffic called "application." If anything, it still needs to be repeated, doing justice to the Bible's intricate art requires a theory and for that matter a history of narrative considerably more developed than the best now available.

Even such questions of method and theory, however, are not in heaven. On the contrary, since the Bible takes measures to render its story accessible to all—here lies much of its originality and my theme—it is only appropriate that a work in biblical poetics should follow suit. This book is addressed to all students of the Bible, professional and other; also to comparatists, narratologists, and lovers of narrative at large. No special expertise in literary or biblical study is assumed. My translations are literal enough, and the transliterations simple enough, to enable even the Hebrewless reader to follow the textual analyses as well as the drift of my argument.

This is a good opportunity to thank the many—scholars, academic audiences, schoolteachers, common readers, not least my students—who have responded and questioned. Perhaps their most important contribution has been the evidence that it still greatly matters how we make sense of the Bible. I owe a special debt to Menakhem Perry, with whom I made the first step (and met the first wave of attack) on the way to this book. Thanks are also due to two other colleagues, Benjamin Hrushovski and Itamar Even-Zohar, for having opened the columns of the literary quarterly *Hasifrut* to the adventure of biblical poetics at a time when editors might well hesitate. The final version of this book would probably still be in the making were it not for Robert Polzin's encouragement and support, far beyond the call of editorial duty; his vision and friendship have made all the difference. To give an idea of my debt to Tamar Yacobi, Proverbs 31 might serve well enough, except that it says nothing about the wife's being a professional helpmate and one as worth listening to as ready to listen.

I want to end where my schooling began and my affections still linger:

with a tribute to the great tradition of Jewish exegesis, originating and to me also culminating in the ancient rabbis. My admiration for their interpretive genius—and I do not use such terms lightly—is only equalled by my variance from their premises and licenses. At a level higher than method, deeper than the ready-made opposition of the scholarly to the creative, their way with biblical language remains exhilarating and liberating. However wild by normal standards of interpretation, their readings do at least practice all the time what Humpty Dumpty with his footling glosses on *his* opaque text merely preaches: that if you make words do your will, you must pay them extra. Whether and how a poetics can improve upon that balance, whether its sense of a system at work can keep the interpreter's will on a tighter rein while offering the Bible's words comparable if not higher pay, this is the question.

M. S.

THE POETICS OF
BIBLICAL NARRATIVE

·1·

LITERARY TEXT, LITERARY APPROACH: GETTING THE QUESTIONS STRAIGHT

The few, by Nature form'd, with Learning fraught, / Born to instruct, as others to be taught, / Must study well the Sacred Page; and see / Which Doctrine, this, or that, does best agree / With the whole *Tenour* of the Work Divine.
                        John Dryden, "Religio Laici"

What goals does the biblical narrator set himself? What is it that he wants to communicate in this or that story, cycle, book? What kind of text is the Bible, and what roles does it perform in context? These are all variations on a fundamental question that students of the Bible would do well to pose loudly and sharply: the question of the narrative as a functional structure, a means to a communicative end, a transaction between the narrator and the audience on whom he wishes to produce a certain effect by way of certain strategies. Like all social discourse, biblical narrative is oriented to an addressee and regulated by a purpose or a set of purposes involving the addressee. Hence our primary business as readers is to make purposive sense of it, so as to explain the *what*'s and the *how*'s in terms of the *why*'s of communication.

Posing such a question in the clearest terms is a condition for reasonable and systematic inquiry, rather than a panacea or a shortcut to unanimity. The answers to it would doubtless still vary as well as agree, since the reticent narrator gives us no clue about his intentions except in and through his art of narrative. To reconstruct the principles underlying the textual givens, therefore, we must form hypotheses that will relate fact to effect; and these may well differ in interpretive focus and explanatory power. But even the differences, including those not or not immediately resolvable, would then become well-defined, intelligible, and fruitful. That they are not remarkable for being so in the present state of affairs is largely

1

due to the tendency to read biblical texts out of communicative context, with little regard for what they set out to achieve and the exigencies attaching to its achievement. Elements thus get divorced from the very terms of reference that assign to them their role and meaning: parts from wholes, means from ends, forms from functions. Nothing could be less productive and more misleading. Even the listing of so-called forms and devices and configurations—a fashionable practice, this, among aspirants to "literary criticism"—is no substitute for the proper business of reading. Since a sense of coherence entails a sense of purpose, it is not enough to trace a pattern; it must also be validated and justified in terms of communicative design. After all, the very question of whether that pattern exists in the text—whether it has any relevance and any claim to perceptibility—turns on the question of what it does in the text. Unless firmly anchored in the relations between narrator and audience, therefore, formalism degenerates into a new mode of atomism.

What, then, does the biblical narrator want to accomplish, and under what conditions does he operate? To answer this question, both the universal and the distinctive features of his communication must be taken into account. Those features combine, in ways original and often surprising but unmistakable, to reveal a poetics at work. Whatever the nature and origin of the parts—materials, units, forms—the whole governs and interrelates them by well-defined rules of poetic communication.

To many, Poetics and Bible do not easily make a common household even as words. But I have deliberately joined them together, avoiding more harmonious terms like Structure or Shape or Art in order to leave no doubt about my argument. Poetics is the systematic working or study of literature as such. Hence, to offer a poetics of biblical narrative is to claim that biblical narrative is a work of literature. Not just an artful work; not a work marked by some aesthetic property; not a work resorting to so-called literary devices; not a work that the interpreter may choose (or refuse) to consider from a literary viewpoint or, in that unlovely piece of jargon, as literature; but a literary work. The difference is radical. Far from matched by whim or violence, the discipline and the object of inquiry naturally come together. And if this claim made for poetics sounds either tantamount to or more extreme than the alternatives just mentioned, that only shows how liable it is to misunderstanding even from sympathetic quarters—or perhaps, judging by past experience, especially from sympathetic quarters.

Since the sixties, I have found myself more often commended than condemned for developing "the literary approach" to the Bible. I was surprised when this description first arose, in regard to a programmatic analysis (written in collaboration with Menakhem Perry) that centered in the David and Bathsheba story.[1] However, my subsequent studies came yet more automatically under the same label, which has gained currency and prestige over the years but only grown more unwelcome to myself. Churlish as it is to quarrel with compliments, it would be still worse to pretend that I have ever advocated quite this kind of program and am happy with all its recent variants, or even those related to my own work. It is not that a biblical poetics and a literary approach must be doctrinally opposed, but that they tend to become so and are indeed on the way to becoming so (still retrievably, I believe) in practice. Nor is it that the literary approach, whatever it may mean and however it may operate, has failed to yield good or at least stimulating results. On the contrary, the small and uneven corpus thus far produced has done more to illuminate the text (and enliven the field) than traditional research many times its size and duration. Rather, the practice suffers from the deficiencies of the underlying theoretical framework, so that both are exposed to serious and often gratuitous objections. Were the theory more on a par or even in alignment with the practical analysis, I would gladly begin this chapter with an exploration of the family resemblance.

As it is, a whole set of problems emerge. To begin with, the very phrase "literary approach" is rather meaningless in view of the diversity of the languages of criticism throughout history, and "*the* literary approach," with its monolithic ring, is downright misleading. Worse, either phrase is also ambiguous between object and method. Whatever the critical mode adopted, there arises the formidable question of its applicability to the Bible. Of course, where there's a will there's always a way of imposing it, as the ancients, misled by Josephus and their own classical bias, already demonstrated in twisting Israelite poetry into hexameter or trimeter form. Such acts of violence can be perpetrated even more easily on the text's world and meaning than on the formal properties of its language: interpretation can take greater liberties than description. The question is only whether we are free to take them with the Bible. Does the literary approach differ from all others in being self-justifying? Or does the expression serve as a shorthand for "an approach to the Bible as the literary text it is"? And if so, why does one so rarely encounter an explicit statement to this effect, complete with an indication of the narrative features that warrant it?

These built-in ambiguities hardly recommend the term "literary approach" and have indeed determined me against it (and its cognates) from the start. On top of them, however, there have gathered a number of strange ad hoc commissions and omissions. Some would appear to relate to the vagueness promoted by the unhappy terminology—above all, the silence on the issue of the Bible's literariness, which one might expect to open and inform every discussion. Others have crept in by different routes. These include the making of claims and assumptions (not always the same ones) that actually fail to establish the relevance of "literary" analysis, let alone the nature of the object, and discontinuities between theory and practice.

Terminology apart, again, the conceptual and methodological weaknesses do not mar the literary approach as such but its few existing formulations (and their implied counterparts in the practice of criticism and teaching). Nor do the weaknesses bear on all these formulations with equal force. What follows should be taken, therefore, as an anatomy of issues—rather than anything like a survey of specific critical performances—and a measure of my belief in their resolvability compared with the chronic ailments of traditional scholarship.

The only thing beyond cure is incompetence. The literary approach may sink to a level as low as David Robertson's *The Old Testament and the Literary Critic,*[2] which undertakes to initiate readers, by precept and example, into its mysteries. This guide betrays all the weaknesses to which I pointed, in their least acceptable form and with no redeeming features except as negative illustration. "The assumption that the Bible is imaginative literature is arbitrary. No one forces us to make it, nor does the Bible itself demand that we make it. We make it because we want to, because literary criticism can yield exciting and meaningful results" (p. 4). Actually, to ensure the divorce between method and object, those aspiring "to study the Bible as literature" are even urged to resist the natural inclination to operate in terms of "its original context" and "original intention" (p. 2). Instead, they must learn to subject it to the tools of criticism or, in the original's idiom, "the conglomeration of procedures and manipulations people have invented to study imaginative literature" (p. 3).

To qualify the novitiate for this task, a sprinkling of general guidelines is provided, e.g., that "the critic operates whenever possible by the principle of synecdoche" (p. 6), that his "final concern is with Beauty, not Truth" (p. 13), or that "literary criticism, conceived of as a language, is more agglutinative than analytic" (p. 7). Shorn of its aphoristic generalities, however, the conglomeration amounts to three procedures. First, the critic assumes "that the text he is interpreting is a whole" (p. 7). Second, he takes everything in the text as fictional and hence "essentially metaphoric" (p. 5). To understand the fiction, third, he picks up clues from "the work itself" and relates them to "the genre to which the work belongs." Since "all contexts are equally valid," the choice of this generic context is entirely arbitrary. Only considerations of what the audience is likely to find more exciting determine whether the critic will perform "a literary study of Biblical hymns" in relation to Mesopotamian or to Methodist hymnody (pp. 9-10).

That such a hodgepodge of vulgarized truisms and plain nonsense should masquerade as a theory of literature, indeed as the distillation and consensus of literary study, might suggest a parody in the manner of F. C.

Crews's *The Pooh Perplex*. The self-contradictions, not to speak of the giveaways, leap to the eye. If the adoption into literature or the exercise of the literary method is a matter of free choice, why will it "go well" with some texts, including the Bible, and "poorly" with others (p. 3)? If "literary criticism, like all sciences, is defined by the nature of the object it studies" (p. 5), how can the defining class of objects be indiscriminately enlarged at will? And if the Bible is to be "wrenched fairly suddenly and none too gently from one context to another" (p. 4), how can the procedure yield "understanding" or "insight"? Insight into what, and, given the recommended variability of the wrenching among readers, for whom?

Still, in view of the claims made for the approach as "a paradigm change" comparable to the shift from Newtonian physics to "Einstein's theory of special relativity" (p. 4), the least one might expect from its application is a crop of provocative readings. But the case proves to be one of the Horatian mountain and mouse. The analyses, operating at the level of extended summary, could hardly be more pedestrian and less unorthodox, except perhaps for verdicts like "reading Greek literature as a whole is better practice for adult living than reading Hebrew literature" (p. 31). By any standard, including excitement, they are not fit to be compared with the insights into the same texts afforded by pre-Einsteinians such as Hermann Gunkel on Psalms or Moshe Greenberg in *Understanding Exodus*. What is worse, the practice leaves behind or contradicts the very precepts introduced with such fanfare. In violation of the holistic imperative, no place is found in the tale of the Exodus for a major character: "Aaron is never well integrated into the story, and just as well could be edited out" (p. 20). The premise of fictionality, bristling with possibilities of interpretive fireworks, never comes into significant play. Conventions, supposedly imported into the text on the reader's whim, often turn out to have been there all the time, firmly embedded and in a controlling position at that. Indeed, phrases like "if this interpretation is correct" or "most readers experience" or the abundant *we*'s betray a yearning for old-fashioned objectivity, a wobbling between the conceptions of biblical literariness as pure fancy and as an inherent, regulative feature. Obviously, if this were what literary criticism has to offer, one could not dispense with its services too soon.

No discipline can insure itself against abuse and misrepresentation, least of all in foreign lands that professionals rarely visit. It would therefore be premature for those ill-disposed toward the whole enterprise to rub their hands. Beyond all questions of theoretical persuasion, this self-appointed spokesman and his like no more speak for literary inquiry, the better sort of its promoters in biblical circles included, than a Thomas Rymer represents Shakespearian criticism. Their vagaries do not and must not reflect on the serious work done, and only betray the proverbial effects of a little knowledge. One would much rather shrug off the whole thing were it not for the danger that in a field where editors judged the book worthy of mentorship, the prospective audience might take it as its own valuation.

Even among scholars whose work commands respect, however, Robertson proves far more exceptional in the level at which he advocates the literary approach than in the doctrines advocated. Almost invariably, the impression that an outsider might get of literary criticism is one of a homogeneous and self-explanatory pursuit, with hallowed articles of faith to which all practitioners do and all aspirants must subscribe. It is as if all that remains is to apply to the Bible the proven tools ready to one's hand. But all too often these invoked articles do not reflect the history or state of the art and would not pass theoretical muster. However laudable their intentions, therefore, not one of the more explicit or missionary statements of belief I have seen outlines a viable framework. Nor do the results achieved in and through the practical criticism always follow from the official platform. It is the consistency of the theory, its continuity with the practice and its relation to the object that form the main, certainly the first, problem. My biblical poetics does, I believe, make a reasonably coherent argument along the lines indicated in the opening paragraphs. But were the points at which it opposes various "literary approaches" of a terminological or even conceptual nature only, my quarrel with them would not go much beyond indicating the moot questions. In the circumstances, the great enemy is not disagreement but darkness, shadowboxing, artificial divisions between traditionalists and innovators, with each side more inclined to differ than to ascertain if and where genuine differences lie. This introductory chapter, I hope, will at least get the issues straight and the lines properly drawn.

Kenneth Gros Louis's "Methodological Considerations," introducing a recent anthology to which he has contributed some fine analyses, may serve as a point of departure. Here are the most basic assumptions[3] supposedly shared by "literary critics of the Bible," myself, alas, included:

1. "Approaching the Bible as literature means placing emphasis on the text itself—not on its historical and textual backgrounds, not on the circumstances that brought the text into its present form, not on its religious and cultural foundations." In short, "our approach is essentially ahistorical" (pp. 14–15).
2. "The literary critic assumes unity in the text" (p. 15).
3. "A literary critic begins by being primarily interested in how a work is structured or organized" (p. 17).
4. "Teachers of literature are primarily interested in the literary reality of a text and not its historical reality," literariness being equated here with fictionality: "Is it true, we ask, not in the

real world but in the fictional world that has been created by
the narrative?" (p. 14).

5. "The literary reality of the Bible can be studied with the methods of literary criticism employed with every other text" (p. 14).

I am sorry to say that, with the possible exception of the second, I do not
share any of these tenets, certainly not as they stand and least of all as
a package deal. Nor do I see how this quintet adds up to an approach
as distinct from a declaration of independence—the less so since almost
all its parts would apply to the study of nonliterary texts, and none legitimates the literary study of the Bible in terms other than the critic's choice
to exercise it. What, if anything, makes the literary critic an overdue arrival
rather than an intruder on the biblical scene? But it may be well to sort
out these matters in a more orderly fashion. So the three following sections
will examine the cruxes that have generated most of the debate between
(and within) the various camps; the fourth will then gather up the threads
into a more systematic argument for a functional poetics.

Discourse and Source

To the student of theory, the list just cited will have a familiar ring and
carry its own note of warning. The literary approaches to the Bible that
would uphold those fiats are for the most part children of the New Criticism,
inheriting its emphasis on the direct encounter with the text and, less fortunately, its professions of faith. This explains a good deal. The New
Criticism, no longer new except in name, arose in the first quarter of this
century (and gained a large following in the second) as a reaction against
the excesses of historical scholarship. One of its foremost advocates, looking back on the scene of his youth, describes his own sensational contribution "as a kind of banner, or rallying cry, for those literary theorists who
would no longer put up with the mishmash of philology, biography, moral
admonition, textual exegesis, social history, and sheer burbling that largely
made up what was thought of as literary criticism in academic circles."[4]
In preaching and practicing close analysis, with particular reference to
the language, the New Critics have rendered an invaluable service to the
study of literature. But theirs has remained a movement of reaction,
iconoclastic, often extravagant, polemical rather than theoretical, speaking in many voices, raising more problems than it would or could handle,
and laying itself open to a variety of charges, with self-contradiction at their
head. Not much has survived, except the practical and educational effect.

History, it is said, repeats itself. In the face of a situation that duplicates
the "mishmash" and bankruptcy of literary scholarship at the beginning

of the century, the New Criticism resurged in the biblical arena. The enemy has remained the same, and so have the issues. But the weapons have already proved ineffective beyond shock tactics in the old campaign and cannot achieve much in the new beyond redirecting attention to the text. For good or for ill, such literary approaches express a reaction, an understandable and timely call for a shift of priorities that overreaches itself and falls short of an adequate countertheory. They advocate the methods and rehearse the manifestoes of the New Criticism, but without duly adjusting them to the theoretical revaluations made since or to the conditions of biblical study or even to their own practice as readers (often shrewd readers) of the Bible. As such, their dismissal of historicism makes an ideological rather than a methodological reorientation: polemics may at best clear the ground but not substitute for a scholarly alternative. At times, indeed, the emphasis laid on the classroom and immediate enjoyment, with the occasional hint that neither requires even a knowledge of Hebrew, gives the impression that the object is rather to save the Bible from the hands of the scholars. Which is not such a bad idea, except that there are hands and hands.

Of this antihistorical bias, the notorious problem of intention affords a miniature. Predictably enough, it heads Gros Louis's list of irrelevancies: "We know, as students of literature, that the author's intention, his goals in writing for his contemporary audience, and his religious convictions, play a small role indeed in literary criticism" (p. 16). One wonders who "we" refers to. So far as this is an empirical matter, it can easily be demonstrated that the overwhelming majority of literary critics have ascribed the greatest importance to the author's intention and that the New Critical attacks only set out and indeed managed to refine the appeal to it. Moreover, if this is a matter of theory, then the question of intentionality has little of its usual bearing.

The affirmation of irrelevance alludes, of course, to Wimsatt and Beardsley's classic attack, "The Intentional Fallacy" (1946). In a retrospect already mentioned, the latter co-author describes it as a "designedly subversive and unpleasantly provoking essay" ("Intentions and Interpretations," p. 188). For all its reaction against the mishmash of scholarship, however, the argument is more moderate than its reputation might suggest. The fallacy actually debunked consists in the reliance on external intention, gathered from the author's psychology or biography or "revelations (in journals, for example, or letters or reported conversations) about how and why [he] wrote the poem—to what lady, while sitting on what lawn, or at the death of what friend or brother."[5]

It follows that biblical study can (indeed cannot but) leave on one side the pros and cons of so-called external intention. About this necessity there is even nothing like the aura of heroism that surrounds the rabbinic choice to the same effect. Though committed to the tenet of the divine author-ship of Scripture, the ancient sages flatly dismissed the ruling of a heavenly voice that intruded on their deliberations in its authorial capacity:

> Rabbi Joshua rose to his feet and said: "'It is not in heaven' [Deuter-onomy 30:12]." What does "not in heaven" mean? Rabbi Jeremiah said: "The Torah has already been given at Mount Sinai, and we pay no heed to any heavenly voice. . . ." Rabbi Nathan met Elijah and asked him: "What did the Holy One, blessed be he, do at that hour?" Elijah answered: "He smiled and said, My sons have defeated me, my sons have defeated me." (*Baba Metzia* 59b)

In the absence of heavenly voices, the question does not arise at all, since none of the biblical authors has left journals or letters or any other bio-graphical matter outside the writings themselves. The writers of narrative, with the possible exception of latecomers like Ezra and Nehemiah, have not revealed so much of themselves as their names. Had the Bible been the whole stock and store of world literature, Wimsatt and Beardsley would not have penned their—or at least not this—New Critical manifesto.

As interpreters of the Bible, our only concern is with "embodied" or "objectified" intention; and that forms a different business altogether, about which a wide measure of agreement has always existed. In my own view, such intention fulfills a crucial role, for communication presupposes a speaker who resorts to certain linguistic and structural tools in order to produce certain effects on the addressee; the discourse accordingly sup-plies a network of clues to the speaker's intention. In this respect, the Bible does not vary from any other literary or ordinary message except in the ends and the rules that govern the forms of communication. Minor dif-ferences apart, however, this is quite compatible with the original Wimsatt and Beardsley position and a variety of others, including the fairly recent pragmatics or speech-act theory. The more so because "intention" no longer figures as a psychological state consciously or unconsciously translated into words. Rather, it is a shorthand for the structure of meaning and effect supported by the conventions that the text appeals to or devises: for the sense that the language makes in terms of the communicative context as a whole.

With the interpreter removed from the Bible's sociocultural context, in-tention becomes a matter of historical reconstruction. And to this some would object on grounds familiar to students of literary and biblical her-meneutics alike: for example, that we cannot become people of the past or that to equate meaning with the original author's intention and his audience's comprehension is to impoverish the text. The problems raised and tangled by this influential minority view, itself far from homogeneous, are too complicated for me to go into here.[6] Nor, despite appearances, is a systematic examination really vital, considering the biblical text and its current scholarly ambiance—the New Critical spirit included. With these provisos let me say, quite simply, that the hard antihistorical line in hermeneutics is too condescending and inconsistent (in varying combinations) to make a viable theory.

It is condescending, not to say arrogant, because it still remains to demonstrate that in matters of art (as distinct from their abstract articulation) the child is always wiser than its parent, that wit correlates with modernity, that a culture which produced the Bible (or the *Iliad*) was incapable of going below the surface of its own product or referring it to the worthwhile coordinates of meaning. (The naive assumption turns grotesque when preached by some of the poorest readers that the Bible has known.) Even worse is the equation of author's and audience's meaning. What text the author made and what sense a reader or public made of it are always distinct in principle; and the Bible's practice brilliantly drives home this variance in that it provides, as we shall see, for all levels of reading through a "foolproof" composition.

Nor is this line consistent. The claim that one has the right to fashion and in effect invent the text anew as one pleases would at least enjoy the virtue of unassailability. But nothing short of this will do. From the premise that we cannot become people of the past, it does not follow that we cannot approximate to this state by imagination and training—just as we learn the rules of any other cultural game—still less that we must not or do not make the effort. Indeed, the antihistorical argument never goes all the way, usually balking as early as the hurdle of language. Nobody, to the best of my knowledge, has proposed that we each invent our own biblical Hebrew. But is the language any more or less of a historical datum to be reconstructed than the artistic conventions, the reality-model, the value system? Given their interpenetration, moreover, where does the linguistic component end and the nonlinguistic begin? Or how does one draw the line between the aesthetic shape of cyclical or symmetrical plot and the "religious" belief in God as the shaper of plot? If the whole network of past conventions is empirically unattainable, then dividing the indivisible is even theoretically untenable.

Once the choice turns out to lie between reconstructing the author's intention and licensing the reader's invention, there is no doubt where most of us stand. This does not exclude the literary approaches that seem to profess otherwise or even vacillate in practice. ("*Conscious* art" is one of their favorite phrases.) There remain differences, of course, but regarding emphasis more than substance. And no wonder they should arise, since the practical difficulties of reconstructing the Bible's code, though they hardly amount to a doctrinal objection, are quite troublesome and procedure still requires considerable attention.

"The age of the text makes no difference. It is from the story of David and Bathsheba itself that we infer its poetics, just as we do with *Lolita,* regardless of what its author or the modern theory of literature may say."[7] This generalization has gained some notoriety by being stood on its head. When the first sentence is torn out of context to make a better slogan or target, indeed, it sounds like a call for setting the text free from the prison-house of history. Actually, by an ironic variation on authorial intention, almost the opposite was claimed *and* demonstrated.

The text's autonomy is a long-exploded myth: the text has no meaning, or may assume every kind of meaning, outside those coordinates of discourse that we usually bundle into the term "context." The appropriate coordinates are historical, and the main trouble with the historical approaches to the Bible is their antihistorical performance. Not even the literary critics that they oppose have subjected the biblical text to so many anachronistic (and often bizarre) norms of unity, social conduct, world order, convention, value judgment. This is largely due to the failure to appreciate the striking systematicity of biblical narrative, which enables the interpreter to derive its poetics from its reticent practice, with some aid (but no dictation) from such extratextual clues as have survived. Historical and literary inquiry thus fall into an unhappy symmetry. In their concern with whatever frames or antecedes the text, the historians tend to overlook the chief body of historical evidence that awaits proper interpretation. In their concern with interpretation, the critics tend to overlook the extent to which their goal involves and commits them to the quest for frames and antecedents. It is for a closer interworking of text and context that the rest of this section, and much of this chapter, will argue.

To begin with the "literary" side, I have already noted that language exposes the Achilles' heel of anti-reconstructionism; and the Bible offers the best case in point. Nobody is likely to regard the grammar and semantics of biblical Hebrew as irrelevant to a literary approach. But are they given "in" the text? Surely not, for the Bible presupposes rather than makes explicit its language system, as every message does its code. To determine the meaning of a word, the syntax of an utterance, the possibilities of stylistic variation, the dividing line between idiomaticity and metaphorical force, the interpreter turns to the linguist and/or turns linguist himself, conducting his own analysis of the underlying system. We thus engage in a historical reconstruction that delimits what the writer could have meant against the background of the linguistic knowledge that, even in artful manipulation, he must have taken for granted. Doing so is evidently as far from reducing the text to extrinsic factors—as if it were a storehouse of verbal data—as it is from the making of a new language at will. Nor is it anything like a compromise between the extremes, but simply the normal business of interpretation.

As with linguistic code, so with artistic code. With a biblical metaphor, for instance, the question whether it is stereotyped or newly coined, dead or live, obviously will make an enormous difference to its meaning and effect. But it has quite a similar (and often more easily determinable) bearing on a compositional measure: dialogue, repetition, omission, ring pattern, temporal ordering, narrative stance. Let us take the last of these, which not only bears clear marks of "literariness" but also must be appraised by all readers, because the sense of the information presented depends on the rules and authority of its presentation. For these reasons, as it happens, I was drawn to this issue from the outset and can now retrace some of the inevitable steps in the process of grappling with it.[8]

Given the biblical narrator's access to privileged knowledge—the distant past, private scenes, the thoughts of the dramatis personae, from God down—he must speak from an omniscient position. This establishes authority but not yet originality. Is the stance of omniscience due to tradition or innovation? The formal systematicity of the narrative from Genesis to Kings still leaves this question open, and the critic has no choice except to turn to the literature of the ancient Orient. There he will deduce the conventional nature of the technique from the extant practice of Sumerian, Babylonian, Egyptian, Canaanite storytelling and, with the net cast even wider, Homeric epic too. The end of the road? No, because a structural convention, just like a verbal cliché, may be revitalized by being put to new uses or into new contexts. The most promising place to look for these is the Bible's original world view: unlike all pagan deities, God is truly and exclusively all-knowing. Does this epistemological novelty in the sphere of world order extend to the epistemology and operation of point of view in the narrative? Does the monotheistic article of faith give a new bearing to the inherited rule of omniscience? Is it, for example, that the narrator assumes omniscience because he could not otherwise do justice to an infallible God and impress on the reader, by appropriate suppressions, his own fallibility? Since the Omniscient inspires his prophets, moreover, does the narrator implicitly appeal to the gift of prophecy, so as to speak with redoubled authority as divine historian? And does this storytelling posture link up with another biblical novelty—human usurpation of knowledge right at the beginning of history?

Whatever the answers—and all evidently bristle with significance—they must also reckon with the fact that books like Nehemiah and (partly) Ezra assume the form of eyewitness narrative. Does that mean that the biblical writer, like his modern or for that matter ancient Egyptian counterpart, can choose between two opposed strategies of narration? If so, his choice of persona would in either case take on new import and require explanation by reference to the specific goals and exigencies that determined it in each book. But is it accidental that the instances of limited ("first-person") narration are all very late writings, which find their equivalents only in apocryphal and gospel literature? Is their divergence from the omniscient perspective, then, a measure of artistic choice or of historical change in the Bible's storytelling? Again, the answers can wait. All that needs emphasizing is that for literary analysts to deal responsibly with a compositional issue par excellence they must engage in a poetic valuation of a whole range of so-called extrinsic evidence: from the art of the Oriental tradition through the premises of monotheistic theology to the dating of the biblical canon. Milieu, world view, history of formation—all untouchables prove indispensable to literary study as such.

The same holds true not only for extraliterary history but even for that taboo called the genesis of the text. Literary analysis, we often hear, has no truck with textual prehistory. This is neither reasonable nor quite true. Why anyone should wish to deny himself a universal resource for explaining a text's incongruities, whether by appeal to its transmission or to any other framework, remains a mystery. Or rather, it would remain one were it not for the incredible abuse of this resource for over two hundred years of frenzied digging into the Bible's genesis, so senseless as to elicit either laughter or tears. Rarely has there been such a futile expense of spirit in a noble cause; rarely have such grandiose theories of origination been built and revised and pitted against one another on the evidential equivalent of the head of a pin; rarely have so many worked so long and so hard with so little to show for their trouble. Not even the widely accepted constructs of geneticism, like the Deuteronomist, lead an existence other than speculative. Small wonder, then, that literary approaches react against this atomism by going to the opposite extreme of holism. But the excesses and fruitlessness of traditional source criticism no more legitimate the waving aside of its available data than they illegitimate its goals.

An example would be another inescapable principle of composition, to which chapter 11 is devoted. Briefly, the repetitions in the Masoretic Text appear in an elliptical or variant form compared with their equivalents in the Septuagint and the Samaritan Pentateuch, which have recently gained support from the Qumran scrolls. The literary critic is hardly entitled to disregard this systematic noncoincidence. Actually, far from threatening his analyses of the received text's variations in repetition, the "external" evidence of verbatim rehearsals confirms it by highlighting the distance between two poetics of repetition within the Bible's line of development. The Masoretic Text's functional structuring contrasts with the others' throwback to the formulaic tradition. While neglect or self-denial will impugn the critic's very method, therefore, the sense of a system may turn the data to poetic account in terms undreamt of by the geneticist bent on harmonizing and purifying versions.[9]

By a triumph of common sense over reaction, moreover, no one practices self-denial all the time. In the face of "Saul was one year old when he began to reign" (1 Sam 13:1), all differences of approach evaporate: the Masoretic version must be corrupt, and the question is only what number fell out. Nor is this a logical—hence automatic and trivial—but a full-fledged hermeneutic "must." Logically speaking, one can easily imagine a world where, by divine grace for example, a one-year-old Saul wields royal power. This is by no means impossible, only implausible and even so only in context. It follows that the dismissal of this possibility constitutes an act of interpretation performed on empirical grounds: it makes more sense to infer a scribal error than a reality-model within which the incongruity will fall into "literary" pattern. The exigencies of simplicity outweigh the postulate of unity-within-the-given-text, which turns out to be a working hypothesis rather than a categorical imperative. The rabbis, predictably, found a way out by twisting "one year" into the figurative meaning of newborn innocence. But then their very wrenching betrays their awareness of the dilemma, and their choice to wrench the sense in order to save the wording dramatizes the antithesis between their doctrinal commitment and the literary interpreter's pragmatic orientation to the received text.

However small this example, accordingly, its implications bear on all the aspects of textual history—glosses, documents, copying accidents, editorial splicing—for the principle is one and indivisible. Far from out of bounds to all but one line of biblical inquiry, genesis as a framework of intelligibility is ever-available to all: it would be as idle for the literary scholar to deny it (and unscholarly to deny oneself of it) as it would be for the traditional biblicist to maintain that genesis comes to light regardless of exegesis. Whatever they may say or think, the only point at issue between them is where and how the appeal to the genetic option serves a purpose.

Indeed, it is in the purpose that the nub of the difference lies. Methodologically speaking, in fact, approaches to the Bible do not ramify into an indefinitely large number of categories distinguished by subject matter, e.g., theological, historical, sociological, anthropological, linguistic, genetic, literary, etc. At a less superficial level, they fall under no more than two heads, which I shall call source-oriented versus discourse-oriented inquiry. Cutting across lines of discipline and resource and vogue, the logic of this bipartition resides in the type of questions asked—in the *object* of inquiry, both in the sense of the thing considered and the goal envisaged by its consideration.

Source-oriented inquiry addresses itself to the biblical world as it really was, usually to some specific dimension thereof. The theologian, qua theologian, dreams of piecing together a full picture of ancient Israelite religion, mutations and conflicts included. The historian wants to know what happened in Israelite history, the linguist what the language system (phonology, grammar, semantics) underlying the Bible was like. And the geneticist concentrates on the real-life processes that generated and shaped the biblical text: the origins and features of the material (documents, traditions) that went into the Bible, the passage from oral to written transmission, the identity of the writers or schools, the modes of editorial work, the tampering by way of interpolation, scribal misadventure, etc. In each case, then, interest focuses on some object behind the text—on a state of affairs or development which operated at the time as a source (material, antecedent, enabling condition) of biblical writing and which biblical writing now reflects in turn.

Discourse-oriented analysis, on the other hand, sets out to understand not the realities behind the text but the text itself as a pattern of meaning and effect. What does this piece of language—metaphor, epigram, dialogue, tale, cycle, book—signify in context? What are the rules governing the transaction between storyteller or poet and reader? Are the operative rules, for instance, those of prose or verse, parable or chronicle, omniscience or realistic limitation, historical or fictional writing? What image of a world does the narrative project? Why does it unfold the action in this particular order and from this particular viewpoint? What is the part played by the omissions, redundancies, ambiguities, alternations between scene and summary or elevated and colloquial language? How does the work hang together? And, in general, in what relationship does part stand to whole and form to function? The thrust here remains determinate and stable under wide terminological, even conceptual variations. To pursue this line of questioning is to make sense of the discourse in terms of communication, always goal-directed on the speaker's part and always requiring interpretive activity on the addressee's. In the framework of an implicit sociocultural code, the one wields certain linguistic and structural tools with an eye to certain effects, the other infers a coherent message from the signals, and the discourse mediates between the two, embodying intent and guiding response.

Thus drawn, in terms of object, the line separating the two inquiries brings out the need for a community or overlap rather than a division of labor. This directly follows from their common exigency as reconstructions of the Bible. I have already suggested why and how the analysis of discourse presupposes, among other things, a reconstruction of various sources—the Bible's language system, cultural milieu, theology, dating, development within the canon, origins, and transmissional fortunes. All these dimensions of the source then operate as parameters of context: the world they compose becomes a determinant and an indicator of meaning, a guide to the making of sense. Accordingly, the more complete and reliable our knowledge of the world from which the Bible sprang, the sharper our insight into its working and meaning as text; and the limits of this knowledge—for example, regarding biblical semantics, politics, rules of parallelism, editorial license, ties with Oriental art—may coincide with the limits of interpretation. But the converse also holds true and, due to the unfortunate limitations under which biblical scholarship operates, with even greater force than usual.

When all is said and done, the independent knowledge we possess of the "real world" behind the Bible remains absurdly meager, almost non-existent when compared with the plenty available to, say, Joyceans or even Shakespearians. For better or worse, most of our information is culled from the Bible itself, and culling information entails a process of interpretation, where source abjectly waits on discourse. There is no escaping this necessity—though, again, many would like to and may even pretend they do. Source-oriented critics often imply that they deal in hard facts and consign "aesthetic" analysis to its fate at the none too reliable hands of the literary coterie. If seriously entertained, this is a delusion, bearing the name of positivism with none of its excuses and facilities. There is simply nothing here to be positive about—no, or almost no, facts concerning the sources of the Bible apart from those we ourselves make by inference from the Bible as source. The movement from text to reality cannot but pass through interpretation.

If the Bible is a work of literature, therefore, nobody can evade the consequences. As reader, for example, the historian must take into account that every item of reality given in the text may have been stylized by conventions and for purposes alien to historical science. The linguist must reckon with the shifts between colloquial dialogue and formal narrative or with the poetic manipulation of the rules of the language, or else he will mistake the liberties taken by art for the encoded norms. The reading lot of the geneticist is perhaps the hardest of all, because the task of decomposition calls for the most sensitive response to the arts of composition. How else will one be able to tell deliberate from accidental roughnesses and identify the marks of disunity in unity throughout a text whose *poesis* covers the tracks of its *genesis*? It is this enforced movement from discourse to source by way of interpretation that allies genetic criticism with that branch of acrobatics known as lifting oneself up by one's bootstraps. But then it's either acrobatics or nothing.

Nor will the denial of the Bible's literariness provide any escape hatch. For the constraint of reading is no more peculiar to a certain kind of text or approach than the search for antecedents. No matter how the writing is viewed, its reading remains the pivotal activity of biblical study as a whole, for a scholar is only as good as his interpretation. Define the Bible as theology, history, myth, or what you will. In each case you have to interpret it in the light of the conventions postulated and defend your interpretation against all rivals who appeal to other frames of reference—literature included—seeing that hypotheses about source stand or fall on the cogency of the analysis of discourse. Indeed, objective lacunae apart, our scanty and chaotic knowledge of the biblical world reflects the interpretive competence of its seekers at large. But this causal relationship may work the other way too, and there are promising signs that it ultimately will.

However this may turn out, the laissez-faire gestures ("You go your way and I'll go mine" or, more belligerently, "You keep off my grass and I'll keep off yours") made occasionally from both sides of the "literary-approach" fence only confuse the issue. They speak as if there were one Bible for the historian, another for the theologian, another for the linguist, another for the geneticist, still another for the literary critic. But there are not enough Bibles to go round, and even Solomon's wisdom cannot divide the only one we do possess among the various claimants. Its discourse remains indivisible for all, and so does its source. Naturally, we may quarrel about its form and meaning and origins—just as we may put different questions to it—but not along predetermined or, worse, insulated lines. Each reading of the text, like each reconstruction of the biblical world, is open to challenge or support from all others, athwart the boundaries of "discipline" sanctified by nothing in reason.

Given their interdependence, accordingly, the two orientations must join forces within each and every inquiry. For the literary critic, success or failure in the reconstruction of the world (above all, the culture) behind the Bible is success or failure as a professional reader, not as an amateur historian. For the historian, success or failure in the interpretation of the biblical text is success or failure as a reconstructor of the past, not as a criticaster or a dabbler in hermeneutics. The actual competence shown by either in the other's branch of learning does not at all affect the principle, and the consequences of its breach only dramatize its validity. Neither inquirer can help making certain assumptions about the source and making some sense of the discourse. Whatever they choose to do with them, the data within and about the Bible await both; so do the tools of analysis.

It is not even true that the one's activity enjoys temporal priority over the other's:

> Historic and literary study are equal in importance; but for priority in order of time the literary treatment has the first claim. The reason of this is that the starting point of historic analysis must be that very existing text, which is the sole concern of the morphological study. The historic inquirer will no doubt add to his examination of the text light drawn from other sources; he may be led in his investigation to alter or rearrange the text; but he will admit that the most important single element on which he has to work is the text as it has come down to us. But, if the foundation principle of literary study be true, this existing text cannot be truly interpreted until it has been read in the light of its exact literary structure. [10]

This claim, made by Richard Moulton (the author of an excellent book on Shakespeare) at the turn of the century and echoed to this day, would be reversed by historicists. There is no "existing text" and hence nothing to be "truly interpreted," they would say, until the best version (and, more generally, context) has been established in the light of its exact historical development. Each claimant thus envisages a two-stage process, where he in effect makes the text that the other then receives for further treatment.

This head-on clash of priorities, however, suggests that such literary and historical approaches entertain an equally unrealistic notion of their independence. The "historic inquirer," as Moulton rightly argues, has little else to go on beyond "the text as it has come down to us"; hence the operations of reading must intervene between the encounter with the extant text and its approval, reshaping, or decomposition. (The same holds true for all other source-oriented pursuits, from the eliciting of historical data to the establishment of the appropriate network of conventions.) But it does not follow that the intervening "literary treatment" enjoys precedence, because it itself rests on a variety of assumptions about the source: the acceptability of the text, the underlying language system, the implied world picture, the operative codes of form and meaning. To the examples already cited, Moulton's own practice offers numerous parallels. It contradicts his "foundation principle" on the very first page of his first analysis, where the historical perspective shows in the surprise expressed at the dramatic effect of Job or in the comparison with Greek tragedy or in the reference to the lack of stage directions in the dramas of antiquity (*Literary Study of the Bible*, p. 25). The next chapter begins with a specifically genetic retrospect, in the form of an attack on the blurring of scriptural verse design for over fifteen hundred years by anachronistic printing and segmentation into units (pp. 45ff.). And so on.

On either side, indeed, the practice is truer than the theory. The common theoretical error has its origin—apart from the spirit of partisanship—in two attempts to accomplish the impossible. One consists in laying down what the philosophy of science would term a discovery procedure, whereby the inquiry will reach its goal through predetermined stages. Obviously, the route is not reducible to law, nor need it bear any relation to the final argument, which is the only thing that matters. (How Saul sought the asses and found a kingdom makes a suggestive parable for all inquirers.) The second impossibility is the linearization of the correlated viewpoints of discourse and source, as if one could read a text out of any context or contextualize it without reading. Both the interpreter and the historian must perforce combine the two viewpoints throughout, incessantly moving between given discourse and inferred source in an endeavor to work out the best fit, until they reach some firm conclusion. The order of this whole process of shuttling has no interest, because it remains as subjectively variable as the process itself is a logical constant of all pattern-making. What actually varies in a systematic way is not the temporal but the conceptual priorities or, in other words, the object that governs the organization of the findings.

Where the object is to make sense of the discourse, all knowledge or conjecture about the source operates as an aid to interpretation and the discovery of its artful rules. In this framework, to pick some examples from the following chapters, the fact that biblical semantics does not lexicalize the distinction between justified and unjustified deceit serves only to bring out the techniques whereby the art of context loads the same words (say, *bemirma*) with evaluative charges divergent to the point of opposition. Conversely, the fact that the lexicon reserves the adjective *bari* ("fat") for animates assumes importance only insofar as it validates the figurative application of the epithet to the ears of corn in Pharaoh's dream. The fact that biblical theology is dogmatic about God's monopoly of absolute knowledge helps to illuminate the art of perspective, for instance, alerting the reader both to the blind spots from which the whole human cast suffers and to the narrator's transcendence of this restriction. Biblical doublets, like Saul's two rejections by God, may have originated in different sources: this heightens our sense of the redundancy or conflict involved in stringing them together and of the possibilities of eliminating it constructively in terms like plot gradation or thematic variation. That so many features (names, customs, movements) of the patriarchal cycle have been verified gives a clue to the rhetoric of historicity in a book where much of the material defies verification. Or, more specifically, the fact that the Mari tablets establish Nahor (*nakhur*) as the name of a place as well as of a person supports the hypothesis that the servant in the Wooing tale (Genesis 24) did not originally intend to go to Abraham's family for a bride. Throughout this list, the source has instrumental value alone, as a pointer to the march and meaning of the discourse.

With the shift of object from contextual sense to the real world, however, the priorities change places too. Each of the examples just given shows its reverse face. To the semanticist, only a proper reading of the text will disclose the lexical gaps in the field of deceit or, in Pharaoh's dream, that *bari* in the context of grain signals neither a chance exception nor an encoded variant but a deliberate breach of rule in the interests of figuration. To the theologian, the art of perspective will reveal that in the Bible's world view the contrast between divine omniscience and human blindness was not simply an article of faith but an ever-operative determinant of vision and action, so much so that not even the prophets ("seers") escaped its ironies. The more the geneticist appreciates how the doublets function as stages (rather than retardations) in an unfolding plot or variations (rather than rehearsals) of a theme, the sharper will be his sense of their diversity and his skepticism about their mechanical adherence to the original traditions. Still more evident, the historian's insight into the Bible's rhetoric of historicity will at the very least alert him to the interplay of hard fact and reality effect.

In the movement from source to discourse, or vice versa, it is not therefore the evidence (given or inferred) that changes but the means–end combinations it falls into. Pragmatically speaking, this may make quite a difference. For one thing, though many of the source-centered ends are unattainable, it is only natural that geneticists, say, will wish to carry their inquiries beyond the point that interpreters will deem even remotely feasible, let alone necessary. An example would be a tale so smoothly composed as to afford the decomposer no opening, or one so ambiguated as to render the historical event completely opaque. In such and other instances, further, the scope of the means brought to bear on the crux may differ as well; and the wider the investigation casts its net, the more perceptible this variety in unity. Discourse analysis, for instance, may find the universals of literature or the devices of modern narrative a more helpful guide than Oriental schemata to certain innovative features of the Bible, like density, multiple views, plot construction, or intricate character-drawing. Just as the contemporary milieu enjoys no exclusive or even preferential status in the quest for the text's design and meaning, so may the Bible's own account of an event give way to a rival version or historical probability in the reconstruction of what really happened. All conventions of writing are to the interpreter what all remains of the past are to the historian and what all textual prehistories, ancient and modern,[11] are to the geneticist: aids to hypothesis-making, serviceable and gradable only insofar as they throw light on the object. If to the historian the Bible is one means ("source") among many—his interest may even center in Egypt or in the international scene of the time—then to the interpreter the Bible constitutes an end in itself. But the findings of each, once reached in accordance with his own scale of priorities, have to meet the standards that govern the operations of all.

Specialization being what it is, terms like "historian," "geneticist," "linguist," and "literary critic," will probably long continue to designate separate inquirers rather than interrelated competences or skills within each. Yet the present state of affairs, with source and discourse made foreign if not inimical to each other, imposes unduly severe constraints on what may be taken on trust from specialists in each field. Consider Leland Ryken's statement that "the literary critic usually doesn't even know the original language" and would anyway remain "dependent on the biblical scholar for his knowledge of the language of the Bible."[12] In view of this sad admission, remarkable for its matter-of-fact tone, one could hardly blame traditional scholars for having some misgivings about his (or the) literary approach, certainly about its relevance to their own work. But neither should he, still less a critic conversant with Hebrew, overestimate the amount of help that may be reasonably expected from traditional scholarship. The interpreter of the Bible must double as linguist far more often than an interpreter of modern literature need do.

For all the exertions of biblical linguists, the quality and range of the linguistics available do not come up to standard. Apart from everything else, they labor under the triple disadvantage of having to derive a language system from a small closed corpus largely governed by artistic norms of which microlinguists have little awareness and even less knowledge. Where do the rules of language end and the conventions of discourse begin? What is the natural syntax or semantics and what the artificial manipulation? When does the code operate and when the context? These problems, always tricky, generally remain shrouded in mystery here, and making poetic sense of the Bible therefore requires a good deal of linguistic spadework. Among the instances that underlie the following chapters are the boundaries of lexical and connotative meaning, linguistic vs. stylistic variation, word order in coordination, levels of speech, social vs. inner language, or the grammar and semantics of free indirect discourse. These and other cruxes await systematic exploration in terms that still have the ring of a paradox: a context-sensitive linguistics.

Linguistics only illustrates an exigency of much wider application. Since biblical study is not a discipline by any stretch of the term but the intersection of the humanities par excellence, the progress it so badly needs is conditional either on all-round expertise, not given to humans, or on a truly common pursuit of knowledge. In the meantime, if we must continue to play double or multiple roles as best we can, we should be all the more on our guard against mixing them up. Genetic criticism most often betrays this mixture. A recent reviewer, having commended my analysis of the Rape of Dinah narrative (Genesis 34) for resolving some pseudo-problems of genesis in poetic terms, goes on to criticize its failure to see that the rape does not belong to the "real" story at all.[13] Now, I would certainly like to know how and when this key incident found its way into the story. But having once arrived there, the proposal to excise it with a view to a better reading must be a joke; and even a joke tends to get a little stale when the changes have been rung on it for two hundred years.

The implications, I trust, are clear. "Literary" approaches have nothing to fear, and occasionally something to learn, from genetic criticism as such, that is, in its source-directed role as an inquiry into the historical processes of composition. Since they do not focus on the same questions, they do not contend for the same prize, except perhaps in terms of academic priorities and prestige. They become rivals only by accident, when the geneticist unwittingly crosses the line between source and discourse, imposing his reconstruction of the process on the structure of the product. I say "unwittingly," because geneticists often operate as if the structure of the discourse (e.g., the pertinence of the rape) followed from the reconstruction (e.g., the supposedly late arrival of the rape). They then fail to realize that they are engaging in a new task from an old viewpoint, switching into interpretation yet interpreting not the text but some conjectural version that may be quite removed from it in purpose and procedure.

Having become a rival, still, the geneticist-as-interpreter must in principle be taken by the literary approach no less seriously than the interpreter-as-geneticist. For every weakness in his position is remediable (which is more than can be said of the objective lacunae in his, and our, knowledge of antecedents). Once the artificial barriers go down, the reading competence of the geneticist may improve in time to meet professional standards, and with it the acceptability of his reconstructions. The wavering between orientations may be brought under control at once. Qua interpreter as well as source critic proper, the New Geneticist—not quite a creature of the imagination even at present—will at least be able to make the best of a bad business. He will then openly put forward an analysis of the discourse, still cutting and remolding with a backward glance at the source, yet no longer by appeal to any special dispensation of the biblicist but to a universal principle of coherence that demands the most wary handling. He will hardly suggest the deletion of a rape that forms the mainspring of the plot and the basis for the operations of meaning, nor expect general assent to the repairing of incongruities less self-explanatory than the accession of the infant Saul. It is in between these poles that the problematic cases will extend: those where an interpretation that dismisses or alters certain elements will clash with another that assigns a constructive role to all. Such fighting on a common ground, the enemy having become "one of us," will not make life easier for anybody. But the study of the Bible will be the gainer.

Fiction and History

It follows that if "literary approach" amounts to "discourse-oriented approach," there is still nothing to warrant or even to distinguish it as such. In terms of method, this orientation forms a necessary means to source-centered inquiry into the Bible. In terms of object, the distinction between source and discourse holds for every text, literary and nonliterary, so that the two orientations must converge on the Magna Carta as well as on *Sir Gawain and the Green Knight*. The method itself does not create its object *ex nihilo*, not even according to theories of literature that appear to shift the locus of literariness from the object to the reader's attitude. "The work has structure and meaning because it is read in a particular way, because these potential properties, latent in the object itself, are actualized by the theory of discourse applied in the act of reading":[14] even this fairly libertarian structuralist view presupposes the actualization of latencies, not their fabrication. Like any other approach, therefore, the literary must choose between total arbitrariness (which of course needs declaring by those who would consider it legitimate) and reference to some textual feature or features that invite it.

Various biblical features have been invoked in vain for this purpose, because they are obviously either not peculiar or not necessary to literature or both. This is the case with qualities (all, perhaps significantly, mentioned rather than argued by their proposers) like great ideas, dramatic effect, rendering of human life, imagery, expressiveness, unified plot, scientific interest. The only serious candidates are fictionality and form.

The view of the Bible's storytelling as partly or wholly fictional often cuts across the lines of approach. In traditional scholarship, the term has long been employed to denote nonhistoricity, of the inventive as well as the falsifying kind. To Robert Pfeiffer, for instance, the "narratives present all the gradations between pure fiction (as in the stories about Adam, Noah, and Samson) and genuine history (as in the ancient biography of David and the memoirs of Nehemiah). . . . The bulk of the narratives . . . transfer the hearers into a romantic world, into a remote past brought to life by fancy—either out of some scanty memories of actual

events or out of the storehouse of a vivid Oriental imagination."[15] Thus
presented, as a type of story rather than an offense against history, fiction
naturally attracts literary notice. Hermann Gunkel's whole form criticism
has evolved from the reasoning that if Genesis is not history, then it is
"saga" and requires critical-aesthetic analysis.[16] Hence the division of the
narrative into subtypes—sagas mythical, patriarchal, heroic, ethnographic,
aetiological, etc.—which his followers have since further split and crossed
and multiplied into varieties that would delight old Polonius. Armed with
more useful tools, literary critics have yet been making the same assumptions, and some even find in the Bible the origins of the novel. Though
the bases of these approaches do not much vary in principle, two are notable
for their verve and forthrightness. What we witness in Genesis and elsewhere, Herbert Schneidau argues, "is the birth of a new kind of historicized
fiction. . . . Its very raggedness and incoherence forces the beholder into
an extra effort of imagination, giving the work a quality of dramatic
vividness—and yet at the same time distancing is accomplished."[17] In
answer to the question whether we "are not coercing the Bible into being
'literature,'" Robert Alter roundly affirms that "prose fiction is the best
general rubric for describing biblical narrative" (*Art of Biblical Narrative*,
pp. 23, 24). Drawing on Schneidau, he gives the thesis a new show of
plausibility by discriminating and illustrating the Bible's fictional range.

To tell the truth, since in his opening chapter Alter so emphatically
excepts the issue of history from his acceptance of my work, it is doubly
surprising to find him in the camp of fiction. This line having once been
adopted, however, it is not at all surprising that he comes to grief. The
case has never been stated so well, and the parts abound in shrewd observations; but the whole suffers from the same fatal flaw as all the previous
arguments for the Bible's fictionality. As so often, the historical approach
is not nearly historical enough and the literary not literary enough, for
one sees fiction only when one loses sight of history and convention.

The trouble goes back to the ambiguity of the key terms *history* vs. *fiction*
between world and word—between the represented object and the discourse
that represents it. On the one hand, each term indicates a different object
of representation, "history" denoting what really happened and "fiction"
the sphere of the imagined or invented. It is in this sense that Schneidau
refers to "the Hebrew habit of looking to history, or experience, for validation of the prophetic message" (p. 25) and Alter to "a whole spectrum of
relations to history in the sundry biblical narratives" (p. 24). On the other
hand, each term may point to a different mode of representation or
writing—"history" to re-creative and fiction to creative discourse. "The
history we find in the Bible is basically concerned with the possibility of
judgment of culture's strivings," while Job is "a great work of self-conscious

fiction" (Schneidau, pp. 210–11, 212). Or, "the Hebrew Bible is generally perceived, with considerable justice, as sacred history" and "the Patriarchal narratives may be composite fictions" (Alter, pp. 23, 24). Each term, then, has a twofold orientation: to the source and to the discourse.

This terminological wavering between world and word would remain a minor affair—most of us perpetrate it, if only for stylistic reasons—did it not tend to get out of hand. No longer innocuous, it then reinforces a conceptual fallacy that is potent and widespread enough anyway. The shift of meaning leads to a symbiosis of meaning, whereby history-writing is wedded to and fiction-writing opposed to factual truth. Now this double identification forms a category-mistake of the first order. For history-writing is not a record of fact—of what "really happened"—but a discourse that claims to be a record of fact. Nor is fiction-writing a tissue of free inventions but a discourse that claims freedom of invention. The antithesis lies not in the presence or absence of truth value but of the commitment to truth value.

The difference between truth value and truth claim is fundamental. If the title to history-writing hinged on the correspondence to the truth—the historicity of the things written about—then a historical text would automatically forfeit or change its status on the discovery that it contained errors or imbalances or guesses and fabrications passed off as verities. Also, its historiographic character would come and go according to historiosophic fashion. But that is not the case, or else there would hardly be any works of history left and librarians would spend most of their time shuttling books between the nonfiction and the fiction shelves. Thucydides and Gibbon and even von Ranke of *wie es eigentlich gewesen* memory have all been caught out or challenged by their successors, but no one would consider relegating them to a genre other than the historical. Whatever its faults, real or imagined, bad historiography does not yet make fiction. For if fiction contrasts with fact, it contrasts even more sharply with fallacy and falsity, which are value judgments passable on factual reporting alone. Falling between fallacy and falsity, therefore, *bad* historiography is bad *historiography*: no more, no less.

Nor does fiction-writing turn on the fictionality of its object. Does the St. Petersburg location of a Dostoevsky novel or the reference of *War and Peace* to historical personages consign them to a genre different from that of a work wholly born of fantasy? Would the discovery that many a Jamesian tale sprang from a piece of dinner-party gossip, or even that some novelistic dialogue replicates a conversation overheard by the author, generate any second thoughts about its category? Or would it be appropriate to mark Dostoevsky's image of St. Petersburg for accuracy, either absolutely or relative to Andrey Biely's? Even where a writer of fiction adheres to the facts, his adherence and the world thereby rendered make different sense from the historian's, because he could always do otherwise. What opposes fiction to historiography is not the writer's breach or avoidance but his independence of factuality: the built-in license to create a world as one thinks fit, which includes the right to bridle or flaunt that license.

Both historiography and fiction are genres of writing, not bundles of fact or nonfact in verbal shape. In either case, then, it all boils down to the rules of the writing game, namely, to the premises, conventions, and undertakings that attach to the discourse as an affair between writer and audience. What kind of contract binds them together? What does the writer stand committed to? What is the audience supposed to assume? What do both sides expect historiography (or fiction) to be and do? This is the question. And as a question bearing on a communicative transaction, it can never be answered a priori. Suppose the account given by the Bible of David's rise has been stamped by later research as false (or true or indeterminate). This would not in the least affect the generic status of the tale, unless it can also be established that the original parties to the discourse were equally aware of the tale's truth value and would consider its determination a sine qua non of acceptance.[18] Otherwise we have at most ascertained the historical worth of the data but not the historiographic force of their representation. The former is a matter of objective factuality ("Did it happen or not?") and therefore subject to a yes-or-no answer; the latter is a matter of sociocultural judgment of factuality and hence infinitely variable according to context.

It is a pity that this distinction has been so rarely observed in biblical study, with little to choose between "nonliterary" and "literary" approaches. In both, the mechanical leap from source (true/untrue, probable/improbable) to discourse (historiography/fiction) produces one non sequitur after another. Equally fallacious, because unmindful of convention and its variability, are the attempts to distinguish fictional from historiographic writing by their form. Gunkel thus launched his whole school on a wild goose chase by his medley of oppositions: *oral* vs. *written, reporter* vs. *eyewitness, poetry* vs. *prose,* as well as the more contentual *incredible* vs. *credible* or *private* vs. *public.* The same holds true of the more sophisticated criteria exercised by modern criticism, which Alter again best represents. He starts, reasonably enough, by insisting on the qualitative difference between works "closely bound to the known historical facts" and others that present "an independent fictional invention" (p. 24). But soon the contrast shifts its ground beyond recognition, on both flanks and along assorted lines.

On the one hand, historiography is no longer identified by its adherence to the *known* historical facts but to the *real* facts (whether or not known to the original participants in the communication act) and/or, shifting (with

Schneidau) from factual to compositional grounds, by its "irregular, 'metonymic' quality" (p. 42). Such substitute criteria are arbitrary and indeed empirically invalid, as well as inconsistent. How, if not by anachronistic hindsight, can historical discourse be defined in terms of its perfect correspondence to its source? And why in the world should the historian conceive of the source, history itself, as describing an irregular rather than a regular or any other movement? All absolutist requirements (truth, irregularity) clash head-on with the relativist spirit of convention. And it is a mystery how Alter, his practice usually notable for entering into the spirit of the text, came to forget this principle.

First defined in terms of invention, correspondingly, Alter's "fiction" often comes to manifest itself in a variety of other features: individuation and realistic psychology, above all, but also thematic shaping, play of language, and conscious artistry in general. All these features do not just specify or subdivide the original criterion of invention. Rather, they sometimes appear as derivative manifestations and sometimes as independent markers of fictionality. Due to "the privilege of invention," for example, the David cycle transmutes "history into fiction" through such measures as imaginative dialogue and characterization (pp. 36–37). Whereas the book of Esther's fairy-tale plot and schematic neatness reveals it as a "comic fantasy" (p. 34). The reasoning may thus go either way, from or to inventiveness.

Unfortunately, all these are neither necessary nor sufficient conditions of fictionality. Not necessary, because fiction is the most protean of literary genres. As Henry James puts it:

> The house of fiction has not one window but a million—a number of possible windows not to be reckoned, rather; every one of which has been pierced, or is still pierceable, in its vast front by the need of the [artist's] individual vision and by the pressure of the individual will. . . . He and his neighbours are watching the same show, but one seeing more where the other sees less, one seeing black where the other sees white, one seeing big where the other sees small, one seeing coarse where the other sees fine. And so on, and so on . . . . The spreading field, the human scene, is the "choice of subject"; the pierced aperture, either broad and balconied or slit-like and low-browed, is the "literary form."[19]

Coming from a great dogmatist, a theorist-novelist with an axe to grind, this declaration of boundless freedom and variety tells the whole story. From some windows, the qualities invoked by Schneidau, Alter, and others, like the Gunkel school, would certainly look attractive. But the house of fiction equally accommodates their opposites: flat, stylized, and archetypal characterization, whether in the manner of Fielding or Dickens; analogical ("musical") at odds with metonymic unfolding, as in the modern novel;

thematic shallowness in the interests of plot (the adventure story) or play (comedy, romance); pedestrian if not graceless language, as often in Hardy; even lapses of artistic control, to which some of the greatest novelists are liable; and what not. So fiction could hardly be born in a narrative that specializes in its nonconstant features.

Nor are those features sufficient conditions of fiction. They can all be encountered in historiography as well, even if we exclude all its so-called primitive varieties to start with the father of empirical history. Are Thucydides' heroes less individualized than the Bible's? His set (and made-up) speeches less revealing? His themes less serious? His overall organization—with its well-known resemblance to tragedy—less masterful? He is very much different, of course, but not on the lines marked by such criteria, in whose light he would be numbered among the originators of the art of fiction. The same holds true for Edward Gibbon's story of the Roman Empire or, in our own day, Garret Mattingly's *The Defeat of the Spanish Armada* (1959), a work of the highest scholarly distinction and a master-piece of historical narrative. Here is an evaluation of his achievement by a fellow professional who also happens to be an expert on the craft of history writing:

> Mattingly believed that though history may be about any number of things—barrel staves and prevailing winds and cannons, canon law and the speed of posts and cryptography—it is also, perhaps it is mainly, about men and women and children, sometimes of necessity considered as aggregates, but often also considered as persons. But if a historian deals with men as persons, he must concern himself with human character. He must bring to play on the understanding of men of whom, in the nature of things historical, the record grants him only fragmen-tary glimpses, all the resources afforded him by his systematic knowledge, his experience of life, his introspection, and such wisdom as God gave him.
>
> The historical record which is all too exiguous is also paradoxically all too full. In order to make human character stand clear of the clutter of routine action which filled the lives of Renaissance men as it fills ours, Mattingly had to practice the art of discerning and reporting the tell-ing detail, the illuminating incident, the revelatory remark.[20]

Note how many of Alter's measures of fictionality are invoked here to define Mattingly's professional excellence as a historian. To say the very least, historiography as well as fiction is a house of a million windows, but all giving on the real world.

With the postulated conditions of fictionality devoid of either necessary or sufficient power, what remains to warrant the ascription of fictionality to the Bible? Apart from its empirical inadequacy, the argument from struc-tural properties also falls into circularity. Consider the strange fortunes of this line of approach in recent times. It all began with Erich Auerbach's appeal to criteria like the agents' "stamp of individuality" or "contradictory motives" or anomalous careers to demonstrate the historical nature of the Bible's storytelling (*Mimesis,* pp. 11–17). Schneidau then applauds Auerbach's idea and criteria, but inadvertently associates them with his own claim that Scripture marks "the birth of a new kind of *historicized fiction,* moving steadily away from the motives and habits of the world of legend and myth" (emphasis added; p. 215). Still, he qualifies this divergence by affirming that "the presence of fiction as a live tradition in the West has its paradoxical generation in the Old Testament's fanatical insistence on historical truth" (pp. 277–78): the Bible would appear to have inspired rather than inaugurated the age of fiction, and even this only by way of paradox. Alter in turn takes up Schneidau's point, but in its extreme form (including the concept of "historicized fiction") and with the reservation that Schneidau's "stress falls on the historicizing, though the fiction deserves equal attention" (p. 25). At the end of the road, then, the features invoked by Auerbach to celebrate the Bible's historicality, if not historicity proper, have transformed into markers of fictionality.

Worked both ways, these supposedly distinctive features work neither way. In their light, one simply cannot tell fictional from historical narrative—still less, fiction from history within the narrative—since they may be equally present in both, equally absent, equally present and absent in varying combinations. So, to the possible disappointment of shortcut seekers, may all other stylistic and compositional features—not excluding factuality versus invention itself. For, as already suggested, fiction may incorporate as many facts as it pleases, but still owes no allegiance to the commitments and constraints binding on a historical equivalent. Obversely, what makes fictional and breaks historical writing is not the presence of invented material—inevitable in both—but the privilege and at will the flaunting of free invention. To develop chronicle into history, after all, the historian must supply a great many missing links—causal connections, national drives, personal motives and characteristics—and the imaginative gap-filling will remain acceptable as long as it operates within the limits of whatever counts as the rules of evidence. Therefore, to demonstrate that the biblical writers allowed themselves some latitude in the treatment of their materials is to demonstrate nothing much about their genre, unless that exercise of invention appeals and amounts to the total license of fictionalizing rather than to the constrained license of historicizing. And while even the first point still needs to be effectively demonstrated, the second is undemonstrable (and untrue).

If this is the case with a prime variable like invention, then others leave the text featuring them even more hopelessly indeterminate between fictional and historical narrative. Individual character-drawing, storytelling posture or pattern, metonymic sequence, richness of detail, credibility: always available and always reversible, none of these has anything like a cutting edge in the discrimination of genre. The sooner we lay to rest the illusion that the matter can be settled by argument from such inherent properties, the better shall we protect ourselves against the rest of the loose thinking into which this crux lures the unwary. The tendency to mix truth value and truth claim, source (the nature of the materials) and discourse (their working in context), standards of literariness, especially literary excellence, and marks of fictionality—all this is only aggravated by the optimistic belief that "the difference between legend and history is in most cases easily perceived by a reasonably experienced reader" (*Mimesis,* p. 16). Surely, the fact that experienced readers have arrived at conclusions opposed to Auerbach's, even by reference to his own standards, proves the very opposite. There are simply no universals of historical vs. fictive form.

Nothing on the surface, that is, infallibly marks off the two genres. As modes of discourse, history and fiction make *functional* categories that may remain constant under the most assorted *formal* variations and are distinguishable only by their overall sense of purpose. For a miniature illustration, think of the Robbing of the Poor Man's Ewe-Lamb in 2 Samuel 12. After the Bathsheba affair, Nathan recounts the tale to David and David fulminates against the rich man's rapacity, whereupon Nathan springs on him the proverbial "You are the man!" Accordingly, as one purpose gives way to another—seeking redress for an anonymous sufferer to passing sentence on the king—the tale transforms from the history of an injustice to a fictional parable of injustice. Nothing in the discourse has changed in reversal—not a word, let alone a structure—except the informing principle. All the parts take their generic orientation from the coordinates of the whole alone. To establish either mode, therefore, one must relate the forms of narrative to the functions that govern them in context and assign them their role and meaning. In communication, typology makes no sense unless controlled by teleology. And teleology is a matter of inference from clues planted in and around the writing, extending from title and statements of intent to conventions of representation that signal the appropriate narrative contract in the given milieu.

So does the Bible belong to the historical or the fictional genre? The mist enveloping the question once dissipated to reveal its communicative bearing, the answer becomes obvious. Of course the narrative is historiographic, inevitably so considering its teleology and incredibly so considering its time and environment. Everything points in this direction. Without going either into the external evidence that has led to such a change in the assessment of the Bible's authenticity or into the details of the internal evidence, let us glance at some broad features of the art of narrative.

As regards cultural value, temporal scope, and persuasive strategy, this art of narrative has no parallel in ancient times. Alone among Orientals and Greeks, it addresses a people defined in terms of their past and commanded to keep its memory alive—which ordinance, judging by the numerous retrospects performed by biblical characters within the drama itself, they religiously observed. (The Hebrew historian, as Arnaldo Momigliano puts it, "only gave an authoritative version of what everybody was supposed to know."[21]) By incorporating the definition and command and observance, the narrative not only illegitimates all thought of fictionality on pain of excommunication. It also uniquely internalizes its own rules of communication, whereby the remembrance of the past devolves on the present and determines the future. It is this cultural imperative that accounts for what a distinguished historian has recently termed "the greatest surprise" in the whole story of history writing. It explains how there suddenly emerged a people "more obsessed with history than any other nation that has ever existed. . . . It was this historical memory that made Israel a people"; why "they stand alone among the people of the ancient world in having the story of their beginnings and their primitive state as clear as this in their folk-memory," in creating the history of a nation and even of humanity itself; whence, in short, this "pocket-size example of the very rise of historiography."[22]

Nor does the Bible content itself with laying down and acting upon its unique rules of discourse. It goes out of its way to anchor them fast in the narrative texture and composition. This involves another landmark in the development of history writing. For if the rules conferred on historiography an unprecedented importance and scope, then the anchorage revolutionized its presentational methods and rhetoric. I have already indicated that the Bible's claim to truth-telling signifies more than the label one may choose to put on the story told. Methodologically speaking, however, the Bible is even the first to anticipate the appeal to the surviving record of the past that characterizes modern history-telling. Such relics abound on the narrative surface itself, appearing as facts to be interpreted and brought into pattern. Recall how often customs are elucidated, ancient names and current sayings traced back to their origins, monuments and fiats assigned a concrete reason as well as a slot in history, persons and places and pedigrees specified beyond immediate needs, written records like the Book of Yashar or the royal annals explicitly invoked. In terms of communicative design and force, it is the novelty of the gesture toward historicity that matters. Whatever the truth value of the references and explanations made, their very making strengthens the truth claim by anchoring the discourse in public and accessible features of reality. "You see how the traces of time that fall within our observation make perfect sense within our account of time," the narrator seems to be saying to his audience. Here, then, the novelties of method and rhetoric coincide: the distributed parts enhance the credibility of the whole, the present witnesses lend an air of truth to the evocation of the past from which they issued.

The new mode and rhetoric of historiography are themselves means to an end that any hint of invention would put in danger. Were the narrative written or read as fiction, then God would turn from the lord of history into a creature of the imagination, with the most disastrous results. The shape of time, the rationale of monotheism, the foundations of conduct, the national sense of identity, the very right to the land of Israel and the hope of deliverance to come: all hang in the generic balance. Hence the Bible's determination to sanctify and compel literal belief in the past. It claims not just the status of history but, as Erich Auerbach rightly maintains, of *the* history—the one and only truth that, like God himself, brooks no rival. Since the principle has given rise to such confusion and since some of its finer implications for the art of storytelling will emerge later, it is well to be very blunt about it now. Suppose the Creation narrative elicited from the audience the challenge "But the Babylonians tell a different story!" or the Exodus cycle met with the protest "But the Egyptians deny the whole thing!" Would the biblical narrator just shrug his shoulders, as any self-respecting novelist would do? One inclined to answer in the affirmative would have to make fictional sense of all the overwhelming evidence to the contrary; and I do not see how even a confirmed anachronist would go about it with any show of reason. This way madness lies—and I mean interpretive, teleological as well as theological madness.

But, it may be objected, how does the narrator's claim to historicity accord with the incorporation of material not just undocumented but undocumentable: the hidden acts of God, the secret thoughts of all the participants, the abundant dialogue scenes? The very query betrays an anachronistic thinking, with a twofold confusion of source and discourse. First, the linkage of history writing to documentation is a rather late arrival, born of an empirical spirit that has not escaped criticism even among moderns and certainly fails to answer to the sense of the real in antiquity. Even if the standard were universally valid, its application might deny the Bible the name of history telling but not the claim (and effect) of truth telling; and it is this claim rather than the label attached to it that dissociates record from fiction.

In the Bible's sociocultural context, second, truth claim and free access to information go together owing to a discourse mechanism so basic that no contemporary would need to look around for it—the appeal to divine inspiration. "The Hebrew historian never claimed to be a prophet," says

Momigliano (*Essays in Historiography,* p. 195). This is true, for interesting reasons to which we shall come in due course. But neither did he disclaim the prophet's range of knowledge, as Herodotus and for that matter Nehemiah in effect did when they introduced themselves by name and offered eyewitness or otherwise restricted accounts of the past, or as Paul explicitly did in his frequent distinctions between the Lord's word and his own (e.g., "What I am saying I say not with the Lord's authority but as a fool" in 2 Cor 11:17). Anonymity in ancient narrative validates supernatural powers of narration; and in Israelite culture, which not only institutionalized prophecy but invested its writings with canonical authority, the narrator's claim to omniscience dovetails rather than conflicts with his claim to historicity. It is no accident that the narrative books from Joshua to Kings fall under the rubric of Former Prophets.

Reserving the detailed argument for the next chapter, I want only to point out that here again "literary" and "nonliterary" approaches strangely meet. Like most people, even religious biblical scholars have always found it awkward to reconcile the doctrine of the inspired word with the factual errors detected in Holy Writ by science and common sense. Hence both the increasing repudiation of the doctrine in the name of historicity and the acrobatics performed in the desperate attempt to salvage it while giving the natural its due. Various literary approaches manifest the same difficulty with the concept of inspiration, but often for the opposed reason: it stands in the way of treating the text not so much as history but as fiction. To Gros Louis, for example, a major obstacle to "studying the Bible as literature" consists in the tradition that it "is divinely inspired. One result of this view is that there is no room for the literary notion of the persona" ("Some Methodological Considerations," pp. 16–17) or, in other words, of the authorially devised speaker who assumes a prophetlike stance.

In either case, however, the problem arises from the misidentification of history writing with historical truth and, correspondingly, of reading postulates with the reader's beliefs. Inspiration is primarily nothing but a rule that governs the communication between writer and reader, licensing the access to privileged material (e.g., thoughts) that would otherwise remain out of bounds and giving all material the stamp of authority. As a compositional and hermeneutic premise of a distinctive kind, it neither substitutes for empirical evidence about what happened in history nor renounces the title to historicity. Inspiration does not substitute for empirical evidence, of course, because it entails a claim to supernatural knowledge that would outrank it in reliability. So where the two diverge, we must each make our own choice or compromise. But if as seekers for the truth, professional or amateur, we can take or leave the truth claim of inspiration, then as readers we simply must take it—just like any other biblical premise or convention, from the existence of God to the sense borne by specific words—or else invent our own text. And to take it means to read the Bible on its own historiographic terms, suspending all the "how do you know?" questions one would automatically address to a historical narrative playing by documentary rules.

This leaves us all free to reject the Bible's inspiration as a principle of faith and, as scholars, to challenge its figures, statements, astronomy, chronology, even historiography.[23] To guard against uncontrolled anachronism, however, it is well to bear in mind that in doing so one is operating from a source-oriented rather than a discourse-oriented position, imposing one's own standards and concerns on a text that would hardly welcome such attentions. There is a world of difference between approaching the Bible as suspect information and as supernatural communication, as a window to and as the last word on history: the first approach is instrumental, the second interpretive.

That literary analysts should perpetrate such shifts in orientation, let alone view the doctrine as a threat to their interests, is all the more surprising in view of their presumed familiarity with a wide range of convention. Why would it not occur to anyone to check Jane Austen's dialogues or interior monologues or descriptions of persons and places against the remains of the past? Surely because one assumes that, like all novelists, she enjoys the privilege of omniscience denied to tellers in everyday life. She invokes different rules, we say. But if it is convention that renders Jane Austen immune from all charges of fallacy and falsity, it is convention that likewise puts the Bible's art of narrative beyond their reach. For the biblical narrator also appeals to the privilege of omniscience—so that he no more speaks in the writer's ordinary voice than Jane Austen does in hers, but exactly as a persona raised high above him—with one crucial difference in convention. Omniscience in modern narrative attends and signals fictionality, while in the ancient tradition it not only accommodates but also guarantees authenticity.

As a rule of narrative communication, inspiration amounts to omniscience exercised on history: the tale's claim to truth rests on the teller's God-given knowledge. The prophet assumes this stance (or persona) explicitly, the storyteller implicitly but none the less authoritatively. And its assumption enables him to bring to bear on his world (and his audience) what would elsewhere count as the poetic license of invention without paying the price in truth claim. Herein lies one of the Bible's unique rules: under the aegis of ideology, convention transmutes even invention into the stuff of history, or rather obliterates the line dividing fact from fancy in communication. So every word is God's word. The product is neither fiction nor historicized fiction nor fictionalized history, but historiography pure and uncompromising. If its licenses yet open up possibilities for literary art, they are built into the fabric of the narrative by a special dispensation: a logic of writing equally alien to the world-centered anachronisms of historians and the novel-centered anachronisms of literary approaches.[24]

Form and Doctrine

A revealing measure of the state of the art is how often the extremes meet in the wrong places. They do so, in fact, on more grounds than the affirmation of their disciplinary self-sufficiency and the Bible's fictionality. Thus, literary approaches tend to concentrate on questions of form and their antagonists on contentual and above all on doctrinal matters. Yet behind this divergence of interest there frequently lurks a common assumption: that the establishment of the Bible as religious and committed writing would disconfirm its eligibility for literary analysis, and vice versa. Widely implicit in the silences and inconsistencies of critical practice, this assumption is at times straightforwardly voiced.

Here are two opposed statements recently made by critics whose performance shows more than a nodding acquaintance with the concerns of the opposition. "What is literary about the Bible at all?" James Kugel asks. "Certainly it does not identify itself as literature, and often such [God-oriented] self-definition as does occur seems clearly to . . . suppose a relationship between speaker and hearer which, we somehow feel, is double-crossed by being looked at *as* literature, as artful composition, as anything more than a faithful and naive recording."[25] The emphasis on "the sacredness of the Bible," Gros Louis asserts, "must, I believe, be rejected by any student of literature," and the author's "goals in writing for his contemporary audience and his religious convictions play a small role indeed in literary criticism" ("Some Methodological Considerations," pp. 13, 16). Both the either/or premise and the operational conclusions drawn from it seem to me false. But they are importantly false, again, and a closer look at them brings out some further characteristics of biblical narrative.

The premise itself need not detain us long. That biblical scholars entertain an extreme "art for art's sake" view of literature, as if it were a machine for pure amusement, only indicates the need for wider horizons of reading. But it is so odd to find literary critics adopting the same position in the name or interests of form that one senses the influence of the New Criticism and the old polemics. After all, they must be aware that literature and thought or use have seldom been divorced in theory, rarely in practice, even more rarely outside lyrical poetry. The question is how rather than whether the literary coexists with the social, the doctrinal, the philosophical.

In ancient times, the two were so closely related as to become indistinguishable. Whatever the differences separating Greek from Oriental culture and polytheism from monotheism, all invested the poet with the mantle of inspiration or prophecy; all drew his writings into the center of ritual; all appear at their imaginative best in works of a sacred or national character. The effects of this linkage have survived all historical and artistic changes and are still very much with us, most often in a secular guise, to the chagrin of aesthetes. "The history of aesthetics," Wellek and Warren insist, "might almost be summarized as a dialectic in which the thesis and counter-thesis are Horace's *dulce* and *utile:* poetry is sweet and useful. Either adjective separately represents a polar misconception with regard to the function of poetry."[26]

One hardly knows what examples to pick. The endless harping on Horace's own formula in the Renaissance and Neoclassicism, or on Aristotle's dictum that poetry is more serious and philosophical than history? The Romantic conception of the poet as prophet and imaginative knower? The "Back to reality!" slogan that eternally motivates literary revolutions? Matthew Arnold's view of literature as "a criticism of life" and the successor of religion? I. A. Richards's recommendation of poetry as emotional therapy? Jacques Derrida's proposal to treat philosophy as a literary genre, and vice versa? Or the far more prevalent recognition of art by moderns, including for example the Russian Formalists, as a social institution? And as for religious art proper, names like Dante and Donne and Milton and Dostoevsky will be enough to suggest that the Bible could find itself in worse company. Not to belabor the obvious, I shall just add one explanatory note. The strange sight of literary believers in form disclaiming interest in the thematic material and load shaped by that form is representative only in one way: literary theory has not yet fashioned the tools for making *poetic* sense of ideas and ideology. The poetics of the Bible yields some vital clues to the interworking; and to this we shall have ample occasion to return.

On thematic-social grounds, at any rate, one argument alone might conceivably justify the exclusion of biblical narrative from the literary sphere, namely, that it makes a didactic work. This claim runs through traditional scholarship, but in formulations so protean and loose that one can seldom tell what exactly it means. And it may bear two very different meanings.

One is that the Bible constitutes ideological writing, anchored in a determinate world picture or value system and concerned to impress it on the audience. If this is the claim, then it amounts to nothing more than the either-literature-or-doctrine premise of which we have already disposed. Far from *sui generis,* the Bible then falls squarely under the universal rule of representation, whereby the represented and the real world always interrelate. In particular, all narratives imply and many advocate some ideology-bound model of reality—sacred or secular, conventional or revolutionary, historical or atemporal, monolithic or dialectical, aristocratic, bourgeois, Marxist, rationalistic, heroic, mythical, aesthetic, and what not. For all that some schools of art and theory have preached to the contrary, it remains a universal of writing that representation is never dissociated from evaluation. If the Bible is ideologically singular—and I believe so—then its singularity lies in the world view projected, together with the rhetoric devised to bring it home. And as long as we adhere to the text's self-definition as religious literature with such and such singularities, we need not even submit to the dictate of identifying ourselves as religious or secular readers. Those who play by the Bible's rules of communication to the best of their ability can keep their opinions to themselves; only those who make up their own rules may be required to lay their ideological cards on the table.

But the claim may also assume a stronger form, namely, that the Bible belongs to that extreme variety of ideological writing known as didactic. Strictly defined, the didactic genre moves beyond commitment to self-immolation: it not only advances a doctrine but also ruthlessly subordinates the whole discourse—the plot, the characters, the arena, the language, their ordering and interlinkage—to the exigencies of indoctrination. Or, in Elder Olson's words:

> The principle of didactic poetry is its doctrine or thesis. . . . Everything in the work mediately or immediately exists only to prove the thesis and is absolutely determined by it. . . . The allegorical incident happens, not because it is necessary or probable in the light of other events, but because a certain doctrinal subject must have a certain doctrinal predicate; . . . and whatever emotional quality or force it may have is determined rather by the emotional attitude which the doctrine must inculcate toward a certain object than by the context of action in which it occurs. Allegorical characters are what they are because we must view virtue or vice or whatever is involved in a certain light.[27]

If valid, therefore, the argument that the Bible is didactic would indeed clinch the issue, since the principle of total subordination leaves no room for other interests, least of all of the literary kind, by nature mistrusted and at best cheerfully sacrificed to the pointing of the moral. But is it valid?

As an empirical question, fortunately, this must and can be resolved by appeal to the Bible's structure and range of interests. Does the didacticist hypothesis explain the features of the discourse? Now, if biblical narrative is didactic, then it has chosen the strangest way to go about its business. For the narrator breaks every law in the didacticist's decalogue. Anything like preaching from the narrative pulpit is conspicuous for its absence. So is its immemorial mate and nearest equivalent—black-and-white delineation of agents, motives, causes, processes. Instead of polarizing the reader's emotional and ethical response in line with some preconceived scheme of values, the Bible habitually generates ambivalence: consider Jacob, Aaron, Gideon, Saul, David, Solomon, Jehu . . . . Rather than aligning divine election and moral stature, it usually foregrounds their discordance. Rather than imposing an automatic or at least intelligible system of rewards and punishments, it undermines every rule of thumb, every simple proportion. Its commissions even radicalize the unsettling effect of its doctrinal omissions, by diverting notice, as it were, from the all-important focus of interest. The characterization is complex, the motives mixed, the plot riddled with gaps and enigmas, behavior unpredictable, surprises omnipresent, the language packed and playful, the registration of reality far more governed by the real and the realistic than by the ideal. In short, where didacticism would insist on subordination, one encounters proliferation; where the discourse should move in a straight line, it weaves a net; where propositions should readily follow from premises, the premises themselves often remain ambiguous or double-edged and the propositions become multiple; where transparence is expected, we have to struggle with opacity on all levels, from word to world to thought. Far from falling under some thesis detachable from its illustration, therefore, the narrative structure renders any such detachment an act of violence.

The closer one reads, moreover, the more do these apparent offenses and incongruities prove to harmonize with the underlying world view. Consider, to mention but a few general coordinates, the principle of free choice, which marks the birth of ethics and of the most complicating force in moral psychology; the total absence of paragons and the scarcity of embodied vices; the prophetic complaints about divine lenience and inconsistency; the respect for the demands of history, whose ragged contours further preclude schematic organization. To my mind, all this shows beyond doubt that the whole idea of didacticism is alien, if not antipathetic, to the spirit of Israelite storytelling and has been imported from later philosophical and religious traditions that it would reject. But the choice presents itself as clear-cut and inescapable: the biblical narrator is either an incompetent didacticist or an artful ideologist.

But doesn't this vindicate the claims of "form"? Again, it depends on what that all-inclusive catchword is supposed to mean; and in the meanings actually assigned to it by the literary approaches, the Bible's formal shape no more establishes its literariness than the ideology rules it out. Lest the statement be mistaken for an antiformalist bias, let me emphasize that this includes the dimensions of biblical form which would (and, as will appear, do) play a central role in a poetics. For example:

1. Temporal ordering, especially where the actual sequence diverges from the chronological.
2. Analogical design: parallelism, contrast, variation, recurrence, symmetry, chiasm.
3. Point of view, e.g., the teller's powers and manipulations, shifts in perspective from external to internal rendering or from narration to monologue and dialogue (often signaled by elements so minute as names and other referring terms).
4. Representational proportions: scene, summary, repetition.
5. Informational gapping and ambiguity.
6. Strategies of characterization and judgment.
7. Modes of coherence, in units ranging from a verse to a book.
8. The interplay of verbal and compositional pattern.

Having pursued these techniques longer than most, I would be the last to slight their importance. The point is rather that this importance is even greater than it may seem: all these are features (and some even universals) of narrative, not differentiae of literary narrative. In varying combinations, they occur in discourse that nobody would regard as literary, including pure didacticism and unadorned history-writing and the stories we tell one another in everyday life. It is precisely their availability to all and sundry that divests them of typological value.

At this level, in general, no element of form has any intrinsic (or empirical) claim to literary status. Since Aristotle, various formal features have been elevated to such a defining position—causal sequence, figurative language, patterns of similarity or equivalence—but none has retained it. Sooner or later, theory discovered that their presence does not suffice to confer literariness, nor their absence to deny it. There are of course reasons for the eternal quest for distinctively literary forms, notably ease of identification and lack of familiarity with the workings of so-called ordinary discourse. Yet since all these quests have turned out not only fruitless but doomed to futility by the protean nature of communication, it is high time to abandon misnomers like "literary form or device." (Not that they are easy to resist: I have often found my terminology, even at its most neutral, "literarized" by colleagues and students who slipped back in all good faith into the comfortable equation of form with artistic form.) The adjective "literary" in these phrases relates, contingently, to the discipline rather than to the object. It just happens, for significant historical reasons having to do with the prestige of the arts, that literary criticism has thought longest and knows most about the formal structure of discourse. Hence, as with the ambiguity of "literary approach" itself, even the universally applicable tools and competences of the method have come to seem distinctive properties of the thing methodized. This deflection of meaning has given rise to no end of trouble and incongruity. It is ironic, for example, that all those who invest too much in the differentiating power of form oppose it in effect to content. However hotly the separation may be denied in theory—and nobody would deny it more hotly than the adherents of the New Criticism—one reinstates it by the very appeal to patterns that accommodate and organize the most heterogeneous materials. The whole line proves self-defeating as well as untenable.

At any rate, if the Bible's particular materials supposedly fail to count and their forms turn out universal, what remains to justify the literary approach? The missing term is evidently the concept of functionality, the purpose or effect that informs (and, from the reader's side, explains) the given organization of the given materials. In the absence of a clear notion of the means and the ends and their interplay in biblical communication, however, not even a sympathetic invocation of this concept on behalf of the literary approach-through-form would salvage it. It is certainly arguable that forms like analogy serve a poetic function: Roman Jakobson might say that they operate to call notice to the design of the message.[28] But even in his scheme the poetic is only one of several coexisting or rival functions and may appear equally in an advertisement and a Shakespearian sonnet. What determines literariness is not the mere presence but the dominance of the poetic function, the control it exerts over all the rest. In the advertisement, for example, the sound pattern ultimately functions to increase the appeal (and sales) of the object announced, not, as in the sonnet, the perceptibility of the words. By this standard, none of the forms mentioned qualifies as poetic regulator.

Chiasm having recently gained popularity as one of the indisputable "literary devices," consider the chiastic pattern that rounds off Samuel:

a_1 Saul's sin against the Gibeonites and its collective punishment (2 Sam 21:1–14)
b_2 David's heroes and their exploits (21:15–22)
c_1 David's psalm (22:1–51)
c_2 David's psalm (23:1–7)
b_2 David's heroes and their exploits (23:8–39)
a_2 David's sin against the census taboo and its collective punishment (24:8–39)

The chief goal of this segment remains informational or memorial; and, pleasing as the ring composition is, it also helps to bind together a miscellany relegated to the end. It is suggestive that the most conspicuous and large-scale instance of chiasm in Samuel applies to a hodgepodge that has the least pretensions to literariness and, even with the artificial design thrown in, hardly coheres as more than an appendix. Granted that form can produce or imply an artistic function, it still cannot enthrone one regardless of context, which includes the matter enformed and the rules governing their union.

The Drama of Reading

To gather up the threads. Biblical narrative emerges as a complex, because multifunctional, discourse. Functionally speaking, it is regulated by a set of three principles: ideological, historiographic, and aesthetic. How they *co*operate is a tricky question, to which we shall soon come back. But that they do operate is beyond question. For at some points—or from some viewpoints—we find each laid bare, as it were, asserting its claims and exerting its peculiar influence on narrative selection and arrangement.

The ideological principle thus leaps to the eye in the segments of law interspersed (say) throughout the story of the Exodus, or in divine and prophetic moralizing, or in thematic structures like promise and fulfillment, sin and retribution. Less obviously, it comes to the fore in the occasional modulations into the genre of exemplum, with its flattened or anonymous or collective hero and its transparent message.

The historiographic function surfaces in the frequent dating, in the commentary on names and places, in the aetiological-looking tales, in the genealogies and other items or even patterns, like chronology, that seem to resist assimilation to any higher order of coherence. For this surface resistance bids defiance to any control other than the intrinsic value of factuality. At a more commanding level, the text even underlines the operation of the principle through metahistorical references—to acts of commemoration, written or ritualistic, to directives to remember the past and transmit it to "thy son and thy son's son," to scenes where characters hark back to the past in relation to the present or the future. All these, again, serve as nodes or notices of larger configurations working below the surface to the same end: recording for its own sake.

As to the aesthetic principle, we have already encountered a good many of its more salient manifestations. There is the abundant material that, without officially appearing as fiction, yet bears the marks of invention and fulfills the roles of imaginative enhancement and probing of reality associated with it. Cutting across the whole Bible, this includes a variety of privileged ("inspired") and in some sense private material: dialogue, motivation, interior speech, heavenly counsel, unwitnessed or even, like Creation, unwitnessable events. There are also the numerous forms of organization just discussed, which cannot guarantee literariness by their very presence but assume new significance in a functional perspective. For their regular occurrence bespeaks and generates a distinctive sense of form that will not be reduced to terms other than aesthetic, just as the lumps of ideology and history may lend themselves to coordination but not to elimination. Symmetry, repetition, wordplay, verbal chains, shifts in perspective or from prose to verse are all cases in point. Thus viewed, even the ring composition imposed on the hodgepodge ending of Samuel grows suggestive, because it contributes nothing to either doctrine or register. On the contrary, it has provoked objections on this very ground. Noting how the complex of public trouble (my a_1, a_2) gets split by the insertion of the hero complex (b_1, b_2) and the latter in turn split by the hymn complex (c_1, c_2), one critic asserts that the text must have met with an accident: "It is incredible that the writer who added the appendix to the book should have so incongruously separated what belongs together."[29] Incongruous, perhaps; but incredible only if you take a gesture toward chiastic composition, with a view to redeeming a sorry stretch of discourse, for an offense of decomposition. The appendix, in other words, deliberately subordinates expository to aesthetic coherence, business to pleasure.

The greater the issue at stake, the more revealing such sacrifices, preferences, compromises, tense and mobile hierarchies. Once the Bible's antididactic moves are recognized as a policy, we gain an insight into the role played in it by aesthetic rules and codes. The narrator may adjust but rarely abandon them even under heavy pressure from the side of history and ideology. Be the issue ever so important or problematic, he will shun extended commentary, let alone homiletics. He will not schematize character, whatever the risk involved in marring the image of the hero or eliciting sympathy for the villainous or the doomed. He will leave gaps for the reader to puzzle over—non sequiturs, discontinuities, indeterminacies, multiple versions—while fully aware of their disordering effect on the shape and lessons of the past. He will conceal and distribute and process meaning to an extent seldom equalled even by storytellers who could please themselves. None of these "incongruous" choices was forced, few inherited from neighboring cultures. Rather, most were invented and elaborated in the Israelite tradition of narrative, so that the whole strategy cannot have been less than deliberate. Far more eloquent than the recourse to particular forms, in short, is the partiality for complex formation in the teeth of constraints that would dictate ready intelligibility. The biblical narrator is determined to operate as an artist even in the radical sense of courting danger and difficulty where he is most anxious for success as a partisan.

Taken together, these central choices and qualities would already be deemed more than sufficient not only to foreground an aesthetic function but also to make a literary work. He is bold indeed who undertakes to define literature these days, when theorists persuasively argue that it forms an open category, whose members need only bear a family resemblance to one another. One must be even bolder to rush into the fray with the load of another inquiry on one's shoulders. Biblical narrative, fortunately, does not require such boldness, still less any special pleading. For, given the features that we have noted, many conceptions of art and literature converge on it from all sides.

The New Criticism, for instance, would be quick to appreciate the artistic qualities of understatement, ambiguity, wordplay, richness of texture. From the side of the semantic definition of literature, as a mode of discourse characterized by the density and implicitness of its meaning, the analysis of a single narrative would clinch the matter. Students of aesthetics would be impressed by the disdain for the line of least resistance, the pursuit of intricate form and representation in the face of deterrents. Audience-oriented theorists would argue from the decisive part assigned to exegesis by the opaque text. Singling out the imaginative projection of reality, the cultural historian would say that the Bible performed the role of literature for its original community. The literary historian proper would further emphasize the originality of the composition and also the fact that ancient literature flourished without the benefit of a special name. (Greek shows the same lexical gap as Israelite culture—Aristotle himself calls literature "the nameless art" [*Poetics* 1447b]; and the Egyptians had no term even for the determinate genre of narrative, yet they practiced it with no less enthusiasm than the duly named genre of "instruction.") The family-resemblance philosopher would wonder at the ado made about the obvious, and so by this time may some of my readers. To reject this chorus of voices—to which others could be easily added, with the exception of the devotee of "pure" art—is to depopulate the republic of letters.

At the present stage, moreover, my argument—that the Bible exhibits the operation of a strong aesthetic (artistic, literary, poetic) principle—even stops short of what this convergence of views might warrant. It is on the pervasiveness rather than on the occurrence of the principle that my claim of the Bible's literariness rests, and with it my case for poetics.

Literature, in other words, is a mode of discourse, and the mere subsumption under it neither exalts nor diminishes the Bible. It does not even pinpoint the text's focuses, let alone its differentiae. The label matters far less than the features that may justify its application. The aesthetic features having been roughly indicated, therefore, two questions arise about the narrative whole that encloses them. First, what relation do they bear to one another? Second, what relation does the overall aesthetic function bear to the historiographic and the ideological?

Significantly, the two questions themselves prove to be related. The part–whole relations they bring to the fore are governed by the same key strategy of the Bible's narrative discourse: the art of indirection or, from the interpreter's side, the drama of reading. In the first case, this common denominator should by now leap to the eye. Take assorted features like gaps in information, neutral-looking posture, complex character-drawing, silent inventiveness, and verbal density. Apart from their general affinity as aesthetic factors, these combine to produce a narrative that makes more sense as an artful network of linkages than as a sequence of bald statements, and accordingly puts a premium on interpretation. But how the aesthetics of this network pervades and orders the communication as a whole still needs to be traced.

I began by speaking of ideology, historiography, and aesthetics as a trio of functional principles and then went on to outline the distinctive manifestations of each. Left at that, their relationship might seem not just one of loose coexistence but of sharp discord. *In the abstract,* they form natural rivals, with different goals in view and different forms of communication to match. Ideology would above all establish a world view and, if militant, a consensus. It accordingly presses for transparent representation that will (and in didactic writing, does) bring the world into the appropriate doctrinal pattern, schematized in equal disregard for the intractability of historical fact and the ordering niceties of art. Historiography has no eye but for the past: at its quintessential, as in chronicle, it would like nothing better than to tack fact onto fact in an endless procession, marching across all artistic and ideological design. For aesthetics, the play's the thing, ideally (as in abstract painting or the fantastic) with no strings attached to what is, was, or should be. Given free rein, therefore, each would pull in a different direction and either win the tug of war or tear the work apart. The annals of writing manifest the first eventuality in the shape of generic diversity—as in the "pure" examples given—and its cemeteries have buried the victims of the second. The choice lies between easy specialization and demanding coordination.

Coordination itself follows a variety of lines. Just compare Herodotus and Thucydides, analytic and narrative history, *War and Peace* and *I, Claudius* and *Henry Esmond.* The first and most ambitious of large-scale coordinators, the Bible is also the greatest. Considering the assortment of its interests, one marvels at the reconciliation of their claims and the interlacing of their teleologies. The three functional principles meet at a junction where they enter into relations of tense complementarity.[30] Some tension remains, of course, explaining the occasional surfacing of an interest that for a moment appears to have taken charge of the discourse and making for a precarious equilibrium throughout. On the whole, however, the rivals are manipulated into operating as a system, a three-in-one, a unity in variety. What, then, forms the basis of their cooperation?

Part of the secret resides in the twofold bearing of biblical history. On the one hand, this history unfolds a theology in action—one distinctively grounded in God's control and providence, enjoining a remembrance of his wonders from Creation onward, with the Exodus as focal point, and therefore inextricably bound to a sense of the past. As the record of God's lordship and his people's indebtedness, history-writing doubles as a sacred contract, uniquely explaining the processes of time by reference to a covenantal relation with divinity. On the other hand, this history makes a story and therefore not only accommodates but also co-determines the rules of narrative. For instance, its passion for the factual (no matter how assumed) so chimes in with objective storytelling as to render it impossible to disengage the historical from the aesthetic motivation for this strategy. Which of the two accounts for the scarcity of commentary or for the foregrounding of external events? In either display of objectivity, the historian's stance coincides with the crafty exploitation of this stance in justifying an opaque, reticent, multigap discourse. The same convergence of functions shows in other key choices. Is the warts-and-all portraiture due to historical fidelity or artistic complexity? Do the manifold patterns imposed on time—analogy, recurrence, cyclical movement, tit for tat, ending where things have begun—reflect the view of history or the coherence of story? Do the hard details form part of the record of the real or of the rhetoric of realism? Does the paratactic style derive from the logic or from the pose of chronicle writing? Does the genealogy come as a lump of pastness or as an oblique intimation of the future? Does the aetiological tale offer an explanation or contrive a pun under its guise? The means thus work both ways to produce an artful story of history, where the most devious maneuvers may find their legitimation or camouflage and the most recalcitrant-looking items their organization. Divergent in the abstract, the trio dovetail in the novel context fashioned by the Israelite tradition.

This already yields a system of relationships where historiography mediates between ideology and aesthetics.[31] But the interaction goes even further and its rationale much deeper than such indirect linkage might suggest. To begin with, all three purposes share certain requirements that the structure of communication indeed meets. Let us review some of the examples given. Does the avoidance of black-and-white portrayal reflect the historian's scrupulosity, the artist's eye for intricate characterization, or the doctrinal tenet that all men exercise free choice, so that no man can be wholly righteous or wholly evil throughout life? Does the imposition of serial or cyclical form on the march of time bespeak an aesthetics of unity, a history repeating itself, or a God in control of the plot? In regard to the fundamentals of character and action alike, then, the various teleologies converge to issue a joint directive to the storyteller.

No less uniquely, moreover, the shape given to history largely results from the combined pressures of the two other forces. To mention only basic configurations, this is the case with the incessant appeal to divine omnipotence, governed by the ideological imperative of celebrating God's mastership and to some extent by the artistic instinct for tight and marvelous plotting, rather than by the demands of the chronicle. To the Bible, history is an affair between heaven and earth, with the heavenly side figuring as a maker and bent on advertising his makership by imposing his will and order on the normal logic of events before the eyes of humanity. Hence the alignment of divine with artistic pattern-making against earthbound recording. Or, in a related partnership, consider the source of the narrator's imaginative ("poetic") license. It is the theology that confers historical status on normally inaccessible materials, in effect suspending the dichotomy between fact and fiction by investing the teller with the privileges of God-given omniscience. Chronicle thus develops into historiography by rules and to ends opposed to the empirical.

This brings us to the most comprehensive ground on which ideology and aesthetics meet to shape history, and with it the narrative as a whole. They join forces to originate a strategy of telling that casts reading as a drama, interpretation as an ordeal that enacts and distinguishes the human predicament. It is here that the three regulating principles merge into a single poetics, where their interests and formations so coalesce that they can hardly be told apart in the finished message.

To start with ideology, theologians bent on defining the originality of the Bible's world view have rightly singled out features like monotheism, the suppression of myth, the rise of ethics and personal responsibility. But what has generally escaped notice is the shift of ground from existence to epistemology, on which I touched in instancing the posture of omniscience as a revitalized convention. Within the Israelite reality-model, briefly, God stands opposed to humankind not so much in terms of mortality—after the fashion of both Orientals and Greeks—as in terms of knowledge. Nowhere in antiquity does the theme of mortality receive so little attention as in biblical narrative; nowhere does the variable of knowledge assume such a cutting edge and such a dominant role. God is omniscient, man limited, and the boundary impassable.

But how to expound and inculcate this new doctrine? Fortunately, both the pragmatic constraints on exposition and the aesthetic preference for indirection ruled out the discursive treatment to which a modern (or a Greek) thinker would almost automatically resort. The solution devised was no less epoch-making (and its genesis no less mysterious) than the philosophy itself: to build the cognitive antithesis between God and humanity into the structure of the narrative. Not the premises alone but the very composition must bring home the point in and through the reading experience. This exigency calls into sacred play all the choices and techniques mentioned earlier under the rubric of aesthetics, for what they have in common is the effect of twisting, if not blocking, the way to knowledge.[32]

Thus, insofar as knowledge is information, the ubiquity of gaps about character and plot exposes to us our own ignorance: history unrolls as a continuum of discontinuities, a sequence of non sequiturs, which challenge us to repair the omissions by our native wit. Through a mimesis of real-life conditions of inference, we are surrounded by ambiguities, baffled and misled by appearances, reduced to piecing fragments together by trial and error, often left in the dark about essentials to the very end. Insofar as knowledge is true judgment, moreover, the scarcity of commentary forces us to evaluate agent and action by appeal to norms that remain implicit, to clues that may have more than one face, to structures that turn on reconstruction, to voices partial in both senses, to models of character that resist polarization. Insofar as knowledge consists in the relations between part and whole, the piecemeal, secretive storytelling makes at best for difficult unity. Far beyond the normal demands of interpretation and with no parallel in Oriental literature, therefore, the world and the meaning are always hypothetical, subject to change from one stage of the reading *process* to another, and irreducible to any simple formula. With the narrative become an obstacle course, its reading turns into a drama of understanding—conflict between inferences, seesawing, reversal, discovery, and all. The only knowledge perfectly acquired is the knowledge of our limitations. It is by a sustained effort alone that the reader can attain at the end to something of the vision that God has possessed all along: to make sense of the discourse is to gain a sense of being human.

Since it has recently grown fashionable to view all literary works as self-reflexive, with their own meaning patterns as theme, it may be well to dissociate the Bible from this trend by making sure of our ground. Let us glance at the ways in which the narrative validates and reinforces the effects of its fragmentary communication. Having already stressed the weight and originality of the epistemological premises, I will only add now that they are often voiced by the dramatis personae themselves: God, prophet, layman. "Man sees what meets the eye and God sees into the heart" (1 Sam 16:7) is a case in point to which we shall return. The term that occurs here on both sides of the opposition, moreover, belongs to a semantic field that the Bible heavily draws on and orchestrates with notable virtuosity. Apart from "see," its key members are words associated with perception and cognition, like *look, looks, eye, hear, know;* and the repertoire of orchestration includes echoing, chaining, recurrence with variation, punning, revitalizing idioms, linkage of verbal to situational and perspectival dynamics. What is more, the narrative that frames this aphorism exemplifies the correspondence devised between external and internal interpreters. The reader's drama is literally dramatized in and through an analogous ordeal of interpretation undergone by some character—for example, Samuel above—with variable success but under the same constraints on human vision. The resulting brotherhood in darkness and guesswork and error thus cuts across the barrier separating participant from observer to highlight the barrier separating both from divine omniscience. Furthermore, God shapes the world plot with a view to getting his creatures to "know" him. Biblical history therefore stretches as a long series of demonstrations of divine power followed by tests of memory, gratitude, inference from precept and precedent, or, in short, of "knowledge," with further demonstrations staged in reward or punishment. God ultimately figures not only as the norm and source but also as the object and tester of knowledge. And by the narrator's art, the historical tests applied to the fathers in the world are perpetuated in the discourse addressed to the sons as a standing challenge to interpretation.

Hence the modernist composition so interrelates with uniquely biblical tenets and focuses as to establish a system decomposable in analysis alone. Where does aesthetics end and ideology begin? How does one differentiate either from history? The finished narrative is all of these and none: it constitutes a whole greater than the sum not only of its parts but also of their regulating forces. But precisely because the materials and forms and goals coordinated into a systematic whole are diverse, it becomes all the more revealing that the system operates by the processes of artistic communication. It makes even theological and historical sense by indirections that would normally count, in the Bible's days and our own, as foreign, if not inimical, to the straightforward expository discourse of theology and history. And it is this privileged status conferred on the art of implication (with its obverse side, the drama of reading) that signals and calls for a poetics of biblical narrative.

The heavy demands such a poetics of composition makes on reader and reading might seem to imply that biblical narrative addresses itself to an elite. Does the "Old" Testament anticipate the opposition proclaimed by the "New" between the spiritual and the carnal among the audience, those who belong inside and those kept outside the circuit of occult communication? "To you has been given the secret of the kingdom of God, but for those outside everything is in parables, so that they may indeed see but not perceive and may indeed hear but not understand; lest they should turn again and be forgiven" (Mark 4:11–12). Critics have always been exercised about this contrast drawn by Jesus in favor of his disciples, and

Frank Kermode has subtly explored it as a paradigm for reading in general. "In all works of interpretation," says Kermode, "there are insiders and out-siders, the former having, or professing to have, immediate access to the mystery, the latter randomly scattered across space and time, and excluded from the elect who mistrust or despise their unauthorized divinations."[33] However true of the gospels and various later counterparts, I believe, this forms only one of the paradigms of communication or "interpretation" envisaged by literary works, even of the more enigmatic sort; and it is certainly not the Bible's rule.

"This commandment which I command thee this day," Moses announces in his valedictory speech, "is not hidden from thee, nor is it far off. It is not in heaven, so that one should say, Who will go up for us to heaven to bring it down to us and declare it to us, that we may do it? Neither is it beyond the sea, that one should say, Who will cross the sea for us and bring it to us and declare it to us, that we may do it? Rather, the thing [or word, *davar*] is very near thee, in thy mouth and in thy heart, so that thou canst do it" (Deut 30:11–14). And again, "Thou shalt read this Torah before all Israel in their hearing. Assemble the people, men and women and little ones and the sojourner within thy gates, that they may hear and learn" (Deut 31:11–12; cf. Josh 8:34–35; Neh 8). The gulf dividing these key statements—one addressed to the Twelve far from the crowd, the other to a whole people for all time—epitomizes the mutual incom-patibility between two ideologies and between two narrative procedures. The Bible has many secrets but no Secret, many levels of interpretation but all equally accessible, so "very near thee" that, given the will, "thou canst do it." By an unintentional yet deeply revealing irony, Jesus in Mark had just been propounding his parables from a boat on the sea to a crowd on the shore. Nothing is more alien to the spirit of biblical narrative than discourse fashioned or meaning hidden across the sea, than speaking in riddles, than the distinction between spiritual insiders and carnal outsiders, than the very idea that anyone with the least claim to inclusion ("men and women and little ones and the sojourner within thy gates") may suffer exclusion. On the contrary, since exclusion figures here not as a sanction against certain readers but as a threat to the writing itself, the need to forestall it comes to regulate the strategy of narration. Where the nation's sense of identity and continuity hangs in the balance, it devolves on the text that forms the national heritage and charter to make sense. Hence the active steps taken to lower the threshold of intelligibility by a poetics thriving on the oblique and the ambiguous.

This paradox finds its resolution in the narrative management. Generally speaking, there are two methods of making a bid for wide appeal across boundaries of interpretative competence. One is the mixed bag technique, whereby the work caters to every kind or level of addressee in virtual isolation from the rest. Herein, according to T. S. Eliot, lies Shakespeare's magic: "For the simplest audience there is the plot, for the more thoughtful the character and the conflict of character, for the more literary the words and phrasing, for the more musically sensitive the rhythm, and for auditors of greater sensitiveness and understanding a meaning which reveals itself gradually."[34] Literature of the highest order, the Bible included, doubtless tends to have something of this appeal or at least the correlated effect of segregation after the reading event. Still, the Bible's thrust and forte rather lie in what I call foolproof composition, whereby the discourse strives to open and bring home its essentials to all readers so as to establish a common ground, a bond instead of a barrier of understanding. The nearest equivalent to what I have in mind lurks in an attractive midrash on "The voice of the Lord is in power" (Ps 29:4). Seizing on the omission of the possessive pronoun ("his or its power"), the rabbis construed the verse as meaning "The voice of the Lord is in *your* power": it is understood according to the capacity of each and every hearer. The divine word is like the manna, which to the young men tasted of bread, to the old of honey, to infants of their mother's milk. But all ate of the manna, and all respond to God's voice (*Tankhuma, Shemot* 25). Unfortunately, the midrash gives no clue to how the miracle works.

By foolproof composition I mean that the Bible is difficult to read, easy to underread and overread and even misread, but virtually impossible to, so to speak, counterread. Here as elsewhere, of course, ignorance, willfulness, preconception, tendentiousness—all amply manifested throughout history, in the religious and other approaches—may perform wonders of distortion. No text can withstand the kind of methodological license indulged in by the rabbis in contexts other than legal, or by critics who mix up their quest for the source with the need to fabricate a new discourse. Still less can it protect itself against being yoked by violence, in the manner of the christological tradition, with a later text whose very premises of discourse (notably "insider" versus "outsider") it would find incomprehensible. Nor can it do much to keep out invidious assumptions about Israelite ethics and culture, of which a relatively mild specimen surfaces in the generalization that the Bible develops "the sort of themes that would appeal to rough humor and rouse the chuckles of the fairly low audience for whom they were designed, who doubled with merriment at the thought of the 'uncircumcised.'"[35] In a hermeneutic and moral as well as a theological sense, interpretation may always be performed in bad faith.

Short of such extremes, biblical narrative is virtually impossible to counterread. The essentials are made transparent to all comers: the story line, the world order, the value system. The old and new controversies among exegetes, spreading to every possible topic, must not blind us (as it usually does them) to the measure of agreement in this regard. The bedrock agreement is neither accidental nor self-evident. Not accidental, because it derives from the Bible's overarching principle of composition, its strategy of strategies, namely, maneuvering between the truth and the whole truth; nor self-evident, because such a principle does not often govern literature operating at the Bible's level of sophistication and interpretive drama.

Consider first the two faces or limits of the regulating principle. On the one hand, the Bible always tells the truth in that its narrator is absolutely and straightforwardly reliable. Historians may quarrel with his facts and others call them fiction; but in context his remain accounts of the truth communicated on the highest authority. In terms of the internal premises established by the discourse—and these alone determine reliability in interpretation—the reader cannot go far wrong even if he does little more than follow the statements made and the incidents enacted on the narrative surface. For the narrator who conveys them to him cannot go wrong himself, unlike so many of the misguided tellers in modern literature, errant in knowledge and evaluation alike. Nor is the narrator mendacious, after the fashion of other modern counterparts, whose pretense and falsehood the hidden author exposes for our benefit and entertainment. Further, just as the narrator is not the victim of irony on the author's part, so does he not indiscriminately traffic in irony at the reader's expense: his ironies, many and diverse, are situational rather than verbal. Still less does he deal in the esoteric: his parables, unlike Jesus' or Kafka's, convey messages that could hardly be less occult to anyone aware of the dramatic situation of utterance. Hence the distance that separates biblical from otherwise kindred narration in all that regards the minimum intelligibility of surface and essentials. Take the governess's account in *The Turn of the Screw* at face value, and you will see ghosts where none may exist outside her imagination. Trust Barry Lyndon, and your judgment of character and plot will go astray in the direction ironized by Thackeray from behind the scenes. Accept Fielding's affirmations without heavy discounting, and you will fall into trap after trap to his amusement. You are either an insider or a dupe. But follow the biblical narrator ever so uncritically, and by no great exertion you will be making tolerable sense of the world you are in, the action that unfolds, the protagonists on stage, and the point of it all.

On the other hand, the narrator does not tell the whole truth either. His statements about the world—character, plot, the march of history—are rarely complete, falling much short of what his elliptical text suggests between the lines. His *ex cathedra* judgments are valid as far as they go, but then they seldom go far below the surface of the narrative, where they find their qualification and shading. His reference to ends and means is conspicuous by its absence, but only to one alive to the novelty and intricacy of their working. As concerns representation, evaluation, and artfulness, in short, if the biblical truth is explicit, then the whole truth is implicit; and the more you bring to this art of implication, the more secrets and prizes it yields. No one goes away empty-handed. But the challenge to the cunning reader is as omnipresent as the solicitude for all.

The device known as free indirect discourse offers an excellent case in point. Generally regarded as a modern innovation, it actually makes a most impressive appearance as a biblical resource for capturing the inner life.[36] Moreover, its Israelite innovators adapted it to their distinctive poetics, where necessary along lines opposed to the rule of modernism. Compare the two following instances, one from the Jael and Sisera episode in Judges and the other from Joseph Heller's *Catch-22:*

> Jael the wife of Heber took a tent peg, and took the hammer in her hand, and went softly to him, and drove the peg into his temple and it went on into the ground. He was fast asleep and weary. So he died. And behold, Barak was pursuing Sisera. Jael came out to meet him and said to him, Come and I will show thee the man whom thou seekest. And he came into her tent, *and behold, Sisera fallen, dead, and a peg in his temple.* (4:21–22)

> Yossarian answered in a collapsing voice, weary suddenly of shouting so much, of the whole frustrating, exasperating, ridiculous situation. *He was dying, and no one took notice.* "Never mind." (chap. 26)

Each of the italicized sentences is a piece of free indirect discourse, where the omniscient narrator refracts a death scene through the viewpoint of a character (Barak, Yossarian). In neither, moreover, is this refraction from within explicitly stated. Quite the contrary, since these sentences are grammatically independent and attended by no internal reporting verb ("he saw" or "thought"), they formally come from the narrator himself. Only in the light of contextual clues—i.e., interpretation—does the objective telling reveal itself as subjective viewing cast in free indirect style.

This similarity brings out three typical and related points of dissimilarity. To begin with, the first statement is true, the second false: Sisera has indeed died, while Yossarian (it later transpires) only thinks he is dying. Second, the amount of guidance offered by the text to the true state of affairs—and hence the play between objectivity and subjectivity—is in inverse proportion to what one might expect. Having recorded the false statement, Heller makes no effort to correct the impression by indicating its figural origin, except perhaps for anchoring the *antecedent* sentence ("weary" etc.) in Yossarian's mind. If anything, he actively misleads the reader by the lurid description of the pool of blood that surrounds the wounded hero.

Having recorded the true statement, on the other hand, his biblical counter-part goes out of his way to signal its true attribution as well. Note the structural clue of repetition: since the narrator has just communicated Sisera's death in his own name, why should he repeat himself? There is also the stylistic clue of the initial "and behold" (*ve'hinneh*), codified as a marker of biblical free indirect thought. And there is also more than one psychological clue, notably the arrangement of the items in a deformed effect–cause sequence (first the death and then the lethal peg) that accords with both Barak's scale of priorities and his order of discovery. Third, the consequences of missing the perspectival indirection or equivocation are sharply opposed. Taken at face value, the Yossarian passage becomes a trap, reversing for the interpreter (here temporarily, elsewhere for good) the actual situation. But Sisera being really dead, the interpreter will come to no great harm if he mistakes Barak's discovery for the narrator's rehearsal of the death. All the clues are amenable at a pinch to an alternative explanation along this line. The repetition is a mere convention of ancient storytelling; the "and behold" drums up excitement; the changed order of cause and effect forms a stylistic variant; and so on.

Given the operation of alternative patterning as camouflage, it is a nice question which of the two arts of ambiguity works more subtly. But the foolproof composition certainly makes a different art from the win-*or*-lose variety, where the reader shares either the narrator's irony at the expense of the misinformed hero or the sting of irony with the hero. Failing to go below the biblical surface results in underreading and below the modern surface in misreading to the point of counterreading.

As with free indirect discourse, so with all the other techniques and strategies we shall be concerned with. Some, equally innovative and even more central, have just been mentioned in passing. The Bible's verbal artistry, without precedent in literary history and unrivaled since, operates by passing off its art for artlessness, its sequential linkages and supra-sequential echoes for unadorned parataxis, its density of evocation for chronicle-like thinness and transparency. Yet those who are taken in will rarely feel the difference, however much they may miss, because they will not feel out of their depth as they would do in Joyce or Nabokov. The structure of repetition, inherited from Oriental culture but metamorphosed into a versatile tool of implication, always makes minimal sense (unlike recent instances of the *Rashomon* design) in terms of plot or the formulaic embellishment it has left behind. The informational gaps—suggesting a bifocal or multiple view of character and motive and event, and announcing the birth of ambiguous narration—need not detain those who run as they read. (The very idiom, it is worth noting, originates in Habakkuk 2:2, where God instructs the seer to make the writing plain, "so that he may run who reads it.") The tale will appear coherent even, or often most of all, to those who unwittingly escape the horns of ambiguity, imposing univocal closures on troublesome omissions and overlooking the rest. The ellipses or non sequiturs that must disturb even such a reader (e.g., the reasons for Joseph's treatment of his brothers) will evoke curiosity and suspense until he manages to repair them after some fashion; other features that he may overlook in running may spring at him later in the form of retrospective disclosures and difficulties too insistent to ignore. So whether the initial choice offered by the gaps is between inference and incoherence or inference and quiescence, there will always remain enough cognitive adventures to give everyone a taste of the drama of reading. Finally, the inner life is kept underground to such an extent—its most complex work-ings rendered by obliquities like dialogue, analogy, linguistic rhyme, free indirect style—that many biblical scholars have pronounced it nonexistent. Ironically, all that their pronouncements establish is how easily poor readers can manage without it, each fashioning his own version of *Biblia Pauperum.* And they can manage without it, indeed with no suspicion of an entire poetics at work, only because the narrative surface—of language, repeti-tion, givens, externals—still conveys a truth that hangs together, if not gloriously then at least sufficiently to pass muster. Such deficiencies of interpretation vindicate the strategy that provides for them. So, within reasonable limits, do the excesses to which professional interpreters are liable in their quest for maximal sense.

But the supreme test of the foolproof composition lies in what ideological writing must do or die: the regulation of distance and judgment. Consider-ing the scarcity of evaluation on the narrator's part—far less in evidence than the fragmentary but ongoing representation—how can a mixed audience be expected to form the proper attitude to the action and the agents, with God at their head? Again, if "proper" means properly differen-tiated and nuanced, they cannot, for the simple reason that the finer points of rhetoric lurk in the art of implication. But if it means properly oriented, then the reader benefits from a set of variations of the same principle, now operating to ensure minimum consensus rather than minimum intelligibility.

One consists in the rule that the complexity of representation is inversely proportioned to that of evaluation: the more opaque (discordant, ambig-uous) the plot, that is, the more transparent (concordant, straightforward) the judgment. Thus, the Purchase of the Machpelah story (Genesis 23) is limited to a dialogue that keeps the intentions of the negotiators hidden; the David and Bathsheba narrative (2 Samuel 11) projects conflicting answers to the questions whether Uriah knows of his wife's affair and why David sends the husband to his death. But then they can afford to play with ambiguity because the moral oppositions are drawn so clearly: our reconstruction of the narrated world enriches and subtilizes but does not generate its judgment. No matter how readers fill in the gaps—even where they see one possibility of the two or more suggested—Abraham will come out in an attractive light and David in disgrace. In normatively problematic tales, however, the essential facts rise to the surface to focus attention and mold attitude. The book of Samuel, for example, counteracts the natural sympathy for the underdog by laying open, if necessary by direct inside view, Saul's murderous intentions in regard to David; while the episode of the Stolen Blessing unfolds a series of fully illuminated encounters to split our sympathy between the ill-fated victims and the ill-doing victimizers in the family conflict.

Another insurance policy lies in the interplay of norms between divergence and convergence. Where the narrative aims at a complex response, it does not hesitate to mix our feelings about the parties to the conflict by increasing (or decreasing) the appeal of each in relation to a different standard of judgment. In the example just mentioned, Isaac and Esau have all the pity on their side, Rebekah and Jacob all the national solidarity. (And if a dogmatic or chauvinistic reader fails to give the victims the sigh due to them, then he at least errs on what is ultimately the right side.) But where bent on a solid judgment for or against a partici-pant—or an act or a cause—the Bible ensures it by combining the frames of normative reference. During his struggle with his brothers, Joseph elicits both emotional and moral sympathy, just as Ahab, instigating Naboth's murder, forfeits both. Or take the chequered career of David. He begins by establishing his superiority to Saul in both divine and social terms; reaches a crisis when he offends against both sets of norms in the Bathsheba affair; and finally, having weathered the terrible storm that his crime unleashed, retrieves his position in the eyes of God and people. It is not merely that two norms count more heavily than one, but that if either misfires with a certain reader, the other will do the job of control.

Still another rule devised for foolproof judgment is retrospective or last-minute clarification. Having presented some drama without any overt com-mentary, though with sufficient clues distributed along the way to guide the alert, the narrative will often enlighten the naive or superficial toward the end. On the better-late-than-never principle, it then retrospectively corrects possible variations from the desired attitude by way of univocal utterance, counteract, or disclosure. Thus, the neutral style of the Binding of Isaac is immediately followed by divine praise, and of the Bathsheba chronicle, by divine thundering. Even one who has been chuckling at Jacob's victimization of his father and brother will not find it easy to view his subsequent encounters with Laban as other than a tit-for-tat judgment.

Most cunning of all is the procedure whereby the narrative lures us into a false impression about a character or event and then springs the truth at the least expected moment. The model for this strategy is the tale of Jonah, which starts by opposing a compassionate Jonah to a wrathful God and ends by switching their portraits round. The unfolding of their true characters must surprise the whole audience, but not to the same effect. The implied reader will be led by the *volte-face* to reconsider some general issues: the relations between God and prophet, power and pride, repentance and mercy, knowledge and judgment. While attaining to less than the whole metaphysical and psychological truth, others will still discover enough about the concrete situation to undergo the ordeal of understanding and place their allegiance on the right side.

Thoroughly typical, all these key measures yet give a better idea of the precautions the Bible takes against counterreading than of the provisions it makes for the reading. It is in the distance between the two, the minimal and the maximal pole, that the Bible's art proper lives. But the safeguarding of the minimum truth forms a distinctive mark of its composition and an index of its ideological basis. Precisely because our main concern will be with the strategies that direct the reader toward the plenary pole, this bid for the widest appeal and its implications for structure need to be kept in mind throughout. I am not at all worried by any impression of flatness or fall below artistic dignity that this early emphasis may give. In our following encounters with the Bible, want of complications will be the least of our problems.

The poetics of maneuvering between the truth and the whole truth, so foreign to the either/or spirit of elitism that informs the gospels and modern art and, by association, the criticism oriented to them, also dramatizes a point I have been suggesting all along. Despite their fewness and tender age, the "literary approaches" are doing a considerable amount of good. But they must soon reach a point of diminishing returns unless they spend less energy on self-assertion vis-à-vis traditional scholarship and more on a systematic examination of their own aims and equipment.

In practice as well as in methodology, the gravest danger to the literary approaches lurks in their importation of models that do not fit the Bible, nor indeed (except maybe for the prestigious or fashionable corpus that inspired them) literature in general. I confess to a horror of the very word "application," no matter how sincerely invoked to express the belief that the universal tools are within reach and nothing could be more simple and productive than exercising them on yet another text. This belief is misguided on both counts, as I have good reason to know. In most of the theoretical work I have done, on narrative and other subjects, the Bible has proved a corrective to widely held doctrines about literary structure and analysis, often a pointer to the formation of alternatives. In my biblical work, conversely, seldom have I found a narrative or a strategy proceeding along the theoretically expected grooves or, after the event, failing to illuminate a host of other corpora and traditions. This, reflected in the interaction of theory and practice throughout the following argument, has no parallel in my experience. If every text is a concrete universal, biblical narrative would seem both more concrete and more universal than most. Considering the unique challenge it presents, it should and I hope will attract producers as well as consumers of literary theory. They can contribute a great deal to the study of the Bible, but no more than they will receive in exchange.

·2·

NARRATIVE MODELS

Moses said to the Lord: "Please, my Lord, I am not a man of words,
either heretofore or since thou hast spoken to thy servant; for I
am slow of utterance and slow of tongue." And the Lord said to
him, "Who has made man's mouth? Who makes one dumb or deaf
or seeing or blind? Is it not I, the Lord? Now therefore go, and
I will be with thy mouth and teach thee what thou shalt speak."

Exodus 4:10-12

Face-to-face communication, the paradigm of language use, underlies the
Bible's prophetic rather than narrative discourse. If prophecy reflects the
forms and intonations of speech even when committed to paper—or
parchment—then narrative operates in and through the medium of writing,
as Scripture in the fullest sense; it also goes from storyteller to audience
without identifying either. Yet the product can hardly be understood apart
from the communicative situation that produces it. Who is the teller? To
whom does he tell? Why does he tell? Whence his authority for telling
what and as he does? Such questions will brook no neglect. They not only
link up with every crux discussed in the foregoing chapter: source vs.
discourse, external vs. internal evidence, fiction vs. history. They also determine the sense of every word and pattern inscribed, the norms and bearing of the tale as a whole. Indeed, new-fangled as these questions of point
of view and storytelling role may look, no reader has ever failed to provide an answer of sorts. The answers, moreover, fall under a definite number
of logics or models of narration, each with its own premises and implications. The issue being so much tangled and so little explored, this chapter
will first sort out and evaluate the models implicit in biblical study, with
a view to developing an alternative that fits the case.

As so often, the raising of the problem, complete with two opposed solutions, goes back to the ancient rabbis:

Rabbi Eleazar says: Esther was composed under the inspiration of the
Holy Spirit, as it says, "And Haman said in his heart." Rabbi Akiba
says: Esther was composed under the inspiration of the Holy Spirit, as
it says, "And Esther found favour in the eyes of all that looked upon

her." Rabbi Meir says, Esther was composed under the inspiration of the Holy Spirit, as it says, "And the thing became known to Mordecai." Rabbi Yose ben Durmaskith said: Esther was composed under the inspiration of the Holy Spirit, as it says, "But on the spoil they laid not their hands." (*Megillah* 7a; translation after Isadore Epstein's *Babylonian Talmud*)

Who wrote the Scriptures?—Moses wrote his own book and the portion of Balaam and Job. Joshua wrote his own book and the [last] eight verses of the Pentateuch. Samuel wrote his own book and Judges and Ruth. David wrote the Book of Psalms, incorporating the work of the ten elders: Adam, Melchizedek, Abraham, Moses, Heman, Yeduthun, Asaph, and the three sons of Korah. Jeremiah wrote his book and the Book of Kings and Lamentations. Hezekiah and his circle wrote Isaiah, Proverbs, the Song of Songs and Ecclesiastes. The Men of the Great Assembly wrote Ezekiel and the Twelve Minor Prophets, Daniel and the Scroll of Esther. Ezra wrote his own book and the genealogies of Chronicles up to his own time. (*Baba Bathra* 14b–15a)

The concerns of these rabbinic statements appear almost as far removed from each other as from the business of poetics. The first sets out to argue for the incorporation of a book—Esther—into the canon; the second, to list the writers responsible for the different parts of the canon. Indirectly, however, the two supply variant answers to a single question that no discipline can afford to ignore. The underlying question is that of scriptural authority: Whence the writer's powers and competence? And the variant answers, standing in hidden dialectic relationship, establish or adumbrate the two basic lines of approach in the millennia to come.

The first passage draws notice to various aspects of what one would call today the biblical writer's omniscience: the ability to penetrate the mind of one character (e.g., Haman) or more (Esther's admirers) and to narrate simultaneous events wide apart in space (the Jews' abstention from looting throughout the empire). From this extraordinary range of knowledge, each rabbi infers the presence of the Holy Spirit behind the composition: hence Esther's claim to canonicity on both doctrinal and historical grounds. The book shows all the marks of divine inspiration, and it also manages to stay on the right side of the dividing line between inspired and uninspired writing, that is, the fall of the Persian Empire, when the Holy Spirit (or its equivalent, prophecy) is supposed to have withdrawn from Israel.

In the second passage, interest shifts to the assignment of earthly authorship. But what forms the basis for attribution? The title appears to serve as the main criterion: note the recurrent formula "x (the eponymous character) wrote *his* book." But this leaves unexplained the attribution of books entitled by theme, like Judges, Kings, Psalms, Chronicles. Correspondingly, it fails to account for the exclusion from authorship of so many title characters. Of course, Job was a Gentile; Ruth and Esther were women. But what about Isaiah, Ezekiel, Daniel, the twelve minor prophets? Even more puzzling would then be the recourse to partial or divided (not joint) authorship. Why are the last eight verses of the Pentateuch transferred from Moses to Joshua (and what makes it "his book" in the first place)?

A closer look will reveal a method in this disorder. In fact, eponymy is here not so much undermined as subsumed by another criterion, one no less implicit but of much wider range and different orientation. I refer to the probability of access to the material (events, society, records) composed into a book. Naturally, the eponymous character—Joshua, Samuel, Jeremiah, Ezra—would be at home in the world where he figured as agent or speaker. So, by an immemorial non sequitur that mars the argument from eponymy itself, the possibility of his authorship is taken for the deed. In effect, the character then doubles as autobiographer, whether he refers to his former self in the third or (as Ezra sometimes does) in the first person. This also makes sense of the attribution of books to figures either not named in the (thematic) title or other than those actually named there. The qualifying principle is that each writer should have a reasonable claim to familiarity with the specific subject or information treated in the book: through personal experience (as with Moses from the Exodus onward), historical proximity (Samuel and Judges or Ruth, Jeremiah and Kings, Hezekiah and Isaiah), and/or access to traditional lore (David and Psalms, the Men of the Great Assembly and Ezekiel, Ezra and Chronicles).

This requirement greatly diversifies the modes of scriptural writing. Apart from the official categories—Torah, Prophets, Hagiographa—the writing shifts between autobiography and biography, eyewitness account and historical inquiry, original and editorial composition. Not in a single instance, however, does the writer nominated by the rabbis overstep the bounds of nature. At the first threat to probability, authorship is either denied or divided. Joshua thus appends the last verses of Deuteronomy, since Moses cannot have recorded his own death. And just as all biblical writing thereby assumes a retrospective cast, so is the retrospection always assigned to a competent writer, namely, a professional wielder of words: prophet, poet, scribe, or man of letters. The related qualifications of access and competence are both measured by essentially human standards.

Hence the most remarkable criterion is the one that entirely fails to appear—the reference to divine inspiration, so crucial to the Esther passage and to the establishment of canonicity in general. Indeed, its sudden invocation in the immediate sequel disrupts the whole argument:

Eight verses in the Torah were written by Joshua, as it has been taught: "And Moses the servant of the Lord died there." Now, is it possible that Moses being dead could have written the words, "Moses died there"? The truth is, however, that up to this point Moses wrote, from this point on Joshua wrote. This is the opinion of R. Judah or, according to others, of R. Nehemiah. Said R. Simeon to him: Can the scroll of the Law be short of one word, and is it not written, "Take this book of the Law"? No; what we must say is that up to this point the Holy One, blessed be he, dictated and Moses repeated and wrote, and from this point on God dictated and Moses wrote with tears. (*Baba Bathra* 15a)

Rabbi Simeon appeals to inspiration ("God dictated") under the pressure of a textual difficulty. Moses' order, "Take this book of the Law" (Deut 31:26), implies that he completed its writing in his lifetime. Therefore, Joshua did not append the final verses relating to his master's death: Moses himself took them down as usual—though "with tears"—at God's dictation. Apparently a simple patch, this in fact opens holes in all that has gone before—and what comes after[1]—for by its logic the reference to human canons of probability becomes not only gratuitous but invalid. Given divine inspiration, Moses could compose the rest of the Bible as well as the Pentateuch to the last letter. So could any of his successors—Joshua, Samuel, David, Jeremiah, Ezra—regardless of their position in history. And just as everyone might then encompass the future no less than the past, so might any inspired amateur outdo the professional writers. After all, as the epigraph to this chapter lays down, is it not God who dispenses eloquence?

Where the Holy Spirit operates, in short, all earthbound notions like access and competence lose their force as criteria of authorship. Either authorship goes by qualification or every single Israelite qualifies. In the face of this inescapable either/or choice, however, the rabbis blithely let the roster of authors stand, without even adducing some ad hoc explanation. Having it both ways is of course a speciality of theirs, but this renders its occasions none the less revealing. What we observe at work here is a split or dialectical tension between two models of writing Scripture that I shall call the inspirational vs. the empirical. In principle, the one suspends or transcends and the other observes the decorums of realistic composition—above all, the constraints that govern ordinary (hi)story telling.

This ancient dialectics (or at least its spirit) later branched out into the two incompatible approaches to biblical composition that have persisted to this day. The inspirational model dominates the line of religious traditionalism, Jewish and, in a far more tormented manner, Christian. The rabbinic tradition has on the whole proved indifferent to the mechanics of divine genesis, on which Christianity expended so much of its energy and fought so many of its battles. From its earliest times, indeed, the issue of inspiration has gained point and urgency as the focus of the most various conflicts: between the "Old" and the "New" Testament, between the attitudes of Jewish writers of the New Testament and Gentile converts to Christianity, between the discrepant gospels or the status of gospels versus epistles, between Roman Catholicism and Protestantism, between faith and science. On each front, the territory wrested from inspiration came under empirical control, though the whole somehow remains in principle of divine origin. In modern scholarship, however, the empirical logic reigns supreme. Here is M. H. Segal on the David narratives in Samuel:

> These chapters were written by a contemporary of David's, who knew the events (at least from II Samuel 9) at first hand and outlived David. Of David's entourage, who was the writer of genius responsible for this marvellous historical work? Some think that it was Ahima'az the son of the priest Zadok. But the work cannot at all be attributed to the young priest who got confused in his answer to David regarding Absalom's fate in the war. . . . And Ahima'az was certainly not so close to the king as to have an intimate knowledge of the secret doings in the palace. Most scholars now think that this source was composed by Abiathar the priest during his exile at Anatoth, after he had been deposed by Solomon. This guess is also very far-fetched. This unhappy old man of eighty or so, David's own contemporary, could not have the desire or strength to produce such a long and detailed and objective work. Throughout these chapters, Abiathar appears as a stranger and in the shade of Zadok. . . . Abiathar would not write thus. And his words would surely betray here and there some resentment for the wrong done him by David and Solomon. And how could Abiathar have been so familiar with the smallest details of the king's political and familial business and of the private conversations between David and his servants and household? Clearly, the writer was one of David's closest servants, always in attendance on the king, with a personal and inside knowledge of all that took place in the house, both public and private affairs; a man who admired David but also perceived the weaknesses of the great king and recounts them objectively for better or worse; a man who served David throughout his reign and also held the same office under Solomon, at least during the early years of his reign. This man was nobody but *Jehoshafat ben Ahilud,* who served both David and Solomon as their *mazkir* (recorder, II Samuel 8:16, I Kings 4:3). We cannot define precisely the functions of the *mazkir.* But it is clear that he was very close to the king, free to come and to go in the king's palace, constantly seeing him and knowledgeable about all his affairs. The *mazkir* of David and Solomon was surely, like those kings themselves, wise and clever and a master of language, which fits the personality of our author.[2]

Except in details like the final nomination (Jehoshafat in place of Samuel) little seems to have changed since the *Baba Bathra* listing. The goal remains the same—to establish origin or authorship—and so does the method. From Segal's argument we can extrapolate three storytelling features, posited as criteria for deciding among the various candidates:

1. privileged access (to intimate scenes, family secrets, official business);
2. writing competence (sufficient to yield "this marvellous historical work");
3. objective presentation.

The candidacy of Ahima'az does not pass either the first test ("He was not so close to the king") or the second ("He got confused in his answer," on the assumption that loss of coherence in life entails lack of control in telling about life). Abiathar is also ruled out, by the combined weight of the first standard (he did not know enough) and the third (he would not highlight his rival Zadok at his own expense, nor could he suppress his resentment against David's house). So the honor falls to Jehoshafat, the royal secretary or recorder, who supposedly meets all the conditions.

In essence, then, this pursues the old line of explaining the storyteller's authority and qualifications in genetic rather than functional or artistic terms—with the difference that the rabbis are always free to locate the efficient cause in heaven, whereas the modern biblicist remains on earth or, more specifically here, in court. Yet, whatever the attractions of earthly genesis, Segal's argument breaks down even in its own terms. Nor would any alternative weighing and nominee, such as offered by his opponents,[3] salvage the approach. What is hopeless about it resides in the logic itself, not just in the application.

Take the main criterion to which all appeal: privileged access to material. Assuming for the sake of argument that Jehoshafat was in a better position than Ahima'az and Abiathar to follow the goings-on in David's circle, this does not yet account for the range of information brought to bear on chapter after chapter in Samuel. However well-informed Jehoshaphat was about the court life around him, how could he know what took place in heaven, including God's mysterious designs? ("Who," in Agur son of Yakeh's sardonic words, "has ascended to heaven and come down?" [Prov 30:4].) And however familiar with external developments, how could he be privy to internals, notably the thoughts of David's enemies—or, for that matter, to the secret life led by any participant other than himself, from the king down? To counter that the writer fabricated or reconstructed or projected himself into these humanly inaccessible areas would not save the argument but rather give it its quietus. For the whole approach hinges on the possibilities of *factual* knowledge. Once the license of imaginative ("fictional") invention is granted, Jehoshafat's advantage over Ahima'az and Abiathar vanishes and all candidacies become equiprobable.

Nor will the other criteria bear scrutiny. The secretary may well have been a master of official and polite language, but this no more invests him with the "marvellous" compositional talents that went into the making of Samuel than does the two priests' (or, to mention the rabbinic nominee, the prophet's) command of liturgical idiom. Just as, from another life-art viewpoint, the incoherence to which Ahima'az is reduced at the sight of the king's anxiety about Absalom does not at all rule out the most fluent storytelling in tranquillity. And if a supposed malcontent like Abiathar gets disqualified for lack of objectivity, why should a partisan (and dependent) like Jehoshafat escape the same verdict? Surely the argument cuts both ways.

Insiders need no telling that such idle speculation passes for scholarship in biblical circles, where it has long occupied a place of honor. (The very term "higher criticism" was coined, in J. G. Eichhorn's *Einleitung in das Alte Testament* (1780–83), to distinguish and promote the inquiry into questions of authorship.) Indeed, this exercise in futility is worth lingering over only because it dramatizes a traditional will-o'the-wisp of source criticism. I have in mind the focus on the real writer (or writership) as a historical figure (or process) at the expense of the author or narrator as an artistic persona, or, worse, the confusion of the two.

In principle, to be sure, there is nothing illegitimate about the endeavor to identify the historical writer(s) with a view to locating the narrative in its proper sociocultural matrix and tracing its rise and fortunes. On the contrary, like all branches of literary history, it has its value not only as an end in itself but even as an aid to biblical poetics and interpretation. Textual history simply makes or enriches contextual knowledge, of which no analyst can have too much. Unfortunately, however, this line of inquiry has yielded over the centuries a prohibitive ratio of fantasies to findings, let alone explanations—and not for want of trying or ingenuity but of data on which to exercise them. On past form, though it may still take the institution some time to assent to such a judgment, the future holds little promise for it. The sad truth is that we know practically nothing about biblical writers—even less than about the processes of writing and transmission—and it looks as though we never will.

Fatally handicapped, such inquiry would still remain harmless if only its object, resources, and above all limitations were perceived and borne in mind. Thus, if the object consists in the historical genesis and generator of a tale like Samuel, no identification can be reasonably made from the telling.

Before casting about for answers, to start with, biblical geneticists (including the rabbis in their empirical vein) might have stopped to consider why answers are so hard to find. Biblical narrative exhibits such a rage for impersonality as must lead to the conclusion that its writers actively sought the cover of anonymity. In this they outdo even the notorious, and somewhat overstated, namelessness of ancient writing.

Like the Greeks, Israel's own neighbors have left various records of attribution, external and internal to the works themselves. Ancient Egypt kept the memory of its great authors alive, so much so that some of the names may still be coupled today with extant writings and others have come down to us (e.g., the famous Imhotep of the third millennium) though none of their works has survived. Take the moving tribute paid to genius in "Praise of Learned Scribes":

> They did not make for themselves pyramids of metal, with the tombstones thereof of iron. They were not able to leave heirs in children . . . pronouncing their names. . . . Their mortuary service is [gone]; their tombstones are covered with dirt; and their graves are forgotten. (But) their names are (still) pronounced because of their books which they made, since they were good and the memory of him who made them (lasts) to the limits of eternity. . . . A man is perished, his corpse is dust, all his relatives are come to the ground—(but) it is writing that makes him remembered in the mouth of a reciter. . . . Is there (anyone) here like Hor-dedef? Is there another like Ii-em-hotep? None has appeared among our relatives like Neferty or Khety, that foremost of them. I cause thee to know the names of Ptah-em-djedhuti and Kha-kheper-(Re)-seneb. Is there anyone like Ptah-hotep, or Ka-iris as well? . . . It is writing that makes them remembered.[4]

This harping on immortality also suggests, of course, what a sacrifice anonymous composition must have been even to ancient man—or rather, since the name figured as the essence of the being, particularly to him.

Nor was Egypt's the only culture to commemorate literary achievement. Mesopotamia offers an even more striking parallel in its scribal traditions and, above all, in the catalogue from the library of the seventh-century king Ashurbanipal.[5] Much like a modern bibliography, it lists and attributes a wide variety of works, including some that circulated anonymously. To mention only a few well-known masterpieces, the *Gilgamesh Epic* is ascribed to "Sin-liqi-unnini, the magician," the *Etana Epic* to "Luanna," and the *Irra Epic* to "Kabti-ilani-Marduk, son of Dabibi."

The last of these items leads us from external to internal attribution, since the catalogue entry manifestly derives from the final part of the *Irra Epic* itself: "Kabti-ilani-Marduk, son of Dabibi, was the compiler of its tablets. / It was revealed to him in the night, and when he spoke it in the

morning, / He did not leave out a single line, nor did he add one to it"
(Lambert, "Catalogue," p. 70). Such incorporated (self-)attribution also
has parallels in Egyptian and cuneiform literature. In *"The Babylonian
Theodicy,"* the writer's name appears as an acrostic: "I, Saggil-kinam-ubbib,
the exorcist, am an adorant of the god and the king."[6] The Hittite *Myth
of Illuyankas* greets us with an open bibliographical announcement: "These
are the words of Kellas, the anointed [priest] of the Storm-god Nerik. What
follows is the cult legend of the *purulli* festival of the Storm-god of Heaven,
(the version which) they no longer tell" (*Ancient Near Eastern Texts,* p. 125).
More usually, the scribe's name is inserted, among other pieces of genetic
or title-page information, into the colophon. Thus the Ugaritic *Baal and
Anath:* "Written by Elimelech the Shabnite. / Dictated by Attani-puruleni,
Chief of Priests, Chief of (Temple-) herdsmen. / Donated by Niqmadd,
King of Ugarit."[7] And the borderline among the scribal roles of composi-
tion, compilation, and copying was fluid in antiquity.

However fragmentary and at times dubious by modern standards, such
references to origin and process of transmission yet deepen the sense of
secrecy given by biblical narrative. Its culture's and its own remarkable
powers of memory encompass everything but the names that produced
it. The canon itself remains the only catalogue, and the few attributions
are obviously exceptional. For whether external or internal, they come too
late to affect the norm or model of narration.

Tradition thus casts Moses in the role of author or mediator of the Pentateuch. Yet the narrative itself makes no such claim. It does refer to Moses
as the writer of certain documents: "The Lord said to Moses, Write this
as a memorial in a book . . . that I will utterly blot out the remembrance
of Amalek" (Exod 17:14); "Moses wrote down their starting places, stage
by stage, by the orders of the Lord" (Num 33:2); "Moses finished writing
the words of this law [torah] in a book, to the very end" (Deut 31:24).
Though they may lend color to the traditionalist argument vis-à-vis source
criticism, however, these fall far short of attribution, even in the Oriental
manner. Nowhere are Moses' recording activities identified with Pen-
tateuchal discourse as a whole, nor always or straightforwardly with the
corresponding parts of the discourse. In short, Moses appears as writing
within the plot rather than as the writer within the narrative, still less as
self-styled writer in the manner of Kabti-ilani-Marduk or the Hittite Kellas.

On the other hand, Nehemiah introduces himself: "The words of
Nehemiah, the son of Hacaliah" (1:1); and so, in the middle of the action,
does Ezra (7:6). But these autobiographical accounts are possibly as fictitious
(and their writing, therefore, as pseudonymous) as Daniel's, certainly late
and divergent in their poetics. So they only prove the rule of narration,
by which self-reflexive language is conspicuous for its absence. No self-

naming, no reference to a speaking "I," no exact clues to the time and place of communication. It is as if, anticipating certain scholarly questions, the writers took good care to frustrate impertinent curiosity. Nothing personal is revealed, little betrayed.

These measures may have failed to discourage the quest for the man behind the book, yet they have certainly brought it up against a wall. For the absence of internal as well as external attribution leaves the handling of the tale itself—the language, the narrative technique, the ideological position, the field of reality—the main if not the exclusive basis for conjecture. How shaky this basis is can be gathered from the interminable quarrels about dating among scholars who appeal to the same body of evidence; and each party to the quarrel usually gives itself a liberal margin of error. Attempts to move beyond such generalities of time and milieu to personalities proper—from a local habitation to a name—are evidently doomed to failure; they would have been abandoned long ago were it not for the conjunction of human drive and institutional inertia. As it is, these detective ventures are kept going only by recourse to unwarranted assumptions, ad hoc epicycling, non sequiturs, and other offenses against logic and common sense that could provide matter for a textbook on fallacies.

Why, for instance, should the author of Samuel be picked from among the dramatis personae? Just because the characters happen to be the only biblical men known by name. And the field thus wonderfully narrowed down, all that remains is to apply to it much the same principle that generated the legend of Homer's blindness by analogy to his Phaeacian bard Demodocus. But there is no reason to believe that either Homer or the biblical writers, both jealous of their private selves, favored the Hitchcock gimmick of making an appearance in one's own work.

Even if such assumptions were plausible, there would still be no way to decide among the candidates. The facts of literary practice disable all the favorite procedures of elimination and choice. Thus, the appeal to "objectivity" is not only, as we have seen, a double-edged weapon. In identifying the person who suffers (or benefits) with the artist who creates, it goes counter to what innumerable studies in biography have established: that even committed writers may rise above their own prejudices for or against their subject. Mercifully, the most objective history of ancient times has come down to us with its authorship undisputed. Or else, by the reasoning from animus that denied the exile Abiathar any share in the composition of 2 Samuel, we might find Thucydides automatically disqualified. Who would attribute *The Peloponnesian War* to a general banished from Athens for his failure to defend Amphipolis?

The appeal to informational facilities is even less warranted. Of course, being a participant in the action affords a character opportunities for direct observation. But an opportunity for observing is not quite a monopoly on telling—neither a necessary nor a sufficient condition, in stricter parlance—or else Homer must have been an eyewitness to the Trojan War and Tolstoy to Napoleon's campaign in Russia. In the biblical context, above all, the invocation of participantship hardly affects the secret of authorship. As long as we have no independent access to the original events (and we usually haven't) and as long as the writer does not explain his access to them (and he doesn't), an eyewitness account remains indistinguishable from one born of, say, hearsay evidence. (This is why the rabbis could so easily shift between autobiographical and biographical or editorial nominees, without fear of empirical contradiction.) The two accounts may be equally true, equally false, equally artful or persuasive or bungled, equally (mis)taken for historical by readers ancient and modern. Whatever the blow to wishful thinking, not even the most sophisticated analysis can tell them apart in such conditions.

These conditions even undergo a drastic change for the worse (if possible) when the narrative conveys information beyond human reach, like internal processes or the workings of divinity. If in regard to observable affairs the "eyewitness" and the "hearsay" or "compiler" hypotheses are equally powerful, then the introduction of privileged material leaves them equally helpless: neither can explain the discourse about humanly inaccessible reality (thoughts, Providence) in terms of empirical access. As a contradiction in terms, this hamstrings the genetic quest for the writer, which must establish a line of realistic access to information or it is nothing. If much of the material is beyond any writer's reach, then it was invented in the writing, whether by way of guesswork or conventional embroidery or for that matter divine inspiration. And if invention is at work, the range of possible writers becomes indefinitely large and definitely irreducible to a single name.

Disheartening as this conclusion may sound, it is inescapable and, what is more, has a constructive side too. It clears the ground for a shift from the doomed line of inquiry to another that does not labor under such hindrance because it involves an entirely different object, problems, methods. I am referring to the shift from composition as *genesis* to composition as *poesis*.

From this new perspective, the facts that have so far proved obstinate readily lend themselves to explanation. To say that the biblical writer exercises or enjoys the license of invention (under whatever guise) is to say that he is omniscient; and to say that he is omniscient is to invest him with a storytelling privilege that the same writer would hardly lay claim to in his everyday life (least of all, if he indeed happens to double as a character, his life within the tale). On laying down the pen with which he had just been tracing the inmost mysteries of God and humanity, a Jehoshafat would no more presume to read his own wife's mind with any approach to certainty than the rest of us do. Or, if tempted into presumption in the teeth of experience, he would meet the usual consequences (from which, as we shall see, not even biblical prophets are immune). Moreover, a Jehoshafat who has just composed with such perfect assurance all the ins and outs of the Bathsheba affair, say, will the next moment fall into irresolution as he considers the snags and exigencies of the Absalom saga. How to characterize Absalom? Why did David fail to control his son? Would it be wise (or effective) to dramatize the king's humiliation en route to the Jordan? Which of the variant explanations of the rebels' faulty tactics makes the best sense? Who might be consulted about the intertribal politics of the time? What form, if any, is God's intervention to assume? And so forth. At last, all inquiries and decisions made, the pen is taken up again to produce yet another masterpiece, complete with motive, background, divine blessing, and, throughout, the stamp of authority. Obviously, its producer is the same man as the waverer, but not in and therefore not of the same capacity.

Whoever the biblical writer was, he did not speak in his own voice and by his natural privileges. Hence the imperative need to distinguish the person from the persona: the writer as the historical man (citizen, partisan, functionary, hunter of facts and records) behind the writing from the writer as the authorial figure reflected in the writing. The person (the object of genetics) may be lost beyond recovery, but the persona (the object of poetics) is very much there, pervading and governing the narrative by virtue of qualifications denied to his historical, quotidian, flesh-and-blood self anyway. Being two faces of the same entity—two modes of authorial existence—these are no more mutually exclusive than identical. Rather, they always remain distinct in principle, and so accordingly do the lines of inquiry oriented to them—the one concerned with the writer's features or portrait as an individual and the other with his portrait as an artist. In fact, they not only preserve but also redouble their essential distinctiveness amidst the mysteries that surround the formation of the Bible while leaving its art of communication in full view. Due to this very contrast in transparence, however, poesis stands to genesis in a more dominant relation than usual.

Normally, the historical writer (Dante, Balzac, Joyce) is a given, relatively speaking at least, whereas his artistic self or surrogate is a construct that the interpreter pieces together from the text as an embodiment of its art. Hence the common interpretive practice of turning to the more or less known quantity for aid in the reconstruction of the unknown. Notebooks, biographies, and early drafts alert us to possible intentions; manifestoes and milieus suggest a range of operative conventions; and, what even strong objectors to "external evidence" would hardly deny, facts so elementary as dating establish the relevant linguistic usage. All that the solemn warnings against the "intentional fallacy" have actually managed to achieve is to delimit and refine rather than eliminate the appeal to such aids to inference. And it is a pity indeed—let me repeat—that enthusiasts about the "literary" approach to the Bible should preach antihistorical doctrines whose brief heyday has long passed and which were never quite literally meant, let alone practiced, even by their New Critical originators. Taken as gospel, such preaching would just duplicate in the field of biblical study the sound and the fury that raged in literary theory within living memory, with none of the lessons learned and to much less purpose. Its imperialistic or isolationist claims for "textual" as opposed to "historical" analysis would generate unnecessary antagonism in those who find their concerns belittled, if not virtually illegitimated, and at the same time mislead the converted.

The question of writing and its models illustrates how this missionary zeal may confuse the issue just where the practicalities of the situation bring the various approaches together, enforcing a community of labor whereby poetics becomes the key to genesis. For the biblical question of authorship, like the Homeric or the Icelandic saga's, bears no resemblance to the normal state of affairs. Here we can find out incomparably more about the writer as an artist than as a man. Therefore, it is not only that both lines of inquiry consist in reconstructions. The very direction of reconstructive activity gets reversed. So far as there are any warnings to be issued against carry-over fallacies, they bear on the movement from the artist to the man: for example, from the skill or objectivity or informational range displayed by the composer of Samuel to the non sequitur that Jehoshafat (or whoever) possessed the necessary qualifications.[8] And so far as there are aids to be invoked, they again concern a similar movement: from the language, the structure, the world view, or the attitudes toward the dramatis personae, say, to the circle or milieu that might reasonably have produced them. The sharper one's insight into what a biblical writer does—the why's and the how's of his communication—the sounder one's guess of who he might or might not be. Indeed, short of miraculous finds, the only chance for this branch of detective work lies in the refining of the interpretive tools brought to bear on the literature that has come down to us. In this sense, the poetics developed in this book has, as poetics, constructive as well as admonitory implications for source criticism. But regardless of the direction of inference, whether we go from the artist to the man or from the man to the artist, the two objects lose none of their distinctiveness. The one remains part of the strategy of the text, the other part of the circumstances that went into the making of the text. Or in the complementary terms I suggested: whether our interest focuses on the discourse or on the source, the writer's two selves—the persona and the person or, when anonymous, his historical framework—have a role to play, but in diametrically opposed means–end combinations.

Nor, to meet a predictable objection, does this difference get blurred by the notorious problematics of the Bible, especially the alleged shift in authorship from book to book or even within the same book. On the contrary, these pluralities (whatever the darkness enveloping them) only throw it into higher relief.

If different narrative books were composed by different hands in different times and conditions, then it becomes all the more remarkable that this mixed array of writers should have cast themselves in essentially the same role or posture as storytellers. Take books as far removed from one another—in subject matter and very possibly origin and date of final shaping too—as Genesis, Samuel, and Jonah. In all three, for instance, the storyteller appears only as a disembodied voice, nameless and faceless. In all three, he avoids all reference to the act of storytelling—to himself as maker, recorder, editor, or even narrator—nor does he betray the least consciousness of facing an audience by way of direct address and the like. In all three, he exercises all the privileges of omniscience, in sharp (because qualitative) opposition to both his dramatis personae and his own everyday self. (Not to mention the concomitant features and practices we shall be discussing throughout.) In certain other respects, of course, like idiom or doctrinal emphasis, each may go his own way to some extent, possibly under the influence of his time and place and commitments. But such divergences only validate and highlight the constancies that persist to establish a literary tradition. As far as the basic narrative traits and tactics that make up a storyteller's portrait are concerned, they all show an impressive family resemblance or, in diachronic terms, continuity: a unity of artistic persona in a variety of historical person.

Far from self-evident, such unity in variety is often absent in comparable corpora old and new, the output of a single writer notably included. Consider a few examples, in an ascending order of proximity to Israelite storytelling. Nobody would be surprised to encounter the most radical shifts of narrative posture and convention in modern writing, notorious for its experimentation and generic diversity. The oeuvre of Henry James is a case in point. In the novels, from *Roderick Hudson* to *The Golden Bowl,* he speaks as an all-privileged superhuman, hampered by nothing except his own choices. In the shorter tales, like *The Aspern Papers* or *The Turn of the Screw,* he speaks through a dramatized and fallible observer, who performs the task of narration under all the constraints humanity is subject to. In the autobiographies, he reminisces in the voice of a Henry James looking back on his own youth and thus under the conventions of real-life rather than fictive storytelling. Whereas in the Notebooks he soliloquizes as an artist struggling with his materials, and in the Prefaces addresses the world in the role of the Master to lay down the laws of his craft.

Well over two thousand years earlier, however, Xenophon appears in *Anabasis* as an eyewitness to the march of the Ten Thousand, in *Hellenica* as a Thucydidean persona rounding off the history of the Peloponnesian War, in *Memorabilia* as a recollector of his teacher Socrates. Earlier still, Oriental narrative shifts between the forms of (third person) impersonality and (first person) autobiography, genuine or fictitious. Occidentally-oriented historians of literature, even when otherwise as wide-ranging as Scholes and Kellogg, attribute the development of the autobiographical stance to the Romans.[9] Millennia before, in fact, this form runs through the modes of Oriental writing: poetry and prose, fancy and history, tombstone inscription and royal letter to the gods, self-contained genre and component of, say, law codes and international treaties. Here are some typical exordiums: "Sargon, the mighty king, king of Agade, am I" (*The Legend of Sargon*); "Anum and Enlil named me / to promote the welfare of the people, / me, Hammurabi, the devout, god-fearing prince" (*The Code of Hammurabi*); "Ah-Mose, son of Eben, the triumphant, says: I speak to you, all mankind, that I may let you know the favors which have come to me" (*The Expulsion of the Hyksos*). Not only does personal outnumber impersonal narration; it also includes masterpieces, like the Egyptian "Story of Sinue" or Esarhaddon's account of his fight for the throne (*Ancient Near Eastern Texts*, pp. 119, 164, 233, 18–22, 289–90).

Even the poetry of the Bible itself reveals similar variations, within as well as across books. Indeed, this marks an important generic distinction between poetry and narrative, certainly one more firm than the sands of parallelism. The Psalter thus operates with a whole range of selves, voices, viewpoints, personae, situational contexts of utterance. Some Psalms are attributed, or even anchored in space and time, and others emerge from nowhere. Some are soliloquies, others appeals, still others dialogues. Some speak with one voice, others with many voices; some in the voice of the individual, others of the collective.

All this bespeaks a repertoire of viable conventions of point of view—of stance, distance, camouflage—to which the writer may appeal in constructing his discourse and the reader must pay heed in reconstructing it. Such multiple options once institutionalized by the genre or culture, there is no way to determine in advance the relations established in a specific work between the composer and the teller or speaker. They may extend all the way from opposition to virtual identity: opposition where the teller's features and privileges are either superior (as with James's novelistic omniscients) or inferior (as with his limited observers) to his creator's, virtual identity where (as with James's nonfictional autobiographies) they are more or less the same. In the latter instance, the distinction may lose its cutting edge, since no practical consequences follow from the separation of the two selves.

But this does not at all apply to biblical narrative, which systematically pursues the line of opposition. The otherwise assorted books conform to a single model of narration, whereby the narrating persona wields powers not just different from but closed to his historical maker, whoever he may be. It is exactly here that Ezra (in part) and Nehemiah, both late works from the Persian period, break with the tradition. If taken as apocryphal memoirs—like the still later Daniel, set in Nebuchadnezzar's court (d. 562 B.C.) but alluding across four centuries to Antiochus Epiphanes (d. 163 B.C.)—then the writer is the first to keep his frontsman on his own level, bestowing on the memoirist no supernatural powers of vision. And if these accounts are taken as real memoirs composed as well as narrated by Ezra and Nehemiah themselves, like Xenophon's *Anabasis*, then the departure from the biblical model even sharpens. As befits autobiography, their telling then brings together subject and object, chronicler and hero, through the nexus of the historical self common to both. Looking back on his own career, each narrates in his own name, in his own person, and hence in the eyewitness mode that assumes no special privileges in the treatment of either God or man—including the man that he himself was as agent and now is as writer. Accordingly, their commissions are the standard biblical teller's omissions, and vice versa. What is more, just as their narrative features group together into a coherent portrait, so do his. For his escape from the real self—from self-identification, from the egocentricity of the "I," from narrow spatiotemporal coordinates—signals and motivates the assumption of another self qualified to perform the telling. Only by disembarrassing oneself of the limitations of personality inherent in human nature can one credibly exercise the superhuman privileges offered by art, religious or secular. Hence the perfect antithesis between "Here is Nehemiah. I was there, and therefore I am competent to tell" and "Here is the voice of narrative. I am everywhere, transcendent, and therefore speak with authority."

As with the *inter*textual, so with the *intra*textual plurality of writers. No matter what the text's process of transmission and through how many hands (writers, composers, editors, interpolators) it is supposed to have passed before hardening into canonical form, the same opposition always holds. Again, the more various the sources of a narrative book, the more tortuous the genesis, and the more diverse the intentions attributed to the line of contributors—the wildest guesswork will do for the purpose—the more striking the adherence to a single model of narration. The contributors might obtrude on the tale the most heterogeneous things—from glosses to philosophies—but not, Nehemiah fashion, their own selves.

Even in modern times, processes of revision do not always exhibit such a religious observance of consistency in point of view, still less an adherence to a single paradigm such as depersonalization in the interests of authority. In reworking *Moby Dick,* for example, Melville so destabilized the point of view that the narrative incongruously shifts between Ishmael's eyewitness testimony and some omniscient perspective.[10] The genesis of Dostoevsky's *Crime and Punishment* and Kafka's *The Castle* went the other way: the early draft underwent a strategic recasting from the first to the third person, whereby the original narrator-agent (Raskolnikov, K.) became a reflector observed from without.[11] Even the exiguous records of antiquity supply parallels. In the passage from the Sumerian to the Babylonian version, the deluge myth thus transformed from the anonymous into the personal mode, with the Noah-like Utanapishtim serving as narrator.[12] Nor is the Bible itself wholly an exception. Having started as an impersonal chronicle, Ezra abruptly shifts into a memoir. On the other hand, Jeremiah begins with a self-introduction ("The words of Jeremiah, the son of Hilkia . . ."), but shuttles between the first and the third person throughout. Yet the exception does not go beyond the works of prophecy and the late prose offshoots: the mainstream of biblical narrative betrays no sign of such wavering in viewpoint. In this regard, then, our distinction between genesis and poetics even cuts across that of process and product. The narrative persona remains constant under all editorial and transmissional as well as personal variations.

For expository simplicity, as students of narrative will have noticed, I have operated thus far with two concepts where three might come into question. Since Wayne Booth's *The Rhetoric of Fiction,* theorists have tended to make a threefold distinction among the actual writer, the implied author, and the narrator. Briefly, the writer is the historical figure who, amidst other activities, composed the work at a certain time and place, from motives ranging from self-expression to financial gain. The implied author is the image of the author projected by the text itself as the creator of its art and meaning and norms, pulling strings to manipulate the reader into the desired attitudes: as such, the implied author forms a construct embodying the overall structure and may vary even from one work to another by the same writer. The narrator, last, is the figure chosen and devised by the author to perform the telling. *The Turn of the Screw* was *written* in 1897 by the expatriate Henry James under the inspiration of an anecdote concerning dead servants with sinister designs on the children of the house; *implies* an author fascinated with ambiguity as an artistic and epistemological issue; and *narrates* the action through a governess who either sees or hallucinates ghosts waylaying her young charges.

Much as it has to recommend it, such tripartition does not quite apply in the biblical context. To be precise, it is both less and more relevant than in certain other models of storytelling. Less, because the implied author and the narrator to whom he delegates the task of communication practically merge into each other here. The biblical narrator is a plenipotentiary of the author, holding the same views, enjoying the same authority, addressing the same audience, pursuing the same strategy, self-effacement included. Like the *Odyssey* or *Emma* and unlike *The Turn of the Screw*, in short, no ironic distance separates these figures of maker and teller. They stand and fall together. And since keeping the two apart yields no practical gain, I shall employ the more univocal term "narrator" to refer to the master of the tale in general.

On the other hand, the distinction crucial to my argument holds with even greater force than ever. In contrast to the merging indicated in the last paragraph, the distance between the historical writer and the implied author/narrator is so marked, indeed unbridgeable, that they not only can but must be distinguished. Nor does their opposition rest on modern (and therefore anachronistic) premises, like unitary composition. The fact that the storyteller's persona retains its essential features throughout the mutations of biblical narrative (and of each specific narrative) demonstrates the contrary. Whether he happens to be a single person or a plurality of hands—a haphazard line, a school, a committee—the "writer" remains the text's genetic originator as against its poetic manipulator. To say that the one embodies the contingencies of the process and the other the regularities of the product amounts to saying that the one lived in history and the other comes to life in interpretation. The author/narrator exists only as a construct, which the reader infers and fills out to make sense of the work as an ordered design of meaning and effect. He is what he does in and through the writing, the embodiment of the sense and the composition and the whole reading experience he has devised for us. This makes him the interpreter's mirror image. Where our interpretations differ, so do our reconstructions of his image—ways, means, and all. But reconstruct him according to our lights we must, all of us, not excluding the most dedicated geneticist. For a moment's thought will reveal that the very fragmentation of a biblical tale into sources, documents, etc. presupposes a unity distinctive of some teller, and the triumphant pointing to some version as *the* original form announces his disentanglement from the overall process of transmission. Even to anatomize, one has first to read; and reading entails the postulation of a determinate artificer as a strategy of coherence.

Concerning the basic model of storytelling, therefore, the Bible raises not conceptual but practical problems, and even these have been blown up out of all proportion. Of course, the implicit authorial figure may vary from one book to another, but hardly so much as does the early from the late Tolstoy. Of course, the possibly eventful genesis of each book must not be lost sight of in interpretation; but neither must that of the *Nibelungenlied* nor, on record for a change, Proust's *Remembrance of Things Past* and Dostoevsky's major fiction. As a matter of principle, referring a textual incongruity to the fortunes of the creative process—known or conjectured—is an explanatory resource to which we can always appeal at need. The question is only where and when that need to shift from poesis to genesis arises from reasons other than an interpreter's bad or set ways.

It is not here, then, that the Bible's uniqueness lies. At this general level, its structure even goes a long way beyond the minimal requirements of narrative toward establishing contact with artistic narrative. Personality suppressed or transformed, situational context and occasion despecified, licenses freely assumed—whether taken as conditions or privileges, these all mark the literary artwork. Indeed, the Bible's narration looks so familiar in this light that the danger is rather that its peculiarities may escape notice.

The danger concentrates in the kind of sense made of the narrator's prerogatives. Whence his authority? In the Esther passage, we recall, the rabbis postulate divine inspiration to account for his unlimited access to knowledge. Given the premise, this covers (as the geneticist's "empirical" model does not) the whole range of departures from verisimilitude: the intervention of the Holy Spirit levels all the barriers that normally divide the far from the near, the private from the public, the interior from the exterior. And just as the ancients' realism in attributing authorship anticipates modern developments, so does their supernatural approach to privilege bear resemblance to the line of explanation that the student of narrative would take as a matter of course. Only, what the rabbis literally affirm to be the narrative situation, i.e., God speaking through an inspired medium, would become in the modern's hands a metaphor for an artistic structure, wherein a godlike author speaks through a narrator invested with all his authority. As a result, what within the inspirational model of narrative serves to validate the Bible's unique claim to truth—divine omniscience—transforms in the quasi-inspirational model into the Bible's recourse to a universal convention of fiction.

Such modernizing (not quite hypothetical, if you recall the Bible-as-fiction line) would be seriously wrong. And since the enthusiasm for "application" is so much in evidence nowadays, I want to emphasize that literary theory has not come to grips yet with the question of omniscience and the automatic assimilation to its rigid typologies would do violence to a novel by Flaubert or Dostoevsky, let alone an ancient original.[13] In the Bible's case, such automatism would certainly erase and distort a set of features that have both distinctive value and sobering implications for the theoretical paradigm itself. If anything, the analogy between the literal and the figurative models of privileged narration might serve to bring out those features by way of contrast. The contrast between inspirational and quasi-inspirational discourse suffices to produce a distinction in nothing less than genre. But this evidently needs some clarification.

In line with his self-effacing policy, the biblical narrator no more lays any explicit claim to inspiration than he makes other mentions of himself and his terms of reference. But the empirical evidence, historical and sociocultural as well as compositional, leaves no doubt about his inspired standing.

In ancient narrative, for one thing, inspiration is the rule of the non-empirical mode, or in other words, all-knowing enjoys supernatural imprimatur. At times, the storytellers themselves articulate these privileged terms of communication. Homer starts each of his epics by invoking the Muse, nor does he hesitate to appeal to her on special occasions, like the mustering of the two armies in the *Iliad*. In the "Hymn to the Muses" that prefaces his *Theogony*, Hesiod celebrates these deities not only as the source and author of his own art ("the Muses once taught Hesiod to sing" and "breathed a voice into my mouth") but also as the embodiment of the universal power of poetry, delighting Zeus with their sweet recital "of things that are, that will be, and that were."[14] As far from the Greek orbit as Mesopotamia, we recall, Kabti-ilani-Marduk describes himself as the mediator of the *Irra Epic*: "It was revealed to him in the night, and when he spoke it in the morning, he did not leave out a single line, nor did he add one to it." More strangely, the Egyptian "Instruction of King Amen-em-het" is spoken by the pharaoh himself from the other world, revealing to his son with the oracular voice of a god the details of the treacherous attack made on him in life.[15]

The Bible would hardly qualify as the exception to this rule. In the Pentateuch, the two figures engaged in writing are God himself (Exod 24:12; 32:16) and more often Moses, divinely ordered to produce written memorials and exalted as one who spoke to God "face to face" (Exod 33:11) or even "mouth to mouth" (Num 12:8). What this linkage of writing and authority implies is not that the author must be Moses but that he must be Moses-like. This hallowed paradigm extends by implication and association to the following narrative cycles as well. The fact that the books that immediately ensue, from Joshua to Kings, have been canonized under the rubric of "Former Prophets" speaks for itself. And in the very last book of the canon, most of the written documents named by the Chronicler are by seers and prophets: the "records" of "Samuel the seer" and "Nathan the prophet" and "Gad the seer" (1 Chr 29:29) or "the prophecy of Ahijah the Shilonite and the visions of Iddo the seer" (2 Chr 9:29).

As with the author, moreover, so with his public. The text not only *implies* its reader as well as its author. It implies the one (as attuned to inspiration) by implying the other (as inspired). And what the discourse implies is in fact supported by the historical record: the tenet of inspiration again cuts across cultural boundaries, including that between polytheism and monotheism. Within each world picture, the evidence indicates the audience's readiness not only to acknowledge such claims but to supply them where left implicit. The Ashurbanipal catalogue thus echoes the *Irra* poet's self-portrayal as a divine vehicle—he "spoke" the tale that "was revealed" to him—just as it directly attributes other works to the god Ea, considered a provider of esoteric knowledge to man (Lambert, "Catalogue," pp. 64–67). Even Plato, who would expel poets from his ideal republic, by no means denies them supernatural gifts.[16] A whole dialogue, *Ion,* explores this theme: "All good poets, epic as well as lyric, compose their beautiful poems not by art, but because they are inspired and possessed. . . . They tell us that they bring songs from honeyed fountains, culling them out of the gardens and dells of the Muses. . . . And this is true. For the poet is a light and winged and holy thing . . . and there is no invention in him. . . . They are simply inspired to utter that to which the muse impels them. . . . God himself is the speaker and through them he addresses us" (*Ion* 533–34; trans. Benjamin Jowett). Plato goes so far as to bring the whole communicative process under the auspices of inspiration. He describes its working in terms of a magnetic field or chain that transmits the divine afflatus from Muse to poet to rhapsode or actor to audience: "Through all these God sways the souls of men in any direction which he pleases, causing each link to communicate the power to the next" (*Ion* 535–36).

As for the Bible's own circuit of inspired communication, its internal positing is the most vivid and its empirical attestation the most impressive and prolonged. By internal positing I mean the audience-response invited and shaped by the discourse itself, notably by appeal to the speaker's authority. It is to this end that the books of prophecy resort to both fiat and dramatization. The call scenes, the staging of vision and vigil, Ezekiel's eating of the divine scroll: these command faith and reverence by doing rhetorical duty for an ambassador's credentials. Its laws ruling out such obtrusion of self and speech-context, biblical narrative yet weaves more oblique parallels into the action. Consider just two, which self-reflexively imply and motivate our distinction of person from persona. The reference to the gift of prophecy as God's bestowing on man "another heart" (1 Sam 10:9) is another figure for Plato's inspiration-as-transformation doctrine.

Whereas God's dismissal of Moses' speech impediment by saying that it is he who gives man "a mouth" literally echoes a topos of inspired composition. Examples would be the Mesopotamian formula "by the mouth of," which expresses the relation between text and author;[17] Hesiod's Muses putting "a voice into his mouth"; and the Platonic argument that it was to demonstrate the heavenly origin of poetry that "by the mouth of the worst of poets [God] sang the best of songs" (*Ion* 534–35). Within Israelite culture, if anything, such norms must have been taken even more seriously than anywhere else. It is inconceivable that a storyteller who keeps in closer touch with God's doings and sentiments than the very prophets who figure among his dramatis personae would operate as their inferior in divine sanction; or that his claim would be challenged by the only society that canonized its sacred writings because it pinned on them faith and hope alike.

Nor, to judge from the surviving records of attitude in ancient times, did they. The book of Kings, for instance, is punctuated with mentions and dramatizations of the reverence in which "the book (or the law) of Moses" was held, along a period that extends from David (1 Kgs 2:3) through Amaziah (2 Kgs 14:6) to Josiah (2 Kgs 22–23). A scene set in the fifth century B.C. describes how Ezra arranged a solemn public reading of "the book of the law of Moses which the Lord had given to Israel" and all the people "bowed their heads and worshipped the Lord with their faces to the ground" (Neh 8; cf. 2 Chr 17:9). "All wisdom is from the Lord": thus, three centuries later, opens Jesus ben Sirah's *Ecclesiasticus.* He goes on to exalt the scriptural writers as recipients of divine wisdom; and in effect claims that privilege for himself as well (e.g., 24:32–34). So, in a more underhand way, did the apocalyptic writings, which resorted to pseudonymity in order to gain recognition as the works of inspired men of earlier times: Abraham, Daniel, Moses, Ezra. One of them, 2 Esdras, gives a vivid sense of the canonical authority to which they aspired. It recounts how, the Scriptures having been destroyed by fire, God inspired Ezra to rewrite the whole twenty-four books, "all that has happened in the world since the beginning," and in addition seventy others reserved for "wise men" (14:19–48). In his *Life of Moses,* Philo takes inspiration for granted: "They know this well who read the sacred books, which unless he was such as we have said, he would never have composed under God's guidance" (II, 11). While Josephus waxes eloquent: "It is not open to everybody to write the records. . . . The prophets alone had this privilege, obtaining their knowledge of the most remote and ancient history through the inspiration they owed to God." There is, he continues, "practical proof of our reverence for our own Scriptures. . . . No one has ventured either to add, or to remove, or to alter a syllable; and it is an instinct with every

Jew, from the day of his birth, to regard them as the decrees of God, to abide by them, and, if need be, cheerfully to die for them" (*Against Apion* I, 37–44). And of course, this is one of the rare issues on which the New Testament agrees with the rabbis. "All Scripture is inspired by God," Paul roundly affirms (2 Tim 3:16). Nowhere along this long chain, finally, does any witness distinguish poetry from prose, visionary from narrative communication. Josephus only gives voice, under polemical pressure, to the ancient view of history writing among the Hebrews as a mode and monopoly of prophetic discourse.

To modern ears, all this may sound odd and remote, not to say superstitious. Which only means that we need to be doubly on our guard against confusing the models of narration and origination, of inspired discourse and empirical source. It is all very well for historians and other empiricists to argue that the Israelite recorders of the past were scribes rather than prophets (or that the "Instruction of King Amen-em-het" was composed in his name after his death). For all we know, this may even be true. But to turn such a genetic argument into a condition and directive of interpretation is to offend against history in the name of history. For here genesis itself has a double face: as real-life origin and as culture-bound fountainhead. The two faces can and must be differentiated, but not along historical lines, because both live in history. The only difference is that one relates to the text's historical composition, where all that matters is how it actually came into being, and the other relates to its historical communication, where all that matters is how it works as a system of rules. So, whether or not inspiration counts for something in terms of genesis-as-source, it establishes a divine genesis for the discourse. In the context of the artist's dealings with his audience, the authority he assumes is neither a fraud nor a fancy but an institutional fact.

A glance at the fortunes of scriptural inspiration will demonstrate how essential it is to keep the two apart. In Christianity, as already noted, the forthrightness of Paul's credo, "All Scripture is inspired by God," soon gave way to a tormented concern with the mechanics and limits of inspiration.[18] Are the "Old" and the "New" Testament equally inspired? Is the human writer a mere penman (veritable amanuensis, in Calvin's phrase), or does he give form to the divine content of revelation? Is he inspired or his words, the meaning or the text, down to vowel points? Does Scripture make literal or also allegorical sense?

Most of these questions, hotly and endlessly debated over the centuries, reflect the pressures exerted on the supernatural doctrine by the "natural" world. One set of pressures came from standards of probability, in whose name a church father like Origen dismissed as false the narrative of primeval history or the cleansing of the Temple by the low-born Jesus. Another issued from the advances made by science, whose findings increasingly clashed with biblical statements of fact. On top of it all, there were old textual embarrassments like the discrepancies among the gospels—does God contradict himself?—and new developments in scholarship, notably the rise and growing influence of source criticism, which challenged the very idea of unitary origination. All these combined to make inroads on the original tenet of inspiration. Obviously, the more separable the human element in the Bible from the divine, the more limited the scope of revelation, and the more approved the nonliteral modes of reading—the easier the reconcilement of supernatural authority with natural modality. For all the concessions made over the years, however, the modern age has become notorious for its crisis of faith.

Of this whole ramified matter, the point that concerns us is that only by mistake has this crisis of faith generated a crisis of interpretation. Dogmas come and go, and opinions about the Bible's real-life authority show infinite variety. But personal opinion about fact or faith is one thing, and interpretive strategy another. Interpreters must either invent their own biblical text or grant the storyteller all the storytelling authority (divine and otherwise) he enjoys in cultural context. Across all doctrinal boundaries, inspiration simply figures as an institutional rule for writing and reading; and it is no more liable to questioning than the Bible's rules of grammar (or the reality of *Hamlet*'s ghost). To make sense of the Bible in terms of its own conventions, one need not believe in either, but one must postulate both. And to postulate inspiration is to elevate the narrator to the status of omniscient historian, combining two otherwise irreconcilable postures or models: the constrained historian and the licensed fiction-maker.

In this light, the approaches to the Bible as inferior history and superior fiction turn out equally anachronistic (and deficient in explanatory power at that). No more viable but far stranger is the dismissal of the whole problem as irrelevant to literary analysis. This line has lately been taken (or rather revived) in Hans Frei's informative survey of eighteenth- and nineteenth-century hermeneutics, *The Eclipse of Biblical Narrative.* His reasonable claim that what biblical narratives "are about and how they make sense" depend on "the rendering of the events constituting them" goes with a set of unacceptable corollaries. First, that this feature of signification distinguishes "realistic" narrative; second, that it brings together realistic and historical narrative; and third, that this "history-like quality" can be "examined for the bearing it has in its own right on meaning and interpretation," without being confused "with the quite different issue of whether or not the realistic narrative was historical" (pp. 13–16). The fatal flaw in this argument lies in its working with two concepts where no fewer than three will do: history-likeness, history telling, and historicity. In accusing his predecessors of "logical confusion between two categories or contexts of meaning and interpretation" (p. 16), Frei himself thus falls into a triple confusion: (1) between history telling, which relates to the truth claim of the discourse, and historicity, which relates to its truth value and therefore has least to do with "meaning and interpretation"; (2) between both and history-likeness, which turns on neither but goes as a rule with fictionality; (3) between the truth claims of history-like and historical narrative, whose variance has a large bearing on "meaning and interpretation" since it determines the presence or absence of fictional license. And what is this if not a variance in genre and generic convention?

Like most "literary" approaches, then, Frei's is well-intentioned, even laudable, but theoretically misguided. He wishes to focus attention on the biblical text by cutting through the hopeless tangle that religious controversy has made of the issues of inspiration and history. But instead of suspending judgment on them as articles of faith oriented to a heavenly source and retaining them as institutional premises (features, coordinates) of the discourse, he tries to neutralize them altogether. And such premises will not be quietly neutralized. Generally speaking, realism or history-likeness never has a bearing "in its own right on meaning and interpretation," because it signifies one thing in a historiographical and another in a fictional context. Even more evidently, neither the omniscient narration nor the supernaturalness of the narrated world, for example, will read the same under these variations in narrative contract; nor will the clashes between the realistic and the nonrealistic. It is exactly to resolve such indeterminacies in truth claim—hence in genre and meaning—that the Bible's inspirational model of narrative operates. It builds the supernatural into the pattern of historiography as well as of history, by crediting God with the authorship or prime movership of both.

With God postulated as double author, the biblical narrator can enjoy the privileges of art without renouncing his historical titles. Here, the line dividing the inspirational from the quasi-inspirational model of discourse becomes most apparent and assumes generic force. Equally institutionalized, they yet refer to very different institutions of writing. The marriage of omniscience to fiction and of restrictedness to factual report is a much later arrival on the scene of narrative, deriving from an earthbound view both of the world and the rules for its representation. Born of a new sense of realism that has established itself as the common-sense norm, it shows an empirical or rationalistic approach in disallowing the supernatural outside the framework of myth, religion, and other fictions. Its spirit is also more egalitarian in that it allows the storyteller no undue advantage over his audience. He must either appeal to supernatural license, thereby sounding the gong of fictional communication, or operate within the human condition if he desires to produce a (real or simulated) impression of factuality. In short, epistemological privilege goes with art, epistemological constraint with authenticity. The assumptions underlying this formula have not gone unchallenged in the tradition of the novel itself, least of all in modernist writing,[19] and lately in the philosophy of history too. But they must be wholly exorcised from the reading of the Bible, where the narrator may freely "cross" the two pairings to have the best of both worlds.

Finally, even if the narrator's privileges were assumed and interpreted only by analogy to the divine order, there would still remain a vital difference from the modern rule. For the Bible collocates throughout the analogized power and the analogue, the figure and its paradigm, the artifice and the real thing. The narrator stands to the world of his tale as God to the world represented in that tale, each reigning supreme in his own sphere of activity. To the extent that the conventional model of narrative applies, therefore, it does so only with a loop that circles back to the starting point of figuration, keeping the literal-figurative relationship alive and its problematics to the fore.

The next chapter will explore the forms and functions of this correspondence, which is at the heart of our subject. This will enable us, first, to correlate the two superpowers of the Bible and, in their light, to bring the human order into the picture. It will also disclose the points at which biblical narration varies from its ancient counterparts (which likewise incorporate the superhuman world) as well as from novelistic realism (where the metaphor alone appears as a residual convention). Most important, it will bring out the unique rationale behind these features and departures: that the divine order provides not only an analogical but an ideological justification for the narrator's exercise of divine powers. And if the analogy would by itself raise him to the status of a god, then the ideology shows him raising himself by art only to serve God all the more effectively.

·3·

IDEOLOGY OF NARRATION
AND NARRATION OF IDEOLOGY

Man sees what meets the eye and God sees
into the heart.

1 Samuel 16:7

"You are my witnesses," says the Lord.

Isaiah 43:10

It is wise to keep a king's secret, but the works
of God should be gloriously revealed.

The Book of Tobit

Omniscience Charged and Monopolized:
The Epistemological Revolution

"Why is the biblical narrator omniscient?" poses two distinct questions,
according to whether one takes the "why" as a request for evidence or for
explanation. In the first sense, the answer is by now simple enough: his
narrative manifests all the privileges of knowledge that transcend the
human condition. For one thing, the narrator has free access to the
minds ("hearts") of his dramatis personae, not excluding God himself
("The Lord repented that he had made man on the earth and it grieved
him to his heart. And the Lord said, I will blot out man" [Gen 6:6-7]).
For another, he enjoys free movement in time (among narrative past,
present, and future) and in space (enabling him to follow secret conversations, shuttle between simultaneous happenings or between heaven and
earth). These two establish an unlimited range of information to draw
upon or, from the reader's side, a supernatural principle of coherence and
intelligibility. For the narrative provides us with an assortment of plot-
stuff that would normally be inaccessible. Any attempt to naturalize it in
terms of human vision and transmission invites the short shrift given by
T. H. Huxley in *Science and Hebrew Tradition* to some of his overreaching

contemporaries. Who, he asks with heavy sarcasm, is afraid of "the supposition that the mother of Moses was told the story of the Flood by Jacob; who had it straight from Shem; who was on friendly terms with Methuselah; who knew Adam quite well?"[1] Indeed, the Bible knows better than to forfeit its claim to truth by catching at this straw of realism. It directs us instead to make sense of the violence done to the constraints on access by appeal to inspirational convention: the narrator speaks with the authority of omniscience.

What reinforces our sense of narratorial omniscience is that the Bible not merely assumes but concretizes the opposition to the human norm throughout, most obviously in the form of dramatic irony that no character (and to rub it in, no reader) escapes. His firm hold on the truth stands out in direct proportion to their blindness, stumbling, wonder, mystification; and vice versa. The rabbis (followed by other religious exegetes) often blur this vital contrast by freely attributing to the characters themselves gifts of divine inspiration, foreknowledge and mind-reading included. Take some examples from *Bereshit Rabba* on patriarchal history. Abraham is supposed to have built an altar between Bethel and Ai (12:8) because he foresaw the violation of the ban that would take place there in Joshua's time. The murderous thoughts Esau entertains "in his heart" (27:41–42) have been revealed to Rebekah by the Holy Spirit. And when Jacob sends his sons back to the Egyptian vizier with the wish "May God Almighty grant you mercy before the man, that he may release your other brother and Benjamin" (43:14), the substitution of the oblique referring term for "Simeon" is taken to mean that Jacob prophetically includes Joseph himself in the prospective reunion.[2]

Apart from the desire to aggrandize patriarchal or other national figures, such pieces of midrash show an urge to impose coherence: to tighten the narrative in terms of doctrinal history, to eliminate incongruities, whether situational (as in Rebekah's case) or linguistic (as in Jacob's), or simply to devise a richer reading. But all indulge this urge at the expense of the Bible's perspectival structure. Even where perspectival coherence is exactly what they set out to establish—How can Rebekah see into Esau's heart?—they heal the part by doing violence to the whole. The "inspiration" is indeed there, but its recipient is, as usual, the narrator rather than the character. To equate the two viewpoints by ad hoc elevation and patchwork is always to confuse the Bible's world view, often to alter the meaning to the point of reversal. This is the case with Jacob, who, even more ignorant of Joseph's survival than the brothers, unwittingly resorts to a term that only those in the know can view as a happy prospect. The ironic discrepancy in awareness contrived by the narrator works through or against but not with the patriarch.

As with local speakers in biblical monologue and dialogue, so with primary tellers like Nehemiah. This sharp line drawn between limited and omniscient discourse exhibits a mastery of point of view where ancient storytelling, whether fictional or historical, often wobbles or falls back on stylization. Egyptian narrative may thus postulate tellers from the other world; Herodotus quotes bedroom talk between Darius and Atossa; even Thucydides dramatizes speeches of which he had no record. But perhaps the worst offender is Luke. Since many others have compiled versions deriving from "eyewitnesses and ministers of the word," he starts by professing, "it seems good to me also, having followed all things closely for some time past, to write an orderly account for you, the most excellent Theophilus" (1:1-4). But his practice flatly contradicts his empirical undertaking and terms of reference.[3] The angel's apparition to Zechariah, the interior monologues of various characters, Jesus' prayer on the Mount of Olives while the disciples are asleep: all these form events accessible only by the privilege of omniscience which Luke virtually disclaims. So the narrative logic breaks down in the telling—and for no reason except inadvertence or, less charitably, a yearning for eyewitness-like authority divorced from any readiness to pay the price in limitation.

Luke's biblical counterparts are neither slipshod nor greedy. They stand opposed to the omniscient narrator in bowing to the same constraints on human vision that he observes religiously (the *mot juste,* this) throughout the discourse of his figures. Thus, Nehemiah cannot and does not know more than the next man; nor does he pretend to omnipresence or omnipenetration. The opening scene of his memoirs already establishes that as long as the narrator remains in Susa, the Persian capital, he depends on others for news about the surrounding world. On the arrival of a delegation from Judah, Nehemiah hastens to make inquiries "about those who had escaped exile and about Jerusalem. And they said to me, Those who remained there in the province after the exile are in great trouble and disgrace; and the wall of Jerusalem is broken down and its gates destroyed by fire. When I heard these words, I sat down and wept: (1:2-4). The narrating-I is essentially restricted to the observations and discoveries made by his experiencing self. Even ostensible exceptions prove to fall within the decorums of realistic storytelling. Having reported how his party of immigrants appealed to God for protection from the dangers along the way to Jerusalem, Ezra immediately adds, "And he listened to our entreaty" (8:23). How does he know? In suddenly ascending to heaven, does he not usurp the privilege of omniscient narration? Certainly not. Ezra tells his story in retrospect, with that journey far behind him; and, since all the anticipated perils have failed to materialize, he piously infers (rather than directly "knows") that God has smoothed his way. Retrospective closure likewise explains Nehemiah's inside views of his enemies Sanballat and Tobiah: "It displeased them greatly that someone had come to seek the welfare of the children of Israel" (2:10), "He was angry and greatly enraged" (4:1), "They intended to do me harm" (6:2). In context, these motivations have nothing superhuman about them. Note how shallow they are, how acceptable to a partisan audience, how passable by the rules of evidence in the human marketplace. Nehemiah simply derives the opposition's thoughts from their vested interests and manifest behavior. Compared with an omniscient narrator's revelation of discontinuities between word or act and thought—as when Judah puts Tamar off with an excuse (Gen 38:11)—this inferential movement from externals to internals is so modest that no one will challenge the end-product on realistic grounds.

The two models of narrative, the inspirational and the empirical, thus contrast most perspicuously where they seem most alike. Here, again, the Bible was the first to systematize a distinction that theory still fails to register. The form of an inside view (or any other privileged information) must not be confused with its authority or warrant, which alone stamps it as omniscient or hypothetical. As long as the context invites us to judge or explain the rendering of inner life in terms of probability, then even the trappings of omniscience may appear without its premises and force. The narrator still remains a limited observer, who for some reason (brevity, convention, the rhetoric of aspersion, as with Nehemiah, or piety, as with Ezra) chooses to invest what he thinks his subject thinks with a show of objectivity. But his show, always open to challenge from our own reading of the situation, is the omniscient's postulate, which may be taken or left but not subjected to empirical questioning.

We may now pass to the more complex, functional rather than descriptive side of the question "Why is the biblical narrator omniscient?" To some degree, his omniscience lends itself to explanation in terms that attach to this feature throughout the history of narrative: the impact of authoritative discourse, the freedom to weave in and out of minds, the widening of the spatiotemporal range, the ready availability of information for any purpose from maintaining continuity through staging a dialogue to tracing a process, and the option to impart or deny it to the reader at will so as to manipulate him into the desired attitude. Yet these universal functions (to appear in action and interaction throughout my argument) still differ from their equivalents outside the Bible, Oriental or Occidental, ancient or modern. For they figure here as means no less than ends, and means to a particular end at that, one which presses narratorial omniscience into the service of its divine analogue within the world itself. This brings us to the ideology of narration and the narration of ideology.

Models of narration, as I suggested, link with models of reality, sacred and profane. It is curious, therefore, that literary scholars should refer to a superhuman viewpoint as an "Olympian narrator," for the model of omniscient narration they have in mind is actually patterned on the Hebraic rather than the Homeric model of divinity. Homer's gods, like the corresponding Near Eastern pantheons, certainly have access to a wider range of information than the normal run of humanity; but their knowledge still falls well short of omniscience, concerning the past and the present as well as the future. In the *Odyssey*'s opening scene, for example, the gods decide to return Odysseus home from Calypso's island. But the nymph herself has no idea of this development and Hermes must make a special trip to inform her; nor does Poseidon, another interested party and a far more senior deity, since his fellow gods have taken advantage of his temporary absence from Olympus to pass the resolution behind his back. Obversely, the Homeric world holds a seer like Tiresias, endowed with supernatural clairvoyance independently of the gods and exercising it where the powers of a divine Circe fail. Closer to the Bible's sphere, the Egyptian king-god offers a parallel: "His majesty knows what takes place," says a courtier. "There is nothing at all which he does not know. He is like Thoth [god of wisdom] in everything."[4] So does the all-too-human Gilgamesh, described in the Babylonian epic as "He who saw everything within the confines of the land; He who knew all things and was versed in everything."[5] Either way, then, the borderline separating divine from human knowledge gets blurred as a matter of expediency or indifference, if not (as in Egypt) of doctrine.

What is more, Homer and Oriental paganism can well afford this blur, since it is above all in terms of mortality that they draw the line between the two orders of existence. Even the variations in knowledge largely stem from the defining trait—the immortals have been longer around—with little theological or normative significance in themselves. Hence the existential distinction retains its qualitative force throughout: an existent is either a god and immortal or a human (even when of partly divine origin, like Achilles or Gilgamesh) and mortal. Whereas the epistemological distinction leaves room for anomalies like humans possessed of superhuman knowledge, or worse—because illogical—gods manifesting informational privilege in one context and restrictedness in another. Far from troubled by such incongruities, an artist like Homer deliberately exploits them in the interests of plot and theme, irony and suspense. The only perfect omniscience is Homer's own, and it reaches perfection only because exempted from the constraints imposed on his Olympians.

Within the same mode of narration—the omniscient—the Bible's reality-model and its compositional status are poles apart from the Homeric or Near Eastern. It all goes back to an epistemological revolution, which shifted the center of gravity from existence to knowledge. The shift (as already indicated in my first chapter) manifests itself all along the biblical line: doctrine, value, interest, plotting, narration, reading process. Nowhere formulated in terms that a philosopher would deem coherent, it yet regulates the whole discourse in ways and combinations systematic as well as original. The regulating principle is what I call the interplay of the truth and the whole truth. And in tracing this master strategy in its various manifestations,[6] we shall have ample occasion to see how the Bible's new departures in poetics and epistemology make the most of each other.

It is thus profoundly revealing that the Garden of Eden should feature not only the conventional Tree of Life but also the Tree of Knowledge, which has no trace in pagan mythology. If the coexistence of the two trees still implies a balance of the old and the new, the plot at once goes on to erect a hierarchy that completes the break with the surrounding world pictures. The demigod Gilgamesh, all-seeing and all-knowing, embarks on a quest for immortality; Eve and Adam hunger for knowledge—literally, in terms of the symbolic action—and consequently bring themselves under the rule of time.[7] Beyond the opening of Genesis, indeed, the issue of human mortality receives little attention in the narrative as opposed to the prophetic and wisdom books (a generic variable that accounts of biblical theology would do well to observe). In contrast, the omniscience of divinity assumes the greatest importance, both as an article of faith and as a concomitant of absolute powers of action and judgment. It is along this dimension that the Bible draws an impassable line between God and man.

This line, moreover, is not only uniquely drawn but also celebrated. Far from undercutting or even merely presupposing divine omniscience, the Bible summons all its craft to dramatize and inculcate it. Precisely here, on the ground of ideological rhetoric, do world view and narrative technique meet in holy alliance. The Homeric narrator stands above the gods, varying their access to knowledge to suit his own requirements. The biblical narrator and God are not only analogues, nor does God's informational privilege only look far more impressive than the narrator's derivative or second-order authority. The very choice to devise an omniscient narrator serves the purpose of staging and glorifying an omniscient God. The means–end combination typical of ancient literature thus gets practically reversed in the framework of monotheistic art.

At first glance, this divine attribute may be established regardless of the speaker's own privileges. The prophets do not hesitate to preach God's transcendent intelligence (e.g., Isaiah 40), and the author of Job has God in person quash the hero's challenge by two chapters of self-glorifying questions: "Who is it that darkens counsel with words without knowledge? . . . Where wert thou when I laid the foundation of the earth? Tell me, if thou hast understanding. . . . Have the gates of death been revealed to thee? . . .

Declare, if thou knowest all this" (chaps. 38–39). Because of generic disparities, such measures are hardly transplantable, since the knowledge claimed is too metaphysical for the plotting of narrative and the claimants too partisan for its rhetoric. But the substitutes that most readily come to mind are those that occasionally appear in narrative proper. A case in point is the dramatic generalization, of the kind made by Solomon when he opposes in prayer the restricted vision of humanity, "each knowing the affliction of his own heart," to the universal range of God, "for thou alone knowest the hearts of all the children of men" (1 Kgs 8:38–39). More indirectly, the same role may be fulfilled by stereotyped modes of expression, whose very conventionality reflects all the more effectively the underlying cultural presuppositions. In the Tekoite woman's address to David, for example, one simile presupposes God's moral inerrancy ("the king is like the angel of God to discern good and evil") and another his omniscience ("my lord has wisdom like the wisdom of the angel of God to know all things on earth"). That the speaker means to praise David rather than God only underscores the powers of divinity, which so unthinkingly surface as an ideal norm and basis for comparison (2 Sam 14:17, 20).

By themselves, however, such utterances are as limited in their rhetorical as in their personal weight. Set into equally limited narrative, they could only express the speaker's subjective belief, but not confer on it even a show of objective truth. And even if the frame were to dramatize their claims by manifesting God in action as well, it would still be a case of the fallible (narrator) supporting the fallible (agents). The plot would lie open to the same epistemological objection as the moralizing: How does he know? Both would remain, in short, a heaven-oriented interpretation of history by earthlings. The Bible therefore postulates a narrator with such free movement through time and space, the public and the private arena, that he invests his dramatizations with the authority of an omniscience equivalent to God's own. Since this omniscience itself ultimately goes back to God, such tactics of validation may not survive logical analysis—but then rhetoric never does, or else there would be no need for it. Its proof lies in the swallowing, and the Bible's art makes resistance difficult, certainly to the implied audience of believers. And whether or not interpreters share this belief, they cannot make proper sense of the narrative unless they take the narrator's own omniscience as an institutional fact and his demonstration of God's omniscience as a informing principle.

This principle has a remarkable explanatory force, since it links together an assortment of apparently disparate, pointless or even incongruous features spread over biblical discourse. Leaving all formulas of divine praise to the characters, the narrator concentrates his own energies on devising a rhetoric of glorification. Thereby God variously enters into patterns of epistemological opposition: overt and covert, actional and formal, expected and surprising, bearing on externals and internals. Divine omniscience is sometimes highlighted by way of contrast to some abstract norm of access that would make it humanly impossible. Take the sequence where the voice of the Israelite stomach ("Who will give us meat to eat?") is first "heard" by Moses and reported to God ("They weep before me and say, Give us meat that we may eat") and then re-echoed by God himself in response ("You have wept in the hearing of the Lord, saying, Who will give us meat to eat?"). The juxtaposition of the original outcry and its two "hearings" dramatizes a clear message: God, whose quotation turns out more accurate than Moses' paraphrase, does not really need an intermediary to keep abreast of developments on earth (Num 11:4–18). As with past so with future, and as with speech and conduct so with access to thought:

> (10) He [Abraham's divine visitor] said, When I come back to thee at about a life's interval, Sarah thy wife shall have had a son. And Sarah was listening at the tent entrance, which was behind him. (11) Now Abraham and Sarah were old, advanced in years; it had ceased to be with Sarah after the manner of women. (12) So Sarah laughed to herself, saying, After I have withered, shall I have pleasure—and my husband old? (13) Then the Lord said to Abraham, Why did Sarah laugh, saying, Shall I indeed give birth, old as I am? (14) Is anything too much for the Lord? At the appointed time I shall come back to thee, at about a life's interval, and Sarah shall have had a son. (15) Sarah denied, saying, I did not laugh, for she was afraid. But he said, No, but thou didst laugh. (Gen 18:10–15)

The scene operates at two levels of awareness. The upper level is inhabited by the divine visitor ("the Lord"), the narrator and the reader, who know everything: the identity of all the participants, the destined birth of Isaac, and the mother-to-be's skepticism. The lower one consists in Sarah's restricted viewpoint. But the tale opposes the two levels not so much to expose the human as to exalt the divine: it even vindicates human blindness to the glory of divine omniscience. With this in view, the narrator is not content to suggest that Sarah has no idea of the company she is keeping. In his interpolated aside on the age of the prospective parents, he goes out of his way to give color to Sarah's laughter at the visitor's forecast: the more natural her doubt, the stronger our sense of God's supernatural prescience. Hence also the otherwise redundant stage direction that she is listening *from* the entrance and the visitor has his back *to* the entrance. Even if Sarah's face betrayed her inner amusement, the speaker could not have observed her expression and must have seen straight into her mind.

With regard to future occurrence or present thought, there is no question here of human methods or contingencies of inference; and the name of Isaac (literally, "will laugh") becomes an eternal tribute to the All-knowing.

Far more often, the transcendent norm finds a concrete anchorage in some observer or antagonist. The most frequent opposition is with the common run of humanity—groping, baffled, laboring under illusions, misled by fear, desire, or plain ignorance—and the Bible unrolls a long procession of multilevel dramas of error and discovery. Each assumes the purely compositional form of contrasted analogy, and may also assume the dramatic form of conflict. In either instance, the confrontation of the human and the divine is often elaborated beyond the immediate requirements of plot and theme in order to bring home the epistemological point.

One measure consists in developing structures of repetition whose features (redundancy, equivalence, variance) gain intelligibility in terms of the perspectival gulf between God and man. It is no accident that such structures abound at the beginning of Genesis, the ideal place to set up premises and generate enduring impressions. Thus, the first interpersonal crime in history is preceded by the notice, "Cain was very angry and his countenance fell" (4:6). Since this inside view conveys the truth on the highest authority, it is strange to find it repeated in the next verse: "The Lord said to Cain, Why art thou angry and why has thy countenance fallen?" For the repetition involves both extreme redundancy in meaning and, despite the change of speaker, parallelism in form. Yet the excesses combine to make rhetorical sense: the twofold equivalence demonstrates God's knowledge—of internals (anger) as well as externals (fallen face)—by maximum reference to the narrator's authority. In turn, this effect sharpens the irony leveled at Cain, who soon plays the innocent in a manner reminiscent of his father's attempt at concealment. Given the recent demonstration, the narrator need not this time repeat his account ("when they were in the field, Cain rose up against his brother Abel and killed him") from his analogue's viewpoint to assure us that God is equally privy to the fratricide. But what the reader now takes for granted Cain has to learn the hard way in the ensuing confrontation. Playing by human rules against a divine opponent,[8] Cain mistakes God's rhetorical question ("Where is Abel thy brother?") for a demand for information, and he therefore pleads ignorance ("I do not know; am I my brother's keeper?"). It must have been quite a shock to discover that he was truly ignorant after all: "What hast thou done? The voice of thy brother's blood is crying to me from the ground!" And what is Cain, like Adam before him and Sarah thereafter, if not a warning or whipping boy for possibly skeptical readers?

Along another line of development, the pattern of confrontation directs the irony at a character supposed either to recognize or to equal divine omniscience. Solomon, we recall, devoutly contrasts man's knowledge of his own heart with God's insight into all hearts. Unfortunately, the king's practice fails to accord with his precept. So, as indicated by the recurrence of "heart" throughout the verse that describes the sin from within and prepares for the retribution, his own phrasing boomerangs: "In Solomon's old age, his wives turned away his heart after other gods, and his heart was not wholly true to the Lord his God as was the heart of David (1 Kgs 11:4). Nor does David himself escape the backlash of the Tekoite woman's compliment—"My lord has wisdom like the wisdom of the angel of God to know all things on earth"—which would do away with the barrier separating the two orders of existence. This is exposed as an empty superlative by way of opposition to reality past (the "David did not know" formulas that punctuate the story of Abner's murder, or his falling into the trap set by Nathan's parable) and to come (including the disastrous results of listening to that effusive complimenter). As with the reports of the Israelite complaint, of Sarah's disbelief, of Cain's anger, or of Solomon's imperfect heart, the narrator's access to the whole truth within the discourse enables him to bring home God's unique privilege within the world.

Most instructive of all is the rough handling meted out in confrontation to figures that do have some title to knowledge beyond the norm. Such shock tactics are an antidote against confusing the prophet and his master, a confusion that bedeviled biblical man and has persisted among biblical scholars. (This can be traced back, again, to rabbinic and christological traditions.) Actually, as scriptural art and ideology alike would lead one to expect, the viewpoints of God and prophet are always distinct in principle and often dissonant in practice. Indeed, since the Bible's precocious sensitivity to point of view attaches to its revolutionary world view rather than being a merely technical accomplishment, it would be strange to find them otherwise—as strange as to find a pagan mythopoet freely dispensing immortality on earth. Of the two drawn lines, if qualitative distinctions be distinguishable, the monotheistic one is even the more jealously guarded because more novel, abstract, and vulnerable. The prophet's occult aura presenting the most serious threat, he (or it) becomes an object of counterattacks designed to reduce him to the ranks. He is just a splendid mortal, the Gilgamesh poet emphasizes by representing the vain bid for eternal life made by a hero one-third human and two-thirds divine. He is just a glorified mouthpiece, biblical narrative points out in demotion of its reputed superknowers. The downgrading metaphor itself emerges from the equivalence between God's two divisions of labor: "I make thee a god to Pharaoh," he tells Moses, "and Aaron thy brother shall be thy prophet" and "He shall be a mouth for thee and thou shalt be a god for him"

(Exod 7:1; 4:16). Elsewhere, this gentle reminder of the language explodes into demoting action.

Whatever his public image, of course, the prophet himself is well aware of his dependent status. All plots against Israel having misfired, the king of Aram suspects treason among his courtiers, whereupon they protest: "None, my lord the king; but Elisha, the prophet in Israel, tells the king of Israel the words that thou speakest in thy bedchamber" (2 Kgs 6:8-12). This is true enough—and disclosed in advance by the narrator—except for the attribution to the vehicle of supernatural powers originating in his employer. (Note the shift in emphasis between the narrator's referring term "man *of God*" and the Arameans' "Elisha the prophet *in Israel.*") But Elisha has no part in the foreigners' misapprehension. As he exclaims in an adjoining context, startled by the death of the Shunamite's boy, "The Lord has hidden it from me and has not told me" (4:27). The two perspectives are hierarchically ordered, so that the subordinate's occult channels of information may be cut off without warning to leave him as fallible in thought and speech as his neighbors.

The trouble is that those neighbors, Israelite as well as Gentile, tend to cast him as a superman; and some prophets, being only flesh and blood, take no special pains to disabuse them of the fallacy. So the Bible performs this image-shattering with a vengeance, at times with a savagery that reveals how deep the rot must have gone and carries the ubiquitous drama of errors to the point of antiprophetic satire. (Indeed, if prophets had any share in the writing of biblical narrative, then their attacks on their own guild would impressively conform to the rule of rising above self in narration. Whoever the writers, on the other hand, they must have assumed a prophetic role in writing—by implicit appeal to inspiration— for an independent omniscience would run counter to their very thesis.) Balaam, the diviner of international reputation who looks a fool beside his own ass until God thinks fit to "open his eyes," has become a byword. Yet, precisely because Balaam is so obviously an enemy and the hatchet-job on him so openly enacted, it may escape notice that his is only a special case of deflation by perspectival cutoff.

The main victim of this ironic counteraction is Samuel, turned butt at two parallel junctures in the rise of the monarchy. While the search for the asses reaches its crisis—Saul about to give up and his servant offering advice—the narrator abruptly disturbs the tale's focus and continuity by drawing attention to niceties of reference:

(6) [The servant to Saul:] Behold, pray, there is a man of God in this city and the man is held in honor: all that he says comes true. So let us go there; perhaps he will tell us our way that we should go. (7) And

Saul said to his servant, And suppose we go, what shall we bring [*nabi*] the man? For the bread in our sacks is gone and there is no present to bring [*le'habi*] to the man of God. (8) And the servant answered Saul again and said, Behold, I have at hand the fourth part of a shekel of silver; I will give it to the man of God and he will tell us our way. ((9) Formerly in Israel, thus said a man when he went to inquire of God, Come, let us go to the seer; for he who is nowadays called a prophet [*nabi*] was formerly called a seer.) (10) And Saul said to his servant, Well said; come, let us go. (1 Sam 9:6-10)

Why does the narrator suddenly multiply and switch referring expressions to prophecy, arrest the dialogue to interpolate a philological comment, revive a term that the speakers could manage without (as they have done so far) and his own audience would find archaic? All these incongruities make sense in terms of image shattering—a thrust against the inflated figure cut by the prophet in the popular imagination, Israelite as well as (in Balaam's or Elisha's case) pagan. "All that he says comes true," the servant believes; and the only question ("perhaps") is whether he "will tell," not whether he can tell. The very term "man of God" has lost its original meaning—as indicated by the wholly secular context, the triviality of the inquiry, the recurrence of the abbreviation "man"—and the stereotype disengages and elevates the man at God's expense. To cut the prophet down to size, the narrator brings to bear on him a series of three referring terms, each pointing to a different side or view of the office and the attack escalating in accordance with the liability to ideological abuse.

The first in line (verse 6) is the appellation "man of God," which gets off most lightly because, once delivered from stereotypical freezing and cheapening, it gives credit for omniscience where credit is due. The contemporary designation "prophet" comes next, but, it turns out, long before its official appearance in the antiquarian gloss. For the narrator's "what is nowadays called a prophet [*nabi*]" links up by wordplay with Saul's "What shall we bring [*nabi*]?", the homonymity insinuating a pejorative etymology for the term: "a man to whom gifts are brought."[9] If the contextual pressures on "man of God" reflected popular misbelief, the twist given to "prophet" debunks prophetic malpractice itself.

But it is the archaism "the seer," most evidently a dead metaphor and most liable to divorce the power of vision from its divine origin, that bears the brunt of the attack. The attack again takes the form of deflationary revitalization by context; and the term has been delayed to a point as close as possible to Samuel's arrival on the scene only in order to maximize the incongruity between the image and the reality.

As the search-party is making its way to the house, the narrator cuts in with the privileged flashback that "the day before Saul came, the Lord had *opened Samuel's ear,* saying, Tomorrow about this time I will send to thee a man from the land of Benjamin, and thou shalt anoint him to be prince over my people Israel" (9:15–16). The aural idiom comes (for the first time in the Bible) instead of the expected visual metaphor for the office; and their interplay connotes that Samuel is less a "seer" (in his own right) than a "hearer" (by God's grace). Next, at Saul's approach, we learn from another privileged comment that "Samuel *saw* Saul and the Lord said to him, Behold the man of whom I spoke to thee; it is he who shall rule over my people" (9:17). Even face to face with the preannounced guest, Samuel would fail to recognize him were it not for the intervention of the divine prompter. Left to his own devices, as Eli was in Hannah's presence (1:12–13) and as Saul is in the ensuing verse, Samuel "sees" (physically) without "seeing" (prophetically). Hence the grotesqueness of Samuel's self-important reply to Saul's inquiry: "He said, Tell me, pray, where is the house of the seer? And Samuel answered Saul and said, I am the seer" (9:18–19). Nothing loath to cultivate his image, he goes on to profess ("All that is in thy heart I will tell thee") those very occult powers with which the popular imagination credits him ("Perhaps he will tell us our way").

Three designations, three denigrations, variously undermining cultural through verbal clichés and culminating in a full-scale exposure of presumption.[10] On the threshold of the monarchy, the outgoing prophet-judge hardly appears in an attractive light. Besides making the timeless ideological point, the narrator so times his critique as to balance the antimonarchical thrust of the preceding chapter: it is not that institution alone that encroaches on divine prerogative. Far from a sop or a fit of pique, moreover, the perspectival opposition encapsulated in "see" is resumed in the corresponding scene of David's anointment (1 Samuel 16), across a distance of eventful years and chapters. And in resumption, the experience the prophet goes through only becomes more humiliating for him and the orchestration of "sight" more admonitory for us.

This time God just directs Samuel to Jesse the Bethlehemite—"for I have *seen* among his sons a king for me" in place of Saul—without identifying the new appointee. Nor, considering their recent disagreement over Saul's rejection and Samuel's ongoing mourning for the rejected king, does this reticence seem accidental. A mark of divine displeasure from the beginning, it soon turns out a prelude to an ordeal. For God having withheld his confidence, the terrestrial "seer's" achievement is in proportion. The great Samuel, whose arrival throws the place into a flutter, helplessly stands oil-horn in hand before the procession of candidates, seeing without seeing whom God has seen for himself:

(5) He consecrated Jesse and his sons and invited them to the sacrifice. (6) When they came, he *saw* Eliab and said, Surely the Lord's anointed is before him. (7) But the Lord said to Samuel, Do not regard his *looks* [*marèhu*] and the height of his stature, for I have rejected him; it is not as man *sees*, for man *sees* what meets the eye and God *sees* into the heart. (8) Then Jesse called Abinadab and made him pass before Samuel. And he said, Neither has the Lord chosen this one. (9) Then Jesse made Shammah pass by. And he said, Neither has the Lord chosen this one. (10) And Jesse made seven of his sons pass before Samuel. And Samuel said to Jesse, The Lord has not chosen these. (11) And Samuel said to Jesse, Are these all the boys? And Jesse said, There still remains the youngest, and behold, he is keeping the sheep. And Samuel said to Jesse, Send and fetch him, for we will not sit down till he comes here. (12) And he sent and brought him in, ruddy with beautiful eyes and good looks [*ro'i*]. And God said, Arise, anoint him; for this is he. (1 Sam 16:5–12)

Worse than his sheer sightlessness in the face of Saul, Samuel now begins with a blunder and ends in paralysis. It is as if God is resolved to teach him a lesson, by demonstration as well as precept, about the gulf separating human from divine vision.[11] Ironically, the prophet commits his worst mistake in the first and easiest test. What would be more natural than to disqualify or at least distrust (with the reader) the candidate who shares the rejected king's most salient feature? But Samuel again puts a favorable construction on physical stature and beauty (cf. 10:24), with ignominious results. Considering the ambiguity of the biblical "said" between thought and speech, he may well have announced his verdict, only to retract it the next moment. Even if he managed to restrain himself in time, he must have smarted under God's inaudible lecture, which ridicules his choice and goes on to bracket him, as a sightless seer, with the rest of humanity. His "seeing" stands to Eliab's "looks" as human "seeing" to "what meets the eye," both opposed to God's "seeing into the heart." And the fact that to respond to his thoughts God must have read them bears out the claim to omniscience in the very act of making the claim.

During the next six rounds, Samuel appears to have learned his lesson, disqualifying one brother after another on (probably) the grounds of over-size and comeliness. But the last round turns the screw again. From Jesse's description David sounds a most promising candidate, if not a sure winner. By both elimination (nobody else "remains") and divine guideline (as the "youngest" or, literally, "smallest"), he fits the bill. The boy once summoned, however, Samuel gets caught between mutually exclusive indices. The "smallness" pulls one way; the hitherto unmentioned attractive appearance (complete with the spurned "eyes" and "looks," both close relatives of "see") pulls the other. Thus paralyzed by the breakdown of his newly adopted rule of inference from surface to depth, he for once falls into an awkward silence, till rescued by God's order to anoint the lad. What meets the eye, then, no more forms a reversed than a straight clue to internals; and the heart remains the monopoly of the All-seeing, to which even official "seers" gain access at his discretion alone. Or to recast the epistemological doctrine in terms of perspectival structure: even the prophet's discourse functions as one of the many voices, all but two potentially unreliable, with and through which the Bible speaks.

But no one finds himself more often at the receiving end of the opposition to divinity than the reader. The only way to spare us the informational trials of the characters would be for the narrator to give us the benefit of his own omniscience. But such vicarious learning ("the whipping-boy rhetoric") has a limited effectiveness, quite apart from the dangers of monotony. Unearned, the godlike vantage point generates an ironic, if not a downright comic, frame of mind; and, especially when sustained, may give a sense of detachment or exemption from the human ordeal below. The narrator therefore varies his techniques of presentation—sometimes revealing, sometimes concealing, most often taking a middle course—in order to cast the reader in the role of participant as well as spectator. Thus dragged by the composition into the human drama of knowledge, we too experience our limitations in the face of the opacities of existence so transparent to God, unless and until the narrator sees fit to open our eyes. This is what makes the Bible such exciting if difficult reading and, as suggested in the opening chapter, forms its main claim to poetic originality and theoretical notice: the transformation of ideological discourse into art of the highest order, without compromising either but enriching both. Since so much of my argument will develop this theme, a single case in point will do for the moment.

Consider the Bible's partiality for springing on the reader accomplished facts of divine choice, with little exposition or none or worse than none. In Genesis, the recurrence of this device even marks an ascending order of incongruity and mystification. God's choice of Noah makes sense in view of his early characterization as "righteous man" (6:8-9; 7:1). But this bare portrait looks ample beside the utter lack of preparation for the next act of choice, which singles out a hitherto faceless member of Terah's clan: "The Lord said to Abram, Go forth from thy land . . . to the land that I will show thee" (12:1). In turn, even this complete surprise assumes an increasingly moderate look as we go further down the line and come to Joseph, whose handling passes beyond reticence to active misdirection. God's future agent and mouthpiece in Egypt could hardly make a worse impression on his first appearance: spoiled brat, talebearer, braggart. Of course, all these elections justify themselves—the last not least—as the omniscient narrator sooner or later establishes beyond doubt and as he could indeed warn us in advance. But the tortuous route to enlightenment is a measure of the extent to which the Bible goes out of its way to complicate ours: to produce curiosity, wonder, even skepticism about God's dispositions in order to trap us into faith on the backswing. The combination of initial blurring and retrospective lucidity demonstrates to the reader, in terms of his own sense-making experience, the force of the generalization that "man sees what meets the eye and God sees into the heart." The world and its management are intelligible, but only to observers properly intelligent.

The Omnipotence Effect:
Control Claimed and Disclaimed

The feature of omnipotence has received even less attention from theorists than omniscience, presumably because deemed irrelevant to point of view. If so, its neglect is regrettable indeed. Surely, it is the exercise or disclamation of omnipotence that separates narrative into its two main classes: fiction, where the author freely creates a world of his own under the aegis of poetic license, and history, where the author re-creates (explores, models, interprets) a preexisting world. Within fiction itself, correspondingly, the same variable draws a sharp line between the author, omnipotent by definition, and the narrator, who may be either invested with the author's own creative power (as in *Tom Jones*) or shaped in the image of the historian, as with all imaginary autobiographies from *The Golden Ass* to *Lolita*.

Hence the implications for point of view of whether the narrated world figures as a creation or a re-creation. It is not just a question of the truth value claimed for the discourse. In all that concerns the legitimate freedom to organize reality from an individual perspective—ideological or artistic— the frank creator stands poles apart from the sedulous recorder, including the one to whom he himself may delegate, as part of the fiction, the role of telling. And the creator stands so even more obviously with respect to the associated privilege of informational access: he knows all because he invents all. By rule, therefore, the authorial viewpoint is expressed by the created world, while kept in check (on pain of dismissal) by the re-created world. From the reader's side, each writing mode calls for a different process of interpretation, one oriented to internal and the other to external givens, norms, probabilities.[12]

Or so it appears till we note the complications and refinements suggested by a text like the Bible. To be sure, the status of the discourse between fiction and history still turns on the license the narrator claims or disclaims, however tacitly. But—and here comes the first anomaly—the criterial license varies. Omnipotence will (or certainly need) no longer subsume omni-science: under such a convention as inspired speech, a narrator unfolding a *historical* panorama may yet, indeed must, speak with the authority born of omniscience. Since the two privileges wedded as a matter of course in the novelistic tradition may be divorced by the ancient rules of storytelling, the biblical narrator's omniscience still leaves his narrative indeterminate between factuality and fictionality. The strength of his claim to truth is in inverse proportion only to his claim to omnipotence.

Here a second complication enters. Whatever the narrator's stance vis-à-vis his world, that world evidently boasts an omnipotent agent. As creator, wonder-worker, lord of nature and society, God is no less in control than in the know: the Bible actually opens with the supreme demonstration of his mastership. But we soon find these two divine powers exercised in sequence and concert, so that it becomes difficult to tell them apart. Thus, the rhetorical question by which God chides Sarah for laughing at the prom-ise of motherhood (Gen 18:14) is construed by some exegetes and translators as "Is anything hidden from the Lord?" and by others as "Is anything too hard for the Lord?" Caught between the omniscient and the omnipotent reading, others still try to have it both ways. Even the great Rashi starts by quoting with approval the Aramaic rendition as "hidden" and then wrenches it in paraphrase into something like "Is anything hidden from me, from doing as I please?" As far as the promise to Sarah is concerned, however, the different readings amount to the same thing, for God's knowl-edge of the future attaches and traces back to the power to bring it about. Elsewhere the text may foreground one attribute rather than another: knowledge, in order to preclude or soften the impression of God's tampering with the human soul, or dominion, to counteract the heresies of accident or (what the pagan world view accommodates) impotent foreknowledge. In principle, however, the two go together as essential features of divinity in monotheism.

But does their coexistence within God's portrait mean that the narrator must or may follow suit in the formation of his own? This depends on the kind of claims he would make for his narrative as an image of the world. In terms of ancient convention, as we have seen, omniscience by itself would leave those claims suspended between the two poles of representation. But if God's omnipotence makes history, then a narrator's makes fiction and, where he introduces God, God himself becomes part of the fiction. Ironically enough, only a dealer in make-believe can play God, and what is more, do so without undermining his model's "real-life" authority. Once the heav-enly model himself appears on stage, however, the balance of power exacts a clear either/or choice that will reflect the generic and doctrinal premises in the heart of the tale. Fictional or historical writing? Artistic or divine stage management? The whole ontological status of the narrative, as a world picture and a mode of discourse alike, turns on the answer. Hence the importance of determining with whom lies the control over the biblical world.

As with epistemology, the monotheistic revolution stands out against the background of the pagan environment. In regard to world order, the differences among the religions of the ancient Orient (or between them and Homer) go with principled uniformity.[13] Within each polytheistic system, the universe is run by a pantheon that divides power and jurisdiction among its members, often along the lines of natural phenomena. Still, the individual gods are subject to the authority of the divine assembly, which makes the important decisions in a fashion less than democratic. The voices of some gods carry more weight than others, and one always figures as leader: the Mesopotamian Anu, god of heaven, the Egyptian sun-god Re, the Greek Zeus, El in Canaan. But the high god's own control is neither absolute nor secure. Sometimes he appears as a rather pale figure or figurehead beside another deity of brute force, like the Mesopotamian Enlil or the Canaanite Baal. Elsewhere he has to deal with external threats, such as the forces of chaos in *Enuma Elish,* or with aspirants for supreme power, as often in Greek mythology; and he does not always emerge triumphant. Even at the best of times, he may have to bow to superior forces like fate. The similarity all this bears to the workings of human society is by no means accidental. (In Egypt there was not even a clear line of demarcation between gods and human beings, so that the pharaoh himself was believed to control all nature that had reference to the prosperity of his land.) Paganism created the gods in man's own image. Hence "the outstanding single feature of the cosmos" was "that no single god is the ultimate source of power and authority, none is truly omnipotent."[14]

It is against this humanizing conception of the divine order and might that the Bible directs much of its narrative energies. It not only assumes or deploys but also inculcates a model of reality where God exercises absolute sway over the universe (nature, culture, history) in conspicuous isolation and transcendence. Again, the ideological thrust accounts for various distinctive regularities of composition and narration—this time, in terms of the rhetoric of omnipotence.

Thus, in regard to no other article of faith (or for that matter technique) does the narrative so richly bring out the difference in persuasive force between statement and stagement, telling and showing. In contrast to the prophetic speakers, the narrator himself will no more preach divine omnipotence than omniscience. He often delegates such statements to the dramatis personae, from God himself through leaders and laymen to foreigners. Their precepts articulate and generalize rather than produce the omnipotence effect, however, and for rhetorical reasons that are themselves constantly dramatized. Words are not sufficient to command belief, least of all in the supernatural newly conceived. When Moses announces to the groaning Israelites that God is about to deliver them from bondage, his speech falls flat: the people simply "did not listen." Whence God draws the right conclusion, instructing Moses not to make another speech but to launch the work of (spiritual as well as physical) redemption by tackling Egypt before the eyes of Israel (Exodus 6). And if this initial lack of faith and response derives from a "broken spirit," others are brought round by deeds where they would not listen to words, owing to ignorance or, from Pharaoh to Jonah, arrogance.

At the same time, these converts are more than dramatic ("whipping-boy") vehicles for the narrator's message to the reader. Within the plot itself, they figure as targets of persuasion in their own right. Far from satisfied with operating behind the scenes—as Jesus forbids the disciples to trumpet his miracles—the Almighty is no less concerned than the narrator to impress his almightiness on humanity. Such is his concern for the image of omnipotence that it motivates omission as well as action. Moses thus dissuades God from wiping out the seemingly hopeless Israelites by an argument from reputation: "Because of his impotence to bring this people to the land which he swore to give to them," the world will jeer, "therefore he has slain them in the wilderness" (Num 14:16). All this harping on public relations, in which modern ears may detect a note of vanity or showmanship, actually springs from a desire to promulgate truth and inculcate faith and ensure right conduct, all subsumed under the biblical heading of "knowledge." "I will get glory over Pharaoh and all his host, and they shall know that I am the Lord" (Exod 14:4). "At twilight you shall eat meat, and in the morning you shall have your fill of bread; then shall you know that I am the Lord your God" (Exod 16:12). "There arose another generation after them, who did not know the Lord and the work that he had done for Israel" (Judg 2:7). The ubiquitous causal link of God's wonder-working and man's knowledge goes to the heart of the biblical world view. In particular, Israel's fortunes throughout history depend on her observance or loosening of that bond.

Once the fact of omnipotence is associated with the display of omnipotence, moreover, there results a clearcut logic of plot and a twofold structure of communication. In terms of plot, God himself must figure as the busiest agent, indeed superagent, bringing his might to bear on the world to make history and flaunting it to the world to publish authority.

Regardless of the artistic merits of telling vs. showing per se, no mere epithet or eulogy would do where the action itself must serve as both the embodiment of divine control and the medium of divine broadcasting. "Signs," the biblical term for those heavenly messages inscribed on the world by the plot, thus bears a well-defined semiotic sense.

From the communicative standpoint, however, biblical demonstrations of omnipotence fall into two types: the asymmetrical and the symmetrical. The asymmetrical situation, whose paradigm is the Creation narrative, arises wherever God works wonders unseen by humanity: he then remains addresseeless, in contrast to the narrator who renders the scene for the benefit of his own addressee, the reader. This brings to mind the typical configuration of the monologist displayed to us by a hidden author, except that here the action takes place in the external world and the agent would welcome the invasion of his privacy. (The gods of *Enuma Elish* or the *Iliad*, in contrast, have little reason to thank the artist for exposing their doings to view; but then the invaded would not much care, as long as their might remained awe-inspiring, and the invaders operate by reference to different standards and designs.) It is hardly coincidental that the paradigm of this type should belong to a time when nobody was around to admire and take note: man was created, it appears, to provide such an audience.

With the advent of man and above all the people of Israel, indeed, the symmetrical situation comes to predominate, as throughout the story of the Exodus. As regards frequency and elaborateness and systematicity, this pattern exceeds anything known in pagan literature, and for reasons closely linked to the break with paganism. Here the narrator constructs a twofold rhetoric, extending to the implied reader the signs and message that God directs at his own refractory clients. God operates and comments to manifest his power in his proper sphere of activity; the narrator, in his guise as objective recorder, stages and preserves the divine manifestations for all time. This finds a telling parallel in God's own strategy of manipulating one agent (say, Egypt) for the good of another (Israel) or delivering one generation in order to leave a record for posterity. The plagues thus come as an object lesson to three different audiences, whom he himself enumerates to Moses: "Pharaoh and his servants," "you," "thy son and thy son's son," all needing to "know that I am the Lord" (Exod 10:1–2).

The symmetry of the two communicative acts—the narrator's frame and God's inset—must not therefore obscure their interpenetration. For one thing, God's addressees are usually the ancestors of the narrator's, but the descendants themselves have long been foreseen and reckoned with by divinity. For another thing, the narrator performs in the service of God; but to do so he must invert their ultimate hierarchical status by incorporating God's performance into his own discourse. For still another, God's operation as self-propagandist affords a number of clues to the narrator's underground maneuvers. In the following analysis of the omnipotence effect, accordingly, we shall trace the relations both between asymmetrical and symmetrical form and, within symmetry, between the tactics devised by the like-minded advertisers.

Man must not exaggerate his imperfections, says Pliny the Elder, since "not even God can do everything. He could not, for instance, if he wanted to, commit suicide, which, in the trials of our mortal life, is his best gift to man. He cannot make mortals immortal, recall the dead, bring it about that one who has lived has not lived, or that one who has borne office has not borne office. He has no power over the past but oblivion, and, if I may be excused for illustrating our fellowship with God by trivial examples, he cannot make it that twice ten should not be twenty."[15] While bitterly opposed to the spirit of this consolation—and bound to dismiss some of the claims as false and others as silly—the Bible provides no counterargument except from history. Wisely avoiding the formalities of logic and metaphysics, it persuades by organizing the past into a rhetoric of faith. And here a sense of a system certainly prevails.

To start with a question that the Bible has bequeathed to religious literature, what makes a display of absolute power? The sine qua non is of course an infringement, preferably a reversal, of natural laws and probabilities. "If these die the death of all men," Moses says of Korah and his crowd, "then the Lord has not sent me. But if the Lord creates something new and the ground opens its mouth and swallows them up . . . then you shall know that these men have traduced the Lord" (Num 16:28–30). The rhetorical need for "something new" explains the Bible's beginning with the quintessence of the new, the story of Creation. The potency of first impressions, already seen to play a key role (the Tree of Knowledge, the Cain affair) in generating a sense of divine omniscience, is also exploited to drive in the equally novel idea of omnipotence. Needless to say, the choice of the earliest event in the text's chronology affords a starting point as natural for a universal history as a man's birth does for his biography. But the virtues of natural arrangement count for less than those of supernatural achievement, which lie in showing God not as he violates but as he makes nature and prescribes its laws. Genesis thus greets us by exposing the very concepts of nature and naturalness as a human fiction, which takes for granted what is to God one of many possible worlds and deifies what God might at any moment suspend or overthrow. This first impression is equally vital for establishing the Bible's value system (the Creator may legislate for and judge his creatures) and its model of reality (the Creator retains control, always able to unmake what he made): since norms and probabilities issue from the same source, it even requires an effort to separate the two. ("He is the Lord," says Eli in 1 Samuel 3:18 on discovering the rejection of his line, "let him do what seems good to him.") So much hangs in the balance, indeed, that the narrative is not content with the tremendous impact of the story-stuff itself, but reinforces it by an array of original devices that are to recur with variations in future contexts.

Nowhere is this art more persuasive than at the very beginning of the beginning: "God said, Let there be light, and there was light." Note first the operation of "Let there be light" as an overt and precautionary foreshadowing, designed to rule out any naturalistic explanation and give credit where it is due. In its absence, the reader (and in symmetrical patterns, the characters as well) might be left in doubt, often allied with wishful thinking. "It [may have] happened to us by chance" (1 Sam 6:9), the Philistines conjecture even though afflicted on all sides (mice, tumors, Dagon's dismemberment) and aware of the possibility that the God of Israel has been at work. Or worse, in case of favorable turns, the exploit might be attributed to a human agency: thin down the army, God orders Gideon, "lest Israel vaunt themselves against me, saying, My own hand has delivered me" (Judg 7:2). Worst of all, the observer is then liable to mistake divine potence for impotence. Suppose God omitted to preannounce (and the narrator to cite) his intention to harden Pharaoh's heart. Would not the tardiness of the Exodus suggest a discrepancy between will and way? As it is, the potential weakness turns into a source of rhetorical strength, because the advance notice ushers in a double demonstration of omnipotence—over the workings of the heart as well as of nature. And with respect to catastrophes, from the Flood to the division of the kingdom and the fall of Jerusalem, the same rule of prophylaxis makes for a special kind of inverted apologetics: the narrator protects God's image by having him forecast and motivate the doom.

From this standpoint, the foreshadowing-fulfillment series at the outset of Genesis has a long-range effect on the formation of our perceptual set. It develops a first impression of a world controlled by a prime mover and coherent to the exclusion of accident. Reinforced at strategic junctures by later paradigms and variants, it also enables the narrator to dispense with the continual enactment of divine intervention that would hamper suspense and overschematize the whole plot.

This offers a poetic alternative to von Rad's thesis about the transformation of the Israelite view of God's activity in history. According to the early traditions, he claims, God mainly revealed himself in marvelous events and interventions; from the age of the monarchy, God also figures as the hidden shaper of the normal-seeming course of events.[16] But this dichotomy has little to recommend it. Of all the narrative books, Esther alone neither stages nor invokes any direct interference by God. This is indeed one reason why it did not always find ready acceptance in antiquity; and the apocryphal Additions actually supply the missing dimension in the form of prayer scenes that in effect launch the canonical foreshadowing-to-fulfillment dynamics. All the other books, however, invariably mix overt and implicit guidance. So the explanation of the diversity lies in a poetic constant rather than in a genetic variable. It above all reflects not a historical metamorphosis of thought but a compositional alternation of treatment, in the interests of plotting and variety. Not only do the artistic gains of omnipotence behind-the-scenes incur little ideological loss, considering the tall letters in which the paradigms write the rule. They find their legitimation in God's own aptness to subject his people to trials of faith by remaining in the shadows. Those subjects (and by implication the audience) disregard the rule at their peril; which may generate the ironic twist of God's manifesting himself to announce the punishment for the failure to read the secret text he has inscribed on the world.

Granting the need for anticipation, its form still remains unexplained. The recourse to direct quotation, to be sure, makes sense in terms like drama and vividness. Compare "God said, Let there be light" with the scene in the Babylonian *Enuma Elish* where the gods lay the garment before Marduk to test the efficacy of his word:

> He commanded with his mouth, and the garment was destroyed.
> He commanded again, and the garment was restored.[17]

The shift into nondirect discourse would no doubt weaken the biblical effect and is wisely avoided at the first-impression stage. But why resort to specific quotation in the first place? Why not simply indicate that God proposed to create light? The reason is that, owing to their divine origin, the quoted words fulfill a double role—performative as well as anticipatory. At the same time as they project an intention within the discourse, they realize it within the world: God's speech is itself a creative act.[18]

This world-making power of the word remains unique to divine omnipotence even in the face of the claims made by speech-act philosophers since J. L. Austin that language functions not only to describe states of affairs but also to bring them about.[19] Austin himself starts *How To Do Things With Words* by exploring the type of utterance he calls "performative," which has the grammatical form of a statement and yet is not true or false: to make such an utterance is to engage in doing something rather than merely saying something. Examples of performative would be "'I name this ship the *Queen Elizabeth*'—as uttered when smashing the bottle against the stem" or "'I give and bequeath my watch to my brother'—as occurring in a will" (p. 5). Austin soon got into glorious trouble, once saying itself proved a kind of doing, and the whole issue has since been much debated. All this minefield need not concern us, however, except as a contrastive background to the singular simplicity of the divine fiat; and it is only to sharpen the contrast that I shall refer to it as performative rather than, properly speaking, formative or creative.

Their approaches geared to "ordinary" circumstances, philosophers of language tend to overlook a point of great importance, certainly to literary communication. Which is that the performative status and role of an utterance depend on the surrounding reality-model, and may therefore vary widely from one (con)text to another. In the biblical framework, for instance, the performatives of the human speakers exhibit all the complications that have bedeviled speech-act theory; but this only throws into relief the transcendence of the divine performative. Like their modern equivalents, for one thing, biblical characters may "perform an act of exactly the same kind *not* by uttering words . . . but in some other way. For example, I may in some places effect marriage by cohabiting." Moreover, as with marriages verbally contracted but sealed by consummation, even where the utterance of words figures as the "leading incident in the performance of the act," taking effect yet requires the performance of "certain other actions, whether 'physical' or 'mental'" (p. 8). But God need not, and throughout Creation does not, engage in any performance other than verbal; and this modus operandi distinguishes him no less than the certainty and magnitude of the results. Hence the immediate continuity in the movement from "'Let there be light'" to "there was light," emphasizing that God did nothing in between, that no sooner had he bidden than his bidding was done. This also goes a long way toward moderating the notorious disproportion between Moses' sin (hitting the rock, twice, instead of speaking to it as ordered) and his punishment (by death in the wilderness). Maintaining discipline is the least consideration. Rather, Moses has indeed supplied the water clamored for by the people, but at the price of diminishing God: that the means lead to the same practical end does not yet invest them with the same communicative value. In robbing the Omnipotent of his hallmark and the demonstration of its grandeur, "you have failed to sanctify me in the midst of the people of Israel" (Deut 32:51).

Even more unique is the absence of any convention behind "Let there be light." For a human performative to function smoothly or at all, it must meet a whole set of conditions: the pre-existence of an accepted conventional procedure, including the utterance of certain words by certain persons in certain circumstances, the appropriateness of these persons and circumstances for the invocation of the procedure, the full and correct execution of the procedure, and various other rules of felicity. This is why so many of our performatives bear a ceremonial or formulaic character. But God need only say the word to accomplish the effect in the world, with no conventional strings attached. It is no accident that throughout Creation he performs in spendid isolation, before the advent of society with its institutions and in asymmetrical contexts where he does not even address anyone. There is simply nothing to enable, nothing to constrain. A divine performative cannot therefore fail to take effect, unless God changes his mind; nor is it subject to "abuse," "misinvocation," "misexecution," "insincerity" and all the other labels for infelicity with which speech-act theory brands offenses against the social contract. Rather, the biblical convention of divine performative works against convention, deriving its affective force from the infringement or the transcendence of all the norms that would govern a human equivalent. If God rises above the laws of nature, how can he be caught in the cobwebs of culture? Here the unity of word and thing—both *davar* in Hebrew—finds its literal apotheosis and perhaps lays bare its roots.

Turning from the speech-act ("Let there be light," *yehi or*) to the enactment ("and there was light," *va'yehi or*), one is struck by the verbatim repetition that apparently carries superfluity to an extreme. Given the performative fiat, what need is there to mention the inevitable result at all? Or, if the first divine utterance constitutes a special occasion, why should this become the standard practice throughout? Besides, why repeat word for word (and there are usually more words than here) where a minimal formula like "and so it happened" could serve the purpose?

Marking an ascending order of redundancy, these features again resist explanation in terms of ideology (or, as I shall argue in chapter 11, conventionality) as distinct from the rhetoric of ideology. There must be repetition to settle any lingering doubt about the causal link between performative and performance. And its force depends on the imposition of equivalence on two terms that could scarcely be more variant: in makeup (verbal vs. nonverbal event), in chronological reference (narrative future vs. present), in perspectival origin (God vs. narrator). The bridging of the first two chasms demonstrates God's power by exposing their irrelevance outside the human sphere (or rather, by turning such human distinctions—like the homonymy between the imperative *yehi* and the preterite *va'yehi*—to the account of the divinity that transcends them). But the effect of the third bridging is entirely due to the narrator himself, who contrives the equivalence in repetition and backs it up with the authority of his omniscience: things turned out precisely as directed. That is why in symmetrical contexts, like the Plagues, the sense of all-powerfulness that such equivalence gives the reader (faced with two matching pieces of discourse) is even sharper than that experienced by God's eyewitnesses (who can only compare a piece of discourse with its nonverbal realization). This also suggests yet another reason for the Bible's preference of direct over nondirect quoting of divine commands: a Marduk-like summary can hardly be matched in repetition. Accordingly, the threefold patterning (sequence, equivalence, shift in viewpoint) imposed by the Bible on these members of repetition is the most effective imaginable: God first appears to voice the performative and the narrator then echoes him to vouch for the performance.

Along another axis of repetition, all these devices may acquire cumulative force by way of serialization. The Creator, free to accomplish his work in an instant, performs by installments distributed over six days. The Deliverer stiffens the oppressor's will in order to "multiply my signs and wonders in the land of Egypt" (Exod 7:3). One likewise thinks of the long series of interventions in the wilderness, of Gideon's catalogue of trials, of Elisha's record of miracles. The narrator no more elucidates the point of serialization than any other aspect of excess or redundancy. But he exploits the symmetrical patterns of communication to make God speak for him, and to us, while ostensibly addressing some dramatized audience. The above quotation from Exodus, for instance, goes on to say that the "signs and wonders" will so abound that "the Egyptians will know that I am the Lord." Earlier, in response to Moses' fear lest the Israelites "should not believe" him, God displays fine psychological insight in providing his ambassador with a whole set of wondrous credentials. "If they will not believe thee and not listen to the voice of the first sign, they will believe the voice of the latter sign. And if they will not believe even the two signs and listen to thy voice, thou shalt take some water from the Nile" and produce a third (4:8-9). However conclusive a single miracle might appear from the logical standpoint, the psychology of faith operates by an algebra that quantifies the qualitative. In the hands of the narrator, therefore, God gives advance notice, then performs, then (often) comments on the performance; and then repeats the sequence all over again. Even so, as the history of Israel testifies, success is not assured and God at times yields to despair. "How long will they not believe in me," he rages on hearing the promised land calumniated, "despite all the signs which I have wrought among them? I will strike them with the pestilence" (Num 14:11-12). Only with difficulty (and partial success) does Moses manage to avert the catastrophe. And the reader, with the historic series of serializations reenacted before him, is expected to take the point: that even an Almighty versed in psychology may weary of playing to an unappreciate gallery.

All these aids to dramatization are common to symmetrical and asymmetrical forms of the omnipotence effect. But precisely because symmetry entails a communicative situation within as well as without the narrated world, it both enjoys certain advantages and also incurs certain constraints.

One difference lies in the widened range of objects for divine manipulation. In asymmetrical contexts, designed for our eyes only, the object is invariably nature. While reducing the point and viableness of asymmetry, however, the birth of society provides God not only with an audience but also with a new target and sphere of action. He may work on nature, as with the Burning Bush or the parting of the Jordan, but with a view to making an impression on society. He may unleash nature on society, for a variety of reasons that come together in the Flood or, even better, the Plagues: impulsion, punishment, deliverance, and, always, spread of "knowledge" among all observers. For similar reasons, he may also operate more directly on society, thwarting its ambitions (the Tower of Babel), resolving its conflicts (the miraculous victory, personal and national), destroying its scum (Sodom and Gomorrah).

Yet the extended range is something of a mixed blessing. Does the Almighty control the human heart? If no, where is his omnipotence? If yes, where is man's free will, hardly less novel in terms of ideology and equally underscored at the beginning of Genesis? Biblical narrative gives no straightforward answer, because the question is unanswerable, and no consistent treatment, except for the consistency of maneuvering between the two extremes. The tampering with Pharaoh's heart illustrates one extreme, but then he is an enemy and its hardening a condition (or, in aesthetic terms, a motivation) for serializing the Plagues and retarding the Exodus with no reflection on God. Rare in general, this kind of pagan determinism is virtually ruled out in Israelite contexts: no wonder the Chronicler replaced "God" (2 Sam 24:1) by "Satan" (1 Chr 21:1) as the agency that incited David to number the people. The Rape of Dinah or the Nabal narrative instances the other extreme, where the human characters and character apparently enjoy free play. This is morally as well as psychologically acceptable—the more so since God is by definition understood to oversee the affair and to retain the privilege of intervening at any moment, as when he throws "terror" into the Canaanites that might take revenge on Dinah's avengers (Genesis 35:5)—but still wanting in omnipotence effect. Hence the centrality of the dialectical handling and, within it, of the recourse to plot "signs" as a means of influencing action. For they always enact a demonstration of power before the characters, and yet, whether suasive or coercive, leave the onlookers a measure of freedom. This enables God (and the narrator) to make up through the omnipotence brought to bear on the world for the suspension of omnipotence over the heart. While offering conclusive knowledge at every turn, God still chooses to let man choose.

Or, passing to a less serious dilemma, take a cultural product like foreign gods. Their very name is obnoxious to God and their exposure required as an antidote to the whoring instincts of his chosen people. Yet it is out of the question to settle the issue after the favorite manner of all pagan (Babylonian, Egyptian, Greek) literature: by test of arms. However decisive the results, the very staging of such a duel would confer on the vanquished the recognition, if nothing more than as entities existing outside the fancy of their worshipers, that the narrative ideologically denies them. And it would be a mockery of omnipotence to show it tilting against fictions ("vanities"). Far from dramatizing, the narrative genre does not even tell about such conflicts in the passing and exultant manner of biblical poetry (e.g., Ps 74:13–14, Job 26:12–13). By the laws of its rhetoric, the opposition is best annihilated by a pregnant silence, broken only to make opprobrious references to idols that carry no presupposition of existence. As well as speaking, moreover, God acts not against those imaginary deities but against their hold over the human mind. Hence the versatility of God's demonstrations—whether the wonders of Creation, the Plagues of Egypt, or the defeat of the Arameans first on the hills and then, when they have taken new courage from the thought that Israel's "gods are gods of the hills," in the plain (1 Kings 20). These are all pointed allusions to a common illusion: their serial form of unity-in-variety argues that the powers and jurisdictions supposed to be distributed among a whole pantheon are actually concentrated in God's hands. Biblical serialization combines the polemics with the psychology of faith.

Hence also the treatment of the three major confrontation scenes, pitting Moses and Aaron against the Egyptian magicians (Exodus 8), the Ark against Dagon (1 Samuel 5), Elijah against Baal's prophets (1 Kings 18). All vary from the norm of direct dramatization, for in none does God appear on stage. He rather delegates power to some representative, human or inanimate. And to show the duel in its proper light, the tone shifts from the solemn to the comic or grotesque: the magicians exacerbating the plagues by multiplying the foul water or frogs, Dagon discovered lying flat on his face before God's Ark with his members spread about, Elijah encouraging the pagan prophets to cry louder to Baal, for he may be lost in thought or fast asleep.

If the widened object raises certain difficulties for symmetrical situations, then its widened communicative bearing amply makes up for them. The fundamental gain lies in the number of roles played by the act of omnipotence. Assymmetry involves a plot function (affecting the world) and a rhetorical function (affecting the reader); symmetry also compounds a rhetorical plot-function (affecting the audience within the world). And this opens further possibilities of extending the range of its services: dramatized commentary or rhetoric, covert serialization, spatiotemporal bounding, and public testimony. Let us glance at them in turn.

Once God himself performs with an audience in mind, the narrator may delegate to a like-minded voice the commentary intended for the reader as well. Through the dramatic communication running parallel to his own, he can make telling speeches while himself remaining silent. Where the performer doubles as commentator—to string together some examples already given—we eavesdroppers learn on the highest authority the point of the marvel, the reason for its serialization, the judgment on misreading or short memory, or the limits of divine patience. But the audience's reaction, right or wrong, also does duty for exegesis that shapes our own. Of course, when duly appreciative, like the Israelites breaking into song on the disappearance of Pharaoh's host, they offer a model for imitation. But they serve the narrator's purpose by more devious routes as well. Even an unreliable attitude or incredulous response may be turned to persuasive account, as in the exchange following God's promise to supply meat for the wandering Israelites:

> Moses said, The people among whom I am number six hundred thousand on foot; and thou hast said, I will give them meat that they may eat a whole month! Shall flocks and herds be slaughtered for them, to suffice them? Or shall all the fish of the sea be gathered together for them, to suffice them? And the Lord said to Moses, Will the Lord's hand fall short? Now thou shalt see whether my word will come true for thee or not. (Num 11:21–23)

The Lawgiver's lack of faith so shocked Josephus that in retelling he transferred the speech to an anonymous Israelite (*Jewish Antiquities* 3.13 §§ 295–300). Shuddering at the very mention of divine impotence, however hypothetical, others have executed interpretive acrobatics to the same effect. In biblical terms, however, all such harmonizing and whitewashing efforts are misguided, even detrimental, on two scores. Their compositional (and ultimately ideological) mistake lies in the automatic equation of the prophet's viewpoint with God's; the rhetorical mistake—to use a distinction that my last chapter will pursue—in confusing the sophisticated with the primitive line of persuasion. In sounding a note of skepticism, Moses echoes and articulates a possible attitude of the reader himself (as Abraham and Sarah do in their internal laughter at the promise of a son, as Homer's Telemachus does in crying out against Odysseus's intention to take on the Suitors single-handed, or for that matter as James Bond does when waving aside the reports of a monumental conspiracy against England[20]). The biblical narrator is too much of a realist and too accomplished a rhetorician to believe, with the biblical prophets and later dogmatists, that incredulity or lack of faith or even heterodoxy can be swept under the carpet. On the contrary, he brings such jarring and inimical views into the open through a dramatic voice that can suitably be dealt with in context, notably by subjecting that misbeliever to a process of discovery that ends in retraction and alignment. Dissonant voices are thus manipulated rather than eliminated in the interests of persuasive harmony.

The tenet of omnipotence specially invites such treatment, because the less credible a marvel before the fact the more impressive its performance. So Moses' very stature actually enhances his value for the narrator. If even he turns skeptic, we reason, then the divine undertaking must be a tall order indeed. We are positively tempted into doubt ("True, will flocks spring up in the desert or the sea be emptied of its fish?") to maximize the effect of the denouement. The earth once covered with quails, Moses never questions God's power again; nor, by implication from our spokesman, should we.

Further, the dramatis personae may offer a contrast as well as a reliable guide or enticing parallel to the reader's viewpoint. Often, they are set up to repel us by their backsliding, mistrust or, worst, flagrant ingratitude condemned by God and prophet. But they may also enlighten the reader by their very blindness, whose exposure involves the technique of serialization in yet another capacity. Thus far I have discussed serialization in its overt aspect, as a preannounced and cumulative sequence of signs: acts of creation, plagues, trials. Where God works from behind the scenes and/or through an intermediary, however, serialization becomes imperative; and so does the tightening of the links among the members of the series. In the absence of prior notice, how else can God make his intervention perceptible to a busy or antagonistic world (and the prophet establish his divine credentials) if not by fashioning an analogical series of marvels too regular for the operations of chance? Of course, the right-thinking require neither advance notice nor incremental occurrence in order to assimilate events to a supernatural plot: a model believer like Abraham's servant will even appeal to God in the paradoxical-looking terms "Devise an accident for me" (Gen 24:12), with the implication of latent design even in manifest coincidence. But then the Bible contains few paragons (and even they cannot manage for long without some direction or encouragement, in the form of recurrence at least). So the dreams toward the end of Genesis, or the signs Moses enacts before the enslaved Israelites or the blows to Dagon, come in pairs. Other manifestations, from the barrenness of the matriarchs to the victories against Aram (2 Kings 13), run to triplets. And the number may further rise in line with the import of the manipulation, as with the ascendancy of the younger brother throughout Genesis or the cyclical progress of Judges from sin to deliverance and back again.[21]

The serial form thus imposed on the action as plotted history is there to be noticed and interpreted by the characters no less than by the reader.

But its significance, if not its very presence, is most often lost on them. This opens a variety of perspectival discrepancies among the characters themselves and between them and the reader: the tracing of the hidden God's figure in the carpet becomes a measure of acuteness and faith alike. Joseph, who interprets the doubling as well as the specifics of Pharaoh's dream as part of the heavenly message, stands head and shoulders above the Egyptian oneiromancers; the captain who pleads with Elijah to spare his life deserves to escape the fate of his two arrogant predecessors (2 Kings 1). When the members appear in a discontinuous sequence, however, their analogy is usually perceived by the reader alone; and in a God-ordered world, analogical linkage reveals the shape of history past and to come with the same authority as it governs the contours of the plot in fiction. Having traced the rhythm of Genesis, for example, we can predict future developments which the agents in their shortsightedness can only yearn for or still hope to block: that Rachel too will be delivered from sterility, say, or that Joseph will get into trouble but finally prevail. The foreknowledge gained from the structure often leads to evaluative as well as informational contrast in viewpoint. As one cycle follows another throughout the period of the judges, the Israelites thus stand condemned for their failure to read the lessons of history: the moral coherence of the series luminously shows the hand of a divine serializer.

While making covertness more than viable, symmetrical communication also widens the possibilities of bringing home overt acts of omnipotence without recourse to commentary. Take the element of preannouncement, whose important (and in nonserialized signs, which are most vulnerable to dismissal as mere chance, decisive) role in commanding belief has already arisen. The effect of prior notice may be redoubled through what I would call spatiotemporal bounding, whereby God commits himself to perform the wonder at a place and/or date appointed either by himself or the prospective audience. Just as when a chess master undertakes to deliver mate on a certain square, the credit for control increases in direct proportion to the risk of failure. And the handicap that would have no point in asymmetry, since God need hardly do precision work to convince himself, enhances suspense and then faith where the world looks on.

As early as the first violence done to nature in the presence of humanity, Noah receives such advance notice: "In seven days I will send rain upon the earth forty days and forty nights" (Gen 7:4). And in enactment, both date and duration duly recur: "After seven days the waters of the flood came upon the earth . . . forty days and forty nights" (7:10–12). Were it not for the Flood's worldwide extension, God might well replace or compound temporal by spatial bounding. Such replacement occurs twice in Gideon's appeal for favorable signs to resolve all doubt about his choice as deliverer or, what lies behind his euphemism, God's powers of deliverance. He presents a spatial challenge, "If there is dew on the fleece alone and it is dry on all the ground, then I shall know that thou wilt deliver Israel by my hand." And his challenge once met, he makes doubly sure by reversing its terms along the same dimension: "Let it, pray, be dry only on the fleece and on all the ground let there be dew" (Judg 6:36–40). The Plagues of Egypt, however, offer ample opportunity for spatiotemporal bounding: "Behold, I will send swarms of flies [?] on thee and thy servants and thy people and into thy houses. . . . But I will set apart the land of Goshen, where my people dwell. . . . By tomorrow shall this sign be" (Exod 8:20–24). Foretelling, two-dimensional bounding, repetition in fulfillment, recurrence within a tenfold series: these combine to maximize the effect ("knowledge") of divine omnipotence on all observers, from God's stricken antagonists through the excepted Israelites to the narrator's audience.

As a focusing technique, whereby the spectator knows when and where to look as well as what to look for, such bounding also maximizes the essential observability of the marvel in its role as persuasive sign. But here this resource for directing attention interacts with another that heightens the impact and value of the fulfillment itself: public testimony. To make an impression, the act must not only be done but seen to be done; and it will carry most weight when most widely attended and attestable. It is therefore in mass scenes that we most often encounter the remark that the sign was enacted not just in the presence but "before the eyes" of the target audience. Take Moses' career. He begins by transforming the rod into a serpent (etc.) *"before the eyes of the people; and the people believed. . . . They bowed their heads and worshipped"* (Exod 4:30–31). The only sin God holds against him is the failure "to sanctify me at the waters *before their eyes"* (Num 27:14). And his obituary, and with it Deuteronomy and the whole Pentateuch, ends in a ringing tribute to "all the signs and wonders . . . and all the mighty power and all the deeds of great terror which Moses wrought *before the eyes of all Israel"* (34:11–12). In the most historic of these mass scenes, the Mount Sinai revelation, there even appears the bold sense-paradox "all the people saw the sounds" (Exod 20:18), which timid interpreters domesticate by smoothing.

The causal linkage of sight and faith or knowledge, like the rhyming of "saw" and "feared"—both *va'yir'u*—gives tremendous rhetorical point to what might appear an empty formula. Having seen with their own eyes, the addressees will (and invariably do) believe the unbelievable.[22] Having believed one wonder or more, they may come to believe others and deduce the logic of omnipotence, whose "knowledge" exposes them to the multiple pressure of warning, reassurance, and gratitude. It is on these that the Deuteronomist's rhetoric skillfully plays. In the reminder of the disaster following the Baal-peor idolatry, he thus harks back to what "your eyes have seen" in warning against transgression (4:3). He likewise derives a model for future reference from the supernatural experience gained since the Exodus: "Remember the great trials which thy eyes have seen" and all fear of Canaanite resistance will be dispelled (7:17–20). He also exacts gratitude for God's past providence ("Has any god ever attempted to go and take a nation for himself from the midst of another nation, by trials and signs and wonders and war, and a mighty hand and an outstretched arm and great terrors, such as the Lord your God did for you in Egypt before thy eyes?" [4:34]); and Joshua's age indeed show it, citing all "those great signs" God has made "before our eyes" as the reason for serving him alone (24:16–18).

But the debt of gratitude should also be paid by transmitting the acquired knowledge to coming generations: "Tell in the hearing of thy son and thy son's son how I have made sport of Egypt" (Exod 10:2), or make "the things which thy eyes have seen . . . known to thy sons and thy sons' sons" (Deut 4:9). The call for appropriate action extends to narration. For an *eye*witness account would sound reliable to the *ears* of posterity—note the care given to the varying modes of apprehension—the more so when told on a national scale and handed down in an unbroken line. Whatever their other omissions, indeed, this is one debt that the Israelites have discharged. As if to testify to the storytelling energy of the fathers, references to the distant as well as the recent past crop up in the speech of the sons, at times in the most unexpected places. As Gideon beats out wheat in the winepress to forestall a new oppressor, he looks back to the Almighty's "wonderful deeds which our fathers recounted to us" (Judg 6:13). Acting out a scenario of David enraged at news of a military fiasco, Joab evokes in detail the inglorious fall of Abimelech (2 Sam ll:21). Even an outlaw like Jephthah, once he opens negotiations with the king of Ammon, exhibits a remarkable but entirely credible command of the minutiae of the ancestral migration from Nile to Jordan (ll:12–28). And what the common people reveal on special occasions is often on the lips of leaders and men of God. Joshua recapitulates history from the days of the patriarchs (Joshua 24); Samuel lists the judges who delivered Israel by the grace of God (1 Samuel 12); Solomon inaugurates the Temple with an oration punctuated by references to the Exodus (1 Kings 8)—not to mention the expertise of the writing prophets.

Such verbal retrospects, moreover, find their equivalent and occasion in nonverbal symbols designed to commemorate some act of God by way of metonymy or iconic reenactment. Examples would be the altars erected by the patriarchs (e.g., Gen 12:8), the celebration of the Passover as a "memorial day . . . for ever" or even "a memorial between thy eyes, that the law of the Lord may be in thy mouth" (Exod 12:14; 13:9, 16), the jar of manna to "be kept throughout your generations, that they may see the bread with which I fed you in the wilderness" (Exod 16:31–34), the bronze censers hammered onto the altar "to be a reminder" of Korah's presumption and fate (Num 16:36–40), the right of gleaning conferred on the landless to ensure that "thou shalt remember that thou wert a slave in the land of Egypt" (Deut 24:19–22), the twelve stones to represent the parting of the Jordan waters (Josh 4:1–9), or in fact the entire law code (Deut 6:20–25). Whether built into the cult or the culture or the scenery, these (human) signs of (divine) signs invite the young to inquire ("Should thy son ask tomorrow"), the old to respond, and all to hark back in the course of daily living.

But the most massive "sign" of all is biblical narrative itself. A variety of writings incorporated in it overtly and dramatically perform this role, starting with the covenantal Ten Commandments, written "with the finger of God" himself (e.g., Exod 31:18; 34:27; Deut 9:9–10; 1 Kgs 8:9), and extending as I said to the Mosaic law code. With less fanfare, however, the whole also exploits the signifying force of more popular attestation. One continuous record of God's lordship of history, the discourse buttresses up its other claims to authority by explicit reference to the nonverbal memorials and implicit appeal to a tradition originating in the eyewitness testimony of a whole people. As the voice of collective memory, Scripture speaks not only of but from the fathers and not only to but for the sons, as much a living monument to Israel's heritage as to her protector's might.

This is an extremely important point, never overtly made but inherent in the logic of composition we have been tracing, and above all in the symmetrical design that projects an unbroken line from eye through ear to writing. The point bears, of course, less on factual genesis than on narrative stance, and therefore has little to do with all the scholarly speculation about oral and written antecedents. Whether or not the Israelites actually did remember (witness, hand down, record) wonders past, the narrator presents them as remembering and himself by implication as the sharer and perpetuator of their remembrance.[23] He thus establishes himself in the strongest position conceivable, one unrivaled in the annals of literature since, again, it uniquely combines the sources of authority attaching to otherwise incompatible models of narration. For he wields the authority of supernatural knowledge and of empirical evidence, of inspiration (or convention) and tradition, of the divine performer and of the human observer, of the mentor and of the "son" meeting other sons on their common ground. To appreciate the strength of this narrative position, just recall some typical counterparts: *Enuma Elish* focusing on the struggles of the gods before the creation of humanity, Homer invoking the Muse while satirizing the whole pantheon, Luke offering an earthly account of Jesus, Herodotus introducing the Greeks to barbarian culture, Thucydides dissociating himself from poetic license in the name of historiography, or the innumerable tellers who have done the opposite under the conventions of fictionality. As far as credibility and persuasiveness go, the Bible would have the best of all worlds, with a special view to incorporating the marvelous into the workings of history rather than fiction.

Poised between God and people, then, the narrator in effect claims to draw on both sides, to represent both and to have the interests of both at heart, of which the most vital is to bring their viewpoints into alignment. Hence the extraordinary care and skill lavished on the omnipotence effect. This includes the pains taken with the asymmetrical situation, by nature unwitnessable, the alacrity with which the opportunities for symmetry are pounced upon, the imaging of God as master semiotician, psychologist, self-advertiser, together with the consistent reference to whatever helps to forge (perhaps in more than one sense) a chain of narrative transmission on earth. This likewise includes the impressive repertoire of more specific devices brought to bear in persuasion. The building of supernatural premises into the action, the preference of the dramatic method over commentary, the foreshadowing-fulfillment structure of repetition, the manifold patterning of redundancy, speech as creative act, the manipulation of sequence in units ranging from the entire Bible to a verse, similarly variable play of perspectives, forms of serialization, shifts between overt and covert providence, spatiotemporal bounding, and so on: the strategy coordinating such an array bespeaks an ideological crux of the first magnitude. Anchored in this composition, moreover, the effect and the narrative stance of intermediacy from which it is generated afford an equally powerful explanation for a set of other measures, great and small. Above all, their ideological imperative accounts for the narrator's drastic self-effacement in the handling of a plot that foregrounds God's omnipotence.

Here, a comparison with modern literature suggests itself. Gustave Flaubert insists in his letters that the author should be in his work like God in the universe: everywhere present but nowhere apparent. In *Portrait of the Artist*, James Joyce's hero draws an analogy between aesthetic and material creation: "The artist, like the God of Creation, remains within or behind or beyond or above his handiwork, invisible, refined out of existence, indifferent, paring his fingernails" (Part 5). The accusation of playing God runs through Jean Paul Sartre's vicious attack on François Mauriac. Like God, "Mauriac is omniscient about everything relating to his little world. What he says about his characters is Gospel. He explains them, categorizes them and condemns them without appeal. If anyone were to ask him how he knows that Thérèse is a cautious and desperate

woman he would probably reply, with great surprise, 'Didn't I create her?'"
In thus offending against relativity and freedom, he has indeed become
God with a vengeance. "God is not an artist. Neither is M. Mauriac."[24]

These influential writers formulate a set of interrelated tenets that govern
the theory and practice of the modern novel. Each shapes or rejects God
to suit an ideal of storytelling whereby the author (or his privileged teller)
should disappear from the surface, if not from the fabric, of the tale. Shorn
of its theological premises, however, their aesthetics would look familiar
to any student of the Bible who has come up against its opacity, reticence,
multiple viewing, problematics of freedom and knowledge. The way of
modernism would doubtless seem to apply to the Bible more than to any
other premodern work. And it is this similarity that gives point to the
dissimilarity.

In marking and explaining those differences, it is hard to separate the
ideology from the art. For the Bible subscribes neither to the moderns'
image(s) of the deity, nor to their deification of certain narrative techniques,
nor to the relations holding between these two models. Like Sartre's, its
reality-model casts God in a role directly opposed to the invisible and
indifferent parer of fingernails, and even exceeds Sartre's portrait of the
absolute sovereign and lawgiver in highlighting the feature of self-
advertisement. Its model of storytelling, on the other hand, shows little
of the modernist dogmatism in that it adopts techniques for their functional value rather than any intrinsic worth. And among the principles
that determine tactical choice, the glorification of God largely figures.

More specifically, another look at the quotations just cited will disclose
that the slogan "Exit Author" involves a denial of privilege (and hence
presence) in four areas:

  i. informational access (e.g., "Mauriac is omniscient about every-
      thing");
 ii. commentary, especially authoritative evaluation ("indifferent,"
      "condemns them without appeal");
iii. expression of personality ("nowhere apparent," "refined out of
      existence");
 iv. plot control or free manipulation ("Didn't I create her?").

Of these commandments, the biblical narrator rejects the first, overrides
the second at will, and bows to the last two but, again, for reasons of his
own. Since his observances and his violations of self-effacement interrelate
within his art, it becomes all the more evident that even the formal similarities between the two corpora arise from a different poetics and lead
to different effects.

We have already seen how and why the biblical artist assumes an omniscience equal but subservient to God's. His reasons are so compelling as

to brush aside any argument to the effect that this position and the result-ant shifts in viewpoint give away his presence. He likewise offers the reader commentary of assorted kinds, including those most frowned upon in the modern tradition. Here are the main varieties of the narrator's own discourse:

1. *Expositional antecedents,* like the preliminaries concerning Job[25] or the delayed mention of the Gibeonites (2 Sam 21:1–3). The exposition may unfold specific or general (Judg 16:4) informa-tion about the world, relate to individuals or groups, consist in external accounts or

2. *Character sketches,* usually in the form of one or two epithets, e.g., "Esau was a skilful hunter, a man of the field; Jacob was a quiet man, dwelling in tents" (Gen 25:27). More variable in length are

3. *Descriptions of objects,* whose upper limit is the meticulous pic-ture drawn of the tabernacle in Exodus and the Temple in Kings.

4. *Interscenic summary:* "He mourned for his son many days" (Gen 37:34), "Absalom dwelt two full years in Jerusalem" (2 Sam 14:28).

5. *Retrospects:* "And this is the reason why Joshua circumcised them: . . . all the people that were born on the way in the wilderness after they had come out of Egypt had not been cir-cumcised" (Josh 5:4–5).

6. *Prospects:* "Samuel did not see Saul again until the day of his death" (1 Sam 15:35).

7. *Genealogies and catalogues,* from "the book of the generations of man" (Genesis 5) to the interminable lists in Chronicles.

8. *Identifications:* "Then Jerubaal (that is, Gideon) and all the people who were with him rose early" (Judg 7:1).

9. *Value judgments:* of agents, like "the men of Sodom were wicked, great sinners against the Lord" (Gen 13:13), or actions, "Thus God requited the crime of Abimelech" (Judg 9:56).

10. *Telescoped inside views:* "Moses hid his face, for he was afraid to look at God" (Exod 3:6), "He went away in a rage" (2 Kgs 5:12).

11. *Notes and stage directions in dialogue:* "All the people answered with one voice" (Exod 24:3), "Michal the daughter of Saul came out to meet David and said" (2 Sam 6:20).

12. *Intrusions into direct discourse:* "He said, Thus and so he spoke to me" (2 Kgs 9:12).

13. *Bibliographical references:* "David lamented with this lamentation over Saul and Jonathan. . . . Behold, it is written in the Book of Yashar" (2 Sam 1:17).

14. *Temporal or cultural bridging,* of special interest in this connection:

> Therefore to this day the Israelites do not eat the sinew of the hip which is upon the hollow of the thigh, because he [the angel] touched the hollow of Jacob's thigh. (Gen 32:32)

> He prophesied before Samuel, and lay naked all that day and all that night. Therefore it is said, Is Saul also among the prophets? (1 Sam 19:24)

> They [the Danites] encamped at Kiriath-jearim in Judah. Therefore is that place called Camp of Dan to this day. (Judg 18:12)

> He [Mordecai] went up to the entrance of the king's gate, for no one might enter the king's gate wearing sackcloth. (Esth 4:1)

> He arrived opposite Jebus, that is, Jerusalem. (Judg 19:10)

> For he who is nowadays called a prophet was formerly called a seer. (1 Sam 9:9)

This looks a mixed bag of intrusions. The first three are aetiological, tracing back the origins of customs, sayings, names. The next explains a concrete event by relating it to a common (foreign) practice. Whereas the final pair clarify reference by the metalinguistic operation of defining an unfamiliar through a familiar term. But all fulfill an elucidatory role by way of mediation—and what is more, one where the narrator is at his most perceptible as commentator, because he verges on the acknowledgment of an audience implicit in all commentary. Note how in each instance the movement from narrative proper to comment involves a shift in sociocultural or usually temporal coordinates: from the time of action (the past in which Jacob struggled with the angel or a man of God was called a seer) to the time of the epic situation (the present in which the narrator faces his contemporaries). Yet even when the narrator overtly identifies himself with one temporal point and viewpoint by way of contrast to another, his intrusion actually bridges the two. Moreover, whether marking a change between past and present ("formerly" versus "nowadays") or establishing continuity ("to this day"), the discourse gives an impression of factual expertise and scrupulosity, even to the extreme of fussiness. Elucidation apart, therefore, these interferences have in common a further effect: the rhetoric of historicity. In this, not despite but because of their heightened intrusiveness, they bring home the biblical rule. The commentary is always a means to an end, and the range of ends excludes nothing except narratorial self-obtrusion.

Contrary to the modern premise, one might add, it is hard to say whether a narrator makes himself more conspicuous by speaking in his own voice or by remaining silent where one might expect speech. But the biblical artist would not much care one way or the other, because to him the whole question is pragmatic rather than doctrinal. He has no hesitation in intruding for a purpose: stage setting, emphasis, intelligibility, economy (where scenic rendering would be wasteful), concentrating interest, plot linkage, historicity effect, or the establishment of a norm as a measure of the characters' subjectivities. Nor will he hesitate to remain "behind or beyond or above his handiwork" where these goals may be equally served by other techniques, disturbing reticence included, or where he has in view other goals altogether. Indeed, this is far more often the case.

The storyteller's instrumental approach to intrusion accordingly explains not only his activity as commentator but also its limits, and not only his commissions but his omissions as well. Most notably, the poetics of maneuvering between the truth and the whole truth calls for a flexible interplay throughout between the revealed and the concealed. Hence—and we shall soon encounter examples—even in commentary the narrator remains less than forthright. He may supply some exposition but not the exposition, sketch character but often leave the essentials out, formulate motive but only in bare outline, pass judgment but with qualifications planted all around it and seldom in the genuinely problematic cases at that. Generally equated in modernism with inartistic lucidity, in short, commentary serves the Bible's art of ambiguity.

Nor does the Bible's free recourse to exegetical "telling" preclude a mastery of the art of dramatic "showing." The very treatment of the omnipotence effect argues to the contrary. The direct citation of God's performative, its rehearsal in fulfillment, and the serialized or bound or publicized signs: these will suffice to illustrate how a well-constructed drama may speak for itself, or rather for the dramatist, saving him the necessity to evoke wonder by way of nudging or so much as exclamation. The more so since the commentary lends itself to plot assimilation, its voicing delegated either to God in person or, less reliably but none the less effectively, to his audience. Where the latter fail to notice or reciprocate, their very failure is eloquent enough. Where they do, their response directly infects their descendants and indirectly fastens the sense of solidarity and the chain of transmission that the narrator epitomizes. Indeed, considering the role played by "seeing" in that process of transmission, dramatic "showing" gains priority as the technique that comes closest to reenacting for the sons the marvelous acts originally eyewitnessed by the fathers.

We shall trace the same functional prinicple at work in spheres other-wise so different as character portrayal, control of judgment, or the render-ing of motive and inner life. But if this whole biblical line of refraining from commentary turns on local considerations, which may lose their force with any shift of context and priorities, two others are categorical. The narrator avoids all commentary that would invest him with the lineaments of an individual person or persona or with the title of a creator.

First, no self-dramatization must threaten the objectivity and authority of the disembodied voice mediating between God and his people. Even where the narrative surface shows the same impersonality, therefore, the underlying motivation has no equivalent in the age of the novel. Nor, as argued in the previous chapter, does such suppression of self follow from the conventions of ancient narrative—Egyptian storytelling and Greek historiography, among others, show the viability of the alternative—nor even of the Bible as a whole. Considering the stance adopted by the proph-ets or the wisdom teachers or autobiographers like Nehemiah, it would be significant enough to find the narrator abstaining from identifying himself by name. But our narrator does not even identify himself in terms of nationality, as a Hebrew, not even through the grammatical means of the first person plural. The self-collocation with Israel in "the land which the Lord had sworn to their fathers to give *us*" (Josh 5:6) and "Solomon held the feast . . . before the Lord *our* God" (1 Kgs 8:65) are the only excep-tions to the rule. Elsewhere the ancestors of Israel always appear as "their fathers," the antagonists as "their enemies," God as "their God"—all forms of self-distancing from the audience where one would most naturally expect self-identification.

This presses objectivity to an incongruous if not counterproductive extreme. Or so it seems till one notices its coincidence with the narrator's recourse to the third person to indicate these referents and Israel herself from God's side of the fence (e.g., "They cried to the Lord" in Joshua 24:7). To maintain his intermediate or double-faced stance between the parties of and for whom he speaks, then, the narrator establishes a system of reference whereby he can apply the same referring terms to and from both sides or indicate each side from the other's viewpoint. For good measure, he makes no pronominal reference to himself or his audience, to the total exclusion of the "I" and the "you" as well as the "we" that fracture even the surface of Homeric impersonality. Since the resulting narrative voice could be either God's or Israel's—which nothing short of such drastic steps could ensure—it reaps the advantages of both.

This does not mean that we cannot draw any inferences about the nar-rator. His poetics invites reconstruction; so do his ideology and histori-osophy; so do even his deictic coordinates vis-à-vis plot and characters, notably the relation of temporal posteriority established by the past tense and the occasional "now" versus "then" or "formerly." All it does mean is that the narrator manifests and defines himself only in the impersonal terms of his unique art of narration. Apart from their hopelessness, therefore, the scholarly endeavors to recover the man from the writing go against the very principle that impelled him to don the mask of anonymity. To a greater extent than God himself, he operates as a disembodied voice. "You heard the sound of words, but saw no form; there was only a voice" (Deut 4:12): no name, no personal antecedents, hardly a local habitation between heaven and earth.

Just as the man effaces his identity, so does the artist his workshop, taking energetic measures to rule out any impression of creative attributes. In effect, he does exercise quasi-divine powers in that he need only say a word to create a piece of world—a character, a dialogue, a situation—and only to distribute points of contact between various pieces to make a law that governs that world. But whatever his practice, it receives no avowal on the narrative surface and no legitimation from the underlying doctrine; hence the contrast between the narrator's shunning and God's pursuit of the image of omnipotence. The narrator's escape from godlike omnipotence would ill-assort with his parade of godlike omniscience were it not for the fact that both positions serve the interests of the same master.

The history of narrative knows a tradition, extending from Petronius and Wolfram von Eschenbach through Cervantes and Diderot to Gide and Fowles, which has inscribed on its banner the laying bare of artifice and in particular the artist's control over his action and agents.[26] No sooner have we settled down to the first dialogue of *Jacques the Fatalist* than Diderot shows his hand:

> You see, reader, that I am well on my way, and that it is completely up to me whether I shall make you wait one year, two years, or three years for the story of Jacques's loves by separating him from his master and having each of them go through all the vicissitudes that I please. What's to prevent my marrying off the master and making him a cuckold? Shipping Jacques off to the islands? Guiding the master to the same place? Bringing them back to France on the same ship? How easy it is to fabricate stories! But I'll let them both off with a bad night and you, with this delay.[27]

"Completely up to me . . . all the vicissitudes that I please . . . What's to prevent . . . I'll let them off": to claim absolute freedom of choice is to claim absolute power, whereby the teller comes to stand in a God-like relation to his world. Henry James branded such a flaunting of artifice as "suicidal," and his judgment would speak with redoubled force for the Bible. A display

of narratorial omnipotence entails a proclamation of fictional license—
"How easy it is to fabricate stories!"—which would undermine all claim
to historicity. By the same token, such a display would have serious ideological implications. In Diderot and others, the waywardness of narration
reflects the waywardness of a world incoherent and out of joint: the artist
is almighty in the absence of an Almighty. With the Almighty actually
present in the action, as in the Bible, omnipotent narration would even
hold him up to mockery. It would overturn the entire world picture by
subjecting the divine to the aesthetic logic of events and reducing the
Creator himself to a creature, plaything, tool of the narrator's imagination. The slightest hint of inventiveness would thus shake the whole system.
Where God appears for the first time on the literary stage to challenge
the fictions of polytheism, the status of the narrative becomes inseparable
from his own, control from existence, ontology from theology.

To be sure, the flaunting of artifice has no place among the earliest conventions of antiquity. Still, were it not for the ideological enterprise, it
would be quite conceivable in the Bible. The refashioning of modes and
molds, the development of a host of new forms, the pervasive concern with
ambiguity and point of view, the high sophistication of treatment, the
intense awareness of audience and communication, the playful spirit
manifested in comedy and satire and punning, the availability of the rhetoric
of omnipotence itself: the aesthetic conditions and resources for self-focused
storytelling are all there, probably for the first time in literary history. Which
makes the absence of the merest gesture toward *that* innovation revealing
indeed.

This brings out anew the contrast between omniscience and omnipotence
as narrative features. The narrator can freely exercise omniscience without
in the least relinquishing his title to historicity. Epistemological license
does not reflect on ontological status, as it would in modern literature,
because given the inspirational convention, the privilege is assumed in
the name and service of divinity rather than art. Far from sealing any
fictional contract, its assumption guarantees the literal truth by its very
supernaturalness, with tradition as co-guarantor on the earthly level. To
flaunt omnipotence in the handling of plot, however, is to speak not for
God in history but as God in fiction, as an analogue rather than voice
of divinity, because absolute power may be delegated to agents—like
prophets—but only imitated by tellers. As tellers, they must either record
God's genuine lordship or fictionalize their own exploits.

The either/or choice explains the impression striven for by the biblical
narrator: that the control he wields is artistic (over his text and reader)
but not existential (over the represented world and characters). In his role
as artist, he does not hesitate to draw our notice to his activity as organizer

as well as commentator. Thus the narrative operates with firm principles of selection. This emerges from the unequal treatment accorded to different figures and plot lines (e.g., Jacob versus Esau), or the alternations of summary and scene, or, tantalizingly, the distribution of such tidbits as the passing reference to "Anah, who found the mules (?) in the wilderness as he pastured the asses" (Gen 36:24), which suggests that a good tale has been consigned to oblivion by the dictates of relevance. As with selectional, so with combinatory indicators: temporal displacement, information withheld, shifts of scene and viewpoint, analogical design, chiastic closure, progression by key words, and so forth. Such signals of artful and masterful patterning are indispensable to the control of the reading process within a reserved and often opaque narrative. But their implications never exceed the license legitimately taken by a recorder concerned to shape a given world into meaningful discourse rather than to create a world in and through the discourse.

To deepen this sense of a given world, the Bible shows a supreme confidence in its facts. Any rival version, it implies, would be absurd, if at all conceivable. And since the historical writer presumably worked with a good many versions, the stance of monopoly and immediate access to the truth in which he placed his narrator becomes all the more revealing. It is as if even collation is ruled out, as an avowal of plurality and a second-order act of creation. Thus, whatever the story told by the royal annals—and it would hardly have been pious—the constant references to them throughout Kings betray no hint of conflict. They rather operate, like the passing allusion to Anah, as a notice of untapped, because irrelevant, resources. "The *rest* of the acts of Jeroboam, how he warred and how he reigned, behold, they are written in the Book of the Chronicles of the Kings of Israel" (1 Kgs 14:19): rhetorically speaking, this not only neutralizes but also makes capital of a possible rival by mentioning it in passing as a further empirical witness to the truth of the main action.

Again, the narrator does not actually invoke such human support, written or oral, any more than he does divine aid. Provided with a double set of credentials, he waves neither for all to see because only by tacit appeal can their authority be combined without loss or friction. To lay claim to inspiration would be to dissociate oneself from the audience; whereas to associate oneself with the audience would be to court dangers even worse than attenuating the divine connection. The reference to documents and traditions as *sources* would inevitably leave empirical gaps in the plot and room for counter-evidence about the whole, thus exposing the narrative to charges of invention and unreliability. Silence alone ensures a firm position astride of origin.

Moreover, traditional speculations about documents and sources and twice-told tales have now piled up so high on the altar of genesis as to obscure the one remarkable fact in sight, which bears on poetics. Granting the profusion of variants that went into the making of the Bible, the fact remains that the finished discourse never introduces them *as* variants but rather strings them together into continuous action. Egyptian mythology embraces incompatible accounts of the creator-god's modus operandi, from thought and command (The Memphite Theology) through naming (The Book of the Dead) or spitting (The Pyramid Texts) to masturbation.[28] In the Hittite *Myth of Illuyankas,* as told by Kellas the priest, the dragon is slain twice: first according to the ancient ("they no longer tell") and then to a newer version.[29] A historian like Herodotus also makes a point of juxtaposing variant accounts between the covers of a single work. He begins by noting that the Persians and the Greeks have different stories of how Io came to Egypt; later he cites the Lacedaemonian affirmation and the Samian denial of the theft of Croesus's bowl; then he pits his own hypothesis concerning Cyrus's crossing into Greece against the prevalent view; and so on to the end of *The Histories.*

In contrast, if the three wife-sister variations in Genesis originate from separate sources (J and E), each has yet been assigned by the discourse to a different phase in patriarchal history. If the account of the conquest in Judges varies from that in Joshua, it formally appears not as a corrective or alternative but as an overture to the record of the next period. If the two divine judgments on Saul reflect competing explanations of his fall, then the doublet has been transformed into two stages along a plot of gradual rejection. Whether the (iffish) stitching into linearity is seamless or discernible may be a measure of the author's skill; that silent stitching is deemed mandatory implies his poetics and the rules laid down for the communication act.

Still less does the narrative surface show any trace of the polemics the Bible supposedly conducts against mythology and heresy. If anything could be more foreign to its spirit than the juxtaposition of discordant gospels, this is Matthew's quarreling with the story "spread among the Jews to this day" that the disciples themselves stole away Jesus' corpse (28:11–15). Nor, as indicated earlier in this chapter, does the narrative favor the prophetic and otherwise poetic onslaughts on idols and the absurd stories attaching to their worship. Students of Genesis have indeed unearthed certain polemical references, like the creation of "the great sea monsters" (1:21) where Oriental myth enacts the struggle of gods against primeval monsters, or the moral rationale of the Flood.[30] But that digging was necessary (and often insufficient) to establish connections between these divergent accounts proves even more suggestive than its results. All the narrative battles against pagan tradition take place underground, by way of allusion and parody detectable by the initiate alone.

The surface itself does accommodate a variety and even clash of perspectives—as in the structure of repetition—about which a dogmatist might well complain. But it is one thing to incorporate alien and erroneous viewpoints (not excluding criticisms of God or appeals to idols) as positions taken *in* biblical history and accordingly open to internal discrediting by action and rhetoric; it is quite another to recognize such viewpoints as independent alternatives, however untenable, *to* biblical history. As the voice of the one and indivisible truth, in short, the narrator formally disavows not just all reconciliation but all knowledge of narratives at odds with his own, since even a distant nod at them would saddle him with the unwelcome title of maker rather than shaper of plot.

·4·

VIEWPOINTS
AND INTERPRETATIONS

"Men work together," I told him from the heart,
"Whether they work together or apart."
　　　Robert Frost, "The Tuft of Flowers"

Point of View and Its Biblical Configuration

The Bible teaches more than one general lesson about narration. Far from a technical choice, point of view has emerged as an ideological crux and force, none the less artful for being thus engaged. And far from a matter of who speaks or sees what, I shall now proceed to argue, it always forms a combination of perspectives—such as the divine, the quasi-divine or narratorial, and the human views of Saul's anointment or Pharaoh's affliction. Curiously, some theoretical approaches to point of view are akin to biblical geneticism in fragmenting the text into bits of discourse and seeking to assign each to its appropriate originator. That the object is to identify the internal rather than the historical sources of transmission only renders this exercise in atomism all the more ill-judged; and its pursuit among so-called structuralists flies in the face of the very notion of structure as a network of relations.

For one thing, whatever else point of view may be or do, it entails a relation between subject and object, perceiving mind and perceived reality. In this sense, all speakers (or viewers) figure as interpreters, their speech deriving from a process of interpretation and reflecting or betraying an interpretive construct that they would regard as the world and others might dismiss as a lie or illusion. Discourse renders a world from a certain viewpoint. The whole text accordingly unfolds as a threefold complex—with the most variable interplay between discourse, world, and perspective—whose disentanglement by the reader forms neither a luxury nor a technicality but the very condition of making sense. Who stands behind this piece of language and what does it project? From what viewpoint does

that action or description unfold, and why? Can the perceiver be identified and evaluated by the field of perception? Where does the subject
end and the object begin? Is this particular reflector ironic or ironized,
reliable or biased or even mendacious, or in short, how does his interpretation stand to the text's and ours? These are among the typical questions arising throughout.

Nor is any of the questions resolvable out of context. As well as inter-
acting with all other components, point of view itself forms a system of
perspectival relations—one constant, most variable, all mutually defining.
Briefly, as I argued elsewhere, narrative communication involves no fewer
than four basic perspectives: the author who fashions the story, the narrator who tells it, the audience or reader who receives it, and the characters
who enact it.[1] Where the narrator is practically identical with the author,
as in Homer or Fielding or indeed the Bible, the discourse therefore operates
with three basic relationships that constitute the point of view: between
narrator and characters, narrator and reader, reader and characters. Of
these relationships, the first alone normally remains constant in its inequality, opposing the omniscient and reliable narrator to his essentially
fallible agents. Whereas the two others are amenable to free variation:
what the reader knows and how well he judges, for instance, depend on
the narrator's strategy of telling. Whether or not he takes us into his confidence will make an enormous difference to the reading, including our
ability to identify or discriminate the perspectives of the dramatized observers and correct their subjective distortions of the implied world and
world view. But regardless of narrative strategy, if we are to make any sense
of the text—to distinguish one refracting medium from another, opinion
from fact, shadow from substance, commitment from irony—we must perform these reconstructive operations as best we can. And we can only
perform them by making inferences about the different perspectives in
relation to one another and above all to the supreme authority that figures
as the contextual measure of their validity. A judgment cannot be located
along a scale of reliablility, nor a description pronounced objective or subjective, nor a character stamped as ignorant or knowing, nor a reading
follow an ironic or straight line—except by reference to the contextual norm
embodied in the all-authoritative narrator. Which is to say that a text cannot
even be decomposed into its perspectival parts without having been recom-
posed into a coherent whole, an orchestration of voices and a hierarchy
of interpretations.

Given these universals of structure and reading, the marks distinguishing
each narrative lie in its treatment of the variable factors and relationships.
And here the biblical configuration of point of view has quite a few claims
to originality. Most notable is its knocking down of the usually impassable

barriers separating authoritative teller from fallible characters to admit God to the position of superperceiver as well as superagent. The reasons having already been discussed, we may now focus on the consequences for the overall art of perspective.

Again, the usual theoretical models and taxonomies fail to apply here. For, as with every structure worthy of the name, the displacement of a part launches a chain reaction that transforms the whole set of relations characterizing omniscient narrative. Where the general model of omniscience in literature dispenses with one of the basic perspectives by virtually equating the author with the narrator, the Bible's introduces a new perspective by dissociating God from the characters and aligning him with the narrator. (Within an inspirational framework, God himself even becomes the author of the book as well as of its plot, without forfeiting his agentlike status.) In so doing, as if to complicate matters further and sharpen the peculiarity of the maneuver, the narrative undermines the normal correlation between a viewpoint's mode of existence (within or without the world) and level of authority (nonprivileged or privileged respectively). Like all commonsensical linkages, this norm may hold in the Bible for the godlike narrator (detached and privileged) as well as for the earthly cast (involved and nonprivileged) but, what is ideologically appropriate, not for divinity itself.

The lines of demarcation are thus redrawn to establish a novel fourfold pattern, involving two assorted and roughly symmetrical couples: the elevated superhumans on the one hand and the erring humans on the other. God existentially inside while perspectivally above the world, the reader wedded in some degree to his fellow men: this structure of point of view acts as a constant reminder of their respective positions in the scheme of things. From this unpromising premise, and not so much despite as because of its theological bearing, there also springs an intricate, flexible, and challenging art of perspective, to which the Wooing of Rebekah in Genesis 24 affords a good introduction.

The Wooing of Rebekah

Positions and Discrepancies Established

(1) Abraham was old, advanced in years; and the Lord had blessed Abraham in everything. (2) And Abraham said to his servant, the oldest of his house, who ruled over everything that he had, Put thy hand, pray, under my thigh, (3) and I will make thee swear by the Lord, the God of heaven and the God of the earth, that thou shalt not take a wife for my son from the daughters of the Canaanites, among whom I dwell;

(4) but to my native land [*el artsi ve'el moladeti*] shalt thou go and take a wife for my son, for Isaac. (5) And the servant said to him, Perhaps the woman may not be willing to follow me to this land; shall I then lead thy son back to the land from which thou camest? (6) And Abraham said to him, Take care that thou dost not lead my son back there. (7) The Lord, the God of heaven, who took me from my father's house and from the land of my birth [*erets moladeti*], and who spoke to me and swore to me, saying, To thy offspring will I give this land, he will send his angel before thee and thou shalt take a wife for my son from there. (8) And if the woman is not willing to follow thee, then thou wilt be free of this oath of mine; only thou shalt not lead my son back there. (9) So the servant put his hand under the thigh of Abraham his master and swore to him concerning this matter.

This is a scene to which the reader has been looking forward for some time, and not merely because the original audience must have known, as every schoolboy now does, that Isaac married Rebekah. The accidentals of the extratextual knowledge brought to the reading are standardized by the internal knowledge built into the reading process. And since narrative tact as well as poetics rules out the baldness of an overt foreshadowing, this internalization takes a form subtle enough to keep even the knowledgeable reader occupied, yet determinate enough to enlighten the less informed.

It is the analogy between Abraham's two sons that first anticipates the marital theme. Ishmael's career shows three landmarks: late birth (16:16), mortal danger averted by a timely divine intervention (21:14-19), and marriage to a compatriot of his Egyptian mother's (21:21). Isaac having likewise gone through the first two stages (21:1-8; 22:1-12), the third is now due by compositional logic. That expectation even gains further point from the tightening of the analogy toward the final stage. The divine promise "I will make him a great nation" (21:18), which came between Ishmael's ordeal and his marriage, now recurs with redoubled force after the sacrificial binding of Isaac: "I will indeed bless thee and I will multiply thy offspring as the stars of heaven and the sand on the seashore, and thy offspring shall possess the gate of his enemies" (22:17). The fulfillment of this promise—significantly echoed at both the beginning (24:7) and the end (24:60) of our tale—again requires a bride. And indeed, as if on cue, she or at least her name makes an immediate entrance:

After these things, it was told to Abraham, Behold, Milcah too has borne sons, to Nahor thy brother: Uz his firstborn, Buz his brother, Kemuel the father of Aram, Kesed, Hazo, Pildash, Yidlaf, and Bethuel. And Bethuel begot Rebekah. These eight Milkah bore to Nahor, Abraham's brother. And his concubine, whose name was Reumah, also bore Tebah, Tahash, and Ma'acah. (22:20–24)

This material could hardly seem less promising: a bare genealogical list of supernumeraries, with none but remote antiquarian value. Yet even catalogues bring grist to the Bible's mill, and the lump of history gets assimilated to the art of the personal story. Inserted under the guise of family news, this digression assumes new shape and meaning in context. The genealogical list falls into analogical pattern, the chronological parataxis ("After these things") stiffens into causal sequence, the retrospect turns round its face to become a prospection. Juxtaposed with God's blessing and placed in structural correspondence to Ishmael's marriage, the report virtually names the bride-to-be.[2] Not, however, in a manner so transparent as to destroy the pleasures of inference. That is why Rebekah gets tucked away in the middle, and a rival candidate, Ma'acah, occupies a far more prominent position. But the camouflage arrests and amuses rather than misleads even the unforewarned reader.[3] Ma'acah is clearly a red herring: a concubine's daughter, in a cycle where mixed descent has played such an unsettling role, she might be a good match for Ishmael but hardly for Abraham's heir. And Rebekah's obtrusive presence amply makes up for her unobtrusive location. In a list supposed to enumerate the "sons" that "Milcah too has borne"—the allusion to Sarah in "too" interprets *banim* as "sons" rather than "children"—why include a female who is not even a daughter? Of Nahor's presumably numerous descendants, moreover, Rebekah is the only grand-daughter mentioned. And as if to italicize the clue, her mention is at once followed by a summative numbering ("These eight Milcah bore to Nahor") that pointedly excludes her. The coherence of that item, the signals imply, must be sought along lines other than genealogical.

The indirections that culminate in this miniature guess-who puzzle, then, serve as a built-in anticipation, elevating the reader to a vantage post from which he identifies Rebekah as the God-appointed bride. But does Abraham, the dramatized recipient of the family news, share this foreknowledge? It is interesting that, where we might expect him to name Rebekah, he does not even direct his servant to her family. This strange failure has often been missed, due to the common fallacy of hindsight reading and specifically a misreading of verse 4. The point needs to be established, therefore, as the groundwork of the tale's play of viewpoints and its overall sense.

It is a fact that the faithful servant does not at all approach the family on arrival, but stops at the well to contrive a test that opens the field to every girl in the town. Indeed, he does not depart for Nahor's house in the first place: his destination is given rather as "Mesopotamia, the city of Nahor." (This reference need not even be to a person but to the place that figures as Nakhur in the Mari tablets.[4]) And the servant's proceeding not only reflects but follows his instructions. Note that Abraham, far from pronouncing the name that is trembling on *our* lips, starts with a general characterization of the bride required and a negative characterization at that: "not from the daughters of the Canaanites, among whom I dwell." And as the dialogue begins so does it proceed and end—with the negative feature of Canaan looming larger than any positive attraction of Mesopotamia, let alone any specific Mesopotamian. Hence the harping on the spatial opposition between "here" and "there" that depersonalizes the whole transaction. In case the woman refuses to settle in "this land," the servant asks, shall Isaac join her "in the land from which thou camest?" No, Abraham insists, he must not return "there": God, who promised my offspring "this land," will see to it that you bring a woman "from there." Yet whatever happens, there is no question of Isaac's settling "there." Which clearly means that, destined to inherit the land, Isaac must on no account marry among those doomed to disinheritance; but since Mesopotamia's recommendation lies in not being Canaan, it would lose all appeal were Isaac to disinherit himself by emigrating. The historical process launched by Abraham's call must no more be reversed by his son's repatriation than subverted by local intermarriage.

No wonder, therefore, that Abraham frames the scenario in the widest ethno-geographical terms; that he makes no mention of his brother Nahor, perhaps even in a deliberate attempt to bring home his point and minimize the danger of emigration; that he impersonalizes the bride into "a woman." He acts from a sense of national destiny rather than from family feeling or nostalgia for his old country. And the servant, who would otherwise appear a disobedient fool or knave, jeopardizing if not sabotaging his mission by his failure to make a beeline for the family address, simply observes his terms of reference.

Within these terms of reference, accordingly, the direction *el artsi ve'el moladeti telekh* in verse 4 does not bear the meaning "thou shalt go to my land and to my kindred," assigned to it by most translators and exegetes.[5] It rather forms a hendiadys signifying "thou shalt go to the land of my kindred/birth" or "to my native land," precisely like the *erets moladeti* of verse 7. In the context of the Abraham saga, as it happens, *moledet* refers to an entity larger than the family anyway. God's very first address to Abraham, "Go forth from thy land and thy *moledet* and thy father's house to the land that I will show thee" (12:1), marks an ascending order of specificity where *moledet* falls between country and kindred. Given the otherwise symmetrical relations between the divinely ordered exodus ("go forth from . . .") and the humanly ordered return ("go to . . ."), moreover, Abraham's omission of the specific "father's house" from the reversed scenario would make little sense were it not for its perfect congruity with the impersonal spirit of the "here–there" opposition. In retrospect, indeed, we note that when the servant rewrites history to cajole the relatives into believing that Abraham expressly directed him to them, he thrice replaces in transmission Abraham's original "land and *moledet*" by "father's house and family" (38, 40, 41). The version revised after the event to narrow down the field only highlights the generality of the original intention.

By the time the servant puts his hand under his master's thigh, therefore, the tale has already established a fourfold (and practically, threefold) structure of point of view, with marked and gradated discrepancies in awareness. God (who promised) and the narrator (who anticipated the fulfillment) stand together at one pole, their supernatural knowledge going with absolute control. The opposite pole is occupied by the patriarch and his envoy, their powers so humanly limited that they can no more foresee than ensure the outcome: to them the issue remains open against their desire, its concrete terms to be disclosed only in historical embodiment, its resolution problematic and fraught with danger. In between stands the reader, privileged enough to foreknow the end as determinate and happy even beyond the characters' dreams, but reduced to ignorance in all that concerns the route leading up to the providential end.

This conforms to the Bible's favorite system of perspectival relations, serving to reconcile the claims of art and ideology into a happy ideological art. God, omniscient and omnipotent by doctrinal fiat, will prove so in dramatic terms as the action translates his implicit will and pledge into the stuff of history: the premise lays the ground for the demonstration and the demonstration vindicates and inculcates the premise—which sounds poor logic but makes excellent rhetoric in the telling. At the same time as the narrator exploits his authority to dramatize and glorify God's, God's own powers invest the compositional foreshadowing-by-analogy with such force as to enable the narrator to canalize interest into the desired grooves without compromising his art of indirection. In turn, the characters' limited knowledge, governed by the realistic norm, first establishes a sharp opposition between the natural and the supernatural spheres and then motivates a progressive discovery of God's benevolent control. The reader's intermediate position, finally, guarantees his awareness of God's superintendence, while leaving the movement from promise to fulfillment dark enough to sustain interest and allow the demonstration to work itself out in human terms. Given the initial sense of divine providence, the interplay of character and event may develop with impunity.

Typical in essentials, this perspectival scheme yet manifests some variables. Above all, the Bible does not often effect such a severance between the informational and the normative axes of point of view. Considered by themselves, the informational tensions might be expected to generate powerful irony at the expense of the least knowing, the dramatis personae. But we actually experience little irony, because the discrepancies in awareness are tempered by parity in values: knowledge of principles always redeems in the Bible any lacunae in the knowledge of facts and contingencies; though not, as evildoers find out the hard way, vice versa. Thus, the implied reader shares—if only by artful courtesy—the narrator's world view. But so does Abraham, who, ignorant of all details and personalities, is still confident that God "will send his angel" to look after them. And so, it progressively emerges, does his servant, who speaks and acts for him throughout as a like-minded ambassador. As he sets out, therefore, the variations between the nondivine perspectives yet go with the question common to all fellow-believers: *How* will God manage the affair?

The Movement from Divergence to Convergence of Perspectives

(10) The servant took ten camels of the camels of his master and went, with all kinds of goods from his master in his hand; and he arose and went to Mesopotamia, to the city of Nahor. (11) And he made the camels kneel down outside the city by the well of water at evening time, the time when the women come out to draw water. (12) And he said, O Lord, God of my master Abraham, make things go well for me this day and show kindness to my master Abraham. (13) Behold, I am standing by the spring of water, and the daughters of the men of the city are coming out to draw water. (14) The maiden to whom I shall say, Pray let down thy pitcher that I may drink, and who will say, Drink, and I shall water thy camels too—let her be the one whom thou hast appointed for thy servant Isaac. (15) Before he had finished speaking, and behold, Rebekah came out, who was born to Bethuel the son of Milcah, the wife of Nahor, Abraham's brother, with her pitcher upon her shoulder. (16) And the maiden was very good-looking, a virgin, and no man had known her. She went down to the spring and filled her pitcher and came up. (17) And the servant ran towards her and said, Pray give me a little water to drink from thy pitcher. (18) And she said, Drink, my lord; and she made haste and lowered her pitcher onto her hand and let him drink. (19) And when she had finished letting him drink, she said, I shall draw for thy camels too, until they have finished drinking. (20) And she made haste and emptied her pitcher into the trough, and ran again to the well to draw, and she drew for all his camels. (21) And the man stood wondering at her, keeping silent to learn whether the Lord had prospered his journey or not. (22) And when the camels had finished drinking, the man took a gold ring, half a shekel in weight, and two bracelets for her hands, ten gold shekels in weight. (23) And

he said, Whose daughter art thou? Pray tell me. Is there room in thy
father's house for us to spend the night? (24) And she said to him, I
am the daughter of Bethuel the son of Milcah, whom she bore to Nahor.
(25) And she said to him, We have both straw and provender in plenty,
also room to spend the night in. (26) And the man bowed his head and
worshipped the Lord. (27) And he said, Blessed be the Lord, the God
of my master Abraham, who has not withheld his kindness and his truth
from my master. I being on a journey, the Lord has led me to the house
of my master's brothers.

Thrown on his own devices on arrival, the servant leaves nothing to chance,
as his mandate entitled him to do, but takes a twofold initiative that weds
good sense to piety. Of the eligible young women in the city, he will not
settle for less than the best. So, appealing to God to bless his principle
of choice, he improvises a shrewd character test. What touchstone could
be more appropriate than the reception of a wayfarer to determine a
woman's fitness to marry into the family of the paragon of hospitality?
And it is a stiff test, too, since it would require far more than common
civility to volunteer to water "ten" thirsty camels. (Note how this initially
descriptive, realistic-looking feature now gains actional and thematic value
as well: from a measure of Abraham's wealth, it transforms into a measure
of his daughter-in-law's worthiness to enjoy it.)

The perfection of the initiative thus continues to moderate the irony
threatened by the discrepancies in foreknowledge. Yet these discrepancies
make for variance even in the application of the perfect yardstick. What
to the servant is a character test of a prospective bride is to the reader
a retrospective (and exhilarating) characterization of Rebekah. Having
already been cast in the bridal role, how can she fail to pass with flying
colors?

Indeed, her entrance could hardly be more auspicious. Where a folktale
would first stage two or three abortive trials, in the interests of variety
and retardation and contrastive portrayal, the Bible brings on the appointed
winner at once. Not that it spurns the effects yielded by a drawn-out
process—we shall see them all generated by oblique means. Rather, the
narrative's primary concern is to show God at his invisible work, and any
serialization of the test would upset the balance between human ingenuity
and divine control. Far from delayed, therefore, the girl shows up even
"before he had finished speaking." She is, literally, God's answer (in the
medium of plot) to the servant's prayer; and so in fact do both he and
we view her. However, we reach that conclusion with much greater certitude, thanks to a sudden widening of the informational discrepancy to
our advantage. Though the new development seems to emerge from the
servant's viewpoint ("and behold!"), the narrator smuggles into the report

three facts inaccessible to any human observer. It is by his privilege and for our benefit alone that the text reveals the water-drawer's name ("Rebekah"), her lineage ("born to Bethuel," etc., to jog the memory of forgetful readers), and, most hidden and reassuring, her morals ("a virgin," etc.). Less favored, the dramatized spectator is also less reassured. The timing is perfect, the good looks a welcome bonus, but what about the character? Only the test can show.

The test does, of course, show. But it performs this role beyond anyone's expectations and with a consummate art that has been mistaken by hard-line geneticists for patchwork and by their modern heirs for "an original narrative prolixity . . . made wordier still by subsequent transmission," with the extenuating circumstance that "the repetitiveness which we occasionally find a bit overwhelming was not so sensed by the authors and editors of the Bible."[6] It is only by the grace of what I called the Bible's foolproof composition that such extreme under-readers yet manage to grasp the essentials of plot and judgment, without suffering anything worse than boredom. If "we" find anything overwhelming, it is not at all the repetitiveness but the fireworks of repetition.

The variations in the passage from wish to fulfillment have a random look, since they manifest the wildest heterogeneity: changes in wording, in continuity, in specification. Below the surface, however, all this formal variety combines into functional unity. All the variations go to dramatize a single point: that the young woman's performance surpasses even the most optimistic expectations. Thus, the increased specificity largely derives from the references to haste that punctuate the narrative: "she made haste and lowered her pitcher . . . she made haste and lowered her pitcher into the trough . . . she ran again to the well." This spontaneous dispatch bears more than the obvious complimentary implications for character and judgment. It echoes nothing less than Abraham's model hospitality, "He ran to meet them . . . Abraham made haste into the tent . . . Abraham ran to the tent . . . he made haste to prepare it" (18:2–7); and the elevating analogy stamps her as worthy of the patriarch himself. Hence also another rise in particularity, from the envisaged "drawing" of water to its actual enactment, "she went down to the spring and filled her pitcher and came up." This meticulous picture of the girl descending empty and then ascending loaded suggests what an arduous chore the drawing of water is, literally uphill work, even in normal conditions; how exhausting when one goes down and up at a run; how interminable when one has to provide for a whole caravan; and all (another recurrent detail) with one little pitcher.

The watering must have taken quite a while; and this is further stressed in verse 21 by the description of the man as "wondering at her, keeping silent to learn whether the Lord had prospered his journey or not," otherwise oddly interpolated between two mentions of her performance. In temporal terms, this discontinuous repetition marks a sequence of "action→regression→progression," and in terms of point of view, a shift from our perspective to the servant's. The reader, who knows that the maiden is destined to complete the service she has undertaken, needs no special telling that "she drew for all his camels." But while she is breaking her back for him, the internal observer can hardly believe what she has already done and only hope ("or not" is for him still on the cards) that she will get through with her task. The descriptive realism, in short, renders the well scene anything but an idyllic encounter: the emphasis rather falls on the correlation between the volunteer's physical labor and moral worth.

That she does more than could be expected becomes doubly impressive in view of the fact that he asks for less. The envisioned request "Pray lower thy pitcher that I may drink" drops to "Pray give me a little water to drink from thy pitcher." So it is she who prolongs the sip into a full-sized drink, just as she thinks of supporting the pitcher for the drinker's convenience and adds the deferential "my lord" in addressing what is to the narrator "the servant" or at most "the man." As for the camels, everyone hopes of course that she will offer to "water" them, but the scope of her initiative again surprises the covert as well as the dramatized observer: "For thy camels too I will draw, *until they have finished drinking.*" And however formidable the undertaking, she means exactly what she says, as the narrator underlines through another subtle (in Hebrew, even punning) repetition with variation. "She drew for *all* his camels" (*kol,* full number) and "the camels *finished* drinking" (*killu,* full belly).

Only at one point, the very outset, does the variation in performance give real cause for concern. Where expected to respond "Drink and I shall water thy camels too," she actually stops halfway through: "Drink, my lord." Even the stoutest heart will miss a beat at this. Is she the type that will oblige at request but offer nothing beyond? Does she overlook the camels thoughtlessly or deliberately? Is it one thing to "lower" a pitcher for a single man and quite another to exhaust oneself on behalf of his thirsty beasts? Owing to the discrepancies in information, these gaps must have troubled the servant even more than the reader: our perplexity about Rebekah may well have been his despair of the first candidate. He may already have written her off when, upon the girl's delivering the second part as well, and to more than perfection, it all turns out to be a false alarm.

In retrospect we discover that the narrator has mixed a little mischief with serious business to extraordinary effect. The mischief consists in retarding the plot with a view to heightened suspense. But the retardation is more cunning and multifunctional than it looks. In playing on our fears, it also serves to insinuate by the backstairs of composition the abortive trial that a folktale would introduce by the front door of the action. Due to our initial ignorance of her personality, Rebekah assumes for a moment the features and fate of a heroine who, if not an utter washout, does not come up to matriarchal standard. Her unfolding thus spread or distributed over two stages, she functions as a two-in-one. Rebekah-of-the-first-half ("Drink, my lord") enriches the plot by indirection and makes the real Rebekah shine by contrast. Far from gratuitous, still less detrimental, the false alarm proves salutary: this is often the case with the piecemeal and tortuous emergence of literary character, and Rebekah affords us the first example of the Bible's command of this art of (temporary or, elsewhere, permanent) ambiguity. We appreciate her true self all the more for not being allowed to take its virtues for granted.

This contrast-in-sequence is enhanced, moreover, by surprise as well as suspense and relief. Not Rebekah's behavior and character alone but even her motives prove contrary to our initial fears. If she responds by installments, it is only because she will not lump together man and beast. Only after she has "finished letting him drink" does she express her readiness to do the same for the camels. Just as she began by injecting into her speech the deferential "my lord," so does she end by showing more tact than could be foreseen or perhaps even required. What threatened failure reveals itself as another God-sent bonus and blessing. She has certainly earned the costly gifts presented to her on the spot.

That the servant must have shared much of our experience (apprehension, enlightenment, character inference) marks a shift in perspectival design and relations. What we have been tracing amounts to a twofold movement that is integral to the Bible's dynamics of point of view. One movement consists in a process of illumination within each of the limited perspectives—the reader's and the hero's—that brings them closer by degrees to the static pole of the omniscient. At this stage, though still not so privileged as God and the narrator themselves, each of the human observers has gained considerable insight into the disposition of things. Relatively, of course, the servant has made more progress since the outset, but that is in keeping with another feature of the strategy. If the first dynamics consists in a progressive narrowing of informational discrepancies vis-à-vis the omniscient, the second involves a convergence of the restricted viewpoints themselves. Having been launched from different starting points along the scale of knowledge, they are then propelled forward not only in the same direction but also at a pace variable enough to allow the one behind to overtake and keep more or less abreast of the one who got a head start.

The narrative began by conferring on the reader an informational advantage over master and servant, through oblique pointers to Rebekah.

Abraham then fades out, and the plot traces the envoy's route to knowledge and success. On arrival, his initiative commands personal admiration and doctrinal assent but, as formerly with the master, it is not at once rewarded with enlightenment. On the contrary, his ignorance relative to the reader deepens owing to the narrator's un-evenhanded treatment of Rebekah's entrance; and the resultant discrepancy leads to further variations in the response to her conduct, dooming the less informed observer to lowered understanding and heightened suspense. The test once under way, however, the two viewpoints begin to converge. Not only do we experience much of his alarm at the threat of failure, but he attains to much of our knowledge when all ends well.

Regarding ignorance and knowledge alike, to be sure, this new alignment is not yet perfect, nor, as a matter of principle, will it ever evolve into strict identity. Apart from all contingencies, it makes an essential difference that, though equally concerned to penetrate appearances and unravel mysteries by way of interpretation, the servant is not a "reader" in the sense that we are. Like all figural interpreters, he directly confronts a world that we receive through the mediation of an artful teller and text. He exercises interpretation on the world of objects; we, on a web of words that projects such a world. And whatever the similarity between these worlds, notably in divine control, each still retains its features and constraints vis-à-vis the interpreter: each, in my earlier formulation, remains a distinct semiotic system, with its own medium, communicator, addressee, and rules of decipherment.

Thus, the servant's knowledge is regulated by God, ours by the narrator, and the two omniscients operate with different means even to the same end. In the absence of explicit foretelling, as here, the reader's foreknowledge and expectations derive from probabilities beyond the agent's ken. The structural anticipations of Rebekah relate far more to the logic (arrangement, coherence, conventions) of the text than of the world; and even if noticed, would hardly carry the same weight for "real life" interpreters as for one facing a verbal artifice. Or consider even the latent parallels between Rebekah's and Abraham's hospitality. The rationale of the test implies that the servant may also have detected them, but only in general outline: since he observes events not words, he could not have been affected by the linguistic echoes of "haste" that clinch the analogy for us. In general—and the following chapters will come back to this key issue—the poetics of the narrative is reserved for the reader's viewpoint and interpretive operations.

Moreover, the dramatized interpreter and his interpreting are themselves part of the represented world and accordingly, like everything else, objects of the reader's interpretation. This builds into the pattern an ironic discrepancy in our favor. But the irony can be sharpened ad hoc, as with Samuel the anointer, through the manipulation of specific perspectival disparities; or it can be attenuated and even neutralized ad hoc, through the reduction of such variations to the point of denying the reader any sense of superiority—not at least beyond that inherent in the position of secretly watching and eavesdropping on a character who goes about his business unaware of being made a show of. Hence the significance of our tale's early alignment of the normative viewpoints and, along the informational axis, its movement from initial tensions to relative harmony. Both go a long way toward bridging the distance between the observers with their distinct posts and sources and procedures of observation. In line with this movement, the ensuing dialogue not only brings them closer but also, though holding far more disclosures and surprises for the servant than for the reader, makes a two-level discovery scene, where he recognizes a set of factors and we applaud his recognitions.

Far from being looked down on for his ignorance of the recipient's identity, the ambassador further endears himself to us by covering Rebekah with gold, because it is exactly his unawareness of the fact that clinches his awareness of the principle: the young woman has earned the gifts, since nothing counts like personal merit. The factual discrepancy itself then gets bridged in the dialogue scene. What is more, the girl's speech affords another chance for perspectival convergence in the observation of her exquisite manners, whose finer points would hardly be lost on an Oriental and a great man's steward at that. She answers the questions in the order but, with the same regard for decorum, not always in the terms in which they are posed. "Whose daughter art thou?" receives the straightforward answer, "I am the daughter of Bethuel," where the omission of her own name spares the questioner, at whatever cost to ego, a detail in which he expressed no interest. But to the inquiry about "room in thy father's house for us to spend the night" she diplomatically replies by stating the objective facilities for hospitality, without extending even to a munificent stranger the invitation that is not hers to extend.

No sooner has this model bride crowned her performance than the reader finds his sentiments and reasoning voiced by the servant, who takes none of the credit for himself but puts it all where it is ideologically due. He does the right thing on the right grounds. Since in a God-directed world there is no room for coincidence, the encounter with Abraham's grand-niece must be an act of providence. (He has started, we recall, with the believer's shibboleth, "Make things go well for me," or in literal paradox, "devise an accident for me.") This declaration of faith thus crowns the meeting of the reader's early anticipation, formed by appeal to the poetic coherence of the text, and the character's later recognition, anchored in the doctrine of the existential coherence of the world. And since the biblical text itself largely depends for its coherence on the assumption of divine control—the narrator playing providence only in God's name and to God's glory—the man's simple piety reinforces rather than just parallels our more complex interpretation.

New Tensions and Final Resolution

Among its other roles, the next phase seals this marriage of true minds:

> (28) The maiden ran and told her mother's household about these things. (29) Now Rebekah had a brother whose name was Laban; and Laban ran out to the man, to the spring. (30) And on seeing the ring and the bracelets on his sister's hands, and on hearing the words of Rebekah his sister, saying, Thus and so did the man speak to me, he went to the man; and behold, he was standing by the camels at the spring. (31) And he said, Come, O blessed of the Lord; why dost thou stand outside? I have prepared the house, and room for the camels. (32) And the man came into the house, and he ungirded the camels and gave straw and provender for the camels and water to wash his feet and the feet of the men who were with him. (33) Then food was set before him to eat, and he said, I will not eat until I have spoken my piece. And he said, Speak.

In terms of plot structure, this episode clearly performs a bridging function. The second movement of the action having been completed with the discovery of the bride, the logic of causality now requires the servant's arrival at the house to launch the movement that will end in the departure for Canaan with the family's blessing. And since protocol forbids the girl's inviting him herself, the narrator packs her off home to summon a higher authority, embodied in Laban. For a causal link between highlights, however, the episode certainly looks overtreated, unrolling at a leisurely pace and with circumstantial detail associated with the Homeric rather than the biblical style. It looks even more so from the reader's vantage point, since foreknowledge presses for a quick transition to the business at hand. Of course, the lingering heightens our expectancy. Yet judged by the economies of biblical narrative, suspense alone does not justify the extent of the retardation—as noted at the foregoing stage—still less the minutiae that compose it. This sense of excess indicates a search for tighter and less obvious coherence.

The whole passage gains intelligibility from its implications for character and perspective. These not only elaborate but also parallel the overt plot function in that they likewise work backward and forward at the same time, linking antecedents to consequents. Thus, the dispatch with which Rebekah

fulfills her plot assignment ("ran" not "went") rounds off her characterization by giving us an insight into her mind: it suggests more than ordinary
goodwill to the stranger and lessens the fear that she may refuse to follow
him. No sooner have we gathered that the obstacles if any will come from
the family, than Laban enters the picture: his immediate role in the plot
(as host) motivates his portrayal in anticipation of his ultimate role (as
guardian).

That portrayal itself looks back to the young woman's, just as it looks
ahead to the negotiation scene. Laban's "running" follows so hard upon
Rebekah's as to give him the benefit of all the favorable effects associated
with her haste throughout: the whole family, it seems, is a credit to
Abraham. No later than the next verse, however, this carry-over impression proves misleading. The initial similarity turns into contrast as the
narrator doubles back in time from the hospitable action ("he ran") to its
ulterior motive (the sight of "the ring and the bracelets"). And when the
action resumes ("he went"), we find the contrast settled through an inside
view in free indirect style ("and behold") where "the camels" prominently
figure, as indeed they are to do twice again in relation to Laban's solicitude.
Accordingly, even his pious address to the stranger as "blessed of the Lord"
sounds an ironic note, sharpened by unwitting allusion to God's promise
to "bless" Abraham by multiplying his descendants (22:17) and to Abraham's
being "blessed in everything" (24:1). Ignorant of antecedents and identities,
Laban twists this charged phrase into homage to material blessing.

This sequential shift in portrayal[7] repeats the technique through which
Rebekah's figure and mind have been unfolded, and insinuates anew the
theme of the abortive test. But its point lies in reversing the earlier movement (verses 18–19) from unfavorable to favorable impression. While
Laban's initial correspondence to Rebekah somewhat dims her virtues by
suggesting a family portrait, the sudden about-face highlights her singularity
more than ever before: she shines in contrast to what her analogue actually
is as well as to what she herself might have been. And while the initial
correspondence bodes good for the servant's endeavors in the coming
negotiations, its breakdown-and-reversal intensifies suspense by disclos-
ing the kind of people he has to deal with. The indirect revelation of
character through details in excess of plot exigencies thus affects our understanding and expectations of the plot itself.

This new disturbing element, however, consolidates the recent perspectival alliance between reader and ambassador. To start with, our relations
with him and with Laban have developed in opposed directions. Laban
has our approval as long as he seems to rush out on instinct, but he forfeits
it as soon as it transpires that his bustle was prompted by knowledge of
the traveler's wealth. The disclosure of informational parity here not only

fails to ensure but actively unsettles his normative alignment with the reader: this makes a telling opposition to the process whereby our moral bond with the servant has counteracted (and foretold the decrease in) informational imparity. Principle always outranks fact, whether considered as dimensions of the Bible's epistemology or its structure of point of view. And in providing a negative illustration of this scale, Laban serves to draw us yet closer to the servant as well as to Rebekah.

Again, not that the two viewpoints perfectly coincide. The insight afforded us into Laban's mind is, as privileged *and* compositional disclosure, beyond the servant's reach; just as the opacity of the servant's own mind puts his current thoughts beyond ours. We are still due for some of those surprises that keep biblical man somewhat less—or, aesthetically, more— than a known quantity even on the closest acquaintance. Yet the emergence of a new, threatening viewpoint reinforces our sense of familiarity and solidarity with the old. While the family is still in the dark, moreover, we are privy to the servant's predicament and intentions, share his hopes and to a lesser extent his fears, and, judging from his past performance with its combination of ingenuity and faith, can even hazard an informed guess as to his general tactics. In retrospect, of course, even the remaining gaps and discrepancies vanish. But hindsight is an aid to rather than a condition of our involvement, inference, irony at the expense of the unknowing. Of all listeners, we alone are in a position to appreciate his maneuvers and motives throughout an address where he rarely speaks straight:

> (34) And he said, I am Abraham's servant. (35) The Lord has abundantly blessed my master and he has become great; he has given him sheep and cattle, silver and gold, manservants and maidservants, camels and asses. (36) And Sarah my master's wife bore a son to my master after reaching old age, and he has given him everything he has. [For expository convenience, I divided the speech into its tactical blocks; but it may be well to read it as a whole first.]

The materialistic exordium shows that the speaker had no need of our privileges to take Laban's measure. The harping on wealth and status begins as early as the formal self-identification, "I am Abraham's servant." For by identifying himself in these self-effacing terms, as though he did not have so much as a name of his own, he at once transfers to his master all the benefits of the impressive entrance: the costly gifts, the ten loaded camels, and "the men who were with him" (their mention reserved for the arrival at the house to suggest the family's viewpoint). It is not he who is "blessed of the Lord," the servant indeed goes on to emphasize in pointed and corrective allusion to Laban's form of address, but Abraham: "The Lord has abundantly blessed my master." So much so, that all they have observed amounts only to a fraction of this blessing. "Sheep and cattle, silver and gold, manservants and maidservants, camels and asses": the items in full view ("gold," "manservants," "camels") are so interspersed as to command belief in their unseen mates; and, against the background of the narrator's shorthand (e.g., 13:2), the range of the catalogue signals the dramatized speaker's reluctance to leave much to his audience's imagination. The opening verse thus marks a steady progression in the inducement of the thought, "If such are his servants, how great must the master be!"

Immediately thereafter, however, the speaker passes to another branch of family news, or so his unforewarned auditors may think. From our vantage point, we easily trace the connection: the next step in the softening-up process is to introduce the prospective bridegroom, display his eligibility, and transfer to him in turn the aura of material blessing. All this gets accomplished without giving the show away. Isaac, the hidden subject of the discourse, comes in only as grammatical object—first of Sarah's "bearing" and then of Abraham's "giving." He even remains nameless, his presence thus subordinated (indeed like Rebekah's on her first appearance amid Nahor's descendants) to the heading of good news about familiar relatives. The audience will be caught all the more effectively if led to believe that they are forming their own conclusions. Hence the sandwiching of the "son" between two otherwise overspecific references to his parents: born by "Sarah the wife of my master" (a reminder of her legal status) to "my master" (harking back to the wealth and establishing legitimacy). Hence also "when she was old," an indication of time ostensibly meant to provoke cheers for the mother but in fact calculated to recommend the son. If she was old at the time, then he is still young now; and if she bore him by a miracle, then he must be blessed and is certainly the only heir. (No mention of Ishmael, naturally.) Indeed, the bland tempter proceeds, his father has already "given him everything he has." This anticipates matters a bit, since Abraham makes over his property to Isaac (in these very words) only before his death (25:5). But since the present company cannot know, the intention may pass for the deed.

The man's art lies not so much in the slight stretching of the facts as in their thorough insinuation. And to mask his drift, the persuader varies his technique from the first step to the second. Abraham's riches can be safely painted in the most glowing colors, under the cover story of "You will be happy to learn that . . ." But when it comes to his deficiency of children, that pretext would hardly serve. Therefore the speaker so wraps up the topic as to invite the deduction that the parent's misfortune is the son's good fortune: to let the thought "What a catch!" steal into the audience's mind before they find him actually offered to them on a hard condition.

(37) And my master made me swear, saying, Thou shalt not take a wife for my son from among the daughters of the Canaanites in whose land I dwell. (38) But to my father's house shalt thou go and to my kindred, and take a wife for my son. (39) And I said to my master, Perhaps the woman will not follow me. (40) And he said to me, The Lord, before whom I walk, will send his angel with thee and prosper thy journey, and thou shalt take a wife for my son from my kindred and from my father's house. (41) Then shalt thou be clear of my oath, when thou comest to my kindred; and if they will not give thee, thou shalt be clear of my oath.

To the unsuspecting materialist, it would indeed prove a catch with a catch. Since Abraham's condition is too operational to be much watered down, the rhetoric addresses itself to pressing for its acceptance. And having already made the most of the worldly blandishments, it now shifts its focus to the familial. What appeared so far the object of a report becomes the frame of reference for an appeal, from one branch of the family to another and with a view to maintaining their kinship. To maximize the force of that appeal, its original terms (verses 3-8) are deftly remolded in quotation, by assorted means but to a single end. The most decisive (and frequent) variation consists in replacing Abraham's "to my native land [*el artsi ve'el moladeti*] shalt thou go" by "to my father's house and to my kindred," with the result that the ethno-geographical opposition between Canaanite and non-Canaanite transforms into the sentimental opposition between non-family and family. Rebekah's guardians would obviously find it much harder to reject a proposal of marriage addressed to them as kinsmen than as Mesopotamians, let alone non-Canaanites. Recast into such positive terms, moreover, the geography takes on a flattering aspect; and to allay its terrors even further, the (mis)quoter personalizes each of Abraham's spatial references to "there" into "my kindred," so as to substitute a tie of blood for a sense of distance.

This crucial variation launches the attack that others either cover or carry forward. Of the preventive measures, the most salient is of course the omission of all reference to the possibility originally raised by the servant ("Shall I then lead thy son back to the land from which thou camest?") and ruled out by his master. While even a negative mention might put ideas into the family's head, silence dismisses them as unthinkable—hence also the elision of Abraham's own exodus *from* Mesopotamia, in a speech that otherwise leans so heavily on past associations as to play down all unfamiliar factors, including the bridegroom himself. Note how "a wife for my son, for Isaac" contracts into "a wife for my son," so as to minimize the threat of the unknown.

Other variations, however, pile on the pressure. It is with this offensive intent that the contingency originally envisaged as "Perhaps the woman may not be willing to follow me" now reappears as "Perhaps the woman will not follow me." The shift from subjective cause ("not willing") to objective result ("not follow") presumably reflects the servant's confidence in the young woman and certainly covers a wider range of obstacles, with family veto at their head. And then we find the shift completed and the implication voiced in Abraham's reply. In retelling, it not only fails to glance at any reluctance on the girl's part but throws the responsibility square on her guardians. "If they will not give thee," in disregard for family claims and heavenly guidance, then "thou shalt be clear of my oath."

With this spot of moral blackmail, so final-sounding in form and message alike, the whole audience (this time, the reader included) might expect the address to close. In fact, however, it brings one line of persuasion to a climax only to usher in another:

> (42) And I came today to the spring and said, O Lord, the God of my master Abraham, if thou wilt prosper the journey on which I go, (43) behold, I am standing by the spring of water; the maiden to whom I shall say, Pray give me to drink a little water from thy pitcher, (44) and who will say to me, Drink thou and for thy camels I will draw too— may she be the woman whom God has appointed for my master's son. (45) Before I had finished speaking in my heart, and behold, Rebekah came out with her pitcher upon her shoulder, and she went down to the spring and drew. And I said to her, Pray give me to drink. (46) And she made haste and lowered her pitcher from her shoulder, and said, Drink, and thy camels I shall water too. I drank, and the camels she watered too. (47) And I asked her and said, Whose daughter art thou? And she said, The daughter of Bethuel, the son of Nahor, whom Milcah bore to him. And I put a ring on her nose and the bracelets on her hands. (48) And I bowed my head and worshipped the Lord and blessed the Lord, who has led me by the true way to take my master's brother's daughter for his son.

The speaker has yet another weapon, skillfully reserved for the last. Again, bringing it to bear marks not so much a shift of ground as of focus and emphasis. The opening itself, we recall, introduced three themes—or, in terms of rhetoric, pressure points—with family bond and divine blessing subordinated to the dominant note of material fortune. The second stage then took up and elaborated the argument from kinship, while still keeping God's involvement in active reserve through Abraham's mention of "the angel" appointed to oversee the mission. Now this reserve force takes over, its pressure judged (correctly, it transpires) best qualified to clinch the issue. Success depends on bringing home the impression that God has been in control all along, perceptibly so ever since Abraham took the initiative.

As the reader knows, this happens to be the literal truth. But truth, alas, does not always have the ring of truth. Just as Abraham's original instructions would not sound flattering enough to the audience, so might the original encounter with the young woman seem too coincidental to establish divine stage-managing. If completely unforeseen, the coincidence that the true believer would read as all the more providential is liable to strike the outsider, let alone an interested party, as the operation of chance. Therefore the servant, like many novelists after him, resorts to invention in order to give the truth a more truthlike appearance. Having just edited Abraham's orders in the interests of moral and sentimental pressure, he now turns the revised version to ideological account: God has realized Abraham's wishes in leading his envoy to the family. The surprise of the encounter is diminished, so that its persuasiveness may increase.

Hence this stage also forms yet another landmark in the development of perspectival relations. The reader's alliance with the servant against the family has so far operated along the informational axis of point of view. Equally in the know about all that has passed since the first scene in Canaan, we have been equally alive (and well-disposed) to the liberties he takes with the facts in repeating them to the ignorant decision-makers: the omission of Ishmael, the premature transfer of property, the delayed disclosure of the reason for the embassy, or the variance between the ambassador's statement and the patriarch's commission. Our initial opposition in viewpoint to the servant has modulated all the way into an alignment against a new opposition exposed to dramatic coaxing and irony. At the back of our minds, to be sure, there has lurked from the start the memory that this new party no more shares the allies' faith than their knowledge. But the ideological division gains point so gradually that one hardly notices its relevance as such. In sequence, the family first appears as an obstacle to patriarchal destiny, but not necessarily for theological reasons; then Laban shows his true colors, but his character still lends itself to ethical as distinct from doctrinal judgment; then the servant shortens Abraham's reference to "the Lord, the God of heaven" into "the Lord" *tout court,* as if to broaden the common ground with idolaters, but how much pressure will this change of terms bear? Only with the overall shift of emphasis at the present stage does this divergence come into the open—though for our eyes only—and the opposition perceptibly extends to the ideological axis of perspective as well. Privilege and true belief now go together, as do their opposites, and the drawing of the line all along the perspectival front explains the servant's last wave of attack. He can manipulate the family because they are his informational inferiors; and he must manipulate them because they are his ideological inferiors. According to their lights, the unvarnished truth would not carry enough weight to induce them to part with Rebekah. It therefore needs refashioning *ad hominem* into a narrative so smooth and well-made as to bespeak divine composition in their own terms. The semiotics of the plot has to be made intelligible to a meaner intelligence.

This secret motive inferred, the new variations in retelling fall into rhetorical pattern. Given the revised instructions, the first problem is to justify the entire well episode. If directed to the family, why didn't the envoy go straight to the family? To forestall this query, he leaves out the sentence "and the daughters of the men of the city came out to draw water" from the quotation of his prayer to God on arrival. With the original range of choice excised, what remains by implication is an appeal for divine guidance in choosing the right kinswoman. It would do him little good to turn to the family without knowing for whose hand to ask; and who except God could do the pinpointing?

Indeed, he proceeds, he had scarcely finished speaking before Rebekah appeared: here he follows events closely enough, but not without recomposition. In divergence from his own viewpoint at the time, he refers to the (then anonymous) girl as "Rebekah," to give an impression of old familiarity with her name and strengthen the sense of her predestination ("It is this Rebekah, here, whom God has appointed!"). For the same reason, he avoids all mention of the temporary doubt and suspense produced by her failure to volunteer service for the camels: despite the triumphant resolution, nothing must complicate the symmetry between his forecast and her performance. If the believer's heavenly plus may look a minus to others, then even scoring is indicated. Nor does the speaker say a word about her good looks, and even her exertions on his behalf assume the telegraphic form "the camels she watered too." This apparent ingratitude no doubt suggests the common bargaining technique of doing less than justice to coveted goods. But it also has a strategic significance, as part of the general depreciation of human in favor of divine agency. The less specified the girl's actions, the more impressive the correspondence between plan and fulfillment; and the less transparent the girl's virtues to the eyes of the beholder, the more visible God's hand.

The well scene loses its original balance, in short, to become less of a character test and more of a manifestation of divine choice. In the interests of the same rhetorical strategy, after all, the servant in his reportorial role cheerfully plays down his own ingenuity in devising the test and his confidence in its results. Reversing the original order, he now puts the inquiry "Whose daughter art thou?" *before* the bestowal of the gifts, as though he would not commit himself as long as there remained the slightest doubt about the alignment of human wishes with divine disposition. And in the ensuing report of his thanksgiving, he appropriately describes the happy coincidence in terms of God's having led him not "to the house of my master's brothers" but "to take my master's brother's daughter for his son."

> (49) Now therefore, if you will deal kindly and truly with my master, tell me; and if not, tell me and I will turn to the right or to the left. (50) And Laban and Bethuel answered and said, The thing issues from the Lord; we cannot speak to thee bad or good. (51) Behold, Rebekah is before thee. Take her and go, and let her be the wife of thy master's son, as the Lord has spoken. (52) When the servant heard their words, he bowed himself to the ground before the Lord.

The course of events becomes so self-explanatory in remodeling that the artificer will not spoil the effect by pointing the moral. Instead, he gathers the human and the divine threads of persuasion into "Now therefore, if you will deal kindly and truly with my master, tell me." Compared with the neutral "If you consent," to which it operationally amounts, the phrasing is so loaded and slanted as to deter noncompliance. On the one hand, the allusion to the recent divine guidance "by the true way" insinuates the meaning "If you will do as God has done" or even the more threatening rhetorical question "Will you go against God?" On the other hand, just as a Fielding's address to "the sagacious reader" punishes dissent with the stigma of witlessness, so is the servant's wording calculated to brand refusal as an offense against morality. Still—and now comes the final pressure— if they do refuse, "I will turn to the right or to the left": I will take my suit elsewhere, to relatives more mindful of God and humanity, kinship and wealth.

Small wonder, then, that Laban and Bethuel declare in response that "the thing issues from the Lord; we cannot speak to thee bad or good." Where God has "spoken" through the design of events, there remains little room for human speech. Nor is it surprising that, though the material and familial considerations must have had some effect, the narrator makes the kinsmen single out the act of providence. Their world picture falls short of the monotheism common to all the Hebrew observers; their morality leaves something to be desired; their knowledge, thanks to the servant's inventiveness, is certainly deficient; and the consent wrung from them, as their subsequent dilatoriness shows, not quite wholehearted even after the event. These manifold discrepancies in viewpoint, whose reconstruction forms much of the business and pleasure of reading, retain their distancing and characterizing force. Yet their imperfect vision also enters into the final movement toward convergence and harmony. Like all the other limited participants—the reader included—the Mesopotamians undergo a process of discovery that brings home to them God's management of the world.

·5·

THE PLAY OF PERSPECTIVES

The Lord knows, and Israel shall know.
Joshua 22:22

The foregoing analysis has sufficiently brought out the constants in the Bible's fourfold structure of point of view. We can now take a closer look at the areas left free for manipulation—relatively free, that is. As well as accommodating a great many local interests and adjustments, the variations are themselves systematic—hence distinctive—in that they proceed from *built-in* discrepancies between the similar and alignments between the opposed. How this enriches the play of perspectives, conferring on it a value beyond the bare necessities of doctrine, may be gathered from the following relations of variety in unity and unity in variety.

Narrator vs. God

It is a nice question whether God's status is more problematic in biblical discourse or in the biblical world. In the narrative, after all, he figures as both inspiring originator and individual viewpoint, as object and subject of representation, as maker of plot and agent, as means and end, as part and reason for the whole. In arranging his relations with God, therefore, the narrator operates under peculiar constraints. To remove the film of familiarity from his predicament, imagine a loyal general driven to employ in the vanguard of his army the king for whom he fights. How to play the master while remaining a subject? How to expose the embodiment of one's cause to the dangers of battle without losing the war? How to exercise military command without encroaching on political strategy? How to perform the tasks to which one's sovereign will not stoop?

If anything, the man of words' lot is even harder than the man of action's. Under the exigencies of his plot, he must, while himself remaining a disembodied voice, personalize an impersonal force, involve divinity in every earthly conflict, expose God's mind as well as his ways to public view. By his terms of reference, moreover, the biblical narrator's modus operandi

153

is limited by the nature of his assignment: he sets out not to destroy an enemy but to redeem and establish control over his own people and, what is more, to manipulate them into the reverential obedience that his lord exacts as his due. By the rules of his art, finally, he will not express his own loyalty except in his dispositions and through the speech of others; nor will he commit those so totally to the business of indoctrination as to exclude his interests as storyteller and historian.

Philosophically unresolvable, the tensions thus generated between the dominant perspectives are not only alleviated or minimized but turned to account in communicative terms. Since point of view forms a system of relations, similarities and dissimilarities assume a contextual bearing: the qualitative opposition in privilege between humans and superhumans dwarfs any variance within either domain. As revealed by our analysis of omniscience versus omnipotence, moreover, the narrator claims or disclaims such privilege with an eye to God's glory. Still, while neutralizing the most dangerous tensions, he will retain or even invent others to serve a wide range of goals.

On the positive side, variety in unity assumes the form of distinctive variations that yet stop short of conflict: the narrator moves beyond or parallel to God's viewpoint without challenging its authority. In the biblical context, what would count as a challenge is the narrator's exercise of powers of knowledge and plotting superior to God's; which, of course, he guards against doing, as a matter of epistemological and ontological principle. But these charged features do not nearly exhaust the axes or dimensions that compose point of view. And the others, precisely because either quantitative or nonideological, license such variations as the narrator requires. The licenses fall into three categories, which mark an ascending order of perspectival distinction: aesthetic interest, rhetorical complication, and expressive opposition.

The first concerns the whole aesthetic dimension of the narrative, that is, whatever might separate it from "pure" historico-theological discourse that straightforwardly presents the divine outlook and lays down the law—an alternative that even Chronicles does not quite instantiate. The aesthetic dimension therefore includes whatever goes beyond or against this degree-zero of writing: from regulating principles (like indirection and the call for inferential activity), through major strategies (like gapping, repetition, external portrayal, dialogue chains, the form of point of view itself), to such occasional devices as the modulation into poetry, parable, or epigram. In the finished product, of course, all these give body and point to the doctrinal argument. But they nevertheless express in concert the narrator's aesthetic perspective, with its distinctive choices or interests, just as the embodied and pointed doctrine establishes his ideological perspective. The more so in that the features of the narrative are irreducible to any simple (aesthetic) means to (doctrinal) end combination. No reductionist formula can explain, for instance, the Bible's manifold departure from the conventions of antiquity, whether by way of renovation or innovation. Nor would it be able to account for the narrator's roundabout methods, sure to baffle the naive reader and hinder even the more sophisticated where a running commentary, say, could make the sense transparent to all. Unfortunately, the history of biblical study has been one long quest for some such formula and a sad demonstration of the trouble if not absurdity in which it is bound to land the seekers: allegorizing, atomizing, decontextualizing, sweeping under the carpet, plain distortion, or the treatment of incongruity as a symptom of genetic interference rather than of engagement and pleasure in the game of art, whose name is difficult coherence. Insofar as the Bible has a poetics as well as a genesis of composition, it establishes a set of norms by which we not only interpret the action but also evaluate the actors by reference to the narrator's perspective as artist.

Where the agents and speakers themselves have artistic pursuits, any discontinuity between their own view of art and the authoritative narrator's carries serious normative implications that may do duty for moral strictures. Artistic norms thus operate as a general measure of a character's reliability throughout James's exposure of the dilettantish Gilbert Osmond in *Portrait of a Lady,* Joyce's citation of Stephen Dedalus's theories in *Portrait of the Artist,* or the debunking of cliché-mongers in a tradition that stretches from Petronius to yesterday's parody. The world of the Bible is hardly so literate. But since its inhabitants employ words or even persuasive tools, they are no less subject to implicit judgment in their role as speakers with certain modes of expression than as agents resorting to certain modes of action. The narrator's laconic style casts an unflattering light on the prolixity of some figures, like Abigail in Samuel; his proper language, on the improprieties and vulgarisms of many; his self-conscious proceeding— and here we move from the humorous to the ironic proper—on the blind spots of all. As the objective standard, in short, his discourse throws into relief the subjectivities of theirs.

Nor does God himself, the Bible's most voluminous speaker, share the narrator's aesthetic norms and practices (with the important exception, to be discussed, of "authorial" management and coherence). But this exclusion renders him neither their victim nor their antagonist. Whatever its surface resemblance to the human order, his discourse does not in principle betray (if anything, it exposes) the same blind spots in knowledge and response; and therefore he escapes the sharper ironies directed against all other subjects. Far from the butt of such irony, he is its beneficiary, ultimately its engineer. Whether the narrator shows up an artless cliché like "seer" or an artful piece of rhetoric like that contrived by Rebekah to impel Jacob to deceive his father, the boomeranging of human speech—the seer proving sightless, the deceiver having to flee for his life into the clutches of an archdeceiver—redounds *ad maiorem dei gloriam.* The superhuman perspectives thus remain united in variety.

As indicated in my first chapter, moreover, the poetic features need not be strictly subordinated to such ends. Rather, it is for their own sake that they are often pursued and everywhere developed beyond the bare necessities. One can hardly think of a biblical narrative that might not be profitably reduced—or lends itself to adequate explanation as it stands—by reference to a narrator with a purely doctrinal interest or viewpoint. But then it would not suffice to cut out some parts (e.g., dialogues, comedies of error, embarrassing complexities of character and judgment) and insert others (commentaries, exhortations, divine appearances throughout). The whole would need to be rewritten to purge the text of its impurities, since too many features still conspire to draw attention to themselves or distract it from "business" to "pleasure": puns, verses, repetitions, ambiguities, surprises, formal equivalences, shifting terms of reference, hidden and unreliable voices, to name but a few regulars. All these become intelligible only if we allow the text to live by its own rules, according to which every pattern fulfills various functions and promotes various interests—historical, ideological, aesthetic—in rich interplay but flexible hierarchy.

Most significant, even where or so far as the ideological and the aesthetic functions (or viewpoints) part company, the Bible recognizes no conflict between them, such that whatever is not all for the heavenly cause must be against it. The presuppoal of this conflict has been the sorriest fallacy and legacy of the "didactic" approach to the Bible, extending with surprisingly few variations and even less opposition from the ancients to the modern scene. Its exponents have never stopped to consider the operational meaning of the term—the dictatorship of dogmatic instruction—or its applicability to biblical practice. Worse, they have imported the very notion of the inevitable quarrel between ethics and aesthetics from doctrines—pietistic or patristic, Platonic or Puritan—wholly alien to the spirit of the Bible. The truth is that the quarrel simply fails to arise, because, except for a veto on graven images, God does not appear as a critic of art. If anything, his management of the world displays a gift for order, timing, irony, repartee, suspense, peripety, neat closure, dramatic effect, sometimes even a grim sense of fun, all incorporated in the narrative under the most respectable warrant. Not only does God have the instincts of a maker. His very articles of faith easily, almost necessarily translate into aesthetic correlates: the doctrine of free will into complex characterization, the equally revolutionary concept of omniscience into dramas of perspective, human restrictedness into studies in ambiguity, omnipotence and providence into well-made plots, control of history into cyclical and analogical design imposed on recalcitrant matter, the demand to infer from past to present into ordeal by interpretation. Beyond this, his viewpoint is neutral in this regard: unlike Homer's or Hesiod's Muses, who embody the universal power of poetry, God remains sublimely indifferent to art as a human product. And just as his operations and requirements positively motivate the aesthetics of the ideological structure itself, so does his indifference confer at least tacit legitimacy on the narrator's enthusiasm for his craft.

As we pass from aesthetics proper to rhetoric, however, this variation of interest threatens to sharpen into disharmony. God has but a limited use for the rhetoric of discourse, since he exerts his influence less through words than deeds or through words as substitutes for or preliminaries to deeds: performatives, forecasts, commands, admonitions. (Having pronounced his intention, for example, he remains silent throughout the Wooing of Rebekah.) Whereas the narrator can operate with words alone and chooses to wield them as a net rather than as a stick: he persuades where God would and does prescribe. Even the symmetrical contexts of the omnipotence effect, with God at his most publicity-minded, bring out these differences. However alike their ultimate ends, therefore, the lawgiver and the persuader mark two distinct viewpoints on the world as object of communication. One is creative, the other re-creative; one often straightforward enough, the other oblique; one formally oriented to past (and at times extinct) dramatis personae, the other to present and future readers.

This disparity shows more clearly in the handling of causes than of persons. Regarding persons, the didacticist myth often goes with the claim that the Bible's character-drawing is flat or one-dimensional to suit with its rigid world view and teaching or its primitive conventions. Actually, the fact that God chiefly concerns himself with man as a moral being does not at all rule out the narrator's psychological interests and human sympathies. On the contrary, the historic birth of man as a free agent entails a problematic approach to character, marks off the doers from each of their deeds and doing from motive, with remarkable complications of response. For this accommodates a range of mixed feeling or viewing: hope for the wrongdoer, from Adam to David in disgrace, pity for the lost and rejected, like Esau or Saul, dissociation from the outwardly well-conducted, like Laban in hospitality, even irony at the expense of God's own ministers and mouthpieces. Polar portraiture thus becomes the exception rather than the rule, finding no welcome even along a single axis of the biblical point of view. Black-and-white rendering is as ill-suited to doctrine and world picture (in terms of the conception of humanity) as it is aesthetically displeasing (because schematic) and rhetorically unwise (because failing to provide sufficient outlet for emotion).

When it comes to causes, however, God is generally so adamant and his judgments so harsh as to make persuasion on orthodox lines next to impossible. It is one thing to adhere to the divine perspective and strategy in demonstrations of vigor, and quite another in demonstrations of rigor, like Moses' punishment or Saul's rejection. Here the very aim to justify God's ways to man calls for some variation from orthodoxy, far-reaching enough to do the rhetorical trick and yet hidden enough to pass doctrinal muster. In the face of these opposed pressures, as I shall argue throughout the last chapter, the persuader coordinates the divine with human grounds for evaluation to facilitate assent and broaden consensus. Saul must go because he is a liar and coward as well as a violator of God's ordinance; David deserves to keep his throne, after all, because he is an admirable as well as a pious king. As with the exploration of character, such avoidance of dogmatism complicates rather than undercuts God's view, which formally retains its supremacy and, though twinned below the surface with a more intelligible and hence more appealing logic, its cogency. The narrator departs from God's perspective to ensure its alignment with ours; to persuade us of God's justice, he brings to bear arguments and methods that God himself would disdain (and his hard-line prophets might even disapprove).

Along the linguistic dimension of point of view, finally, the variety passes even beyond complication to opposition; and this opposition is subsumed by the larger one that marks off the agents' discourse from the narrator's. Just like the human dialogists and monologists, the divine speaker resorts to an array of expressive modes conspicuously absent from the frame: rhetorical questions, figurative language, imperatives and other forms of command, vocatives, references to the first and second person, oaths, emotionalisms, verbal irony.

In general, this opposition yields a double gain: expressive mimesis of an order unprecedented and long thereafter unrivaled in literary history, and reinforcement of the narrator's impersonality by way of contrast.[1] The richer the figures' speech-palette, the more does his restraint assume the authority of the spirit of narrative. In regard to God, however, the balance sheet gets entangled by ideological credits and debits following from his incorporation into the plot. The image of an active, involved, omnipresent God, neither Flaubert's invisible nor Joyce's fingernail parer, risks the proverbial effects of familiarity. Therefore we find some counter-measures taken even along this least sensitive of perspectival dimensions. Within the primary opposition that brackets the whole dramatis personae, the Bible draws a secondary line between the two levels of the world, so that, though the narrator still discourses with divine accents, God does not altogether speak in a human voice. Thus, he is spared the vulgarisms that pepper human speech; and correspondingly, on solemn occasions, he rises to the stately language reserved for prophecy. As befits an omniscient, his questions are all rhetorical rather than (as Cain belatedly discovers) information-seeking. And in line with his omnipotent status, he has a monopoly on creative and other performative utterance. In a sense, such unique functions as relate to God's attributes and viewpoint are none the less impressive for being performed through the commonest speech patterns of the biblical world.

Narrator and Reader vs. God and Characters: Spheres of Communication

The perspectival variety-in-unity just outlined brings to the fore the whole issue of what I called modes of existence. This is, after all, where the trio of distinctions (in aesthetics, judgment, expressiveness) meet. God operates within and the narrator without the represented world; so do their respective addressees, the characters and the reader. As record of fact, to be sure, the Bible maintains a spatiotemporal (as well as a thematic) continuity between the textual and the extratextual world denied to fictional writing. The heroes are the ancestors of the teller and his reader, God their God, the stories their history, and the stage their land. The teller even alludes to those ancestors as his sources, and God to the reader in his calls for handing down the tradition from father to son. For all their manifest and secret bonds, however, the two pairs have no direct dealings with each other across the existential dividing line. The narrator would not dream of apostrophizing the characters, in the manner of the *Iliad* or Sumerian epic or for that matter Nehemiah (e.g., 13:31); nor do they, again including God himself, show the least awareness of his existence. Each remains in his own sphere of influence and communication, facing his proper partner.

What this seeming formality means is that the "insiders" deal only with the world round them and the "outsiders" with that simulacrum of the world that we call biblical narrative. And however close the correspondence between the real thing and the image, they are kept apart by the mediation of the image-maker: the narrator interposes a network of representational premises, conventions, strategies that shape the represented world into meaningful discourse about the world. Insofar as they engage in expression as well as in action, of course, the characters themselves do much the same in every speech or thought. What do these exhibit if not representations—attempts to make sense of the world from a certain viewpoint or impress that sense on others according to cultural schemata, the arts of address included, and personal forms of desire? Even so, owing to the basic disparities in perspective, the different sets of representational transactions widely vary both in convention and in intention.

The sharp line separating the privileged from the nonprivileged—not to mention the variability within the latter group itself—makes for the clearest divergence in representation and interpretive cogency, amounting to an antithesis between the objective and the subjective views of the world. The seer proves blind to the signs of election; Cain misrepresents his deed, Sarah her thoughts, from false optimism; even comparatively informed observers like the reader and the servant in the Wooing tale must guess their way through mysteries (of circumstance, character, fate) transparent to the narrator and God. Yet we find this distinction cut across by several others that relate each member of the privileged pair to the fallible humans with whom he cohabits and communicates. Of these, the contrast between the restrained narrator (with his face to the nonspeaking reader) and the highly expressive agents, from God down to Balaam's ass, draws the most palpable line in terms of the verbal resources available for discourse. Given two viewpoints on the same event—say, the objective and the subjective account of Pharaoh's dream—the narrator's representation will accordingly carry more weight but, often, less color. Only God's utterance gains such color without loss of authority; which enables him to communicate naturally from a supernatural position. So naturally, indeed, that some of his addressees mistake the common forms of discourse for common norms of discourse, like those who deduce ignorance from God's recourse to questions; others, like Samson's parents, do not at all recognize the voice of divinity when they hear it, and therefore distrust its message.

Even more far-reaching is the concomitant difference in evaluation and persuasion. Not that the agents' normative outlook is necessarily incongruous or skewed: that is the case with Samuel's admiration for Eliab's looks, but hardly with God's partiality for the omnipotence effect or even the servant's rhetoric in the family circle. Rather, their status between reliability and unreliability is conditional on the narrator's implicit norms: even God's attitude, as I indicated, remains subject to contextual qualification from a wider or more sensitive perspective. They all form part of the narrator's discourse and it is through as well as about them that he speaks to us, often in a voice artfully distorted in transmission by flaws in the channel. To reconstruct his (hidden) vision, we must therefore scrutinize theirs—juxtaposing, discriminating, integrating, complicating, checking for deviances and correcting them where necessary to produce the authorized standpoint.

This relation of part to whole, inset to frame, holds equally true for dimensions of viewpoint other than evaluative. Due to the figures' mode of existence, the correspondence in world-imaging between them and the outsiders must not be pressed too far. For the characters look out on their world from within that world, and therefore their very outlook forms stuff for the narrator's registration and our exploration. To the pair of outsiders, the figural subjects are themselves objects, their subjectivity often no less central and problematic than the field of reality on which it operates. What does God see in Abraham that he elects him? Where does Samuel go wrong in the anointment scenes? Why does Laban rush out to the wayfarer? To maintain contact with the narrator, the reader has to review the agents' viewpoints, interpret their interpretations, make sense of their sense-making, judge their judgments, along with and in the light of the facts that serve as the common object of representation.

Nor do those facts (Abraham's character, David's beauty, the servant's munificence) come into view under the same conditions or fall under the same conventions. For each superhuman manipulates the perspective of the human interpreter by means appropriate to his own arena and repertoire. Common to the two sets of means are shifts in communicativeness: between guidance and bafflement, direction and indirection and misdirection. Both God and the narrator may proclaim or conceal their standpoint, in various degrees, according to their plans for their respective addressees. In concealment, moreover, they not only manifest similar designs—from thwarting to testing the interpreter by leaving him to his own devices—but expect the interpretation to proceed by certain rules and assumptions.

The most distinctive is the premise of coherence, which we have seen at work throughout the sections on omnipotent display and the Wooing of Rebekah. Coherence depends on the presumption of control; and biblical history marches under double control, artistic and divine. Uniquely, such doubling means parallel (not just reinforced) coherence within two different frameworks, which in principle leaves no room for chance in either. From Homer to Robbe-Grillet, the universal assumption that literary *discourse* coheres often goes with a *world* (mis)governed by fortune or caprice or accident or plain human muddle: the very theme may lie in the opposition between the discipline of art and the existential chaos that it brings out. Given the Bible's divine controller, however, equivalence takes the place of opposition. That Abraham should receive family news from Mesopotamia just after God's promise to multiply his offspring becomes no more coincidental than that the two announcements should be juxtaposed by the narrator. And if the narrator conceals his hand, as he can well afford to do, then God flaunts his own to school his creatures, by precept and precedent, in the ways of interpretation. Hence the emissary (and, suitably nudged, the bride people) views the encounter at the well as an expression of divine will. And so would all qualified observers, pointedly excluding unbelievers like the afflicted Philistines or waverers like Gideon. Thus constituting a sign-system regulated by intrinsic principles of coherence, the biblical world itself functions as a text or medium of discourse: history *makes* sense, effects presuppose supernatural causes, the plot bristles with meaning for natives as well as outsiders, even in the absence of speech and direct revelation. From all four viewpoints involved, communication goes beyond language to become an exercise in semiotics, complete with aids to intelligibility (foretelling, juxtaposition, serialization, the lessons of the past) and rewards and penalties for decoders.

On this divine text, however, and in its best interests, the narrator superimposes his own, designed for the reader's eyes only. And here the correspondence so far traced in the means and ends of shaping viewpoints gives place to divergence between the two pairs. I am not referring to local variations alone (such as the fact that while the rhetoric of omnipotence shows a deep community of interest, elsewhere the narrator may strive for effects that God disregards, reveal what God conceals, persuade where God commands). Owing to the different spheres of existence, even the same object may (in principle, must) elicit different interpretations from the dramatized and the implied subject. However comparable their access and doctrine, each brings to bear on the world the rules governing his own framework of communication. The characters can reasonably make sense of their text only by appeal to "real-life" schemata and probabilities—not excluding the supernatural—whereas the reader, his text at one remove from theirs, also gets the benefit of poetic guidance, coherence, inference.

Thus, the world of things confronting the dramatis personae reaches us through the mediation of words, selected and combined to form their own logic. The anointments in Samuel indicate how interscenic echoes (e.g., the recurrence of "see") or the choice of referring terms ("seer," "prophet," "man of God") may afford disclosures or judgments or continuities inaccessible to the agents themselves, faced with the unaltering objects rather than with their alterable labels. Even where much the same conclusion is simultaneously drawn, as with the analogy between Rebekah's and Abraham's hospitality, the verbal links give our reading superior precision and certitude. More generally, the narrator's mediation offers the reader a pre-interpreted image of reality where his fellow interpreters find the raw materials on their hands. From the characters' standpoint, for example, repetition is an inevitable (and often imperceptible) part of life. To achieve his goals, the servant must first devise a plan, then set it in motion on the girl's arrival, then recount to the family both plan and performance. To the reader, however, the plot function of the two last stages could as well be fulfilled by the briefest summary. So the one's minimum becomes the other's excess, impelling him to look round for an explanation that will establish an artistic coherence that lies beyond the envoy's ken and, as it happens, provides an insight into that ken. This suffices to formulate the principle that we shall trace at work throughout. Though the Bible may in practice balance matters, the characters' data and interpretive operations are essentially all available to the reader, but not vice versa. And if meaning turns on choice, then the meaning reserved for the reader's viewpoint has an extension as wide as the range of choice marking biblical poetics.

Three Reading Positions

From still another side, the double pairing of viewpoints—according to authority on the one hand and existence on the other—entails dependency relations within each framework of communication. Just as the characters depend for guidance on God, especially regarding privileged matters, so does the reader depend on the narrator's communicativeness. That God chooses to enlighten or mislead his creatures does not at all affect the reader, unless the narrator elects to follow suit. Within his own sphere of operations, God's opposite number may deny us the perspectival benefits that God himself grants his conversational partners, as when he delays or withholds divine revelations to prophets; just as he is free to mitigate divine silence by disclosure, opening or (as with the identity of the bride-to-be) foreshadowing what the characters are to find out later or not at all. This applies with even greater force to the handling of information that is not only privileged but originally noncommunicative, like secret thoughts and designs. In each case, our position relative to the other observers—facing the represented world and world view, past and future, act and motive and personality—turns on the strategy of narration. And since two of those other viewpoints form constants, the strategic variables bear primarily on the relations between reader and character: whether the narrator is reticent or forthcoming determines which of the human interpreters stands closer to the authorized version.

These variations fall into three basic strategies, which may be called reader-elevating, character-elevating, and evenhanded. Each launches a play of perspectives and a reading experience of its own; but equal determinacy does not go with equal frequency. Again, while displaying its precocious command of the universal resources and permutations of narrative, the Bible specializes in those most congenial to its ideology and most adaptable to its goals.

The two "elevating" strategies mark polar extremes, the one's superior intelligence figuring as the other's victim of irony. Within the reader-elevating configuration, the discrepancies in awareness are so manipulated in our favor, at the expense of the characters, that we observe them and their doings from a vantage point practically omniscient. The narrator's disclosures put us in a position to fathom their secret thoughts and designs, to trace or even foreknow their acts, to jeer or grieve at their misguided attempts at concealment, plotting, interpretation. The Bible's interior monologue encapsulates this situation of dramatic irony: Haman in miscalculation ("Whom would the king delight to honor more than me?") or Abraham in skepticism ("Shall a child be born to a man who is a hundred years old?") betrays both factual and metaphysical ignorance of his world (Esth 6:6; Gen 17:17). But similar patterns abound elsewhere. Cain prevaricating with God, the brothers pulled about by Joseph, Jethro's daughters mistaking Moses for "an Egyptian," Pharaoh determined to stick it out, the Gibeonites tricking Israel into an alliance, Samson's parents failing to recognize the angel, Eli accusing Hannah of drunkenness, Saul hoping to derive comfort from David, Adonijah's party celebrating a victory that has already fallen to their enemies, Boaz asleep with Ruth at his feet: these are typical situations where the reader knows better.

Even beyond changes in context and dramatis personae, such situations manifest remarkable variability. In magnitude, for instance, they range from short snatches of monologue or dialogue, as with the reference to Moses as an Egyptian, to full-fledged scenes or even, like the affair between Joseph and his brothers, cycles. In generic tone, they extend from the comic if not satiric, like Balaam's quarrel with his ass; through the serious or pathetic, like the theft of the blessing from the blind Isaac; to the cruel "irony of fate" whereby Jacob's unwitting curse falls on the head of his beloved wife or the vindictive hoist-with-his-own-petard effect generated by the Philistines' making jubilant arrangements for their destruction at Samson's hands. The privileged disclosures we receive may consist in information about the past or the future, externals or internals, earthly or heavenly schemes, in concrete facts or general canons of probability or normative truths. And the perspectival design may so juggle with the material as to elaborate the most various correspondences and oppositions. It may thus ally us with one character against another (with the servant against Laban, with Esther against the unsuspecting and villainous Haman or, more complex, with Jacob against Isaac and Esau along the informational axis but also with the victims against the victimizer along the axis of judgment); or it may privilege us at the expense of all, as when the Judah and Tamar story lays bare throughout the deceptions and counter-deceptions that the two schemers in conflict practice upon each other. In turn, this flexibility of alignment promotes further complications in response, notably through the enactment of a paragon in the dark or the splitting of the irony between a well-informed wrong-doer and a less informed well-doer. For of the two aspects of biblical "knowledge," as argued in the foregoing chapter, right principles always outrank but never quite void right information. Still, what remains constant under all these varia-tions is the reader's omniscient-like superiority to at least one dramatized viewpoint. Though the strategy accommodates the whole gamut of effects from laughter to tears, they all exhibit signs of this imbalance in awareness and evaluation between humans.

The character-elevating procedure reverses this discrepancy. Through a piecemeal release of material, it propels the reader from initial ignorance (or at best mystification) to ultimate surprise, usually two-pronged because it springs on us both new facts and, no less inglorious, some character's long-standing awareness of them. It is from this vulnerable position that we first misinterpret and then, on the emergence of the backward-looking inside view, reinterpret Laban's motives for hastening to welcome the stranger. Examples on a larger scale (to be treated in chapter 8) include the belated surfacing of the reasons behind Abimelech's restoration of Sarah to her husband, Gideon's violence during his pursuit of Midian, Jonah's flight from God—all antecedents as familiar to the agent concerned as to the reticent narrator himself. Here, each agent enjoys the same kind of superiority over the reader as God does in his incongruous-looking election of Joseph or David.

There is one marked difference, though, even apart from the temporari-ness of the elevation. As regards the human perspectives, informational superiority vis-à-vis the reader may well go with or eventuate in normative inferiority. Gideon produces an impression of gratuitous savagery as long as we remain ignorant of his personal bereavement, just as the approval elicited by Laban's hospitality does not survive the disclosure of its causes. Indeed, the point of the early withholding of information is to lure us into a false sense of emotional or ideological disharmony with the character so as to twist it into harmony with redoubled effect, or to reverse apparent harmony into disharmony, or to combine the two perspectival shifts. That such tensions between and along different axes of point of view have their counterparts in the reader-elevated position (e.g., the blessing scene) should be evident. So should the compositional gains and pleasures—from nar-rative interest to control of response—yielded by both interplays. But behind it all there lurks the rhetorical argument peculiar to the Bible. To share

God's knowledge is to think well of him and judge properly of others. Sharing the knowledge of a human agent need not produce either result. On the contrary, whether because the shared knowledge is incriminating or fragmentary, such parity may only lead to dissociation and misvaluation. The deeper the insight we gain into Laban or Absalom or Jonah, the greater the distance created; and the more we adhere to one figure's view of another, the greater the danger of taking the part for the whole and the image for the character. Ignorance itself, then, might lead to judgments less unfavorable or less unjust than limited knowledge. The repeated dramatization of this point, freely modulating between anticipatory and retrospective enlightenment, generates a reading experience with clear implications for everyday life, where one normally is in the confidence neither of God nor of one's fellow men.

However serviceable the polar strategies of elevation, neither is yet entirely in keeping with the spirit of the Bible. In purely artistic terms, one might say that the narrator is too secretive to keep the reader informed by an endless stream of asides and too mindful of perceptual verisimilitude to draw characters who keep themselves informed by their own efforts. On closer inspection, however, these two reasons show a common anchorage in a ground where the Bible's art and doctrine inextricably fuse together. The position of cognitive authority simply offends against man's natural state, and it would be idle, indeed risky, to pretend otherwise. Characters cannot be long maintained in such a position without making impossible demands even on an irreligious story, let alone a history geared to the unique privileges of divinity. Nor can the reader, by special dispensation and artificial spoon-feeding, be allowed to keep the narrator company throughout. The heights of ironic observation may go to his head, loosening his bonds with humanity and giving him an illusion of immunity from the constraints that inhibit the agents below, all exposed to suspense, wonder, error, suffering. To the Bible, nothing would be more unthinkable than Anthony Trollope's poetics of lucidity, whereby "the author and the reader should move along in full confidence with each other," allied from start to finish against the blundering and struggling characters.[2] It has created *ex nihilo* a poetics of ambiguity, with reticence taking the place of confidence, in order to fix rather than blur the line of demaracation between heaven and earth: unless the reader undergoes the drama of knowledge himself, the whole tale will have been told in vain.

This explains the Bible's tendency to eschew both extremes in favor of the intermediate strategy, where evenhandedness is at times so scrupulously observed as to give one a sense of bumping against life itself. The ends and the means involved paradigmatically emerge from the narrative of Solomon's Judgment, following God's promise to grant him supreme wisdom:

(16) Two women, harlots, came to the king and stood before him.
(17) And one woman said, O my lord, I and this woman dwell in the
same house, and I gave birth with her in the house. (18) On the third
day after I had given birth, this woman also gave birth; and we were
together, there was no stranger with us in the house, except we two in
the house. (19) And this woman's son died during the night, because
she overlaid him. (20) And she arose at midnight and took my son from
behind me—thy maidservant was asleep—and laid him in her bosom,
and her dead son she laid in my bosom. (21) I arose in the morning
to suckle my son, and behold, he was dead! Then I looked at him closely
in the morning, and behold, he was not my son whom I had borne!
(22) But the other woman said, No, the living is my son and the dead
is thy son; and the first one said, No, the dead is thy son and the living
is my son. Thus they spoke before the king. (23) Then the king said,
This one says, The living is my son and the dead is thy son, and this
one says, No, the dead is thy son and the living is my son. (24) And
the king said, Bring me a sword. And they brought a sword before the
king. (25) And the king said, Divide the living child in two, and give
half to one and half to the other. (26) Then the woman whose son was
the living one said to the king, because her bowels were moved on
account of her son, O my lord, give her the living child and by no means
kill him. And the other one said, He shall be neither mine nor thine.
Divide him. (27) Then the king answered and said, Give her the living
child and by no means kill him; she is his mother. (28) And all Israel
heard of the judgment that the king had given and they feared the king,
for they saw that God's wisdom was in him to render justice.
(1 Kgs 3:16–28)

The effect of this tale depends on its blending of genres. Thematically,
it enacts a test and a riddle—a puzzle-solving exploit by which an untried
youth made a name for himself as a possessor of divine wisdom. Perspectivally, however, it operates with conventions (or rather inventions) that
were to be codified only as late as the detective story. The most basic of
these is the fair-play rule, whereby the reader must be given the same data
to make inferences from as the detective himself. So if the thematic materials
foreground the puzzle-solution movement to the glory of Solomon, then
the superimposed perspectival equality drives his achievement home by
contriving a two-level riddle and a double test: it challenges us to match
wits with Solomon and, indirectly, with his heavenly source of inspiration.

Hence the correspondence devised between the two lines of inquiry.
Having introduced the litigants as harlots, the narrator sees to it that the
recital—notably the emphasis on solitude in childbirth—should at once
divulge their profession to the judge as well. The only common ground
between them—that there is one living and one dead baby—likewise forms
common knowledge. As with facts, moreover, so with gaps, which ambiguate all the rest. Neither Solomon nor the reader has had any previous

acquaintance with the two whores, who are appropriately termed "the one woman" and "the other woman." Neither has had the slightest advance warning of the point at issue—not even that it lies *between* the two women—which unfolds in and through the dialogue alone. And when the case does begin to unfold, neither could foresee what an impasse it will reach and how little hard evidence will emerge in the process.

Having done with the expositional preliminaries of verse 18, the first woman seems to plunge into a straightforward narrative of events: the fatal accident, the substitution, and then, with "thy servant was asleep," comes the reversal. Far from a factual or even an eyewitness account, it has all been a reconstruction without a shred of supporting evidence; and worse, it soon transpires, one affirmed by an interested party and denied outright by her opponent. As such, it turns out worthless. The two versions, just like the professional unreliability of their sources, cancel out each other. Even the frankness of the speaker's reference to her uninterrupted sleep does not count in her favor, since the very logic of her tale forces this admission. How else could she explain her failure to resist the switch? Nor does the circumstantiality of her tale, for all its emotional appeal, give it any real advantage over her neighbor's curt no. For the defendant's strongest point is that she has no story to tell: she did nothing, saw nothing, suffered no loss, and would not care to advance any theories about the death of another's child.

The only clues beyond dispute are of a negative kind, bringing into play another (future) convention of the detective genre: the hermetic sealing of the scene of the crime, so as to keep suspicion within the circle of insiders. Hence the insistence on their being alone in the house during the night, thrice repeated by the speaker to throw the guilt squarely on her neighbor and by the omniscient teller to focus hesitation between the two of them. But the exclusion of outside interference also excludes outside confirmation or disconfirmation, which underlines anew the inferential stalemate. Of this whole line of reasoning the king shows himself no less aware than ourselves when his summing up discounts the complainant's lengthy protestations: "This one says, The living is my son and the dead is thy son, and this one says, No, the dead is thy son and the living is my son." Indeed, that is what the evidence boils down to: "the one" prostitute's word against "the other's."

Where, then, does the truth reside? Himself baffled, the reader might be tempted to scoff at his fellow inquirer's apparent variation on the cutting of the Gordian knot. Divine sagacity, indeed! Yet by a surprising turn—more surprising, though, to a waverer than to a believer, let alone a detective story aficionado—the appeal to the sword reveals itself as a trap, and not for the reader alone. It is a false solution deliberately put forward to trick the culprit into self-betrayal: in default of clues, they must be elicited by shock tactics. In fact, the extreme responses provoked are as good as a confession; and the narrator clinches the matter in his unobtrusive way.

Lest the snare be mistaken for a fluke, he establishes it as the judge's design all along by the brilliant twist given in verbatim repetition to the mother's outcry. What judge caught off guard would have the presence of mind to transform a shriek of renunciation ("Give her the living child and by no means kill him") into a verdict of restoration ("Give her the living child and by no means kill him") by a simple shift in reference? To leave no doubt about the correctness of the solution, moreover, the narrator departs for once from the objective mode to put his whole authority behind the designation of the renouncer as "the woman whose son was the living one." Nor is it an accident that this label conceals as much as it reveals: we never find out for sure which of the harlots ("the one" or "the other") is the mother. By a final anticipation of the detective story manner, attention is thus focused on the inquirer—his predicament, acumen, triumph—at the expense of the suspects. All that matters is that he succeeded where everyone, given an equal opportunity, would fail—as we have reason to know. It is therefore both fair to the winner and comforting to the loser to deduce, with all Israel, that "God's wisdom was in him." From an illusion of equality to an admission of inferiority with a loophole for self-esteem: this is the route marked out for the reader by the dynamics of point of view. Having started by putting us in Solomon's place, the tale concludes by putting us in our own.

Like some other dialogic occasions, Solomon's Judgment occupies the exact middle of the scale leading from the reader-elevating to the character-elevating position. The evenhanded treatment establishes a parity in both the raw information and the modes of processing, since the two detectives must weigh the same evidence by the same lifelike standards. It is precisely this that rubs in the ultimate superiority of divinely inspired over native wit; and, with the withdrawal of supernatural inspiration from the pattern, this may also reverse the cutting edge of the irony. The joke is on Samuel when, thrown on his own devices in the face of Jesse's sons, his interpretive performance turns out much below par; or more grimly, on Adonijah as he supplies the pretext for his own execution by making a bid for Abishag, his father's bedfellow. Whom God wishes to undo, we say, he first strikes blind.

Where the intermediate differs from the polar strategies, then, is in the equal opportunities provided for observation and inference rather than in the use made of them by the observers concerned. The possibilities of variance and ranking and irony further increase with the decrease in evenhandedness. For most often the imbalance derives not so much from the relative skill of the interpreters as from the resources available for interpretation. Abandoning or loosening the rules of fair play, the narrator then stations one human viewpoint closer to the privileged norm than its fellow. A matter of degree, this unequal positioning lends itself to innumerable gradations and, no more realistically than aesthetically objectionable, may elevate either side or even both at once along different dimensions, without yet polarizing them.

As far as their secret selves are concerned, for instance, characters may act from motives that we can only guess at and judge by criteria too heroic to be other than ideal, as throughout the Binding of Isaac, or too individual to be anticipated, as often with David. Generally speaking, the more complex the figure, the more perceptible our inferior understanding of his inner life even with his speech and action in full view—indeed, even where the shape of his future stands revealed to our eyes alone. Uriah going to his death with his private thoughts undivulged illustrates the form and effects of this two-way inequality.

On the other hand, the Wooing of Rebekah has suggested a variety of modes and axes in which the perspectival imbalance works in the reader's favor. The simplest way of tipping the scales is for the narrator to cut in with a privileged scene or comment, sharpening our vision through some inside view, retrospect, foreshadowing, or glance at the divine order. And as long as our resulting advantage over the figural perceiver stops short of contrast, this need not blur the distinction between the first strategy (where Pharaoh sees a troublemaker we see a deliverer) and the third (where the servant observes a girl we receive an identification *cum* portrait). Or in regard to the future: while all Israel admires the young David's bravery, we alone know whence it comes and where it leads. Significantly, such tensions in viewpoint coincide with the thematic distance between the truth and the whole truth. No less privileged but more artful is the Bible's complex of indirections. A perspectival domain out of bounds for the characters, it yet forms a source of inference about matters of common interest. I have already instanced the elevating role of the predictive and retrospective analogies in the Wooing tale, the redundancy patterns, the shifts in sequence, the verbal echoes and chains. And if this tale sustains a normative parity in informational disparity, to shield the faithful servant, elsewhere our counterpart (Saul persecuting David, Haman on his way to Esther's second garden-party) labors under a twofold disadvantage. Still, these discrepancies remain quantitative. The appointed victim suspects the truth; and, even while we foresee the end of the affair, we are not quite in a position to determine how what must come will come.

Furthermore, the tendency to moderate perspectival tensions controls, rather than just shades off into, the sharper disharmonies of "elevation" themselves. For the Bible multiplies but does not often polarize opposi- tions, except to the divine order. A closer look at the examples of the elevating strategies will usually reveal measures taken to spoil the polarity, as it were, by reducing or complicating the distance between the outer and the inner observers. Along the informational dimension we find our- selves aligned with Jacob against the manipulated Isaac, but we hardly condone the trickery, nor indeed does God. From the most advantageous position, we may be troubled by certain spots of opacity or incongruity that are child's play to the participants themselves. What can lie behind Balaam's apparently docile behavior to justify God's waylaying him en route to Moab and going to the lengths of staging a comedy of errors, with a drawn sword for an epilogue? Conversely, the narrative may afford us some measure of knowledge denied to a character who is otherwise our superior. However false our impression of Jonah's mind turns out in retrospect, we at least remain with the satisfaction of having shaken our heads over the démarche of flight from God. Or consider the perspectival ups and downs along the sequence. No matter what our elevation at one phase, the next may pull us down with a vengeance: having savored the irony of Joseph's brothers prostrating themselves before the Egyptian vizier, the reader finds himself sighing for clues to the workings of their mind as Joseph begins to turn the screw. Just as our initial disadvantage vis-à-vis the secretive Absalom transforms into manifold irony. With so many promising can- didates impelled toward the middle ground, the heights can boast only a very limited membership.

The reason is not far to seek. While the polar extremes are a liability to the Bible, as already indicated, the freedom to range between them has everything to offer. In terms of world view and aesthetics alike, its norma- tive implications are not just acceptable but constructive, since no midway configuration leaves either human interpreter fully or permanently allied with the scriptwriters. On the contrary, the assorted variations I have out- lined inculcate those thematic norms more powerfully than any amount of lecturing would do, since their variables always interact with (and often pale into insignificance beside) the constant, qualitative opposition between the human and the superhuman. At the same time, they allow the nar- rator the flexibility necessary to meet his contextual exigencies and shape the most dynamic reading process, where we shift from position to posi- tion within a single book, cycle, tale, even verse. From one position, we enjoy a grandstand view of divine history in the making; from another, we form hypotheses and impressions only to be proved wrong and inferior even to our natural peers; from still another, we can puzzle out the truth given to humanity. With the change of position, there goes a change in the company we keep: sometimes the best, sometimes the worst, sometimes just average, most often a mixed lot, always unforeseen but explicable after the fact. As the Wooing of Rebekah suggests—and so will each of the analyses to come—it is largely due to this incessant dynamics that the Bible's reading makes a drama no less eventful and memorable than its action. The agents, of course, interpret by different rules and routes; but then, in a way, our interpretive adventures subsume as well as run parallel to theirs. Let us turn now to the logic and design of their ordeal.

From Plot to Perspective

The "characters' perspective" differs from all the others—God's, the narrator's, the reader's—in its multiplicity. Each character observes the world from his own perspective. And it is their divergence—in interest, interpretation, world view, scenario, hope and fear—that keeps the action going, just as their convergence makes for its resolution. Balaam quarrels with his ass because he is insensible of the angel blocking their path. The servant maneuvers to bring Rebekah's family to see things his (and God's) way. Jacob loves Joseph, the brothers detest him. From their first encounter, Moses and Pharaoh get locked in a conflict of national interests, prolonged by the Egyptian's undervaluing the opposite camp and resolved by a blow so terrible as to enforce a revaluation of the issue. What such diverse figural perspectives have in common is the inherent limitation of knowledge and liability to misjudgment, which motivate the progress of the tale. Accordingly, even apart from all ideological and aesthetic determinants peculiar to the Bible, the interfigural play of viewpoint is dictated by the most basic exigencies of narrative: for the characters to clash and make peace as dramatic agents, they must clash and make peace as fallible subjects.

This vital link between plot and perspective is only obscured by the common tendency to reduce plot to externals and mistake perspective for less than the whole self finding its expression in speech, thought, *and* action. Aristotle's *Poetics* thus singles out two lines of dramatic change. One traces the movement of characters from happiness to unhappiness or the reverse; the other, from ignorance to knowledge, climaxing in a recognition (*anagnorisis*). But Aristotle deems only the first movement a universal of plot, assigning to the second an optional role in the "complex" plot. Wiser words proceed from a critic-novelist who made a lifelong study of human ignorance as the stuff and theme of narrative. "If we were never bewildered," Henry James insists, "there would never be a story to tell about us; we should partake of the superior nature of the all-knowing immortals whose annals are dreadfully dull so long as flurried humans are not, for the positive relief of bored Olympians, mixed up with them."[3] An actional sequence (even of the "happiness to unhappiness" type) cannot go far, if at all, without some impetus from "bewilderment" on the part of the agents: cross-purposes, miscalculation, overconfidence, hope and fear, inability to read the mind of others, or penetrate the past and the future, etc. Where else would the complicating and propulsive forces come from? Indeed, *pace* James—who typically yokes together the Hellenic concept of divinity as immortality with the Hebraic concept of divinity as omniscience—it is exactly because Homer's Olympians are *not* "all-knowing" that they escape "boredom." With humans, the formula is even simpler. No ignorance, no conflict; and no conflict, no plot.

Like Greek tragedy in the dramatic genre, however, the Bible is the first narrative to develop this necessary condition for plot into a focus of interest and a compositional principle. In historical context, its break with standard Near Eastern plot-making gains weight and perceptibility from an interrelated set of factors. Generally speaking, we have the new doctrinal load carried by the opposition between divine omniscience and human restrictedness; the two faces of "knowledge" as world viewing and world view; and the overall interplay of perspectival tensions. More specifically, where the minimal requirement for plot would be one "bewildered" agent or party vis-à-vis God, the Bible opts for the multiplication and complication of viewpoints on the human side. It is hard to say what the popular reference to "the inability of the narrator to catch and depict the actual distinctions among individuals"[4] betrays most: the modern judge's preconception about ancient man and writing or his own reading competence. Even in a world still hardly populated, the serpent is kept apart from Eve in informational terms, and Eve from Adam along the axis of judgment as well. And the cast once expanded, a single issue like the Joseph affair may be refracted as well as forwarded through a whole gallery of observers: Joseph himself, the ten brothers—among whom Reuben figures as an old dissentient and Judah as a new beginning—Jacob, the majordomo, even Pharaoh.

Nor are all such variations of ignorance, not even the nuclear discrepancy between Joseph and his brothers, subordinated to the immediate exigencies of the plot. Some have long-range effects, as when Pharaoh's attitude throughout initiates processes extending to the Exodus. Others carry the widest ideological as well as historical implications: the superior insight and leadership shown by Judah vis-à-vis the older Reuben as persons ultimately motivates the reversal of their natural positions as tribes. Still others move even further beyond the minimal plot function, their movement suggestively correlating with that from more to less predictable disharmonies in outlook. Human nature being what it is, certain patterns of conflict occasion no surprise: man against God, leader against people, prophet against king, let alone ordinary material squabbles and international affairs. Less expected types arise from the peculiarities of biblical thematics, such as the familial splits due to the favoritism of God or/versus man: husband against wife, father against son, brother against brother, with fortune and judgment but not necessarily limelight turning on the relative distance from the divine viewpoint. Even Cain, his plot role over with the murder of Abel, remains on stage to betray his blindness; and so does Saul, David's metaphorical father, throughout his long struggle against the inevitable. In its passion for differentiation, further, the Bible also explores variety within pairs or groups of subjects who have been acting in unison and would seem to merge into a single or collective viewpoint. By a sudden shift of position along some axis, the narrative thus opposes man to his own favorite (as when Jacob scolds Rachel or Joseph), brother to his natural ally (as when Judah rises above his peers or Aaron sinks into complicity in the Golden Calf outrage), prophet (Moses, Samuel, Jonah) to God. Here the perspectival opposition moves further away from dependence on plot exigencies, since it need not lead to enduring dramatic or even ideological opposition and, the viewpoints having at one juncture diverged to their mutual illumination, they may soon reconverge into normal harmony. Located between two states of harmony, the device I would term "splitting the common front" invests disharmony with intrinsic interest. And the functional autonomy of the device grows in inverse ratio to its productiveness and predictability in terms of causation, so that the limiting case would be the clairvoyance of Balaam's ass, which generates nothing except satire at the expense of the seer reduced lower than his own beast (Num 22:21–35).

As regards the Bible's fascination with point of view in the human sphere, Balaam's ass has yet another claim to notice. Not only is the perspectival incongruity of the episode, like that of prophetic omniscience, motivated by appeal to supernatural interference; its very incongruous effect derives from a violation of the Bible's rule of naturalism. As with the access to knowledge, so with the more common lack of access that gives rise to varying degrees of ignorance: both fall here under a norm of perception grounded in reality not artifice. Even the ass owes her powers of speech and sight not to any convention of talking animals[5] but to supernatural naturalism ("the Lord opened the mouth of the ass"). And in a narrative where the supernatural governs the world, one would hardly expect to encounter such a concern for perspectival verisimilitude amidst plot marvels. We recall the scenes of David's anointment or Sarah's laughter; but there are far more dramatic instances. However marvelous Elijah's translation to heaven in a whirlwind, it emerges from the viewpoint of his disciple, Elisha, whose eye proves unequal to the speed of events and barely manages to register the disappearance: "As they were going on and talking, and behold, a chariot of fire and horses of fire! And they separated the two of them" (2 Kgs 2:11). Later, Elisha's luring the Aramean army into a Samaria defended by invisible "horses and chariots of fire" occasions a manifold play of human perspectives, some enlightened and others in blinkers, yet all following from the same "real-life" premise, namely that normal laws of perception are in force unless God chooses to tamper with them for better or worse (6:14–23). It is as if the Bible were looking ahead to those modern theories of narrative that infused new life into the ghost story by preaching that "the extraordinary is most extraordinary in that it happens to you and me";[6] or in other words, the more supernatural the rendered object, the greater the need for rendering it through some natural or naturalized subject(s). The human attestation contributes not so much to the movement of the plot itself as to its impact and credibility.

The less supernatural the object, moreover, the less does the observance and exploration of constraints on subjectivity heighten any realism other than that of perspective proper. Why does the suspicious Isaac bless Jacob after all? Whence the different views of David among his contemporaries? How does Boaz discover the identity of the woman lying at his feet? Drawing further away from the naive or stylized epistemology of its time and place, then, such ubiquitous concern with the state of fallibility develops into an end in itself—an epoch-making study in the conditions and processes of apprehending the world. The epistemological antithesis between superhumans and humans dovetails with, and apparently generates, the concern with perception in the human sphere. Later chapters will amply show how far the Bible goes in exploring this uncharted territory of the mind: how it distinguishes words from things as percepts and physical from psychological obstacles to vision, with a play on the meanings of "blindness"; how it relates clairvoyance and blind spots to normative schemes; how it unfolds the same object from various positions; or how it fashions special forms of narration, like repetition and free indirect discourse, to accommodate its perceptual interests. Not to run ahead of my story, I shall only emphasize now that all this inside-viewing displays features too marked and systematic to be reduced to any other framework, plot and ideology included. While the human play of perspectives may certainly serve these functions, it retains a measure of autonomy by exceeding and even exploiting them in turn—plot and world view often operating as determinants of vision—to produce the two-way traffic between means and end so dear to the Bible's art.

From Ignorance to Knowledge

To crown it all, the inside views offered go beyond isolated glimpses, locally motivated and opposed, to trace a dynamics of perception. So far, in other words, I have explained how and why the "freezing" of the action at any given moment reveals a crisscross of perspectival variations among the dramatis personae as well as between them and the three other observers. In fact, however, such variations are anything but static. They so develop along the sequence of plot as to mark discrepancies even within a single figural viewpoint as it moves from beginning to end: its progress through time correlates with a progress in knowledge. Samuel or Abraham's servant discovers at last the identity of God's chosen; Balaam, the reason for the ass's antics; Isaac, the trickery practiced on him by his younger son; Pharaoh, the full extent of divine might; Delilah, Samson's secret, and Samson, Delilah's perfidy.

As we pass from the single agent-as-interpreter to the entire cast, the static variations among them assume dynamic form and force. Often, different characters attain to knowledge by different routes (as with the processes by which Balaam and Balak learn that God will not have Israel cursed), or at different paces (Eli identifies the mysterious voice addressing Samuel in the shrine long before the novitiate himself), or to different degrees (like the envoy and his audience in the Wooing of Rebekah), or even in regard to different objects (Jacob finds out the truth about Joseph, the brothers about themselves). Moreover, some (like Joseph) seek knowledge, others (like his brothers) have it forced on them, others still (like Jacob) abruptly gain or stumble on it. And the perspectival picture takes on even greater intricacy owing to the simultaneous yet independent movement of the reader along his own obstacle course. With surprisingly few exceptions, however, in each tale at least one character goes through a drama of discovery, complete with *anagnorisis* if not with a whole series of them, and none ends as unenlightened as he began. The passage from ignorance to knowledge, one of the great archetypes of literature, is another Hebraic innovation, for which the Greeks got all the credit.

For all its universal applicability, this innovation yet preserves its native features. To say, as an Aristotelian might, that biblical narrative unfolds a succession of "complex" plots is to cast a net with holes far too large; and not just because the *Poetics,* point of view hardly being its forte, would capture very few of the variables and subtleties that attend these processes of discovery and transform instrumental into self-focused changes in awareness. As a matter of art and doctrine alike, the Bible simply establishes a different relation between the external ("happiness to unhappiness" or the reverse) and the internal ("ignorance to knowledge") movement of the plot, whereby the former enjoys no poetic priority over the latter and the distinction itself is scarcely recognized at all. Rather, external and internal plot fuse together into a movement in which history turns on discovery—failures, zigzags, relapses and all—and the progress made by an agent emerges by reference to both equally developing counterparts and the two static superiors. Roughly speaking, so far as personal and national fortune goes by merit, then merit itself consists less in innate virtue than in the capacity for acquiring *and* retaining knowledge of God's ways: less in a state of being than in a process of becoming, by the trial and error of experience. That is why *anagnorisis* gets promoted from an optional to an omnipresent and foregrounded element of plot; why it recurs throughout in the form of the omnipotence effect; why it so often undergoes a stretching from point to process; why it may combine a specific object (say, an identity) with a global or abstract truth (usually involving God's place in the world); why it admits of quantitative variations among different observers; why it figures as a component as well as a determinant of "happiness," which thus comes to lose its purely external bearing. That is also why so many biblical plots (e.g., Balak's hiring of Balaam) contrive discovery scenes that, far from meeting the Aristotelian requirement of "producing love or hate among the personages marked for good or evil fortune" (*Poetics* 1452a 30–32), would seem to lead nowhere: the knowledge acquired forms its own closure, point, recommendation.

Again, some of these biblical *differentia* anticipate the art of modern fiction, with its turn inward to focus on the workings of viewpoint and consciousness. So do quite a few others. One is the correspondence devised between the processes of discovery undergone by the reader and the hero—Strether in James, Marlow in Conrad, K. in Kafka, Humbert in Nabokov, among the famous literary detectives—each pursuing his own route but equally anchored in the human condition. Another is the thematic charging of the process, which dramatizes the way to knowledge in the wider sense rather than, as in the detective story proper, a quest for facts. Still another is the self-reflexive exploration, in and through the drama, of perceptual and epistemological limits, interpretive success and failure—in short, of whether and how one knows.

Even more modern, if possible, is the conception of discovery. Considering the thematic value and long procession of ignorance-to-knowledge plots, one might expect some moral about the enduring effects of learning. In line with its rather somber view of humanity, however, the Bible shows little of the facile or pretended optimism of the didacticist, least of all in regard to knowledge of God. No matter how hard-earned, how deep-felt, how sincere its expression at the time, learning tends to evaporate with frightening speed and regularity. All biblical characters lapse, but many live to relapse as well. Instead of marking a reversal of character and often fortune too, as in Greek tragedy or the classical novel, biblical discovery, like Joycean epiphany, comes up as a momentary illumination that may well be followed by a backsliding into darkness. Having bowed to God's will in the evening, Rebekah's family yet make difficulties the next morning; Pharaoh's heart softens again and again under the impact of a plague only to harden anew upon its lifting; the Israelites never retain long the spiritual lessons (even when they do the memories) of God's acts of deliverance; no sooner has Gideon received one sign of divine favor than he petitions for another. But the most telling example rounds off the Bible's longest and most excruciating drama of recognition, namely, Joseph and His Brothers. The fraternal ordeal apparently a thing of the past, it suddenly resurges after Jacob's death, when the brothers voice the fear that Joseph is at last free to take his revenge (Gen 50:15-18). No wonder Joseph bursts into tears. It is as though the whole ordeal has been in vain: if they have learned anything about him beyond externals—and the fear may well have haunted them all those years—the effect has evaporated. God-like to the last—and himself among the handful of genuine learners—Joseph repeats his assurances in the hope of implanting the knowledge for good. Only a hope, this time, since he has just discovered the biblical rule ("Hard come, easy go") concerning the problematics of discovery.

As in the Aristotelian analogy, however, the dissimilarities to modernism prove no less revealing than the similarities. In purely compositional terms, the most salient relate to the method designed to ensure that the process of reading should run more or less parallel to the process of living. To this end, Henry James preached and practiced the "limited point of view," whereby one of the characters serves to refract and interpret the world throughout either as a vessel of consciousness (Strether in *The Ambassadors*) or as a restricted narrator (the governess in *The Turn of the Screw*). In each case, the reader receives only such and so much information as the fallible subjects gather from one point to another in the drama: "Their emotions, their stirred intelligence, their moral consciousness become thus, by sufficiently charmed perusal, our own very adventure" (*The Art of the Novel*, p.70). Neither limitation is, however, viable in the biblical context: the first, because it entails a turning inward undreamt of in ancient narrative and also goes ill with such requirements as panoramic or historical range; the second, because it clashes with the very model of authoritative narration. Hence the recourse to two substitutes that often do analogous duty in modernism. One consists in the dialogic technique that, in Solomon's Judgment as in Hemingway's short stories, leaves the situation equally opaque to all observers. The other turns from formal to pragmatic correspondence en route. The omniscient narrator so shifts the point of view as to establish the desired perspectival relations between the fellow interpreters: whether equivalence (through evenhanded disclosure and withholding) or reader-elevation (through privileged disclosure) or character-elevation (through the withholding of, say, common knowledge).

If these substitute forms for the limited point of view do not result in quite the same functions, this is mainly because the most salient difference is not yet the most radical difference. The real variety in unity lies beneath the formal surface of the narrative, buried as deep as the ideological foundations. Why does the Bible freely switch the reader from position to position, whereas the modern novel, except in its rare comic moods, increasingly favors the middle ground of equivalence? Why does the Bible postulate two authoritative perspectives, whereas modernism would cast doubt on the knowledge and general reliability of the author himself? Why does the biblical plot move from ignorance to knowledge—however qualified—and modernism, especially post-Jamesian, from ignorance to ignorance, leaving the heart of the matter ambiguous to the reader as well as the hero? (Marlow never fathoms Lord Jim's nature and K. dies without an inkling of his guilt, not to mention the total breakdown of the quest in a Robbe-Grillet.) Taken together, these distinctive features suggest not that biblical narrative is a pale version of things to come—as some recent fashions in criticism might have it—but that it follows its own code in suiting a poetics to a world picture. In view of what I have been arguing, the structural implications can now be phrased as a series of blunt fiats.

The Bible must have an omnicompetent God and a privileged narrator to serve his cause. It must draw a qualitative line between their authorial perspectives and the human interpreters. Given God's relation to man, it must propel the characters toward enlightenment: to spread knowledge, influence choice, validate the election of learners, justify the fate of backsliders, as well as to guarantee the foolproof composition whereby not even the slowest in the uptake among the audience will be left unenlightened at the end. And in the interests of rhetorical effect, it must preserve the greatest freedom in manipulating the reader's journey and the least freedom in establishing his terminus, which in principle coincides with that of the better sort of characters. (Hence the convergent dynamics of point of view.) Within these limits—and all great art thrives on the challenge presented by constraint—enough can be achieved by way of complication, ambiguity, play if you will, to satisfy the most fastidious. But the limits themselves, whether viewed as ideological or rhetorical premises, are sacrosanct. For to violate them would be to undermine the very idea of divine order: that the world is intelligible, because providentially controlled, however mysterious if not offensive its workings may appear to dim eyes.

Privilege and Performance

The exigencies of discovery, finally, affect the privileged as well as the fallible viewpoints. Not that the superhumans can gain from the plot developments any knowledge or control they did not have before, but that they must limit their own privilege in order to lead their limited addressees through the ordeal of learning. Revelation presupposes concealment, and concealment self-restrictedness. Hence the tensions within their own perspective between what they know and what they tell, what they are capable of and what they opt for doing, what their powers vis-à-vis their interpreters enable and what their designs on those interpreters require. By thus distinguishing potentiality from performance in biblical communication, we can gather up some threads of the argument in the last three chapters and pave the ground for what follows.

Doubts about the absoluteness of God's knowledge and control have been variously expressed in the last two thousand years. The notorious removal of anthropomorphisms by ancient translators betrays the anxiety that the original has not properly dissociated God from the human condition. To shield God's prescience, for example, the Aramaic translation of Onkelos twists the phrase that the sins of Noah's generation "grieved him to his heart" (Gen 6:6) into a decision to break the sinners' strength; to free him from any dependence on sense data, it will euphemize "God went down to see the city" (11:5) into an act of revelation or transform verbs like "see" and "hear" into the passive. Historical scholars have often taken such phenomena as traces of pagan thought: Gunkel's note that God learned of Abel's murder from the crying of his blood (see chapter 3, n. 8) is a small but typical case in point. With no theological axe to grind, Steven Brams's amusing *Biblical Games* roundly denies God both omnipotence and omniscience. From this game-theoretic standpoint, "He can perform miracles and even endow others with great powers. But . . . human beings *do* have free will and can exercise it. . . . Consequently, God, powerful as He is, is sometimes thwarted in His desires." And, "though unique in His ability to plan his moves over an extended series of games," there are limits to his knowledge.[7]

Carried thus far, the whole method of taking the variety of heavenly doing as a reflection on heavenly being can be disposed of quite summarily on both general and empirical grounds. In general, God's portrait as more than human and less than superhuman has so little internal consistency that it simply fails to hang together. It leaves God one absolute feature (omnipresence) while divesting him of its closest relations (omniscience, omnipotence). Worse, it subjects those related absolutes to quantitative partitions, whereby God enjoys foreknowledge and inner knowledge without all-knowledge, dominion over nature but not or only occasionally over the mind. This logical monster (and its family) bears little resemblance, moreover, to the God of the Bible as glorified by the rhetorics of omniscience and omnipotence. These rhetorics not only drive home the principle of divine transcendence by strategies that make light of dogmatic scruples about the language of personification. They even build certain divergences (variations, self-restrictions) into the portrait and the world picture. Recall the pretence of ignorance as a dialogic gambit; the suspension of control over the human heart; the change of mind following repentance; the shift between overt and covert interference; or the recourse to serialization where a single act could produce the same effect on the world but not on the observer. Being choices rather than constraints, these are all reversible at will and, not excluding free choice, reversed in fact. Every limitation is self-imposed and motivated, none permanent. So even what appears a failure or discontinuity in terms of inherent privilege makes excellent (as well as favorable) sense in terms of divine performance and communication.

As to the narrator, however, the control he exerts over his plot and world is not much in danger of attack from interpreters these days. On the contrary, the vogue of regarding him as a fiction-maker exaggerates his latitude and dominance as much as his earlier source-critical portrait as a tradition-bound compiler underrates them. It is rather his omniscience that has been challenged, recently on literary as well as on the age-old historical grounds.

The historical challenge bears of course on the narrator's facts: the world was not created in six days; Abraham's migration involved whole clans rather than a single family; the alleged miracles have natural explanations; the casualty figures are inflated; and so on. Whereas the literary devaluation bears on his supposed failure to transcend God's own vision or to rise to a godlike height of understanding. "Not that any of the writers deify themselves!" Herbert Schneidau claims, "They don't even assume what we would call an 'omniscient' point of view. But they do identify with Yahweh's interests."[8] He also approvingly quotes A. E. Speiser's view that only through ignorance have certain patriarchal narratives been kept mysterious—the wife-sister triplet, the shift of the birthright to the younger brother, Rachel's theft of the household gods—although perfectly explicable in terms of Hurrian law. "The full meaning of these episodes . . . had already been lost to the narrator himself; otherwise he would surely have taken the trouble to enlighten his reader. . . . The narrator no longer knew the explanation, yet set down the details. . . . His aim was not to question or to reason why, but only to record faithfully what tradition had handed down to him."[9] At a more sophisticated level, even a work so alert to point of view as Robert Polzin's *Moses and the Deuteronomist* takes a similar line in accounting for the narrator's supposedly inadequate comment on, for example, a place name. If the Samson story emphasizes how the characters "who appear to have all the answers are naively mistaken and misguided, the narrator who apparently displays an omniscient control of the story then undercuts his own omniscience by his careful use of ambiguous phraseology. . . . In addition to the voice that names names and explains events, there is the voice that cries out to Yahweh for understanding. In this regard, Samson and the Deuteronomist are one."[10]

As in no other supernatural context, this line creates problems where none actually exist. For instance, the questions of the biblical narrator's control over his plot has its intricacies, resolvable only by appeal to rather slippery distinctions—between making and shaping or fictional and inspired license—whose tracing makes demands on our historical imagination. In regard to omniscience, however, the most basic conventions of artistic and even everyday storytelling distinguish the teller's powers from his performance.

First of all, the knowledge a narrator possesses can only be inferred from but never equated with the knowledge he imparts to his addressee. These form two separate axes of point of view: the first bears on the narrator's innate (or in literature, authorially delegated) privileges; the second, on his choices and designs in communication. To realize how common and varied the disparity between those axes is, it suffices to think of a few biblical speakers in action: God pretending ignorance to Cain or withholding from Abraham Sodom's doom and then ("Shall I hide from Abraham what I am about to do?") changing his mind; the servant schematizing the past for the family's benefit; Potiphar's wife accusing Joseph of rape; the whore laying a false claim to the child; Saul informing his uncle about the asses but suppressing the matter of kingship. Some would say that only such discontinuities between the known and the told make life tolerable. They certainly render communication flexible and meaningful, showing their rich play in the Bible's world itself, notably throughout the dramatized structures of repetition.

When it comes to omniscient narration, second, this universal duality within a single perspective gains extraordinary force. In a limited speaker's case, the failure to tell the (whole) truth may remain ambiguous between withholding or lying and ignorance, choice and constraint. After the campaign against Amalek, Saul greets Samuel with the words, "Blessed be thou to the Lord; I have performed the commandment of the Lord" (1 Sam 15:13). Does he hope to cover up the looting by this report, or does he mistake violation for observance? In contrast, the narrator's all-knowing rules out by definition the thought of any informational lapse or shortage. Whatever the cogency of the historical objection to his statements, the quarrel in terms of source does not affect their supreme authority within the discourse, that is, in relation to the other viewpoints converging on that piece of world. (To give an extreme example: were a biblical character to voice the modern historical understanding of an event, the contextual truth-value of his account could still vary all the way from positive to negative, depending on the narrator's own view.) And within the discourse, his silences must take their reference from the same authority as his statements.

The narrator's omniscience once postulated—and there is no escaping it—the consequences for the interpretation of dissonance logically follow. In the face of an omission or some other strange recounting on his part, it would be unthinkable to deny him the benefit of indeterminacy—between suppression and confusion—that he himself grants the characters. And in the face of such an indeterminacy, it would be unreasonable to bracket him with the characters by considering a resolution of his viewpoint in terms other than knowledgeable silence and maneuvering. For omniscience is a qualitative and therefore indivisible privilege. If a narrator shows himself qualified to penetrate the mind of one of the characters and report his secret activities—a feat impossible in everyday life—he has established his competence to do so in regard to all other inaccessibles as well. The superhuman privilege is constant and only its exercise variable: it is precisely the distance between them that cries out for explanation. And whatever line the explanation takes, it always starts from the premise that the narrator could do otherwise if he chose. In other words, if the motivation for the characters' reticence and incongruities may be lifelike in its appeal to human fallibility, the motivation for the narrator's must be communicative: withholding for a (rhetorical, aesthetic, structural) purpose. It is in the interests of communicative effect that the omniscient teller opted for a mode less than omnicommunicative.

Accordingly, from the narrator's failure to provide the Hurrian background to the wife-sister motif or the bypassing of the older son or Rachel's theft of the figurines, it does not at all follow that "his narrative reflects puzzlement" and that he "no longer knew" the reasons but simply parroted the tradition. Genetically a non sequitur, Speiser's claim makes no interpretive sense. For example, how can the teller be expected to ground the transfer of the blessing from Esau to Jacob in the discretion left to the father under Hurrian law, if in his tale the father would never make the transfer willingly and must be bamboozled into it? Rather, throughout the patriarchal cycle the narrative supplies a human and implies a divine reason for these reversals of status—the former increasingly elaborated and the latter increasingly hidden as we progress from Abraham's offspring through Isaac's to Jacob's. This systematic interplay of disclosure and concealment goes to show that what might possibly count as a lapse in a cultural history bespeaks a deliberate choice in an ideological art concerned to dramatize how seniority shifts in a certain direction regardless of the parent's will. In terms of his strategy, then, it is the narrator's communication rather than possession of knowledge that varies. He knows all that he wants to know, conveys what we need to know in order to infer the rest. The only reason why he does not "know" foreign custom is that he has not the least desire to know it, far less to make it known as the mainspring of his national plot.

Though Polzin's argument impugns the narrator's omniscience to explain the workings rather than the genesis of discourse, it runs into straits of the same order and ultimately defeats itself. Granting all that he claims about the ambiguity of naming in the Samson tale, the sting of its ironies cannot yet be turned against the teller (or the Deuteronomist) himself. To put it at its briefest: if the narrator devised the ambiguity, he perforce could, if he would, devise lucidity or what would count as such in context; and if he could devise lucidity, he must be credited with it no matter what his actual choice of tactics. "We find ourselves in the midst of obscurity because the Deuteronomist has led us there"[11]: precisely, and for that very reason we must not equate him with the dimness and the dim-sighted of his own making. The less so because high privileges tend to go together, and it would be a very strange narrator who would show himself in full control of his reader without being in the know as well. He would become still stranger, if possible, when conceived of as omniscient in some contexts (e.g., Samson's mind) and benighted in others (e.g., Samson's geography). As superhuman attributes are not divisible, worst of all, any attempt to divest the narrator of omniscience in one place would reflect on his status in all others, certainly reducing him to unreliability concerning the mysteries of heaven and earth. If he cannot explain so much as a name, how can he explain the world and its fortunes? Can the blind lead the blind? To undercut the narrator's cognitive authority is thus to launch a chain reaction that ends by undercutting God's own—whose exaltation by antithesis to humanity motivates Polzin's hypothesis in the first place. Rather, for God to be exalted, the narrator must be equally exempted from the darkness that he throws about human action and vision.

This will suffice to indicate the rule of duality in communication that the following chapters will systematically explore. Generally speaking, there are three areas or dimensions of narrative where the narrator does not evenly or fully exercise his privileges, with an eye to opacity or even downright incoherence. He abstains from (1) sharing with the reader all the plot information accessible to him; (2) elucidating structure and signification; (3) passing judgment by way of commentary. However wide the resultant variety of mode and combination in his narrative performance—I shall argue—it all falls under the strategic principle of maneuvering between the truth and the whole truth. And however wide the range of effects, they are all subsumed by the play of ambiguity and the processing of meaning. Let us start with a tale that radicalizes all three departures from straightforward communication.

·6·

GAPS, AMBIGUITY, AND
THE READING PROCESS[1]

Leave (as in despair)
Moral and end and motive in the air;
Nice contradiction between fact and fact
Will make the whole read human and exact.
Robert Graves, "The Devil's Advice
to Story-Tellers"

The Literary Work as a System of Gaps

To understand a literary work, we have to answer, in the course of reading, a series of such questions as: What is happening or has happened, and why? What connects the present event or situation to what went before, and how do both relate to what will probably come after? What are the features, motives, or designs of this or that character? How does he view his fellow characters? And what norms govern the existence and conduct of all? It is the set of answers given that enables the reader to reconstruct the field of reality devised by the text, to make sense of the represented world.

Yet a closer look at the text will reveal how few of the answers to these questions have been explicitly provided there: it is the reader himself who has supplied them, some temporarily, partially, or tentatively, and some wholly and finally. The world of situations and dramas constructed by the reader—causal sequence and all—is far from identical with what he encounters in the form of overt statement. From the viewpoint of what is directly given in the language, the literary work consists of bits and fragments to be linked and pieced together in the process of reading: it establishes a system of gaps that must be filled in. This gap-filling ranges from simple linkages of elements, which the reader performs automatically, to intricate networks that are figured out consciously, laboriously, hesitantly, and with constant modifications in the light of additional information disclosed in later stages of the reading. Even genres considered far from sophisticated— say, children's literature—demand such gap-filling. A well-known nursery rhyme in Hebrew, "Little Jonathan," goes like this:

Every day, that's the way
Jonathan goes out to play.
Climbed a tree. What did he see?
Birdies: one, two, three!

Naughty boy! What have we seen?
There's a hole in your new jeans!

How did the jeans get torn? The reader is quite sure that the tree is respon-sible for the big hole in little Jonathan's trousers; it hardly occurs to him that the hole could, perhaps, be from some fence that the boy crawled under the previous evening. The reader automatically opts for the first of the two possibilities, even though there is no explicit statement in the song to the effect that the trousers got torn in tree climbing or that there had not been any hole in them before Jonathan approached the tree. The hole could have been mentioned, after all, simply as part of a description of Jonathan's jeans. But the reader prefers the hypothesis that the tree is to blame, because it enables him to link the tree (just indicated in the song) and the hole into a causal chain. This hypothesis offers the simplest and most probable explanation for the coexistence and unfolding of the different givens in the text: it creates maximal relevance among the diverse features and levels (that's what happens to children who climb trees to harm little birds—even the pointed "What have we seen?" is thus justified) and brings together more elements than the alternative hypothesis (the hole was already there before the boy climbed the tree). Hence its appeal and validity. All the same, this still remains a hypothesis, whose preference over others entirely derives from the logic of gap-filling. The closure of the central gap in "Little Jonathan" is (a) automatic (so that it is absurd to discuss it at such length); and yet (b) essential to the reader's making sense of the "poem" as a whole.

In works of greater complexity, the filling-in of gaps becomes much more difficult and therefore more conscious and anything but automatic. The reader cannot take in his stride such problems as: Why do the two Hemingway gangsters, Al and Max, want to kill Anderson the Swede? What was Abraham's state of mind while answering the question "Where is the lamb for the burnt offering?" put to him by his son Isaac? Why does Faulkner's Emily Grierson murder her lover? What has Tristram Shandy's crushed nose to do with his character and fortunes? Or how does a nose, wrapped up and thrown into the river, appear "in various places in the form of a state councilor. . . . And then too, how could the nose have got into the roll of bread, and how could Ivan Yakovlevich himself? . . ."[2]

To emphasize the active role played by the reader in constructing the world of a literary work is by no means to imply that gap-filling is an arbitrary process. On the contrary, in this as in other operations of reading, literature is remarkable for its powers of control and validation. Of course, gap-filling may nevertheless be performed in a wild or misguided or tendentious fashion, and there is no lack of evidence for this in criticism ancient and modern. But to gain cogency, a hypothesis must be legitimated by the text.

Illegitimate gap-filling is one launched and sustained by the reader's subjective concerns (or dictated by more general preconceptions) rather than by the text's own norms and directives. A case in point is the readings to which the rabbis subject biblical stories. The hypotheses they frame are often based on assumptions that have no relevance to the world of the Bible (e.g., that Jacob and Esau went to school), receive no support whatever from the textual details, or even fill in what the narrative itself rules out. Where there's a will, the midrash will always find a way.

The David and Bathsheba story, for example, confronted the rabbis with what was to them a formidable problem: How is it possible that a king of Israel, and the author of the Psalms at that, should be guilty of adultery? The most prevalent of the solutions devised (and they all form instances of gap-filling) is that David did *not* commit adultery, because Uriah had divorced Bathsheba before leaving for the front line. As Rabbi Shmuel Bar Nakhmani contends, "Whoever says that David sinned is totally mistaken. . . . How could he fall into sin while the Divine Presence rested upon him? . . . Under the house of David, whoever went forth into battle would give his wife a letter of divorce" (*Shabbat* 56a). But this whitewashing still leaves unexplained the sharp rebuke delivered by the prophet Nathan, the parable of the Poor Man's Ewe-Lamb and all, and David's own confession of guilt. So some interpretive rule like "If you can't ignore it, then minimize it" is brought to bear on the narrative: David gets off with the most venial sin possible under the circumstances. "Still, the thing was ugly," one traditional commentator says, "because the custom was that the husband would remarry her on his return from the war" (Metsudat David on 2 Samuel 11:8). David's sin accordingly shrinks from adultery to wife-stealing.

As often, the questions troubling the rabbis here are certainly legitimate and indeed point to a central gap in the tale. But their answers, as hypotheses, stand or fall on their congruity with the text's own norms. Thus judged, the presentation of David as an offender against decorum rather than morality shows up as tendentious and idealizing. Such a reading, designed to reconcile David's conduct in the Bathsheba affair with the favorable (and ideologically vital) impressions he produces in other parts of Samuel, betrays the typical marks of an arbitrary hypothesis. It imposes on the world represented in the tale a socioreligious law (pre-battle divorce) consonant with the culture and world view of the reader; it has no anchorage in the textual details, and even clashes with some givens.

Far from arbitrary, then, the process of hypothetical reconstruction is variously directed and circumscribed by such factors as:

a. the different materials—actional, thematic, normative, structuring—explicitly communicated by the text;

b. the work's language and poetics;

c. the perceptual set established by the work's generic features;[3]

d. the special nature and laws and regularities of the world it projects, as impressed on the reader starting from the first page;

e. basic assumptions or general canons of probability derived from "everyday life" and prevalent cultural conventions.

It is "natural" or "probable," we reason by appeal to (e), that such and such a person should act in such and such a way. The reader tends to "adjust" the narrated world, as far as possible, to such premises and models, since the hypothesis that is most conventional in terms of his own culture also yields the simplest and certainly the least demanding answers and linkages. But the reader will often abandon (e) in favor of (d) and the like under the pressure of criteria other than simplicity. The most obvious is the historical sense and context or, negatively speaking, the deterrent of anachronism. Another, also mentioned, lies in the appeal of the hypothesis that organizes the maximum of elements in the most cohesive patterns. And there is always the attraction of the gap-filling that presents things in the most interesting light. So whenever the work fails to provide an explicit answer to the reader's questions—that is, to the questions it itself raises—these struggle to form the mimetic basis for the adoption or rejection of hypotheses.[4]

All these factors and criteria will soon appear in dynamic and often conflicting action. At this stage it is sufficient to introduce them as the dramatis personae of literary reconstruction.

The immediate sequel proposes to do two things. We shall first trace the narrative technique that shapes the story of David and Bathsheba (2 Samuel 11). Although the story is part of an extended cycle—the history of David's reign—the techniques traced are especially distinctive of this particular link in the chain. We shall above all be concerned with the gaps in the tale's world: their nature, their location, their equivocation, and their effects on the reader from opening to closure. The final section will then move from the particular to the general, so as to bring out some of the implications of the analysis for the reading process and the structure of the literary text. This in turn will pave the way for some further exploration of biblical poetics in later chapters, with special regard to a set of intimately though not obviously connected principles: suppressive narration under the constraints of truth-telling and intelligibility, the relevance of absence, the arts of temporal displacement, the ambiguation of character and event, not to mention the overarching law of meaning as quest and process.

The Story of David and Bathsheba

On the Narrator's Reticence and Omissions

2 Samuel 11 tells a brutal and shocking story, which exposes the king's twofold crime. But the chapter does not call the ugly deeds by their names. The chain of events is presented in a neutral manner, as it were, without comment or judgment; these the narrator leaves to the reader. Such a method does not simply follow from the biblical norm of narration. Compare this chapter with, say, the opening of Job. There the narrator time and again resorts to moralistic epithets ("perfect and upright, one that feared God and eschewed evil") and value judgments ("in all this Job sinned not"); here, he gives no *direct* moral characterization of David or his actions. Nor does he delegate this task to his dramatis personae. After all, a narrator averse to direct and explicit condemnation of the hero's villainy can still put the words of judgment into the mouths of other characters and use their reaction to mold the reader's. Such a delegation of judgment indeed marks the immediate sequel to the Bathsheba affair: the rape of Tamar by her brother Amnon. Tamar brands her brother's assault as "outrage," upbraids him for the "great wrong" he has done her, and departs weeping aloud, with ashes on her head. Nothing of the kind fractures the surface of the David and Bathsheba narrative. Up to verse 27, which ends the chapter and effects a transition to the ensuing developments, not a voice is raised against the king. Even Uriah himself—*if* aware of his master's doings—prefers a charged silence to crying out against injustice. It is as if nothing has happened, and the narrative flows on briskly, without interruption.

Omniscient but far from omnicommunicative, moreover, the narrator limits himself in another direction as well. He presents external occurrences alone, deeds and words, leaving his agents' inner lives opaque[5]—

even though in a dramatic narrative of this type it is precisely the motives and thoughts of the characters that interest the reader most. To understand what is going on, the reader must assume here the existence of emotions, passions, fears, and scheming; but he can infer them, if at all, from externals alone. He must puzzle over enigmas like: Does Uriah know?—and this is not easy to resolve—as well as provide answers to relatively simple questions like: Why does David summon Uriah to Jerusalem? The narrator himself, however, evades all explicit formulation of hidden thoughts and designs, thus creating the central gaps in the plot sequence.

Again, this reticence on the narrator's part is not the law of biblical narrative. The Bible, to be sure, does not linger on mental processes, nor, except by indirection, does it go so deep as to expose their undercurrents. Still, it is interspersed with inside views like "David understood that the child was dead" (2 Sam 12:19) or "Then Amnon hated her exceedingly; so that the hatred wherewith he hated her was greater than the love wherewith he had loved her" (2 Sam 13:15).[6] In contrast, the tale of David and Bathsheba not only elides those states of mind (e.g., the king's designs on Uriah) that are as crucial to its plot as to its morality. What is even more striking, it also dwells on minor episodes and details, which seem grotesquely overtreated in a tale otherwise so frugal. Coming after the statement that Uriah has been killed and that Joab has sent a messenger "and told David all the things concerning the war," for example, verses 19–25 cannot but appear superfluous, because the information about the central line of development is already in our hands and needs no rehearsing. The scene of Joab's instructions to his messenger looks especially wordy and redundant. This elaboration of details throws into high relief the skimping of essentials: the main story is for the most part implied rather than stated.

No overt judgment, from without or within the world, no going behind externals and, on top of it all, not even an intelligible proportioning of emphasis. Intimations of modernism? Perhaps. Certainly not standard novelistic, let alone ancient, practice. The suppression of essentials, the narrator's pseudo-objectivity, and the tone rendering the horror as if it were an everyday matter: all these create an extreme ironic discordance between the tale's mode of presentation and the action itself, as reconstructed and evaluated by the reader.

Biblical narratives are notorious for their sparsity of detail. Yet our chapter—especially because it leaves mental states and causes and processes opaque—is frugal to excess even relative to the biblical norm. And the resultant gaps have been left open precisely at key points, central to the discourse as a dramatic progression as well as a structure of meaning and value. Hence their filling in here is not automatic but requires considerable attention to the nuances of the text, both at the level of the represented events and at the level of language; far from a luxury or option, closure becomes a necessity for any reader trying to understand the story even in the simplest terms of what happens and why.

The extremes to which the David and Bathsheba narration goes will emerge more sharply against the background of the Binding of Isaac, an episode celebrated for leaving details in obscurity. Indeed, the Bible gives us no access to what passes in Abraham's mind after loading the firewood on Isaac's back (Genesis 22). A close reading of the exchange between son and father ("But where is the lamb for the burnt offering?"—"God will provide himself the lamb for the burnt offering, my son") may enable us to fill in the gap and reconstruct the father's thoughts after a fashion. (After a fashion, because the reconstruction will remain dim and fragmentary, even if it exploits the well-known ambiguity—between a vocative and an appositional reading of "my son"—in the response). But the focus of interest lies in Abraham's supreme obedience regardless of any possible thought. His state of mind thus becomes of secondary importance. An insight into it would doubtless enrich the drama, and the reader concerned with realizing the text's potentialities in full will cast about for clues; but this will at best round things out. The point will be made and taken even with this gap left open. The main omissions in the Isaac story stand opposed, then, to their centralized and inescapable counterparts in the story of David and Bathsheba. In between these poles falls the Wooing of Rebekah, where closure makes quite a difference—but more to thematic than to plot intelligibility. Narratives are thus distinguishable by the position assigned to their system of gaps.

Far from reducible to a single mechanical norm, the functionality as well as the weight and peremptoriness of the numerous gaps in the Bible widely vary from one context to another. This function depends on the relations between the suppressed and the given. In the Isaac ordeal, the system of gaps is so fashioned as to play down anything which might disturb concentration on the main point; it operates to foreground the father's admirable conduct at the expense of "all the rest," sacrificing thought to action just as the hero himself does. Here, therefore, it is the essentials that are given, and the subsidiaries correspondingly held back in more than one sense: the Binding of Isaac resorts to systematic omission in order to establish (and impress on the reader) a hierarchy of importance.

In the David and Bathsheba context, however, the essentials are precisely what the narrator chooses to withhold. Crafty and devious, he takes advantage of the fact that the reader himself will have to provide whatever has been left out. And the system of gaps, developed primarily to direct attention to what has *not* been communicated, becomes the central device whereby the narrator gradually establishes his ironic framework. The incongruity between the scales of importance and representation makes for ironic understatement. And the David and Bathsheba imbroglio gives him an opportunity to carry this favorite mode of narration to a rare extreme.

The Ironic Exposition

The tale's opening verse (see next paragraph) appears purely expositional, serving no other purpose than to impart some necessary background data: the time of the incident, the war then being waged, the location of the characters. But this seemingly innocent information warrants a second look, for what is smuggled into it already marks the beginnings of the ironic perspective.

This exposition falls into two main parts, conspicuously asymmetrical:

> (1a) At the turn of the year, at the time when kings go forth to battle, David sent Joab and his servants with him and all Israel, and they ravaged the Ammonites and besieged Rabbah,
>
> (1b) and David stayed in Jerusalem.

Of the two, the first part stands out, not only by reason of its length relative to the second, but also due to the piling up of details, far in excess of the narrator's norm in the book. For example, the list "Joab and his servants with him and all Israel" could be justified in informational terms were it to appear as prelude to a war story centering in Joab and his army. But in an opening to an episode from king David's private life—where the war figures only as background—these minutiae parade their superfluity and call for motivation.[7] This brings into play a basic strategy of reading.

In a sentence where, as here, a short segment follows an exceptionally long one and the two correspond in some way, we tend to draw out our reading of the shorter segment in order to make it equivalent (at least perceptually) to the reading time of its longer mate. Therefore, while the leading part of verse 1 is quickly assimilated (the more so as we perceive how it goes on and on), the short counterpart arrests our attention. The reader lingers over each individual word, creating significant pauses in between:

veDavid	*yoshev*	*birushalayim*
and David	stayed	in Jerusalem

The device of dilatory progress activates and foregrounds a complex of implicit meanings that go far beyond geographical stage-setting.

These features of the opening direct the reader to view the king (who tarries at home) in ironic contrast to all the others (whom he has sent to make war): "David" as against "Joab and his servants with him and all Israel"; "stayed" (literally, "sat") as against "ravaged . . . and besieged": "Jerusalem" as against "Rabbah." The contrast also exploits all the seemingly redundant detail of the first part: the listing of "Joab and his servants with him and all Israel" produces the momentary impression that no one at all remained in Jerusalem except David. This makes an effective introduction to a story where one of the central ironies is: What is the king doing in his city while the nation is fighting in the field?

Note that the covertness of the irony is in inverse proportion to the solidity of the cultural norms to which it appeals. In the world of Samuel, actual military leadership figures as a (and in the eyes of the people, even as the) major criterion for evaluating a king. After all, the monarchy owes its very rise, in the face of the prophet's most awful warnings, to the Israelite determination to have a king "go out before us and fight our battles" (1 Sam 8:19). And the observance of this social contract, in suggestive correlation with the divine scheme of values throughout, indeed proves to make and break the king. Though officially elected and anointed, Saul's hold on power remains shaky until he achieves his first victory (11:5–15). Later, his falling out of divine favor goes with a loss of nerve and initiative: the morbid hate for David stems precisely from envy of the young man's daring leadership, which increases his prestige at the expense of the stay-at-home king. "All Israel and Judah loved David, for he went and came in before them" (18:19); and when the people offer David the throne, they bluntly state that even during Saul's nominal kingship, "thou wert the one that led out and brought in Israel" (2 Sam 5:2). It therefore leaps to the eye that this is the first war in which David fails to lead the army in person. Nor, in view of the contract and the precedent, is it accidental that this war marks his decline in the esteem of man as well as God. Only because the underlying norms are so univocal can the narrator radicalize indirection and ambiguity without compromising his moral any more than his artistic code. At one point, indeed, he slyly alludes to the governing norm itself.

"At the time when kings go forth to battle" (literally, "at the time of the kings' going forth") seems to be no more than an expositional indication of time. It is either a ready-made phrase that refers to the season of spring by way of periphrasis (a season when it does not rain, the roads are in good condition, there is plenty of fodder for war horses, and hence the time of year usually chosen by kings to lead out their armies) or a reference to a particular historical date (one year after the kings of Aram went forth to join the Ammonites against Israel). In either the idiomatic or the literal sense, this time-reference has no direct bearing on David. But the emphasis laid on "David stayed in Jerusalem" in the sequel builds a thematic bridge of irony between the beginning and the end of the verse. The dynamic norm foregrounds the static exception; the phrase that speaks of kings going forth to war turns a spotlight on the king who "is sitting" at home. The narrator thus devises an oblique and subtle exposure. The incongruity would have been glaring had its two members been placed in immediate succession: "At the time when kings go forth, David stayed in Jerusalem." As it stands, the text refines the effect by keeping these incompatibles as far apart as possible and filling the in-between space with who-what-where details which give the impression of innocent adherence to the factuality of a chronicle.

The numerous occurrences of the coordinator *ve* ("and") in the leading part of the verse reinforce the impression of an artless and strictly informative account. For they encourage the reader, by force of inertia, to take the *ve* of "veDavid yoshev" ("*and* David stayed") as yet another coordinative "and," which merely tacks a final piece of information on to the list. Although the ironic patterning soon turns this *and* into a *but,* this reading does not implicate the "innocent" narrator.[8]

On the face of it, then—and in terms of a naive reading—the details of the exposition combine into an additive structure, linking item to factual item by way of loose conjunction. In fact, they are tightly organized as a contrastive analogy, projecting a different, implied, charged meaning.

The ironic line established at the beginning will be further developed to the very end under cover of that synchronous action: the war. The story of the war is not collocated with the David and Bathsheba story merely because it happened to occur at the same time (although this supplies a "realistic" pretext or motivation for their interweaving). Nor is its relevance to the David and Bathsheba affair confined to the dimension of metonymic linkages (or patterns), as a state of affairs that makes possible both the king's dalliance with Bathsheba as grass widow and, later, the murder of Uriah. It also serves to construct metaphoric linkages—based on parallelism—by turning an ironic spotlight on what takes place in the city. If in the first role the war operates along the sequence of plot, then in the second it deploys a network of oppositions that interpret that sequence.

This interpretive function of the war materials controls their distribution along the text. The narrative opens (11:1) with a reference to the campaign; it concludes (12:26–31) with a description of the victory. Thus the war story frames the personal drama. This positioning of the victory, however, is not at all due to chronological exigencies. Before he comes to mention it, the narrator traces a whole chain of family events: the birth and death of the baby, Bathsheba's new pregnancy, and the birth of Solomon. And the victory surely antedates (part of) this chain of events, for the siege of Rabbah did not last two years. In fact, the tale's principle of montage sacrifices chronology to structural-thematic considerations, and the narrator so manipulates the sequence as to introduce the victory only *after* bringing the personal story to an end. It is only then that he doubles back in time and reveals the antecedents, which assume greater significance by being deferred to this late point:

> Joab fought against Ammonite Rabbah and captured the royal city. And Joab sent messengers to David, and said, I have fought against Rabbah, and also captured the city of waters. Now therefore gather the rest of the people together and encamp against the city and capture it: lest I capture the city, and it be called after my name. And David gathered all the people together and went to Rabbah and fought against it and captured it. And he took their king's crown from off his head, its weight a talent of gold and precious stones in it; and it was set on David's head. . . . Then David and all the people returned to Jerusalem. (12:26–31)

The delay of the victory to the end preserves narrative continuity in the personal sequence of events. Moreover, the victory (unlike the outbreak of the war) is not a necessary condition for the management of the David and Bathsheba plot. But its telling in the context of the main plot raises it above mere chronicle: the war story becomes an indirect means of shaping and elucidating the David and Bathsheba story itself. Here the selection of materials becomes as revealing as their distribution. Why does the narrator vary from the book's norm of keeping down military tactics to a minimum? And given this sudden disproportion, why does he devote his account of the final stage not to the real conquest of Rabbah by Joab but to David's (literally) nominal conquest, spoils and all?—Because the slanted details of the victory fashion a wry counterpoint to the personal doings of the victor. The king has stayed in Jerusalem, others have waged his war, he reaps the fruits of a subordinate's campaign and gives the city his own name: a fitting last note of ironic commentary on the tale of a king who steals a subordinate's wife and sees to it that she "be called after his name."[9]

What Is the King Doing in the City?

> (2) One evening, David arose from his bed and walked about upon the roof of the king's house and saw from the roof a woman bathing; and the woman was very good-looking. (3) And David sent and inquired about the woman. And one said, Is not this Bathsheba, the daughter of Eliam, the wife of Uriah the Hittite? (4) And David sent messengers and took her, and she came to him and he lay with her, and she was

purifying herself from her uncleanness, and she returned to her house. (5) And the woman conceived, and she sent and told David, I am with child.

In verse 2, with its movement from the general to the concrete ("One evening"), the exposition gives way to the narrative present itself. Again, the narrator "innocently" relates external events: the king rises in the evening and walks about on the roof. Yet the reader cannot but see this verse in the light of the preceding one and go on to develop the ironic oppositions set up there. In contrast to the nation fighting at Rabbah, the king is leading a life of idleness in Jerusalem, taking his leisurely siesta, getting up in the evening, and strolling about on his roof.

Now, for the first time, the failure to communicate the thoughts and feelings of the characters becomes perceptible. David observes "a woman bathing" from the roof and makes inquiries about her. Yet Bathsheba's beauty is presented in the narrator's impersonal style—"And the woman was very good-looking"—even though it is the protagonist's emotions that matter at this point, since they cause and explain his actions. Instead of finding the inner life specified in the interests of plot coherence, the reader can only infer their general drift *from* the plot (in the light of "David sent and inquired about the woman and . . . sent messengers and took her").[10]

Does David fall in love with Bathsheba, to the loss of mental balance, or is he seized by a momentary passion? The narrator leaves this crux indeterminate and our curiosity unsatisfied in order to exploit both later. Furthermore, having adopted an "objective" posture as ironist, he leaves to the reader both the inference that David lusts for a married woman and the condemnation of the king,[11] while himself saying nothing at all.[12] His matter-of-fact registration, far from speaking out against the king's conduct, pretends that the narrative traces a natural and ordinary chain of events, devoid of any special interest:

> David sent and inquired about the woman. And one said, Is not this Bathsheba, the daughter of Eliam, the wife of Uriah the Hittite? And David sent messengers and took her, and she came to him and he lay with her . . . and she returned to her house.

The note or pose of "there is nothing much to tell" mainly arises from the paratactic series of verbs, which make up the bulk of the passage and laconically unroll a rapid sequence of external actions in almost assembly-line fashion: David sent, inquired, sent, took, lay—"and she returned to her house"; nothing seems to have happened. The clash between matter and manner in the discourse greatly sharpens the irony, which develops by steady escalation. It starts with a king who does not go to war, moves on to a king who leads a life of idleness, then to a king who commits adultery with the wife and lays traps for the husband, and will reach its climax with a king who perpetrates murder.

The verses just quoted present the assembly-line of events in their chronological order. But "and he lay with her" is actually followed by an exceptional conjunct that I omitted to quote: "and she was purifying herself from her uncleanness." This unit, whose location and grammar signify not an action but a description of Bathsheba's state, breaks the otherwise chronological line of development. What is more, not only does it seem out of place in terms of dramatic logic, but the reference to "purification" (and as an ongoing process at that) after "he lay with her" is simply absurd. So the reader must wonder: Why is this information necessary? And why here of all places? That the sentence is so perceptibly incongruous (and superfluous) launches another search for coherence.

The reader's immediate move is to relate this item to "from the roof he saw a woman bathing" of verse 2, as a retrospective motivation for the bathing. But even making sense of it in terms of plot does not yet explain the unnatural order of presentation: Why has the flashback been torn out of place and delayed to verse 4 only to be so oddly conjoined? In trying, nevertheless, to justify its position, we wonder: does the text wish to show a meritorious side of David, who has indeed slept with another man's wife but did not transgress the laws of menstrual purity?[13] Such a justification, replacing one incongruity by another, has, of course, an immediate ironic effect.[14]

Only in retrospect, when verse 5 comes to Bathsheba's pregnancy, does the relevance of "and she was purifying herself from her uncleanness" emerge. This detail, ostensibly so pointless in context, enables the reader to infer and nail down David's paternity. Even though the omniscient narrator (remaining true to his suppressive method) does not say this in so many words, there is surely no possibility of Uriah's being the father. This gap-filling wholly resolves the collocation of the troublesome phrase with "and he lay with her," and what was previously taken as an objective and impartial recording of external facts now turns into a covert indictment. Even more ironic, the very detail that might at first have been interpreted as the sole meritorious feature of David's act ("and he did not transgress the laws of menstrual purity") twists around to condemn him. Yet once again the indictment is pieced out by the reader, while the "innocent" narrator can deny having had any hand in it.

This again shows how the Bible exploits the fact that literature is a time-art, in which the textual continuum is apprehended in a temporal continuum and things unfold sequentially rather than simultaneously. In its withholding and gapping of information, the text makes use of the reader's reluctance or inability to wait until the end for closures that may never come. Instead, he endeavors at each stage to pattern the materials already presented as logically and completely as possible, even to anticipate what the future holds, constantly attempting to infer from the given to the hidden. It is in order to illustrate this dynamics that we shall reconstruct the gap-filling process step by step, through a "linear" reading.

Uriah the Hittite Recalled to Jerusalem

> (6) David sent word to Joab, Send me Uriah the Hittite. And Joab sent Uriah to David. (7) And Uriah came to him and David asked how Joab fared, and how the people fared, and how the war fared. (8) And David said to Uriah, Go down to thy house and wash thy feet. And Uriah went out of the king's house and there went out after him a gift from the king. (9) And Uriah slept at the door of the king's house with all the servants of his lord, and did not go down to his house. (10) And they told David, saying, Uriah did not go down to his house. And David said to Uriah, Hast thou not come from a journey? Wherefore didst thou not go down to thy house? (11) And Uriah said to David, The Ark and Israel and Judah dwell in booths, and my lord Joab and the servants of my lord are encamped in the open field; shall I then go to my house, to eat and to drink and to lie with my wife? As thou livest and as thy soul lives, I will not do this thing. (12) And David said to Uriah, Stay here today also, and tomorrow I will let thee depart; and Uriah stayed in Jerusalem that day and the next. (13) And David invited him, and he ate in his presence and drank, and he made him drunk; and in the evening he went out to lie on his bed with the servants of his lord, and did not go down to his house.

Uriah is summoned to Jerusalem. But why? Again, the narrator's strategy of confining himself to externals, chronicle fashion, leaves David's plans hidden and indeterminable, even though they are undoubtedly at the center of the reader's interest. Does the king wish to confess to Uriah? To ask for his forgiveness? To bully or perhaps to bribe him? The informational gaps leave room, at this stage, for various conjectures—some of them "positive"—about the king's motives. His true intentions once clarified, however, the positive hypotheses will boomerang; and this shift from the meritorious to the villainous will then help to sustain the chapter's overall ironic thrust. This is an example of *potential* gap-filling, artfully exploited even though it does not become actual. For the effect produced on the reader by a literary text does not rest only on the final conclusions he reaches on turning the last page; it embraces all the impressions, true or false, generated in the course of his reading. Even though our tale will later eliminate the "positive" hypotheses, they will in the meantime have played their role. Both their evocation and their elimination thus contribute to the overall effect.

Take the (relatively) detailed reception scene:

> Uriah came to him, and David asked how Joab fared, and how the people fared, and how the war fared.

While what really matters (even on the simplest level of plot intelligibility) has been withheld, this polite conversation is accorded liberal ("how . . . how . . . how") treatment. For a moment the reader is impressed by David's friendly attitude, and the positive hypotheses come to the fore. When David ends the audience with "Go down to thy house and wash thy feet," this impression hardens further. The king's concern for his weary soldier seems beyond doubt, and something like affection is expressed in the "gift" he sends after him.

Hence the tendency to interpret the reception scene as a preparatory delay on the king's part, for Uriah would not have been summoned to Jerusalem just for a friendly chat. For a moment, even Uriah's being sent to his home looks like an additional delay: the main business has, understandably enough, been put off to the next day. And meanwhile let Uriah go down to his house, wash his feet, rest from the fatigue of the journey, regale himself with the king's delicacies, and . . . And here comes the shock of enlightenment. Once we bring this course of relaxation to its natural climax, a different pattern altogether forces itself on us. What was taken as a mere delay, prior to the main encounter, is now revealed to be the king's real and diabolical scheme in its full force and extent: Uriah has been summoned to Jerusalem and sent to his house for no other purpose than to lie with his wife and thus cover up the king's paternity. The irony rises to one of its peaks when, by another of the tale's cutting reversals, it turns out that the king's scheme lurks within the very words that seemed to express his friendship and affection. But it is not the narrator who has formulated that scheme. All the responsibility for condemning the king rests with the reader alone.

Uriah does not object to the king's suggestion: "Uriah went out of the king's house, and there went out after him a gift from the king. And Uriah lay . . ."—with Bathsheba? For a moment it looks as though the king's plan is going to work, but the text immediately veers around: "—at the door of the king's house with all the servants of his lord, and did not go down to his house." Again, with units small as well as large, the sequence of the text is exploited to arouse expectations which will be immediately dashed in an ironic collapse. The narrator will repeat this miniature device of inversion further on, in verse 13, when he comes to the third night. On that night, David gets Uriah drunk and the chances of success appear to increase. Indeed, "in the evening he went out to lie on his bed"—on his own bed at home? With his wife? No, on his bed of the past two nights, "with the servants of his lord, and did not go down to his house."

Note that making these value-laden inferences is not just a license that the reader may take or leave at will. Given the pressures of coherence, it is a responsibility that he must assume. For to one who contents himself with what the text states outright, the meetings between David and Uriah will appear rather strange, if not comic. Having summoned Uriah to Jerusalem at a critical juncture, the king chats with him politely but to no purpose, and waves him home to rest. On the next day he expresses further concern about his guest's welfare and asks why instead of going home he made do with an uncomfortable bed in the palace. He suggests that Uriah should spend another day in town, without yet saying anything material to him, and promises that the next day he will send him back to the front. But for no apparent reason, this pointless stay of Uriah's drags on for yet another day. On the third evening the king comes to treat his subordinate with the greatest familiarity, carousing with him and getting him drunk. Still no hint of business. Only on the fourth day does he send him back, with "new instructions," which is something he could have done three days before. Uriah himself, if he does not know of his wife's infidelity, must have wondered at this tardiness in the middle of a war.

It is the sheer frivolity and irrelevance of these goings-on that direct the reader all the more forcefully to the implicit linkages, which he must work out for himself. As always, the incongruity between the appearance of the events and their true nature, radicalized by frequent inversions, has a distinctly ironic effect. The king's solicitude for his guest appears to grow from day to day, reaching a climax in the wining and dining. But what actually increases is his anxiety to bring off his villainous scheme. Stage by stage this hope fades and David goes from bad to worse.

Does Uriah Know about His Wife's Doings? The Twofold Hypothesis

The surprising "did not go down to his house" opens a gap at another focal point. The question why Uriah fails to make a beeline for home links up with a more central enigma: *Does Uriah know of his wife's infidelity and pregnancy?* The text does not permit any univocal answer: both affirmative and negative hypotheses arise with a legitimate claim to gap-filling. Each of these hypotheses is indicated and reinforced by a good number of arguments, while other arguments draw attention to its flaws and support the rival answer. And each hypothesis sheds a different light on details in the text and organizes them into a different plot. The narrative deliberately creates this impossibility of deciding between the two alternative systems of gap-filling. It demands that both be maintained simultaneously, and thus profits from their tense interaction. (Later we shall see that such composition is not peculiar to the Bathsheba story, but forms a basic principle of the literary text and a key to biblical ambiguity.)

The possibility that Uriah knows nothing appears to the reader quite reasonable at the end of verse 8, in view of the secrecy that has cloaked the love affair between the king and Bathsheba ("and she returned to her house"; cf. also the later words of Nathan, "thou didst secretly"). For Uriah, encamped far away from home, to know of his wife's doings, there has to be someone to bear tales, in the army camp or at least in Jerusalem. But if the news of Bathsheba's adultery and pregnancy has leaked, there is not much point to David's cover-up operation, designed to make it appear that Uriah is the child's father. The fact that Uriah is summoned to Jerusalem argues that David is convinced of his ignorance. The reader is thus encouraged to assume the same.

Yet, however reasonable, these considerations do not rule out the opposed hypothesis. It is possible that though David assumes that the affair is not generally known in Jerusalem, he may not be up-to-date on the current gossip. It is even possible that David *knows* about the gossip circulating in the city and realizes that suspicion will turn into certainty when it becomes apparent to all that Bathsheba is pregnant even though her husband has been away for months; and precisely for this reason, to squelch what is at the moment no more than rumor, he tries to get Uriah into bed with his wife. Furthermore, that Uriah, on his arrival in Jerusalem, has learned of the affair (and if not of Bathsheba's pregnancy, then at least of her infidelity) is not at all impossible. A number of people are in the secret, for David used messengers to summon Bathsheba to him, and so in turn did Bathsheba to inform him of her pregnancy. So during his three days (and nights) at the palace, Uriah may have picked up some news. If the narrative wished to establish his ignorance, finally, it would resort to some formula like "and Uriah did not know," whose equivalents disambiguate even characters and contexts of far less significance.

The decision between these incompatibles, "Uriah knows" versus "Uriah does not know," is of great practical importance for David and may also be sought (in vain) by readers whose entire concern is the historical event. But to the reader who approaches this story as the work of art it is, any clear-cut choice between the two possibilities matters far less than a clear view of the *ways* in which the text produces an undecided fluctuation and interplay between the hypotheses, and of the *functions* of this undecidability. Rather than inviting himself to the narrative on his own terms, he will accept the narrator's invitation in the spirit in which it is extended: as a challenge to participate in the *making* of sense under a well-defined and demanding set of rules.

Notable among these rules is the seesaw movement of gap-filling along the sequence, the ups and downs appointed for each hypothesis vis-à-vis its rival(s). With ambiguous cruxes, the reader must no more expect (and impose) a quick than a facile resolution, not even one in the form of the permanent ambiguity of stalemate. Avoiding such premature closure, the Bible achieves its finest effects by drawing out the play of meaning through constant variations, from shift to reversal, in the balance of power. Thus, when the reader reaches verse 9, the "Uriah does not know" hypothesis seems to collapse entirely. If Uriah has no suspicions, why does he not go home? And to make sense of the new fact, the assumption that he knows of his wife's infidelity is not enough—he must also know of her pregnancy!

At *this* point, then, it is hard to form any alternative explanation for Uriah's strange refusal to go home after a long and arduous campaign. Even readers thus far so convinced of Uriah's being in the dark that no other reconstruction has occurred or appealed to them at all, will surely discover now that there *is* another possibility. Indeed, for a moment that possibility becomes something like an absolute certainty. But the balance is soon redressed. Verse 11 already enables the reader to reinstate the first hypothesis—that Uriah does not know—provided that we take Uriah's words at their face value:

> And Uriah said to David: The Ark and Israel and Judah dwell in booths, and my lord Joab and the servants of my lord are encamped in the open field; shall I then go to my house, to eat and to drink and to lie with my wife? As thou livest and as thy soul lives, I will not do this thing.

Taken literally, Uriah refrains from going home out of "idealistic" solidarity with his comrades and reverence for God's Ark. This projects the figure of Uriah as an exemplary soldier, a man of noble spirit and uncompromising conscience. When the reader comes to verse 13, his amazement grows further at the sight of the loyal soldier who, even in his cups, exhibits the same unwavering *esprit de corps.*[15]

Such a view of Uriah coheres with one of the ironic lines that goes back as early as the exposition: the contrast between the king in the city and the nation at war. So far the tale has developed this irony by opposing David's concrete behavior to the abstract concept of kingship (the kings, including David's former self, going forth to battle) and through the timing and location of his activities vis-à-vis his people's. Now this ironic line is carried forward through the indirect opposition drawn between the king and the perfect figure of a *concrete* warrior, Uriah. The hypothesis that Uriah is an idealist and that his words mean what they say thus fits in with tendencies long established in the text, and this argues in its favor.

In this light, Uriah's response to the king can be seen to contain a disguised but well-aimed thrust—one that goes home no matter whether the attacker is Uriah himself, who under a show of innocence delivers a sly blow, or whether the responsibility devolves on the narrator, who exploits Uriah's innocent outburst as a vehicle for his own criticism. Uriah declares he will not so much as approach his house while his comrades are encamped in the open field and "the Ark and Israel and Judah dwell in booths"; and the reader—prepared for the theme from the beginning—cannot but apply this norm to the king who dawdles at home in those very circumstances. What Uriah says about himself thus bears in context on the king's aberration and serves to evaluate it afresh.[16]

Moreover, verse 11 turns to new account the catalogue presented as early as verse 1, about Joab and his servants with him and all Israel besieging Rabbah. In the opening, with its nominal chronicle-like framework, this material figured as pure information; whereas here it appears as a reason in the framework of an argument against staying at home. Therefore, the irony at this point stands out more sharply. And if in verse 1 the ironic camouflage derived from the artless-looking exposition, here it lies in Uriah's professing to speak about himself, with no glance at the king. Like verse 1, finally, verse 11 goes into excessive detail ("Israel," "Judah," "my lord Joab," and "the servants of my lord," where "Joab and the army" would suffice). And this relisting further heightens the earlier ironic effect: the impression that no one in the entire nation is "staying at home"—and to judge by the absence of names throughout, certainly no one that counts—except for the adulterous king.

Note also that, in failing to go home, Uriah fails to comply with something not far from a royal order. From the hypothesis that insists on a literal reading of Uriah's explanation, it follows that because of his solidarity with his comrades and his commander (Joab) he is not prepared to bow to the authority of the supreme commander himself.[17] Seen in this light, even the details of Uriah's language become vehicles of irony. Uriah speaks of Joab as "my lord Joab," which is indeed how one makes a deferential reference to one's commanding officer. But in this particular context, the words "my lord" draw the reader's lingering attention, for they sound dangerously like "To me, *Joab* is my lord; and it is with *him* that I identify." Uriah even refers to the army by the ambiguous term "the servants of my lord": Joab's servants or David's? Is the army, to him, really Joab's?[18]

This question about loyalty gains further point in view of the wider linguistic context. In verse 9 the narrator speaks of the "servants of his lord" (meaning "David's servants," but deliberately avoiding specification), and he repeats the same phrase in verse 13 ("and in the evening he went out to lie on his bed with the servants of his lord"). These verbatim echoes— reminders that Uriah's formal lord is David—bring out by force of contrast the ironic sting in the nearby phrase "my lord Joab and the servants of my lord," with its two pieces of impertinence, one certain and the other ambiguous. Later, verse 24 will even dramatize a model for addressing royalty: "The archers shot at *thy servants* from off the wall; and some of the *king's servants* died, and *thy servant* Uriah the Hittite is also dead." The messenger's speech, with its phrasal variations on the theme of the people's "servanthood," Uriah's included, concretely establishes the norm of reference to the king.

Nor does Uriah rest content with a general negative. He proceeds to illustrate more specifically what to "go down to my house" means to a warrior on leave: "To eat and to drink and to lie with my wife." On the hypothesis that Uriah does not know, the innocent idealist has no idea that by this declaration he is stinging and defying the king to an even greater extent than he intended. But the reader, aware that David has made his suggestion only because he really wants Uriah to lie with his wife, goes on to construct this irony too. What the speaker contemptuously dismisses is the addressee's secret hope.

The hypothesis that Uriah does not know derives additional support from the fact that Uriah himself does not say that he knows. Why else does Uriah not raise an uproar about the wrong that has been done him and force a showdown with the king?[19] And this hypothesis, based on the possibility of viewing Uriah as a man of conscience, gains further probability if we consider David's behavior. David himself apparently believes that Uriah does not go home only out of solidarity with his comrades, and for this reason he detains Uriah in Jerusalem for two more days in the hope that earthly longing will finally prove stronger than idealistic commitment.[20] When this does not happen either, he gets Uriah drunk, apparently following the same line of reasoning (a man who is drunk is more liable to forget his loyalties to his comrades than his wife's betrayal). If a character who has directly observed Uriah's behavior and has come to know him not through the mediation of a multigap text but as a man of flesh and blood, is persuaded that Uriah is an "idealist," then the reader's willingness to endorse this interpretation grows by analogy.

Accordingly, if we assume that Uriah knows nothing, we must also assume that Uriah believes he has been summoned to Jerusalem to report on the military situation (verse 6) and transmit new orders (verse 14). It would seem that only a man who does not suspect the king's present intentions (now that his scheme has come to nothing) would bring a letter to Joab without examining its contents. A man aware that he has been deceived and that the king must be getting desperate at the thought of public exposure, would have opened the letter and then fled far beyond the reach of David's power.

But verse 9, we recall, encouraged the reader, at least temporarily, to make the opposite hypothesis, that *Uriah knows about his wife's infidelity.* And the reader cannot easily free himself from (sup)positions induced at earlier points in the reading. The less so since the conjecture that Uriah indeed knows has a good deal to recommend it. To start with, as we have already seen, there are quite a few people who must know about the affair—the pregnancy as well as the adultery—and if one of them has tipped Uriah off, this will readily explain several disturbing features in Uriah's behavior.

Uriah does not immediately respond, as a man acting from noble and even aggressive solidarity would have done, to the king's suggestion that he should go home to rest from his journey. Instead, he makes his declaration of faith only on the morrow, after the king has left him no other course. This looks like the behavior of a man forced into offering an excuse for actions he has performed for other reasons. Moreover, Uriah's "idealistic" behavior, taken at face value, is strange and unrealistic. It seems *too* heroic to be true. It is incredible that a soldier lucky enough to get leave should keep away from a beautiful wife, even if he draws the line at eating and drinking and lying with her. Does even a look-in appear to Uriah a breach of solidarity with the comrades besieging Rabbah? Recall, further, that Uriah lives very close to the palace, for otherwise the king could not have espied Bathsheba's charms as she bathed herself. And this topographical fact only underlines the strangeness of Uriah's conduct: he spends three nights at the entrance to the king's house, when a few more steps would bring him to his own.

On the reading that he knew of his wife's adultery, therefore, Uriah emerges as a more realistic and, above all, a more *complex* character. He does not hurl accusations at the king, does not raise an uproar, nor indulges in any extravagant behavior. It is hardly believable that he chooses this course in order to save his skin (the disrespectful address and the failure to open and read the letter suggest otherwise). Uriah opts for a response that is perhaps the most effective and impressive of all: an obstinate, proud silence. Even in the framework of this hypothesis there is—as we shall see—an ironic barb in Uriah's words to the king. But if coming from a man who "does not know" such irony is a piece of impertinence, then on the part of one who "knows" it is the least that could be expected. The reader can now construct the figure of Uriah as a complex personality torn between his sense of betrayal and his sense of duty. Uriah, on this reading, accepts his fate with an awe-inspiring dignity. He does not rebel against royal authority; he does not even open David's letter to Joab, despite his suspicions about its content. He has nothing left in life but a code of honor that equally forbids playing and exposing the king's dirty game. Except for an oblique protest against the king, therefore, he imposes silence on himself. But perhaps it is exactly by omission that Uriah takes a quiet revenge. For the king, unable to decide whether the man standing before him knows or not, is forced into his next and most heinous crime.

The Uriah who "knows" is a more alluring character, in the tensions and stresses he lives through, than the flat figure of the idealist. Not for the modern reader alone but also for the reader guided by the Bible's amazingly modern conceptions of character, the psychological appeal is another reason to cling to this hypothesis.

Even under the "Uriah knows" closure, we still find the indirect irony that attaches to the rival hypothesis, with several shifts of emphasis and perspective. The flick at the king dispatching others to wage his war changes its whole context once attributed not to a soldierly paragon speaking from the viewpoint of abstract solidarity but to a doubly betrayed man speaking from personal pain. Uriah's excuses for not going home then take the guise of matters of conscience. But when he details and illustrates his viewpoint ("to eat and to drink and to lie with my wife"), his specification no longer coheres in terms of a narrator who exploits a speaker's innocent outburst to slip in an irony of his own. It transforms into an innocence assumed by the speaker himself for ironic purposes. So the phrase "to lie with my wife" now reads not as just another item in an illustrative list but as the main point, which the whole list has been fabricated to disguise. The implication seems to be, "You want me to lie with my wife? Not a chance!" And in this light, the next sentence ("As thou livest and as thy soul lives, I will not do this thing") also takes on deliberate ambiguity. Overtly "this thing" refers to his going down to his house, but covertly it indicates "to lie with my wife." And now the dig at the king who stays at home also shifts its context and becomes a slap in the face. It is as if Uriah were saying: "I will not violate my solidarity with my comrades encamped in the field; I will not 'do this thing' and 'go to my house, to eat and to drink and to lie with my wife.' But *you* are the man who has been doing 'this thing,' sitting at home, eating and drinking and lying with 'my wife.'" The arguments that support the first hypothesis weaken the present alternative, and vice versa. These arguments have not been exhausted here, and additional ones can be produced for either side.[21]

In order to preserve his pseudo-objective tone and assumed artlessness, the narrator does not pass direct judgment on the king's actions, nor does he even turn his characters into overt normative mouthpieces. Yet Uriah is deftly employed as an agent of an implicit (and thus two-pronged) irony. And he performs this role no matter whether he himself shares this irony *with* the narrator (in which case the artful structure of meaning is motivated through a parallel lifelike pattern) or whether the narrator operates behind Uriah's back, manipulating the overt speaker's ignorance to communicate to the reader an ironic picture of David. If so far the irony has arisen only from the narrator's own discourse, then with Uriah's appearance a new kind of irony is introduced into the story: "motivated" irony, the ironic portrayal and judgment of one character by means of another. (Later on Joab will serve in a similar capacity.)

On the one hand, the narrator needs an agent who will show David up as an "idler" in the city, at home, while the nation is out at war. For an irony of this kind to produce the maximal evaluative effect, it must come from the viewpoint of conscientious "idealism." And in the framework of the "Uriah does not know" hypothesis, Uriah is indeed such an idealist. On the other hand, the narrator also needs an agent who will brand the king as a double-dyed deceiver, an adulterer-*cum*-schemer. And who could be more suitable for this purpose than the deceived husband himself, aware of the adultery and thus qualified to comment on the scheme of maneuvering him into self-deception? This husband's mode of commentary is all the more effective because it combines the force of indignation with the dignity of restraint.

Uriah as an agent of the first kind is, of course, incompatible with Uriah as an agent of the second kind. For us to interpret his words as those of a heroic idealist, he must not know of his wife's infidelity; while for us to see his words as the outcry of a deceived husband, his idealistic reason for refusing to go home must be a smokescreen. But the narrator, who settles for nothing less than the best of these two worlds, still yokes them together for maximum effect. *He builds up a multiple and hence multifunctional character.* Because of the reader's inability to decide between the two mutually exclusive portraits, the figure of Uriah comes to operate in both directions at once.

By manipulating both together, moreover, this elusive narrator, so concerned to keep up the facade of innocence and disclaim any malicious intent, can easily cover his tracks (as he also does when placing the irony in the mouth of a character). For any irony that shows in one direction meets with a counter-irony from the other direction. As soon as you notice the thrust from the "idealistic" point of view, the "defiant" reading immediately vies for your attention; and vice versa. The sharper the ambiguity of event, character, and position, the more hidden the narrator's true face.

Finally, since the features of the represented action and of the narrative discourse are organized differently within each of the alternative hypotheses or systems, they cease to be "automatic." There is here nothing like a one-to-one correspondence between the details and the generalization (or umbrella hypothesis) which they manifest, or—on a different level—between the text and the reality projected by it. For two contrasting versions of reality are being projected at one and the same time by a single order of words. So the constant and unresolved vacillation between the possibilities achieves what every literary work strives for: again and again it brings the reader back to the concrete texture of the details, making each one prominent and interesting.

What Does David Think That Uriah Thinks?
The Three-Way Hypothesis

David sends Uriah back with a death-warrant in his hand:

> (14) In the morning David wrote a letter to Joab, and sent it by the hand of Uriah. (15) And he wrote in the letter, saying, Set you Uriah in the forefront of the hardest fighting, and retire from him, that he may be smitten and die.

The effect is macabre. Yet the narrator does not abandon his dry, factual tone and records this with maximum brevity, as if it were a matter of daily occurrence. Again, evaluative and informational reticence go together. If the failure to comment at this key point is a new invitation to judgment, then the silence on David's motives opens yet another gap which, to understand what is actually happening, the reader must close. Still pretending innocence, the narrator will neither condemn the king openly nor lay open the king's plot. And since he states nothing, the reader has no choice but to puzzle out for himself what David hopes to gain by having Uriah murdered. The choice is not between inference and quiescence, but between inference and incoherence.

Nor can this gap be filled in automatically. The reader must consciously weigh the pros and cons of each reconstruction of the inner life. It should be borne in mind that the king's information about Uriah is, roughly, identical with the reader's. And similarly equipped, or rather ill-equipped, the internal and the external interpreters face a similar opacity. For the reasons given earlier, the king can no more determine with any certainty whether Uriah knows how things stand. In principle, David may have decided in his own mind in favor of one of the hypotheses; but then it is also possible that, like ourselves, he is unable to make univocal sense of Uriah's strange behavior. The difference is that we are supposed to interpret his interpretation as well, which launches another play of ambiguity. At this point, the reader oscillates among three hypotheses about what is happening in David's inner world:

1. One possible hypothesis is that David thinks that Uriah does not know. David may have arrived at such a conclusion through many of the arguments that have given rise to it in the reader's own mind.[22] And we have good grounds for supposing that David indeed thinks so. For had David, after the first night, suspected that Uriah knew of the Bathsheba affair and seen through the cover story, he would not have detained him for another two days in Jerusalem in the hope that Uriah would nevertheless succumb to the temptations of homecoming. Such a hope, as already argued, would be natural with Uriah as an unwitting idealist rather than as a witting cuckold. The strongest argument for the hypothesis that David thinks Uriah ignorant is the sending of the letter to Joab by his hand. It stands to reason that only if the king believed that his messenger knew nothing (and did not suspect that he was going to certain death) would he give him his own death-warrant to carry, confident that the letter would reach its destination unopened.

If this is what David thinks, what will he gain by killing Uriah? David's reasoning goes in a straight line. Since Uriah has refused to go down to his house, a new whitewashing operation must be devised. Bathsheba is now in her second month of pregnancy. (She came to David "purified from her uncleanness": the apparently irrelevant detail of verse 4 pays yet another dividend in closing this new gap as well). If Uriah is killed now, at once, and if the king takes Bathsheba to wife after the period of mourning, then she will give birth in the palace about seven months after entering it by the front door and it will be possible to hush up the scandal of her having conceived while still Uriah's wife. For the cover story to work, the king *must* of course marry Bathsheba since it is common knowledge that Uriah has long been abroad and that even when he did show up in Jerusalem he kept away from his house.

In the light of this hypothesis, some further aspects of the tale spring into prominence. As we have seen, the opening verses do not allow the reader to determine with certainty David's feelings toward Bathsheba. What has got him into trouble—a great and lasting love or a momentary lust of the flesh? If the former, then we have a *crime passionel* drama, and the king, never infatuated before, may evoke a certain understanding and sympathy in the reader despite the immorality of his actions. But the fact that instead of seeking to take Bathsheba for himself from the moment of her announcement "I am with child," David concentrates his energies on a switch of paternity, thus in effect conceding Bathsheba to Uriah from the start, does not exactly suggest a schemer on fire with love. On the contrary, this is the behavior of a man who regrets his involvement and is now trying to evade the consequences. An intoxicated lover, and a king at that, would not have given up Bathsheba so readily.

If David is now acting on the assumption that Uriah does not know, then his marriage of the widowed Bathsheba signals not an ardent lover but a direct continuation of his previous course in summoning Uriah to Jerusalem, that is, an attempt to conceal the adultery. True, he certainly takes into account that by killing Uriah he will also be taking revenge on the man who had dared to sneer at him for neglecting his duty in wartime. He doubtless also knows that this killing will yield him a further benefit—Bathsheba herself. Yet under the "David does not think that Uriah knows" hypothesis, David is not primarily the figure of a lover who elicits some understanding. Rather, he is a colorless character, the thoughts uppermost in his mind all concerned with dark plots and all aimed at extricating himself from personal disgrace. Viewed in these terms, his conduct looks particularly ugly. To "save his own skin," David is sending to death a person whom he himself sees as an innocent idealist and a man of conscience.

2. A second possible hypothesis is that David has decided that Uriah knows. Again, if David has reached this conclusion, he has done so on the strength of, among other things, some of the arguments that recommend it to the reader. In all likelihood, the king settles on this interpretation after realizing that Uriah, even when drunk, will not go down to his house. And David too is likely to suspect that Uriah's professed idealism is "too good to be true."

Such a state of mind appears inconsistent with David's readiness to entrust the letter to Uriah himself. But this troublesome fact can still be assimilated to the present line of reading, with a contribution to the reshaping of the king's image.[23] When, under Hypothesis 1, we reasoned that David would not put the letter into Uriah's hands if he thought that Uriah knew, we automatically assumed that David was acting from cold calculation. Now, in the framework of Hypothesis 2, David's character must be differently constructed. His reputation at stake, his desperate gamble foiled again and again, his pride smarting under Uriah's mockery, David loses his head and overlooks (or dismisses) the possibility that Uriah may open his letter to Joab. He does not believe Uriah will suspect him, the king, of such treachery.

This assumption of a loss of judgment under psychological pressure may seem a bit artificial, as if produced ad hoc to salvage Hypothesis 2. But before rejecting it out of hand, consider one point: This assumption is independently necessary, for there is no escape from the inference that the king has indeed lost something of his balance. Take the contents of the royal letter, ordering that Uriah should be assigned to "the forefront of the hardest fighting" and then abandoned. For this plan to be carried out, all the soldiers must be let into the secret or at least receive a bizarre order that Uriah is not to hear. To the meanest intelligence, any such order will give away the intention of having Uriah killed. If to this one adds the urgent need for the king to wed and bed Bathsheba in his palace, immediately thereafter, the thing must become a matter of public scandal; and then what need could there be for the whole conspiracy in the first place? If it is to come to light anyway, then why not have Uriah killed in Jerusalem? David, the brilliant general and the veteran of a hundred battles, cannot have been in his right mind when he issued such an order. And in case there is still a lingering suspicion of our having somehow read into the text what is not there to be read, let us observe that Joab, the commander of the army himself, shares this opinion of the king's plan, as we shall immediately see. It is therefore probable (though of course not inevitable) that he who writes an ill-judged letter will also, in the same ill-judged manner, place it in Uriah's hands.

In terms of this hypothesis, David must assume that there is no sense in hiding his liaison with Bathsheba; whoever has today revealed the secret to Uriah may reveal it tomorrow to all Jerusalem.[24] If so, why does he send Uriah to his death? One answer may be that, even if it fails to squash rumors, Uriah's death will enable David to marry Bathsheba. While on Hypothesis 1 Bathsheba's becoming David's wife is a by-product of the plot to disguise the sin, here Uriah is killed expressly in order to clear the way for the king's marriage. While Hypothesis 1 played down David's love, Hypothesis 2 presents David as having reached the conclusion that it would be useless to curb his passion any longer, now that the affair has leaked out. This hypothesis casts the king in the role of the great lover, even though there is no ignoring the fact that such an image is somewhat tarnished by his previous hesitations, his reluctance to take Bathsheba under his wing at once, his concern with saving face. Furthermore, now that putting Uriah out of the way is not an act of "self-defense," it becomes a tyrant's cruel revenge on a man who has dared to mock him. These feelings of anger and frustration find their expression in David's ill-advised order. And the view of the murder as an act of insane vengeance again attenuates the impression of David's love for Bathsheba, which loses further ground as the exclusive motivation for the murder. Still, within the framework of Hypothesis 2 the character of David emerges as that of a ruthless but passionate and heroic king—a figure of grandeur and drama conspicuously unlike the colorless schemer of Hypothesis 1.[25]

The two hypotheses are of course mutually exclusive, and their object therefore, like Uriah, irreconcilably ambiguous. Each shows David in an ironic light, since he has failed to realize that the other is equally warranted. Each transforms our conception of the king's state and personality as framed in terms of its mate. By simultaneously manipulating both possibilites, between which the reader constantly wavers, the narrator has refined each of these portraits of David by means of the other: he has projected an intricate character that does not lend itself to univocal formulation, the weak, pale figure cohabiting with one of cruel majesty.

3. In principle, there is also a third possibility: that David, like the reader, cannot tell whether Uriah knows or not. Under this hypothesis, David's considerations are many and varied. On the one hand he may be saying to himself: "I think that Uriah does not know, in which case his death will help to bury the whole affair" (and, for all his uncertainty, he is prepared to throw away a man's life on this)—"but even if Uriah knows there is nothing to lose, and at least I will have Bathsheba and avenge myself on her insolent husband." (This kind of internal argument projects a "colorless" David.) On the other hand, he may be saying to himself: "I think that Uriah knows, in which case I need no longer curb my love for Bathsheba nor my desire to win her and to avenge myself on Uriah; but even if he does not know, then, in addition to all these gains, the whole affair will be buried." (This reading brings out a more "colorful" figure.)

Accordingly, in the framework of Hypothesis 3 we have much the same interplay as marks the relations between Hypothesis 1 and 2, because Hypothesis 3 forks into two subhypotheses similar to Hypotheses 1 and 2. Still, Hypothesis 3 has its own claim to interest and effect, since it turns the two others into conflicting sides in David's mind. Such a dramatization changes once again our view of what happened, at least in the protagonist's inner world. It also modifies our attitude to him by narrowing down one ironic discrepancy in awareness: the two interpreters reach the same irresolution in face of the same puzzle. And it also gives some realistic color to the aesthetic logic of ambiguity. While preserving the effect of alternative gap-fillings, such as multiple characterization, this hypothesis anchors as well as mirrors their interplay in David's own psychology. Indeed, the following stage applies a variant of this technique to Joab at Rabbah.

How Joab Fails to Carry Out David's Order

(15) [David] wrote in the letter, saying, Set you Uriah in the forefront of the hardest fighting, and retire from him, that he may be smitten and die. (16) And when Joab invested the city, he assigned Uriah to the place where he knew that valiant men were. (17) The men of the city came out and fought with Joab; and there fell among the people some of the servants of David, and Uriah the Hittite died also.

Ostensibly, the narrator just records (verses 16–17) how Joab acted upon David's order (verse 15). Once again the text gives the impression of a purely additive sequence, tacking the incident of the execution on to that of the death-warrant. The account of the military murder thus seems almost completely redundant. Since the plan is laid down in the order, it should have been enough to note that Joab implemented it, and there is no need to dwell on the predictable manner of implementation. But a closer look reveals subtle differences between the order and the performance, and this encourages the reader to take the additive structure as another camouflage for a structure of opposition.

The hidden opposition is precisely between the two apparent counterparts: the order of execution and the execution of the order. For what the narrator intimates is how and why David's plan has *not* been followed. True, his scenario requires a minimum of casualties—one, to be exact. But we have already picked more than one hole in this ill-advised order. And it now turns out that Joab, likewise disturbed by those holes, makes improvements on the plan, implementing it in spirit rather than to the letter. A born pragmatist as well as an experienced soldier, he realized that the saving in casualties, however desirable in itself, is also the weak spot in the king's plan. It is better for many to fall, he decides, than for the conspiracy to stand revealed. He therefore provokes a sharp battle in which many are killed, Uriah *among* them. Uriah's comrades do not "retire from him"— they fall together with him ("and there fell among the people some of the servants of David, and Uriah the Hittite died also").

The narrator has laid bare the shortcomings of David's plan with consummate artistry. Not a word is spoken against it: its lack of considered judgment stands out in eloquent relief against the background of Joab's modified enactment. And the point is so subtly made that a hasty reader may pass through these verses (as traditional exegetes since Josephus in *Antiquities* have done) without even noticing the discrepancy and its implications for the whole plot.[26] An additional ironic feature is that, juxtaposed with Joab's cool and cruel revision, the king's plan appears for a moment as the more humane of the two. The narrator, as it were, maintains his objectivity by adducing the "strongest" arguments in David's favor, until we recall that this humaneness bears on the treacherous murder of an innocent man.[27]

How the Messenger Fails to Carry Out Joab's Order

Now Joab has to notify the king of Uriah's death and of the variation from the original plan:

> (18) Joab sent and told David all the matters of the war. (19) And he instructed the messenger, saying, When thou hast finished telling all the matters of the war to the king, (20) and if the king's wrath arises and he says to thee: "Wherefore did you go near to the city to fight?

Did you not know that they shoot from the wall? (21) Who smote Abimelech the son of Jerubbesheth? Did not a woman cast a piece of millstone upon him from the wall, so that he died in Tebez? Why did you go near the wall?" Then say thou: "Thy servant Uriah the Hittite is dead also."

Verse 18 covers all the required information (i.e., "the king has been duly notified"). But the narrator, so reticent about essentials, suddenly goes out of his way here to specify Joab's instructions to his messengers at Rabbah (and later, the exchange between the messenger and David in Jerusalem).

Unlike David, Joab communicates not by letter, but orally, through a messenger. This fact is covered by a good realistic motivation: Joab, with the whole war on his hands, has no time for epistolary composition. Yet the narrator also makes artistic capital out of the double shift in the form of communication, the word of mouth relayed by a fallible go-between. And the coaching scene makes it possible to reconstruct the exigencies that he devises for the characters to further his own ends.

Joab has performed his task so well that he got Uriah killed without giving the show away. Now he must effectively disguise his report to the king, concealing from the messenger the true purpose of his mission. While the messenger believes that he is carrying news about the abortive battle, Joab smuggles into the message the crucial item about Uriah's death. At the same time, Joab does not miss this chance to play a harmless but stinging joke on the king. He orders the messenger to start by reporting "all the matters of the war," numerous casualties and all. David, who has no idea that this fiasco has anything to do with the liquidation of Uriah (for the original plan provided for no such carnage), is almost certain to fly into a rage. And he must be given every opportunity to inveigh ("Why did you go near the wall?" etc.) against the commander's disastrous error of judgment. Only then will the messenger (according to Joab's scenario) let the cat out of the bag and, instantly, the wind out of the king's sails: "Thy servant Uriah the Hittite is dead also." Now the king's anger will doubtless cool down.

To Joab as stage-manager, all this mixes business with pleasure: it keeps the go-between insensible of the main object of his mission, and baits a seriocomic trap for the king. But the same envisaged dialogue also serves the narrator's own purpose: to stage an exposure—distanced and indirect, and thus all the more effective—of the king's ruthlessness. The abortive battle with its many casualties is sure to infuriate the king, but only so long as he fails to spot the connection with his private affairs. Once he discovers that the battle was deliberately mismanaged and that Uriah is among the fallen, all is well: the king raging at the death of so many soldiers can be wonderfully pacified by news about the death of one more soldier.[28]

In actual fact, Joab's scenario does not come true. But this only renders the judgment more trenchant. The new stage begins, quietly enough, with the strictly informative

> (22) The messenger went, and came and told David all that Joab had sent him to tell.

Again, given this summary, verses 23–24 appear redundant, since they merely detail how the messenger told David "all that Joab had sent him to tell." And again, redundant information in this frugal text draws attention to fine points and discordances. And once again it turns out, on a closer reading of these features, that the narrator has in effect "innocently" conveyed how orders (this time, Joab's) were *not* implemented.

By Joab's reasoning (and that of anyone else who, like the reader, has been let into the secret), the information "Thy servant Uriah the Hittite is dead also" certainly ought to allay the king's anger. But this reasoning is at variance with anything an ordinary man living by conventional norms is likely to think if ignorant of the king's scheme. The messenger must have considered Joab's logic to be twisted and strange. It is surely difficult for the messenger to understand how the king, tearing his hair about all these needless casualties, can be soothed by means of a follow-up about an additional casualty: such an addition would seem most likely to prove the last straw. Therefore, the messenger tries to forestall this danger and save himself from the king's wrath. And how can danger and wrath be averted except by deviating from Joab's text? It must seem to him that in this way he would be fulfilling the spirit of his orders:

> (23) And the messenger said to David, Indeed the men prevailed against us and came out to us into the open field, and we drove them to the entrance of the gate. (24) And the archers shot at thy servants from off the wall, and some of the king's servants died, and thy servant Uriah the Hittite is dead also.

In actual fact, we recall, it was Joab's troops who provoked the battle. They approached the Rabbah wall, and the defenders counterattacked them *beside the wall.* Had not this been the burden of Joab's message, there would have been no reason for the king to retort: "Why did you go near the wall?"

But the messenger, having decided to play it safe, manipulates a few points; and the result is a somewhat different story, which, even if short of downright distortion, certainly gives a twisted account of what happened. In the messenger's version it was the people of the city who initiated the attack, at first breaking through the front line of their besiegers ("the men prevailed against us") and pushing on as far as "the open field"; and only then, in driving them back, did Joab's troops approach the gate. Such a report leaves no room for the complaint "Why did you go near the wall?", since there would have been no way of repulsing the enemy except by going "near the city to fight."

The story told so far is nowhere given explicitly in the text. Yet this is the story the reader must infer to make sense of the disparities between the assorted versions: the messenger's version, the version of the fighting as it actually went (verses 16–17), and the version in which Joab coaches the messenger. The gaps forced open by these unexplained disparities call for a motivating closure; and this is possible only if we "reconstruct" the messenger's reasoning. This messenger serves to dramatize the contrast between the ordinary man's and the king's viewpoint—a contrast that highlights the extent to which the king's character has deteriorated under the stress of his private emergency.

In this light, even the summary, "The messenger went, and came and told David all that Joab had sent him to tell," takes on an ironic ambiguity in retrospect. This verse is formulated either from the standpoint of a narrator who feigns innocence or from the perspective of the messenger himself, who feels that his editing of Joab's instructions has in effect *improved* the message he bears. For now the item about Uriah's death comes as part of the information about the casualties, where it belongs, and not as a reply to an angry king. From the messenger's logical (as opposed to Joab's psychological) viewpoint, only while speaking of the casualties does it make sense to add "Thy servant Uriah the Hittite is dead also." But in such a framework the reference to Uriah's death becomes incidental and could just as easily have been omitted altogether in the editing. Not only has Joab's "joke" misfired, but it is by chance that the crucial piece of news has reached its destination at all.

The analogy between Joab's "improvement" of the king's orders and the messenger's "improvement" of Joab's orders is therefore ironic too. For Joab knew what he was doing and really did salvage the king's plan; while the messenger, with the best intentions in the world but in the wrong world, spoils Joab's point in transmission and might thwart the whole costly plot by omission.

Still, as it happens, he does mention Uriah's death. And David who now employs the same messenger to carry back his reply, must in turn ambiguate the message, to keep up Joab's pretense: that the whole exchange bears on the military setback. This constraint enables the narrator to play on the incongruity between David's righteous-sounding words and his secret intentions:

> (25) David said to the messenger, Thus shalt thou say to Joab, Let not this thing be evil in thy eyes, for the sword devours now one man and now another: make thy battle stronger against the city, and overthrow it. And encourage him.

That David, instead of flying into a passion, replies "Let not this thing be evil in thy eyes," is surely taken by the messenger as the success of his diplomacy. What this innocent hears are words of comfort and encouragement, directed by a forgiving king to the commander of his army after a temporary setback ("Don't take your failure to heart"). But to us these words ironically signify almost the reverse: a disguised appeal to that commander not to bear his master any grudge ("Don't take my transgressions, and your involvement, to heart") nor to regret the number of casualties he has been forced to suffer in order to satisfy a king's caprice. Or else words of comfort indeed, but with a view to consoling the commander in the field for having been driven to *stage* an abortive battle and to make unnecessary sacrifices. Whatever the nuances, the king's covert message certainly indicates retroactive approval of the change of plan.

Moreover, "Let not *this thing* be evil in thy eyes" nominally refers to the fortune of war; but the reader, knowing what lies behind this battle, shifts or widens the reference. For he spots a closer (and ironic) linkage between the end of one message and the beginning of another: "Thy servant Uriah the Hittite is dead also"— "Let not this thing be evil in thy eyes." Hence the words purporting to bring comfort ("Don't take it to heart") show another face as understated congratulations ("Good!" or "Thanks!"). As in verse 11, the narrator has opted for "this thing," because, being indeterminate in reference, the phrase allows him both to pinpoint and to elaborate the scenic ambiguity.

Next, "for the sword devours now one man and now another" will likewise be taken by the innocent messenger as a sigh of fellow-feeling on the king's part: "What can you do? . . . These things happen . . . In war many good men are killed; don't lose heart, but carry on and win." But to anyone in the know, these elegiac-sounding words convey a cynical subtext: "Do not grieve overmuch at the loss of good men. No matter how you look at it, the sword greedily devours soldiers. Why should you care, then, if a few more have been devoured together with Uriah?" If, previously, David appeared in a "humane" light in comparison with Joab, now even this dubious merit has finally been taken away from him.

The ending then goes on to unfold, with no break in the cool tone, the final stages of the villainy. The show goes on:

> (26) Uriah's wife heard that Uriah her husband had died and she made lamentations over her husband. (27) The mourning passed and David

sent and brought her into his house, and she became his wife and bore him a son.

And now, at the very end of the sin-and-concealment story, come the only words of moral evaluation in the entire chapter:

(27b) The thing that David had done was evil in the eyes of the Lord.

Yet even here the narrator has, as it were, not said a thing. Not on his own authority, at least. For the attitude expressed is God's, and though it carries sufficient weight to open the eyes of the naivest reader, the narrator is still careful to quote it with due (and distancing) acknowledgment.

The Analogy to the Story of Abimelech and the Woman

Joab's message also invites construal from another perspective. He anticipates David's spontaneous reaction to the report and provides his man with a clincher. Yet instead of contenting himself with a succinct outline of the future dialogue—which is all that the messenger needs—Joab gets carried away by his flow of words spoken in David's name. His utterance is lengthy and disordered:

Wherefore did you go near the city to fight? Did you not know that they would shoot from the wall? Who smote Abimelech the son of Jerubbesheth? Did not a woman cast a piece of a millstone upon him from the wall, so that he died in Tebez? Why did you go near the wall?

These words suggest a picture of a general who not only gives his messenger the contents of the king's anticipated response but also acts the part of the king, expressively mimicking the intonations and speech patterns of royalty in rage. What Joab utters (in his assumed role) stands out for a number of reasons: (1) the "life" which Joab's imitation infuses into the words; (2) their prolixity relative to the narrator's norm; (3) their formal incoherence (repetitions, etc.); and (4) the fracturing of the tale's impersonal surface by the citation (in David's name) of another incident as an explicit analogy to present concerns.

The divergence from factual dryness, culminating in the appearance of this analogy, finds its realistic motivation in the context of utterance. After all, the speaker imitates the mode of speech appropriate to a king agitated by a military reverse: such news will naturally elicit a royal diatribe, including a reference to the "classic" example in this connection. Thus motivated, the analogy performs different functions in the characters' dialogue and in the narrator's text.

The analogy-by-retrospect indeed forms a striking parallel to developments in the narrative present. It is not just that both stories deal with a war leading to a siege; in both the besiegers approach the city and as a result suffer losses beside the wall. This is what the messenger surely understood, and what Joab meant him to understand.

But to appreciate the role played by the same elements within the narrator's text, we must make a distinction between an open and a closed analogy. In a closed analogy, at least one point of similarity between the members is explicitly stated in the discourse. This is the case with the analogy before us: the king's anticipated words themselves indicate ("close") the equivalences between the base story and the analogical story.[29] Now in an open analogy or simile ("He made the world like a desert"), the likened materials are autonomous, and only the context determines the relevant aspects of similarity, that is, those which participate in the parallel. But even a closed analogy or simile, where the relevant aspects of similarity are stated, still leaves some aspects open. For every analogy contains a number of autonomous and loose elements (some irrelevant and some even incongruous), which "officially" remain outside the play of equivalences. Unstructured within the limited context, such elements may yet gain relevance from the broader context.

This may be formulated in another way. A perfect, one-to-one correspondence entails "transparency" and automatic response. The details of the parallel incidents or expressions are apprehended only insofar as they enter into equivalence-relations, and have no perceptibility in themselves. What makes an analogy concrete is the presence of features that resist assimilation to the "official" equivalence, or to any equivalence. Still, the reader is always apt to hesitate, to wonder just how far the analogy extends and to try to draw into it the autonomous materials as well. The official linkage or integration is made within the local context; but since a literary text is an enclosed world and hence invites maximal patterning— on the fundamental assumption that this world is controlled and unified— the reader tends to anchor even the loose details in the immediate or some wider context of similitude.

Consider the materials that do not "officially" enter into the analogy between the Abimelech and the David and Bathsheba battle scenes: the status of the fallen besieger (king ≠ commoner), the identity and sex of the person who fells him (woman ≠ archer), the place of the action (Tebez ≠ Rabbah), etc. But these outsiders beautifully fall into pattern within the broader context, so as to promote the tale's general ironic tendencies. The story of Abimelech, formally invoked as a parallel to the story of the war at Rabbah, also turns out an ironic parallel to the story of the king in his city. Both kings, David and Abimelech, fall because of a woman. (So, in still another sense, does Uriah.) What is more, the notorious incident of Abimelech's death bears—for both Joab and the reader—connotations of a disgrace brought on royalty at a woman's hand:

> A certain woman cast a piece of a millstone upon Abimelech's head and smashed his skull. And he called hastily to the young man his armour-bearer and said to him, Draw thy sword and slay me, lest it be said of me, A woman killed him. (Judges 9:53–54)

These pejorative connotations of Warrior King Laid Low by Woman are shared by the David and Bathsheba and the Abimelech stories, to the exclusion of the military setback at Rabbah, centering in Uriah's honorable death. Moreover, Abimelech tried to cover up the disgrace for fear that the rumor would spread among the people ("slay me, lest it be said of me . . ."); but to little avail. The very reference Joab now makes to the incident attests that what Abimelech feared most has indeed befallen him: he has become a byword for a king's shameful downfall at a woman's hands. This feature likewise recurs in the David story, but *not* in the Joab and Uriah subplot. David too makes desperate efforts to save face, but with so little success that the whole inglorious episode has been perpetuated (in the text before us) as an even more classic memento.

"Unofficially," then, a telling analogy to the David and Bathsheba affair emerges here. Yet even with the unofficial linkages performed, some autonomous materials remain. For example: (1) the different time and place; (2) the king's "fall" in one case assumes the form of being killed by a woman and in the other of killing because of a woman; (3) David, God's anointed and a great king, is otherwise poles apart from a petty thug like Abimelech. The effect of concreteness produced by these recalcitrant elements gains further strength from the fluctuation of parts of the analogy between the explicit and the implicit linkage. The official linkage subordinates several details to the pattern of equivalences while leaving others autonomous (and therefore concrete). And yet the very materials that in this light appear irrelevant leap into central relevance in terms of implicit structuring—except that now the materials that fall under the official analogy have become autonomous and therefore concrete.

Even the features that look totally autonomous, however, have some role to play in developing the ironic implications of the analogy. For example, that David is likened to Abimelech has—because of the very distance between them—the effect of diminishing his image. The more so since

Abimelech fell at a woman's hands while at the head of his army: David falls at a woman's hands precisely because he plays truant from war.

Of course, the narrator will not make an ironic analogy in his own name. The peculiar thing about it is that it stands twice removed from him: it forms a "dramatic" analogy made through a "second-level" conversation (the narrator quotes Joab who quotes David's predictable response). Since the narrator does not reveal the inner world of his characters, there is no telling to what extent Joab himself appreciates its implications. Does Joab know of David's personal imbroglio and slips into his mime—which seems to be directed at something else—another concealed barb (again, as a completely private joke, since the messenger does not suspect a thing)? Or does Joab make an innocent imitation and the omniscient narrator quotes it in order to construct, together with the reader, an additional pattern behind Joab's back? This would yield a perspective (the omniscient ironist's) behind a perspective (Joab as dramatized ironist) behind a perspective (Joab's official stance) on the analogy. In either case the irony sharpens, since the barbed analogy is placed in David's own mouth.

Joab may then be serving either as a conscious agent or merely as an unwitting vehicle of the text's machinations. If previously Uriah was exploited as a conductor of irony, now Joab performs a similar function. Only that Joab is not an idealist, nor a moral paragon, nor a deceived husband. The irony in his words is irony for its own sake. And as for the narrator, he has again managed to leave himself the loophole of artless reporting.[30]

On Mutually Exclusive Systems of Gap-Filling: Turning the Screws of Henry James and Others

In contrast to what its neglect in criticism and theory might lead one to expect, the phenomenon traced in our biblical paradigm—the establishment of *dual or multiple systems of gap-filling*, mutually incompatible and yet coexistent—is hardly a rarity in literature. Not that this extreme form of ambiguity runs to a single pattern. Certain literary texts develop multiple systems of gap-filling as a dominant compositional principle, which makes it impossible to give an adequate account of the work's shape and meaning without reference to them. In other texts, this multiple system applies to points few in number but crucial to interpretation. In others still, the indeterminacy concerns gaps of relatively minor importance or local interest only (though even here it subtly affects response and understanding).[31]

It would be no exaggeration to claim that such ambiguity is, at least as a secondary feature, typical of literary discourse. If critics tend to pick one (not always the same one) of the relevant systems of gap-filling to the exclusion of the alternative(s), wrenching it from context and squabbling among themselves over the matter, their practice only demonstrates the commonness and the irreducibility of the principle. True of the Bible, this holds equally true for literature throughout the ages.

Take Henry James's short novel *The Turn of the Screw*. Since 1924, this narrative puzzle has given rise to endless argument over the question of ambiguity and the establishment of a single valid hypothesis to resolve it. Scores of critics have suggested solutions to the puzzle of "what really happens" in this story, each attempting to give some unitary interpretation to the "world" represented in it. Interpreter after interpreter has triumphantly "solved" the problem and, what is more, eliminated rival solutions and/or the ambiguity itself. Yet the problem remains unsolved. Thus far, no simplex reading has won the day—someone else invariably turns up to give the screw one more twist.

For all their assortment of views and approaches, the three hundred or so interpretations generated so far by this one narrative can be divided into two main camps. (Many readings offer little more than a variation on previous ones by raising yet another argument, by throwing some new light on familiar details, or by introducing additional details into the hermeneutic arena.) These two camps are divided over the status to be assigned to the ghosts of the servants reported by the governess. Are the apparitions real, which would make this a "ghost story," or does the governess only hallucinate them and her report makes a psychological story?[32]

"The governess who is made to tell the story is a neurotic case of sex repression, and . . . the ghosts are not real ghosts but hallucinations of the governess," says Edmund Wilson, the most influential exponent of the second hypothesis. While Robert Heilman, waving aside that Freudian interpretation, typically counters: "At the level of action, the story means exactly what it says: that at Bly there are apparitions which the governess sees, which Mrs. Grose does not see but comes to believe in because they are consistent with her own independent experience, and of which the children have a knowledge which they endeavor to conceal."[33]

As always, the ideal of English criticism on this subject is to reach some unequivocal decision between the two alternative hypotheses or approaches: the Apparitionist vs. the Non-Apparitionist. James's notebooks and other statements have proved a happy hunting ground for critics of both persuasions, each trying to clinch matters through an appropriate citation from the master's writings. But whatever the substantial and methodological variations—ghosts or fantasies, external or internal evidence—the interpretive ideal remains constant.

Beardsley thus pounces on what he takes to be the final vindication of the Apparitionist hypothesis. As he puts it:

> But the final scene cannot be explained by Hypothesis 2, for in that scene Miles shows that he has seen Peter Quint's ghost before, and would not be surprised to see it again. . . . In the final analysis, one hypothesis is far more probable than the other, and there is therefore no "ambiguity of Henry James" in this story.

By this he believes to have disposed of the whole troublesome problem: what to do with a text that leaves room for two mutually incompatible elucidations, without resolving the issue.

Twentieth-century criticism has a great deal to say about "paradox," "pluri-signation," "ambiguity," "multiple meaning," (etc.) on the verbal and thematic levels of the literary work and in the dimensions of tone or attitude. In contrast to an earlier ideal of univocal and consistent signification, it has elevated plurality of meaning to the status of a, if not the, literary value, indeed a distinctive feature of literary language. Yet this very same criticism shows signs of acute discomfort when faced with the ambiguity of the "world" of events, with the resultant multiple readings of the field of reality represented in the work; and, to say the least, does not tend to consider it a distinctively literary phenomenon. In all that regards this level of the literary text, it is upon an unequivocal choice that criticism insists.[34]

It is the ideal of univocal gap-filling, then, that has generated and maintained the argument about James's story. And critics have failed to draw the obvious conclusions from its interminability. One article, giving up in utter exhaustion after half a century of controversy, leaves the decision between the two hypotheses to the individual reader: "The question whether *The Turn of the Screw* is a ghost story or a psychiatric case history will probably never be answered to everybody's satisfaction. There is enough evidence to convince proponents of either side of the controversy, and I suspect that it is not so much the evidence as the predilection of the proponent that determines his choice."[35] The reader with a taste for fantasy will see ghosts in the story, and the down-to-earth person will talk of hallucinations. This laissez-faire is still a far cry from declaring invalid any gap-filling that will establish one of the two hypotheses to the exclusion of the other.

Even if the one-gap-one-closure dictate were reasonable, the critics would yet have no justification for overlooking both the effect produced on the reader by the temporary emergence of the ultimately invalidated alternative and by the interplay between the hypothesis endorsed and the one rejected. This interplay constitutes one of the basic features and appeals of literary art. In actual fact, however, the regulating principle of *The Turn of the Screw* is the impossibility of choosing between the alternative readings. This is why the debate over it will perpetuate itself as long as each interpreter hopes to enthrone a single hypothesis. For the very composition elaborated by James sees to it that arguments for and against each gap-filling should be producible: the text itself devises a manifold clash between elements supporting the Apparitionist hypothesis and undermining its rival and other elements that perform a diametrically opposed role.[36] Demonstrating this would require a close step-by-step analysis of the tale, but one or two points will have to do by way of illustration here.

By providing sufficient clues to shake both hypotheses, the text discourages the interpreter from committing himself to either; however plausible it may look at a certain moment, before long something always turns up to discredit it in favor of the other. The first section of this chapter outlined a set of criteria with which the reader operates (consciously or unconsciously) to judge between alternative hypotheses. As in the Bathsheba story, the application of these criteria to the Jamesian masterpiece results in stalemate. A complex machinery has again been set up to prevent the reader from reaching any definite verdict. Thus, one gap-filling ("There are no ghosts") is "realistic," that is, consonant with the normal logic of reality; and this inclines the reader in its favor from the start. But the second possibility—although it requires a suspension of disbelief, a shift from the familiar world of the reader's everyday life to the strange world of fiction—is the one explicitly maintained by the narrating governess; and this serves to redress the balance. And so on. The reader who endorses either hypothesis will be driven to make a narrow and tendentious selection of materials from the text, in disregard of all clues pointing the other way. An adequate reading of the tale must reject each individual hypothesis in isolation and admit them only in tense concert.

As with general factors, so with particular clues and features. According to Beardsley, what establishes the Apparitionist view is that in the last scene Miles betrays his familiarity with Peter Quint's ghost: "Peter Quint—you devil! . . . Where?" Beardsley thinks, as the governess did before him, that the "you devil" in the boy's last words is addressed to the ghost—and as a result concludes that the boy does see it. But Non-Apparitionists would say that the boy, terrified to death by the hysterical behavior of the governess, answers her question "Whom do you mean by 'he'?" with the words "Peter Quint," and addresses the "you devil!" to the governess herself. On this reading, the boy—who has never seen the ghost—dies of fright.

James's *nouvelle* is not at all an exceptional case. Gogol's "The Overcoat" has long been read as a story about a poor downtrodden clerk, Akaky Akakyevitch, who is robbed of his overcoat, dies of grief and cold, and then haunts St. Petersburg to avenge himself by stripping overcoats from people's backs, notably including the General ("the person of consequence") who has done him wrong during his lifetime. More recently, however, certain critics have raised another, more "realistic" possibility: it is no ghost that is stealing overcoats throughout the city, but the same resourceful gang of thieves that has relieved Akaky of his own. It is mere rumor—though one that the thieves take full advantage of—that a vindictive demon-spirit is on the prowl.[37]

Instead of a story with the causal sequence of "an eye for an eye," this reading yields a story about analogical cases of overcoat robbery: Akaky's and (among others) the general's. The supernatural element would then be dismissed in terms of (real or pretended) confusion on the narrator's part. Having picked up the rumors circulating in St. Petersburg (he takes care to note that the ending of his story is just that), the narrator tells a fantasy with no factual basis in the represented world.

This attractive hypothesis can be reinforced by various details. Indeed, those people who actually saw the ghost did so from a distance, or for some reason or other did not manage to get a good look at it, or have never met Akaky himself. The behavior of the ghost shows evidence of unusual vitality; and the technique of overcoat snatching is precisely that devised by the moustachioed thieves, who took possession of Akaky's overcoat on the pretext that it was theirs. The general, the only witness who comes face to face with the robber and actually hears him speak, has unfortunately been suffering from hallucinations brought on by pangs of conscience, and is haunted by Akaky's face. Worse, at the time of the robbery he is slightly drunk. Even this face-to-face encounter can, then, be explained in terms other than fantastic: he saw the overcoat thief and fancied he was seeing Akaky. Finally, at the very end we hear about a ghostly apparition seen by a sentry "with his own eyes." But, as usual, the narrator is careful to leave things open. By describing the apparition as tall and (like the thieves) adorned with immense moustaches, he hints that this must be someone other than the dead clerk. Could he be wrong?

The emergence of such a reading, of course, sheds an ironic light on all the interpretations of "The Overcoat" that reconstruct its world and events in terms of Akaky's vengeful return. But the critics who exclusively adhere to this hypothesis are no less one-sided than their predecessors. The realistic closure is simply a possibility existing alongside the fantastic. Only a reading that simultaneously activates both hypotheses (and takes their interplay into account) qualifies as a valid reading.[38] Although the multiple system of gap-filling in "The Overcoat" organizes the events of one part alone—what happens in the end?—it determines the whole interpretation, from genre to meaning to tone.

S. Y. Agnon's "Another Face," to cite a final example of narrative ambiguity, has an open ending. In the few hours they spend together after their divorce, Tony and Hartman gain such an insight into their situation as years of marriage have not afforded them. And the question that arises at the end is, Are they going to return to each other?[39] This links up with another and even more important gap: What is Tony's attitude to Hartman? Does the action pull her toward or away from him? Predictably, the answers given by critics have been univocal one way or the other. But Agnon himself invites quite another reading: he distributes throughout *two-faced clues* (pointing in both directions at once) and sees to it that neither of the alternative reconstructions should gain overwhelming support.[40] As gossips and sensation-seekers, we should all like a clear answer to the question of what the characters are ultimately going to do. As readers, we must be concerned here with other questions. How does Agnon construct the multiple hypotheses? To what uses does he put them? And what would the text lose in their absence?

James's *The Turn of the Screw*, Gogol's "The Overcoat," Agnon's "Another Face": these multiple systems of gap-filling sufficiently differ from one another (and from our paradigmatic case, the David and Bathsheba story) to give an idea of the scope and implications of this principle. One could easily multiply examples from all literary genres—epic, novel, drama, poetry. The endless critical warfare about their interpretation misses (as well as, unwittingly, establishes) the poetic point. And so do the attempts to resolve the quarrel by blaming the work itself: the incoherencies that derive from its history of transmission—the staple of biblical source criticism—or from its sloppy execution or even from its disregard for clarity.[41] It is not that any of these explanations of incoherence may be ruled out a priori, but that their abuse obscures the scope and working of ambiguity as a constructive force.

The multiple system of gap-filling must not be equated with confusion, sloppiness, or vagueness. Where a text accommodates various closures merely because certain relevant data happen to be discrepant or lacking or obscure—that is, where interpretation has failed to find a place for their variety—there is no point in talking about "interplay" and "tension" between alternative possibilities. What plays no role can have no interest, except of a negative kind. In themselves, generally speaking, gaps and indeterminacies have no aesthetic value. They may turn out a crux or a misadventure, an integral part of the work's organization or a measure of its failure. Only when each hypothesis performs some definite function, illuminating the elements from its own particular angle, and only when the multifold linkage integrates with the other features of the discourse into an overall complex pattern—only then does ambiguity operate as a distinctive principle of literature.

Apart from the light it throws on the Bible's genius for processing our experience, the David and Bathsheba story triumphantly manifests this operation. The coexistence of two (or more) mutually exclusive hypotheses—concerning action, motive, character—always enables the author to kill two birds with one stone, using the same materials for different ends. Above all, it enables him to base sequence and effect on the tensions between the two possibilities. Each reading may serve to balance and ironize the other. The emergence of such a hypothesis in a text that equally validates its contrary renders each quite unlike a similar hypothesis appearing unchallenged. A simultaneous reading of a text from two unresolvable perspectives, with its constant movement between the rivals, not only enriches every doubled construct, actional or psychological. It inevitably makes for heightened perceptibility. It sharpens our awareness of the work's verbal art, foregrounds the modes of expression, and brings out the more subtle features of the represented events. Each detail assumes importance, deriving from the support or resistance it offers to the hypotheses and from the coincident pleasure afforded by its double reading. In short, the ambiguity calls attention to the literary texture as such.

To be sure, in everyday life people also construct hypotheses and fill in gaps. They work out the doings and motives and personalities of others and, on the basis of whatever information they have at their disposal, guess at what remains hidden. No one can otherwise possibly exist as a rational creature. David asks: Does Uriah know?—exactly like the reader, and David, too, must deal with the gap. But, as our biblical paradigm suggests, there are some essential differences between gap-filling in real life and in literary experience. Even in a literary structure that imitates the ordinary business of living, the process of making sense is directed by aesthetic clues and conventions. These include such factors as the implications of the work's poetics, the tendency to opt for the hypothesis that will bring the elements of a text into the most interesting or attractive pattern, or that will present a character in a richer and more complex light, etc. Other dimensions of the text—rhythm, style, form—likewise control the process of hypothesis-making, so that the reader of the literary work operates with a great number of models and variables that in everyday life would be considered irrelevant.

We also construct *multiple* systems of gap-filling in real life, with one crucial difference. In a specific real-life situation, a person torn between two conflicting hypotheses knows only too well that only one hypothesis "fits" the case, that only one can be right, and it is only for lack of sufficient wit or knowledge that he (or she) remains powerless to decide. One can only continue to hope for additional information to turn up in due course and resolve the issue. In a literary work, on the other hand, two contradictory hypotheses may both be valid, since their coexistence may be motivated and legitimated in terms of artistic intentions. Hence the Bible and its reader can luxuriate on the Gordian knot that David must cut.

·7·

BETWEEN THE TRUTH
AND THE WHOLE TRUTH

He who knows, why should he keep it hidden?
Sumerian proverb

Foolproof Composition in Ambiguity

Arising from a lack in the telling, gaps give rise to a fullness in the reading: the Bible presses this universal of literary communication to extremes undreamt of before modernism. But the comparison with modernism also throws its peculiar features into relief. What emerges from the inquiry into perspectival structure in chapters 2 to 5, notably the handling of discovery, applies to the related issues of gapping and sequence as well. Like the resemblance, again, the difference from modern literature is one within the family. It does not lie where prejudice might expect to find it: in sophistication, range, or indeed historical evaluation.

As regards sophistication, the Bible is second to none and no allowances need be made for it. The opening and timing of gaps, the processing of information and response, the interlinkage of the different levels, the play of hypotheses with sanctions against premature closure, the clues and models that guide interpretive procedure, the roles fulfilled by ambiguity: all these show a rare mastery of the narrative medium. The Wooing of Rebekah, the David and Bathsheba affair, and other episodes to be discussed, could even give moderns a few useful hints—about the art of maneuvering in small compass, for instance.

Nor does range, in any of the senses material to the comparison, exhibit much disparity. Thus, the examples considered and to follow are all models rather than freaks. Whatever the features distinguishing each tale and the occasion for its analysis, it still manifests the Bible's rule and poetics of ambiguity no less than *The Turn of the Screw* or *The Ambassadors* does Henry James's. As with frequency, so with versatility. If the David and Bathsheba story focuses attention on what I shall call permanent gaps, then the Wooing

230

of Rebekah manipulates a set of temporary counterparts, from the identity of the bride-to-be through her qualifications to her family's amenability. And the tentative inferences made from the servant's rhetoric to his designs even show how uncertain and certain closures may go together in a single narrative.

Likewise, if the David and Bathsheba tale makes capital out of mutual exclusiveness, then others vary the relations between the hypotheses. Thus, Uriah must be either in the know or in the dark; but Joseph may be both vindictive and redemptive in his dealings with his brothers, Samuel torn between belief and disbelief in the election of the red-haired lad, David a strong man who once succumbs to a weakness of the flesh or, later, a great leader who mismanages his own family. With the Bible's partiality for complex character and motive, in short, its multiple systems of gap-filling describe a whole range of logical relations in ambiguity.

The Bathsheba narrative itself, moreover, illustrates how such married rivals at times leap at the reader simultaneously (as with the nature of the king's feelings for his mistress) and at other times in succession, the one remaining in undisputed control (e.g., "Uriah acts from idealism") till the sequel brings up an alternative explanation. Elsewhere we find the options realized in a purer form. To take examples from David's own career, "He mourned for his son day after day" (2 Sam 13:37) at once leaves the reference to the object of mourning indeterminate between nothing less than the murdered Amnon and the murderer Absalom, the favorite now in exile. Whereas the double account of how David came to Saul's notice affords an equally pure instance of the "successive" or dynamic ambiguity. Having first been summoned to court as an accomplished musician, David then kills Goliath before the eyes of a king who does not seem to recognize him (1 Sam 16:15–23; 17:1–58). Are these variant accounts of the "first" meeting of the two men or a sequential development of their relationship? The narrator's typically two-faced clues permit no resolution of the incongruity, and for good reason: to launch David on his public career with the blessing of both humanity (in peacetime) and God (in wartime).[1]

Temporariness vs. permanence, incompatibility vs. complementariness, simultaneity vs. successiveness in hypothesis-making: these will do for the moment to suggest the range covered by the Bible's ambiguation of the world.

Historically speaking, finally, from the vantage point of modernism one espies here not precursory explorations but a full-fledged kindred spirit. Working independently, the Bible and Homer created a remarkable art of sequence, with the possible difference that the Bible broke with time-honored conventions of narrative in the process and the certain difference that its artistic revolution correlated with an ideological revolution. How this triple miracle happened in Israel, God only knows; but there can be no doubt that it did happen.

Even a cursory comparison of biblical narrative with Homeric epic (as I analyzed it in a previous book[2]) will reveal an unmistakable similarity in the management of sequence. It includes deformation of chronology, playing on the resultant gaps, baited traps and false impressions, rise and fall and yoking together of hypotheses, use of uncertainty for effects stretching from plot interest to intricate characterization. (To say nothing of related correspondences, whether the technique of repetition or the capacity for extended storytelling.) The Bible's art is on the whole richer and craftier, its surface incomparably less formulaic, its play more serious, and its view of meaning and experience as a process built rather than incorporated into the composition. But nothing like the famous antithesis drawn by Erich Auerbach between scriptural darkness and Homeric illumination has a leg to stand on.

No more tenable is the claim of similarity between biblical and Near Eastern literature, increasingly and often triumphantly made by Orientalists. Hard as one looks at those texts—in Pritchard's magnificent collection, for example—one discovers little in common beyond occasional phrases and formations. Nothing in them begins to explain how even these forms shed their schematism and developed new functions, how others were invented—dechronologized sequence included—how all came to be orchestrated into a mature art of signification by reticence and dissonance and ambiguity (or for that matter linguistic virtuosity). On the contrary, the surface similarities only heighten the wonder and conviction of strategic novelty: the Bible's poetics appears to have sprung full-blown. And if anything can account for such a radical break in aesthetics, this is I believe the coincident break with pagan metaphysics.

How one marvel explains another has already been suggested by the linkage of the innovations in point of view and in epistemology. It is but a short step from opposing divine and human insight in the plot to dramatizing the opposition further by confronting the human interpreters inside and outside the plot with the opacities and enigmas of sublunary existence. Samuel, Abraham's envoy or David on the one hand and the reader on the other undergo what is essentially the same ordeal: making sense of a world impenetrable except by divine eyes or grace. Indeed, the ideological thrust (exigencies, priorities, motivations) of the drama of reading indicates where and why biblical gaps do vary from those in Homeric epic and the modern novel.

Consider first the choice of objects for gapping. What aspect of the world is it that the informational omissions and discordances blur, ambiguate, reduce to hypothetical status? Even the few examples given above manifest an impressive variety. The gapped object may consist in a piece of action, e.g., What happened between the two whores during the night? Another type of gap concerns the temporal sequence of events: Did the servant present the gifts before or after having inquired about lineage? Are David's two "first" encounters with Saul consecutive or alternative? A more common type bears on causal linkage (as when events that follow one another in the telling do not follow *from* one another in the happening). Another relates to character: Is Rebekah ordinarily or divinely elected, Uriah an idealistic soldier or a stubborn husband, Joseph a tormentor or a redeemer, Jehu a madman or a zealot? Still others that we have encountered contrive indeterminacies about designs, motives, viewpoint, speech event, or personal relations. Only one sphere, and the most comprehensive at that, remains essentially outside the Bible's operations of ambiguity: the world order itself, the laws governing reality as a whole.

Homer may leave basic uncertainties and incongruities in his world picture to suit his varying purposes; modern literature deliberately plays on gaps of the "ghosts or hallucinations?" scope to exclude any univocal reality-model. Far from offering equivalents or anticipations, however, biblical narrative goes here to the opposite extreme of elaborating rhetorics of divine transcendence in order to inculcate an objective frame of reference. God knows and controls all, and humans must learn their limitations, including the impossibility of fully comprehending God's way with the world. Even at this level—as I have already argued and will soon show anew—the Bible allows itself considerable room for maneuvering between elucidation and implication. The narrative thus keeps open part of the gaps regarding divine omnipotence because they would be tedious or, as with the issue of control versus freedom, because they would be awkward to close outright. But the principles of gap-filling and their application to specific cases are so forcefully impressed on the reader's mind that he can be trusted to deal with the remaining indeterminacies in their spirit, the sense of mystery included. In the Bible's scale, it is well to remember, knowledge of principles stands higher than knowledge of facts and mechanics, and the two dimensions of knowledge need not coalesce even at the moment of discovery.

This also explains another distinctive feature, concerning the relations between fact and judgment. In modernism, ambiguity of plot often not only goes and dovetails with but also generates ambivalence in response. *The Turn of the Screw* is a paradigm of this twofold bifurcation. If the narrated world is abnormal, then the narrating governess is normal; but if the world is normal, the governess herself must be abnormal, whether hallucinating out of power hunger or sexual repression. And since the existential polarity defies resolution, the evaluative follows suit. Elsewhere, as in Kafka or the *nouveau roman,* the world may assume such incoherence as to preclude not just the application of a value system to the dramatized acts and agents but even the reconstruction of any coherent value system.

That biblical narrative rules out the latter extreme goes without saying. As a matter of ideological principle, however, it ensures rather than undermines practical evaluation even amidst dramatic ambiguation. Not that its poetics favors univalence—on the contrary—but that its ambivalences must ultimately cohere as judgment.

This coherence may be realistic, as with mixed motives: Joseph wants to teach his brothers a lesson in more than one sense; Rebekah's family is influenced by the material as well as the spiritual blessedness of the match. Here, the ostensible opposition is resolved by appeal to both the complexity of the world (i.e., the human heart) and of the effect (the character's mixed feelings leading to our mixed response). Elsewhere, the discourse resists existential only to clinch evaluative coherence. Every irresolvable ambiguity throughout the Bathsheba affair reflects further discredit on David, just as the double account of the meeting with Saul redoubles his credit. The less compatible the rival hypotheses are in terms of plot, the greater is their convergence in terms of judgment: this forms the biblical rule of ambiguity. Thanks to this rule, even the reader who altogether misses the ambiguity—and with it the ironies, double meanings, psychological insights, verbal design, shifts of position, almost everything of value—will still take the moral point. Morally as well as artistically speaking, of course, such underreaders or misreaders will yet fall below the implied reader. Underreaders will respond only to one of the two or more stories narrated and learn little in the process, unless they need to be reminded about the ethical status of adultery or murder. As long as they do recognize the premises, however, their flattening will no more misdirect them about essentials than will their superior's ingenuity. The wilder the play, in short, the wider the margin of safety.

This manifests in the most radical way the Bible's foolproof composition. We have already observed in other contexts how it provides for minimum intelligibility: by concealing everything but essentials between the lines of repetition, by staging discoveries at a point where the reader is already supposed to have made them, or by keeping the world order gap-free. Nowhere does this constraint assume such heaviness as in the management of ambiguity, and the performance under it such brilliance. Its effortless appearance will not, I trust, obscure the consummate art required to invent and sustain it. But the prime condition remains the same: the transparence (however illusory and spotted with opacities) of the reality-model, the plot line, and the judgment. In turn, for this condition to be fulfilled, unreliable narrative in the modern manner, where not a single report or value can be taken on trust and ambiguity pervades the whole discourse, must be avoided. However far from omnicommunicative, the Bible's narration yet remains omniscient and authoritative and intelligible on different levels of reading. The narrator may play games with the whole truth for the pleasure and benefit of the cunning few, but he must communicate the truth in a fashion accessible to all.

The Relevance of Absence

The distance between the truth and the whole truth, then, correlates with the distance between minimal and implied reading. The indispensable minimum of truth is ensured by the foolproof composition. But what leads the implied reader (which most of us, doctrinal anachronists excluded, aspire to become) from the truth to the whole truth: from the givens to the rounded understanding that will bring one as close to the narrator's as humanly possible? To bridge the distance, we must make inferences throughout the reading; and to make inferences, we must first know their proper objects and conditions. What is it that needs rounding out to make contextual sense of the text? Hence the necessity of establishing the relevance of the absent material—from abstract rule through plot-stuff to judgment— which in the immediate connection means recognizing a gap when we see one. In view of the numerous contenders for gaphood, the identification is not quite so easy as it may sound. Nor can the biblical interpreter look for guidance to literary theory in its present state.

So let me start with some basic definitions not given thus far.[3] A gap is a lack of information about the world—an event, motive, causal link, character trait, plot structure, law of probability—contrived by a temporal displacement. Like the objects displaced, the forms of displacement vary. What happened (or existed) at a certain temporal point in the world may be communicated in the discourse at a point earlier or later, or for that matter not at all. Absalom's defeat is foretold, and its circumstances accordingly gapped, well in advance of the battle (2 Sam 17:14). The facts of the nocturnal affair at the whores' house emerge only as late as Solomon's judgment. And whether or not Uriah knew is a secret that he takes with him to the grave. Prospective, retrospective, irresolvable gaps: these varieties (and others to be discussed) have a structural feature in common. They all result from a chronological twisting whereby the order of presentation does not conform to the order of occurrence. The sequence devised for the reader thus becomes discontinuous—with causal as well as merely temporal non sequiturs, since the gappy events follow rather than follow from each other—and gap-filling consists exactly in restoring the continuity that the narrator broke. For all our attempts at restoration, however, the breaches remain ambiguous—and hypotheses multiple—as long as the narrator has not authoritatively closed them. The storyteller's withholding of information opens gaps, gaps produce discontinuity, and discontinuity breeds ambiguity.

So far, so straightforward. The trouble is that the world, every piece of it inexhaustible, will not lend itself to coverage by discourse. Nor would discourse cover it, even if it could, because meaning and value depend on selection. All other things being equal, for instance, an event dramatized into a scene will assume greater importance than one telescoped into a summary, though there is nothing intrinsically important or unimportant about either. For the message to signify, there must be omissions, absolute and relative. But if this criterion operates to foreground and rank what the narrator leaves in, it entangles the problem of subdividing what he left out. Why does David have Uriah killed? When did this solution occur to him? Whence Bathsheba's readiness to commit adultery? How long did it take Joab to carry out the order? And what color were the messenger's eyes? All these questions point to aspects of the David and Bathsheba world or plot omitted from the David and Bathsheba narrative. And yet they mark—everyone will agree, I'm sure—a descending order of importance. But on what basis? How do we, under the Bible's guidance, manage to draw value-laden distinctions within what is not there?

Two conclusions follow. The first concerns the need to separate omissions or lacunae into relevancies ("gaps") and irrelevancies ("blanks"). This is a universal of reading that no one can escape for a moment, including those who shudder at the very mention of interpretation. To make sense is to make distinctions between what was omitted for the sake of interest and what was omitted for lack of interest: between what I called, for short, gaps and blanks. Only the former demand closure, while the latter may be disregarded without loss, indeed must be disregarded to keep the narrative in focus. The things a writer may wish to communicate about the world, like the questions the audience may wish to ask about it, are limitless. But since the whole of anything can never be told, the whole truth is always the contextually relevant truth—including the filled gaps but exclusive of the innumerable blanks.

In practice, however, the distinction turns out as problematic as it is inescapable, since it can appeal to no formal (and thus automatically applicable) marker. The gap and the blank show identical characteristics in all that regards temporal structure. So any informational lacuna may in principle give rise to either, and one reader's gap may prove another's blank. In biblical studies, indeed, this has often been the case. Professionally bent on wringing from the text every bit of information, historians have posed (and sometimes answered) questions that find little if any anchorage in the text's own concerns and management. Overreading, though by a different logic and to other ends, is of course the occupational hazard of interpreters as well. On the other hand, geneticists are apt to explain away discontinuity in terms of misadventure in transmission, especially when assuming the writer's lack of interest in psychology or his general incompetence. The first procedure tends to elevate blanks to gaphood; the second, to downgrade gaps to blankhood.

Hence, second, the need for criteria other than impressionistic. If temporal displacement along the lines I outlined forms the necessary condition for a gap, these criteria will provide the sufficient condition. I speak of criteria in the plural because, as everyone can convince himself by reviewing a miscellany of examples, no hard-and-fast rule of validation obtains in the Bible any more than it does in other artworks. Still, the set of validators I shall propose share an important feature. All bring to bear on the missing piece specifically biblical operations and principles, of which the most regulative is the subject of this chapter. To validate the relevance of the absent is to heighten the reader's sense of suspension between the truth and the whole truth.

Temporary and Permanent Gapping

All gaps result from discontinuities between the order of narration and the order of occurrence, with its straight chronology. But it makes a considerable difference whether what happened at a certain point in the action emerges in the narration later or not at all. Compare the following passages:

> (1) Samson went down to Timnah, and at Timnah he saw one of the daughters of the Philistines. (2) He came up and told his father and mother, saying, I saw a woman at Timnah, of the daughters of the Philistines; now get her for me for a wife. (3) And his father and mother said, Is there not a woman among the daughters of thy kinsmen or all our people that thou goest to take a wife from the uncircumcised Philistines? But Samson said to his father, Get her for me; for she pleases me. (4) His father and mother did not know that it was from the Lord, for he was seeking an occasion against the Philistines. (Judges 14:1-4)

> (25) The man seized his concubine and put her out to them [the people of Gibeah who demanded to "know" him]. And they knew her and abused her all night until the morning, and as the dawn began to break, they let her go. (26) As morning appeared, the woman came and fell down at the door of the man's house where her master was, till it was light. (27) And her master rose up in the morning and opened the door of the house and went out to go on his way, and behold, the woman

his concubine was lying at the door of the house, with her hands on the threshold. (28) He said to her, Get up and let us be going. But there was no answer. Then he put her on the ass; and the man rose up and went away to his place. (29) When he entered his house, he took a knife and seized his concubine and divided her, limb by limb, into twelve pieces, and sent her throughout all the territory of Israel. (30) And all who saw it said, Such a thing has never happened or been seen from the day that the people of Israel came up from the land of Egypt. (Judg 19:25–30)

In the Samson passage, the chronological order of occurrence that we reconstruct at the end of verse 4 goes as follows: (a) God, bent on delivering Israel from her oppressors, seeks to make trouble between Samson and the Philistines; as a result, (b) Samson falls in love with a Philistine woman; naturally, (c) he asks his parents to arrange a marriage, and no less naturally, (d) they raise objections; but (e) without avail. Yet this sequence, which would prepose God as the initiator of a naturalistic-looking plot, gets twisted in the actual telling into another that withholds and delays the first link to the end. With the divine architect kept out of view, the order we encounter in the reading greets us with an odd piece of information that at once produces a gap about antecedents. How come that a born deliverer of Israel should want to enter into an exogamous marriage, and with a member of the oppressing nation at that? Samson's parents then voice the incongruity; and his own recalcitrance, closing all interpretive loopholes like youthful thoughtlessness, deepens it further. Only at this late point does the narrator reveal what none of the three human subjects knew and two (Samson and his parents) still do not: "that it was from the Lord." Our wonder having been aroused, echoed, and drawn out, it proves *in resolution* justified if somewhat short-sighted: we should have looked for an explanation not (and certainly not only) in Samson's but in God's mind. And the true cause having emerged at the end, we must go back to the beginning to reshape the sequence and (because of the shift in level and motivation from human character to divine plan) the meaning and the scale of the action. We reread on enlightenment, and with redoubled attention, what we read before in artful darkness. In terms of validation, therefore, the gap's multiple effect from opening to authoritative closure only enhances the sense of relevance given by its temporariness. Its very closure, in perceptibly belated retrospect, establishes that it was there in the first place.

This does not hold for the Gibeah story. Was the raped woman alive or dead when addressed and later dismembered by her master? Was her lack of response to the man's marching orders ("Get up and let us be going") due to exhaustion, shame, or merciful release? The tale's own phrase applies to the reader's question as well: there is no answer. Not at once, nor ever. The cause and time of death remain a permanent gap, the information having been elided to open an ambiguity for the reader to puzzle over throughout.

We cannot help puzzling over it, because the answer would make quite a difference to our judgment of the other participants. And in fact, the resolution never comes exactly because the narrator wants to prevent our drawing any sharp line between them. By the device of permanent elision, forcing on us the two mutually exclusive readings, he manages to blacken both parties to the crime at once. On the one hand, the woman died of pain and shock while still lying at the door, which exposes the townsmen to the odium of murder as well as gang rape. On the other hand, though speechless or unconscious, she was alive till dismembered; and this gives the finishing touch to the portrait of her sanctimonious spouse, who pushed her out into the arms of the gang to save his own hide and then spent the night in bed while she was being subjected to horrors. His doings extend from "seized his concubine and put her out" to "seized his concubine and divided her, limb by limb." (In retelling, of course, he lays the death at the others' door; but his version is hardly reliable.) With the ambiguity pointing an accusing finger both ways, there is much less to choose between the hypothetical killers than the Levite's outraged appeal to the nation would suggest. Each thus functions to illustrate the narrator's lamenting refrain, "In those days there was no king in Israel; every man did what was right in his own eyes."

Why does Tamar disguise herself as a prostitute (Gen 38:13–19)? Who is the roaming priest acquired by the Danites (Judg 17:7; 18:30)? What lies behind Solomon's order to divide the baby (1 Kings 3)? How does Boaz mean to fulfill Ruth's hopes (Ruth 3:9–13; 4:1–13)? These figure among the Bible's temporary gaps. They contrast with the permanence of the ambiguity shrouding the reason for Moses' reluctance to assume the office of leader (Exod 3:4), the identity of Jacob's nocturnal assailant (Gen 32:25–31), the inner life throughout the Bathsheba affair.

It is not that the difference is immediately apparent or that multiple hypotheses are reserved for the permanent variety. As long as the information remains fragmentary, any gap counts as virtually permanent; and to make sense of what happens, the reader cannot wait to find out whether or not the narrator will in the end supply the whole truth about Tamar's motives or Boaz's plans. Rather, the reader fills in the gaps himself to the best of his (limited) ability, forming and revising and if possible deciding between alternative closures as he goes along, till the end either resolves or fixes the play of ambiguity. Prior to the terminal point, therefore, the distinction between temporary and permanent gaps does not much signify.

The less so considering the surprises often held by the intermediate route: the abrupt reopening of gaps ostensibly closed before, such as the motivation of Laban's hospitality, or the last-minute closure of gaps apparently destined for openness or even blankhood, like the wandering priest's name.

In retrospect, however, the disparity between the two types of suppression comes into force. Each has its own resources for establishing the relevance of absence. Since the temporary gap arises from an artificial disordering of the naturally ordered sequence, its closure raises a combinatory question. Why has the narrative chosen to distribute the information that belongs together, to deform a coherent plot only to reform it into proper chronology at a later stage? In short, why fabricate an ambiguity destined for resolution, and why conceal and reveal the truth at exactly these stages? This leads to the kinds of explanation I instanced in the foregoing analyses and will generalize in what follows. On the other hand, forming a causal-chronological breach in the reconstituted as well as in the actual sequence devised for the reading, the permanent gap generates a different question: Why has the narrator chosen to omit this information altogether?

In principle, the latter question admits of a simple answer, namely, that this information happens to be irrelevant. That a question about the narrated world *can* be posed does not yet legitimate its posing and resolution in terms of the narrative discourse. Hence the need for corroboration, in at least one of the forms to which we now proceed. If the temporary gap may (and does) receive such contextual support, the permanent gap must receive it to be distinguished from a mere blank in which some reader or approach happens to take undue interest.

The Echoing Interrogative

Apart from its temporariness—and at a point where the filling is still kept back—the gap concerning Samson's behavior derives validity from its articulation by interpreters other than the reader. "Is there not a woman among the daughters of thy kinsmen or all our people," his parents object aloud, "that thou goest to take a wife from the uncircumcised Philistines?" In less reticent styles, such pointers may come from the narrator himself. The opening dialogues of Henry James's *Tragic Muse* having suggested that the hero approaches some crisis, the narrator intrudes to tantalize us with the comment, "Why a crisis—what was it, and why had he not come to it before? The reader shall have these things in time if he care enough for them" (chap. 2). There can be no stronger support for the question revolving in our own mind, but the Bible would not pay the price in obtrusiveness. It prefers, even to a higher extent than with other types of commentary, to delegate the voicing of the hitherto implicit gap to the agents and observers within the drama itself. "What hast thou against me that thou hast come to me to fight against my land?" Jephthah's messengers ask the Ammonite king; whereupon the invader's reply straightens out this long-standing chronological deformation by unfolding his territorial claims on eastern Israel (Judg 11:12–28). "Why hast thou not gone down to thy house?" David interrogates Uriah, only to elicit the equivocation about the Ark and the warriors in the field that deepens rather than closes the gap. Even more so does the inquiry Jacob makes of his nocturnal assailant, "Tell me, pray, thy name" (Gen 32:29), which meets with point-blank refusal. Whether the enacted gap remains temporary or permanent, therefore, the question-and-answer enactment doubly highlights its relevance: the question always echoes and the answer either dispels or perpetuates our sense of mystery, incongruity, discontinuity.

In terms of point of view, each voiced gap signals equality in ignorance between the coupled interpreters, the dramatized (Samson's parents, Jephthah, Jacob) and the implied (the reader). Faced with the same lack of information, each tries to make sense of events by casting about for the missing link: the reader, by looking back on the past; the character, also by directly tackling the logical informant. Not that the question-and-answer form is confined to the egalitarian relationship. Often it displays the characters as troubled (and enlightened) about puzzles that we have been spared by the orderly chronology of the omniscient narration. If Jacob's acknowledged ignorance of the attacker's identity parallels ours, then Isaac's interrogation of the disguised Jacob in the blessing scene is a measure of inferiority: the blind man's suspicion is our certitude, his gap our fact. With questions coming out of the blue, the reverse discrepancy in awareness arises. Take the surprise question that Ishbosheth addresses to Abner, "Why hast thou gone in to my father's concubine?" (2 Sam 3:7). It springs on us a situation where one agent reproaches another for a full-blown and explosive affair of which we have had no inkling, let alone any queries. Accordingly, what all three reading positions have in common is that the dramatized question encapsulates the appropriate play of perspectives and foregrounds a crux in the plot or the meaning. Only in the intermediate as opposed to the two polar strategies, it serves the additional purpose of forcing some recent suppression on the notice of the least alert reader and confirming by echo the initiate's sense of distance from the whole truth.

Opposition in Juxtaposition

Gaps of either kind and their expression heighten our sense of disharmony: they bring out the missing link in the chain, the oddity of conduct, the inconsistency or looseness of the official record. Each procedure makes some further ado about the lacuna, redoubling the disturbance so as to call attention to what might otherwise pass unnoticed. This is how they sift the gaps from the numberless blanks, whether by way of selectional clues, temporal distribution, or perspectival underlining. But the same validating effect may be generated (or reinforced) by other combinatory patterns, notably juxtaposition-turned-opposition:

> Jacob said to Laban, Give me my wife that I may go in to her, for my term is completed. Laban gathered together all the men of the place and made a feast. In the evening, he took his daughter Leah and brought her to him; and he went in to her. Laban gave her, his daughter Leah, Zilpah his maidservant to be her maid. In the morning, and behold, it was Leah! (Gen 29:21–25)

> Cain rose up against his brother Abel and killed him. And the Lord said to Cain, Where is Abel thy brother? And he said, I do not know; am I my brother's keeper? (Gen 4:8–9)

> Esau said, Let us start on our journey and I will go alongside thee. And [Jacob] said to him, My lord knows that the children are frail . . . and if they are overdriven even one day, all the flocks will die. Let my lord pass on before his servant and I will proceed slowly . . . until I come to my lord in Seir. . . . So Esau turned back that day on his way to Seir. And Jacob journeyed to Succoth and built himself a house. (Gen 33:12–17)

> Michal, David's wife, told him, saying, If thou dost not save thy life tonight, tomorrow thou wilt be killed. Michal let David down through the window, and he went and fled and escaped. . . . Saul said to Michal, Why hast thou deceived me thus, letting my enemy go, so that he escaped? And Michal said to Saul, He said to me, Let me go; why should I kill thee? (1 Sam 19:11–17)

> Joab knew that the king's heart went out to Absalom. So Joab sent to Tekoa and fetched from there a wise woman . . . [and through her manipulated David into recalling his favorite from exile.] Then the king said to Joab, Behold now, I grant this thing; go, bring back the lad, Absalom. Joab fell on his face to the ground and did obeisance and blessed the king; and Joab said, Today thy servant knows that I have found favor in thy sight, my lord the king, in that the king has granted the request of his servant. (2 Sam 14)

In each instance, the narrative juxtaposes two pieces of reality that bear on the same context but fail to harmonize either as variants of a situation or as phases in an action. Taken at face value, event clashes with event, speech with event, speech with speech, or interior with vocal discourse. And the fact that the pieces appear in quick succession highlights their semantic distance. Later chapters, especially those on temporal disconti- nuity and repetition structure, will concentrate on the modes and roles of such fractures. Now I only want to indicate, with the aid of a few simple examples, how this principle contributes to the grounding and fore- grounding of gaps.

The wedding night sequence begins by disturbing both Jacob's and the narrator's consistency. Jacob bargained for Rachel, so why does he settle for Leah? The midposed reference to Zilpah then leaves the question suspended, to the enhancement of our sense of time (a busy night) and of inconsistency alike. The retardation over, the non sequitur abruptly extends to the narrator himself, who expresses wonder ("and behold!") at a fact that he plainly recorded before: the bedfellow's identity. This exten- sion, however, serves to disentangle the whole affair. Instead of attributing the surprise to the omniscient narrator—incoherence and all—one would in principle much rather anchor it in Jacob, especially since the biblical "and behold" (*ve'hinneh*) operates as a clue to subjectivity in the form of free indirect thought. But why should Jacob himself experience surprise? Here the contrast between the incidental details "In the morning" and "In the evening" comes to the rescue, opening up the possibility that Leah was smuggled into the bridal bed under cover of darkness and identified too late. The leading account, then, contains an imperceptible gap and the follow-up a retrospective disclosure of the switch: the chronology has been so deformed as to align the reader's viewpoint and process of discovery with Jacob's. Indeed, the tricked trickster at once confirms our entire re- construction of the twofold plot—Laban's and the artist's—by echoing our own query: "What is this thou hast done to me? Did I not serve with thee for Rachel? Why then hast thou deceived me?" With all the other validators present—temporariness, unusual selection of detail, dramatized inter- rogative—it is still the juxtaposition that pinpoints the incongruity and launches the quest for harmony by gap-filling.

In the examples that follow, the opposition having once drawn notice to the gap, there is even no need to conjecture figural subjectivity and interference in transmission. For at least one of the opposing members formally originates in a character. Given the reliable account of Abel's mur- der, we thus resolve the murderer's outrageous plea of ignorance by supply- ing an in-between motive: fear of punishment *cum* hope of concealment.

The same reading operation foregrounds and interprets the obverse sequence as well. If Jacob's speech fails to cohere with his subsequent action, this is because he puts Esau off with a promise of reunion in Seir that he has no intention of keeping. Their past relations and the circumstances of their present encounter make such duplicity far more probable than a later change of mind. Just as the contrary is true of the night scene where David first instructs Abishai to remove the spear and the canteen from beside the sleeping Saul and then—with no reason given but presumably in sudden distrust of his lieutenant's impulsiveness—removes them himself (1 Sam 26:7–12). In both cases, of course, the permanence of the gap leaves the hypotheses multiple and the preference decidable on contextual grounds alone. But either filling would establish as well as repair the causal breach, and in similar terms: the overt discontinuity between speech and action gets bridged by appeal to the covert workings of the psyche behind both.

So do a variety of jarring movements from one speech to another by the same speaker. Since Michal saved David's life on her own initiative, why should she tell Saul the opposite of the truth if not from fear? It is actually her father, not her husband, who may "kill her" for treachery. Again, the missing psychological link in the dialogic chain may relate not so much to hidden as to second thoughts. Consider how the Reuben and Gad tribes first apply to Moses for exemption from crossing the Jordan and then do an about-turn and volunteer "to go before the people of Israel" throughout the conquest. The leader's intervening (and explicit) tirade must have precipitated another intervening (but implicit) development, in the form of a conviction on the part of the would-be Transjordanians that to achieve their tribal goal they must spearhead rather than shirk the national campaign (Numbers 42). And when the sequential opposition holds between inner and vocal speech, this line of resolution comes even more naturally to the fore. The distance that separates Joab's thinking how to do the king a favor from Joab's thanking the king for having done "his servant" a favor coincides with the distance separating interior from social discourse. Judging by the zest with which he plays the grateful petitioner, Joab himself must have savored the irony.

Just as the members of the opposition may vary—between act, speech, and thought—so may its sharpness and hence the perceptibility of the resulting gaps. Dissonance varies with distance, and along several lines. One is simply textual. All other things being equal, the more adjoining the members, the more glaring their divergence as variations and their non sequitur as actions. God's sanction against Moses in Numbers (19:12, 24) versus Moses' throwing the blame on the people in Deuteronomy (1:37; 4:21), the envoy's report in Genesis 24 of Abraham's transfer of his property to Isaac versus the narrator's reference to that transaction a chapter later,

Cain as murderer in one sentence and innocent in the next: these trace an ascending order of perceptibility in opposition. Hence the significance of the Bible's tendency, manifested in all the examples just cited, to deploy such inconsonants within the limits of a single episode, often even cheek by jowl. Hence also, inversely, the question whether mismatches straddling whole books indicate a gapping design or a change in authorship, a poetic or a genetic discrepancy.

In its semantic aspect, distance varies with the logical relations between the members juxtaposed. The fuller the opposition, the more incongruous the juxtaposition. At their most distanced, the pieces of reality hold relations of mutual exclusiveness: either Cain murdered Abel or he has no idea of his whereabouts; Saul's association with David began either in the palace or on the battlefield; or, speaking of *implicit* ambiguity, Uriah either knows or does not know. At their least distanced, short of verbatim equivalence, the opposition assumes a general-particular form—as when the narrator mentions that the Philistines captured the Ark and then, having interposed Eli's response to the catastrophe, picks up the thread to render a more detailed account (1 Samuel 4-5). Between the peremptory and the minimal gap there extends a dense continuum of breaches, variously establishing a marked departure in terms of correspondence and/or a marked rupture in terms of plot. The servant's description of the well scene does not *coincide with* the narrator's. Solomon's judgment hardly *issues from* the empirical data. Given Jacob's promise to Esau, his journey to Succoth fails to *follow* in either sense.

Unless, of course, the semantic or logical distance is bridged along some other axis, which invites the reader either to postulate an intermediate link (the servant's rhetoric, Solomon's inspiration, Jacob's guile) or a mere blank. It is exactly here that perspectival variations come in to radicalize some discontinuities, moderate others, and validate the gappiness of either type by implying lines of closure. Within each member of the opposition, who says what to whom? Its relevance ensured by the Bible's sensitivity to point of view, this question brings into play the qualitative differences between the two orders of vision. Due to its superhuman authority, for one thing, the discourse anchored in God and the narrator overrides any human opposition. This encourages us to explain the representational in terms of perspectival distance: to make the most of discrepancies in awareness (knowledge versus ignorance) or in telling (e.g., truthfulness versus mendacity). Such an explanation of the gap will repair even the widest breaches. Jacob as bridegroom may safely be assumed to diverge from the narrator in what he sees, Cain in what he thinks fit to communicate, Michal in both. By the same token, however, even a slight appearance of inconsistency within the narrator's own account will strike us far more forcibly than its logical status would warrant. And attuned to the strategic principle of maneuvering between the truth and the whole truth, the reader tends to resolve it in functional rather than genetic terms—as a clue to inference rather than as a symptom of interference. The non sequitur, we are then led to conjecture, marks a withholding of information to be supplied in its proper chronological place by reference to an agent's mind, God's own included. The variant repetition, alternatively, signals a shift in treatment—from, say, a cursory to a full-scale account—or again in viewpoint, from objective to subjective rendering. The gap once subjectified and transferred to a figural consciousness, its closure becomes a problem of choice among the host of available motivations: blindness, fear, irony, spite, mendacity, dialogic face-saving, monologic license, perceptual conditioning, change of mind or attitude. As shown by the ambiguity enveloping Uriah—and accounting for so many of the narrative tensions— this choice need not even be clearcut. The heart of biblical man is intricate enough to accommodate the most diverse sentiments and the most conflicting motives.

More generally speaking, the sharpness of the representational discontinuity between the "juxtaposed" members is proportionate to their continuity in all other respects. Perspectival continuity is one important factor: opposition from the same viewpoint, as with Michal's discrepant speeches, looks far more incongruous than opposition with shift of position. Therefore the interpreter always seeks—above all, within the narrator's privileged discourse—to convert one into the other. Michal, we say, changes addressees (Saul in place of David); Joab, expressive contexts (dialogue in place of monologue); the narrator, voices and tactics. Another variable is temporal continuity, its maintenance likewise operating to fix gaps and its hypothetical disruption to resolve them. The plot non sequitur, so disquieting as long as taken to reflect the order of occurrence, makes sense as soon as we infer and close an in-between hiatus: David's despair of tricking Uriah, say, comes between the warm welcome and the liquidation order. (With temporary gaps—like Jacob's sleeping with Leah—this movement from continuous truth to discontinuous whole-truth even shows on the narrative surface.) Similarly, troubled by finding the same object differently rendered by the same speaker on the same occasion, the reader looks around for some intervening development: such is the Transjordanian tribes' change of mind between their two proposals to Moses.

As with continuity in perspective and time, so with character, intention, even genre. In the framework of biblical prose, sequential opposition remains much more conspicuous and disturbing than when the narrative shifts its generic gears. Once the tale modulates into or from parable (as with Jotham's sermon from the mount) or poetry (Deborah's or Hannah's song) or dream (as often in Genesis), divergences from the prose version find their coherence in the laws of the genre: formal constraints, poetic license, stylized expression, the language of symbols or morals. It makes no sense, therefore, to ask why Hannah sings of the barren woman bearing seven children while she herself bore only six; nor to dovetail every reference in Deborah's paean with the foregoing tale of the victory; nor to wed all items of the dream or the parable to realistic correlates. Generic goes with representational variation, convention goes against conjecture. Along this axis, then, variety exceptionally blocks or at least plays down (because it replaces) the operations of gap-filling. But the general interpretive rule still remains in force: continuity in opposition makes for the establishment of gaps, discontinuity for their resolution.

Coherence Threatened and Fortified

From another side, all the measures discussed so far establish the relevance of withheld information on pain of incoherence. Incoherence will result if we fail to account for the belated emergence of God's designs on the Philistines, to distinguish between the claims of scene and summary, to associate ourselves with the questions puzzling the dramatis personae, to take notice of variants or non sequiturs, and so on. Thus viewed, these invitations to hypothesis-making have several counterparts in the Bible's repertoire.

The most basic consists in plot value or function. In general, the reader's interest in missing antecedents and transitions depends on the extent to which he is made conscious of their role within the causal sequence, where past is ineluctably linked to present and future. The centrality of a gap accordingly becomes proportionate to the havoc it plays with (or the other way around, the contribution its filling would make to) the intelligibility of the plot. Even on the simplest level of reading, what happens makes little sense unless we reconstruct the chronological order to supply such omissions as why Joseph plays with his brothers or why David summons Uriah to Jerusalem. Contrary to the oft-made claim that the Bible neglects the secret life in favor of higher interests, the gaps thus foregrounded by the plot bear on the characters' psychology rather than overt actions. But then so do most biblical gaps, including those that the "havoc" criterion would stamp as relatively innocuous (because the questions they raise concern minor agents, or single events, or the beginning and ending rather than the heart of the causal chain, or even cruxes sufficiently resolved on the surface to pass muster, like why Abraham's servant retells his adventure). It is on these gaps, as if to compensate for the smallness of their intrinsic nuisance value by giving them other claims to attention, that the Bible will most often bring to bear the validators mentioned earlier. Delayed disclosure, scenic rendering and echoing, opposition in juxtaposition: each works by its own means to transform even a tiny into a big question mark and a faint into a nagging discomfort about the plot.

Needless to say, these also rouse the reader to action by threatening values associated with plot, notably the coherence of character and reality-model. But much the same effect derives from an incentive other than the structural problematics of the world. A gap may force itself on the reader's notice by virtue of its implications for theme and judgment. Puzzling over David's move and Uriah's countermove is dictated by the need to make agents and acts intelligible, but it is equally vital for their evaluation. David who summons Uriah in order to confess is one man; David who machinates to add insult to injury is quite another. These two interpretive pressures—from world and world view—need not even go together. When exactly did the raped woman in Judges die? So little does such a question affect the overall course of events that it might escape attention were it not for the difference the answer makes to our view of the murderer and the whole thematic pattern.

The gap's relevance and centrality, then, depend more on the magnitude of the threat it presents to narrative integration than on the quarter from which the threat comes. Such magnitude may in turn depend on combinations of minor threats, varying in scope, origin, target, sequential emergence. Not surprisingly, considering its art of relations, the Bible even prefers the cumulative to the big-bang method of exciting notice. Hence, again, the frequent coincidence and interlinkage of diverse signals in our examples; hence also their flexible coordination with still other devices, notably the progressive harping on an enigma or oddity as the tale unfolds. On Sarah's first appearance, the narrator observes with no special fanfare that she "was barren; she had no child" (Gen 11:30). Abraham once called, however, this feature grows increasingly discordant. It is not only that the generic context of Genesis invests the issue (in more than one sense) with tremendous ideological and historical weight. In his very first address to Abraham, God promises "I will make of thee a great nation" (12:2). The ensuing reference to the patriarch's age ("five and seventy years") indicates the need for urgency in fulfillment. The constant presence of Lot as his uncle's fellow traveler rubs in the absence of a son, and their growing estrangement and ultimate parting even quashes the possibility that "the great nation" will issue from an adopted rather than a natural heir. Each new development thus sharpens the non sequitur between God's promise and Abraham's plight. Has God failed or has he delayed to keep his word? Or, what seems less probable, is it just that the narrator has failed or delayed to record how God had kept his word, due to the pressure of other business—just as he chose to pursue the story of Eden to the final expulsion before doubling back in time ("Adam had known Eve his wife and she conceived") to inform us of the childbearing? Though the incongruity has been studiously ignored on the narrative surface, therefore, Abraham's eventual complaint ("What wilt thou give me, when I go childless?") finds us fully prepared, voicing an old question rather than springing a new.

This crux gains its perceptibility from the arts of sequence. But later equivalents in patriarchal history derive theirs from the suprasequential forms of analogy as well. The theme of mysterious barrenness having once been announced, making sense of its variations (How? Why? Till when?) enjoys relevance, affords interest, develops meaning, gives a sense of a system, and generally yields a superior, because more integrated, text. If the negative face of gapping consists in its operations as a disruptive force, demanding attention by threats of incoherence, then its positive face extends an invitation to synthesis beyond the bare necessities of reading and offers a point of maximum convergence.

Norms and Their Violation

To return once again to Samson's first love. Note to what an extent the gap-producing oddity of his conduct derives from its running counter to an established norm: the fiat or custom of endogamous marriage, which of all Israelites would be most binding on a man of God. But this is only one of a whole set of norms that regulate the biblical gap—all subsumed under the general norm or presumption of coherence. To see why they must be thus inferred and subsumed, imagine a text or a reading where no such presumption obtains: where the model of reality may change its laws from moment to moment, the dramatis personae change character, the ideology change sides, the language change rules, and the discourse or poetics change conventions. (Or to extend this lawlessness to the indicators just discussed: where information may be suppressed and then revealed at haphazard or the enigmas troubling the agents bear no relation to the reader's concerns.) Obviously, this way chaos lies; and even a narrative so fluid as Robbe-Grillet's *La Maison de rendez-vous* or an analyst so dedicated to atomism as a radical source-critic does not approach this extreme. In all discourse, whether viewed from the author's or the reader's side, the making of sense hinges on the postulation of constancies—laws, rules, regularities, continuities, or, in short, norms—if for no other purpose than to make divergence perceptible and meaningful. Coherence is inseparable from norms.

Given this universal of communication, particular works (or styles or genres or periods) may still widely differ in the techniques for implementing it: in the frames of coherence, the areas and limits of incoherence, the roles performed by the interplay between the coherent and the incoherent, etc. This whole book is exactly a study in the principles of biblical coherence, emphatically including the coherence of deliberate and systematic incoherencies, or in other words, of the difficult coherence regulated by the maneuvering between the truth and the whole truth that the search for the facile click has mistaken for incoherence. My immediate concern, however, is with a set of underlying norms whose violation operates to establish informational gapping throughout biblical narrative.

Since those norms look more assorted than they actually are, let me first indicate their similitude in dissimilitude. It consists in a protean law of reading that I would call, for short, the breach-to-gap-to-norm movement: a cultural breach always points to an informational gap, whose closure will either restore or replace the norm originally broken.

To be sure, all norms are cultural, but this does not make them equipollent even within the same culture. In the Bible's system, for reasons already considered, the *epistemological norm* that opposes divine to human knowledge is the most binding and its infringement, accordingly, the most perturbing. Why does the Omniscient start some conversations with a profession of ignorance, and what is more, about matters to which even we are privy, like the question of Abel's whereabouts? Whatever our hypothesis, the interpretive process then follows the same route. It will begin by detecting a gap in God's conduct against the background of the supernatural norm and end by resolving it through an explanation that preserves that norm: he intends to trap the sinner, to elicit a confession, or merely to set a dialogue going. All these entail a shift, not nearly so imperative in pagan literature, from the axis of potentiality to performance. To close the gap, that is, we deduce some motive for God's masking a rhetorical as an information-seeking query.

By the same law, the crossing of the epistemological borderline by a human also assumes enough incongruity to open a gap:

> Esau said to himself, The days of mourning for my father are approaching, and then I will kill my brother Jacob. But the words of her older son Esau were told to Rebekah. She sent and called her younger son Jacob, and said to him, Behold, thy brother Esau consoles himself with the thought of killing thee. Now therefore . . . flee to Laban my brother in Haran. (Gen 27:41-43)

How have Esau's secret designs ("said to himself") reached Rebekah? The midrash appeals to divine inspiration; but then, to meet interpretive exigencies, it deals out far too liberally and ad hoc a privilege that the Bible itself often withholds from full-time prophets. The naturalistic inference that the plan leaked out because Esau could not keep his own counsel is both simpler and more in character. Either way, however, it is again the apparent violation of the norm that opens the gap; and, whether we choose to elevate one character (Rebekah) to the divine order or to consign another (Esau) to the all too human, it is its reaffirmation that closes the gap.

In the absence of such violation, significantly, dozens of comparable lacunae remain inert unless *otherwise* activated. Take the leakage of secret activities performed outside the mind. How did Pharaoh learn about Moses' killing of the Egyptian, or the king of Jericho about the infiltration of Joshua's spies? Nothing could be of less interest and relevance to the tale. And the Bible often shrugs off such questions through linguistic markers: the addressee-oriented verb, e.g., "Pharaoh heard" (Exod 2:15), or the passive equivalent, "Saul was told" (1 Sam 22:13), the conspiracy "became known to Mordecai" (Esth 2:22). The norm thus plays a role in the disqualification as well as the qualification of temporal discontinuities for the honors of gaphood.

With the predictable exception of omnipotence—which authorizes gaps like why God fails to interfere or how humans can work miracles—no other biblical norm rests on a qualitative, ungradable opposition. In principle, still, they all operate according to much the same breach-to-gap-to-norm logic. And to make up for the loss of absoluteness—to the detriment of perceptibility—they often converge on a single temporal displacement.

A variety of *moral and social norms* compose one important subset. It is not easy to tell where morality ends and mores begin in biblical culture; but their power to guide the reading, singly or in concert, is beyond doubt—and I refer not to the making of judgments alone but of sense in general. Whatever Samson precisely offends against in going to the Philistines for a wife, his offense is serious enough to antagonize and disturb the reader together with the parents, who express the national view of exogamy. In the face of Amnon's dishonorable intentions, Tamar likewise speaks in the voice of her culture: "No, my brother, do not abuse me; for such a thing is not done in Israel; do not commit this outrage" (2 Sam 13:12). Unlike Samson's behavior, Amnon's does not come as a total surprise. Yet the girl's remonstrance so brands and pinpoints its incongruity as to serve as a measure of the rapist's passion and character, thus filling out our knowledge.

Even where left implicit, such norms are potent enough in the Bible's rule-governed world to force open gaps about the antecedents of disorderly acts. How come that Solomon has Joab struck down while he is gripping the horns of the altar (1 Kgs 2:28–34)? How dare Uriah (2 Sam 11:11) and later Joab (19:6–8) address their king with such disrespect? How is it possible that a traveler should find no hospitality in the streets of Gibeah, unless, as the narrator indeed confirms later, the townspeople are "base fellows" (Judg 19:22)? And considering the solemnity of anointment, why does Elisha instruct his messenger to "open the door and flee" (2 Kgs 9:3) as soon as he has poured the oil on Jehu's head? As with antecedents, more-over, so with consequents. Amnon's rape of Tamar focuses attention on the unnatural silence of her brother and natural avenger, Absalom; so do Joab's harsh words bring out David's wordlessness. Since passivity or acquiescence on the injured party's side would aggravate the breach of rule, his silence assumes an ominous meaning; and his ultimate retaliation—restoring cultural equilibrium by murder in one case, dismissal from high office in the other—does not quite take us by surprise. Itself attended by a gap with a normative anchorage, the action in turn opens another, which the counteraction then resolves in accordance with decorum and expectation.

Note, finally, how often the narrative makes doubly sure by dramatiz-ing the operative norm, especially when left unvoiced, in an action *juxta-posed* with the infringement itself. Thus, the custom of sanctuary gets dramatized in the executioner's hesitation about doing his business at the altar; the laws of hospitality, in the traveler's refusal to spend the night in a non-Israelite town; the decorums of anointment, in the question posed by Jehu's comrades, "Why did this mad fellow come to thee?"; and, by straight causal linkage, the misdemeanor of rape or lese-majesty in the vengeance that overtakes the misdemeanant. The firmer the cultural ground, the prompter and more warranted the interpreter's response to every tremor.

The cultural norm bearing on the gap may, accordingly, range all the way from ethics to etiquette. As concerns explicitness, it may be pre-supposed, dramatized in speech and action, or, usually when foreign, stated. Its violation may strike us as outrageous, daring, or, as in the anointment that prefigures Jehu's frenzy, grotesque—though not always in line with the viewpoint of the participants. (Guided by the Bible's ideological frame—which may well disapprove of the social norm itself—the reader's response to the breach accords with the dramatis personae's more in inter-pretation than in judgment.) And the violating act may raise questions about past causes or future effects; just as it may direct notice to the character and inner life of the agent (Samson, Amnon, Solomon) or the patient (Jehu) or both (the wonder about Joab's state of mind during the showdown soon giving way before David's quietness). All along the line, however, there arises a well-defined sense of incongruity crying for resolution in terms of some hidden link that will explain, if not vindicate, the breach of social rule.

What distinguishes the Bible's *psychological system of norms* from the social is its level of generality or what I would rather call "scope." This distinction brings out a principle of high interest. Generally speaking, a norm may govern the behavior (and foreground the divergent behavior) of various bodies of people, from humanity as a whole through certain types or groups or communities to specific persons. Let us designate these *scopes* as universal, typal, and individual respectively. In the light of this tripartition, the world view underlying biblical poetics reveals notable flexibilities and peculiarities.

The *social* norms just discussed concentrate in the *middle* range, bearing on Israelite culture in disregard of and often in emphatic opposition to its neighbors. So far as ideologically determined or colored, it is as a matter of principle that they do not lend themselves to application beyond the Chosen People; so far as they relate to decorum, the question of what others do simply fails to arise. Accordingly, where foreign customs do enter the picture, the narrator will go out of his way to formulate them—"for Egyptians might not eat bread with Hebrews" (Gen 43:32) to explicate the odd seating at Joseph's feast, "for one might not enter the king's gate wearing sackcloth" (Esth 4:2) to elucidate Mordecai's stopping at the gate—as if resolved to preclude any distraction by incidental puzzles. All this is a far cry from Homer's imposition of homogeneity, whereby the Greeks and Trojans have the same gods, arms, manners, codes of honor. Homer's cultural scope is universal, the Bible's typal.

In contrast, the *psychological* norms brought into play in the Bible are either universal or individual, to the pointed exclusion of the intermediate scope. We may thus encounter "the devisings of man's heart are evil from the first" (Gen 8:21) and "the driving is as the driving of Jehu the son of Nimshi, for he drives like a madman" (2 Kgs 9:20), but nothing comparable to, say, Balzac's favorite type-generalizations: on the ways of duchesses, old men, provincials, bankers, criminals, and what not. Nor is the absence of explicit formulation any accident, for characterological norms of this scope are not tacitly postulated either. Indeed, as I shall argue in chapter 10, each biblical character is *sui generis,* a unique combination of universals and idiosyncrasies. His behavior is therefore referrable to no psychological (and with the exception of a few villains, no moral) character-type: neither of the Israelite, nor of the Benjaminite, nor of the Woman, nor of the Deliverer, nor of the Prophet, nor of the Righteous or the Rich or the Lovelorn or the Vainglorious, nor even, coming down to heredity, of the Patriarch. The agents may have features in common but not clusters; and it is clustering that makes (stereo)types.

The fashion of sneering at intricate character portrayal in the name of art comes and goes in literary theory. I for one am convinced that the secret of the spell exercised by the Bible over numberless readers through the ages largely resides in its haunting portrait gallery. But the portraiture involves such art as must satisfy even the sneerers. It calls for distinctive and complex operations of reading: to establish coherence between behavior and personality, deed and motive, the reader must overleap rather than, as is far more usual, appeal to the middle range of stock character. In terms of this revolutionary world picture, if normal behavior may simply follow from some cultural convention, then divergence resists assimilation to any model (norm, rule, type, frame of reference) lying between human nature and individual psychology. Instead, the poles—including the traffic between them either way—yield four basic strategies whereby gaps are validated and closed so as to lead us from the truth to the whole truth about character.

Two of these four inferential logics operate within the confines of the poles themselves: the incongruity is brought out by reference to one (universal or individual) feature and then resolved by appeal to another of the same scope. Take first the inconstancy shown by that collective character named "Israel" throughout his history from Exodus to Exile. It is in the light of omnipresent tensions dramatized as early as the rise of humanity— and articulated by God in, for example, "sin crouching at the door, desiring thee, yet thou canst be its master" (Gen 4:7)—that we register and make sense of Israel's oscillation between faith and doubt, confidence and fear, thanksgiving and ingratitude, recovery and relapse. (According to the Bible's psychology, we recall, the presence or absence of the omnipotence effect may tip the collective scales. A case in point is the otherwise inexplicable decline from steadfast "mastery" in Joshua's age into recurrent "sin" throughout the Judges': it correlates with the decrease of the eyewitnesses to God's mighty acts [Josh 23-24; Judg 2:7-12]. History thus turns on a mass psychology determined by perceptual as well as ethical forces.) Personal (mis)conduct becomes intelligible in similar terms. Consider how David "untypically" falls into lust and murder but redeems himself in the end; or, in perceptual terms of similar generality, how the visitor's ascent to heaven "in the flame of the altar while Manoah and his wife looked on" (Judg 13:19-22) propels the dramatized observers from skepticism to fearful belief. In each instance, the movement from gapping to gap-filling is oriented throughout to universal points of reference that compose the image of man.

But since biblical man is so rarely Man, his opacities (divergences, non sequiturs) far more often take their reference *and* resolution from his own character as a unique interplay of universals. All that would figure as "in character" then becomes the operative norm; some act "out of character," the gapping violation; and the bringing of that act "into character," the resolution. Given David's loathing for "the lame and the blind" since the war against the Jebusites (2 Sam 5:6–8), one is brought up short by his decision to give Jonathan's son Mephibosheth, "lame in both feet" (9:3, 13), a permanent seat at the royal table. That the man could be shown favor in any number of ways and that appointing him a dining-room fixture would be enough to spoil all future meals for the king, carries this beyond ordinary inconsistency. Is David willing to undergo such a daily ordeal just in memory of his friendship with Jonathan, as he himself declares, or as the price for keeping an eye on the last of Saul's line? Considering David's genius for aligning the proper with the expedient, he may even be acting from both motives. No matter which of the three hypotheses we favor, however, our hypothesis-construction goes through the same process. What leaps out of character by reference to one peculiar trait falls back into character and intelligibility, and not without dividends, once orientation shifts to another.

Two further operations, distinct but often complementary, assume the form of cross-relating the universal and the individual scopes—appealing under interpretive pressure, so to speak, from one to the other. In the process, the range gets either narrowed or widened and the character, accordingly, either specified or generalized. Consider first the passage from gapping to closure in Abraham's binding of Isaac: what looks unbelievable in terms of a universal instinct (parental love) makes difficult but good sense in relation to a feature peculiar to the agent from his first appearance (heroic faith, obedience, selflessness). Conversely, a piece of behavior inconsistent with a figure's given or dramatized portrait may cohere in terms of some human fundamental. It would be strange to hear Obadiah, "who greatly feared the Lord," refusing to deliver Elijah's message to Ahab, were it not for the inference that he fears for his life even more (1 Kgs 18:1–14). Just as the movement from the universalist validation of the gap to its individualized closure brings out Abraham's transcendence of the human norm, so does the opposite movement suggest Obadiah's ultimate conformity. Both put to an acid test, each shows his true colors.

Other sets of norms bear not on the represented world that the agents inhabit—the models of divinity, society, character—but on the representing discourse encountered by the reader. *Linguistic rules or codes,* for one thing:

> Samson turned aside to see the remains of the lion, and behold, a swarm of bees in the carcass of the lion, and honey! (Judg 14:8)

> Pharaoh drew near, and the people of Israel lifted up their eyes, and behold, Egypt [was] marching after them! And they fell into great fear. (Exod 14:10)

Ben-hadad [king of Aram] sent out scouts and they told him, saying, Some men have come out from Samaria. And he said, If they have come out for peace, take them alive, and if they have come out for war, alive take them. (1 Kgs 20:17–18)

Each of these illustrates an anomaly with respect to a different axis of language: the syntagmatic, the paradigmatic, and the contextual. In the final sentence from Judges, the syntax is anomalous not so much due to the elliptical predicate as to the order imposed on the two subjects. Instead of appearing in succession, as befits coordinate members, one ("a swarm of bees") occupies its proper place at the beginning, while the other ("honey") comes late to make an infelicitous end. Thus left dangling, the second subject assumes the look of an afterthought. But if so, whose? Since the "and behold" opening signals free indirect thought in the Bible, the narrator is a less likely candidate for ownership than Samson himself. Indeed, we infer, it stands to reason that the hero should first have noticed the swarm of buzzing bees and only then caught the (less visible and more attractive) implications of their presence. Forcing the free indirectness on our attention, the syntactic discontinuity thus impels the reader to anchor the statement in the proper mind and fill it out into a two-stage train of thought. Our process of discovery within the narrative ends by reconstructing Samson's within the world.

In the Exodus passage, by contrast, the gap in the free indirect thought following "and behold" is highlighted through a selectional rather than a combinatory incongruity. The foregoing verse having twice referred to Egypt in the plural (*they* "pursued" and "overtook"), why the abrupt shift ("Egypt [was] marching") to the singular? Is it because the Israelites have eyes for nobody except Pharaoh, "drawing near" at the head of his army and personifying the might of Egypt? Or because they suddenly feel their military inferiority to the compact formation heading for them as one man? However that may be, the selectional deviance once identified as an index to a psychological gap, it will also find its resolution in the closure of that gap.

In the last example, the direct form of quotation gives the reference of the incongruity to a character something like factual status. Why does Ben-hadad issue such a nonsensical order, rendered all the more so by the deliberate-looking variation in repetition? If for peace "take them alive," but if for war, "alive take them": incoherent in terms of the state of affairs spoken about, the change in sequence must cohere in terms of the speaker. And so it does, once we link it to the narrator's sly glances at the goings-on in the Aramean headquarters on the eve of the war (20:12, 16). Not to put too fine a point on it, Ben-hadad is so drunk that he hardly knows what he is saying. With the missing antecedent supplied, the consequent order makes sense as a mockery of an order.

At the same time, these examples combine to suggest not only the fluidity of the line separating linguistic rules from *poetic norms and conventions* but also the proper hierarchy between these systems. That all these passages encompass units beyond the sentence and appeal to contextual parameters—speaker, speech vs. thought, decorums of relevance—would prevent traditional linguistics from capturing their violations and explaining their effects. A telling measure of this impotence is the fact that in contextual terms our examples mark an ascending and in grammatical terms a descending order of incongruity. (As well as failing if not disdaining to make sense of all three, the grammarian would describe the word order in the coordination as unhappy, the switch from the plural to the singular as a license granted to collective nouns, and, with a shrug, Ben-hadad's gabble as a vagary of individual performance.) What is more, the reading procedures launched turn on the reader's awareness that the Bible *institutionalized* discordance—including free indirect discourse, another of its major claims to originality—within its artistic repertoire. The linguist's very exceptions, let alone his omissions, fall into rule within the art of implication whereby the Bible processes meaning and response. As long as the examples are divorced from poetic rule—or for that matter approached under the prevalent illusion that the free indirect style rose as late as the novel—their features must be missed and, if noted, dismissed as irregular. Indeed, professionally debarred from missing anything, translators often string together Samson's two coordinates, render "Egypt" as grammatical plural, excise the "behold's," unfold Ben-hadad's two commands in the same sequence. Who stops to consider random irregularities, except perhaps to regularize them in passing? Only these (and many others) happen to be regular irregularities, inviting full regularization in the mind not on paper and by reference to poetic not linguistic code.

As with linguistic form, so in principle with any other system and device, including all the measures of validation discussed earlier. Even those ostensibly effective and artful in their own right derive their force from the regulation of the poetic whole of which they are parts. What makes a temporary gap, for instance? Certainly not that temporal displacement whereby an element is wrenched from its chrono-logical position and revealed at a subsequent point. However determinate-looking this twofold manipulation, it forms only a necessary not a sufficient condition of the gap effect. For it does not yet suffice to mark off temporary gaps from other chronological latecomers: the delayed reason for Samson's affair with the Philistines, say, from the delayed mention of Job's friends (2:11). Formally similar, they are totally dissimilar in function. Of the existence of Job's friends we have (and need have) no idea until they actually arrive on the scene; nor does their emergence from nowhere, after the catastrophe, illuminate in retrospect what has gone before. Though they belong to Job's expositional past no less than do his family or his riches, they get mentioned only when the need for their presence on stage arises. On the other hand, Samson's Philistine connection at once troubles us, its gapping effect produced by reference to specifically biblical rather than inherent or universal norms of storytelling. His conduct bears the mark of individualism, and the Bible's models of character together with the line of unique figures in Judges draw attention to the nonconformist. It goes against national custom and interest, and the Bible's outlook is nothing if not patriotic. It jars against his foretold destiny as a liberator, and God's predictions ensure fulfillment. It evokes a protest from his parents, and figural wonder always sounds a gong. All along the line, then, what in other normative contexts might appear trivial or even perfectly coherent operates within biblical poetics as a marked discontinuity and a call for inference. (And, of course, vice versa.) So the eventual disclosure of God's involvement only confirms our suspicions of a manipulated chronology by repaying them in the coin of altered and enhanced understanding. In short, that piece of information got delayed not because it was irrelevant in its natural slot but precisely because it was relevant and with a view to focusing its relevance in retrospect. It is this context-dependent feature alone that makes and breaks a temporary gap.

All other validators likewise need and receive validation from the poetics. By itself, the voiced question may count for little or, in genres like comedy or satire or the absurd, produce ironic or even grotesque effects by dramatizing the incongruity of the agents' concerns. It becomes such a forceful gapping measure due only to poetic directives, especially the high seriousness with which the Bible correlates the characters' drama of living and our drama of reading. So—due to their sheer frequency and the interest shown in motive—do the juxtaposed oppositions. So do the distinctions between central and peripheral gaps, resting on inferred scales of value and norms of plot intelligibility. So do the apparently nonpoetic norms, from the epistemological down: nowhere stated in the reticent discourse, they and their gap-producing violations must be reconstructed from its art. Ultimately, therefore, all these regulators of communication go back to the arch-regulator: the interplay of the truth and the whole truth.

From Gapping to Closure: The Functions of Ambiguity

The reader's discontent with the given truth once aroused, how is he supposed to advance toward the hidden whole truth? The first thing to remember is that if gapping operations are normatively determined—hence context-sensitive and hypothetical—so must gap-filling operations be. As stages in a continuous process of interpretation, the two even become mutually determinative. The opening of a gap (Does Uriah know? Is the woman alive or dead?) not only legitimates but also launches the activity of closure. Further, it even guides this activity, since a norm violated calls for rescue or replacement—often, as with biblical epistemology and psychology, by fairly clearcut mechanisms. In turn, closure not only repairs but also (re)validates the gap by assigning to it a place in the structure. The question looks forward to the answer, and the answer looks back to the question. The bidirectionality of the reading process could not be more evident and inescapable than in this movement.

Apart from these general principles, then, what governs the interpretive movement along the Bible's sequence? The problem can be approached through the means supplied for closure: directions (e.g., the narrator's filling of a temporary gap), half-directions (fillings voiced by characters, often unreliably), indirections (like metonymy, analogy, verbal echo, generic frame). Yet these are, precisely, means; and as such their enumeration will not by itself lead us very far. It can explain how the process of ambiguity is controlled but not why: why it gets launched in the first place, why it is sustained in a certain manner, why it goes through certain phases, why it ends by way of resolution or fixture at a certain point, why it exhibits uniformities and variations in different contexts. These forms will receive due notice in what ensues, but since their working and relevance are themselves subject to higher control, the best place to start from is the functions that *in*form them.

Among these functions of ambiguity, the most basic consist in the manipulation of narrative interest: curiosity, suspense, surprise. The withholding of information about the past, especially if it deforms the plot line—the effect appearing before or without the cause—at once stimulates the reader's *curiosity* about the action, the agents, their life and relations below the surface, the world they inhabit. To make sense of them, he will try to resolve the gaps; failing that, he will look forward to new disclosures; so that a gradual release of clues will keep him happily busy on the horns of ambiguity. The opposed temporal displacement by way of foreshadowing generates *suspense*. A conflict lies ahead, with an outcome uncertain in nature or in route, with sympathies divided between the two sides to heighten the clash between hope and fear or polarized to make a certain resolution desirable and its retardation enjoyably frustrating. *Surprise,* finally, catching the reader off-guard due to a false impression given earlier, brings all the pleasures of the unexpected as the elements spring into new shape. The dynamics of the three vary according to their dislocation of chronology. As tortuous forms of experience, however, each invests the reading with drama, excitement, adventure, entertainment value if you will.

The next chapter will do more justice to these primary narrative interests. But we must first deal, briefly, with two general misgivings about their very applicability in the biblical framework. One concerns the "original" audience's prior knowledge; the other, the Bible's hierarchy of values.

To start with the first question. Given the temporal distance separating the represented events from their representation, even the future naturally hidden from the characters (and by assimilation to their temporal co-ordinates or viewpoint, also from the reader locked into the narrative present) is in fact to the audience a thing of the past. This disparity in temporal position is almost a universal of narrative, fictional and historical, since the standard use of the past tense establishes a retrospective mode of narration. In all fictional and some historical writing, however, the tense-pattern simply indicates that by the time of narration the narrated events have worked themselves out, but does not assume that we know of them. In contrast, it might appear, the Bible's subject matter directly relates to the antecedents of a public with a long national memory and a strong sense of identity. And if they brought their knowledge to the reading, what room would be left for narrative interest? Can one be curious about what one knows, in suspense about what one foreknows, surprised by the expected?

Scholarly opinion about the audience's prior knowledge shows wide divergence. Its presuppositions extend from virtual omniscience to virtual virginity, owing to mass ignorance on the audience's part or mass fabrication on the storyteller's. But all this is pure guesswork, and never systematically argued at that. To cut the matter short, let us again distinguish historical mysteries from poetic realities.

As I showed in chapter 3, the narrator forges a chain of narrative transmission from fathers to sons, from eye to ear to writing. But this may well be a forgery rather than a forging: a storytelling posture, adopted in the rhetorical interests of authenticity and solidarity, with the most flimsy anchorage in genetic and public history. The only hard evidence that has come down to us, from a culture even more notorious in scholarship for the reworking of traditional material, certainly points this way. "Even subjects that are known," Aristotle testifies, "are known only to a few, and yet give pleasure to all" (*Poetics* 1451b 37–39). As theorist, moreover, he confirms what he declares from personal experience, for he goes on to recommend the incorporation of surprising (i.e., unknowable) events into the complex plot. Even on the assumption that the familiarity with the national past was more intimate and widespread among the ancients Israelites than the Greeks, it could hardly have been so complete as to rival the narrator's and prevent him from exploiting its lacunae for the arousal of narrative interest.

Indeed, to leave speculation behind, their knowledge could not possibly rival the narrator's in his narratorial capacity. As an inspired omniscient, he has access to a whole range of information that remains closed to the unprivileged audience unless and until he pleases to disclose it. Much of his history would elsewhere count as invention, and accommodates the same management. As a cunning artificer, moreover, he so ambiguates parts that they lend themselves to no resolution even when the last plot twist has been rounded. Privilege and performance thus combine to allow the narrator sufficient, virtually fictional latitude in playing on gaps and uncertainties.

Whatever his pose of a shared heritage may imply, further, the narrator does not in practice assume even sketchy knowledge on the reader's part. Of the various features of his practice, the most revealing is a technique that we first encountered in the Wooing tale: the internalization of premises, however elementary. Few things would appear more safely presupposable than Rebekah's marriage to Isaac, and yet it becomes the object of elaborate compositional foreshadowing and suspense. So do numerous equivalents, from Joseph's reunion with his brothers to Solomon's accession to the throne, all half-revealed and half-concealed beforehand in the service of ambiguity.

This building of information into the dynamics of the narrative is accountable in more than one way. Is it that the narrator cannot or that he will not take much for granted, preferring to make a self-contained whole with a view to both artistic roundness and insurance-by-leveling against variations in historical awareness among the audience? No matter what the reason, it leads to the same conclusion and to the decisive point, namely, that the whole question is incidental to poetics. Narrative interest, like all response and hypothesis-making, is primarily a matter of internal or structural rather than external relations. It turns not so much on the knowledge brought to the reading as on the informational tensions generated in the reading by the mechanisms of sequence and discourse. Suspense thus arises when conflicting clues project two future scenarios, and dies with the enactment of either in the plot.

Far from a special case, then, the importation of extratextual lore into biblical reading—by those possessed of it—falls under the same rule that governs an event no less common than the importation of textual hindsight into a second reading of a novel. It is an odd but widely attested fact that on a second or tenth reading of *Crime and Punishment* we still find ourselves asking whether Raskolnikov will murder the old woman. On a corresponding perusal of *The Brothers Karamazov*, we have no doubt that the murder of the old man is only a question of time—or narrative timing—but then this tragic crime has been anticipated by the narrator as early as the opening paragraph. Such acts of self-induced amnesia (or remembrance) testify to our general ability and readiness to suspend whatever is extraneous to the artful release of information from moment to moment, producing those interplays of ignorance and knowledge that make or break gaps and their effects. In our experience of the irreversible sequences of life, once curiosity or suspense or surprise is past, it is gone forever; in story, once interest is conjured up by imitation of life, it is reproducible at will with each return to the beginning.

Narrative interest may also come under attack in the name of value or viability. Is it conceivable that the Book of Books should seek to produce a succession of thrills? And if by any unfortunate chance or necessity it does produce them, are they not peripheral to its main concerns—thematic, ideological, historical—and better forgotten? Such attitudes, by no means hypothetical, find their equivalents among literary Puritans outside the study of Scripture and betray the same misapprehension. Significantly, they are prevalent among critics rather than writers, even of the most highbrow order. It is hard to think of a novelist of higher seriousness and fastidiousness than Henry James. Consider, then, the superlatives he heaps on the "love of 'a story as a story.'" It is "the vital flame at the heart of any sincere attempt to lay a scene and launch a drama." The storyteller has failed to do his duty if he has not let it "fire his fancy or rule his scheme." The "appeal to wonder and terror and curiosity" are for him "the very source of wise counsel and the very law of charming effect . . . a strange passion planted in the heart of man for his benefit, a mysterious provision made for him in the scheme of nature."[4]

The roots of this divergence go far deeper than literary taste, deeper than the respective scales of value, deeper even than the artist's awareness of the need to seize and sustain narrative interest if he is to carry the reader with him toward the achievement of the "higher" goals as well. It is a matter of insight into the structure of narrative and the control of response and understanding in a time art. Where discourse unfolds along a sequence, all elements and all sense-making are regulated by the processes of sequence: ideas or character or the meaning of a word are no less liable to shifts and twists than the plot itself. Owing to the interdependence of the elements, moreover, the various shifts and twists determine one another: the theme of the Wooing story, for example, surfaces in line with Rebekah's personality, the meaning of "sight" undergoes a process of charging and revision as Samuel's ordeal goes forward and in turn helps to shape our response to Samuel. Narrative interest, therefore, is "primitive" in the honorific sense of "fundamental," because its varieties bear on the tortuous unfolding of the world, and in narrative the represented world is the most determinative part within the whole. Its conception, and therefore its misconception and ambiguation and final disclosure, exerts a crucial influence on how and when the reader understands everything else. The rise of curiosity signifies that the past has been deformed; suspense entails a future opaque and open; surprise is a measure of false understanding and a call for a repatterning of what has gone before. Few strategies boast such control over the emergence of world and meaning.

The Bible's interrelation of assorted interests and effects to realize its distinctive goals will be traced throughout the next chapter. Each narrative interest, I shall argue, has its own temporal form and its own dynamics of reading, but performs a variety of functions. No primary interest is wedded to any specific function, as we shall see, though the argument will focus on some typical couplings in order to bring out the general point. I shall thus demonstrate how the manipulation of suspense yields ideological gains, how curiosity serves the cause of characterization, and how surprise operates to mold attitude and judgment. The more variegated and decisive their functions, the more intelligible their role as the vital flame at the heart of narrative.

·8·

TEMPORAL DISCONTINUITY, NARRATIVE INTEREST, AND THE EMERGENCE OF MEANING

> He has revelled in the creation of alarm and suspense and surprise
> and relief, in all the arts that practise, with a scruple for nothing
> but a lapse of application, on the credulous soul of the candid or,
> immeasurably better, on the seasoned spirit of the cunning reader.
> Henry James, Preface to "The Altar of the Dead"

Suspense and the Dynamics of Prospection

In art as in life, suspense derives from incomplete knowledge about a conflict (or some other contingency) looming in the future. Located at some point in the present, we know enough to expect a struggle but not to predict its course, and above all its outcome, with certitude. Hence a discontinuity that extends from the moment of prospection on the unknown to the moment of enactment and release. Hence also the state of mind that characterizes the intermediate phase: expectant restlessness, awareness of gaps, gap-filling inference along alternative lines, with the attention thrown forward to the point in time that will resolve it all and establish closure by supplying the desired information. Often, moreover, we have a stake (ethical, emotional, practical, doctrinal) in the event that hangs in the balance. The play of expectations then escalates into a clash of hope and fear, which engenders the sharpest form of suspense, because these rival hypotheses about the outcome are both loaded (hope with a positive charge, fear with a negative) and mutually exclusive. "Human life," says Lucian, "is ruled by a pair of tyrants called Hope and Fear. . . . The one thing people want, the one thing they must have, when they're oppressed by either Hope or Fear, is information about the future."[1] But if in human

264

life Lucian's crooked diviner makes money out of these tyrants, then the narrative of human life employs them to make interest and sense.

As an intersection of objective time and subjective knowledge, suspense is inescapable in life but manipulable in art, not excluding historical discourse. For in all representation the future has already been determined—by nature or by poetic license—and only its mode of disclosure remains to be fixed upon. The variations in disclosure fall between two polar dynamics, contrasting in the viewpoint and experience allotted to the reader. The narrator may choose to construct the reading sequence so as to imitate (or even to worsen) the conditions of our suspenseful advance from present to future in life, exploiting the opacity of time to human vision in order to multiply gaps, pit hope against fear, and delay the resolution to the last possible moment. But he may equally exploit his retrospective posture and conventions like omniscience to turn the natural opacity of the future into artful transparency: to play down suspense by revealing at an early point some normally inaccessible information about what lies ahead, whether by way of explicit or implicit forecasting. By this shift in the relations between time and knowledge, perspectivally speaking, the reader comes to occupy an elevated rather than an equivalent position vis-à-vis the unprivileged characters. Either way—as also with all the mixed dynamics of reading between these extremes—the actual choice about suspense gains point from the range of options behind it and reflects the broader aims and strategies that govern the text as a whole.

The Pros and Cons of Suspense in the Bible

Biblical narrative is an illuminating case in point. Rather than opting for either extreme, it maneuvers between them to reconcile two divergent sets of goals and constraints. On the one hand, there is an array of weighty factors that press for carrying suspense even beyond the minimum indicated by the universal desire of narrative to capture and sustain the reader's interest. Of all narrative interests—to begin with an aesthetic pressure—suspense would appear the most congenial to a literature concerned to hide its artfulness, since its arousal requires the least (certainly the least overt) meddling with temporal sequence. An omniscient narrator may be expected to start by unfolding the expositional past and then to lead the reader through a succession of narrative presents as each comes into being; but he cannot reasonably be expected to anticipate the future, which would amount to a trumpeting of artificial license. Predictably, the Bible seldom resorts to such perceptible anticipations. And when it does, their normal function is to mark the closure of a side issue—Esau's future offspring

(Genesis 36), the duration of the manna (Exod 16:35), Michal's lifelong childlessness (2 Sam 6:23)—not to resolve a crux that is yet to work itself out on stage. To a narrator bent on self-effacement, it makes a considerable difference whether his operations on sequence are of a retrospective or a prospective nature. With regard to the forestalling of narrative ambiguity, to preclude gaps about the past through timely disclosures of what happened and why (e.g., that Judah puts Tamar off out of fear for his son) is to follow the story line, whereas to volunteer information about the future is to thrust oneself forward. With regard to the perpetration of ambiguity, correspondingly, to unfold a sequence with gaps about the past is to deform chronology; to leave gaps about the future, however intriguing their effect, appears natural because it accords with chronology. This, as it were, is the way life goes and the particular action went: first crisis, then seesawing, then resolution. From either standpoint, therefore, the order of suspense is the order of self-effacement.

The plot structure would also seem to invite such prospective gapping and to reinforce its naturalness. For the Bible need not go out of its way, as some "plotless" moderns do, to fabricate or coax the stuff of drama. It deploys a world in incessant conflict—God against nature and culture, man against God, Israel against her neighbors, man against man, man against himself—with morality and history as the result. Whatever the other reasons for shaping the march of time as a cavalcade of protagonists in bitter strife, suspense accrues by the very terms of the case.

From the perspectival side, moreover, exploiting that suspense would dovetail with the biblical line of making our hypothesis-construction run parallel to the characters'. Since suspense turns on information and information determines understanding and judgment, to devise such a parallel in restrictedness is not just to adopt a favorite ("evenhanded") structure of point of view. It is, as chapters 3 to 5 argued, to promote empathy and insight in the way best calculated to drive home a point of the greatest thematic importance: the continuity between the human condition inside and outside the world of the text. In its perspectival aspect, then, this narrative interest counteracts facile irony, secures solidarity, heightens self-awareness, and universalizes the ordeal of interpretation.

Doctrinally, last but not least, suspense pays a moral as well as an epistemological dividend that the Bible can hardly afford to forgo. What gives a sharper sense of the agents' freedom of choice than the uncertainty of their ultimate fate? The two issues may not be logically interdependent, since the one (freedom vs. determinism) relates to the makeup of the world inhabited by the characters and the other (chronological vs. anticipatory order) to the unfolding of that world to the reader. Yet, as suggested by the attack made even by a professional philosopher like Sartre on authorial manipulation, these two are rhetorically interdependent, since an early prospection appears to seal or foreclose the agent's destiny in advance of his own choices. And just as narrational connotes existential predeterminism, so does a future left open in the reading imply a future open for living. The gaps about the outcome are waiting, as it were, for the dramatis personae to enact their closure without undue influence.

This set of constraints and incentives is, however, opposed by another powerful coalition of anti-suspense factors. All revolve round the article of divine order: God's involvement in the world and the overriding need to publish his supremacy. Clearly, the generation of suspense throughout the tale would militate against our sense of the divine control of history: to alternate between hope and fear is to postulate a world of divine laissez-faire, of natural contingency or, perhaps worse, of contingency subject to the regulation of art alone. Since the reader forms hypotheses and calculates probabilities by reference to general laws, the ambiguation of future closures would leave him in doubt about the very way of the world. And even the disambiguation after the fact—revealing the true architect once the action has run its suspenseful course—might prove too late to eradicate that doubt, certainly to exploit the incremental rhetorical effects of foresight.

A telling measure of incompatibility is that the pros and cons of suspense fall into oppositional pairs. Thus, the narrator's self-effacement advocates lifelike openness and darkling movement toward the future; but the highlighting of God's omnipotence calls for anticipatory resolution, preferably in the teeth of both natural and cultural probabilities. Although biblical plot-making thrives on conflict, it cannot reap the gains in seesaw hypothesis-making if God becomes a side. And since nothing falls beneath his notice, no amount of ingenuity can reconcile dramatic participant-ship (which implies equality amid antagonism) with cosmic directorship (which entails transcendence). As with actional, so—to turn from omnipotence to omniscience—with perspectival structure. For the attractions of demonstrating the human state of ignorance are at odds with the need to demonstrate superhuman knowledgeability. How can this need be met without giving the reader some share in omniscience, through scenes where God penetrates what is to the dramatis personae the opacity of things to come? In turn, while suspense correlates with agents free to make or mar their destiny, its quashing by divine fiat threatens a reduction of the human order to puppethood, with characters and character turned into instruments or pulling in vain against foregone conclusions. So if the three previous clashes between desirables have ideological implications, this one bears straight on essentials.

Self-effaced vs. obtrusive narration, genuine or fixed conflicts, empathetic parity or ironic discrepancy, free will or the omnipotence effect: each of these symmetrical extremes would appear to follow from the choice between a "realistic" and a "prospective" handling of sequence. Forced into making a choice, the Bible opts for lowered suspense but, far less predictably, without overlooking the claims and advantages of the alternative dynamics of composition. Since the ideological as well as the aesthetic positives do not all lie on one side, the narrator skillfully avoids or minimizes the consequences of an either/or choice. He still maneuvers between the extremes, if not to have the best of both worlds, then at least to incorporate as much as possible of the surrendered into the chosen one. And this reconciliation of apparent irreconcilables largely determines the art of biblical storytelling and sense-making.

Modes of Shaping the Narrative Future

To begin with, the constraint of prospection yet leaves the mechanics within the artist's discretion. And of the two primary modes, the overt and the covert, the narrator typically appeals to the one that will keep him in the shadows. Within his generally reticent discourse, *fore*telling would yet seem the least congenial form of telling, expositional *back*telling definitely included. Rarely, as already noted, will he anticipate the outcome on his own authority. Indeed, the contrast drawn by Erich Auerbach between the suspenseless Homer and the suspenseful Bible could hardly be more unfortunate.[2] Not only do the facts disallow his contrast. The example he picks, the Binding of Isaac, even happens to be one of the rare exceptions to the norm of self-effacing anticipation. "God tested Abraham," the narrator states by way of preface, the urgent need to soften the shock of the coming dialogue impelling him to lay bare God's intentions in advance. As a rule, however, the foreshadowing assumes one or more of three forms variously distanced from narratorial foretelling: analogy, paradigm, dramatic forecast.

The first, and most lifelike, consists in analogical organization designed to launch inductive reasoning from known precedent(s) to some present counterpart facing an uncertain future. The manifold analogy between the ambitious Adonijah and the dead Absalom, constructed at the opening of Kings, directs the reader to apply the lessons of the past to the imminent conflict: to look forward to the new pretender's downfall while he appears at the zenith of his fortunes. The correspondence in sexual hospitality emerging between Sodom and Gibeah toward the end of Judges promises the collective destruction of the latter-day Sodomites: the equivalence turns out to extend even to the marital straits of the few survivors (Lot and his daughters versus the six hundred wifeless Benjaminites).

And the fact that each precedent openly stages divine interference also brings God into the later reenactment by the backstairs of association. The narrator thus effaces himself to good ideological as well as aesthetic effect.

Such prospective coupling may recur often enough to signal a divine law or logic that governs the march of history, even where, in default of explicit generalization, less frequent recurrence might be attributed to the workings of art or chance. As argued in reference to the omnipotence effect, this motivates the various techniques of serialization, continuous and discontinuous. Take the "unnatural" rise of the younger above the elder brother throughout Genesis—also evident in later additions to the series, like Moses, David, Solomon—rendered increasingly providential and decreasingly accidental from one manifestation to another. As the chain of analogy unfolds along the sequence, extending from Cain and Abel to Manasseh and Ephraim, the cumulative lessons of induction solidify into a general rule or historical paradigm, which grows in predictive determinacy and ideological force with each new successful application. By the end of the book, all our prospections having come true, those structures of incertitude known as nature and culture have been exposed as powerless in the face of God's controlling design.

Sometimes, however, the foreshadowing by paradigm assumes a deductive rather than an inductive form. The parade example appears at the beginning of Judges, immediately after Joshua's death: "The people of Israel did what was evil in the eyes of the Lord and served the Baals. . . . The anger of the Lord was kindled against Israel . . . and he sold them into the hand of their enemies. . . . They were in sore straits. . . . The Lord raised up judges and they delivered them from the hand of their plunderers. . . . Still they did not listen to their judges, for they whored after other gods" (2:11-19). Disguised as a summary introduction to the period, this actually offers a schematic outline of things to come. It projects a four-stage scenario of Evildoing→Punishment→Outcry→Deliverance that will enact itself in instance after dramatic instance, with Deliverance followed by a backsliding ("Still they did not listen") that launches a new round and motivates the cyclical pattern of history.[3]

To be sure, the deductive and inductive methods of paradigm formation significantly vary: the one preliminary and overt, the other gradually revealed in and through the action and hence modifiable to the last twist. The implications of this difference for the reading will soon come up in specific analyses. Nevertheless, the two methods have in common a distinctive relationship between precept and example—or, in modern parlance, type and token—that invites joint consideration. This is what empowers each to form an architectonic principle of coherence, its logic of recurrence so superimposed on temporal sequence as to shape chronicle into history and assimilate human to divine causality. This is also what produces such a rich interplay of unity and complexity throughout: the paradigm in both Genesis and Judges figures as constant theme, and its analogical enactments as illustrative, incremental, exploratory variations. In terms of reading experience, finally, this is also what establishes each paradigm as a system of expectations, determinate enough to outline in advance each plot instance and yet general enough to leave room for gaps and opacities, traps and shocks of discovery. The mandatory distance between the truth and the whole truth thus finds a new tactical correlate in the distance between schematic paradigm and unique filling.

The occasional recourse to "deductive" prospection testifies anew to the importance ascribed to the proper handling of suspense. In the given ideological context, it appears, the strongest point of the inductive shaping of the future is also its weakest. Its implicit and distributed form, artistically so appealing, carries with it two dangers. The pattern is liable to be (as indeed it has been) missed in whole or in part, and even if traced, attributed to the wrong pattern-maker: the narrator rather than God. Not that the clues to analogy will escape the initiate, but that when it comes to the few vital matters of doctrine, the narrator will leave little to the chances of inference and will write in letters tall enough to catch the eye of the most dim-sighted. Therefore, still reluctant to speak or even to paraphrase in his own voice, he sometimes calls on God himself to forecast the paradigm destined for serialization, as on the eve of the ten plagues of Egypt (Exod 7:2–5). By the same rule of foolproof composition, God often forecasts in our hearing specific crises and resolutions that fall under a generally hidden paradigm. The prenatal oracle of fraternal conflict between Jacob and Esau or the assurance of a safe return given to Jacob in flight exemplifies such spelling out for good measure. And when the drama about to unfold has no (or no univocal) precedent to guide our sense of the ending—and this is most often the case from the creation of light to the fall of Jerusalem—no wonder that the divine stage-manager should play prologue and epilogue himself or delegate the roles to some mouthpiece, with the whole repertoire of the omnipotence effect behind them.

Darkness in Light, or: Zigzagging toward Sisera's End

It is hard to exaggerate the cumulative impact of such prospection, perhaps most forceful when least consciously registered, on our grasp of the Bible's world and world view. It is easy, though, to underestimate its artfulness. Does it not play the ideology safe to the point of artistic suicide, carry the multitude along at the expense of putting the alert readers to sleep, bring the truth so close to the whole truth as to allow no room for the drama of meaning to play itself out? Let us look at Judges 4, a narrative that combines all three modes of prospection and yet manages to leave enough of the future and the sense opaque to keep the shrewdest interpreter busy and guessing till the final twist has been rounded:

> (1) The people of Israel again did what was evil in the eyes of the Lord, and Ehud had died. (2) And the Lord sold them into the hand of Jabin king of Canaan, who reigned in Hazor; the commander of his army was Sisera, and he sat in Harosheth of the Gentiles. (3) And the people of Israel cried out to the Lord, for he had nine hundred iron chariots and oppressed the people of Israel hard for twenty years. (4) Deborah, a prophetess, the wife of Lapidoth, was judging Israel at that time. (5) She sat under the Palm of Deborah, and the people of Israel went up to her for judgment. (Judg 4:1–5)

In context, the oppressor's overthrow is foreshadowed by paradigm and analogy even before Deborah lifts a finger. Chapter 2 drafted the cyclical plot of Evildoing→Punishment→Outcry→Deliverance; chapter 3 then serialized some instances of the pattern, where the variations in the identity of the deliverer (Othniel, Ehud, Shamgar) and the enemy (Mesopotamia, Moab, the Philistines) only bring out the paradigmatic constancies. So the three opening members of the paradigm having recurred in our exposition, verbal echoes and all, the fourth ("Deliverance") must soon ensue in the action. Nor is this a purely formal or "aesthetic" expectancy. According to the value system built into the paradigm itself, national fortune waits on moral choice, redemption following as hard upon penitence as subjection upon idolatry.

Yet for reasons of narrative interest—among others, like novelty, realism, thematic complication—the book of Judges never allows the predictive logic to adumbrate the happier of these futures beyond the general scenario. The variations prove no less integral to structure and effect than the uniformities. Indeed, their enrichment motivates the book's repeated and otherwise disproportionate lingering over the terminal link in the chain. The three antecedents may enjoy moralistic superiority; but it is in the Deliverance that the stuff of drama lies, that the figure of each judge waits to be explored, that the plot brings God and Israel into concerted action, that the theme may freely move between the actors and the cycle between historical generality and specificity.

In terms of the reading process, all this latitude in dramatization profoundly affects the shape of the future, since just as the uniformities afford light and certitude beforehand, so does variance make for opacity and suspense. Hence the interaction between the sequential unfolding of the whole book and of each component episode. Given the deductive force of the paradigm, of course, the ending is never in doubt. But its details do not remain entirely indeterminate either. For only in retrospect do we discover that the paradigm consists in no more than what the narrator started by outlining: a quartet of bare bones that each tale fleshes out in its own manner, changing not the date alone but also the oppressor, the deliverer, and the modus operandi. With the advantage of hindsight, the reader would doubtless be wiser in his operations as literary fortune-teller. In its absence, however, the gradually emerging pattern invites application to the case at hand: induction from precedent closes gaps left by deduction from the paradigm. Equipped with the scheme abstracted from earlier episodes, we naturally attempt at each new stage to maximize certitude and intelligibility by projecting it onto the future, only to find our expectations disappointed and the scheme further whittled down by the concrete features of the narrative. (The process appropriately culminates in Samson's bundle of incongruities.) Often the narrator will deliberately tempt us into such premature forecasts of uniformity with a view to springing all the more effectively the variants that thwart them for our entertainment and edification.

(I say "our," because the course is open to all. In paradoxical fact that forms the Bible's rule, however, the more active and cunning the reader, the greater is his vulnerability to the traps set by the narrative all along. But then so is his enjoyment of the game of art, and so is the insight he carries away with him. Underreaders may get things right, but at the lowest level and for the wrong reasons. In contrast, so far as the implied reader falls victim to the text's misdirections, he gains in understanding even or especially where he went astray: he does right to go wrong and will be rewarded accordingly.)

The tale launches this intricate paradigm-precedent dynamics as early as the exposition. On the appearance of Evildoing, Punishment, and Outcry in the orderly and quick succession familiar from the preceding episodes, we look forward to meeting the hero who (now that "Ehud had died") will deliver Israel in the impending conflict. But here comes the first of the tale's surprises: it is a deliveress this time, the judgess-prophetess (*nebi'a, shof'ta*) Deborah. It is she, "sitting under Deborah's palm," who emerges as the opposite number not so much of King Jabin as of his general Sisera, "sitting in Harosheth of the Gentiles." At the sequential position reserved for the deliverer, she springs at us from nowhere, complete with husband, national role, foreign antagonist, seat of judgment bearing her name: all expositional features calculated to bring her sex into marked dissonance with her offices past and to come. However unexpected in the light of both cultural code and historical precedents—Othniel, Ehud, Shamgar—that dissonance yet makes good sense after the fact, as a variation on the theme of the incongruous deliverer. To flaunt his omnipotence, after all, God has already picked his instruments in contempt of human norms of seemliness and efficacy; and if the left-handed Ehud and the oxgoad-wielding Shamgar have worked wonders, Deborah promises to do no less against Sisera's nine hundred iron chariots. In terms of the structure of expectations, then, the antecedents so unfold as to fulfill a double role. The recurrence of the initial items of the paradigm allays suspense about the final outcome, while the twist given to the concluding item heightens retardatory suspense about the ways and means of deliverance. For the first time in history— we rub our hands in anticipation—a woman will lead Israel into battle.

No sooner has this expectation arisen, however, than the reader finds it undercut:

> (6) She sent to call Barak the son of Abinoam from Kedesh in Naphtali, and said to him, The Lord God of Israel has commanded, Go, draw toward Mount Tabor, taking with thee ten thousand men from the Naphtalites and the Zebulunites. (7) And I will draw Sisera, Jabin's army commander, and his chariotry and his multitude against thee at the Kishon river; and I will give him into thy hand. (8) And Barak said to her, If thou wilt go with me, I will go, and if thou wilt not go with me, I will not go. (9) And she said, I will certainly go with thee. However, there will be no glory for thee on the road on which thou art going, for into the hand of a woman will the Lord sell Sisera. Then Deborah arose and went with Barak to Kedesh.

As the exposition gives way to the action proper, then, the first reference (verses 6–7) to the ways and means produces another surprise, which compels us to remodify the modification. For the action starts by reverting to normal pattern: Deborah seems to have made an appearance only to bow out at once with her appointment of Barak to be deliverer in God's name. For all its sociological interest, this unprecedented division of labor between judicial-prophetic and military office is a comedown in terms of narrative interest. The sudden shrinkage of the variation from precedent diminishes expectancy to a level well below the standard, to say nothing of the expositionally promised extras. It is disappointing to find the prophetic amazon giving place to Barak's colorless figure, introduced with no other distinguishing feature than parentage ("son of Abinoam") and locality ("from Kedesh in Naphtali"). Worse—and equally without parallel in what has gone before, though common enough elsewhere—much of the remaining suspense is dissipated by the scenario where Deborah spells out the tactics and assigns to God the leading part in the battle. Paradigm, precedent, forecast: all three modes of prospection now combine to rob the conflict of its mystery and interest.

As if determined to keep us on our toes by making each step along the sequence both a revelation of the past and a reprospection on the future, however, the narrator goes on to spring a third, multiple surprise. Interest rekindles as the whole picture changes. For one thing, Barak captures our attention with his very first words: "If thou wilt go with me, I will go, and if thou wilt not go with me, I will not go." The flat character gains rotundity with a vengeance as soon as he betrays his lack of self-confidence. Barak thus becomes typical in revealing himself as untypical. He falls into pattern, after all, but so oddly that we must further stretch the paradigm to accommodate the figure of the faint-hearted deliverer. Of the two leaders, it is he who plays the woman; and having been summoned to do a man's job, he refuses to act unless the woman who delegated it to him comes along to give him moral courage.

This stipulation, moreover, has a prospective as well as a retrospective effect. For Barak's timidity motivates Deborah's continued and felt presence in the action from which she seemed about to withdraw. The sudden dynamization of her role even finds a subtle correlate in the shift from static to dynamic verbs. She was introduced "sitting under Deborah's palm," her immobility underscored by her seat's forming a point of convergence for the movements of others—the people arriving for judgment, Barak for instructions. Hence the force, literal and symbolic, of "Deborah arose and went with Barak to Kedesh." (Indeed, *arose* marks such a turning point that her claim in the victory song that the nation had been in straits "till I, Deborah, arose, arose a mother in Israel" (5:7) reads, by virtue of this echo from the narrative, as a statement of fact rather than a piece of credit grabbing.) Moreover, to judge from her prophecy that Barak will reap no glory because "into the hand of a woman will the Lord sell Sisera," she is yet destined to play a role almost as decisive as that misleadingly assigned to her by the expositional pattern. With this authoritative foreshadowing, the generic scheme that underwent a change on Deborah's first appearance and then resumed something like its normal shape on Barak's, now falls into a divergence sharper than any before. The battle will be waged under the leadership of two unconventional deliverers, one a strong woman and the other a weak man, with the credit going by merit rather than sex.

Hence also the repatterning of the interplay between narrative interest and doctrinal thematics or persuasion. Narrative interest requires constant disclosures, developments, shifts and turns along the sequence. But from the standpoint of ideology, all this tortuous-looking progression carries straight forward the rhetorical line established as early as the paradigmatic dissipation of suspense. Just as the overt foretelling of both the outcome and the tactics of the war reinforces our sense of God's control of history—where foretelling by paradigm and analogy might by itself suggest the narrator's control of his medium—so do the shifts in the role of the human deliverer. The more numerous and unexpected these shifts, the less important do they look; the more they upset from moment to moment our prospections about the immediate future, the stronger is our sense of their amounting to the same thing in the end, given the firmness of the ultimate result. The human deliverer, we generalize from our very reading experience, is an embodied instrument in the hands of the divine, who can equally well accomplish the work of redemption through the agency of a woman or a man, of the normal or the incongruous, of the determined or the hesitant, of one figurehead or two or, by implication, none.[4]

Yet the very twists that propel the dynamics of faith in a straight line introduce fresh complications into the dynamics of suspense. The last-minute change of plan appears negligible in terms of divine omnipotence and, hence, of suspense as the clash between hope and fear; but it has crucial implications for the human arena and hence for retardatory suspense. What dwindles to a footnote *sub specie aeternitatis* makes the whole story as enacted history; and the Bible, as often, has it both ways. Does the joint leadership imply a change in the foreshadowed tactical scenario as well? Will Barak's courage hold now? What part will each of the mismatched associates play? How will God deliver Sisera into "a woman's hand"? These newly opened gaps not only revive the expectancy just dulled by the articulation of the future. They sharpen and concretize it beyond any previous phase, so as to pitch our attention forward to the battle scenes.

(10) Barak summoned Zebulun and Naphtali to Kedesh; and ten thousand men went up at his heels, and Deborah went up with him. (11) Now Heber the Kenite had separated from the Kenites, the descendants of Hobab the father-in-law of Moses, and had pitched his tent as far as the Oak in Za'ananim, which is near Kedesh. (12) And Sisera was told that Barak the son of Abinoam had gone up to Mount Tabor. (13) Sisera summoned all his chariotry, nine hundred iron chariots, and all the men who were with him, from Harosheth of the Gentiles to the Kishon river. (14) And Deborah said to Barak, Arise, for this is the day in which the Lord has given Sisera into thy hand. Has not the Lord gone out before thee? Then Barak went down from Mount Tabor and ten thousand men after him. (15) And the Lord confounded Sisera and all the chariotry and all the host at the edge of the sword before Barak; and Sisera went down from his chariot and fled away on foot. (16) And Barak pursued the chariotry and the host as far as Harosheth of the Gentiles, and all Sisera's host fell by the edge of the sword; not one was left.

While seeming to concentrate at each point on the exciting narrative present, from muster through battle to pursuit, this account fulfills the past and covertly prepares for the future. The gaps of retardatory suspense find their closure as Deborah's prediction turns by degrees into historical reality. By degrees, because contrary to her own oracle, the prophetess initially plays a minor role beside Barak's. She first departs "with" him for Kedesh, then ascends "with him," just like ten thousand others, to the hill country. Then, from the enemy's viewpoint, Sisera's intelligence report ("Barak the son of Abinoam had gone up to Mount Tabor") makes no mention of her who was introduced as his opposite number in Israel. One cannot even shrug off this omission as a typical piece of male chauvinism, destined to a hard fall, since it is Barak who has lately shown all the leadership.

Just as the reader may begin to wonder whether and where his expectations have gone wrong, however, they triumphantly come true. At the critical moment, when the Israelite infantry must be led down from the safety of the mountains to the "nine hundred chariots of iron" deployed on the plain, Barak falters and Deborah once again emerges from the sidelines to prod him into action. Nowhere stated, this is yet the inference to be drawn from the joint bearing of memory and forecast on the narrative present. For Barak's old lack of confidence reappears in a set of new clues: the fact that he has made no move since concentrating his forces on Mount Tabor three long and wide-ranging verses ago; the repeated description of the Canaanite war machine; and the details of Deborah's exhortation. She starts with the loaded verb "Arise!", already invested by her own case with the sense of shifting from prolonged immobility into action and now framed in the imperative mood to highlight the need for external rousing. Quick to transform the menace of the chariots massed at the Kishon river into positive reassurance, she proceeds to assert that this is the day foreseen (4:7) in her prophecy. (In line with the reversal of normal roles, moreover, the formula of reassurance she addresses to Barak echoes the one used in the previous tale (3:28) by a truly brave leader, Ehud, to move the people to follow him down another mountain to confront another oppressor.) To hearten the man, she now reverts ("the Lord has given Sisera into thy hand") to her original promise in verse 7 ("I will give him into thy hand"), diplomatically forgetting the revised oracle ("into a woman's hand will the Lord sell Sisera") that his ultimatum provoked. And she ends with a fresh injection of courage: God not only backs him up but leads the way before him.

Barak thereupon descends, but he pays dearly for hesitancies old and new. Part of the glory having already fallen to the prophetess even before battle is joined, God himself now appropriates much of what remains, as if to exact payment for the need to do the earthly work of deliverance as well. Since God has "gone out before" Barak, Barak's eventual descent "and ten thousand men after him" sounds a mocking note: the nominal leader is himself a follower. Nor does the divine role turn out to be merely a figure of pious speech. Contrary to the patterns of expectation hitherto set up in Judges, God actually intervenes to ensure the victory; and the ambiguity of "God confounded Sisera and all the chariotry and all the host at the edge of [*leꜰi*] the sword before Barak" only leaves doubt about his mode of intervention. Does the unusual association of "confound" with "sword" imply that God drove the enemy onto the edge of the Israelite sword or, figuratively, that he wrought the havoc himself through some divine equivalent of the human edge of the sword? Does the final (and syntactically awkward) "before Barak" denote spatial anteposition (he drove them in front of Barak) or temporal anteriority (he smote them before Barak did)? In either case, Deborah's prophecies reach their fulfillment before the eyes of posterity. She has initiated and forced the battle; God has won it; and Barak remains with a mopping-up operation to his credit.

Or does he? After all, the sweeping "not one was left" refers to "Sisera's host." Sisera himself, who would be the feather in anyone's cap, is still on the run. But who will net him? With the opening of this new question, suspense and conjecture suddenly revive at a point where all seemed over bar the shouting. By one of the paradoxes of reading, moreover, once our attention has been given a prospective turn and thrown forward to the opaque future again, we revert to the known past for clues, precedents, guidance. And, to one attuned to the Bible's temporal art, not in vain. Two cruxes—one hidden from view so far, the other a long-standing incongruity—show new faces in retrospect and fall into this newly devised pattern of expectancy.

The resurgence of expectation at this late point brings us back to an issue of general interest: the license amidst constraint. Under the pressure of the anti-suspense factors, as we have seen, the biblical narrator is compelled to foreclose the future. Only seldom will he allow himself to construct a "naturalistic" plot, without any determinate (and determinative) interference of the divine with the human order. Will Rahab the harlot be spared? Will David kill Nabal for his insolence and ingratitude? How will the conflict between Micah and the Danites end? With the future suddenly turned opaque, the dynamics of suspense enjoys free play, and we start calculating the chances for and against the alternative resolutions by appeal to natural probabilities. Like the characters themselves, we then form and shift our hypotheses by reference to the social context, the relative strength of the parties involved, their personality and antecedents; and, like them, we may fail to achieve closure before the event. Typically, however, such episodes are neither central nor, with the notorious exception of Esther, drawn out. Elsewhere the plot not only shows God's controlling hand. The ideological requirement of lucidity even bears on the means of showing: the indirect modes of anticipation by precedent and paradigm are often spelt out, if not replaced, by way of divine forecast.

With genuine suspense so circumscribed, retardatory suspense would appear to become the staple of divination. To judge by the foregoing analysis, indeed, the Bible makes the most of this enforced shift from "what" to "how" hypotheses about the future by multiplying the adventures of meaning and experience en route to the predetermined end. Due to the manipulation of sequence, the plot constantly twists and turns, character emerges, the theme develops, the paradigm now falls out of and now into historical shape, so that the reader never knows what the next moment will bring and how its unfolding will affect past inferences. As long as the forecasted end is never in question, all these adventures of reading still remain tactical. But even forecasting affords two loopholes for strategic changes of direction, whereby the narrator may spring an unexpected prospect or closure without undermining the authority of the divine forecaster.

First, the future may change with God's change of mind. As such divine repentance follows human repentance, it incurs no ideological loss and even highlights man's freedom and God's justice. (We shall have occasion to consider two fine instances of this strategy—Jonah's tale and Saul's rejection. In the latter, the closed future reopens only to reclose on the offender's proving hopeless.) Just as the first strategy is motivated by a new development in the plot, so is the second by a new disclosure about the plot. The forecast, it suddenly turns out, did not really mean what we (and possibly the addressee too) took it to mean at the time of utterance. It was equivocal from the beginning. As early as the Eden narrative, the God-announced penalty for eating of the Tree of Knowledge—"thou shalt surely die" (2:17)—thus changes in retrospect from death to mortality (3:17). But Sisera's fate offers a much subtler case of prospective equivocation.

Sisera's escape upsets the reader's sense of the end. And this ambiguation of the end lays bare a hitherto unsuspected ambiguity in the forecast that announced and shaped it in the first place: "I will certainly go with thee. However, there will be no glory for thee on the road on which thou art going, for into the hand of a woman will the Lord sell Sisera." At the time of utterance, Deborah's prophecy compelled interpretation as a taunting self-reference, cast in sexual ("a woman's hand") rather than pronominal ("my hand") terms to rub in the antithesis and the price. Why should it occur to anyone—Barak included—to look elsewhere? Note how elaborately the reading trap has been baited. Deborah was introduced as deliverer and, now that her male substitute has appeared, seems even more qualified for the role. Her very presence at Barak's side will (and does) suffice to tarnish his glory. So far as her oracle looks forward as well, the tale's horizon contains no other woman. And the causal or conditional force of the opposition between "I will go" and "thou art going"—because or in case of my going, your going will suffer—springs the trap. Later, therefore, Deborah's exhortative "God has given Sisera into thy hand" (14)—going back to her original forecast (7) as though the in-between reference to a woman to be covered with glory (9) is being fulfilled in the very need for her encouragement—even gives the impression that the worst is over for Barak.

Only when the unitary line of suspense branches out without any warning into two separate issues, the army's fate and Sisera's, does this univocal reading of the oracle collapse and the anticipation turns out double-barrelled. Where the reader saw a foregone conclusion, there now yawns a gap. In terms of the present action, of course, Barak as the leader of the pursuit seems to have the best chance of dispatching Sisera; but then the prospective reference to a woman's hand denied him that honor in advance. If anything, he has even less chance than any man under his command. For his failure would be the narrative's success. It would be in keeping with his record as a character who lets opportunities slip through his fingers. Marring even his achievement as pursuer, it would be the final judgment on that record. His failure would likewise crown the sexual theme, in which he has cut such a poor figure all along, and also the implicit antithesis to his predecessor Ehud, who initiated and performed the whole work of redemption, starting with the assassination of the enemy leader, to his everlasting glory. For the converse reasons, Deborah would admirably fit the part, but then she is again immobilized on a mountain.

With the action's most likely candidate ruled out by the composition and the composition's by the action, the ambiguity dormant in the authoritative forecast rears its head. In retrospect, each of the key expressions turns out to have a double reference, the overt one bearing on the national and the covert one on the personal level. The indefinite term "a woman" now reads not only as a provocative self-reference, amply justified by intervening developments, but also as an enigmatic reference to some other female participant yet to appear. And the proper name "Sisera" reads not only as a synecdoche for the enemy army now wiped out—just as "Barak had gone up to Mount Tabor" covers the whole Israelite side—but also as a literal designation of its fugitive commander. The double references thus combine to foreshadow a reenactment of the fortunes of the war on the personal level, with Sisera as prize, Barak as eager contender, and some woman as dark horse. Has Deborah herself contrived an equivocal prophecy to maximize Barak's discomfiture? Or has God, who confirms his servant's word, intervened to extend the application of her words beyond her own ken? Ambiguous to the end, the closure of this gap no more affects the function than the authority of the prophecy. The two-faced forecast is so projected onto the narrative sequence as to compose a two-phase action and suspense strategy—its referential range ("a woman"; "Sisera") first camouflaged and then unveiled, first narrowed and then widened, to enrich the overall dynamics of expectation. Having so far divided interest and merit through the seesaw movement between Deborah and Barak, the narrative now diminishes both protagonists by shifting its focus to a third.

Even with a future newly illuminated to promise another race for glory, the dark horse still remains dark all round except for her sex. Yet that single clue suffices to bring out another, equally retrospective but at once more subtle and more substantial, whose emergence makes sense of an otherwise troublesome piece of delayed exposition. Why has the narrator interposed between Barak's and Sisera's mobilization the (for him) extended retrospect, "And Heber the Kenite had separated from the Kenites, the descendants of Hobab the father-in-law of Moses, and had pitched his tent as far as the Oak in Za'ananim, which is near Kedesh," that seems to have nothing to do with either? Scissors-happy as usual, genetic critics have been quick to dismiss the note as a remnant of an independent and poorly integrated tradition ("the Jabin strand"). But whatever the accidentals of source, they have been replaced by the laws of discourse. The answer rather lies in an important principle—I call it the proleptic exposition or future-directed retrospect—where the Bible's strategies of economy, sequence, and foregrounding meet. According to this convention, retrospective incoherence signals (guarantees, invites) prospective coherence. The interpolation concerning the Kenites, that is, should yield plot dividends in what follows. In this, it bears a negative analogy to the earlier cryptic retrospect, "And Ehud had died," similarly lopped off as an excrescence by traditional harmonizers, starting from a number of Septuagint manuscripts. Just as the Ehud comment functions to neutralize a possible line of expectation by establishing absence—he cannot play the deliverer again—so does the Kenite comment generate one by marking presence and keeping it in reserve.

Disappointingly, however, this presence has not had the slightest effect on the course of the battle. So our long-delayed (11–16) interest is about to sink or die for want of nourishment, when the general revival of expectation induces another quest for coherence. Since that obscure promise has not been made good so far, its proleptic force is apparently reserved for the finale of Sisera's pursuit and dispatch. But how can the narrative bring the Kenite connection into effect?

Here, by an interpretive chain reaction, one clue leads to another. Paradoxically, the ambiguation of Deborah's explicit prospect disambiguates the narrator's implicit retrospect-turned-prospect, so as to link the two into a continuous outline of the future. The one having reopened the future for a new female participant to enter, the other proceeds to give her a local habitation if not a name. Of course, this retrospect on the Kenites makes no mention of a woman. But the encampment at "the *Oak* in Za'ananim" does invoke one by sly analogy to the seat at "the *Palm* of Deborah." The immediately following reference to Kedesh completes the pattern by introducing Barak through the backstairs of his native place.[5] And once the reader catches the intimations of the analogy by wordplay and geography, he finds them reinforced through analogy by theme—and one that figures as the tale's thematic hallmark at that. The contrast between the foregrounded chieftain Heber and the woman lurking between the lines would ill accord with their relative status in the action anticipated did it not bring to mind that between Barak's nominal leadership and Deborah's hidden power. In the Kenite as well as in the Israelite sphere, sexual protocol clashes with historical role. All that remains to be discovered is the precise who and how of the resolution.

> (17) Now Sisera had fled away on foot to the tent of Jael, the wife of Heber the Kenite; for there was peace between Jabin king of Hazor and the house of Heber the Kenite. (18) And Jael came out to meet Sisera and said to him, Turn here, my lord, turn here to me; have no fear. He turned to her, into the tent, and she covered him with a rug(?). (19) And he said to her, Give me, pray, a little water to drink, for I am thirsty. She opened a skin of milk and gave him to drink and covered him. (20) And he said to her, Stand at the entrance of the tent, and if any man comes and asks thee, Is there any man here?, say, None. (21) Then Jael the wife of Heber took a tent peg, and took the hammer in her hand, and went softly to him, and drove the peg into his temple and it went on into the ground. He was fast asleep and weary. So he died. (22) And behold, Barak was pursuing Sisera! Jael came out to meet him and said to him, Come and I will show thee the man whom thou seekest. And he came into her tent, and behold, Sisera fallen, dead, and a peg in his temple.

The last act does fulfill the reader's expectations and puts an end to suspense, but not before leading them another merry dance by way of retardation and false alarm. The sequence of the very first verse abruptly veers round from the resolution to the sharpening of doubts. "Sisera had fled" thus uniquely corresponds in grammatical form to "Heber had separated"— both pluperfects marking a spatiotemporal shift of scene vis-à-vis an antecedent string of imperfects, and the parallel serving to reaffirm the Kenite connection. The implied convergence of plot lines then takes place at once, to our full satisfaction, in "to the tent of Jael, the wife of Heber the Kenite." The mysterious woman, so far a creature of our hypotheses alone, indeed exists in the flesh at the spot foretold. The appositional reference to her as "Jael, the wife of Heber" fastens the inferred link with "Deborah, the wife of Lapidoth," not least because of the thematic irony that both husbands are conspicuous by their absence throughout except in the titles of their heroic spouses. And, we recall, the location of her "tent" in Kedesh provides another thematic link—with the third term of the analogy, Barak "of Kedesh Naphtali."

All this looks so conclusive that we are caught off-guard by the alarming note that the narrator sounds through the reference to the peaceful relations between Jabin and the Kenites. Instead of carrying the plot forward to unfold the manner of Sisera's liquidation, then, he doubles back in time to unfold another piece of exposition that threatens the whole prospect of liquidation. It is not for nothing, we suddenly fear, that the clan's first appearance came between Barak's and Sisera's mobilization: the temporal sandwiching, especially of the immobile ("pitched his tent") amid feverish movement, implies neutrality. Far from closing the gaps, the new disclosure reveals new ones and tangles the old.

The two ensuing verses progressively heighten suspense by tracing Jael's solicitude for the fugitive: the warm invitation, the reassurance, the concealment from view, the hospitable offer of milk instead of plain water, followed by a mindful re-covering. But the third already dynamizes our hopes by harping afresh on the sexual theme. Is it not ironic that Sisera starts by addressing Jael with the masculine imperative "Stand [*amod*] at the entrance of the tent"? Or that he casts his order in terms of male roles alone ("Should any man come and ask thee, Is there any man here?"), little dreaming that the real threat lurks in a woman, still less in this cooperative woman? Does not that perspectival incongruity reenact in small compass the blindness betrayed by his preparing for war against "Barak the son of Abinoam," as if armed conflict were an affair between men only? If so, the whole recent sequence beginning with the encounter in verse 18 twists round again to suggest the kind of invitation extended by the spider to the fly.

Jael, we now realize, felt no more committed to the unholy peace arranged by her husband ("the house of Heber the Kenite") than Deborah did to the status quo vis-à-vis the same enemy. And since she could expect no help from her menfolk, she disarmed Sisera with a woman's weapons: soft words and strong drink. (Another double bond, this, with the prophetess, who used strong words because *her* man needed rousing, not doping.) Indeed, she also deals the fatal blow with a woman's camping utensils—tent peg and mallet, their wielding rendered in slow motion to bring home the point. But the slow motion enhances three more general features as well: the drama of the climax, the literal fulfillment of the prophecy that God will deliver Sisera "into a woman's *hand*," and the parallel with Ehud's cunning (and similarly drawn out[6]) assassination of Eglon king of Moab in the preceding chapter.

It is only then that Barak arrives in hot pursuit, a good second as usual, too late for getting any credit but just in time to be the first to survey the enemy general pierced by a big wooden nail from his own neighbor's basket. (That "Sisera fallen, dead, and a tent peg in his temple" echoes "all the host of Sisera fell by the sword" only foregrounds the variation of the lethal instrument, humiliating to both victim and viewer.) And the inglorious figure cut by both leaders in this final tableau redounds of course to Jael's glory.

Barak thus ends where he began, in Kedesh Naphtali, with little to show for his trouble except a junior partnership in a female enterprise. In tactful (and typical) restraint, however, the narrator voices neither that sense of frustration nor, didacticist fashion, the moral of the three-way partition of glory. Instead of gloating over the discomfiture of the unworthy, he makes his point by encouraging us to read it as the human effect of a divine cause. Even the credit he gives to the power behind the scenes ("On that day God subdued Jabin king of Canaan before the people of Israel") might sound like a formulaic salute were it not for the abruptness of the shift to the divine plane and, above all, the telling opposition to the closure of Ehud's exploit in the previous chapter ("Moab was subdued that day under the hand of Israel"). The trivial-looking variations from the passive mood ("was subdued") to the active ("God subdued") and from "under" to "before" assume ideological meaning in context. Encapsulating the overall variations—in expectancy, plot structure, personal merit—the exit lines recollect in triumph the suspenseful interplay between the first two enactments of the paradigm.

Curiosity and the Dynamics of Retrospection

Curiosity has much in common with suspense. Both are interests that derive from a felt lack of information about the world, give rise to a play of hypotheses framed to supply the missing link, and generate expectations of stable closure. Unlike suspense, however, curiosity bears on things past relative to the moment of their becoming of interest. Which of the harlots is the baby's mother? Does the servant intentionally edit his report to the family? Why does Samson insist on marrying a Philistine woman? How did David come to meet Saul? Is Uriah an idealist or a resentful husband? What induces God to replace Elijah by Elisha? In each case, the answer may yet (and, the reader hopes, will) surface in the discourse, but the question relates to an accomplished fact in the world: an incident, relationship, motive, character trait, plot logic, which has already played some part in determining the narrative present. So whether provided by the text itself in due course (as with Samson) or by our own inferences, the closure takes the form of a retrospect.

Curiosity thus stands opposed to suspense in the temporal direction of interest—past vs. future—and therefore in the artistic structure of arousal as well. Since the dramatic future is naturally opaque and its conflicts naturally open till resolved by events, the artist need do little more than adhere to the order of occurrence in order to create suspense gaps about if's and how's. The various modes of foreshadowing are in principle options and intensifiers rather than necessary conditions. To produce curiosity, on the other hand, the artist must perceptibly deform the chronological order: suppress and entangle and delay information in order to open gaps about what has already come to pass in terms of the natural time-line. Through timely disclosures, the omniscient narrator could not only resolve but forestall all enigmas—the mother's identity, the servant's designs, the oddity of Samson's conduct, the secret of Uriah's character—did he not choose to make an ado about them. He disorders where he could follow the natural order, conceals where he might reveal, twists a coherent action into incoherence, challenging the reader to straighten out the incongruity by his own efforts. In short, while the ambiguation of consequents essentially arises from the dynamics of the action, the ambiguation of antecedents requires the dynamics of presentation, artfully manipulating sequence so as to turn what is chronologically past into a hoped-for textual future.

Structural contrast, as the Bible impressively demonstrates, is no bar to the richest interrelation. The sharper the suspense generated by the Sisera narrative, for instance, the prompter and closer the reader's scrutiny of the antecedents in the hope of unearthing some aid to the resolution of the plot. Conversely, the more lively the curiosity stimulated by the two whores' versions, the more opaque and eagerly expected the ending that will resolve both interests at once. In terms of the Bible's world view, the inferential movement back and forth along the plot line even assumes the status of a rule, for to be in suspense about what looms ahead is to be curious about the divine scenario for it. The uncertainty of prospection, then, puts a premium or a strain on retrospection, and vice versa. But even the interplay on top of the similarity does not yet equate the two dynamics whereby the art of sequence processes effect and meaning and comprehension. Suspense gaps ambiguate the shape and sense of the future; curiosity gaps, of the past.

In biblical poetics, accordingly, the manipulation of curiosity does not labor under the heavy ideological constraints on suspense. The clearest measure of the difference is the relative frequency of resolution. Suspense, as we have seen, is for the most part retardatory rather than genuine, and the foreshadowed outcome sooner or later translates into history; whereas curiosity turns out far more often permanently than temporarily unsatisfied, and its objects depend for their coherence on the reader's own gap-filling. If anything, the enigmas mentioned in my opening paragraph unduly increase the proportion of questions that find a definitive answer in the text; nor do they reflect the mutually complicating effect of lacunae arranged, in the David-and-Bathsheba manner, as a chain or a network.

Rather, both the pros and the cons of curiosity are mainly of an aesthetic nature. The only ideological constant is the veto on global ambiguation, which might blur and undermine the laws of a God-ordered world. All other factors and strategies may be ideologically oriented but not predetermined. The recommmmendations of maneuvering between the truth and the whole truth about the past should by now be fairly evident: narrative interest, the rhetoric of epistemology, the drama of interpretation running parallel to life, the molding of response to character and event by way of piecemeal or fragmentary disclosure, the exploration of the mystery of man. On the debit side, the only serious consideration is the obtrusiveness of withholding and displacing plot-stuff that omniscience could unfold in a natural order. Still, the narrator covers even his disingenuous sequencing with a show of innocence. This motivation turns to account the distance between the hidden interests and the official posture. Most of the curiosity gaps bear on internals—motives, schemes, personality—which the narrator is under no obligation to communicate in his guise as historian. It is the public life that he professes to record, and the secret life that his recording secretly twists into prominence for the reader to unravel. Nowhere is the process of retrospective unraveling so complex and the stakes so high as in the Joseph narrative, the Bible's siren and sphinx rolled into one.

Joseph and His Brothers: Making Sense of the Past

Plot intermediacy goes with plot indeterminacy: so much follows from biblical rule. Joseph's rough handling of his brothers causes the reader no undue worry about their ultimate fate. Apart from any extratextual foreknowledge of a happy ending, the Genesis system of prospection (already observed in the Wooing tale) again makes for reassurance. The youthful dreams, on their way to fulfillment and promising a reunion with the father himself, augur well. So do Joseph's recent maturation and his enjoyment of divine as well as royal favor. And so does the absence of any precedent for violence on the part of God's elect against a fraternal antagonist. The compositional indirections thus reflect and establish the same scale of interest as the more usual foreshadowing by divine forecast. Real suspense, as the clash of hopeful and fearful expectations about the future, gives way to the retardatory play of how-when-why hypotheses, which leaves our mind free for the manipulation of curiosity about the past. Attention shifts from terminus to route, from long-range effect to intermediate causes, from plot as such to its motivation through the tangle of God's providence and human character that makes biblical history. The very early promise that the brothers will come to no harm in the end, therefore, doubly foregrounds the interim ado made about the conflict. And the gratuity of this retardation brings out the extent to which the whole ado turns on one gap of motive that sustains the cat-and-mouse drama in both artistic and psychological terms: why does Joseph torment his brothers?

Since this gap forces a choice between inference and incoherence, no reader can afford to ignore it; and many have left their closures on record.[7] Their motivations of Joseph's conduct have always proceeded along four main lines: punishing, testing, teaching, and dream fulfillment. Predictably enough, however, each line is wrong because all are right. In characteristic biblical fashion, no hypothesis can bridge the discontinuities and resolve the ambiguities by itself; nor can the joint explanatory power of all four—and a few others to be suggested—unless brought to bear on the narrative in a certain order and shifting configurations. The need to combine inferences brings out their common features: all revert to the past not only as the key to the mysterious present but also as the object of the characters' own concern. At the same time, the combinatory variations reflect the changing pressures of the past on the present and the movement toward a happier future. Taken together, combination and variation focus interest on the (re)shaping of the past as a dramatic and psychological as well as an interpretive process. It is above all the emergence of that orchestrated sense of the past—the reader's, Joseph's, the brothers', even Jacob's train of retrospection—that my analysis will be tracing.

> (3) Joseph's brothers, ten, went down to buy grain from Egypt. (4) And Benjamin, Joseph's brother, Jacob did not send with his brothers, for he said, Lest he should meet with disaster. (5) So the sons of Israel came among the comers, for there was famine in the land of Canaan. (6) And Joseph was the governor over the land, it was he who did the selling to all the people of the land. Joseph's brothers came and bowed before him, face to the ground. (7) Joseph saw his brothers and recognized them, and he made himself a stranger to them and spoke to them harshly. He said to them, Where have you come from? And they said, From the land of Canaan, to buy food. (8) Joseph recognized his brothers and they did not recognize him. (9) And Joseph remembered the dreams that he had dreamed about them. And he said to them, You are spies; you have come to see the nakedness of the land. (10) And they said to him, No, my lord, it is to buy food that thy servants have come. (11) We are all of us the sons of one man. We are honest. Thy servants have

never been spies. (12) And he said to them, No, it is the nakedness of the land that you have come to see. (13) And they said, We, thy servants, are twelve brothers, the sons of one man in the land of Canaan; and behold, the youngest is now with our father and one is gone. (14) And Joseph said to them, It is just as I said to you, you are spies. (15) By this shall you be tested: you shall not leave this place, by the life of Pharaoh, unless your youngest brother comes here. (16) Send one of you and let him bring your brother, while you remain under arrest, that your words may be tested, whether there is truth in you. Or else, by the life of Pharaoh, you are certainly spies. (17) And he put them together in the guardhouse for three days. (Gen 42:3-17)

Why, then, this harsh speaking? The first inside view supposed to elucidate the dialogue—"Joseph saw his brothers and recognized them, and he made himself a stranger to them"—rather poses than resolves the question. It begins by skimming over the surface and concludes with a twist. (This surprise ending is weakened by the common misrendering of the final "and," which keeps expectation alive, as the openly contrastive "but.") And the second glimpse only offers information that more perceptibly conceals the workings of the mind it pretends to reveal. First repeating verbatim what we already know ("Joseph recognized his brothers"), this inside view goes on to state the one-sidedness of the discovery ("and they did not recognize him"), likewise redundant because safely inferable from the innocence of the brothers' response to the harsh inquiry ("From the land of Canaan, to buy food"). Drawn out not to satisfy but to whet curiosity, the rephrasing from within actually signals a pause in the action, motivated by Joseph's need to pull himself together, take stock and plan ahead. It is as if, his direct thoughts rendered in grammatical transposition, Joseph were saying to himself: "So I know them and they don't know me; now what?" And the answer immediately follows, though in a mental shorthand intelligible to him alone: "Joseph remembered the dreams that he had dreamed about them. And he said . . ." To him obviously a logical progression from internal cause to externalized effect, to us the passage from recollected dreams to accusations of spying makes a non sequitur: a narrative chain with a gap for a middle and an opaque mind for a bridge.

The discontinuity between inner and outer events thus widens from one pairing to another. The mystery thickens, incoherence threatens, retrospective deduction alone can yield some light; but clues are scarce, and those available, far from reassuring. That it takes Joseph time to recall the dreams suggests his general state of mind since his rise to high office, confirming the implications of studied forgetfulness carried by the names bestowed on his sons (41:50-52). But does not this insight into his psyche link up with his ensuing words to allude to the kind of plans he has in store for his brothers? Now that the past has forced itself on him, we fear, those who have made him wish to suppress it will become the victims of his pent-up fury.

The hypothesis that Joseph is bent on revenge gains further psychological support from the object of remembrance—the dreams, whose narration led to the crime and whose fulfillment enables the punishment—and more subtly from the playacting that follows. The trumped-up charge makes sense not only as a prelude to retribution but also as the first step in the tit-for-tat process itself, for it reenacts the final phase of Joseph's own suffering: vilification, by Potiphar's wife, leading to imprisonment. Even so, why charge the brothers with espionage of all crimes? Ostensibly picked at random, this accusation affords in context an intricate and ominous view of the accuser's mind; it ties up with both his recent and his remote past to suggest a double casting of roles. On the one hand, it imposes on the brothers an ignoble and dangerous role that comes as close as possible to the one he himself was reduced to by the woman's slander: hence his appositional exegesis of "spying" in terms of "seeing the nakedness of the land." By figurative analogy, the ten are thus branded as the would-be Hebrew rapists of Egypt. At the same time, the charge of spying harks back to childhood, when the young Joseph endeared himself to his brothers by bearing tales about them to Jacob; and, need I say, the present inversion of the roles of spy vs. victim betrays a sense of guilt that only adds fuel to the psyche's flames.[8]

In ethical terms, moreover, such vengeance has a rough justice about it that might appeal even to one who has not gone through, and just relived, a series of traumatic experiences: attempted murder, enslavement, seduction followed by a charge of attempted rape and three years in jail. To clinch matters, the crime-and-punishment reading finds a fast anchorage in the tit-for-tat design of the language. At first glance, the wordplay in "Joseph saw his brothers and recognized them [*va-yakirem*] and made himself a stranger to them [*va-yitnaker aleihem*]" radicalizes the contrast between perception and behavior. But the whole inside view also rhymes with the brothers' own scheming in the distant past, when "they saw him from afar off and they conspired [*va-yitnakelu*] against him to kill him" (37:18). *Va-yitnakelu* then; *va-yitnaker* now. The rich pun (*l* and *r* interchange in biblical Hebrew) not only draws together the starting points of criminal action and punitive counteraction. Nor only does it effect such a change or increment in the latter term—from dissembling to plotting—as to encapsulate the reversal of fortune and shape the two conspiracies into a causal chain of sin and retribution. By analogical extension from the specified ("to kill him") to the unspecified member, it would also appear to validate anew the ominous closure of the gap concerning Joseph's intentions: their life for his life.[9]

That this gap-filling shows Joseph in a rather ugly and (given the fore-shadowed happy end) ironic light does not at all disturb the reader. On the contrary. Besides its psychological appeal, in a context where a saint would not find it easy to resist the onrush of memory and desire, such a characterization has an encouraging precedent: our very first view of the youthful Joseph at home. The spoiled favorite had not only looked but been unlovely, before misfortune, the Bible's teacher and touchstone, made a man of him. Dovetailing with the whole pattern of clues, the analogy between his youthful and his mature self only gives hope for better things to come without varnishing the rawness of his spontaneous emotion. In other words, the motive gets resolved within what I called the *individual* scope of character; which makes the ugliness a point in its favor. Rather, the weak spot of this hypothesis lies in its failure to explain the dissembling. If Joseph meditates revenge, why is he denying himself the immense satisfaction of crushing his brothers with the disclosure of their nemesis?

As the dialogue unrolls, however, the solution to this enigma abruptly emerges with the ultimatum to produce the youngest brother, "that your words may be tested, whether there is truth in you." Joseph, it appears, is playing an even deeper game than his double talk has so far led us to believe. Still intent on having his revenge, he must for the time being forgo its pleasures to settle one terrible question mark. It would be gratifying to find oneself designated as "brother," perhaps for the first time, were it not for the implied definition of brotherhood in terms of common parentage: "Thy servants are brothers, sons of one man in the land of Canaan." In his own experience, after all, it was precisely that reductive orientation to the father that made the fraternal relationship less than worthless, a breach rather than a bond. And if so, Benjamin's ensuing collocation with himself takes on a portentous look indeed. What fate (Joseph asks himself) has this gang of fratricides devised for Benjamin, his full brother and the next object of jealousy, allegedly at home now but quite possibly likewise put out of the way? Perhaps they have said that he "is now with our father" only because the reference to two missing brothers might lead to awkward questions, whereas the circumstantiality of their actual account (ten here, one left behind, one gone) would invest it with an air of truth?

In retrospect, this suspicion elucidates anew the cryptic inside view regarding the dreams, especially the non sequitur from remembrance to accusation. Since each dream showed all the brothers doing obeisance to him—and the second even numbers them as "eleven"—Joseph must have been terrified by the absence of the one closest to him and most hateful to the rest. So if "spies" is his cover name for unnatural brothers, then the challenge to produce Benjamin indeed serves to "test their words": to determine their guilt on this recent account and maybe also their punishment for the long-standing crime. But such an inquiry calls for dissembling to ensure the suspects' cooperation and penetrability. The emergence of a new motive would thus seem to close the gap left by the old.

But not for long, though the next phase does start by confirming our recent inferences:

> (18) On the third day, Joseph said to them, Do this and you shall live; I am a God-fearing man. (19) If you are honest, let one of you brothers remain under arrest in your guardhouse, and you go and bring grain for your famished households. (20) And your youngest brother bring to me, that your words will be verified and you shall not die. This they did. (21) And they said to one another, Indeed, we are guilty concerning our brother, in that we saw the distress of his soul when he pleaded with us and we would not listen. That is why this distress has come upon us. (22) And Reuben answered them, saying, Did I not tell you, saying, Do not sin against the boy? But you would not listen, and now comes a reckoning for his blood. (23) They did not know that Joseph understood, for there was an interpreter between them. And he turned away from them and wept. (24) Then he returned to them and spoke to them. And he took Simeon from them and put him under arrest before their eyes. (25) And Joseph gave orders to fill their bags with grain and to return every man's money to his sack and to give them provisions for the road. This was done for them. (26) They loaded their asses with the grain and departed. (42:18–26)

Joseph has apparently launched his course of retribution—their otherwise pointless three days' arrest corresponding to his three years in prison—as if determined to exact at least a symbolic measure for measure. But the technique of juxtaposed opposition at once unsettles this reading; it highlights and gaps the reversal of the original terms, whereby nine were to remain as hostages and one to depart for home. By itself, indeed, this could still be taken to reveal how deep goes the anxiety to ascertain the truth about Benjamin. (Drastic pressure may frighten off the sole returner for good, and, if Benjamin is yet living, a chorus may persuade the father to let him go where a single voice would plead in vain.) Yet the reference to their "famished households," whom the grain carried by a single returner would hardly keep alive, reflects a more general concern; and the thought that the shock of a mass detention may kill Jacob could not have failed to occur to Joseph in the meantime. The change of terms thus suggests an intervening change of mind, all the more encouraging because it consists in a threefold psychological movement: from death- to life-thoughts, from a fixation about the past to shaping the future, and from egocentricity through selective fraternity to a sense of familial responsibility. Joseph's horizon has widened. And the ensuing developments, culminating in the secret tears, make it less and less probable that he still entertains punitive designs beyond a token revenge, of the kind just exemplified by the imprisonment.

Not that the originally signaled desire for revenge now proves illusive but that it proves short-lived: Joseph has checked and outgrown the temptation. Indeed, this underground development is one of the tale's subtlest psychological touches. The very primitiveness of the initial urge renders the hero's later magnanimity all the more credible, and his change of mind or heart parallels his overall change of character in the growth from adolescence to maturity. The change is even more plausibly motivated. The three days' interval gives Joseph as well as his brothers the time necessary to adjust to a shattering experience and do some soul-searching. As it transpires, they repent openly of their evil treatment of him—"we are guilty concerning our brother"—and so does he, by implication, of his evil designs against them. The hints given by this equivalence are even fortified by its causal sequence, for what draws tears from Joseph is his brothers' avowal, capped by the (to him) startling revelation that the eldest has been innocent all along. So the new development of motive and character eliminates the leading hypothesis—certainly in its portentous and egocentric form—as effectively as would any new disclosure. The process of gap-filling having started in the first encounter with the action inducing retrospection, the retrospective hypotheses are then superseded in the next encounter by the dynamics of the action.

They are not entirely superseded, however, because the effects of reconstruction persist, as I have just noted, and so does at least one reconstructed motive. What remains constant under this shift in the action *and* its reading is the anxiety about Benjamin, now promoted to chief gap-filler and replacing Joseph's own grievances as a reminder of the past and a cause for vindictive thoughts about the future. To this extent—and the narrator takes advantage of Joseph's ignorance to spin out his process of discovery in the interests of credibility—the relenting is strictly conditional. However humanized, the original plan remains in force, tears or no tears. This even interprets the curious and ostensibly arbitrary choice of surety. As Leah's second son, Simeon makes the perfect hostage for Benjamin, Rachel's second. Having turned aside to weep, thus sealing the renunciation of personal vengeance, Joseph reappears to arrest Simeon, as if to enact both his shift of interest and the continued dependence of future relations on past conduct. To him it is not so much coming as past events that cast their shadows before them: shadows in the plural, because the past itself still bifurcates from his anxious viewpoint.

Therefore, it is not (as some think) because Joseph's purpose lies in bringing his dreams to fulfillment that he compels his brothers to reappear with Benjamin, so as to have all the fraternal "sheaves" bow down before him.

The antecedent assumption about Joseph's purpose is itself dubious, and the causal relationship between that purpose and the Benjamin maneuver far more intricate. We must again dig into the past to reconstruct the on-going causal chain that leads from thought to speech and action. Note, first, how brilliantly the Joseph story exploits that ever-potential discrepancy between the reader's perspective on dreams (as authoritative foreshadowing devices within the text's system of conventions) and the characters' perspective on dreams (as "real life" events within the world's web of contingencies). Of the three figural views of Joseph's dreams—including his own, the main object of the reader's gap-filling efforts—two clearly regard them as less than infallible guides to the future. The brothers dismiss them as projections of the favorite's power hunger, and believe they can quash the dreams together with the dreamer ("We shall see what will become of his dreams"). Jacob does take the dreams more seriously, but not too seriously, or else he would never jump to conclusions about Joseph's death. Nor does their skepticism look unreasonable. For the second dream (37:9–11) contains a glaring incongruity that troubles the reader as well. Rachel ("the moon") being long dead, how can she ever do obeisance to Joseph in company with Jacob ("the sun") and all the brothers ("the eleven stars")?

Joseph himself must have mulled over this impossibility—its weight increasing with his expertness at dream interpretation, notable for making sense of every detail—but with no apparent success. Taken together with the series of misfortunes launched by those supposed to recognize his ascendancy and with the speedily-fulfilled dreams of his Egyptian clients, the failure would discredit his own youthful dream or at least its surface meaning. Far from buttressing his confidence, therefore, the sudden arrival of the brothers undermines it even further, since it throws into question even the first, hitherto straightforward dream. Eleven bowing sheaves foreshadowed, but only ten appear before him. It is strange, then, that each dream turns out to have numbered one participant too many. Stranger yet, each dream-extra stands in a special relationship to Joseph, one being his mother and the other his full brother. Most perturbing of all, the double correspondence in absentness and family tie links up with other indicators to engender a horrible suspicion: just as Rachel is dead, so is Benjamin.

How, then, can anyone hypothesize a wish to fulfill the dreams and causally relate it to the insistence on Benjamin's showing himself? In fact, the dreams make no sense to Joseph, either singly or paired, except for the ominous implication that Benjamin is no more. So he extorts from the brothers the commitment to produce Benjamin, not in order to realize but to test and elucidate the dreams. If Benjamin proves to have died—so Joseph's reasoning goes—then the dreams are not what they seem and the confirmed fratricides will be treated accordingly. If on the other hand Benjamin is alive, then the first dream will after all have been fulfilled on his arrival, however belatedly, and accounts can thereupon be settled on firmer ground. To him, again, the shaping of the future waits on the resolution of the past. The whole internal action and the whole gap-filling process come to turn, for the enlightened reader, on the doubt about Benjamin's survival that torments the benighted hero.

As its partiality for gradual and multiple unfolding could lead one to expect, however, the narrative soon divests this motive of explanatory monopoly. The eventful third day ends with yet another gap, arising from another strange act recorded without an antecedent cause and therefore producing another stab of curiosity. Why "return every man's money to his sack"? However softened his heart, Joseph can hardly seek to reward the criminals. Nor can this be meant as a gesture of goodwill, for then he would make it openly; and the discovery after the event indeed frightens ("What is this that God has done to us?") rather than heartens the recipients. Nor does it make sense as a trial of honesty, for thievery would pale beside their known and suspected crimes.

Yet the hiddenness of the act does suggest a new test or trap, and a retrospective scrutiny of the text enables the reader to puzzle it out. Joseph's train of thought may be reconstructed as follows. "If Benjamin is gone, they will never dare to show their faces in Egypt again and, though I can then do with the hostage as I think fit, I will never find out whether they truly repent of their evil ways. But what if they can easily produce Benjamin—how will I know their hearts then? What is their breast-beating about me really worth? So let me see how these professed penitents will now treat a brother in circumstances brought as close as possible to my own at the time. To reproduce the past, I will put the life of one of them into the hands of the rest and plant temptation in their bags to equal or exceed the profit they hoped to make by selling me into slavery. Will they now opt for the brother or for the money? Will they return at once to redeem the hostage or play a waiting game till hunger forces them back, in which case undue delay may become as revealing as outright desertion? True, Simeon cannot be hated by them as I was; but then to keep this money they do not have to dirty their hands—they can simply abandon him to his fate at mine. So if they do not show up, there are other ways of ascertaining Benjamin's fate. And if they do show up with the utmost dispatch, there is so much insight gained, the first dream will reach its fulfillment, and I can proceed accordingly." If concerning Benjamin the future hinges on whether the brothers have repeated their crime, then in regard to Simeon the question is whether they are capable of repeating it.

Throughout the drama of retrospection, Joseph figures as stage-manager as well as player, exploiting his superiority to assign roles to his brothers along two lines.[10] One consists in *role-reversal*, whereby he gives them a taste of his own suffering—helplessness in the hands of a bully, false charge with death in the offing, imprisonment, abrupt commutation of sentence—by forcing them to go through it in experiential order. Whether motivated in punitive or redemptive terms, this is what his policy has seemed to amount to. With the slipping of the money into the bags, however, there emerges another line of stage management: *role-duplication*, whereby he compels them to relive not his past but their own, reproducing something like the old temptations to find out whether they will now make the same criminal choice. Simeon's arrest pinpoints the modulation from the reversing to the duplicating policy. It begins as a show of arbitrary power, akin to both the brothers' and the Egyptians' changes of mind about Joseph. But then it veers round all the way from a new memento or lesson of victimization to a character test imposed on the old victimizers, complete with bait (the money) and deterrent (the report to the father). Whether this shift in role assignment marks a turning point in the ordeal remains to be seen; that it goes beyond the Benjamin-centered inquiry into the facts is certain.

In its tortuous unfolding of Joseph's motives and designs, the narrative has so far managed both to keep him in the foreground of the reader's attention (as the object of curiosity) and gradually to narrow much of the distance between our viewpoint and his (as the subject of consciousness). Looking back on those three days that began with the heavy dramatic ironies of the first encounter, we are no less struck by Joseph's than our own progress toward the order of vision normally reserved for the hidden superhumans. In moral stature, he has grown from the none too noble figure of the avenger driven by a personal grievance into a responsible kinsman, still tormented but in control and more sinned against than sinning. Attuned to the divinely predetermined movement toward the future, he now operates more as the agent than as the antagonist of the historical process that will reunite the whole chosen family in Egypt. And with regard to knowledge of the past, he has already discovered a good deal (Jacob's survival, Reuben's innocence, the others' regrets) and has taken steps to clear up the remaining gaps, notably the one that still troubles us as well: the character of the brothers. Having started as an object of judgment, he thus establishes by degrees his right to play the judge himself; from the victim of dramatic irony, he evolves into its master, manipulating his relatives according to a covert and well-planned scenario that increasingly coincides with the narrator's. This manifold dynamics, partly actional (developments in Joseph) and partly revelatory (developments in our insight into Joseph), controls the Egyptian scenes. It marks him as the center of interest and heightens his psychological reality for us and our sympathy for him.

As soon as the ten leave, however, they seem to carry away with them the drama and the interest:

> (26) They loaded their asses with the grain and departed. (27) Then one of them opened his sack to give his ass provender at the lodging place and he saw his money, and behold, it was at the mouth of his bag. (28) And he said to his brothers, My money has been returned and, behold, it is in my bag. Their hearts stopped and they turned trembling to one another, saying, What is this that God has done to us? (29) Then they came to Jacob their father in the land of Canaan and told him all that had befallen them. (42:26-29)

This marks a transition in more than geography. With the shift of scene from Egypt to Canaan and of theme from plan to fulfillment, a corresponding shift of focus would appear to be indicated. The space (42:27-43:15) and the time (weeks? months?) devoted to this phase certainly exceed the reasonable limits of an interlude. The narrator cannot just mean to keep all the parties concerned in suspense—the reader, Joseph, Simeon, the brothers, Jacob, each with his own hopes and fears—by retarding the promised second encounter. Is it, we wonder, that the narrator has in effect done with Joseph, as hero at least? The final revelations having brought the Joseph-centered play of events and hypotheses to a satisfactory conclusion, does the text now want to explore the brothers' side of the case? To give them, too, a fair hearing? To penetrate their mystery, thickened in and through the unraveling of his? To demonstrate how the two lines of action converge according to divine plan? The answer, it turns out, is yes and no.

Yes, because the brothers now come to the fore to be subjected to an intensive process of unfolding, remolding, or what I would term *crystallization*. Our own curiosity having been aroused by the incongruity between their early callousness and their recent penitence, we are pleased to find our (and Joseph's) suspicions dispelled by the favorable closure assigned to this character-gap throughout, from departure to return. Of course, the reader has long known that they have not laid a finger on Benjamin. But what their behavior now settles is that they are incapable of doing so, still less of deserting Simeon for any consideration short of parental veto; which in turn lends credence to their sense of guilt about Joseph as well, and by the very logic of his test.

But do this and related inferences we now make about their character arise from its development in the action or its disclosure in retrospection? Is it they who change or only our knowledge of them? The question raises a nice point, central to the view of man in the Bible, notably including the recent portrayal of Joseph himself. These two dynamics of sequence—character development and character disclosure—combine to suggest a realization of existing but hitherto dormant or stunted potentialities, moral and psychological. (Taken as a collective psyche, we now recall, the ten have long ago manifested their potential for brotherliness in Reuben's scruples and for self-criticism as well in Judah's vindication of Tamar.) So the favorable traits of character that resolve the discontinuity between their past and present behavior are not so much either created or unveiled as brought out by the pressure of events. Destabilizing routine and forcing clear-cut choices that the old balance of power within man cannot accommodate, the test *crystallizes* personality. And this internal process finds a subtle external equivalent in the shift of hierarchy within the family. Judah, who has already shown himself capable of admitting mistakes, replaces the well-meaning but ineffectual Reuben as leader and spokesman. That social regrouping goes with psychological crystallization is a measure of the importance assumed by the interlude in Canaan; that both must be traced (and correlated) without the slightest overt guidance, of the attention it demands.

At the same time, the shift in focus occurs amid such continuity that we hardly lose sight of Joseph and his viewpoint. It is as if the discourse were proceeding on two levels at once. Given his dual role as family victim and foreign victimizer, the others often have occasion to mention and more often to remember him. On top of his dramatic presence as lost son and brother there is his compositional presence as analogue and architect. The invocation by analogy derives from the narrator's patterning the brothers' character and characterization on the Joseph model. Thus, the brothers and our first impressions of them also undergo a surprising change for the better. Not only the overall reconstruction of their portrait but also its details and clues and very gaps keep ringing a bell. Consider the change of heart from fraternal enmity and vindictiveness to solidarity, the repentance of evil done or contemplated, even the sudden recognition of the Omnipotent's control ("What is it that God has done to us?") that has constantly been on Joseph's lips since his arrival in Egypt. The brothers' process of crystallization shows them following in Joseph's footsteps, slowly and belatedly yet surely, as if to make them worthy of him at the end of the course.

But this course is not just parallel to but devised by Joseph, as the instrument of the authors of text and history. On the dramatic level, it is Joseph who reproduces the past, maneuvering the brothers into situations that will cast them again in their old roles and give them a firsthand experience of his. And these stage-managed analogies in role (duplicated or reversed) help to produce by degrees the analogy in character. This causal link between situational and psychological analogy has already surfaced in Egypt, where the reenactment of the false charge leading to imprisonment elicits the first words of self-reproach. On the road, subsequently, the discovery of the money occasions the first reference to God. And the same type of manipulation, whereby one equivalence brings out another, then keeps the manipulator before our eyes in Canaan as well, bridging the geographical distance and giving the physically absent an architectural presence.

Hence the multifold continuity of plot and design and gap-filling amidst apparent discontinuity. The focus widens while seeming to shift. The brothers draw closer to Joseph while kept apart from him. Their retrospection on the distant past coexists and even deepens with the anxiety about the immediate future, as if to actualize the saying that it is not by *bread* alone that man lives. The upset balance of dramatic irony between the brothers (their character now dynamic, their awareness sharpened, their opportunities for direct observation ample) and Joseph (marking time, a prey to doubt and ignorance) is redressed by the reminders of his hidden influence and superiority. Even the complex of gaps and hypotheses surrounding him remains alive throughout our adventures with the secret life of his family: the reading of his schemes gains in validity and plenitude as we observe them realized beyond his fondest hopes.

On arrival, to trace the process briefly, the brothers must needs perform a familiar role vis-à-vis Jacob: breaking the news of another missing son. This time they tell the truth but, anxious to spare him as much distress as possible and ensure his cooperation in the release of the hostage, not the whole truth. In retelling, for instance, the mass arrest gets elided, Simeon's detention played down, and (most fatal but so unobtrusive as to escape the notice of commentators) the reappearance of the money in one load wholly omitted. Ironically, this very editorial solicitude for the addressee thwarts their efforts to convince him that all will go well if Benjamin only shows himself in Egypt. While Jacob's initial lack of response to their assurances suggests indecision—so that they begin unloading to give him time—the shock of the money turning up everywhere tips and almost breaks the scales.

(35) As they were emptying the sacks, and behold, every man's money bag was in his sack. They saw their money bags, they and their father, and were afraid. (36) And Jacob their father said to them, You have brought bereavement upon me: Joseph is gone, and Simeon is gone, and Benjamin you would now take away. It is upon me that all these things fall. (37) Then Reuben said to his father, saying, My two sons thou mayest kill if I do not bring him to thee; put him in my hands and I will return him to thee. (38) And he said, My son shall not go

down with you, for his brother is dead and he alone is left. Should harm
befall him on the journey you are to make, you would bring down my
gray hairs with sorrow to Sheol. (42:35–38)

Once more we receive from the Bible that pressing invitation to inference:
the non sequitur between act and act, act and speech or, as here, mental
state and vocal expression. In contrast to the psycho-logical transition from
external cause (startling discovery) to internal effect (fear), the movement
from that effect to the speech presumably generated by it looks strangely
discontinuous. For Jacob makes no reference at all to the pivotal money.
Instead, he lashes out at his sons as authors of his endless bereavement,
sandwiching the present victim (Simeon) between unforgettable retrospect
(Joseph) and unthinkable prospect (Benjamin). The whole chain makes
little sense unless we repeat the interpretive operation launched in a recent
corresponding scene by the non sequitur between Joseph's review of his
dreams at the sight of the brothers and *his* attack on them: the operation
of positing a gap in the very inside view supposed to bridge the two events
that flank it. Confronted by the money, are father and sons "afraid" for
the same reason?

Jacob's outburst, I would argue, implies that his fear differs from their
uneasy sense of mystery. It is less obscure and more terrible. Two strange
disclosures having been sprung on him in quick succession—Simeon's disappearance and the money's (re)appearance—Jacob refuses to accept them
as coincidences. A tight causal explanation, clearing up one mystery in
terms of another, suggests itself to him: the brothers have sold Simeon
into slavery and are now pretending to be dismayed only to cover their
tracks and lay the ground for yet another coup.

For Jacob, indeed, this suspicion is too terrible to voice. And for us it
might well be too terrible to attribute to him, were it not for the seeds
planted through Joseph's forethought (the Simeon-or-money test) and now
germinating between the lines of the dialogue. In the light of this reconstruction, what otherwise sounds like an irrational panic and a callous aban-
donment of a son becomes sadly intelligible. Jacob not only begins and
ends with the "upon me" that denies his sons all share in his grief. He
also insinuates the reason by interposing a threefold analogy. The equivalence in wording between "Joseph is gone" and "Simeon is gone" connotes
an equivalence in fate: inferring (falsely) from Simeon's case, Jacob now
(correctly) reinterprets Joseph's and finds the two mutually reinforcing.
"This mysterious money explains why sons of mine keep disappearing from
your company. Would you have me now entrust my youngest to you as
well? No, I had better cut my losses."

The brothers, with their awakened sense of guilt about Joseph, at once catch and smart under this aspersion. Hence Reuben's appeal, widely mistaken for a mere index of recklessness. Its extravagance makes sense as a desperate response to an accusation that admits of no straightforward denial—not just because it is left unspoken but mainly because it happens to be half-true. How could he say, We (or *they*) have indeed done away with your favorite and lied to you, but this time our hands are clean and our hearts pure? Or could one repeat the old falsehoods about a crime that lies at the root of the new trouble? Caught in this grotesque visitation of the past, Reuben tries the indirect father-to-father approach: "My two sons thou mayest kill if I do not bring him to thee." But such facile talk about the killing of sons only makes Jacob dig in his heels. Every phrase now bristles with dark suspicion. Having already excluded them from the grief of bereavement, he will not give them any credit for brotherhood, with the exception of the patently innocent Benjamin: "My son [rather than 'your brother'] will not go down with you, because *his* brother is dead." Then, "he alone is left": of the sons of Rachel, that is, and therefore a more tempting victim than either of his predecessors. And "should harm befall him," not in Egypt at the hands of the foreign lord but "on the journey which you are to make," then you "would bring down my gray hairs with sorrow to Sheol," thus finishing the work begun with Joseph's elimination (cf. 37:35).

While bringing the action in Canaan to a standstill, however, the money scene dynamizes into retrospective life our hypotheses about Joseph. For one thing, it confirms the reader's inferences about his hidden motives. If Jacob can believe his sons guilty or capable of the most heinous crimes against Simeon and Benjamin, Joseph has even better ground for misgiving. That *we* know the brothers to be for once blameless in deed and thought does not at all rule out the suspicions entertained by their judges. It only gives us a new measure of the distance separating their past from their present self and of the shadow cast by the past on the present. Retribution is largely a matter of the offender's old image overshadowing his new self: this message beautifully emerges from the two adjacent and parallel sequences where the group's appearance before a relative, with an expected brother missing, evokes secret fear about the absentee's fate and his substitute's prospects.

But the more recent sequence fillips as well as gratifies our curiosity about Joseph. Did he mean the money to serve a double purpose—a temptation for the brothers and an eye- or gap-opener for the father—or is it God that put the test to another use? The cause remains permanently ambiguous—as with Deborah's oracle—to suggest anew the blurring of the borderline between the agent and the lord of history. Yet the plot effect is one of a beneficial chain reaction that shakes the entire family. By unsettling Jacob's certainties about the past and exciting present mistrust, the discovery of the money prepares him for future discoveries. In turn, the mistrust gives the brothers another taste of false accusation, rendered all the more bitter by its true ingredient and affording them food for thought in the period of inactivity that lies ahead. And that accusation provokes Reuben to shoot his bolt, thus clearing the ground for the rise of a new order under Judah's leadership.

It is indeed Judah who, the famine having compelled Jacob to reopen the subject, finally breaks the stalemate (43:1-14). His persuasion works backwards as well as forwards, since it also reflects the progress (in empathy, self-control, family feeling) made by the brothers during the otherwise blank period of waiting. It does not betray the slightest resentment of the aspersion cast on them; nor any countercharge of the kind made by Simeon and Levi (34:31) in a former case of paternal indifference to the fate of a child of Leah's; nor even a trace of Reuben's verbal violence. Jacob's timid gambit ("buy us a little food") simply meets the response that it all hinges on Benjamin's accompanying them. Judah's double conditional amounts to an if-and-only-if proposition that the addressee can take or leave but, since it originates in the Egyptian lord, not haggle about. When Jacob counters with a vain plaint about their having mentioned a younger brother, Judah patiently explains the obvious: that no one could foresee the consequences. And Jacob once reduced to silence, Judah seizes the initiative and forces the issue by a newborn combination of vigor and insight. Alluding to his father's secret fears, he points out that the choice is between certain death for all, Benjamin included, and possible danger to one. To minimize even that danger, he harps on the fraternal bond with Benjamin ("our brother," "the lad") and offers as surety not yet another hostage, but his own filial piety: "I shall stand guilty before thee forever." For all its incongruous coupling with the realities of starvation and violent death, this moral commitment inspires trust by its very intangibility.

Not that Jacob's mistrust has evaporated. The restored money is, grudgingly, "perhaps an oversight"; with a barely concealed suspicion that Benjamin may be exchanged *for* Simeon, he prays for the return of both; and he finishes by resigning himself to bereavement. Yet he does recognize their brotherhood and does lift his veto. This promises a shift from retardation to acceleration toward the foretold happy end, with all goals accomplished. The more so since, by another doubling, the "present" Jacob instructs his sons to carry down to the Egyptian lord (43:11) rhymes with the merchandise imported by the Ishmaelites who sold Joseph into Egypt (37:25). The wheel seems to have come full circle. The plot movement that started with a brother leaving home in all innocence to join his brothers, only to find himself the property of a trading caravan bound for Egypt, now presses for closure once the brothers leave home in a caravan to rescue a brother in Egypt.

Astonishingly, however, Joseph shows no emotion, still less any intention of revealing himself, when he "saw Benjamin with them." He even seems too busy to stop for a greeting, and it is his majordomo who keeps the Egyptian side of the bargain by releasing Simeon. Have we utterly misread his mind? Is he content with having verified Benjamin's survival? Ignorant of the recent crisis at home, has he read a sinister meaning into the delay? Or is he merely putting off the recognition scene to the banquet announced? Just when we find the gaps reopened, there follows an assortment of digressions and frustrations that tease curiosity. And as if to underscore the denial of inside views, the narration of externals assumes a rare leisureliness and circumstantiality. With our minds anxious for some interim retrospection, the plot creeps forward (43:18–44:3) to apparently little effect except to worsen our anxiety.

First comes a wordy dialogue with the majordomo, whose contribution to intelligibility remains purely negative: there is no catch in the returned money. Owing to the discrepancies in awareness, the brothers alone can take this reassurance at face value and look forward to their host's arrival without any misgivings. But gradually the reader himself is lulled into a false sense of security. Repeating the tactics of the first encounter, the narrative begins the second by demoting genuine in favor of retardatory suspense. As the meal progresses, all fear of Joseph's intentions is dispelled and the unraveling of the mystery seems imminent. Joseph at once inquires after his father and must rush out of the room to hide his tears at the sight of Benjamin. (Weeping, we recall, signals relenting, if not regret about wrong suspicion. In terms of the consonantal Hebrew text, there is even an ambiguity about whether he was overcome by feeling for "his brother" [*akhiv*] or "his brothers" [*ekhav*].) Anticlimactically, however, the convivial banquet leads not to the expected reunion but to another parting, and along familiar lines.

> (1) He commanded his house steward, saying, Fill the men's bags with food, as much as they can carry, and put each man's money in the mouth of his sack; (2) and put my goblet, the silver one, in the mouth of the bag of the youngest, with his money for the grain. And he did as Joseph told him. (3) With the first light of morning, the men were sent off, they and their asses. (44:1–3)

Our whole structure of inference undermined, we hardly know where to turn. Does Joseph have another delay in mind, and if so, to what purpose? Or is this the final goodbye, and if so, why expend all this energy and then withdraw just when things have gone according to plan? Or again, did he only seek to meet Benjamin without having to reveal his own identity? Since none of these alternative hypotheses will cohere with the facts distributed along the narrative sequence, the reader must wait on events for enlightenment. Given the uninformative text, only fresh developments can resolve the ambiguities of retrospection. Mercifully, the sudden acceleration of the tempo does not keep us baffled overlong. Departure, pursuit, accusation, search, arrest, return: these follow hard upon one another (44:3-14), and at last we know where we are. No change of plan, this, but its high point, leading us past the final bend in the corridor of Joseph's mind to the brothers' decisive test.

> (4) When they had gone but a short distance from the city, Joseph said to his house steward, Up, go after the men; and when thou hast overtaken them, say to them, Why have you repaid good with evil? (5) Is it not from this that my master drinks, and by this that he divines? You have done wrong in this. (6) He overtook them and spoke to them these words. (7) They said to him, Why does my lord speak such words as these? Far be it from thy servants to do such a thing. (8) Behold, even the money that we found in the mouth of our bags we brought back to thee from the land of Canaan; how then should we steal silver or gold from thy master's house? (9) Of thy servants, he with whom it be found, let him die, and we also will be my lord's slaves. (10) He said, Well, let it be as you say: he with whom it be found shall be my slave, and you will be clear. (11) They made haste and every man lowered his bag to the ground and every man opened his bag. (12) And he searched, beginning with the eldest and ending with the youngest; and the goblet was found in Benjamin's bag. (13) They tore their clothes, and every man loaded his ass, and they returned to the city. (14) When Judah and his brothers came to Joseph's house, he was still there; and they fell before him to the ground. (44:1-14)

Joseph's role-assignment has progressively emerged as the key to his own role-playing. And whether manipulated into retracing their own or his career, the brothers appear to have given an excellent performance. But to an observer in Joseph's particular position—combining an outside view of the present with an inside knowledge of the past—the Simeon test has been too easy and inconclusive at that. Too easy, because Simeon is no object of general hatred. Also inconclusive, because the (to Joseph, suspiciously) long delay in the brothers' return to Egypt leaves their motive ambiguous between starvation and affection; and even Benjamin may owe his survival first to his father's vigilance and then to the Egyptian's ultimatum. Viewed in the most charitable light, the test proves only the solidarity among the ten malcontents. But does fraternal solidarity now extend to Rachel's sons as well? Have they come to terms with the father's preference? This still remains in question, even to the more privileged reader.

Hence Joseph's final test, the supreme exercise in "real life" gap-filling. It consists in turning back the wheel of time to the original crime against himself, with the circumstances reproduced and the ten ranged against Benjamin. Rachel's youngest, as his absence from the first encounter suggested to the experienced observer, has (if alive) taken his brother's place as paternal favorite. To exacerbate the brothers' jealousy, Joseph now shows him special favor during the banquet— "Benjamin's portion was five times as much as any of theirs"—rubbing it in through the contrast with the order of natural seniority in which he has taken care to seat them. (Even the slipping in of the silver goblet on top of the restored money gives the impression of a parting mark of favor; only in retrospect—nicely counterpointed, again, by the search in order of birth—does it reveal itself as a frame-up.)

The experiment thus proceeds under something like laboratory conditions. On the one hand, the subjects (re)cast in the role of victimizer have been put at their ease: mission accomplished, all fears gone, dined and wined, as though in compensation for ill-treatment. They are even prevented from suspecting any trickery on the way. For the replacement of the money on the previous visit would now neutralize the effects of any accidental discovery; the search follows the hierarchical order; and Benjamin appears the least likely object of a conspiracy on the part of their gracious host.

On the other hand, the appointed victim is at his most vulnerable. With Simeon released, the brothers have their hands free. The (jogged) memory of lifelong favoritism presses for making use of that freedom while they can. The search party's indifference to the money in *their* bags suggests that by doing so they could, once again, mix profit with pleasure. And the opportunity for theft afforded by the long stay in the Egyptian's house combines with the incriminating evidence so fairly turned up to invite them to wash their hands of the thief with an easy conscience. After all— they may piously sigh—how can we save him?

This cruel trap once baited, Joseph hastens to spring it ("Up, go after the men"). But the narrator takes his time in divulging the results. The grand climax, resolving past doubts and leading straight to a happier future, arrives only after three inconclusive rounds, where the narrator's adherence to the dramatic method leaves even the most promising bits of dialogue and action under some shadow of ambiguity. Of course, the restriction to externals mimes the dialogists' own viewpoint and interpretive difficulties. Yet each side knows its own mind at least, while the reader must grope his way throughout with nothing to aid him but his experience with both.

That experience raises the reader's hopes to a new height. Is not the deviser of the test anxious and its subjects ripe for success? As the prospect gains in certitude, so does the whole shape of the action as a process that began with dissembling and will end in recognition. But this growing lucidity is not uniformly spread over the discourse, nor will it be even in retrospect. However transparent the start and finish, operating as reference points along an "unhappiness-to-happiness" line to safeguard foolproof composition, the causal movement that bridges them by reversing the one into the other retains much of its opacity. And it is of course no accident that the delimiting reference points consist in externals and the bridging or motivating forces in internals. The principle that the secret life remains secret history, that plot intermediacy goes with plot indeterminacy unless the reader determines it for himself, governs the narrative to the very climax.

As shown by their argument from minor to major in verse 8, the brothers meet the charge of theft-with-ingratitude with utter disbelief. Their consignment of the offender to death and themselves to slavery is accordingly yet another mode of expressing incredulity—this time, by way of extravagant prospect rather than logical retrospect. Still, as with Reuben's offer to have his two sons killed, a character's verbal extravagance is revealing precisely due to its spontaneity. Hence the merit in the brothers' assumption of collective responsibility. It is freely undertaken by all, as a matter of course and for the first time in a cumulative series of false accusations. It also betrays how the Joseph affair has come to pervade their very modes of thought and judgment, now unmistakably governed by the logic of retribution. Note the automatic causal linkage between theft (as crime) and death and slavery (as punishment), and the virtual equation of death and slavery: both expose a whole network of psycho-moral relations, associations, correspondences. And their response looks even more impressive against the background of Jacob's hyperbolic outburst— "any one with whom thou wilt find thy gods will not live in the presence of our brothers" (31:32)—when accused by Laban of having stolen his figurines. A thief envisaged as falling in the presence of his brothers as against brothers falling together with the thief: the recurrence with variation, backed by related gap-filling clues, offers both an inside view of the otherwise opaque mind and an evaluation within an otherwise detached narrative.

Speaking for his master, however, Joseph's steward will have none of this package deal—certainly not as long as undertaken under the illusion that it will never be put to the test and in ignorance of the identity of the test case. Politely declining their offer, in effect treating it as a verbal flourish, he nevertheless seizes on the element that will clinch the equivalence with Joseph's actual history. Yes, he answers, let the thief incur slavery and the rest go free. Indeed, once the goblet has been found in Benjamin's sack, his refusal to take their words seriously no longer appears gratuitous. Far from reiterating their commitment to stand or fall together, the brothers say nothing at all. So the gap of character, never definitely closed, yawns at us again. Does their solidarity exclude Benjamin, as it did Joseph, or are they struck dumb with horror? (Or in terms of narrative dynamics: does their silence operate to undercut the implications of their recent statement, as an ironic exposure, or to prolong curiosity and sharpen expectation by deferring the full disclosure of internals to the climactic showdown with Joseph?) If their silence points one way, their actions point the other way. All now tear their clothes, as Jacob alone did in Joseph's case. Though free to go, all turn back. Having left the city as "the men," they return as "Judah and his brothers": a shift in designation that augurs well both as a reminder of the newly dominant figure and as a hint of solidarity with the brother who has gone surety as well as with the one in obvious trouble. And rather than doing their usual obeisance to the Egyptian lord, they now "fell before him to the ground" in expressive speechlessness.

> (15) Joseph said to them, "What deed is this that you have done? Do you not know that a man like me can divine things? (16) And Judah said, What can we say to my lord? What can we speak, and what can we do to clear ourselves? God has found out the guilt of thy servants. Behold, we are my lord's slaves, both we and he in whose hand the goblet was found. (17) Then he said, Far be it from me to do this. The man in whose hand the goblet was found shall be my slave, and as for you, go up in peace to your father. (44:15-17)

As if a partaker in our remaining doubts, Joseph does not rest content with outward gestures. Having finally cornered his brothers, he will let them off with nothing short of a full-scale inquisition where he plays the tempter. By starting with the collective charge, "What deed is this that you have done?" he resumes the test just where the narrator (and, dramatically, the steward) left it off. If, as their silence since Benjamin's arrest may imply, the brothers have gone back on their word and are now merely keeping up appearances, then they will be quick to disclaim responsibility ("Not we, only he") as soon as matters come to the crunch. Judah's stout reaffirmation of a common fate, therefore, must have enlightened and pleased him. So must have its attendant features: the disdain for excuses, stopping short of any actual admission of guilt; the oblique glance at Joseph's ill-treatment and the submission to God's justice; even the skill with which, under the guise of shared responsibility, the death sentence originally pronounced on the thief gets commuted in repetition to enslavement.

For all the progress it reflects, the speech does not yet satisfy the inquisitor, for reasons unstated but deducible from his overall approach and his probing counterspeech. To him, Judah does not so much fail as deflect the test, and in two ways. In moral terms, first, Judah's words sound far more ambiguous and problematic to one with inside knowledge of the past, like Joseph, than they would to an outsider like the Egyptian nobleman to whom they are nominally addressed. The Egyptian would take the reference to God's having "found out the sin of thy servants" as a euphemistic confession to the theft, and leave it at that. But Joseph, aware of being the hidden topic of that reference, deciphers it as an expression not so much of present solidarity with a brother as of guilt concerning the past betrayal of another brother. What would they do, the question remains, if their conscience were clear and the exigency of adhering to a Benjamin (or indeed a Joseph) first arose? Worse, the verbal rhyming of "God has found out the sin of thy servants" with the "he in whose hand the cup has been found" so patterns the workings of divine retribution as to saddle Benjamin with a large share in the crime against Joseph, of which he is wholly innocent. Is Benjamin included in their collective responsibility only at the price of being included, if not as agent then as scapegoat, in their collective guilt? As the tale moves toward its climax, the moral distinctions become as fine (the late Henry James produced no finer) as those that sustain the David and Bathsheba irony are broad. But then their drawing is motivated in terms of character and psychology. For at the moment of truth Joseph must have the whole truth, however ruthless its eliciting, and Judah by now can (and, it turns out, does) supply it under pressure.

To disambiguate the ethical outlook, therefore, Joseph turns the screw. He shifts his ground from collective to individual responsibility. There is no question of bringing anyone to book except the actual thief, he now affirms, presumably waiting to see whether they will cling to Benjamin simply in virtue of brotherhood. Put another way, Judah has sidestepped the trap by casting the situation in terms of role-reversal, as (divine) tit for (human) tat and theft revealed for theft concealed. So Joseph puts the trap in his way again by foregrounding and improving the chances of role-duplication: to absolve the others from blame is to tempt them to desert Benjamin and betray their fraternal bond once again.

To judge by other clues, at the same time, Joseph finds Judah's reply even more deficient in feeling and empathy than in morality. Why, of all the parties concerned, has the father received no mention? And however gratifying the egalitarian reference to Benjamin (included in the "we"), his parity as brother goes with no recognition of his peculiarity as son. To Joseph, ignorant of the developments at home and Judah's part in them, this twofold omission rings an ominous bell. He interprets it as a total lack of understanding, let alone acceptance, of the paternal sentiments that have torn the family apart and, unless the bonds of brotherhood withstand every strain, may yet do so again. Joseph's reference to "the man in whose hand the goblet has been found" thus plays the brothers' game by pretending that Benjamin is just one of a crowd. While the terminal "As for you, go up in peace to your father" prods for a response to an old-new scenario that leads them back to Jacob "in peace" to report his last favorite gone for life.

To this challenge Judah magnificently rises, in a retrospect that at long last floods the brothers' side of the case with light and winds up their process of crystallization (44:18–34). Overtly intended to move the Egyptian addressee by rehearsing the story of their dealings with him, this retrospect encapsulates the history and portrait of an unhappy family from the viewpoint of a member passionately committed to it for good or ill. It is as though Judah has seen straight into his interlocutor's mind and detected its weakest spot. For he also shifts his ground to meet the issue squarely: from moral to personal relations, from fraternal bond to interfamilial tangle, from the fiat to the feeling of responsibility. The neutral reference to Benjamin gives place to the loaded "child of old age," "our youngest brother," and, most often, "the lad." Even more novel, the old father's sentiments now receive not just a mention but repeated and preferential treatment. His brother having died, that child of old age "is alone left of his mother's children and his father loves him." Again, "should the lad leave his father, he would die." And again, this time quoting the father himself, "two sons has my wife borne to me; one left me and I said, Surely he has been torn to pieces. . . . If you take this one also from me and harm befalls him, you will bring down my gray hairs in grief to Sheol." The youngster equally loves his father, moreover, as suggested by the referential ambiguity in the second quotation above: who "would die" out of the other's company, the father or the son? How can one decide—as so many exegetes and translators have done—considering that "his soul is bound up with his soul?"

It is thus the multiform (and reading between the lines, inexplicable and often unfair) play of family feeling—the ten's for the youngest brother, his for his father, the father's for him and his brother and their mother—that knits them all together. And in his final plea to be allowed to take Benjamin's place, Judah associates himself with this whole network of relations:

> (30) Now therefore, when I come to thy servant my father and the lad is not with us, and his soul is bound up with his soul, (31) then as he sees that the lad is gone, he will die; and thy servants will bring down the gray hairs of thy servant my father in grief to Sheol. (32) For thy servant has gone surety for the lad to my father, saying, If I do not bring him back to thee, I shall stand guilty before my father forever. (33) Now therefore, let thy servant, pray, remain instead of the lad as a slave to

my lord, and let the lad return with his brothers. (34) For how can I
return to my father if the lad is not with me? I fear to see the evil that
would overtake my father. (44:30–34)

The critical point is reached by a gradated movement all along the line
of discourse. In regard to the viewpoint expressed, Judah modulates from
spokesman to speaker: having so far articulated the voice of the ten ("we,"
"thy servants"), he now goes on to assume a special position ("when I come")
within the group ("with us" etc.) and ends by sounding an individual note
("thy servant," "I"). The shift in person from plural to singular correlates
with a shift from their collective to his personal responsibility and therefore,
it is hoped, judgment. The personal note itself first evokes the speaker's
moral responsibility to his father ("thy servant has gone surety," "I shall
stand guilty"), but culminates in a purely emotional appeal. It is no longer
a matter of obligation; nor, appropriate as it looks that the initiator of
the sale of the first favorite into slavery should enslave himself to set the
second free, of justice and conscience. Simply, Judah so feels for his father
that he begs to sacrifice himself for a brother more loved than himself.
Nothing could do more to establish the depth and genuineness of this feeling
than the abrupt loss of control reflected in the switch (verse 34) from
ceremonial language to a cry from the heart: he cannot bear to see his
father stricken.

To Joseph, of course, the speech again reveals even more than the speaker
intended: the official version of his own death ("torn to pieces"), the reason
for the delay in the brothers' return, the pain his testing as well as his fate
must have given. Most important, if to a listener ignorant of the family
situation and record, the brothers' attitude as expressed by their leader
would appear admirable, then to one in the know it surely manifests nothing
short of a transformation, from subnormal to abnormal solidarity. That
the sons of the hated wife should have come to terms with the father's
attachment to Rachel ("my wife") and her children is enough to promise
an end to hostilities and a fresh start. That the second of these children
should enjoy his brothers' affection is amazing. But that Judah should
adduce the father's favoritism as the ground for self-sacrifice is such an
irresistible proof of filial devotion that it breaks down Joseph's last defenses
and leads to a perfectly Aristotelian turning point, a discovery with peripety.
Nor is this a one-sided but rather a double and causally motivated enlightenment: having discovered their character, Joseph discloses his identity. One
anguished cry about the patriarch draws out another, "I am Joseph. Is
my father still alive?"

Surprise and the Dynamics of Recognition

Both suspense and curiosity are active interests, generated and sustained by felt discontinuities that interpretation does its best to repair. We know that we do not know, and behave accordingly. In contrast, the production of surprise depends on the reader's being lured into a false certitude of knowledge. In structural terms, therefore, the discontinuities in chronology, especially between cause and effect, must assume here the appearance of continuities, so that the gap will surface only at the moment of its filling. For the new information to perform its unsettling effect, the old must look settled. In short, the dynamics of recognition is characterized by a sequence where imperceptible disordering sets us up for unpredictable reordering.

Consider the following excerpts, one from Elisha's dealings with his liberal Shunamite hostess and the other from the siege of Samaria:

(12) [Elisha] said to Gehazi his servant, Call this Shunamite. He called her, and she stood before him. (13) And he said to him, Say now to her, Behold, thou hast taken all this trouble for us; what is to be done for thee? Wouldst thou have a word spoken for thee to the king or to the commander of the army? But she said, I dwell among my own people. (14) And he said, What then is to be done for her? And Gehazi said, Well, she has no son and her husband is old. (15) And he said, Call her. He called her, and she stood in the doorway. (16) And he said, At this time, at about a life's interval, thou shalt embrace a son. And she said, No, my lord, O man of God, do not delude thy maidservant. (2 Kgs 4:12–16)

(1) [When the Aramean siege had reduced Samarians to cannibalism,] Elisha said, Hear the word of the Lord. Thus says the Lord, About this time tomorrow a bushel of fine flour shall be sold for a shekel and two bushels of barley for a shekel, at the gate of Samaria. (2) And the aide-de-camp on whose arm the king leaned answered the man of God and said, If the Lord should make windows in heaven, will this thing come to pass? And he said, Behold, thou shalt see with thy own eyes, but thou wilt not eat of it. (3) Now there were four men, lepers, at the entrance of the gate, and they said to one another, Why do we sit here until we die? (4) If we say, Let us go into the city, then the famine *is* in the city and we shall die there; and if we sit still here, then we shall die also. Now therefore come, let us go over to the camp of the Arameans: if they spare us, we shall live, and if they kill us, we shall die. (5) So they rose at twilight to go to the camp of Aram, and they came to the edge of the camp of Aram, and behold, there was no man there! (6) For the Lord had made the army of Aram hear the sound of chariots and the sound of horses and the sound of a great army, and they said to one another, Behold, the king of Israel has hired against us the kings of the

Hittites and the kings of Egypt, to come against us. (7) So they rose
and fled in the twilight, and left behind their tents and their horses and
their asses in the camp just as everything was, and fled for their life.
(2 Kgs 7:1-7)

Before Gehazi divulges the Shunamite's misfortune, it would no more occur
to the reader to wonder whether she was childless than whether she was
handsome or popular with the neighbors. Not that the question is not important to her, but that the tale has thus far done nothing to make it so
for us—to force open a gap—and therefore it simply fails to arise. In fact,
its very importance within the Bible's world (in terms of social norms) erects
the silence on it into a mark of irrelevance within the Bible's art (in terms
of contextual norms). Wherever childlessness does assume poetic relevance,
we find it noted at an early stage in our acquaintance with the heroine.
Sarai enters Genesis as "barren; she had no child" (11:30); soon after
Rebekah's marriage, it transpires that "she was barren" (25:21); so is Rachel
(29:31); and the rule of making an ado early if it is to be made at all extends
to Manoah's wife in Judges (13:2) and Hannah in Samuel (1 1:2). In each
case, then, the information comes in advance of developments rather than
in retrospect, focusing attention on the narrative future (in the interests
of suspense) rather than the past (with an eye to curiosity or surprise).

Given this artistic norm, the gap as to the Shunamite's childlessness
becomes doubly concealed and hence doubly surprising once revealed.
The surprise involves a retrospective illumination of all that has gone before,
notably of the woman's character as well as her state. No ulterior motive,
the discovery establishes, has lain behind her "taking all this trouble."
Reserving for the man of God's use a room "with a bed, a table, a chair
and a lamp" (4:10) is no prelude to a petition but a spontaneous act of
piety. Even when the thankful Elisha gives her an opening, inviting her
in effect to name her own reward, she passes up the chance to "have a
word spoken" for her to one still closer to the prophet than "the king or
the commander of the army": indeed, to tell the wonder-worker that her
relief is right in his line. And even when the prophet (his persistence a
measure of both her hospitality and the novelty of finding his good offices
in so little demand) uncovers her trouble and volunteers help, she does
not seem to put much confidence in his undertaking. In brief, where an
anticipatory disclosure of the Shunamite's plight would first render her
motives suspect and then her skepticism implausible—"too good to be
true"—its temporary withholding and abrupt emergence maintain throughout an attractive yet credible portrait of a woman who deems virtue its
own recompense.

In the other passage, the hidden gap concerns an aspect of the represented world very different from the Shunamite's long-standing state—an in-between event—but its disclosure in closure proves equally unexpected. The discovery of the Arameans' flight startles the reader no less than the personages. Nothing in the text gave away the secret that such a reversal has or might have intervened between the two successively ordered and to all appearance sequent occurrences that in reality flank it: the prophecy of relief (verses 1–2) and the venture of the lepers (verse 3). Unlike the investment of Jerusalem in Hezekiah's reign, for example, the divine word does not even foretell the lifting of the siege ("By the same way that he came, he shall return" [2 Kgs 19:33]) but only an end to the famine ("a bushel of fine flour shall be sold for a shekel"). And instead of reporting the miracle after the prophecy, where it temporally belongs, the narrator pretends that it has not yet taken place at all: he goes on to trace the lepers' counsel of despair, arousing the expectation that they will somehow figure as the instruments of God's deliverance, and only on arrival ("behold, there was no one there!") reveals them as its first witnesses. What looked at the time like a tall order to come—and it will not come, the officer adds for good ideological measure—proves in retrospect an accomplished fact; what looked like a suspense pattern, retardation and all, emerges as a bait for surprise; what looked like a straight chronology reverses into a multiply discontinuous ordering, with a camouflaged gap and an overdue resolution.

Elsewhere, the dynamics of recognition shifts its focal point from initial lulling to misdirecting. The order devised for the reader's surprise temporarily camouflages less the very existence of a gap in the narrative chronology than its true closure or significance, which later springs up to shatter and replace the false:

> (18) [Gideon] said to Zebah and Zalmunah [the captured kings of Midian], Where are the men whom you slew at Tabor? They answered, As thou art, so were they, like the same man; all with the looks of a king's sons. (19) And he said, They were my brothers, the sons of my mother; as the Lord lives, if you spared their lives, I would not slay you. (Judg 8:18–19)

The information sprung by this exchange is so unforeseen as to alter our understanding of the whole sequence of events that leads up to it. As early as verse 4 ("Gideon came to the Jordan and passed over"), the question arises why Gideon should cross the Jordan after his defeat of Midian. But this gap between occurrences is anything but troublesome, since the answer at once suggests itself: he pursues the enemy in order to complete his victory. What could be more natural? This automatic hypothesis even grows in contextual force from one verse to another. For the sequel minutely renders the jeers ("Is the fist of Zebah and Zalmunah in thy hand?") with which Gideon's call for bread meets en route from the people of Succoth (verses 5–6) and then of Penuel (verse 8), the dire threats he utters in response (verses 7, 9), and the carrying out of the threats after the second battle (verses 14–17). The progress of the tale thus foregrounds the national issues, impressing on our mind how hollow the victory is (or would be) and how precarious Gideon's leadership as long as part of the Midianite army, having withdrawn in good order beyond the Jordan, remains operational under the kings' command.

Hence the surprise now occasioned by the surfacing of the familial motive for the pursuit—the slaughter of Gideon's brothers, who have so far played no role in the narrative. Gideon, it turns out, has not even entertained any hope of rescuing those brothers. "Where are the men you *slew* at Tabor?" he asks his royal captives, an inquiry whose apparent senselessness has elicited from scholarship the usual crop of textual emendations. But what really needs emending is the scholar's sensitivity to the expressiveness of biblical dialogue. For the question is not intended to make sense as a demand for information: indeed, the addressees themselves (to dispose of another scholarly pseudo-crux) show their perfect understanding of its rhetorical drift in making no attempt to meet it. The very incoherence of the question betrays the questioner's raging pain and indicates vengeance as the mainspring of his actions all along.

The switch from a national to a private motivation not only reopens and closes anew a gap that has long appeared settled. It also impels us to review the intervening developments. The disproportionate violence with which Gideon has just treated the uncooperative citizenry of Succoth and Penuel—the lashing with briers, the pulling down of the tower, the mass execution—suddenly makes psychological as well as political sense. Whereas the relative mildness of Gideon's dealings with the real enemy, again caught off-guard, now shows itself as less accidental and less justifiable than it did before. His mind has been fixed on capturing the two kings whom he holds responsible for his bereavement ("Zebah and Zalmunah fled, and he pursued them and took [them]"), so much so that he did not exert himself to wreak havoc on their army beyond "throwing it into panic." The manipulation of antecedents thus launches a surprise chain reaction from the point of retrospective (dis)closure, whereby Gideon's personality emerges as more complex and less admirable than before.

This surprise turns not so much on the imperceptibility of the gap as of its true filling. Unlike the Shunamite's childlessness, the question of Gideon's pursuit does arise at once. In the absence of any clue to the contrary, however, the hypothesis of a single-minded Gideon gains an initial monopoly: any other explanation, alternative or even complementary, would be so far-fetched that we do not "see" (expect, look round for) it until the informational turning point. So perceptibility is a matter of probability, and probability is a matter of degree. The less automatic the early filling, the sharper our awareness of the gap and our expectancy of a or the ultimate resolution; or in other words, the stronger our curiosity from the point of opening and the milder our surprise at the point of closure. This enables the Bible to vary the proportions of surprise and curiosity from one narrative (or stage or verse) to another by appropriately manipulating the reader's sense of temporal discontinuity.

Consider four successive episodes in 2 Samuel: (1) David's response to the death of the baby (12:14–33); (2) Amnon's rape of Tamar (13:1–14); (3) Absalom's murder of Amnon (13:22–29); (4) Joab's scheme to have Absalom recalled from exile (14:1–23). None of these follows the chronological sequence, whereby one would learn beforehand how or why the protagonist acts, but rather opens with a gap concerning his character or designs and releases the information only later. Still, the four episodes mark a steady shift in the dominant interest: a descending order of surprise and, proportionally, an ascending order of curiosity.

David's appeals to God to spare his boy exhibit such violent grief—the fear is even voiced that he "may do himself some harm" on discovering the catastrophe—that the speed with which he resigns himself to the inevitable cannot but bring us up short. His intimates' question *echoes* our own: "What is this thing that thou hast done? Thou didst fast and weep for the child while he was alive, and when the child died thou didst arise and eat bread? And he said, While the child was still alive, I fasted and wept, for I said, Who knows, perhaps the Lord will be gracious to me and the child may live? But now he is dead, why should I fast? Can I bring him back again? I shall go to him, but he will not return to me." Nobody, then, could predict David's reaction in the absence of an exhaustive character sketch, and its very unpredictability enhances the insight into his extraordinary mind. Though Amnon's mind remains equally opaque before the fact, his violation of Tamar is more predictable, because his earlier maneuvering for a tête-à-tête implied some design on her virtue. That he should not stop at rape may come as a surprise; but, given his desperate passion and the whole build-up for at least a seduction scene, it would be even more surprising to find him letting her go in peace. A volte-face indeed ensues—love turning into hate—but it forms a development rather than, as with David, a revelation of the initial state of mind: an effect rather than a cause of the surprising event. In the case of Absalom, who "hated" Amnon, one is even more prepared for the violent outcome, because he can have only one reason for inviting the rapist to a feast and only one way of avenging himself on him. The only gap that remains open concerns the mechanics of execution. And in Joab's initiative to return the exiled favorite, even the means receives some advance notice: he summons and coaches the wise woman on stage, so that her actual address alone is reserved for the dialogue with the king.

This goes to show that those basic temporal effects I name surprise and curiosity may interact not only in a single biblical narrative but within a single gap. Such mixtures, however, do not blur the peculiar contours of either as a compositional strategy and a dynamics of reading. Arising from a marked suppression of antecedents, curiosity involves a play of no fewer than two gapfilling hypotheses. Uriah either knows or does not know; Joseph means to settle accounts with his brothers or to ascertain Benjamin's survival or to forge real fraternal bonds; Absalom may kill Amnon in any number of ways. So the interpreter looks forward to new information and looks back to the gap as each new piece crops up, his retrospective engagement lasting till the ambiguity is definitively closed or (if permanent) left open at the end. While surprise, dependent on a reduced awareness of antecedents withheld, involves a threefold process of interpretation. The reader first moves forward unsuspectingly across the gap, which he misses altogether or settles in passing; then the shock of recognition throws him back to the gap with an alternative answer; finally, he retraces his steps from the newly filled gap to the point of recognition in order to reinterpret (check, repattern, disambiguate) all that intervenes. All our three dynamics of meaning proceed by trial and error, but only here does the error come first.

In this strategic unity that keeps surprise distinct, we have so far noted three aspects of variety. The first concerns the object in the world about which the reader is misled to be enlightened: event, personality, motive, causal linkage—again, to the exclusion of the underlying reality-model, which modernism so likes to play with but the Bible keeps stable on ideological principle. The second concerns the purity of the effect, which by nature adheres to every new disclosure but, as just exemplified, need not govern its working. The third concerns the functionality of the surprise ordering. The roles already traced—from the pleasures and exigencies of retrospective adjustment through memorable characterization to doctrinal emphasis—suffice to indicate that the operation of surprise differs from the two other narrative interests in arrangement but not in range. Still, I want to consider those variations by reference to one central function, namely, the control of judgment. How does the tortuous emergence of the object determine its evaluation?

Recall how the favorable impression made by the Shunamite's hospitality gains depth and realism from the late unfolding of her childlessness, whereby the woman's conduct gets dissociated from her state. Conversely,

Balaam's portrait as Balak's hireling (Numbers 22–24) assumes an even darker color with the abrupt report of his execution some chapters later (31:8). Abrupt, because it is hard to understand why he should be put to the sword during the campaign waged against Midian in reprisal for the sin and the plague they brought on Israel. What has Balaam to do with this affair, and has he not, however reluctantly, blessed Israel after all? But another surprise lies ahead, in the form of the retrospect that Midian has been guided "by the counsel of Balaam" (31:16); and the second surprise resolves the first, closing the breaches to make the whole sequence intelligible in terms of psychology and morality as well as plot. Balaam, we now recognize, has been an enemy all along, even more so than suggested by our previous encounter with him. It is not for nothing that God took drastic measures to prevent him from cursing Israel in Moab's employ. But his malignity having been checked in one instance, he soon found another opportunity to express it, in a different place and by different means. The otherwise redundant specification of the manner of his death even pinpoints the continuity in theme and characterization between the discontinuous episodes. Having disregarded the warning against mischief given him en route to Moab by an angel "with his sword drawn in his hand," he now appropriately dies "by the sword" in the aftermath of the Midianite plot.

As the Bible avoids formal character-sketching, such touches are very common. In a more drastic form, however, antecedents unexpectedly arise not to enhance and clinch an initial impression (portrait, response, assessment) but to qualify and complicate it, sometimes to the point of reversal. This often serves to bring home the tangle of motivation or to demolish a self-righteous posture. Our view of Gideon thus undergoes a twist for the worse with the disclosure of the personal stake he has in the capture of Zebah and Zalmunah, especially since his quest for revenge appears to have affected his judgment as leader. In revision, therefore, the newly-constructed character gains in depth at the expense of stature; his mixed motives evoke from the reader a mixed feeling, normative distance increases together with psychological complexity.

But this distributive strategy yet leads to a moderate revaluation compared with Abimelech's in Genesis 20. For the duration of no less than sixteen out of the text's eighteen verses, Abimelech enjoys the appeal of the injured party, more sinned against than sinning, and impresses us by his upright and generous behavior. Since he brought Sarah into his harem under the impression that she was Abraham's sister, we feel for him when he counters God's threat of death ("for she is a man's wife") with the dismayed protest, "Lord, wilt thou slay the innocent? Did not he himself say to me, She is my sister?" We are then relieved to find God acknowledging the king's innocence, empathetic when he indignantly upbraids Abraham for having led him into "great sin," and filled with admiration when he restores the woman to her husband laden with gifts ("sheep and oxen, male and female slaves"), not least an invitation to settle wherever they please.

But just as our sympathy reaches its height, the narrator brings it all down by a sensational disclosure: "God healed Abimelech and his wife and his female slaves, so that they could bear children. For the Lord had closed fast every womb in the house of Abimelech on account of Sarah, Abraham's wife" (20:17–18). The surprise ending drives home to the reader that Abimelech is after all just another Pharaoh, likewise prevented from violating Sarah only by "great plagues" inflicted on him by God (12:17). The difference lies not so much in the characters of the two kings as in their narrative unfolding. With Pharaoh, the divine preventive measure appears in its proper causal-chronological place, between the taking and the restoration of Sarah, while here it is quietly withheld to be sprung by way of retrospect at a point where the affair seems all over. The chronological deformation has produced and sustained an interpretive deformation, finally set right with a vengeance. And if the king remains an injured party, sexual scruple has nothing to do with it. His spirit was willing enough, only the flesh turned weak.

As we look back on the narrative from the closural point of vantage, moreover, details as well as contours assume new shape, meaning, determinacy—usually with an ironic twist. At the time, for instance, the seizure of Sarah (verse 2) and the appearance of God in a dream (verse 3) seemed as continuous in the action as in the narration. But if the intervening period demonstrated the sterility of the whole household, then Abimelech must have kept Sarah much longer, probably waiting for a respite from impotence. That "he had not approached her" (verse 4) is accordingly due not to some lucky accident but to divine providence. It was to this—we now perceive behind time—that God was obliquely referring by "I did not let thee touch her" (verse 6) and "thou shalt surely die" (verse 7), which signifies less a threat about the future than an allusion to a present state. The address to Abraham ("What hast thou done to us? . . . Thou hast brought on me and my kingdom a great sin") likewise scales down from moral to physiological reproach; and the gifts, from compensation to a husband to a bribe to an intercessor. The key once provided, in short, everything conspires to strip his credit down to technical innocence.

The order of surprise thus leads us to revaluate Abimelech's character and conduct more thoroughly than Gideon's, the retrospect on whom mixes with rather than subverts the first impression. Just as Abimelech's unmasking is still less drastic than David's, whose solicitude for Uriah turns out a base trap. These three variants mark an escalating clash between stages in interpretation, and accordingly a progressive dynamics of judgment: from qualification through complication to reversal.

But the evaluative change of direction may be for the better as well as for the worse. What is more, we have already seen the two directions co-ordinated in the Wooing tale: from negative to positive in the case of Rebekah, who first seems to fail the test in disregarding the thirsty camels and then puts the test itself to shame by surpassing its terms, and from positive to negative in regard to Laban, his mask of hospitality torn off in flashback to disclose a calculating face. Other instances of favorable recognition have been noted in passing. Recall the gappy (if not downright misleading) sequences of election throughout Genesis, whereby the un-known Abraham or, further, the unlovable Joseph establishes himself as a paragon. For some closer analysis, however, let us turn to a book whose art is generally undervalued.

Why do the two and a half tribes (Reuben, Gad, and half of Manasseh) build a "big-looking altar" (Joshua 22:10) as soon as they settle across the Jordan? The explanation that immediately comes to mind is that voiced by the embassy sent to remonstrate with the Transjordanian tribes in the name of a people armed for war: "Thus says the whole congregation of the Lord, What is this treachery which you have committed against the God of Israel . . . by building yourselves an altar this day in rebellion against the Lord?" (16). To our as well as the delegates' amazement—the two human viewpoints continuing equal in enlightenment as in ignorance—the answer made by the Transjordanians brings to light a diametrically opposed motive. Far from rising against the Lord, they have striven to perpetuate their claim to his worship:

> "The Lord is god of gods, god of gods! The Lord does know, and Israel shall know. If it was in rebellion or in treachery toward the Lord, spare us not today. . . . Nay, we did it from fear that in time to come your children might say to our children, What have you to do with the Lord God of Israel? For the Lord has made the Jordan a boundary between us and you, you Reubenites and Gadites; you have no part in the Lord. Thus might your children make our children cease to worship the Lord." (Josh 22:22–25)

So they built an altar as a defensive rather than a provocative act against the bulk of Israel, one meant "not for burnt offering nor for sacrifice" but to bear eternal "witness" that they equally belong to God's congregation. In fact, it is not even an altar at all but a model ("copy") of the only real one standing before God's tabernacle.

Some acquaintance with the play of first and last impressions, one of the glories of the Bible's art of sequence, might have prevented critics from jumping to the conclusion that the Transjordanians knuckled under in the face of superior numbers. The dramatic reversal of the charge not only rings true. It also coheres with otherwise disturbing precedents, like the spirit shown by those tribes throughout the Conquest, and even illuminates otherwise submerged or ambiguous features in the manner integral to the process of recognition. Why, if not to pave the way for a shift from a cultic to a memorial reading of the altar, did the narrator describe it at the outset as "by the Jordan" and "big-*looking*"? As usual, all these confirmations and adjustments and alternative patternings are deliberately kept in abeyance till the moment judged proper to bring them to retrospective life. Like the whole of Israel, however, the reader is "well pleased" to find himself in the wrong. Here, indeed, lies the very point of this device of misdirection. It was worth falling into gross error to elicit and appreciate such a touching declaration of faith.

In this regard, finally, the tale of Jonah has a fourfold claim to notice. First, though not much longer than some of the other sequences through which we have been twisting, it is the only biblical instance where a surprise gap controls the reader's progress over a whole book. From the ideological standpoint, second, the narrative plays a dangerous game in misleading the reader almost to the end about the relations between God and prophet, especially as concerns their respective features or characters. Third, both the false impression produced at the start and its ultimate reversal work in two directions at once. And fourth, the whole tortuous process of interpretation bears on the nature not of the agents only but also of the framework (doctrinal, thematic, generic) in which they operate.

Why does Jonah flee when God orders him to "go to Nineveh, that great city, and cry against it, for their wickedness has come up before me" (1:2)? The narrator does not say, but apparently only because the reason is self-evident: Jonah is too tender-hearted to carry a message of doom to a great city. He obviously protests against a wrathful God not with words, like Abraham or Moses or Samuel, but with his feet.

This contrastive impression gradually solidifies into certainty. The prophet's humane image deepens, touch by attractive touch, as his character unfolds in action. He warns the sailors beforehand that "he was fleeing from the presence of the Lord," resigns himself to misfortune (his inertia amid the tempest suggesting an act of defiance and certainly an awareness of what he had let himself in for), urges the sailors to save their lives by throwing him overboard, and holds out for three days and nights in the belly of the fish before surrendering. At the same time, God's image grows more and more forbidding as he pursues Jonah with relentless violence from land to ship to sea to fish, till he cows the fugitive prophet into obedience. In the process, he thinks nothing of endangering the lives of wholly innocent bystanders, whose conduct, too, favorably compares with his. Why do the sailors bombard Jonah with questions ("What is thy occupation? And whence dost thou come? What is thy country? And of what people art thou?"), when he has already informed them that he is on the run from the Lord? Surely, because they find it incredible, heathens as they are, that God should go to such lengths to persecute a conscientious objector; and so they proceed to dig deeper. Whatever their suspicions, they heroically stand by their passenger as "the sea grew more and more tempestuous," until the mounting pressure breaks their spirit, as it soon will Jonah's, and they consign him to his fate under protest ("Lay not on us innocent blood"). This fixes the image of the God of Wrath. It is fear alone that he inspires in the dramatis personae (Jonah identifies himself as one who "fears the Lord" and the sailors thrice fall into "fear"); and it is by brute force, with some moral blackmail thrown in, that he imposes his will.

By the time the original embassy scene repeats itself ("The word of the Lord came to Jonah the second time, saying, Go to Nineveh, that great city . . ."), therefore, what began as a conjecture has hardened into certainty. Confident of his grasp of character and motive, the reader infers the future from the past and sees destruction ahead. What mercy can Nineveh, a city of sinners and Gentiles at that, expect from a God who stopped at nothing to have her doom announced? Hence the shock experienced once the announcement induces repentance (fasting, prayer, sack cloth, and all) throughout Nineveh:

> God repented of the evil which he had said he would do to them; and he did not do it. This displeased Jonah exceedingly, and he was angry. And he prayed to the Lord and said, I pray thee, Lord, is not this what I said when I was yet in my country? That is why I hastened to flee to Tarshish. For I knew that thou art a gracious and merciful god, slow to anger and of great kindness and repentest thee of evil. Therefore now, Lord, take my life from me, pray, for it is better for me to die than to live. (3:10–4:1–3)

This series of informational thunderbolts shatters the entire model of the narrative world and world view, so that the reader cannot find it easy to get his bearings at once. Hardly has he recovered from the surprise of God's repentance, contrary to all expectations about the future, when he discovers his reading of the past turned upside down. Not that the plot and the participants are suddenly transformed, but that they are suddenly recognized for what they have always been; and if they look transformed, that is only because the narrator has passed in misleading silence over what the prophet actually said "when [he] was yet in [his] own country" in response to God's original command. What appeared at the time as a one-sided speech event, all too common in divine transactions, now emerges as a genuine dialogue, to which Jonah harks back in his outraged "I told you so" or "I knew I couldn't count on you to keep your word." With this master gap disclosed in closure, God and Jonah prove opposites indeed, but with the roles and portraits and normative loads reversed. Of the two, Jonah has been the ruthless one all along and God the merciful; Jonah so proud that he would rather flee or die than lose face by a divine pardon of the doomed, and God so forbearing that he thinks more of the sinner's repentance than of his own prestige. In fact, he has pursued (and will continue to pursue) his prophet so relentlessly not in order to break but to temper his spirit: to teach him a much-needed lesson in love as opposed to self-love. But this sea change, from which God comes out even better (as well as more realistic) than from the straightforward portraiture of a hymn, also involves a broader dynamics of theme and genre. Beginning as a punitive affair between God and Nineveh, temporarily interrupted by the go-between's recalcitrance, Jonah evolves before our eyes into a story of a prophet's education.

·9·

PROLEPTIC PORTRAITS

> When I first met Miss Coplestone, in this room,
> . . . . it was obvious
> That here was a woman under sentence of death.
> That was her destiny. The only question
> Then was, what sort of death?
> T. S. Eliot, The Cocktail Party

The whole of anything, said Henry James, is never told. But the converse surely holds true as well. The whole of anything is never suppressed. Even discourse as reticent as the Bible's neither attempts nor craves the impossible. "No straw is given to thy servants, yet they say to us, Make bricks!" (Exod 5:16): the Israelite protest to Pharaoh is the one complaint that the reader cannot fairly make about his taskmaster. While doubtless on the skimpy side, moreover, the building material provided is of the finest quality. It comes from or at least through the mediation of the biblical narrator himself, rather than an unwittingly or cold-bloodedly or whimsically unreliable persona in the modern style. Though anything but omnicommunicative, he is not only omnicompetent by privilege but also responsible and systematic in performance. The art therefore turns on authoritative relations between the told and the withheld or, from the interpreter's viewpoint, the given and the hypothetical: between the *truth* and the *whole* truth.

The foregoing chapters have brought out the essentials and variations of this all-embracing principle. But exactly because its working has so far been shown to cut across all forms and all matter enformed—dialogue, commentary, plot, character, theme, language—I would now like to trace it in a more delimited sphere. The next two chapters, therefore, will round out the picture by demonstrating how a certain body of "truth" develops in the reading into "the whole truth" regarding that particular area or arena of the biblical world. That the inquiry may not sink into a mere exercise, the object must be worthwhile as well as determinate and challenging. So let the truth be the explicit statements made about character, the whole truth the secrets and consequences of character, and the bridge, accordingly, the models of character and characterization. In view of the text's general reticence, this may appear a tall order. The more so since the Bible's staple of overt character-portrayal consists in the least promising material: epithets, and in none too liberal supply at that. The promise rather lies in the lessons acquired so far, from the systematicity and resourcefulness exhibited by biblical poetics in general to the memory of a narrative like Joseph and His Brothers, a triumph of subtle characterization achieved even without recourse to epithets.

Character and Characterization: From Divine to Human

The most startling thing about the Bible's opening words, "When God began to create heaven and earth," is that God comes on stage with a complete absence of preliminaries. Who is God? What is God? Where does he hail from? How does he differ from other deities? Such questions are anything but a matter of idle (or scholarly) curiosity. They gain point in the Oriental context, with its medley of divine bodies and biographies, and must be resolved to make sense of the world and the world view even on the simplest level. Yet the narrator no more provides late than anticipatory answers by way of direct characterization. The complex of features making up God's portrait emerges only by degrees and only through the action itself, starting with the creation of light by terse fiat.

In the absence of overt exposition, the reader must piece it together for himself by extrapolating features from dramatic givens. We infer divine motive (as cause) from act or response (as effect); check that inferred motive against later acts supposed to issue from it; generalize recurrent instances or lines of action into attributes and the various attributes into a theocentric world picture, subject at any moment to further retrospective adjustment as well as deepening or specification. For though God himself does not change—even this, by the way, is an inference—our acquaintance with him frequently and at times surprisingly does. With the advent of humanity, and later of Israel, we discover that the hitherto homogeneous portrait of God—omnipotent, omniscient, well-disposed, equable—must be stretched to accommodate no end of problematic stuff: wrath, guile, self-limitation, communicative exigencies, retribution, change of mind. Crisis and choice bring out complexity; complexity multiplies unpredictability, which in turn darkens the next crisis; and so on. It is only by such a process of reconstruction, working back from the dynamics of events to the static but tense antecedents that govern and produce them, that the reader gradually closes the gaps to form something like the character sketch that classical narrative (or the novel) so often provides right at the outset.

Though God is the Bible's hero, his portrayal may yet appear a special case. After all, most dimensions associated with character—physical appearance, social status, personal history, local habitation—do not apply to him at all. They are meant to be conspicuous by their absence, which impresses on the reader from the very beginning the message that the whole Bible will dramatize with variations: the qualitative distance that separates God from humans *and* pagan gods, both existing in matter and time and space and society. So nothing "material" is told, by way of preliminaries *or* retrospect, because for once there is nothing to tell; and the mind must attune itself to radically new coordinates of divinity.

Divine attributes other than material do indeed apply. But if they are communicated not in an orderly form at the start but piecemeal and in their dramatic manifestations, this may still be due to the unusual object of portrayal. For one thing, it would be awkward if not offensive to open by introducing to the audience the God of their fathers, however dim or even misguided their actual conception of him. Only a Pharaoh, as it were, requires information on "Who is the Lord, that I should listen to his voice?" (Exod 5:2). The rhetoric of solidarity indicates a more oblique line of unfolding, whereby the narrator first pretends to assume his reader's knowledgeability and then slips in the necessary premises, under dramatic guise and often with corrective or polemical intent, as the need for them arises. For another thing, it would be equally bad policy to reduce God to a series of epithets, as if he were one's neighbor rather than a unique and enigmatic power, knowable only through his incursions into history. Suggestion again proves more effective than statement and open-ended showing than finite listing, because this reveals enough to make the divine order intelligible and impressive while concealing enough to leave it mysterious, transcendent, irreducible to terms other than itself. Besides, it is doubtful whether the biblical artist could at all replace his favorite indirections by a strategy of orderly analysis. He has as little competence as taste for abstract theologizing: like Henry James's little Maisie, he has more "conceptions" than "names." So whatever the combination of reasons for God's abrupt entry—rhetorical, ideological, expressive—none would seem to hold for the rest of the dramatis personae.

Nevertheless, the hero's case turns out not so much an exception as a harbinger of the rule. The special reasons indeed remain valid and distinctive but not exclusive. They are subsumed by the general strategy of disclosure whereby the given does not suffice and the sufficient is not given in time or at all. In its application to character portrayal, this strategy manifests itself in a distributed, often oblique and tortuous unfolding of features. So reading a character becomes a process of discovery, attended by all the biblical hallmarks: progressive reconstruction, tentative closure of discontinuities, frequent and sometimes painful reshaping in face of the unexpected, and intractable pockets of darkness to the very end.

Governing the whole cast, this principle draws a secondary but important line between the divine and the human in terms of both character and characterization. In terms of character proper, even the salient differences in make-up have less obvious poetic implications. One concerns the features of material existence: their withholding may open a gap about a human (as with David's looks while he is being summoned for inspection by the anointer) but only establishes a marked absence in God. Another bears on motivation. The mainspring of God's actions throughout history is the spread of "knowledge" (in the sense defined in chapter 3). Only when his creatures threaten or frustrate that desire do other motives, like retribution, come into play; and along fairly determinate lines. For all its surprises, even the Jonah narrative follows this rule. None of the motives it implies for God's behavior, from wrath up, is new; neither is their dominant new—inculcating knowledge, if necessary by violence. The unpredictability rather lies in the change of God's target and priorities: Jonah, it turns out, needs a lesson more than Nineveh. But there is no similar key to human motivation, which, contrary to expectations about ancient literature, shows an infinite variety in direction and priorities and psychological mechanism. Compare even such analogues as Rebekah and Laban, Barak and Deborah, David and Uriah; or shifting selves like Samuel in the two anointments, Joseph jockeying his brothers into a succession of roles, Gideon with his objective reversed in midcourse. But it is character proper, as well as motivation, that is subject to change. God's mode of action shifts from one moment to another, yet his nature remains static; while human personality, as the Joseph cycle so impressively demonstrates, may itself develop or crystallize under pressure. Due to his transcendent vision and control, finally, God's performance reads against his privileges where the behavior of a limited human might remain ambiguous between choice and constraint. God must be pretending ignorance to Cain, but is the accused harlot to Solomon or Uriah to David?

Material features, psychological motive, the equilibrium of the self, epistemological and existential power: all along this line, God's character tends to constancy and man's to variability. It follows that a given amount of information will reveal far more about the workings of divinity than of humanity. As far as the interests of the narrative go—to the chagrin of theologians—the gaps about God concentrate in what exactly he is up to at this or that moment in time; those about man, in what he is in the first place or has become in the process. Neither the magnitude nor the ineffability of the heavenly superagent must obscure this crucial fact.

Created in God's image with a vengeance, biblical man is not much less unique than God and more mysterious.

As we go on from essence to rendering in portraiture, this distinction gains further weight. For the modes of character-drawing validate and radicalize the implications of character at the points of divergence. God's continuing presence throughout evidently makes for transparence relative to the human cast, each of whom comes (to occasion a new quest for character) and then goes (with his enigma less than solved but his successor's ready to take its place). The narrative, moreover, singles out certain divine features for extensive treatment in period after period—hence the rhetorics of omniscience and omnipotence—while in the human sphere its individuals will retain and often flaunt their individuality. This difference manifests itself in the handling as well as the selection of the features portrayed. Though the Bible does wonders with God's figure, its presentation still remains far more uniform than man's due to normative constraints on technique. Consider how seldom the text employs the rise and fall of first impressions to illuminate God. One does not play tricks with God's image: the writer of Jonah shows exceptional courage as well as craftsmanship in twisting order and response. But even he draws the line at temporary misdirection, with a view to ultimate enlightenment reinforced by the dynamics of surprise. Permanent ambiguation of character, comparable to the doubling of Uriah, is out of the question in the divine sphere. Paradoxically, divine otherness itself breeds familiarity ("knowledge") by ideological fiat. Taken together, then, all these practices of characterization dovetail with the essentials of character: God's ways may remain mysterious but man is himself a mystery.

Why the Truth about Character Does Not Suffice

Only at one point does this relative difference in opacity seem to work the other way. Disallowed in God's case, characterization by epithet is applicable and indeed applied to humans. As the most explicit and authoritative mode of portrayal, this might counterbalance all the restrictions put together. But nothing so far-reaching happens, in fact, because the human epithets and the portrait they compose are themselves restricted in the service of ambiguity.

Since Chapter 5 has already opposed the Bible's poetics of ambiguity to Anthony Trollope's poetics of lucidity, it may be well to pursue the opposition in the techniques of character-drawing. Trollope's novelistic portraits follow from his doctrine of "straightforward storytelling," where "the author and the reader should move along together in full confidence with each other" (*Barchester Towers,* chap. 15). The exposition accordingly introduces the dramatis personae as psychological, moral, social, physical existents, concentrating more on features than on facts and fortunes in order to realize character for us in the strongest terms. It is precisely to forestall surprises in the coming drama that the opening description—complete with trait lists, analysis of intricacies, examples, judgment—gives such a firm sense of personality. "Each full-length portrait," as I summarized it elsewhere, "is designed to impart to the reader all the data necessary for a thorough comprehension of a certain character: it forms an authorially stated general-ization of which the action or 'plot' itself is only a particular dramatized manifestation. And it is his possession of the sum-total of portraits that elevates the reader to his quasi-divine observation post, from which he can catch more than a glimpse of the future as well as see the present in the round."[1] Trollope thus starts by communicating what is, in context, the whole truth about the secret selves of his agents.

With biblical man, in contrast, there is usually a distance—and often a clash—between the impression produced on his first appearance and the one left after his last. What is more, the very presence or absence of an early character-sketch does not make a crucial difference to the reading of character, because its presence does not bridge and its absence need not widen this distance.

At its most rounded, such a portrait consists of five interlocking sets of features. The glowing testimonial given to David by Saul's servant shows all these ingredients that make up the Bible's conception of character. "I have seen a son of Jesse the Bethlehemite, skillful in playing, able in deed, a man of war, wise in counsel, a man of good presence, and the Lord is with him" (1 Sam 16:18):

1. Physical ("a man of good presence");
2. social ("a son of Jesse the Bethlehemite");
3. singular or concretizing ("skillful in playing" or, usually, just a name);
4. moral and ideological ("the Lord is with him");
5. psychological in a wide sense ("able in deed, a man of war, wise in counsel").

Portraits that cover all or most of these dimensions are far more prevalent in biblical history than is usually thought, extending even to quite a few minor agents. The portraits also compose those elements into a whole far more integrated and artistic than my rough decomposition and labeling might suggest. But they are the product of the reader's cumulative and gap-filling activity along the sequence where the portraitee figures rather than of the narrator's solicitude from the outset. A formal and orderly character-sketch such as David's, conveyed as a string of summary epithets (or some equivalent) before the hero goes into action, departs from the biblical rule of characterization; or perhaps, since even here the sketch falls short of completeness and the narrator delegates the sketching to another agent, only proves it. Even when one or more epithets are given, they turn out less than helpful and sometimes downright misleading in relation to subsequent disclosures. Not that such epithets are unreliable—at least when they come from the narrator—but that even at their most reliable they do not go far and deep enough. They yield a partial picture of the figure and we must round it out by our own efforts, usually at the most essential (intriguing, problematic) spots.

How come, then, that truth authoritatively imparted by way of block characterization should count for so little? The answer lies, first of all, in the position of the given versus the gapped features within the contextual scale of interest or significance. Considering the human view of character, it is predictable enough that the five sets of characteristics that I have distinguished should widely recur throughout literature. But they as widely vary in, among other things, their relative importance within the overall model of character.

In the biblical framework, with its theocentric ideology and ethical concerns and endless situations of choice, the first two sets are definitely subordinate to the last two. (I shall soon return to the intermediate category, which is usually present in the minimal form of a *name*.) Physical appearance or prowess and social status do not begin to assume the importance they enjoy in epic and saga, romance and novel of manners. Both are not only bestowed by God but also subject to neutralization or reversal at will. "The bows of the mighty are broken, and the feeble gird on strength. . . . The Lord makes poor and makes rich; he brings low, he also exalts" (1 Sam 2:4–7). What Hannah sings, others enact. Abraham suddenly turns warrior in his pursuit of Lot's captors; Goliath falls by David's hand; the younger son or the lowborn Jephthah rises above his social superiors; the reliable servant must have welcomed both Rebekah's beauty and lineage as auspicious extras, but it was a character test that settled the issue.

These features and their like, accordingly, serve more to identify and variegate characters than to define character. And yet it is precisely such externals that the Bible tends to specify by way of introduction, while leaving the internals opaque and penetrable, if at all, by trial and error. On the whole, the givenness of character stands in inverse proportion to the ultimate characterological relevance or centrality of the given character traits.

This explains why moral and psychological portraiture by epithet is so rare or, in occurrence, spare. It most often schematizes collective or marginal agents:

The men of the city, base fellows, beset the house round about and beat at the door. (Judg 19:22)

The sons of Eli were base fellows, they knew not the Lord. (1 Sam 2:12)

The name of the man was Nabal, and the name of his wife Abigail. The woman was of good understanding and good-looking; the man was churlish and ill-behaved. (1 Sam 25:3)

The whole personality gets crammed into one or two adjectives, with clear evaluative import but little else: The Gang of Rapists, the Sinful Priests, the Churl married to a Paragon. The processes of character-flattening are carried to the limit in order to turn the various citizens of Gibeah into a homogeneous mob, Eli's sons into idential twins in iniquity, Nabal into a living incarnation (cf. 25:18) of his name. We know that people "are not really like this," that they have more sides to them; but so does the Bible, which does not resort to such formulas and abstractions except when shifting its generic gears to pure ideological narrative, with ideological character-drawing to match. The stylization operates not just to invite unequivocal responses to its objects but also to discourage for once any further inquiry into makeup and motivation. In context, it implies, the omitted features should be taken as blanks rather than gaps: details and complications would only sidetrack the issue, since nothing can justify the agent's conduct. Were it not for this signaling or directive function, the preliminary adjectives could be eliminated without loss, since the ensuing plot transparently dramatizes them. Thus, where we need the exposition of internals to elucidate character and event, it is not provided; and where provided, we do not really need it.

The Art of the Proleptic Epithet

It emerges that while indirect characterization may follow any number of lines—as illustrated by the foregoing analyses, notably of the Joseph story, and summarized in chapter 12 below—direct characterization falls into three varieties. One affords an early and complete but stylized insight into a simple or simplified character. Another consists in a partial revelation of a complex and otherwise opaque character (as when the narrator extols Solomon's wisdom but keeps his disastrous malleability hidden). The third is the depiction of externals, for which the transparent and the intricate are equally eligible. Of these, the truth overtly communicated about character leads straight to the whole truth only in the pattern where the two are virtually (and uninterestingly) identical.

Hence two questions. The first, to which the next chapter will address itself, is how the process of discovery works in the more interesting cases. The second is whether the given "truths" of the different varieties have anything in common. They do in fact share an important principle, wherein the Bible's portraiture varies from that favored by some arts of narrative—above all, the so-called realistic tradition.

Notorious for its general courting of the redundant detail, the nineteenth-century novel intersperses its block characterization with assorted features that perform no other role than realistic fullness. These extras particularize the character, plant him upright on his feet, impressing him on the mind as an existent in his own right and part of a world of irreducible specificity. This technique endlessly recurs in the pages of the masters of character—Balzac, Dickens, Trollope, Dostoevsky, Henry James—whether in order to enhance or to salvage verisimilitude. But it occurs much earlier too, even in narratives packed with action. When introducing Gunnar, for example, it is only natural that *Njal's Saga* should describe his prowess at length: "a tall, powerful man, outstandingly skilled with arms. He could strike or throw with either hand. . . . He was excellent at archery. . . . He could swim like a seal. . . ."[2] He is the greatest of its heroes and, as the sequel discloses, each expositional trait prepares for his exploits. But why should the saga then go on to depict him as "a handsome man, with fair skin and a straight nose slightly tilted at the tip. He had blue eyes, red cheeks" etc.? Irrelevant in terms of the action, these characteristics yet produce solidity of specification. And where epithets have not grown formulaic to the point of referential emptiness, even ancient literature shows equivalents of this purely descriptive function.

The great exception is the Bible, which does not *reserve* so much as a single characterizing epithet for solidity of specification. Not that this type of realistic effect is shunned or disdained—quite the contrary—but that its pure manifestations arise from other means, less obtrusive and therefore more congenial. Of these realistic indirections, the one more predictable by now lies in dramatizing a character beyond the point required for making him intelligible as an actional and moral agent. Every story we have considered will supply examples, from Samuel's small vanities to Joab's wry humor. Considering the range of the Bible's portrait gallery, it is amazing how distinct and memorable its figures remain, without benefit of formal portrayal. And this is largely due to the surplus inner life expressed in act and speech.

A related and even more widespread indirection is the use of names. The Bible's system of personal reference differs from most of its ancient and modern equivalents, certainly from those of comparable scope, in consisting almost entirely of unique names. That is why it boasts the largest onomasticon in literary history. While the Icelandic saga (for example) has only a limited repertoire to draw on and the realistic novel must strike some balance between the singular and the typical appellation, the Bible assigns to each character a name of his own. The choice it recognizes lies not between singularity and typicality but between singularity and anonymity.

Anonymity is the lot (and mark) of supernumeraries, type characters, institutional figures, embodied plot devices. Its ranks comprise wise women, messengers and other personified voices—including single-action prophets and even Abraham's envoy to Mesopotamia—collective figures like gangs or courtiers. To remain nameless is to remain faceless, with hardly a life of one's own. Accordingly, a character's emergence from anonymity may correlate with a rise in importance. It is no accident that the text consistently withholds David's name—referring to him instead as "one of Jesse's sons" or "the youngest" or "he" or even "him whom I will tell thee"—till the very moment of anointment and elevation; nor that Saul, desperately attempting to turn back the wheel, persists in calling him "Jesse's son." By analogy to the biblical world, where the absence or the blotting out of a name implies nonexistence, the abstention from naming in biblical discourse thus implies the individual abeyance of the nameless within the otherwise particularized action.

If worthy of naming at all, on the other hand, biblical man receives a proper name in the fullest sense of the word. Apart from its uniqueness—by itself possibly a mnemonic aid—it also exhibits some opacity, arbitrariness, irreducibility to anything beyond itself, notably including the kernel of character. A name confers being, even status, without defining personality. It is in this intractability that biblical naming, rather than going the way of allegory, offers a parallel to the epithetic redundancies of realism. Many biblical names, like "Ehud ben Gera" or "David," have defied all the efforts to make etymological sense of them. Many others are indeed explicable after a fashion—Joshua, Samson, Abigail, Rehoboam—but significantly left unexplained by the narrative itself, as if to avoid imposing on them any relation to their bearer except the purely referential. Some do receive an explanation, most often in Genesis, but as a rule well short of coherence or transparency. These overt etymologies are not fully coherent because they seldom click together with the name in question to the degree of exhausting its diverse (phonic, morphological, semantic) features. Abraham, Jacob, Levi, Moses: each of these preserves some linguistic roughness, equivocation, idiosyncrasy. Nor do such explanations lead even to relative transparency, since what they extract from the name is the bearer's role or status or destiny or prenatal antecedents rather than his secret self. So far as they reveal character, the revelation concerns the giver rather than the bearer, who has no voice in the matter at birth and no recourse to deed-poll thereafter. The most memorable case in point is the reflection of Leah's ever-frustrated yearning for her husband in and through the naming of her sons (Gen 29:31–30:19).

Hence even surface etymologies do not divest biblical characters of their individuality and existential otherness, let alone their mystery. A person's name may be the essence of his being, but that essence is more ensured, if not veiled, than expressed by the name. So even protagonists may be introduced by name alone, sometimes followed by the briefest reference to local habitation, without detriment to their solidity and centrality. The male deliverer in Judges 4 makes his appearance as "Barak son of Abinoam from Kedesh in Naphtali"; and the prophet who dominates the middle of Kings bursts into the tale as "Elijah the Tishbite" (1 Kgs 17:1). If for a biblical agent to come on stage nameless is to be declared faceless, then to bear a name is to assume an identity: to become a singular existent, with an assured place in history and a future in the story.

It is the naming and dramatization of biblical chatacters, then, that do duty for the redundant epithets that elsewhere specify character in the interests of realism. All formal epithets, in contrast, enter into tight relations with the patterns that surround them, fulfilling at least one role beyond direct characterization. That invariable function consists in laying the ground for plot developments, so as to enhance their predictability or at least their intelligibility after the event. Ostensibly descriptive of the statics of character, all these epithets are implicitly proleptic within the dynamics of action. Not even the most idiosyncratic trait fails to cohere, sooner or later, with the processes of history.

The story of Ehud offers a masterly case in point. According to the book's fourfold paradigm, he duly appears after the Israelites have sinned, then suffered under the yoke of Moab, then finally cried out to God:

> (15) The Lord raised up for them a deliverer, Ehud the son of Gera, a Benjaminite, a left-handed man. And the Israelites sent tribute by his hand to Eglon, king of Moab. (16) And Ehud made for himself a sword with two edges, a cubit in length; and he girded it under his clothes on his right thigh. (17) And he presented the tribute to Eglon king of Moab; and Eglon was a very fat man (Judg 3:15–17)

This forms a memorable exposition to the first tale of deliverance in Judges. Each of the three participants introduced, two human and one inanimate, is deviant in some respect. Ehud is left-handed, the sword is short and double-edged, Eglon is very fat. Besides jarring against the appropriate sociocultural norms, these peculiarities rarely appear in the world of biblical narrative. And the context maximizes their perceptibility through happily incongruous juxtaposition and cross-reference, phrasing and wordplay.

The undersized sword thus contrasts with the oversized king, while its "two mouths" (the Hebrew for "two edges") slyly brings to mind the source of his corpulence: to get so fat would require more than a single mouth. Nor is the hero himself excluded from the punning composition. Against the background of Ehud's role, the Hebrew idiom for his distinctive mark— literally, "a man handicapped in his right hand"—springs to life and galvanizes the whole opening into a crisscross of tensions. Unprecedented in the Bible, the feature itself would stand out even if denoted by a neutral term like our "left-handed." But the normative circumlocution radicalizes our awareness of Ehud's physical peculiarity and also, given the cultural associations of right vs. left, our wonder at God's choice of such an ill-omened deliverer. The sinister redeemer would appear a contradiction in terms. As well as going counter to the social model of his role—or the reader's sense of fitness—the phrase literally clashes with the hero's adjoining epithet and activity. In the first place, Ehud's tribal origin is juxtaposed and rhymed but out of keeping with his physical hallmark: "a man of the right"—a Benjaminite (see Gen 35:18)—with a weak right hand makes a rather strange portrait. By another flick at our sense of inverted directions, he wears his sword "on his right thigh," which is of course the wrong side for normal drawing. And to cap it all, it is "by his hand" that the Israelites send their tribute to Eglon—a left-handed tribute indeed.

Good fun apart, this interplay of epithets stamps the expositional trio on our memory as concrete, if not unique, entities: the Left-handed, the Short, and the Fat. But the reader versed in the Bible's norms of formal characterization cannot rest content with intelligibility in terms like vividness or realistic effect. By internal convention, these epithets are charged with kinetic power straining for release. They are bound to carry some actional as well as descriptive implications: their coincidence and interlinkage even suggest that they somehow belong together in this capacity too. And again, just as the art of relations enhances the effect of the epithets as particularizing features by turning (statistical) rarity into (contextual) incongruity, so does it shape our expectations of their plot relevance and coherence.

Along this dimension, the ordering of the sequence proves the most helpful guide. The anticipatory notice that Ehud is a God-sent "deliverer" from the yoke of Moab encourages the reader to integrate each of his traits and actions and concomitants into a prologue to an approaching feat of deliverance: to linger and puzzle over the assorted curiosities with a view to turning them to properly narrative account. And the order in which the three objects are depicted gives linear shape to this integration by foreshadowing a sequence of events: Ehud as Agent, the sword as Instrument,

Eglon as Oppressor-cum-Target. It is not only that each static portrait assumes dynamic force, that retrospect transposes into prospect, that cause heralds effect. By a further reversal of temporal directions, the *order* of antecedents projects an *order* of consequents leading to a political murder.

As causes loaded with future effects, moreover, the particular features thus ordered serve to validate and fill out by degrees this line of expectation. We already noted that the switch of temporal directions, governing the Bible's portraiture and exposition as a whole, finds a spatial equivalent in the switch from right to left peculiar to Ehud's figure. But the scheme behind the narrative presupposes yet another switch, this time of an ideological nature: from human to divine logic. And this third term now intervenes to bring the two counterparts into active relation. In a context of predetermined deliverance, left-handedness sheds the connotations of ill-fortune. Its semantics undergoes such a metamorphosis that, far from negating the other proleptic clues, it confers on them the supreme imprimatur. For by a reversal of normal probabilities built into God's operations on history, the weakness ("handicapped") promises to become a source of strength and the omen marking the hero bodes ill for the antagonist.

By the same token, the right-thigh girding and the left-handed tribute only raise our hopes. So, from feature to concrete feature, does the appearance of the sword. Ehud fashions the sword at a critical point: after the election by God but before the journey to Moab. This at once associates it, as Instrument, with the imminent act of redemption. Its "two mouths," already analogized to Eglon through one pun, come to yawn at him through another that pursues the same line of dietary figuration. In biblical idiom, swords not only have "mouths" but also "eat" (e.g., 2 Sam 11:25) their prey: the realized metaphor thus predicts that the two-mouthed sword will make short work of the large feeder. (Since *Eglon* also puns with *egel,* calf,[3] the satiric etymology projects the encounter to come in an even lower key: a fatted calf eaten by a blade specially designed for it, or in terms of orders of being, a man eliminating a pretentious animal by recourse to a clever weapon.) The "cubit in length" then goes on to confirm the implied prediction by harping afresh—this time, as later in the David and Goliath story, in the language of physical size—on the theme of divine operation-by-reversal. And the strapping of the sword under the clothes on the right thigh—whose very wrongness by normal standards now makes it perfect, indeed "right," from the tactical as well as the symbolic viewpoint—gathers up the clues into a humanly workable plan. By projection into the future, a left-handed hero about to confront the oppressor of his people with a miniature sword hidden where nobody would suspect it equals a story of assassination.

Everything so falls into place, therefore, that Eglon is already as good as dead even before he grants the ambassador a private audience. But has the whole story died with him, told and killed by way of anticipation? This has certainly not been the effect of the other techniques that compose the poetics of foreshadowing: neither the dreams in the Joseph saga, nor the analogy that heralds and blesses the Wooing of Rebekah, nor even the paradigm *and* precedent *and* oracle in the Sisera tale. Amidst the greatest diversity, these testify to the skill with which the Bible counteracts the dangers of redundancy and boredom, by turning even the reader's fore-knowledge to inferential account. The device of proleptic portraiture, which completes the repertoire, is no exception to this subrule of maneuvering between the truth and the whole truth. However close the reading and the synthesis, there remain impenetrable enigmas, opacities, ambiguities.

This holds true for both expositional disclosures and suppressions. Of the various epithetic features, for example, Eglon's corpulence remains least projectible into action. Will the fat make it difficult for him to evade the blow or easy for the weapon to plunge in? We cannot yet tell, and must leave the trait unwedded and unfulfilled—a cause still hesitating among possible effects. Elsewhere, the cause or antecedent is itself gapped, so that the future consequence becomes doubly obscure. Owing to the opacity of Ehud's mind and character, thrown into relief by the manifest externals of activity and appearance, much of his immediate scheme and all the ensuing developments are shrouded in darkness. How will Ehud get past the bodyguard? And if he does, provided his is not a suicide mission, how will he come out alive? And supposing he manages that too, how will he exploit the confusion of the leaderless enemy to set Israel free?

The future stretches in our mind as a chain of contingencies. And this yields the double gain so precious to biblical art: ideology built into the very structure of narrative, its message arising from independently necessary and desirable operations of reading. On the one hand, the contingency of each issue along the way to liberty renders overall success so doubtful by ordinary probabilities as to draw attention to the only agency that transcends and controls them. Though God does not at all appear on stage, his leading role shines through the drama of indeterminacy. At the same time, since God has raised up Ehud as deliverer and the choice (unlike Barak's) seems justified, the tale of deliverance still promises to enact complication and resolution as well as exposition in human terms. So the Bible's two logics of history join forces to cast our interest forward to the action proper, its course packed with activities and satisfactions.

(18) When he had finished presenting the tribute, he sent away the people that carried the tribute. (19) And having returned from the sculptured stones (?) near Gilgal, he said, I have a secret word for thee, king. And

he said, Silence, and all his attendants went out from his presence. (20) Then Ehud came to him, as he was sitting in his cool roof-chamber, alone, and Ehud said, I have a word of God for thee; and he rose from his seat. (21) And Ehud reached with his left hand and took the sword from his right thigh and thrust it into his belly. (22) The hilt also went in after the blade and the fat closed over the blade, for he did not draw the sword out of his belly; and the filth came out. (23) Then Ehud came out into the vestibule, and closed the doors of the roof-chamber upon him and locked them. (24) He had just gone out when Eglon's servants came and saw, behold, the doors of the roof-chamber locked! And they said, He is only relieving himself in the cool chamber. (25) They waited a long while, and behold, he did not open the doors of the roof-chamber! They took the key and opened them, and behold, their master fallen on the floor, dead! (26) Ehud had escaped while they were tarrying; he had passed beyond the sculptured stones and escaped to Seirah. (27) On arriving, he blew the horn in the hill country of Ephraim; and the Israelites went down with him from the hill country, and he went before them. (28) And he said to them, Hasten after me, for the Lord has given your enemies, the Moabites, into your hand. So they went down after him and seized the fords of the Jordan against the Moabites and let no man cross. (29) And they smote the Moabites at that time, about ten thousand men, all stout and all warlike; not a man escaped. (30) So Moab was subdued that day under the hand of Israel, and the land had rest for eighty years.

The whole course of deliverance runs so smooth, after all, as to convey with increasing force the idea of divine stage management that Ehud finally voices in his exhortation: "The Lord has given your enemies, the Moabites, into your hand." In the Bible's typical manner, however, doctrinal uni-linearity goes with tortuosity of sequence and inference. Some developments are so predictable as to generate a *déjà vu* effect. With regard to arrange-ment, the key items in "Ehud said, I have a word of *God* for thee, and he *rose* [*va'yakom*] from his seat; and *Ehud* reached with his *left hand* and took the *sword* from *his right thigh* and thrust it into his *belly*" follow the same order as their emergence in the expositional scenario "*God raised up* [*va'yakem*] for them a deliverer, *Ehud* . . . a *left-handed* man. . . . He made for himself a *sword* . . . girded it on *his right thigh* . . . Eglon was a *very fat* man." With regard to selection, note the recurrence of the loaded epithets and the whole slow motion unrolling of what must have been a blow struck with lightning speed. Falling below the threshold of plot relevance, the excess details cohere in terms of inferential drama: the anticipations pre-figured in our mind now figure forth into the world and history.

Other occurrences reverse this dynamics in that their present enactment allays rather than gives body to past expectancy, usually in unforeseeable ways. Such is the case with the series of answers provided for the "if" and especially the "how" questions, concerning the mechanics of assassination, then extrication, then liberation. Far from anticipated by the exposition, these mini-dramas retrospectively fill out and illuminate the exposition, revealing one by one the secret designs that it has so thoroughly concealed that their fruition now piles surprise on surprise. Take developments like the private interview, the dilatory escape, the swooping down on Moab at the head of a premustered army. These cannot be said to meet expectation, except insofar as the reader has had some general grounds for hope; nor to foil expectation, since the premises hardly suffice to project any determinate forecast. As effects that disclose their causes only after the event, they amount to a multiple bolt from the blue, a *jamais vu* series.

Between the figuring forth of prospection and the gap-filling of retrospection, there extends a range of mixed dynamics, characterized by an active *two-way* traffic along the reading sequence. Here each epithet plays its part or some additional part. Unlike the *déjà vu* causality, governed by the epithets as firmly as plot is elsewhere by dreams or divine commands, the advance from expositional promise to actional fulfillment is here less than wholly predictable. Nor, unlike the epithetless *jamais vu* movement, do events come as a total surprise because totally deprived of antecedents. Rather, the initial epithets generate some fairly determinate expectations, which the sequel so resolves or ramifies as to shape afresh our understanding of the entire causal chain.

Within each member of the trio, as it happens, the epithets perform a different prospective-retrospective dance. Eglon's obesity, the only feature whose causal implications have eluded the reader so far, now pays the least expected plot dividend. His paunch swallows up the sword and with it the cause of death, thus making the enemy's confusion worse confounded and gaining Ehud precious time for escape and surprise attack. While bringing the hitherto unattached characteristic into pattern, moreover, this discovery also repatterns the otherwise multiply attached characteristics of the sword. Its small size matches the big belly of its target in yet another, quite literal way, foreseen by the hero as early as its making. The seed of "two mouths" likewise germinates anew into a punning, metaphorical action where the Sword "eats" the Fat Man only to be eaten up by him in turn. This Eglon, the macabre joke goes, will feed on anything. And if the concluding *va'yetse ha'parshedona* means "the filth came out," then it carries the situationally realized wordplay to new lengths. It insinuates a network of rather obscene connections (which I invite readers to figure out for themselves) between natural and figurative nourishment, upper and *middle* and lower mouth, eating and excreting.[4] Last, by a synecdochic twist—the only mode of figuration not encountered so far—the peculiarities distinguishing the two leaders and their fortunes prove to extend to their respective nations. At the time, the divinely reversed significance of Ehud's left-handedness and Israel's choice to present the tribute "by his hand" to the "very fat" Eglon appeared to bear on the coming assassination. But the battle then reenacts the private scene on a national scale. It opens with Ehud's cry to his troops that God has delivered the enemy "into your hand," ends with the notice that Moab was subdued that day "under the hand of Israel," and consists in the destruction of the whole Moabite army, ten thousand "stout" men (with the same ambiguity between "fat" and "strong" as in English). Sequential fruition, retrospection, extension: each turns on the play of determinacy and indeterminacy launched by the forward-looking epithets.

Epithets and the Rule of Forward-looking Exposition

The Ehud narrative richly illustrates the Bible's art of prolepsis in both general and specific terms. In general, because it typifies the regulating principle of exposition, which cuts across the boundaries of expositional content: event-stuff, character-stuff, historical fact, interpersonal relation, state of affairs, spiritual or sociocultural condition, laws encompassing reality as a whole. In each case, the poetic rule goes against description for its own sake, with a view only to introducing, articulating or realizing the object described as part of the furniture of the world. Rather, not the object alone but its given features and concomitants must transpose from a world at rest into a world in motion. And if incapable of initiating motion, they will at least enable and foreshadow it. Hence the future-directed retrospects in the Sisera tale: the pluperfect references to Ehud's death and Heber the Kenite's migration. These antecedents even carry the practice to an extreme since they are superfluous in their formal role, as descriptions of a state, and assume coherence only by projection into the axis of time. But this only brings out the principle by disturbing the balance between the two functions that other instances maintain. Ostensibly conveyed to specify Noah's figure as "the first tiller of the soil," the mention of a vineyard turns out to generate a story of inebriation (Gen 9:20–28); from an epitome of an ideological state, the comment "the word of the Lord was rare in those days; there was no frequent vision" transforms into a dramatic motivation of the young Samuel's puzzlement in the face of God's abrupt address (1 Samuel 3). The principle is still one: exposition, by nature descriptive and retrospective, also turns kinetic and prospective by convention.

But nowhere does this rule of prolepsis operate so uniformly as in portraiture. In this respect, the Ehud exposition is most illustrative. A biblical epithet serves at least two functions, one bearing directly on the character it qualifies and the other bearing indirectly on the plot where he figures as agent or patient. One has its face to a state of affairs that endures or recurs till the expositional past gives way to the narrative present; the other, to a unique process to be launched in the future. If in its overt characterizing role the epithet renders a static feature, then in its covert guise it assumes a twofold dynamic force. It shapes the sequence of our expectations (as a foreshadowing device) because it is bound to shape the sequence of events (as a developmental factor). This unusual premise to a coming proposition, then, appears as a cause that signals some effect yet unborn in the world but already a presence to be reckoned with in the reading.

Here resides another claim to notice. As befits a forward-looking antecedent, the biblical epithet is normally preliminary: it precedes rather than follows the action it doubly governs, so as to form a straight chronological line from cause to effect. The late retrospect that Eli broke his neck in falling because he "was an old man and heavy" (1 Sam 4:18) runs counter to the norm. Far from predictable, as it would be within Trollope's poetics of lucidity, this norm has a distinctive value. For it contrasts with the temporal discontinuities, non sequiturs included, which the Bible multiplies when arranging information in forms other than epithetic.

All this remains stable under the widest variations in epithet content and context. In semantic filling, for instance, the epithets of the deliverance tale ("left-handed . . . double-edged . . . very fat") relate to physical traits. Given their otherwise lowly status in the Bible's hierarchy, it is not very surprising that they should find parallels in other epithets of the same category. However trivial in themselves, these may have (and foretell) tremendous consequences. Esau's hairiness (Gen 25:25) interacts with Isaac's failing sight (27:1) to motivate the drama of sibling rivalry. Asa'el's swiftness of foot (2 Sam 2:18) brings about his death at the hands of Abner, who is himself soon killed in revenge and long thereafter avenged in turn by Solomon. Na'aman's leprosy (2 Kgs 5:1) leads first to a royal panic, then to a miraculous cure by the prophet and a religious conversion of the patient, and finally to a curse on the greedy servant. Provided they assume the same linguistic form, however, characteristics belonging to higher sets bear exactly the same proleptic function. Consider the serpent's subtlety (Gen 3:1), Noah's piety (6:9), Moses' meekness (Num 12:3), Nabal's churlishness (1 Sam 25:3), Solomon's wisdom (1 Kings 3-4).

The Ehud epithets, moreover, are remarkable for their infrequency in the Bible and hence their particularizing effect. Yet their lesson holds equally good for other cases of idiosyncratic portrayal, like Asa'el's speed, and for recurrent features like old age, evildoing and, most common, good looks. As with variations in reference and distribution, so with structure. In fact, the Ehud model itself is so intricately structured that it covers many of these variations; for example, regarding the interplay of expositional epithet and actional fulfillment, prospect and retrospect, knowledge and ignorance, curiosity and surprise and suspense. In the textual distance that separates the birth of expectation in the reader's mind from its resolution in the plot, however, the Bible shows greater flexibility than our model might suggest.

Sometimes the epithetic cause immediately precedes and produces its effect, as with the straight continuity of "the men of the city, base fellows, beset the house round about" (Judg 19:22) or of Tamar's beauty and Amnon's infatuation (2 Sam 13:1–2). Elsewhere the epithet may take whole chapters (as well as, in plot time, years) to germinate into action. One thinks of Sarah's barrenness (Gen 11:30→15:2), Esau's hairiness (Gen 25:15→27:11), Mephibosheth's lameness (2 Sam 4:4, 9:3→19:25). The effect is so long delayed that the impatient reader may begin to suspect that it will never materialize. The more so since the causal implications of such traits are often less followable and the future more opaque than usual. Is Mephibosheth's lameness only designed to show David so resolved to keep faith with the dead Jonathan that he will have the son dine at his table regardless of his own proverbial aversion for the lame? Is this feature not a dynamic cause but, on the contrary, an obstacle overriden by a more powerful cause? Is it, after all, a discloser of character rather than a generator of plot? But the narrative adheres to its rules and keeps their promise. Having exploited the retardation to dramatize character and prolong suspense, it unexpectedly turns the epithet to proleptic account during Absalom's rebellion, when Mephibosheth's disability costs him half his fortune and very nearly his life. As always, therefore, the epithet is a ticking bomb, sure to explode into action in the narrator's (and God's) own good time.

Thus, a woman described as good-looking will sooner or later become an object of love or lust. Of if a man is introduced as specially endowed, then, be he hunter or sage, we confidently expect his skills to come into demand. What fruit such characteristics will bear depends, however, on internal canons of probability, attaching to a theocentric reality-model and deliberately brought into conflict with normal or natural logics of action.

We have so often encountered the ideological clash between probability-registers that this new manifestation can be readily appreciated. The seeming discontinuity between the initial epithet and its consequences brings out in miniature how normal expectation must give place to the divinely informed. In terms of the reading process, giving place subsumes a whole range of adjustments, from qualification to reversal. The portrayal of a woman as barren promises that her sterility will come not only to a crisis but to an end. The very self-confident strength of a man (the minute depiction of Goliath as a war machine at once suggests itself) guarantees his defeat. A new arrival described as a villain—Nabal, the Gibeah rapists, Eli's sons—will be struck down in due course. Whereas one characterized as pious, like Noah or Job, will come through his ordeal, if not unscathed, then at least alive and possibly triumphant.

Lest this should give the impression that here for once the Bible sacrifices art and verisimilitude to rank didacticism, we should keep in mind the broader picture. There are certain natural probabilities—especially concerning matters of the heart—that God himself will not interfere with. Whatever his silences may imply, the gentlemanly narrator calls no woman ugly. But one described as beautiful will never want for attentions; nor, as with Rachel versus Leah, will she take second place to a less attractive rival, however well-deserving. Most neutral epithets, moreover, are subject to no determinate predetermination and therefore engender multiple futures. Further, even moral epithets predict the "what" rather than the "how" of their bearer's destiny, which leaves room for intermediate twists of suspense in the human condition. Most important, the epithet is only part of the Bible's repertoire of characterization, and all its fellows show much less regard for the dictates of "poetic justice." Not only indirections but even modes of direct commentary other than epithetic avoid all straight correlation between merit and fate.

Consider the morally inconsistent fortunes of five successive kings portrayed and evaluated without restraint in a book as ideology-laden as 2 Kings (chaps. 18–23). Hezekiah, who "did what was right in the eyes of the Lord" and "trusted in the Lord" more than any other king of Judah, indeed dies in peace. But so does his son Manasseh of odious memory, whose catalogue of atrocities gives the impression that he spent his life trying to make himself into his father's opposite. His own heir Amon, a pale replica of the archsinner, perishes by the hand of conspirators. Yet his son Josiah, a God-fearing man like his grandfather and the author of the famous religious reformation, does not fare much better: he is mortally wounded in a battle against Pharaoh. And his son Jehoahaz, a typical evildoer, is deposed by the same Pharaoh and dies in exile. Evidently, this sequence makes no moral sense. It appears to go out of its way to thwart any attempt to establish a pattern of expectation, least of all in terms of retributive justice. Indeed, the corresponding series in Chronicles imposes such facile intelligibility on the plot by resolving the two anomalies: it has Manasseh repent his ways (2 Chr 33:11–20) and Josiah dig his own grave (35:20–24). But this only encapsulates the opposition between ideological and near-didactic history writing.

In this light, the two modes of direct characterization emerge as alternative options that enable the narrator to reconcile the competing claims of aesthetics, history, and ideology. Each affords a determinate logic of action and hypothesis-making. Portrayal by means other than epithetic leads the portraitee through an opaque action subject to the constraints of factuality and God's mysterious designs; but his epithets determine or even seal his fate along ideological lines, equally incorporated into the poetics. Even under double constraint, again, art manages to retain a freedom of choice by inventiveness and alternation.

·10·

GOING FROM SURFACE TO DEPTH

For the adequate comprehending of Claggart by a normal nature these hints are insufficient. To pass from a normal nature to him one must cross "the deadly space between." And this is best done by indirection.

Herman Melville, *Billy Budd*

Character as Action, Character in Action

The art of prolepsis systematizes and facilitates the movement from the truth to the whole truth within the plot. Epithet prefigures drama. But does it extend the same service to the intelligibility of character proper? As well as leading from past to present to future and from cause to effect along the axis of time, does it lead, by a vertical interrelation, from surface to depth? Does the epithet make personality, artistically speaking at least, as it makes history?

The Bible's economy certainly raises this possibility, for the epithet is multifunctional anyway. Apart from its two constant roles, the portraitistic and the proleptic, it may fulfill a variety of others. We have already seen the epithet pressed into ideological service by the non sequitur between feature and fortune that implies supernatural resolution. We have also seen it yield the pleasures of wordplay above the call of other duties. In the interests of cohesion, moreover, the puns of the Ehud tale assume the shape of a network and a line of development.

Of this range of variable functions, however, the most important but also the most tricky is *indirect* characterization, that is, portrayal beyond the feature or facet specified by the epithet. What gives this function its importance is that it affords access, if not a key, to those depths of personality that the Bible's world view holds so central and its narrative surface so jealously guards. This also makes it tricky to go below the surface epithet. What the Bible will not straightforwardly articulate into an epithet (or some equivalent direction) it will not often transparently reveal through

342

the epithets that it does articulate. Like all the keys offered by biblical poetics, the inference from the givens to the gaps of personality enjoys no magical facilities. In certain cases it will open no new door of character at all; in others it will open only too many and leave us wondering which leads to the real man.

For the first of these predicaments, consider again the assassination story. That Eglon is described as "very fat" tells one much about his destiny but nothing further about the man himself, least of all about his inner self. Nor does the reason for this blockage lie in the irrelevance of anything below the corporeal attribute. For we also experience it with participants whose character does assume contextual interest, signaled by early gaps or retrospective disclosure. What suggestions about the inner person arise from, say, the swift-footedness of Asa'el, who rushes headlong into danger and death? Or from Na'aman's leprosy, which leads him first to question and then to acknowledge God's power? Or from the initial reference to the barrenness of Sarah, later to unfold as quite a colorful lady?

Insofar as these epithets do characterize by indirection, moreover, the character revealed is not that of the personage who bears and exercises the attributes but of another who feels their results. By a typical shift from agent to patient, Asa'el's speed as pursuer brings out the anxiety of the pursued Abner to spare his life unless his hand is absolutely forced. Sarah's barrenness throws favorable light on Abraham, growing old without a murmur against either the wife who leaves him childless or the God who promised to make a great nation of him. While Mephibosheth's lameness evokes the characteristic mixture of David's motives. And if all these surface epithets fail to reflect depths just because they denote morally and psychologically neutral features, take a charged physical feature like leprosy. Though a staple of divine punishment (Num 12:10; 2 Kgs 5:27; 2 Chr 27:20), it has no opprobrious connotations in Na'aman's case. He emerges as an admirable foreigner and his malady as a piece of fortunate misfortune.

However wide we cast our net for the deep correlates of biblical externals— and internals, I shall argue, follow much the same rule—we come up with nothing like a table of association: a law of metonymic inference from (given) surface to (hidden) depth in character. Of course, the fact that a man depicted as fat remains a fat man, a barren woman a barren woman— and so on with every feature that resists conversion or extension into terms other than itself—reinforces our sense of their particularity. The trouble is that it also heightens our sense of their opacity in the face of disturbing gaps or sometimes, worse, of their transparency where, as we later discover the hard way in the face of surprise gaps, they are really opaque.

But, it may be objected, Ehud's portrayal does invite the reader to go below the surface epithet of left-handedness. After all, does it not round out the figure by suggesting his bravery and resourcefulness? In fact, that inference is doubtless there to be made, but it does not follow *from* the overt characterization, which simply states a physical peculiarity. Rather, the surface characterization (together with other proleptics and circumstances) looks ahead to a course of action; and it is only this course of action that suggests, and in fulfillment validates and elaborates or if necessary qualifies, the additional facets of character required to accomplish it. For a hero to plan and execute an assassination in enemy headquarters, turning to tactical account both his victim's idiosyncrasy and his own, he must be fearless and cunning; just as for Eglon to rise at Ehud's mention of God, despite the effort it must have cost a man of his girth, he cannot be wholly impious. The epithet as cause prefigures and motivates a dramatic effect that in turn harks back to further causes in the form of the character-traits supposed to have motivated it in the first place. Within all such chains of causal reasoning, then, the action figures as a vital bridge or mediating term between direct and indirect characterization: the need to make psychological sense of it, whether as scenario or as accomplished fact, impels the interpreter to look round for features that will close in retrospect the gaps of character left open by the initial exposition. This again brings out the contrast between arts such as Trollope's and the Bible's. The poetics of lucidity, with its exhaustive portraits and static portraitees, launches a one-way movement from character to the action that both follows and follows from it in dramatic shape. The poetics of ambiguity involves a two-way traffic, but with significant variations. Thus, if in the absence of any preliminary givens ("truth") we first move from the action to the agent's character and then back and forth till his exit—as with God, Abraham, Moses, Samson, Jonah—then epithet-oriented inference goes from character to action to character.

Like prolepsis itself in the sphere of history, this busy and uncertain movement from the truth to the whole truth about personality cuts across the line dividing externals from internals. Moreover, the two cross-cutting dynamics interrelate. For the action limned by prolepsis and in turn fleshing out the proleptic skeleton remains at least partly opaque to the last twist of its enactment. As long as the suspension lasts, art and ideology combine to prevent any straightforward, let alone automatic, inference from the given to the gapped trait associated with it by nature or culture: whether from Sarah's barrenness or Na'aman's leprosy or Solomon's wisdom to their moral being. With internals, on the contrary, the given feature is itself subject to retrospective adjustment, by way of character change or redefinition under the pressure of events.

The epithetic reference to wits sharply manifests the gap concealed in the given. The agents who prove sagacious—from Jethro teaching Moses effective administration to Hushai outmaneuvering Ahitophel—are rarely called so by the narrator. Whereas those called sagacious do not usually turn out a recommendation of sagacity. The serpent "was more subtle [*arum*] than any other wild creature" (Gen 3:1), but the abuse of that subtlety boomerangs on the abuser as well as undoes his victims. The "very crafty [*khakham me'od*]" Jonadab, Amnon's friend and adviser, only leads the prince into dishonor and death (2 Samuel 13). And if Egypt's "wise men [*khakhamim*]" (Gen 41:8) do not manage to harm either themselves or others, this is only because Pharaoh wisely rejects their interpretation of his dream. In Solomon's unfolding, the retrospective twist is most pronounced. The opening chapters of Kings give an overwhelming impression of his wisdom: they trace its divine origin, dramatize it through illustrative scenes, even allot to it a whole descriptive paragraph unrivaled in specificity and superlatives (5:9–14). Exercised to intellectual rather than moral ends, however, that unique genius suffices to establish a reputation but not to secure a kingdom. With the serpent or Jonadab, the feature is revaluated and placed by the action; with Solomon it develops or crystallizes. In each case, however, the initial epithet serves not so much to guide as to lure and frustrate normal expectation: to drive home in retrospect the ironic distance between the character's auspicious potential under God and his miserable performance in opposition to God.

Even morally directed epithets turn equivocal as the plot goes forward. If negative instances ("base fellows") cover flat or flattened characters by way of evaluative shorthand, then positive counterparts often give an impression of flatness only as a step toward later complications. The label makes the unrighteous transparent and the righteous *appear* transparent. In view of the expositional emphasis laid on Noah's piety, for example, the revelation of his drunkenness, which brings him down to the level of a Lot or a Ben-hadad, comes as a surprise. In retrospect alone can we appreciate the force of the temporal adverbials that qualify Noah's complimentary epithets, first in the narrator's "Noah was a righteous man, blameless in his generations" and then in God's "I have seen that thou art righteous before me in this generation" (Gen 6:9, 7:1). Further, Job's portrait as "blameless and upright, one who feared God and eschewed evil" (1:1) looks so categorical as to leave no room for the subsequent emergence of the bold inquirer into God's ways. The clash between Job's epithetic and dramatic characterizations threatens the unity of his character and lends some color to the friends' (and Satan's) insinuation that the upright Job is little more than the public image exposed by adversity. But if they are right, what are we to make of the narrator's commitment about the old Job? And if the narrator's word stands, what are we to make of the new Job? The unfavorable explanation, in short, has the virtue of psychological continuity; the favorable, of narrative authority; but neither enjoys both strengths. Only with God's approval of Job toward the end is the apparent contradiction resolved as an extension of the initial portrait: the dramatic disclosures form a whole with their antecedents within an unsuspected, because deliberately gapped, complexity of character and world view alike. Moral perfection no longer subsumes but opposes unquestioning acceptance. As with Noah, the flat epithetic image rounds itself out in actional sequence by gaining dissonant features that would seem to belong to another type of character altogether. Unlike Noah, however, Job acts counter to expectation not despite but because of the qualities specified on his first appearance; and his character gains in complexity not by appeal to new factors but to the new and newly assessed manifestations of the old. The non sequiturs of prolepsis, personality, and perspective fall into coherence together. The dissonance here is more illusory than real, laudatory rather than ironic, intended not just to modify our view of a certain righteous man but to redefine the concept of righteousness itself. And yet, no matter how tremendous the consequences, the gap-filling process does not essentially vary from that set in motion by the lowliest biblical externals: from given character to action provoked to deeper character implied.

The Composition of Character and the Limits of Metonymic Inference

That this inferential movement goes from character to action to character means that the features given by epithetic characterization are discontinuous with their hidden complements in two ways. First, surface and depth are discontinuous in terms of presentational order. Apart from being rendered by different means—direction vs. indirection, commentary vs. enactment— they occupy different, sometimes far removed positions along the narrative sequence. However coexistent within the character they portray, the two sets of traits yet emerge in a successive and distributed form within his characterization. Even the most static characters—quite a few, to be sure, change or crystallize—thus reveal themselves by a dynamic process. And that process generally assumes a distinctive temporal shape, whereby the action mediates between the truth and the whole truth. We first encounter the epithet serving as prospect and then deduce from the intervening developments, by way of retrospect, whatever lies behind or beside it.

This reading exigency would still be fairly easy to meet were it not for the fact that the biblical discontinuity extends from the art of characterization to the model of character. The features belonging to surface and depth no more go together in the personality (as fixed concomitants) than they run together in the portraiture (as immediate sequents). They are separated by the world view as well as along the discourse.

Were the discontinuity a matter of textual arrangement alone, the reader could bridge it without much trouble by reference to the appropriate character-types. For the very idea of such types, whether adopted from life or fabricated by art, entails the codified linkage of a certain number of traits to produce some stock figure: the Miles Gloriosus, the Knight-errant, the Miser, the Ingénue, the Noble Savage, to mention but a few. And since the traits form a determinate set, we can always infer the presence of one or more from the explicit mention of the other. By the conventions of the classical detective story, to take a simple example, the entrance of a policeman arouses deep misgivings about his intelligence even before he manages to do or say anything. Or by the code of the Victorian novel, the introduction of a heroine as dark or fair is enough to subsume her under a well-defined moral pole. Each character type, then, associates the component features by *strong metonymy,* interrelating them into uniform contiguity within the world; and such association renders the associated features mutually implicative.[1] Given one, the others follow by metonymic kinship, correlation, or, as with outside-inside traffic, projection.

In its commitment to the mystery and the dignity of man created in God's own image, however, the Bible will not allow any ready-made law of association. The *scopes* it operates with, as I argued in chapter 7, are the universal and the individual to the exclusion of the typal. Not that the Bible's characters are universals, for such personified characteristics, allegory fashion, would make the flattest types of all. Nor are their characteristics so individual as to exceed the bounds of human nature. Rather, each personality forms a unique combination of features, the parts common or recognizable enough to establish universality and the whole unusual enough to exclude typicality in favor of individuality. Many biblical characters share isolated attributes or drives; no two characters, except those patently stylized, are alike in overall makeup. (Hence, again, the unique names.) In Melville, to revert to the epigraph, Claggart exceptionally departs from normal nature; in the Bible, there is no norm of human nature to be embodied in a character, not even by way of contrast, and to gain insight one must always cross "the deadly space between."

In rendering each character sui generis, this inherent discontinuity undermines all characterological package deals and all regularities of metonymic inference from the given to the gapped. Features will not correlate but only relate in the particular case and in a manner discoverable only after the particular event. Far from reducible to and even further from predictable by type, new manifestations will often even fall out of character, that is, out of the particular image given or formed earlier. For the Bible takes no less delight in non sequiturs of personality than of plot, interweaving the two for maximal incongruence and variety.

The metamorphosis of a single feature, as when Job's righteousness is subjected to a process that extends from celebration through challenge and ambiguity to reaffirmation, marks the limiting case. Less radical, but much more frequent, is the surfacing of an attribute that goes ill—psychologically or morally speaking—with its established antecedents. Of the many forms taken by this dynamics of surprise, already thoroughly discussed, just recall the interplay of pure and impure motives in the unfolding of Joseph, Gideon, David, God as against Jonah. Or take the distance between divine choice and the formation of the chosen, pointed out by Erich Auerbach in what remains the most penetrating account of the Bible's approach to character.[2] In terms of my own concerns, this distance entails a threefold process, whereby the given character is brought into discontinuity with the feature of electness and then by degrees outgrows the discontinuity. Even though the process repeats itself, little else does: neither the initial figure nor the processing nor the finished product. Least incongruous, but still unforeseeable because unclassifiable, is the disclosure or development of traits that do not so much revise as fill out the overall image of a person: Joab's sense of humor or Moses' meekness under calumniation. However diverse the relations between the old and the new character, then, they all retain enough uniqueness and surprise value to block any straightforward gap-filling by metonymy.

Like all the Bible's models of life and art, this is nowhere formulated for the reader's convenience but is driven home in and through the reading. For ease of reference and understanding, of course, the reader tends to generalize character and assimilate it to type. And the Bible encourages this tendency with a view to its ultimate discomfiture. Many personages show on arrival a surface that looks smooth or familiar, but sooner or later fractures under the blows of the plot beyond easy repair. As suggested in chapter 7, we may then have to appeal to the individual scope in order to repair the breach of a universal, or vice versa; we may have to reinterpret a facet of personality or rearrange the whole, sometimes into permanent ambiguity. But never can we retain the original picture of the self, with its associated metonymic implications. It is by trial and error, as always, that the reader learns the lessons of complex character and difficult coherence.

These operations bear on surface epithets of all kinds. But the kind with the strongest claim to analysis are those that present a surface in a double sense: externality as well as givenness and explicitness of portraiture. And of all external features, the most common and instructive are the Janus-faced pair: old age and good looks.

Old Age in Genesis

The sequence of Genesis launches and frustrates the reader's quest for the correlates of old age. It shapes history into a zigzag line, where the concomitants of and inferences from the same datum change beyond recognition from the life of one patriarch to another. Not even divine election and natural heredity on top of declining years can bring them under a rule or "code" of character.

Significantly, the narrator's ascription of old age by way of epithet is reserved for the three patriarchs on the point of winding up their earthly affairs. In a book so packed with Methuselahs that a mere centenarian might count as a stripling, the first patriarch is yet the first character to receive the epithet: "Abraham was old, advanced in years, and the Lord had blessed Abraham in everything" (24:1). "Everything," we soon learn, includes not only great wealth but also a new lease of procreativity and the retention of all spiritual powers. Dismissed by his first wife, half a century before, as too "old" (18:12) to beget children, he now takes "another wife, whose name was Keturah, and she bore him Zimran, Yokshan, Medan, Midian, Yishback, and Shuah" (25:1-2). Yet so blessed is Abraham that he can spend his last years raising a new family while taking measures (with his characteristic wisdom and foresight and fairness) to safeguard the interests of his old and divinely appointed one. Putting his house in order, he arranges a non-Canaanite marriage for his heir, makes over to him all the property and, to obviate fraternal strife, loads the concubines' sons with gifts and sends them away "from his son Isaac while he was still living" (25:5-6)

Appropriately, all this crowns the lifelong opposition to Lot, termed "old" (19:31) in figural rather than narratorial discourse. Of Lot we catch a last glimpse as he holes up in a Dead Sea cave, drunkenly siring a new family on his own daughters. In contrast, even the parting from Abraham (25:7-10) sketches an idyllic picture. It leaves an impression of the most natural death ("in a good old age, an old man and full of years"); familial harmony between the sons ranged in the hierarchical order predetermined by the father ("Isaac and Ishmael his sons buried him"); and, to screw down the antithesis, a reunion with the proper mate ("Sarah his wife") in their own "cave of Machpelah."

Epithetic old age thus associated with all the blessings of character and fortune, it becomes their overt metonymy. Surface and depth appear to establish in concert the type of the Departing Patriarch. So the reader naturally looks forward to the recurrence of this typal precedent in the next generation. But history does not repeat itself, except to dissociate externals from internals. Contrary to expectation, "Isaac was old and his

eyes were dim so that he could not see" (27:1) turns out to be a prologue
to a very different tale. Here old age goes neither with admirable character
nor with happiness and success but with failing powers all round, notably
spiritual as well as physical decay ("blindness"). The day having come for
Isaac, too, to put his house in order ("I am old, I do not know the day
of my death"), he only manages to create disorder, ranging himself openly
against his wife and exacerbating fraternal tensions to a point never reached
since the days of Cain and Abel. He puts himself in the wrong from his
opening words to his favorite son: "Go out to the field and hunt game for
me and prepare for me savory food, such as I love, and bring it to me
and I will eat, so that I may bless thee before I die" (27:3–4). Even if he
does not know that Jacob is the destined heir—and nothing suggests that
he does—then his blindness stands in telling contrast to his own father's
as well as to the reader's foreknowledge. Besides, his own wife having been
imported from afar, who could (or should) have known better that Esau
with his Canaanite wives—that "made life bitter" for both parents-in-law
(26:35)—has disqualified himself for patriarchal blessing? Yet he gives way
to his affection for his firstborn, wild, devoted, and a provider of savory
food. (A subtle echo of Lot's self-indulgence, this, just as the blindness
harks back to the drunkenness in terms of plot and indirect characterization alike. Neither knows what he is doing.)

It is ironic that only Isaac's physical blindness makes it possible for others
to retrieve the mistakes of his spiritual decline. Some of the consequences,
however, remain irreversible: the trickery to which his wife is driven, Esau's
bitterness and fratricidal plans, Jacob's flight to Mesopotamia, straight
into the arms of an archdeceiver who will play tricks on him for decades.
To protect his successor, Abraham sent away all his other offspring; while
Isaac has brought things to such a pass that the heir must run for dear
life, bound for a land that his grandfather rejected out of hand as a dwelling for *his* son. The unflattering contrast between his lot as son and his
adminstration as father can hardly have escaped Isaac himself.

Thus we leave the second patriarch: sightless, baffled, feelings in clash
with reason, self-image eclipsed by paternal example, ill at ease with every
single member of his family, all (like himself) sinning and sinned against
as a result of his folly. We leave him with painful memories of the past,
a disheartening present (Esau going Canaanite, Jacob's fate unknown),
and nothing settled about the future. In his old age Isaac has made such
a mess of a hitherto uneventful career, patterned on his father's, as to jeopar-
dize his whole heritage. And it is none of his doing that Jacob survives,
prospers, *and* returns. Nor that the brothers are at last reconciled. Nor
that—though what became of the property remains gapped to the last and
the reunion with Rebekah after death is left unmentioned and Esau plays

chief mourner ("Esau and Jacob his sons buried him")—he eventually rests in something of the peace that Abraham carved out for himself (35:29).

Faced with this reversal of metonymic direction, one is tempted to explain it and salvage a principle of inference by focusing on the variation in patriarchal analogy. The reference to old age, it now seems, does carry favorable implications for character, except when overriden by failing vision, with all its charged figurative suggestiveness. In each case the quality indicates, in either/or fashion, a determinate pole of character; and the two poles make two subtypes of the patriarchal figure.

This revised norm of gap-filling looks so motivated, in terms of prolepsis and portrayal alike, that we approach Jacob's deathbed scene with some confidence. And the antecedents given in chapter 48 not only justify but reinforce it from one touch to another. We find Jacob ill, bed-ridden and, climactically, so blind that he fails to identify his own grandchildren. Though younger than either of his predecessors, his physical decay is yet more advanced than his father's in the corresponding prologue to disaster. Even their common affliction is more underscored than before, "Israel's eyes were dim with age: he could not see," and so shaped as to relate the failing eyesight to old age in both causal and synecdochic terms. By the logic of inference from surface to depth just constructed, the descriptive focusing-with-repetition signals a proportional worsening in mental and moral decrepitude. When Jacob offers to bless the two lads, therefore, the reader knows what to expect—the worst. The more so since such gap-filling by metonymy and precedent and character type also recommends itself on other grounds. It derives support from Jacob's record of favoritism— i.e., the individual scope of character—brought to mind anew by his sudden animation ("Israel summoned his strength and sat up in bed") at the prospect of a visit by his lifelong favorite. And it also gives coherent shape, aesthetically if not otherwise attractive, to patriarchal history as a whole: a line of steady physical *and* spiritual deterioration.

But, again, the sequel cuts the ground from under our feet. For once, at the last and least expected crossroads, Jacob shows true patriarchal foresight and responsibility—including the impersonal spirit that distinguishes the makers from the pawns and driftwood of biblical history. For his decision runs counter to his beloved son's wishes and authority. Jacob's main concern is to do the proper rather than the pleasing thing by his grandchildren, in the interests of a design greater than any individual and to realize a vision that rises above personalities. Remarkably, therefore, his action is both in and out of character: he still imposes his will on his deathbed, but only to redeem a life of self-will.

To maximize the surprise value of these disclosures, the narrator devises a cunning route to enlightenment. On hearing that Joseph has brought his two boys along, Jacob predictably volunteers to "bless them." This at once evokes not only the past series of choices between brothers that has punctuated the course of Genesis, but future developments as well: future, that is, in relation to the scene enacted by the dramatis personae, as opposed to the narrative situation that frames this scene. Just as from the vantage point of structural retrospection we know that throughout Genesis the choice always fell on the younger, so from the vantage point of external hindsight do we know that the younger tribe of Ephraim has outstripped Manasseh. Paradigm thus combines with fact, historical probability with historical reality, to establish Ephraim as God's elect. But where does the decrepit Jacob himself propose to bestow the blessing?

Far from resolving the gap, the omniscient narrator goes out of his way to suspend and darken it (48:10–13). It is exactly at this point that he interpolates the ominous as well as retardatory portrayal of Jacob's blindness. He then activates its implications for character and plot by reporting, with a backward glance at Isaac's pre-blessing kiss (27:26–27), how fondly Jacob "kissed" and "embraced" the boys. By a further delay charged with prospective force, Jacob's "I did not expect to see thy face again, and behold, God has let me see thy offspring also" bristles with ironic significance. It harks back to the speaker's twofold sightlessness, through the interplay of literal and figurative sight, and betrays to what degree his pleasure in "thy offspring" is an extension of his love for Joseph. And as if to confirm our worst suspicions, Joseph then firmly stage-manages the blessing scene for his doting father. "Joseph took them both, Ephraim in his right hand to Israel's left and Manasseh in his left hand to Israel's right, and led them to him": the unusual detail, which invites the reader to visualize movement and position after the manner of a Sterne or a Joyce, would appear to clinch the antithesis to the patriarch enveloped in darkness. Everything appears set for a reenactment of Isaac's folly, but this time with no Rebekah in the wings to save the situation.

Incredibly, however, the old man saves himself, crossing his hands so as to place the right "upon the head of Ephraim, who was the younger" and the left "upon the head of Manasseh . . . the firstborn." Is this last-minute retrieval due to blindness, as in Isaac's case? Or to senility? (Or even less charitably: having just adopted the lads, is Jacob at his old tricks of favoritism again?) So the whole buildup may lead one to think, together with the displeased Joseph, who forcibly tries to straighten the crossed hands: "Not so, my father, for this one is the firstborn; put thy right hand upon his head." But the prompt response to the voice of natural precedence quashes both his hopes and our doubts: "I know, my son, I know. . . . Nevertheless his younger brother shall be greater than he." Jacob, then, does the right thing for the right reason, in the face of heavy pressure and without any human or divine agency having exploited his disability to twist around his intention into a tragicomedy of error. Acting in the spirit of the divine logic of election manifested in the past, the blind patriarch shows an insight into the future denied to his clear-sighted (and occasionally clairvoyant) but for once earthbound son. His reversal of the order of seniority, in short, enforces our reversal of the correlation between physical and inner vision.

Nor is the reversal of expectancy and meaning confined to Jacob's powers of sight. Our view of his whole character, based on personal antecedents and interpersonal precedents, suffers the same fate as we observe him approaching death in a manner reminiscent of Abraham as opposed to Isaac. In subtle allusion to Abraham's sexual prowess, the apparent wreck manages to increase his family, though by way of adoption rather than procreation: "Ephraim and Manasseh shall be mine, as Reuben and Simeon are." The fact that these are Egyptian-born involves another allusion—to Ishmael's maternal origin ("an Egyptian maidservant whose name was Hagar")—which implies superiority even to Abraham. Far from driving sons away, as a result of historical necessity (like his grandfather) or personal bungling (like his father), Jacob redeems his own past and ensures the national future by keeping them all around him.

As his career draws to an end, moreover, Jacob leaves no thread loose and no patriarchal decorum unobserved. He extracts a promise from Joseph not to inter him in Egypt; goes on to establish the appropriate hierarchy among his descendants; and despite his lifelong passion for Rachel, buried on the way to Ephrath, chooses to rest with his fathers at the side of Leah. With a similar regard for propriety and historical continuity, he avoids at the close his father's hugger-mugger method, but takes formal leave of all his sons. And if his parting words to them sound at times overfond and at times overharsh, then it is at least the verdict of biblical history that each receives "the blessing suitable to him." In psychological terms, indeed, the fact that he cannot rise to perfect impartiality even then—just as, in a wonderfully revealing touch, he cannot bring himself to refer to Leah as his wife (49:31)[3]—serves to keep an otherwise startling deathbed "crystallization" in character.

The disclosure that Jacob dies a better man than he lived thus transforms in midcourse our reading of the central deathbed scene and redefines his figure for posterity. But this twist, false clues and all, also launches more global retrospections and repatternings. As concerns character, to begin with, it sharpens our sense of the foregoing patriarchs as unique individuals: Abraham, who leaves life exactly in the way he lived it, and Isaac, whose old age all but shamed his youth. It is precisely the breakdown of expected unity, first in Isaac's and then even more dramatically in Jacob's case, that creates meaningful variety among the trio. As the narrative twists its way from one concrete universal to another, it demolishes all fond hopes of reducing the patriarchs to type.

As with portraiture, so with temporal paradigm. These shifting relations compose our understanding of patriarchal history and the shape of Genesis as a whole. The reader having been tempted into simplistic views of history—it first seems to repeat itself, then to trace a straight line of personal and familial deterioration—the complex scheme that actually regulates the process emerges with redoubled force. The patriarchal age moves from the ideal through decline to a rise coinciding with a new beginning: a course that highlights the misfortunes of the past, to the extent of insinuating them into developments up to the turning point itself, and yet ends the book on an optimistic note.

In still more general terms, finally, the same reversal thwarts for good the reader's long-drawn endeavor to extrapolate a logic of inference from surface to depth. In dashing our expectations about Jacob, it makes nonsense of any anticipatory passage from exterior to interior, including the refined distinction between old age and sightless old age. If Abraham's end implies a straightforward positive correlation and Isaac's complicates it into a twofold system of linkage or gap-filling, then Jacob's leaves nothing to be salvaged from the ruins of the pattern. His body in a state of decrepitude exceeding even his father's, his deeds yet show him to take after his grandfather. With Abraham, physical vigor is in harmony with spiritual blessedness, so as to maximize, if not to idealize, the favorable connotations of old age. With Isaac, physical is in harmony with spiritual collapse, literal with metaphorical blindness, producing an image of old age at its worst. With Jacob, physical breakdown is in *dis*harmony with spiritual invigoration, a coupling encapsulated in a paradox that makes its début in literary history: the blind turning out clairvoyant where the seeing prove benighted. The fact that metonymic transfers from appearance to personality and conduct may follow the logic of either reflection or inversion means that their ambiguity defies foreclosure. The oscillation between the extremes can be resolved only at the end of the process of discovery. And this in turn means that in the Bible not merely gaps but principles of gap-filling are objects of sequential manipulation, sources of curiosity and surprise, agents in the overall drama of reading.

Good Looks in Samuel

Just as the feature of old age leads the reader a fine dance in Genesis, so does that of good looks along Samuel. It even radicalizes the unsettling effect of the zigzag progression. For the temporal line of development goes not only with a firmer analogical linkage of the ambiguated characters but with a verbal ambiguity between their alternative readings. Consider the series of handsome men deployed, all kings or pretenders to the throne: Saul, David, and Absalom (of whom Adonijah is a pale copy). Everyone knows how dissimilar these are in character and fate, but only by the wisdom of hindsight. Reading in sequence, with each new arrival a bundle of gaps and the future uncertain, one has to make the best sense one can of the hints given by assimilating them to some tentative structure of probabilities. Throughout this search for intelligibility, we are invited to grasp each member of the trio as both a precedent and a foil to the next good-looker in line; and cannot help wondering which of the analogical patterns of characterization and foreshadowing will materialize in the end. More generally, again, does the Bible postulate a type of the Good-Looking Man or King?

Thus, Saul's expositional portrayal sounds definitely auspicious. "Saul"— the traditional rendering goes— "was a handsome [*tov*] young man. There was not a man among the people of Israel more handsome [*tov*] than he; from his shoulders upward he was taller than any of the people" (1 Sam 9:2). Not only does he enjoy royal appearance; he may well have the character to go with it. For the key epithet *tov,* translated in automatic fashion as "handsome," originally means "good" and only by extension "good-looking." So the two readings of the character are prefigured in miniature by the two-faced epithet. Does Saul owe his election to his being the best or the best-looking of the Israelites? Since the two possibilities are compatible and their encapsulation in the same word hardly ominous, however, the question remains submerged for the time being. And so far as it does arise, the ensuing action seems to resolve the ambiguity in the most complimentary terms. All the character traits it brings out in episode after dramatic episode—modesty, self-restraint, inspired leadership in the war against Ammon—count heavily and unequivocally in Saul's favor.

No sooner have we formed these impressions and expectations, however, than the narrative proceeds to reverse them. The campaign against the Philistines in chapter 13, where Saul fails to observe the prophet's command due to what is theologically lack of faith and psychologically loss of nerve, marks the turning point. The "sparing" of Amalek, in flagrant violation of norms human and divine, consumes most of the remaining sympathy. And David's advent generates a series of conflicts and comparisons that leave Saul little appeal other than his shell. To some of the steps in this process I shall return in due course. Note, meanwhile, that the narrative's indeterminacy between disclosure and development of character renders its treatment of Saul another classic instance of biblical crystallization. But whether he himself or only the reader's insight into him undergoes a change, the change is (even more deeply and antithetically than Isaac's) for the worse at every point. Modesty gives place to tyranny, self-restraint to fits of homicidal rage, personal leadership to remote (and ineffective) control, not to mention the loss of sanity under pressure that even at its most touching evokes responses scarcely fit for royalty to evoke. In retrospect, it emerges that the information about character has been so distributed along the sequence as to inveigle the reader into error, with a view to hammering home in enlightenment the negative correlation between goodness and good looks.

While this lesson in metonymic inference is still in progress, we encounter the next in line. David figures more clearly as a personal choice of God (16:1), but his abrupt introduction sounds more than one note of warning. Like Saul at the time, he is yet an unknown and untried quantity; and even more than Saul, he presents only an attractive exterior. "Ruddy with beautiful eyes and good looks [*tov ro'i*]" (1 Sam 16:12). The "heart" to which God refers here as his monopoly is, if possible, less in evidence than before. For the quietly ambiguous epithet *tov* now modulates into the portentous univocality of *tov ro'i*, which literally signifies "good-looking." How does this shift tally with the intervening statement, addressed by Samuel to Saul at the moment of his rejection, that God has transferred the kingdom of Israel to someone "better [*tov*] than thou" (15:28)? While the three rhyming adjectives establish continuity in royal portraiture, the sudden imbalance in favor of externals hardly ensures a change for the better.[4]

However, just as the original inference from Saul's outside (by way of straightforward correlation) proved overoptimistic, so does the revised inference from precedent (by way of negative correlation) happily turn out a false alarm. As David's character unfolds in and through the action, the reader does not long waver between the hypotheses. As a proleptic feature, naturally, his good looks affect the course of events. (They motivate Goliath's contempt and Michal's love, perhaps Saul's and Jonathan's too.) As suggested by its incorporation into the glowing portrait drawn to recommend the young Bethlehemite to Saul (16:18), however, this trait also has intrinsic value. It fulfills a properly characterological role in forming the image of an all-round paragon. And as to its metonymic equivalent, David establishes himself as good, though anything but simple, by all biblical standards of devoutness, humanity, and kingship. Indeed, we conclude, God "sees into the heart," whether concealed or reflected by man's outer shell, but no one else can tell in advance which way the coupling will go. After all, the similarity between the two kings in one set of features only highlights their diametric opposition in another.

Or so it seems till David, too, suddenly gets into trouble with God and society. Even the implications of the antithesis to his predecessor, marking two clear-cut (because polar) though unforeseeable logics of metonymic association, are then subjected to a twist that renders these logics less clearcut and accordingly less foreseeable than ever. This reopening of the gaps starts with the Bathsheba affair and extends, with ramifications, to the end of the book.

In appropriately metonymic guise, David's liaison with the "very goodlooking" (*tovat mar'eh me'od*) but disloyal Bathsheba stands in opposition to his past dealings with Abigail "of good understanding and good-looking" (1 Sam 25:3). Surely the two women, with the tell-tale epithets adhering to them, call to mind the basic relations between exterior and interior previously dramatized through the two kings. And by the old rule *noscitur e socio,* David's own character would appear to be reflected in each instance or stage by the female company he chooses to keep, let alone the terms and consequences of the involvement.

In a way reminiscent of Saul's decline, moreover, the sequence now works both backward and forward. Its movement thus brings to light hitherto unsuspected flaws in David's personality. Weakening of personal leadership, lust or vulnerability to infatuation, abuse of royal power for the murder of antagonists, a taste for costly spoils, mismanagement of children, lack of foresight: most of these newly revealed features hark back to Saul at the corresponding phase and all betray the familiar syndrome of reason overruled by ego. But this process of discovery goes with a process of social demotion, for the king's unkingliness motivates a reversal of fortune that threatens utter ruin. The onetime darling of fortune, with an unbroken record of success as both private and public figure, now suffers one catastrophe after another, in all spheres of life and with no end in sight. First exposure to divine wrath, death of Bathsheba's baby, son raping daughter, rapist murdered by another, favorite son, murderer living in exile, rebellion, flight from Jerusalem, incest perpetrated on the royal harem before the eyes of the people, civil war ending in terrible personal bereavement, swallowing lectures and menaces from subordinates, reduction to wooing the fractious tribes all over again, new rebellion . . .

How come? Amidst unsettling retrospection and suspenseful prospection, the interpreter must yet go back again and again to the turning point in an attempt to uncover some principle that will make sense of all these incongruous developments. Either the old logic of reading must be salvaged or a new one puzzled out in order to explain the collapse of established relations, to relink character with action and action with character and both with the ideological scheme, to bring the past into causal alignment with the present and the future. Are David's acts of adultery and murder, say, in or out of character? If out of character, do they signal a temporary lapse from virtue and accordingly, though visited with fury, qualify rather than demolish his past image and mar rather than break his career? If in character, does this disclosure reverse the linkage between his exterior and interior from harmony into disharmony, as implied by the switch from Abigail to Bathsheba? If the positive metonymic correlation still remains in force, what are we to make of the dissonant gaps, traits, insights, catastrophes divinely proportioned to moral guilt? If it no longer does, these dissonances indeed become consonant, but what are we then to make of God's initial claim to see into the "heart" and of the narrator's misleading techniques of characterization? Has David changed or finally revealed the (or at least a) self that he has concealed so far? Is he after all another Saul, God at his most inscrutable, and we dupes of appearance again? Given the lessons of the past, one need not be a specially close reader to find these questions troublesome.

As if to pile novelty on confusion, however, it is while David has by no means weathered the storm and the reader feels less sure of his bearings than ever that Absalom makes his appearance. And to a far greater extent than did his predecessor and father in Saul's lifetime, he makes it in a way calculated to intensify the reader's sense of disorientation. Consider first how the narrator subjects us again to his artful modes of informational delay and distribution, but with a notable variance in ordering: he exhibits the new arrival in action (2 Sam 13:20–14:24) before referring to his beauty. The drama extending from Tamar's rape through Absalom's revenge to his recall, moreover, unfolds a character that is neither unattractive nor unfamiliar. Absalom shows pride and passion tempered by amazing self-restraint, a gift for secret planning followed by resolute action, and loyalty to his own regardless of consequences. What is more, since his only problematic act comes in response to the assault on his sister, he gets the benefit of our polarized attitudes to the victim as against the rapist. And to maximize this emotional transfer, the cause of Absalom's act of violence affords a new and for once unambiguous variation on the exterior-interior theme: Tamar is beautiful *and* good, but so unfortunate that her very attractiveness proves her undoing.

Only at the end of this affair does the narrator release the information about Absalom's looks, with a perfect timing that the reader grimly smiles at in later recollection: just before the prince crosses the line separating the man of honor from the malcontent and rebel. It emerges, in other words, at a strategic point so as to catch the reader at his most charitable and vulnerable. Absalom has paid dearly for his crime—three years of exile, present disgrace at home—and we have been led to think that we already know the worst about him and the worst is not so bad after all. Even the delayed features of appearance, precisely because they ring more than one bell, do not enforce a view of character so novel as to unmake his past record or to foreshadow the enormities to come:

> (25) In all Israel there was not a man so much to be praised for his beauty as Absalom; from the sole of his foot to the top of his head there was no blemish in him. (26) And when he cut the hair of his head (at the end of every year he would cut it; when it was heavy on him, he cut it), he weighed the hair of his head, two hundred shekels by the king's weight. (27) There were born to Absalom three sons and one daughter, whose name was Tamar; she was a good-looking woman. (2 Sam 14:25–27)

This unusually specific portrait forms a junction where different echoes (attributes, precedents, lines of inference) meet only to neutralize one another. Even more striking, the descriptive microsequence is so ordered as to retrace the broad actional sequence that has unfolded the career and character of Absalom's handsome predecessors. Composed of three parts, that is, it not only links up with three analogues. Each part also looks back to a correspondingly placed analogue, so that the implications of the spatial (analogical, suprasequential) linkage are reinforced and their conflict sharpened by means of temporal patterning.

The opening tribute to singular beauty thus couples Absalom with Saul, likewise the handsomest man of his generation. But the next verse suddenly shifts orientation to the next in line, smuggling David into the picture by omission and inclusion. Just at the point where Saul's portrayal went on to describe his height—by now an established metonymy for worthlessness and inglorious fate—Absalom's switches to his magnificent hair, an attractive feature hitherto reserved for David. Nor is there any trace of the two-faced *tov*. In view of recent (and still unresolved) developments, however, to which David does the link point as a suitable precedent for character inference? If to David before Bathsheba, then the shift in surface description signals a favorable turnabout or at least balance in overall characterization. If on the other hand the reference is to the later David, then the analogy validates the suggestions of a flawed nature and a punitive future made by its antecedents.

Moreover, just as the optimistic reading gains support from further correspondences to David—the recurrent self-control, fall from favor, flight into exile—so does its pessimistic mate derive encouragement from the common association with a "good-looking" woman. But this final (and otherwise superfluous) mention of beauty also points in a third direction: the daughter Tamar recalls the sister Tamar, handsome and virtuous but ill-starred. It therefore opens an entirely new avenue. The pairing with Saul directs the reader to oppose exterior to interior and hence to fate; the auspicious face of the David precedent turns the opposition into harmony, and its ominous face leaves the whole metonymic traffic under a question mark. But the association with Tamar makes it possible to divorce the reading of character from the expectations about fate: exterior reflects interior in opposition to (mis)fortune. Does the reference to a good-looking Tamar, then, predict another cycle where Absalom is driven to violence by someone else's criminality?

The descriptive montage of externals thus projects three different Absaloms (bad, good, problematic) and, kinetically, three different lines or outcomes of action involving Absalom (unhappy, happy, problematic). Which is the real man? Which his destined fate? Though nominally offered new information, we find ourselves more in the dark than ever, with gaps forced open and curiosity and suspense excited rather than allayed. For the network of relationships centered in it envelops every crux with ambiguity: the logic of appearance, the truth about the past self, the chances for the future, the causal movement from past to future and its ideological rationale. The lingering over the surface, in brief, proves less than useless for the resolution of depths and plot contingencies—this being exactly the point of its marvelous design.

Lured into this maze by the overt portraiture, the reader again looks to the action for guidance. And the action, in the form of the rebellion story, indeed comes to the rescue. With lucidity and economy, the two complexes of gaps opened in quick succession—one bearing on David, the other on Absalom—are now resolved together. For the rebellion so interweaves these tangles as to effect a mutual as well as simultaneous disentanglement. So far linked in terms of analogy, the two figures now come into open conflict and thus illuminate each other by way of double opposition. In dramatic and compositional terms alike, David diminishes Absalom while Absalom elevates David. More generally, good fortune brings out the worst in Absalom and ill fortune the best in David. So even while Absalom's strength appears to be on the rise and David's on the wane, their moral-psychological powers move the other way. And this in turn accounts for the ultimate reversal of worldly fortune, to the reestablishment of overall coherence.

In adversity, briefly, David reverts to his pre-Bathsheba self: devout, resolute, far-sighted, self-controlled, a shrewd judge of men, and yet a loving parent to the last. At the same time—and the constant shifts of scene make for near-simultaneity in juxtaposition—Absalom in prosperity forfeits whatever appeal he had as victim of circumstances. His behavior increasingly marks a contrast both to his antagonist and to his own former self. It is not only that he raises his hand against God's anointed, who in his time would rather suffer hardship than touch a hair of Saul's head, and against a father who takes risks to spare his life. He proves no match for his father's craft or charisma and surpasses him in sexual depravity alone. The throne once seized, the combination of qualities required to secure it—the independence, self-restraint, and decisiveness manifested in the Amnon affair, the acumen and single-mindedness that brought off the political conspiracy—does not once show. And the good looks now suggest an overweening vanity, as in the insistence on seeing "the king's face" (14:32) or when Hushai, playing on the usurper's narcissism, gets Ahitophel's wise counsel dismissed by promising victory if "thy face goes to battle" (17:11). Indeed, by the time battle comes Absalom is little more than a pretty face; and it is appropriate that his magnificent hair, like Tamar's beauty, should in the end prove his undoing. Quite literally so, in a situation that realizes the implicit metonymy under a proleptic guise: "Absalom was riding on a mule and the mule went under the thick branches of a great oak tree and his head caught fast in the oak and he remained dangling between heaven and earth," soon to be dispatched by Joab (2 Sam 18:9-15).

Both put to the test of changed fortune and fight for survival, then, each crystallizes at long last. David's sin at the turning point defines itself as a lapse after all, sufficiently grave to complicate his character as well as his life—he will never be the same again in our eyes or the people's or God's or, one suspects, his own—but not to overturn it. The origins of that sin remain obscure to the end. Yet, whether because they were not deep-seated in the first place or because David has learned his lesson, they have in effect been counteracted for good. And this relegates them to the periphery of the portrait we carry away with us, its center occupied by such features as will persist to the very death scene, like the old qualifications for kingship and the newly disclosed mishandling of children. On the other hand, Absalom takes on complexity only to deteriorate in the process. His initial attractiveness gradually turns (or turns out) skin-deep, sufficient perhaps to explain his temporary success and his father's love but not to make either a moral being or a king. The Bible's verdict on him thus lurks in the references to hair that frame his decisive trial, the first propounding a question and the last enacting the answer.

With the closure of the character gaps, moreover, the broader ambiguities also find their resolution. In terms of doctrinal as well as causal intelligibility, character aligns itself with fortune: Saul, David, and Absalom get their just deserts. Not that the whole clicks together into a neat moral. It is, as usual, difficult coherence that the narrative favors. Each of the three handsome men meets with his deserts through a process whereby he becomes more rather than less complex; and as a further antidote against schematism, the trio of female counterparts (Abigail, Bathsheba,Tamar) leave a sense of imponderables by jarring even against the moral pattern.

"Truth uncompromisingly told," the ending of *Billy Budd* reminds us, "will always have its ragged edges." And such residual tensions, so abhorrent to the moralist even where they cannot upset the overall balance, are less the Bible's concession than its contribution to art, made in order to reconcile the claims of aesthetics, ideology, and history.

Last, while the relations between surface and depth in character still resist univocal (unitypal, unimetonymic) fixture, they no longer remain open-ended either. Rather, as with old age toward the end of Genesis, good looks assume a determinate indeterminacy. With Saul and Absalom lodged at the extreme of disharmonious correlation and David at the harmonious extreme, the rule establishes itself as one of mutually exclusive ambiguity that may keep oscillating till the character bows out of Samuel but will finally come to polar rest. The good-looking king may crystallize as good and successful *or* bad and doomed, but, except in transitional phases, not as neither or both.

There is nothing arbitrary about the Bible's choice to cast good looks and old age—rather than stoutness, say—in the role of Janus-faced metonymies. It is a device anchored fast in both world and world view. In the world, because either of these surface features has been associated from time immemorial with two "deep" extremes. Old age thus relates to the two faces of time: its fruits (wisdom, experience, providence, objectivity) on the one hand and its ravages (infirmity, senility, suggestibility) on the other. And good looks make the index but also the façade of virtue. There-fore, either coupling of surface and depth forms a natural or naturalized mode of characterization—or, from the reader's side, of inference about character—with instances ranging throughout the history of literature. But if the linkage with either polar extreme has a basis in nature, then the Bible's shifting or ambiguous linkage with both is a matter of ideological culture, where poetic strategy takes its regulation from the norms of a distinctive world view. I am referring, of course, to the epistemological theme, which coordinates action, viewpoint, and sequence into the human ordeal of reading.

Rarely does the marriage of aesthetics and ideology show to such advan-tage as in the artful discontinuities between the outside and the inside of character. The inverse proportioning of givenness to significance, the mul-tiple lines of resolution, the tortuous unfolding contrived to discourage early and punish easy closure, the sense of mystery left when all has been said and done, together with the sense of community with the dramatized interpreters, who have nothing but externals to go upon in their dealings with fellow humans: these make the reading of character by indirections a paradigm as well as a crux of biblical strategy. The approximation to real-life conditions of inference from opaque surfaces can hardly go any further.

Of all externals, however, old age and good looks form the exemplar of exemplars. For one thing, both strike a perfect balance between the rationales of sense-making. As happens even in the best marriages, that balance is elsewhere disturbed on either side. Thus, that the exterior opposition strong/weak metonymically connotes or translates into the interior opposition bad/good marks an imbalance in favor of the theocentric ideology, especially since the key includes the counterrealistic plot opposition unsuccessful/successful as effect and evidence. A corresponding imbalance in favor of aesthetics manifests itself in an opposition like barren/fertile, kept morally neutral and hence free for attribution in the interests of vivid portrayal and drama. Looks and age alone take a middle course between the Scylla of univocality and the Charybdis of untrammeled ambiguity. Anchored in natural probabilities either way, they can align ideology's clamor for instructive wonder with aesthetics' yearning for realism and free play. Unpredictably shifting the surface–depth relations back and forth from the pole of harmony to that of conflict, they also mediate between the one's insistence on pregnant and the other's on individual characterization.

For another thing, the two features make natural complements. While sharing the status of double-edged metonymies for personality, each yet attaches to a different extreme of the life span: the Bible, alas, reserves good looks for the young. This variety enables the narrator to apply the same two-faced portraiture to characters of any age, not excluding the same character as his life unrolls. It is no accident that David comes on the public stage only to be despised by Goliath for his good looks (1 Samuel 17) and exits with a painful lesson to all, notably the handsome Adonijah, who have written him off as a dotard (1 Kings 1).

Moreover, since old age often goes with failing sight, the two properties are also naturally associated with two complementary sides of *vision*, the good-looker serving as the object or focus of observation and the aged as the observing subject as well. "Do you *see* him whom the Lord has chosen?" Samuel asks the people as Saul's impressive figure comes into view. "And all the people shouted, Long live the king." Later, Goliath "*looked and saw* David and disdained him, for he was a youth, ruddy and good-looking." These contrasting inferences from and by the visual prove equally wrong, just like Joseph's when he "saw" his old father elevate the younger above the elder son. The seeing as well as the seen do not go below the surface. But while Saul and David are looked upon, Jacob also looks in turn, with the blind eyes of his own father yet with a clairvoyance that puts the human optic to new shame and gives the appearance-and-reality theme its crowning twist. In the context of old age, this paradox encapsulates the regulative opposition of human sight and divine *in*sight that God himself spells out in the context of good looks: "Man sees what meets the eye, but the Lord sees into the heart." Short of God-like privilege, it is only by the trial and error of experience, enformed in the plot, that one can advance from the visible truth to the whole truth about the mystery of man.

· 11 ·

THE STRUCTURE OF REPETITION: STRATEGIES OF INFORMATIONAL REDUNDANCY[1]

One thing has God spoken; two have I heard.
Psalm 62:12

Everything that I command you you shall be careful to do:
thou shalt not add to it nor take away from it.
Deuteronomy 13:1

Similarity Patterns and the Structure of Repetition

The way of repetition seems to clash with one biblical principle we have been tracing and to fall under another. In its aspect as superfluity, it will not easily cohere with the dominant logic of gapping. How does loquacity go with reticence, overtreatment with undertreatment? In its aspect as recurrence, on the other hand, it will no more easily escape assimilation to analogy. Still, one of the main aims of this chapter is to demonstrate the interplay of these three structural logics: how repetition forms a whole with elision and more than a part within similitude.

To begin with the latter, biblical narrative certainly abounds in patterns of similarity, all based on the principle of analogy.[2] Analogy is an essentially spatial pattern, composed of at least two elements (two characters, events, strands of action, etc.) between which there is at least one point of similarity and one of dissimilarity: the similarity affords the basis for the spatial linkage and confrontation of the analogical elements, whereas the dissimilarity makes for their mutual illumination, qualification, or simply concretization. In several respects, however, the Bible's similarity patterns do not essentially vary, in form or function, from their counterparts elsewhere. In its art, for instance, they manifest themselves on all the levels (and combinations of levels):

1. On the levels of sound and linguistic sense, similarity patterns verbal units into or according to such relations as verbatim

equivalence ("Abraham, Abraham!" in the Binding of Isaac, the root "bless" in the Wooing of Rebekah), synonymity ("man of God" = "seer" = "prophet"), antonymity ("older" and "younger" in fraternal struggles), homonymity (*nabi* in Saul's first encounter with Samuel), syntactic parallelism (the wrangling of the prostitutes in Solomon's Judgment), etc.

2. On the level of plot, it assumes the form of equivalences and contrasts between events, characters, and situations (Ishmael's and Isaac's ordeals, Deborah and Barak, anointment scenes).
3. On the thematic level, it consists in more abstract linkages: variations on a theme, like the younger brother's ascendancy.
4. On the generic level, it ties together the pieces of verse (e.g., Hannah's song at the beginning and David's at the end of Samuel) set into a prose frame or contrasts the straight rendering of an event to its rehearsal as parable (e.g., Jotham's on Abimelech and Shechem), and so forth.

This multilevel recourse to the principle of analogy is integral but not peculiar to biblical composition, even against the background of ancient literature. So are most of the other biblical features and practices along this dimension. Examples would be the size of the analogized units (from a sound to a plot strand), the textual distance that separates them (from immediate juxtaposition to book-length chiasm), the equivalence relations between them (straight and contrastive, static and dynamic), or the roles served by their suprasequential patterning (unity, emphasis, expectancy, mutual illumination, play of viewpoints, thematic or persuasive generalization).

But though the differences revealed by such a comparison are quantitative and variable rather than qualitative, their cumulative weight is yet significant. As regards the textual levels, for instance, consider the generic linkages and tensions just noted. They do have equivalents throughout the history of narrative, whether the Icelandic saga's distribution of complex bits of poetry along its prosaic sequence or the sobering digressions in Fielding's comic novels. Still, these equivalents are neither frequent nor orderly enough to weaken the distinctive force of the Bible's generic shifts and counterpoints. This is also true of the aesthetic perceptibility and relevance of the similarity patterns on the various levels. On the level of sound, for example, poetry radically differs from prose. Poetry is marked by a systematic organization of sound elements, quantitative (notably meter) and/or qualitative (rhyme, orchestration). In prose, even where we come across such patterns, their relevance is as a rule incomparably lower, because they are sporadic and our attention focuses on the larger units of sense.[3] In this respect, too, the Bible diverges from the rule of prose narrative, and along more than one axis: miniature proportions, intercalation of verse segments, and an intensive working of the features and potentialities of language.

This holds even truer for the mode of equivalence or overlapping between the analogical components—above all, within what I shall term *the structure of repetition*. Every pattern of similarity is by definition based on the recurrence of at least one element—a sound, semantic feature, word, situation, theme, generic quality—that serves to link together the components of the pattern. In the Bible, however, this necessary similarity is often carried to a high degree of equivalence in form and meaning. In the "book of the generations of Adam," for example, each item in the list derives from the productive pattern "X lived a years and begot Y; and after he begot Y, X lived b years and begot sons and daughters; and all the days of X were $a + b$ years, and he died" (Genesis 5). Later, the same principle generates the three wife-sister tales, their analogy so close as to produce on many the impression of variants of a single myth. Numbers deploys a series of twelve identical offerings made by the leaders of the tribes (7:10–88). And these are only a few extreme instances of the protean principle of analogy that we have encountered everywhere: whether in the form of echoes, allusions, verbal chains, parallels, catalogues, or serializations. But nowhere is similarity pressed to such an extreme of redundancy as in the structure of repetition. For this structure consists in the repetition not of elements designed to link larger units but of those large units themselves; not in setting up points of contact between events that remain discrete even at their most equivalent—as do the affairs where a wife is passed off as a sister by different patriarchs or at different times—but in what comes close to a repeated account of the very same event. We first observe how Abraham's servant acts and then how he reports his action to Rebekah's family; we first learn of Pharaoh's dream from the narrator and then from Pharaoh himself; we first have the dialogue between Ahab and Naboth and then Ahab's retelling of the scene to Jezebel.

For the moment, this will suffice to indicate the special problematics of the structure of repetition compared with more familiar patterns of similarity in literature. Standard patterning by analogy raises a *combinatory* question in the reader's mind. Why has the text established such a network of parallels and oppositions as to couple the apparently dissimilar (David and Abimelech, say, or Eglon and the short sword), to disjoin the apparently similar (Laban and Rebekah), and/or to elaborate symmetries that (as with the wife-sister plots) already inhere in the materials themselves? Here neither of the analogized units is redundant, because their similarity stops well short of identity—unless, ascending to a higher level of abstraction, we say that Abraham and Isaac underwent "the same marital trial."

With the structure of repetition, however, the same material (event or utterance) recurs in a straightforward rather than thematic sense. And since its recurrence therefore incurs redundancy, the question it poses is primarily *selectional*. As the "second" occurrence seems to add nothing to the "first," what is it doing in the text and why have they been collocated by way of analogy?

Formulaic Convention or Functional Principle?

The rabbinic tradition of exegesis has always been sensitive to biblical redundancy, and not in legal contexts alone. The sages themselves focused on overlaps within the units of the phrase and the sentence. Their medieval followers (notably Don Isaac Abravanel) and more recent traditionalists (like Nehama Leibowitz) often scrutinize the larger blocks of narrative as well. For all their insight and ingenuity, however, such ad hoc comments hardly amount to a reasoned analysis of the structural and hermeneutic operations involved. They do not even come to grips with the fundamental problem that stands in the way of any treatment of specific cases of repetition: Does this technique at all signify as a functional principle and interpretive guideline?

Repetition is not peculiar to literary discourse, and the theory of communication has long been grappling with the concept of redundancy.[4] Human communication is subject to all kinds of "noise" that interfere with the exchange of messages, from external disturbances in the conditions or channel of discourse through mispronunciation to excitement or absence of mind. Hence the need for redundancy as a counterbalance designed to ensure a full and unambiguous reception of the message. Some redundancy already inheres in the structure and conventions of language—syntactic rules, word order, ready-made phrases—that impose constraints on the speaker and proportionally heighten the predictability and followability of his utterance to the receiver's advantage. The prior information encoded in the language system, moreover, usually goes with material redundancy in the makeup of the discourse itself.[5] In conversation, for instance, far more than the bare minimum gets said. We reformulate previous statements; we clarify, emphasize, sum up—in short, we "repeat ourselves."

Yet any comprehensive theory would do well to approach the problem in a comparative light. For the nature and status of informational redundancy vary from one communicative framework to another, notably from speech to writing and from ordinary to literary discourse. Since the literary text is characterized by rigorous selection and arrangement, with corresponding demands on attention, the dismissal of its redundancies in terms of "noise" is the reader's last rather than first resort. After all, the general presumption of coherence applies to redundancy no less than to any other literary feature, dissonance, or incongruity. Even what would count in ordinary discourse as an instance of noise transforms here into a simulation or mimesis of noise. The chances therefore are that this redundancy, too, is deliberate and functional—in fact, no redundancy at all. The text has devised a redundancy on some level with an eye to a definite effect; that is, in order to impel the reader to transfer it to another level (pattern, context, framework) where it will duly fall into place. Disturbance, shifting, synthesis: this is the course taken by the interpretive process launched by redundancy from emergence to elimination.

These general assumptions and expectancies gain special force in biblical narrative. And their force does not at all turn on the rabbinic belief in the text's divine origin and hence perfection, a belief that, right or wrong, has been of service as an incentive to close reading. We can leave dogmatics on one side and consider the empirical evidence. Take the striking frequency and diversity of the Bible's variations in repetition. Far from enhancing, these diminish predictability and thus go against the very *raison d'être* of redundancy in ordinary communication. But it is exactly this offense against the workaday norm that increases the probability of their having a different and covert role to fulfill. From a broader viewpoint, neither the reticence of biblical narrative, nor the ubiquity of informational gaps, nor the miniature scale, nor the reign of economy, nor the combinatory artfulness, nor the demand for alertness—none of these accords with a wasteful handling of the structure of repetition. Hence a prima facie case, even better than usual, for a functional approach.

Such a line of argument would, however, meet with a challenge from a persistent tradition of biblical commentary, no less ancient and certainly more vocal than the opposite party originating in the sages. Of its many voices, consider first three discerning exegetes, two (Abraham Ibn Ezra and Radak) medieval and one (Umberto Cassuto) modern:

> Said Abraham the author: the practice of the speakers of the Holy Language is at times to explain their discourse thoroughly and at times to say whatever necessary in brief, so that the hearer will be able to understand their meaning. And you should know that words are like bodies and meanings are like souls, and the body is like a vehicle for the soul. The practice of learned men in all languages, therefore, is to preserve the meanings without worrying about the change of words, since they are equivalent in meaning. Let me give you some examples. God said to Cain: "Thou art cursed from the soil; when thou tillest the soil, it shall no longer give up its strength to thee. A restless wanderer

shalt thou be on the land." And Cain said: "Thou hast driven me today
from the face of the earth." Who is so senseless to think that the meaning
is not equivalent because the words have changed? And then Eliezer
[the Wooing Servant] said, "Pray give me a little water," and he said,
"I said to her, Pray give me to drink." . . . The rule is that in everything
repeated, like Pharaoh's and Nebuchadnezzar's dreams and many others,
you will find different words, but equivalent meaning. (Ibn Ezra on
Exod 20:1)

The truth is that he [Abraham's servant] laid before them [the relatives]
all the things as they happened, and we cannot give meaning to all the
numerous omissions and fullnesses. . . . And when these things get
repeated, there occurs a change of words but the meaning is one, for
such is Scripture's way with repetition: it preserves the meanings but
not the words. Indeed, even when Deuteronomy repeats the Ten Commandments, the fundamentals of the Torah, it changes their words but
the meaning is one. (Radak on Gen 24:39)

The epic poetry of Ugarit, like all epic poetry, Eastern or Western,
evinces a love of repetition. The listeners are very pleased when the singer
begins a familiar and favorite section; they find it easier then to follow
the singer and, as it were, to participate in his telling or song. It is common in the epic, therefore, that whole sections should repeat themselves.
Though a general phenomenon, not peculiar to Canaanite epic, it still
seems to me worth attending to. For we have already discovered that
the Bible's narrative prose continues in some ways the tradition of
Canaanite epic. So if we also find in it epic-like repetitions, we may
conclude that in this matter, too, it is the tradition of Canaanite epic
that is at work. . . .
    Usually, when the subject is not so technical as in the work of the
Tabernacle and does not require great exactitude of detail, the repetitions in prose are not word-for-word equivalents. Prose is designed for
reading more than for listening, and the reader does not have the listener's craving for what he already knows by heart. On the contrary,
exact repetition may sometimes be burdensome to him. When reverting to a given subject, therefore, prose is inclined to modify the expressions or abbreviate them or change their order, with artistic skill. The
principle of repetition, however, remains in force. . . .
    An interesting example of a subject repeated four times, with varia-
tions, occurs in Genesis 24, in the story of Abraham's senior servant
and his meeting with Rebekah. It is first narrated how the servant prayed
to God for a sign (verses 12–14), then how the sign was given him (verses
17–21), then how he told Rebekah's family about his prayer (verses 42–44)
and the given sign (verses 45– 46). A similar case is the story of Pharaoh's
dreams.[6]

Common to all these statements, ancient or modern, is the reduction of
the technique to normative rule: the rule of language as such ("the practice of learned men in all languages"), of Hebrew ("the practice of the

speakers of the Holy Language"), of the Bible ("Scripture's way"), or of the tradition of Canaanite epic to which the Bible supposedly belongs. Not that the explanations offered are identical either in their factual grounds or in their scope and bearing. Ibn Ezra and Radak are mainly concerned to account for the changes that take place in recurrence: with this in view they devise a punning link between the two words (*lishnot*→*leshanot*) to fortify their claim that repetition simply goes with variation. Cassuto, on the other hand, accounts for the repetitions in terms of epic rule and for the variations in terms of the difference between written and oral literature. Further, Ibn Ezra and Radak fail to assign to the convention any role whatsoever, not even one so automatic and generalized as the accession of pleasure invoked by Cassuto. (Nor for that matter any practical service, as do those approaches to ancient narrative that appeal in effect to something like the theory of "noise" in ordinary discourse. They would explain the repetitions not as a choice made to indulge the taste of the contemporary audience but as an exigency born of the disorderly conditions in which oral literature was performed.[7])

Still, each of the three nullifies in advance the semantic import of biblical repetition and variation on the strength of two associated premises. They all assume that words stand to meanings as "body" to "soul," so that meaning remains constant under verbal variation. And they also postulate a dictatorial, mechanical, and flattening convention of redundancy—linguistic or literary, atemporal or historical, general or generic.

Such doctrines, moreover, do not govern exegetical practice alone. At least two ancient sources reflect their influence on the formation and ramification of the biblical text itself: the Samaritan Pentateuch and the Septuagint. Nowhere does the Samaritan version's rage for harmony and explicitness show so clearly as in its handling of the structure of repetition. Here this policy assumes the form of what I would call *fore*smoothing and/or *back*smoothing, both operating to resolve clashes and variations into correspondence.

Thus, we only have to open our Bibles to see that the Masoretic Text may show a character referring back to an event or speech that has not been previously rendered at all. In contrast, the Samaritan version will make a point of inserting the original occurrence in its proper chronological position. If Jacob tells his wives a dream in Genesis 31, then by the process of backsmoothing the dream will be enacted in the chapter that precedes its narration. The Plagues of Egypt are especially notable for their diversity of closure (and also for the equivalent that the Samaritan recension finds in the Exodus scroll discovered at Qumran[8]). Here this law operates on the series to fill out the tripartite causal scheme leading from God's message to Pharaoh through Moses' delivery of the message to the fulfillment of the prediction. Sometimes the breaches are closed by way of backsmoothing, as in the plague of locusts or the slaying of the firstborn. The Masoretic Text starts the episode with Moses thundering at Pharaoh; the Samaritan, with God's dictation of the speech to Moses. Elsewhere foresmoothing comes into demand: the Masoretic Text jumps from God's threat to inflict blood or frogs on Egypt to the infliction, while the Samaritan pedantically fills in the intermediate stage of the threat announced to the king. Likewise, where an incident or utterance in the Masoretic Text recurs with variations, the Samaritan may impose harmony by casting the two occurrences in the same mold. In the Ten Commandments themselves, the notorious disparity between "Remember the sabbath day" (Exod 20:8) and "Observe the sabbath day" (Deut 5:12) does not at all trouble the Samaritan recension, which cuts the knot by reading "Observe" in both places. And if here the smoothing goes in one direction, i.e. backward, then the harmonization of the Israelite wanderings in Numbers with Moses' retrospective survey in Deuteronomy shows a constant two-way traffic.

The Septuagint follows a kindred policy. Delilah having moaned over the lies that Samson fed her and reiterated her question about how he might be bound, the Masoretic Text proceeds:

> He said to her, If thou weavest the seven locks of my hair with the web. She made them tight with the pin and said to him, The Philistines are upon thee, Samson! And he awoke from his sleep and pulled away the pin, the loom, and the web. (Judg 16:13-14)

But the Septuagint will not tolerate such an elliptic narrative, however easily the missing bits may be supplied in reading. So it fills out Samson's reply by drawing both upon his words in previous rounds and Delilah's next move, and then goes on to round out Delilah's action as well in conformity with Samson's present avowal and his future reaction on awakening. The multiple closure yields the smoothest progression:

> He said to her, If you weave the seven locks of my hair with the web and make it tight with the pin, then I shall become weak, and be like any other man. So while he slept, Delilah took the seven locks of his head and wove them into the web. And she made them tight with the pin and said to him, The Philistines are upon you, Samson! But he awoke from his sleep, and pulled away the pin, the loom, and the web.

This translation of the Greek comes from the Revised Standard Version, but I could have quoted from any number of others. Like modern scholarship in general, translators incline to the fullness of the Greek (even though the two great uncials themselves offer variant readings here) on the grounds that the Masoretic Text has lost the intervening parts by haplography. The spirit of the Septuagint is very much alive in scholarly dealings with repetition.

Concerning poetics and interpretation, then, such tendencies lead to much the same result as the dismissive references of Ibn Ezra, Radak, or Cassuto to the variations along the story of Pharaoh's Dream or Rebekah's Wooing. Take the claim that there is in fact no disagreement between the narrator's and the servant's ordering of the presentation of gifts to the bride and the inquiry about her descent:

> If he found out that the girl who had given him and his camels to drink was of another family, he would leave her without any loss, since "He said, Whose daughter art thou?" means 'He had said before giving her anything.' So indeed he told [her relatives]: "I asked her and I put the ring" (Ibn Ezra ad loc.).

> "He took": in order to give her after having asked whose daughter she was, and if it turned out that she was of Abraham's family, to make the gift. And so it appears in his narration of the event, that he first asked her and then gave her. (Radak)

This is a clear instance of backsmoothing. There emerges an "undesirable" incongruity between the occurrence itself and its reporting after the fact. And since the lucidity of the report disallows foresmoothing, it remains to backsmooth the occurrence itself in its light. Only what the commentators do by explaining away the points of variance is carried to its logical conclusion in the earliest stage of the same tradition by editing them out (a practice that many biblicists would and do applaud,[9] with the possible exception of Cassuto, who might view it as a throwback to the simple harmonies of oral literature). Insofar as the Samaritan and Septuagint readings follow a version independent of the Masoretic, they establish a poetics of their own, whose compulsive tidiness bespeaks a form of narrative neurosis. Insofar as they are superimposed on the Masoretic, they betray the same neurosis by way of embodied interpretation. Either way, their antiquity must count for something.

A tradition extending from the Second Temple era through the Middle Ages to the present day would thus stamp the Bible's structure of repetition as a formulaic scheme, with no room for play and meaning. The grounds adduced or presupposed may vary: the corruption of the source, the conventions of discourse, the pressures or pleasures of oral delivery, even the generic assimilation to nothing less than children's literature.[10] But the operational consequences remain much the same. Unwelcome, if not naive, as this approach may look to those impatient to get on with the business of close reading, it is too much in evidence to be dismissed out of hand and too resilient to be easily quashed. The lines of attack that immediately suggest themselves prove less than conclusive on reflection.

One is to centralize all those instances where even the most determined levelers make contextual sense of repetition or abstain from smoothing away variation.[11] This will bring to light not so much their inconsistency, which by itself settles nothing, as the constraints that pressed for such departures from the official rule. But the argument from inconsistency, however revealing, does not yet cover the whole ground. Another possibility is to analyze a number of specific instances with a view to extrapolating the functions of redundancy and the uses of variation. In what follows we shall appeal to this method, too, but to put too much weight on it would be to beg the major question. However impressive the sense made and the regularities brought out in analysis, the very legitimacy of the reading operations that yield them remains questionable in view of the formulaic alternative. Insofar as the body-soul relationship between form and meaning may conceivably govern the Bible, any quest for more artful and flexible transactions will be vulnerable to charges of anachronism.

There is nothing for it but to take the bull by the horns: to start by reconstructing from internal evidence the norm of repetition that underlies biblical narrative. This makes the logical starting point because it escapes the circularity threatening the oblique avenues; it alone offers a chance of clear-cut decision between the opposed frames of intelligibility. But this is also a more promising line than may seem at first glance. For all the champions of minimalism—versions, translations, commentaries, source criticism—inevitably betray a fatal flaw. Those committed to the schematism of the repetition structure—like the Septuagint, the Samaritan Pentateuch, and their scholarly following—leave unanswered the question why so many variations remain in the Bible even according to their philosophy. Whereas those who build variation into the system—like Ibn Ezra, Radak, or Cassuto—leave unanswered the question why so many exact repetitions have slipped through. This double hole urges afresh the need to inquire whether the invocation of ancient rule carries more than declaratory weight. And whatever the findings, the inquiry will afford us the best opportunity we have had as yet in this book of reconstructions to conduct a full-scale search for the poetics of an art retrievable mainly from its practice.

What, then, are the features of the biblical structure of repetition as compared with its relatives, ancient and modern? Are these features constant? As constant as their equivalents elsewhere? Constant to the point of rigid formulaicness? Or are they variables? And if so, in what do they vary and is their variability so free as to follow no preconceived scheme whatsoever? With these questions in mind, we shall initially concentrate on formal aspects—as distinct from semantic and rhetorical effects—in order to avoid the whirlpool of circularity.

Constant and Variable Factors

Neither literary nor biblical study has developed the tools required even for a formal analysis and typology of repetition structures. So, having started by delimiting this from related principles of composition, we now have to make a further step toward a theory of redundancy by anatomizing the delimited area. I shall suggest how its forms and features may be discriminated, their flexibility within various periods or genres or models traced, and both regularities and divergences explained. Fortunately, the Bible's poetics of repetition is so versatile that there is no need here for more than occasional glances in other directions to round out the theoretical picture. The variables of one corpus may become the constants of another, but the factors themselves retain their centrality.

Formally speaking, the biblical structure of repetition exhibits five more or less constant features:

1. Referential bearing: The plot of repetition in world and discourse
The members of the structure assume a representational character. What they have to tell (and retell) bears directly on the narrated world: as distinct from all other textual levels (which would benefit from the recurrence of a sound pattern, a verbal figure, a thematic comment, a generic paradigm) but also from the narrative situation in and through which the world unfolds (like recurrent self-references on the narrator's part, such as "I don't know" in Ford Madox Ford's *The Good Soldier*). Their field of reference is even more determinate than that. For these repetitional units generally yield not descriptions of a certain state of affairs (as does, exceptionally, the fourfold statement "In those days there was no king in Israel" in Judges), but full-fledged occurrences that affect the overall course of the action. Furthermore, it is not only the event told about but also its telling and retelling within the biblical world—i.e. by a character—that plays this active role in the dynamics of the action: the servant's retelling of the encounter with Rebekah to the family makes a causal link no less important than the original encounter itself.

The referential-dynamic orientation just outlined in an ascending order is anything but inevitable or, in literary practice, standard. Typological value apart, however, does it not neutralize the significance of the repetitional members? Once they fall into a causal chain, the tightness of the ensuing synthesis might appear to do away with the redundancy, since the repetition then serves a plot function. This is what Cassuto in effect argues (inconsistently, by the way) when the plan of the Flood, "The Lord said, I will blot out man whom I have created from the face of the earth, man and beast and creeping things and birds of the air, for I repent that I have made them" (Gen 6:7), recurs in God's address to Noah, "I have decided to make an end of all flesh, for the earth is filled with violence because of them, and behold, I will destroy them with the earth" (6:13). Actually, Cassuto says, "this is not an unnecessary repetition of vi 7; there the Bible tells us of God's decision, and here of its announcement to Noah."[12] But such reasoning mixes up redundancy within the narrated world and redundancy within the narrative discourse confronted by the reader. Within the world, the dramatic auditors (Noah, say, or Rebekah's family) may of course stand in need of the entire report, which for them contains new rather than repetitive information. Within the text, however, this news is by then ancient history; and the fulfillment of the plot function accordingly requires no more than a summary formula like "he heard all these things" or "he did so"—which indeed sometimes do duty for the whole retelling. So the question remains why the Bible does not always take this shortcut but sees fit to re-detail "all these things" or the "so" or even to concatenate summary and re-detailing. The causal movement lessens rather than lifts the pressures of repetition.

2. Filling and constitution

The biblical structure of repetition woven into this plot dynamics is composed of no less than two of the three following types of member:

　　i. *the member of forecast* (command, prophecy, scenario), defined in terms of expectation about the narrative future: God resolves to strike or deliver; David plots Uriah's murder; Abraham instructs his steward to negotiate for a Mesopotamian bride;

　　ii. *the member of enactment* (performance, realization, or, rarely, state of affairs), which focuses on the narrative present and may causally derive from (i), as Uriah's murder does from David's orders, and/or lead to:

　　iii. *the member of report* (about "forecast" or "enactment"), defined of course in terms of retrospection on the narrative past: the prophet conveys God's decree to a sinner; the messenger breaks the news about the war to David; the steward transmits Abraham's proposal to his kinsmen. When the report itself opens a prospect of further action, as clearly in the last example, it serves at the same time to sharpen or diversify expectation about the future.

The whole chapter will reveal what varied and subtle permutations a combinatory art like the Bible's can wring from these members. At this stage, the rough outline will suffice to bring out five additional characteristics.

First, the biblical member of forecast generates expectations (though, as I have shown again and again since the analysis of Rebekah's Wooing, not perforce the same expectations) in both characters and reader. Both receive or entertain it, one directly and within the world itself and the other through the narrator who quotes the forecast in his text: both accordingly visualize the future at the same time. This is a distinctive feature, since nothing prescribes such a coincidence of dramatic and reading anticipation. Each by itself suffices to establish a forecast. On the one hand, the expectation may remain the exclusive privilege (or torment) of the reader, to whom the narrator opens the future behind the backs of the unenlightened dramatis personae: as when Nabokov in *Laughter in the Dark* greets us with a plot synopsis that covers the hero's whole change of fortune. (This is the way the Bible itself manipulates its indirect foreshadowings— through analogies, paradigms, proleptic epithets, formal expositions— but not the explicit forecasts within repetition.) Alternatively, the narrator may reverse privilege and hence irony by temporarily withholding the vision of things to come that an agent forms or communicates to another: only in retrospect does the reader of *Njal's Saga* discover Njal's foreknowledge of his trial by fire. Rejecting both one-sided or "elevating" options, however, the Bible's structure of repetition prefers a two-level forecast, usually with two simultaneous addressees. This choice partly derives from general poetic norms: the multifunctional use of materials, the fair play between the interpreters within and without, the keeping of intrusion to a minimum. Yet other reasons specifically concern the poetics of repetition. The first "elevating" option would go against the tendency to assimilate the members to the plot; the second, against the tendency (see [3] below) to arrange them in chronological sequence.

Nor, second, is there anything self-evident about the biblical rule of combining members that are variant in their temporal direction—let alone opposed, like prospects and retrospects. The refrain in poetry follows no such rule of direction; nor does narrative, ancient or modern. In the Sumerian work "The Scribe and His Perverse Son," for example, the whole structure of repetition consists in two members of forecast: the father issues a series of commands and then, to make sure they were taken in, has the youth repeat them.[13] The *Odyssey,* conversely, evokes Agamemnon's murder no fewer than five times, but only by way of report after the fact: Zeus's, Athena's, Nestor's, Menelaus's, Agamemnon's own. Empirically as well as logically, then, the requirement for a structure of repetition is minimal:

the occurrence of two members, even of the same type. The Bible raises the threshold to two members of different types.

Third, such filling and constitution go on to tighten the links between the members even beyond the point indicated by their referential bearing. They not only coexist in the same framework and dynamize the same plot but also enter into causal and expectational patterns among themselves. A divine forecast guarantees, and a human one at least envisages, actional fulfillment. Here biblical composition differs again from the *Odyssey*'s harping on Agamemnon's murder. Each of these five reports is woven into the world of the epic—motivated by a dialogue scene where some character looks back on the past—but their effect on the action is negligible, to say nothing of their power to generate or even to anticipate one another.

Fourth, that the members differ in plot role and temporal direction already raises serious doubts about the formulaic view of biblical redundancy and variation—certainly far more serious doubts than homogeneous structures would warrant. Human nature and the pressures of existence being what they are, one does not have to be morbidly suspicious to predict (and detect) tensions between forecast and enactment or enactment and report.

Fifth, the frequency with which the member of enactment is heralded by a forecast or retold after the event, or both, also has typological significance. Like the other features, this tendency is not predetermined by life or art, nor is it routine literary practice. True, some premises of the biblical world have a bearing on the incidence of repetition—the activity of an all-powerful and interfering God or the need to communicate by messengers for reasons of decorum as well as technology[14]—but that bearing stops well short of dictatorship. After all, ancient literature often postulates worlds that are not dissimilar, and even the world of modernist writing abounds in predictions or schemes on the one hand and reports or gossip on the other—but without any corresponding effects on artistic design. These existential constraints and opportunities, that is, do not engender the same poetics in all that concerns the very appeal to repetition, still less the rate of its occurrence, and least of all specific traits like the filling and permutation of the members. The Bible's reality-model does not so much enforce as enable its compositional model; it answers rather than makes demands.

3. Order of presentation

The order in which the members appear usually reflects their chrono-logical sequence: planning before performance, decree before fulfillment, action before its reporting as a thing of the past. Far from being the rule in modern counterparts of the device, as it is in ancient literature, this correspondence between the orders of occurrence and presentation is not even habitual in the Bible itself. We have by now traced quite a range of chronological manipulation, in units extending from the sentence to the book. It leaps to the eye, therefore, that the structure of repetition alone shares with the proleptic epithet the privilege of something like immunity from temporal displacement. With the understandable exception of prophetic messages, it rarely happens that the utterance of a forecast or the occurrence of an event emerges only from a later scene of report. So much so that when the reader finds the natural order subverted, he is entitled to take it as a question mark about the reliability of the report or the reporting character. Given the unique norm, temporal comes to imply perspectival divergence.

Take the retrospect sprung on Joseph (and ourselves) by his brothers: "Thy father commanded before he died, saying, Thus shall you say to Joseph, Forgive, pray, the transgression of thy brothers and their sin, for they did evil to thee" (Gen 50:15-17). There has been no hint of such a deathbed prospection, nor indeed of Jacob's discovery of the crime for which he allegedly urges forgiveness. Taken together with the emphasis on the brothers' fear of revenge, therefore, their unsupported report makes sense as a desperate fabrication. So does the self-quotation of the Israelites panic-stricken at the approach of Pharaoh's chariotry, "Is not this what we said to thee in Egypt, Let us alone and we shall serve the Egyptians? Better for us to serve the Egyptians than to die in the wilderness" (Exod 14:12). Typically, the Samaritan Pentateuch backsmoothes the "elliptical" structure, dramatizing a scene of complaint in Egypt so as to pre-position the forecast in its "proper" chronological slot. The very same gap-filling operation assumes exegetical form in Ibn Ezra's claim (ad loc.) that the Israelites' original speech "is not given, but we know that this is what happened." How or why we are supposed to know, except by formulaic fiat, he unfortunately neglects to say. Cassuto, on the other hand, is driven to offer a "psychological" explanation for the Israelite retrospect[15]—thus impugning his own doctrine together with the reality of the invoked forecast and the motives of the invoker. Faced with an incongruity that threatens the very norm of mechanical repetition, in short, its exponents are caught between two evils. They must either maintain formulaic consistency by inventing an episode that will bring the incongruity under the preconceived norm, or sacrifice consistency to functional coherence by making the reporter himself invent the episode and thus assimilating the incongruity to his subjective viewpoint.

That the Bible invites the latter approach (and not just as a last resort) also emerges from another fact: it sometimes carries the question mark about the unbacked report beyond a permanent gap and the reader's sense-making beyond a plausible suspicion. The gap turns out to be temporary, and the hypothesis of unreliable retrospection, the simple truth. While fleeing from Jerusalem, David hears from Ziva that his master Mephibosheth has stayed behind, "for he said, Today the house of Israel will restore to me the kingdom of my father (2 Sam 16:3). True or false? Is the master the traitor or, as seems more likely, the servant? Our distrust of Ziva is vindicated after the quelling of the rebellion. Not only does Mephibosheth then give him the lie ("My lord the king, my servant deceived me. For thy servant said to him, Saddle an ass for me and I will ride on it and go with the king. For thy servant is lame. And he has slandered thy servant to my lord the king"). The narrator himself harks back to describe the man's loyal conduct throughout the period: "He had neither dressed his feet, nor trimmed his beard, nor washed his clothes, from the day the king left to the day he came back in peace" (2 Sam 19:25-31).

Again, the suspicious divergence from the time-line does not consist in withholding the contents of an earlier member—nobody will suspect the Tekoite woman of misrendering the plea that Joab "put in her mouth" (2 Sam 14:2-3), though his instructions come to light only in her address to the king—but in withholding the very existence of an earlier member. And the departure from chronology again coheres, in terms of perspective, with specific contextual indicators. Where these are too weak to undermine the character's reliability, indeed, the narrator may have to fall back on explicit discrediting. Given the credibility of prophetic utterance, for example, no wonder that as soon as the Bethel prophet startles his guest with the report "An angel spoke to me by the word of the Lord, saying, Bring him back with thee to thy house that he may eat bread and drink water," the narrator edges in the corrective aside "he lied to him" (1 Kgs 13:18).

4. The sources of presentation: Between objectivity
and subjectivity in point of view

The credibility of reports attended by temporal displacement, real (Ziva and his master) or apparent (Joseph and his brothers), brings us to a wider issue concerning the sources of presentation. Who supplies the information for what? Here, too, the Bible's structure of repetition adheres to a set of rules, all self-imposed and luminously opposed to the paradigms of modern narrative. First, the different members originate from (at least two) different sources of information. Second, at least one of the members ("the enactment") will come on the highest authority: that of the omniscient narrator himself. And third, if the additional member(s) derives from a character—who expresses it in a monologic or dialogic scene—then at least its expression will be vouched for by the narrator in his role as authoritative quoter.

As just indicated by the examples of fabricated repetition—and the same principle, we shall find, governs a spectrum of less drastic cases—this does not at all mean that all members are consonant and reliable. On the contrary, the heterogeneity of sources joins with the heterogeneity of fillings to sharpen our expectations of dissonance. The point is rather that these three rules operate to bring the structure, dissonances and all, under objective control. And this reveals anew, in small compass, where the ways parted in the history of narrative.

The question concerns the limits of ambiguity. A modernist like Joyce or Robbe-Grillet will go so far as to throw into doubt the very occurrence of an act of speech or communication (hence the frequent blur between real and imaginary dialogue); whereas the Bible will draw the line at ambiguating the message conveyed by the speaker. Given the narrator's word ("He said: . . .") for it, the character's speech-event assumes factual status; but are the statements that the character makes (or reports) true, wholly true, nothing but true? This is precisely why the generation of more radical indeterminacy requires special measures and indices—like chronological deviance in repetition, which deprives the alleged speech-event of narratorial support and leaves its reporter to the mercy of context.

Moreover, a modern novel like Frisch's *Homo Faber* or Ford's *The Good Soldier* may restrict the reader throughout to the viewpoint of a fallible (if not mendacious) narrator-agent or, as in Faulkner's *Absalom, Absalom!*, trap us into such a maze of conflicting versions that we find it impossible to tell objective truth from subjective prism. In contrast, the Bible's structure of repetition conveys the truth about its essentials through the most authoritative source. Modernist writing, in other words, may show no interest in the truth as such or even dramatize its inaccessibility to humans; and therefore the member of "enactment" has no existence apart from the subjective "reports" from which both characters and reader attempt, often in vain, to reconstruct it. In the Bible, the very distinction between the members hinges on the differences in authority between the sources of information. When the narrator presents an event in his own name, we have "a member of enactment"; when a character presents it—and the narrator only quotes his presentation—we have "a member of report."

This manifests anew the strategic tendency to objectify reality that informs biblical narrative as a matter of principle, anchored in a definite world view and serving definite (epistemological, aesthetic, thematic, historical, rhetorical) ends. Like every other aspect we have considered, this structure of repetition maneuvers between the truth and the whole truth, establishing the one as an indispensable ("foolproof") safeguard and composing the other by an art of implication second to none. It would be a mistake, therefore, to evaluate it by reference to fashionable models and ideals of narrative. Its objectifying rules do not rule out a concern with personal motive and viewpoint, informational gaps, clashes of fact and invention, or the tangle of reliability. They only set a limit to the interplay of the certain and the dubious, the real and the imaginary, the external and the internal, the objective truth and its subjective reflections and refractions. Whatever the ambiguity of the parts, the whole must retain a determinate shape and sense.

5. *The formal boundaries of the structure*

Regarding its boundaries or range of deployment, this structure of repetition tends to concentrate its members within the unit of the episode, intermediate between the single scene with its spatiotemporal concreteness[16] and the historical or biographical cycle. The resultant continuity in terms of both text and plot has its exceptions. The prospective curse laid by Joshua on the man who will rebuild Jericho (Josh 6:26) does take effect to the last detail, but only a few books and centuries later, during Ahab's reign (1 Kgs 16:34). Still, the rule of episodic deployment suffices to mark biblical practice in two ways.

No book in the canon depends for its effect on such distributed repetition as the series of reports about Agamemnon's murder that punctuate the *Odyssey;* or in the "forecast → enactment" sequence, Gudrun's dream and its progressive fulfillment throughout *Laxdaela Saga;* or in the "enactment → report" sequence, the initial rendering of the crime and its progressive reconstruction by the detective in certain types of thriller, *Crime and Punishment* included. Nor does the Bible's structure of repetition show the same elasticity as its own forms of analogy, which may extend from a single verse to an entire book, as with the ring composition of Judges or Job. Of course, the two modes of construction are anything but mutually exclusive. Their family resemblance as similarity patterns has already been argued in my opening comments, and their interplay will soon appear in action. Yet I would hazard the generalization that the large role played by analogy in shaping the biblical book has its counterpart in the rhythm of repetition along the plot of the episode.

Looking back on these five constants, we note that they are all so marked and regular as to form a distinctive structure. On the other hand, for all its typological value, this systematicity is not to be confused with formulaicness. Not only does each constant tolerate or even encourage variations, but some actively raise doubts about the redundancy of the repetitions.

And the latter conclusion gains powerful support from the variable factors, of which I shall now outline four:

6. Combinatory latitude

This aspect of variety in unity is the obverse face of the constant that the Bible strings together at least two out of three possible types of member: forecast, enactment, and report. The combinatory constraint still leaves plenty of room for choice in regard to the identity, number, and linkage of the members available for combination. And the narrative indeed takes such advantage of this variability as to make it worth specifying.

The structure of repetition may issue from various dual choices out of the threefold option: *forecast* → *enactment* (as throughout the Creation story) or *enactment* → *report* (as in the movement of 1 Samuel 4 from Israel's defeat to the tidings brought to Eli). It may also combine all three types, and into different plot sequences. One basic sequence is *forecast* → *report* → *enactment* (the rhythm of the Ten Plagues of Egypt); another permutation is *forecast* → *enactment* → *report* (as in the tale of the Golden Calf, where Aaron asks for gold, the people supply it, and God denounces them to Moses). Each may even assume further complexity with the doubling or tripling of one of the members, most often the report. Consider repetition-within-repetition series like *enactment* → *first report* → *second report* (as when Potiphar's wife plays seducer and then, twice, accuser) or *forecast* → *report* → *report* → *report* → *enactment* (Pharaoh dreams → tells the magicians → tells Joseph → Joseph retells in interpretation → the famine comes) or *forecast* → *enactment* → *forecasted report* → *report* (David orders Uriah killed → Uriah is killed → Joab contrives a message for David → message transmitted).

All this assorted opting for elaboration argues against the theory of mechanical treatment. But so, even more powerfully if less obviously, does the opting for reduction. After all, each and every member of enactment can be paired with a report or yet more easily with a forecast, which does not require the staging of an additional scene but may appear as an inside view of the agent's plans. The frequency of repetition in the Bible, by modern standards, is liable to blind us to the fact that the narrator actually forgoes the device much more often than he employs it. And the weight of abstention confers perceptibility and significance on the favored minority.

7. Representational ratios

The Bible also goes further than any other corpus I know in varying the specificity of the different members. Sometimes they receive more or less uniform treatment: equally circumstantial (Jacob's proposal and Laban's implementation in Gen 30:31–36) or equally foreshortened ("The child died . . . and David perceived that the child was dead" in 2 Sam 12:18-19). Elsewhere the representation upsets the balance, possibly even to the point of eliding one of the members altogether and leaving its reconstruction to the interpreter. This happens throughout the Plagues of Egypt (not in the Samaritan telling, of course) or in a shorter example, where the prospect appears to the exclusion of its enactment: "He [Reuel] said to his daughters, And where is he? Why have you left the man? Call him that he may eat bread. And Moses was content to dwell with the man" (Exod 2:20-21).

Between the uniform and the exclusive treatment comes a spectrum of more moderate disproportions, some of them widely recurrent. At times, one member gains scenic foregrounding—as dramatized act or verbatim quotation—while another shrinks into a phrase or formula. In the *enactment → report* sequence, for example, the scene of Tamar's rape gives way to the bald summary "King David heard all these things" (2 Samuel 13); and in *forecast → enactment* pattern: "God said, Let the waters under the heavens be gathered into one place and let the dry land be seen. And it was so" (Gen 1:9). Here the summary takes the form of an anaphora ("these things," "so") that refers back to the opening member, but it may also appear as a selection *from* the opening member. Rebekah commands Jacob, "Go to the flock and take me from there two good kids." In enactment, however, the narrator repeats only the key verbs to produce the telegraphic "He went and took and brought to his mother" (Gen 27:9, 14).

The ratio of representation varies even further because of three unusual licenses. The telescoped member need not be the last (and hence apparently redundant) in the series, but may also lead the way. Joab's coaching of the Tekoite petitioner thus receives the most enigmatic summary, and her performance the most liberal dramatization (2 Samuel 14). Still more curious is the foreshortening whereby all the members become so gapped that none can be reconstituted except by appeal to its neighbors. In response to the census, God orders the prophet Gad: "Say to David, Thus says the Lord, Three things I hold over thee; choose one of them." But what are these "three" afflictions to be chosen among? The answer emerges only from the actual address to David, which ellipts the opening we already know from the forecast (and now have to fore-supplement) but fills in the message itself (which we now have to back-supplement into the original order): "Gad . . . said to him, Shall seven years of famine come to thee in thy land? Or shalt thou flee three months before thy foes and they pursue thee? Or shall there be three days' pestilence in thy land? Now consider and decide what answer I shall return to my sender" (2 Sam 24:11-13). In the Samson and Delilah affair, we recall, the Septuagint explicitly closes such gaps, its "neurosis" being intolerant of ellipsis.[17]

These two practices depart from the chronological norm that governs the plot of repetition, and accordingly invite explanation in terms of effects like suspense or surprise. But the third license overrides a far more widespread convention of well-formed narrative. The narrator often flaunts his contempt for mechanical repetition by interpolating his summary within the character's (forecaster's, reporter's) direct speech: "Hushai said to Zadok and Abiathar the priests, *Thus and thus* did Ahitophel counsel Absalom and the elders of Israel; and *thus and thus* have I counseled" (2 Sam 17:15).[18]

8. Generic modulation

Unlike most works, old and new, the Bible does not always maintain generic homogeneity in repetition. Side by side with its normal practice of casting all the members in the same (artistic, conceptual, verbal) register of narrative prose, we encounter an assortment of generic tensions. The sequence may collocate a "prosaic" and a "poetic" member, as with Sisera's defeat and Deborah's song of victory. It may likewise shift from a "realistic" to a "symbolic" member (from Abimelech's massacre to Jotham's parable) or vice versa (from Pharaoh's dream to its fulfillment); or even from a "realistic" to a "pseudo-realistic" but in fact "symbolic" counterpart (the Poor Man's Ewe-Lamb). On top of all this, discontinuities abound in the mainstream of repetition itself: between the narrator's writing and the characters' speech, between their own monologues and dialogues, between formal and colloquial style. The further one progresses along this list of uneasy couplings, the harder it becomes to dismiss the resultant variations in genre by appeal to mere variety.

9. Semantic correspondence

Reserving some further variables (notably the modes of divergence or the represented object) for later treatment, I now want to approach the heart of the matter: the semantic relations between the members. It is on this factor more than any other that the question of informational redundancy turns, that the whole formulaic platform stands or falls.

"When these things get repeated, there occurs a change of words but the meaning is one, for such is Scripture's way with repetition: it preserves the meanings but not the words": this claim, where Radak articulates what his tradition implies in practice, is theoretically dubious and empirically untenable. Theoretically dubious, because it presupposes such an extreme divorce of content from form as to see no obstacle to preserving the semantic equivalence ("the meanings") of the members while freely disturbing their verbal and structural equivalence ("the words"). To modern ears, no doubt, the argument that meaning remains constant under all formal variation sounds preposterous. As already indicated, however, this does not yet constitute sufficient grounds for dismissal, owing to the possible counterchange of circularity and anachronism: of the imposition of modern semantic doctrine on an ancient formulaic text. To clinch matters, therefore, the theoretical line needs validating in empirical terms, and this can be done from three converging directions.

To begin with, the degree of variability exhibited by the (purely formal and hence indisputable) factors discourages a monolithic view of the semantics of biblical repetition, whatever its legitimacy in ancient art elsewhere. Some of these factors—like the heterogeneity in temporal reference and viewpoint—even build semantic discordance into the pattern. Only in a world where all sources of information enjoy equal privileges, where neither God nor the narrator towers above the human agents, where every forecast comes true and every report is ideally accurate, where all accident, cross-purpose, wishful thinking, and existential pressure have disappeared—only in such an imaginary world, possible perhaps but certainly not biblical, can the iron law of semantic equivalence prevail in repetition.

Nor, finally, is this "Scripture's way with repetition." Here, in fact, the conventions of biblical poetry and prose strikingly diverge. In transition from one member to another, the versified structure of equivalence preserves the core of "the meanings" but not "the words"; whereas narrative repetition operates with far greater flexibility. Sometimes it preserves both the meanings and the words ("God said, Let there be light, and there was light"). Sometimes, as in the representational or generic variations cited, it alters the words but carries over much of the meaning. And sometimes it transforms the meaning as well, to an extent that must shake even dogmatic smoothers, conventionalizers and other beneficiaries of the narrative's foolproof composition:

> The Lord God commanded the man, saying, Of every tree of the garden thou mayest freely eat; but of the tree of the knowledge of good and evil thou shalt not eat, for on the day that thou eatest of it thou shalt die. . . . And [the serpent] said to the woman, Even though God said, You shall not eat of any tree of the garden . . . you will not die (Gen 2:16–17; 3:1–4)

> Sarah laughed to herself, saying, After I have withered, shall I have pleasure—and my husband old? Then the Lord said to Abraham, Why did Sarah laugh? . . . And Sarah denied, saying, I did not laugh, for she was afraid. And he said, No, but thou didst laugh. (Gen 18:12–15)

These are among the variant repetitions that even the Septuagint or the Samaritan dare not harmonize and that like-minded interpreters find it necessary to motivate. Radak himself could hardly number the addition or omission of the little word "not" among surface changes.[19] On the contrary, the words are patterned into formal symmetry only to dramatize the reversal of meaning: "thou wilt die" → "you will not die," "Sarah laughed" → "I did not laugh" → "No, but thou didst laugh." This applies with even greater force to the forecast → enactment sequence. No semantic theory can possibly relegate to the sphere of "words" the variation from God's order ("Speak to the rock") to Moses' performance ("struck the rock"), which barred the great leader's way into the land of Canaan. And once the possibility of semantic reversal in repetition is admitted, there is no stopping half-way. One must then recognize the principle of semantic variation in all its forms and degrees, from near-equivalence to head-on collision and mutual incompatibility.

Variations in makeup, particularity, genre, semantics: these build so much latitude and dissonance into the system, especially when taken together with the loopholes afforded by the constants, as to silence all talk of stereotypical or even typical handling. (Or in the terms introduced in chapter 7: both as plot and as analogy, repetition forms a system of *juxtaposed opposition*.) The more diverse the variables and the wider the range of choice, the more imperative the need to consider each instance of repetition in its own terms with a view to explaining how and why it has been put together—to making sense of its peculiar configuration of rule-governed and free elements. The question now confronting us is no longer whether the Bible's structure of repetition adheres to some formal scheme but whether its patterning manifests functional regularities: informing principles, determinate means–end combinations, or what I call strategies of informational redundancy.

Verbatim Repetition

In the absence of an overall binding norm, then, not even a single case of biblical repetition is self-explanatory. As with other aspects of storytelling, the range of available options invests each choice with significance against the background of rejected might-have-beens. Here, unlike the Gilgamesh epic for example, it is not the case that variant repetition gains a particular claim to notice as a stranger in the land of verbatim repetition. Instead, given the mandatory shift in, say, time and perspective, a structure exhibiting verbatim repetition needs to be accounted for no less than another that couples repetition with variation.

Nor does verbatim repetition itself play the same role within an utterance made by a single speaker as within a plot that unfolds a number of discrete utterances. In the former case, which lyrical poetry amply exemplifies, the recurrence of a unit (word, phrase, statement) along the sequence may operate in the interests of cohesion, enrichment or reversal of meaning, or the mimesis of disorderly speech and thought. Biblical narrative will also use such doubling for dramatic emphasis. Judah thus opens and concludes his refusal to go back to Egypt with a quotation of the Egyptian lord's warning "You shall not see my face, unless your brother is with you" (Gen 43:3, 5). This situational motivation likewise applies to utterances where the speaker underscores the point through synonymic rather than formal equivalents, as when Ruth overrides Naomi's dissuasion: "Press me not to leave thee, to turn back from following thee. For wherever thou goest I will go, and where thou lodgest I will lodge. Thy people are my people, and thy God my God. Where thou diest I will die, and there will I be buried. May the Lord do so to me and more also, if even death will part me from thee" (Ruth 1:16–17). Internal repetition of this type thus shows a diversity of form and function. But verbatim repetition within different speech-events, even where performed by the same speaker, raises problems of another order, because it entails a confrontation of different contexts of utterance. This sharpens our sense of a double incongruity: the superfluous presence of repetition and the curious absence of variation. Both redundancy and equivalence come to the fore with the decline of the situational logic, which can no longer assimilate them to the dramatized speaker's goals or speech patterns.[20] And if so, how come that different utterances and utterers say "the same thing"?

The answer varies from one context to another—for instance, according to the membership of the series. In the *forecast* → *enactment* sequence, verbatim repetition may serve as an indirect means of characterizing the giver or the addressee of an order or their relations. What makes Noah "a righteous man"? Why has he alone of his generation "found favor in the Lord's eyes"? These queries remain suspended till the Flood story closes the gaps by replicating the divine order in the favorite's execution. The fit between "Thou shalt come into the ark, thou and thy sons and thy wife and thy sons' wives with thee" and "Noah and his sons and his wife and his sons' wives with him came into the ark" (Gen 6:18; 7:7) is even tighter in the Hebrew original. Enacting and filling out what has so far been stated, it implies that Noah is so obedient that he even leads his family into the ark in God's order of reference. When the same agent utters the forecast and acts on it, however, this very form of doubling comes to perform a different function. The informational redundancy, italicized by the full equivalence between the members, no longer coheres in terms of interpersonal or theological relations; it rather has the effect of throwing light on the accomplished action and the actor. One could hardly ask for a more impressive example than "God said, Let there be light, and there was light." The structure of repetition does here duty for the explicit (and expensive) commentary by which the narrator sometimes drums up enthusiasm for a supernatural feat, e.g., "The Lord visited Sarah as he had said, and the Lord did to Sarah as he had spoken" (Gen 21:2). The laconism of order and fulfillment (suggesting "God need not exert himself to work wonders"), the textual continuity of the members ("Word became world without any delay"), and above all their perfect symmetry ("Vision actualized to the last detail") produce the tremendous rhetorical impact saluted by a professional like Longinus as early as the first century B.C.

In *enactment* → *report* series, on the other hand, the Bible often devises the correspondence to generate a favorable attitude to the reporting character. When Sarah complains to Abraham about Hagar—"Since she saw that she had conceived, I have become contemptible in her eyes"—the reader might suspect her of inventing a grievance to expel a dangerous rival. As part of the rhetoric of complication, therefore, the text prefaces this scene with an identical statement coming from the narrator himself, "Since she saw that she had conceived, her mistress became contemptible in her eyes." Sarah's ultimatum, however cruel, at least rests on the simple truth (Genesis 16). Apart from conferring factual or normative reliability on the speaker, this form serves to establish his insight and knowledge. Just as the equivalence within the creation of light celebrates God's omnipotence, so does the twin movement from "Cain was very angry and his countenance fell" to "'Why art thou angry and why has thy countenance fallen?'" bring out his omniscience, soon to be hammered home by irony at the expense of the optimistic fratricide. In this sequence too, then, the members cannot be omitted, shortened, or otherwise modified without detriment to the effect resulting from their confrontation. For the information that looks redundant within one framework (the rendering of the world) finds its coherence within another (the judgment of the world).

Finally, the strategies just traced appear even in the tradition of the novel. Take the stricture that the character sketch of Mr. Collins in chapter 15 of *Pride and Prejudice* is "superfluous"[21] because the reader could have deduced it himself from the action. In fact, this sketch operates within a covert structure of repetition. Two chapters earlier the Bennets received the first of Collins's epistolary gems, which elicited from them a range of typical inferences about the writer's nature and designs. Of the five sisters, Elizabeth alone finds the style pompous and the man ridiculous, an attitude voiced in the rhetorical question she addresses to her father: "Can he be a sensible man, sir?" Events soon vindicate her judgment and draw a flattering contrast to the erroneous impressions formed by others. But Jane Austen, concerned to establish her heroine's expertness in reading simple characters, is not satisfied with dramatic vindication. She offers a portrayal in her own name, opening with a complimentary allusion to

Elizabeth's insight: "Mr. Collins was not a sensible man." Despite certain differences from the Bible's structure of repetition—for example, concerning the limits and hence the perceptibility of the series—this follows the same principle. Troubled by the redundancy of the discourse within its immediate frame of reference (Collins's characterization), we integrate it with a more hidden pattern (Elizabeth's characterization) that fully exploits the verbal and semantic equivalence between the members.

Repetition with Variation: Forms and Functions of Deviance

Strictly speaking, even verbatim repetition falls short of reproduction. In a theoretical study that underlies this chapter's argument, I distinguished four types of ready-made or "bound" linguistic units according to the possibility of reproducing them in a text.[22] This possibility attaches only to the two types of unit that have acquired institutionalized status in the language system by virtue of the frequent collocation of their parts in discourse: the literal ("knife and fork") and the idiomatic ("turn an honest penny") stereotype. Being relatively context-free, both may appear in any number of environments without the least deviation from the norm. Two other types, however, have come to be bound not by sociolinguistic fiat but by a specific textual choice to fix certain words in a certain order. I refer to pieces of discourse whose cohesion results from their having occurred in an earlier text (allusive fixture) or earlier in the same text (internal fixture). Here every new use entails deviant use, every repetition a variation. For the original is rooted in its native ground—tone, genre, situation—so that even to reiterate it word for word is to uproot and transplant it. Given this shift in context, divergence can be adjusted (in form, extent, role) but not avoided.

The structure of repetition presents a special case of the internal (or intratextual) bound unit. In the Bible, the contextual variations between the members are not limited to position along the sequence—though even this minimum has its effect in a time-sensitive art—but extend to what I would call narrative transformation. These fall under two heads, each sharpening the sense of deviance produced by the other. One transformation consists in varying the member's reference and plot function within the dynamics of events (forecast, enactment, report); the second, in varying the coordinates of the speech-event (speaker, addressee, time, place) from which each member arises. Both kinds of shift mark and affect verbatim repetition—as in the examples from Noah, Cain, Sarah, or for that matter Elizabeth Bennet—no less than any other; and therefore verbatim repetition is not precise repetition. It is precise only in the sense that its members vary in contextual rather than physical (verbal, grammatical) features. Indeed, what demands an explanation is the oddity of physical similitude in contextual dissimilitude; and this is what the foregoing analysis began to supply.

Very often, however, the operations on context go with one or more forms of physical deviance in repetition:

1. *Expansion or addition*
The Lord God commanded the man, saying, of every tree of the garden thou mayest freely eat; but of the tree of the knowledge of good and evil thou shalt not eat, for on the day that thou eatest of it thou shalt die. . . . And the woman said to the serpent, Of the fruit of the trees of the garden we may eat, but of the fruit of the tree in the middle of the garden God said, You shall not eat of it *and you shall not touch it,* lest you die. (Gen 2:16-17; 3:2-3)

[Isaac to Esau:] Hunt game for me and prepare for me savoury food, such as I love, and bring it to me and I will eat, so that I may bless thee before I die. . . . And Rebekah said to her son Jacob, Behold, I heard thy father speak to thy brother Esau, saying, Bring game for me and prepare for me savoury food and I will eat, so that I may bless thee *before the Lord* before I die. (Gen 27:2-7)

2. *Truncation or ellipsis*
Pharaoh's daughter said [to the mother of Moses], Take this child away and nurse him for me, and *I will give thee thy wages.* And the woman took the child and nursed him. (Exod 2:9)

Eli said to Samuel, Go, lie down; and if he calls to thee, thou shalt say, Speak, *Lord,* for thy servant hears. And Samuel went and lay down in his place. And the Lord came and stood forth and called as at other times, Samuel, Samuel! And Samuel said, Speak, for thy servant hears. (1 Sam 3:9-10)

3. *Change of order*
Doeg the Edomite . . . said, I saw the son of Jesse coming to Nob, to Ahimelech the son of Ahitub; and *he inquired of the Lord for him and gave him provisions and gave him the sword of Goliath the Philistine.* And the king sent to call Ahimelech the priest . . . and said to him, Why have you conspired against me, thou and the son of Jesse, in that *thou gavest him bread and a sword and hast inquired of the Lord for him?* (1 Sam 22:9-13)

The messenger came again and said, Thus says Ben-hadad, I sent to thee, saying, Thou shalt give over *thy silver and thy gold, thy wives and thy sons.* . . . And the king of Israel called all the elders of the land and said, Mark, pray, and see how this man is seeking trouble, for he has sent to me for *my wives and my sons, my silver and my gold.* (1 Kgs 20:5-7).

4. *Grammatical transformation* (e.g., between active and passive)
The heaven and the earth and all their host *were finished.* And God *finished*
on the seventh day his work which he had done. (Gen 2:1–2)

The Amalekites had made a raid on the Negeb and on Ziklag. They
overcame Ziklag and *they burnt it with fire* and *they took captive* all the women
in it, both small and great. They killed no one, but carried them off
and went their way. And David and his men came to the city, and behold,
burnt with fire and their wives and sons and daughters *taken captive!* (1 Sam
30:1–3)

5. *Substitution*
Reuben returned to the pit, and behold, *Joseph was not* in the pit, and
he tore his clothes. And he returned to his brothers and said, *The child
is not* [there] and I, where shall I go? (Gen 37:29–30)

She [Potiphar's wife] called to the men of her house and spoke to them,
saying, Look, he has brought us *a Hebrew man* to play games with
us. . . . And she spoke to him [Potiphar] according to these words, saying, There came in to me *the Hebrew slave* that thou hast brought us to
play games with me. (Gen 31:14–17)

Beyond distinguishing contextual from physical variation and indicating
the Bible's favorite modes of effecting them, I see no point in developing
the argument along these lines. And a look at the categories just drawn
will suggest the reason. They expose once again the limited value of the
formal typologies that so often pass for the business of literary theory and
analysis. One must not expect much from the classification of modes of
divergence under the heads above or into still more inclusive terms like
syntagmatic (e.g., expansion, ellipsis, change of order), *paradigmatic* (lexical
substitution), and *contextual* (narrative transformations). Such a taxonomy
will doubtless reveal something: that the Bible operates with a far wider
range of variation than, say, Homer or the Gilgamesh epic; that it favors
some modes of deviance (like expansion, substitution, transformation) and
eschews others (like shift of meaning through homonymy); or that it is
more partial to some (like ellipsis) than to others (like change of order).
These findings afford us another perspective on the variables involved in
repetition and characterize the narrator's repertoire by separating practical from theoretical options. By themselves, however, they tell us very
little about the role fulfilled by variant repetition in biblical poetics or in
a specific narrative.

Take the five categories of variation illustrated above. However hard one
looks at the paired examples within each, no common denominator
emerges. Beyond the fact of expansion itself, what does Eve's addendum
"and you shall not touch it" (reflecting the speaker's attitude) have in

common with Rebekah's "before God" (designed to affect the addressee's attitude)? Beyond the fact of ellipsis in the passage from forecast to enactment, what links together the shortened recurrence of directives in (2): that of Pharaoh's daughter (with its ironic flick at the offer of wages to the mother) and that of Eli (with its insight into the novitiate's state)? What has Saul's change of order to do with Ahab's? And do the grammatical transformations make the same sense in the Creation and the Ziklag tales, or the shifts of referring term with Reuben and Potiphar's wife?

Moreover, the functional similarity conspicuous for its absence between these formal brothers in deviance may and does hold between formal strangers. Eve's addition thus bears a marked resemblance to Samuel's omission, for both betray the speaker's feelings (discontent and awe respectively). So does, in terms of one character's attempt to influence another, the syntagmatic operation of expanding Rebekah's address ("before God") to the paradigmatic measure of substituting "slave" for "man" in that of Potiphar's wife. And Reuben's substitution of "the child" for "Joseph" corresponds in perspectival role both to Samuel's timid ellipsis and to the change of order made by the furious Saul: each does duty for an inside view of the variant repeater.

It follows that the bearing and effect of variation can be determined only in context. This rule holds even for verbatim vis-à-vis frankly deviant repetition. That the echoing of a forecast by the action brings out the actor's power, for instance, does not mean that verbatim iteration enjoys a monopoly on this rhetorical effect. Given the appropriate context, deviant repetition may equally serve for this purpose, as when the narrator elaborates the member of action in the interests of realism and vividness:

> [God to Moses:] Lift up thy rod and stretch out thy hand over the sea and divide it, so that the people of Israel may go through the sea on dry land. . . . Moses stretched out his hand over the sea and the Lord drove the sea back by a violent east wind all night and made the sea dry land, and the waters were divided. And the people of Israel went through the sea on dry land, with the waters a wall to them on their right and on their left. (Exod 14:15–22)

Formal unity in functional variety as against formal variety in functional unity: this two-way divorce establishes the need for a properly communicative approach, one that will accommodate the interplay of means and ends in sophisticated art and relate the principle of repetition to the working of the narrative whole. The rudiments and gains of such an approach have emerged from every story we have considered. To gather up the threads and carry the argument forward, however, I want to turn to a narrative that presses the structure to a luminous extreme.

Repetition and Communication: Pharaoh's Dream

(1) After two whole years, Pharaoh dreamed, and behold, he was standing by the Nile. (2) And behold, there came up from the Nile seven well-favoured and fat-fleshed cows, and they grazed in the reed grass. (3) And behold, seven other cows came up after them from the Nile, ill-favoured and lean-fleshed, and stood by the cows on the bank of the Nile. (4) And the ill-favoured and lean-fleshed cows ate up the seven well-favoured and fat cows. And Pharaoh awoke. (5) Then he fell asleep and dreamed a second time, and behold, seven ears of grain, fat and good, came up on one stalk; (6) and behold, seven lean and east-wind-blighted ears sprouted after them. (7) And the seven lean ears swallowed up the seven fat and full ears. And Pharaoh awoke, and behold, a dream! (8) In the morning his spirit was troubled and he sent to call all the magicians of Egypt and all its wise men. Pharaoh told them his dream, and there was no one who could interpret them to Pharaoh. (9) Then the chief cupbearer spoke to Pharaoh, saying, My faults I remember today. (10) Pharaoh was once angry with his servants and put me in custody in the house of the captain of the guard, me and the chief baker. (11) And we dreamed a dream the same night, I and he, each dreaming according to the interpretation of his dream. (12) And there was with us a Hebrew lad, a servant of the captain of the guard; and we told him and he interpreted our dreams to us, interpreting to each according to his dream. (13) And as he interpreted to us, so it came to pass; I was restored to my office and he was hanged. (14) So Pharaoh sent to call Joseph; and they rushed him out of the dungeon and he shaved and changed his clothes and came in before Pharaoh. (15) And Pharaoh said to Joseph, I have dreamed a dream and there is none who can interpret it, and I have heard it said of thee that when thou hearest a dream thou canst interpret it. (16) And Joseph answered Pharaoh, saying, It is not in me; God will give Pharaoh a favorable answer. (17) And Pharaoh spoke to Joseph, In my dream, behold, I was standing on the bank of the Nile. (18) And behold, from the Nile came up seven fat-fleshed and well-formed cows and grazed in the reed grass. (19) And behold, seven other cows came up after them, miserable and very ill-formed and thin-fleshed—I have never seen their likes for poorness in all the land of Egypt. (20) And the thin and ill[-formed] cows ate up the first seven cows, the fat ones. (21) And when they had consumed them, no one could know that they had consumed them, for they were still as ill-favoured as at the beginning. And I awoke. (22) Then I saw in my dream, and behold, seven ears of grain, full and good, came up on one stalk. (23) And behold, seven withered, lean, east-wind-blighted ears sprouted after them. (24) And the seven lean ears swallowed up the seven good ears. I told it to the magicians, and there is none who can explain it to me. (25) And Joseph said to Pharaoh, The dream of Pharaoh is one; God has declared to Pharaoh what he is about to do. (26) The seven good cows are seven years, and the seven good ears are seven years: it is one dream. (27) And the seven thin and poor cows that came up after them are seven years, and the seven empty, east-wind-blighted ears will be seven years of

famine. (28) This is just the thing that I have spoken to Pharaoh: God has shown to Pharaoh what he is about to do. (29) Behold, there come seven years of great plenty in all the land of Egypt. (30) And after them will arise seven years of famine and all the plenty will be forgotten in the land of Egypt, and the famine will devour the land. (31) The plenty will be unknown in the land owing to that famine thereafter, for it will be very severe. (32) And as for the dream having recurred to Pharaoh twice, it means that the matter is fixed by God and God will shortly bring it about. (Gen 41:1-32)

The tale unrolls a long and variegated string of repetitions: dream → first report (summary: Pharaoh to the magicians) → second report (summary: interpretation dismissed) → third report (scenic: Pharaoh to Joseph) → fourth report (scenic: Joseph's solution) → enactment (dream fulfilled). Of these, the leading member is of decisive importance, since it comes from the biblical narrator himself. Predictably avoiding all overt commentary, he yet encourages the reader at once to do his own deciphering of the enigmatic dream by reference to its context and design. That oblique communication both puts us in the dreamer's own place and challenges us to elevate ourselves above him by making the most of the submerged clues.

The context of Genesis, notably Joseph's own history, elucidates the dream's existential status within the represented world and its compositional status within the discourse. The modern view of the dream as the expression of internal states and stresses has its precedents in antiquity. One thinks of Homer (Penelope's ambivalent attitude to the Suitors surfacing in the dream where she sees herself crying because the eagle-Odysseus has killed off her flock of geese); of rabbinic thought ("A man is shown in a dream only what is suggested by his own thoughts" [*Berakhoth* 55b]); or even of the Bible's own prophecy and wisdom books (e.g., "A hungry man dreams, and behold, he is eating, and he awakes with his hunger unsatisfied" [Isa 29:8]). Yet this conception is alien to the spirit of biblical narrative.[23] Here, as always in the Icelandic saga, the dream is not an internal but an external sign; not subjective and questionable ("the dreamers talk false dreams and give empty comfort," says Zechariah) but objective and infallible; not an illumination of the past and the present but of the future. In terms of the Bible's reality-model, the dream projects a divine scenario, and in compositional terms, a foreshadowing on the part of the narrator. This is the case with the dreams of the young Joseph (chapter 37) and of the imprisoned ministers (chapter 40); and Pharaoh's dream follows suit.

This has an immediate bearing on the dream's intelligibility within the structure of repetition. What in a modern text would figure as "enactment" or "report" operates here as "forecast," though not necessarily an easily decipherable one. In point of temporal direction, therefore, the reader's view of it coincides with the characters'.

But interpretive correspondence or parity by no means extends all along the line. In respects other than the basic premise, the reader has from the start exclusive access to a variety of clues—reminiscent of those sunk round and into the Wooing of Rebekah or the Humiliation of Barak in being likewise indirect, but even more context-dependent and effecting a far greater distance from the bewildered fellow interpreters. Figuratively speaking, if Abraham remains unaware of the bride's identity, Pharaoh and his magicians have no idea that a marriage is impending. Our perspectival superiority results from a close interaction between the book and the tale itself as guides to understanding. The wider context, which has already established the dream's status and reference as dream, also provides three aids to decoding. And the narrow context validates and fills out each of these aids, whether by way of anchorage in specific details or of new patterning to the same effect.

First, the most serious obstacle to interpretation, the reader's included, lies in assigning the proper (i.e., temporal) value to the key number seven. Not that the dream entirely fails to point in the right direction. Thus, the emergence of both the lean cows and the lean ears "after" the fat ones acts out a two-stage *process* in the language of time itself, sending a message that Joseph is indeed to catch and articulate: "After them will arise seven years of famine." But such pointers would remain too generalized and ambiguous—for anticipatory if not retrospective deciphering—were it not for the interaction of contexts. Of the two foregoing series of dreams, one (the ministers') suggests that the recurrent number seven signals a time unit. And the tale itself increases the probability of this hypothesis. It contrives a double plot-link between those dreams, first casting Pharaoh as agent in the ministers' dreams and Joseph as intermediary between them and Pharaoh's intentions, and then casting the chief cupbearer as literal intermediary between Pharaoh and Joseph. The link further tightens owing to a double organization of the sequence. In terms of the world's own calendar, Pharaoh's dream occurs on the anniversary ("After two whole years") of his ministers'; and in terms of the reading process, the occurrences are continuous. The deliberateness of this multiple interweaving emerges, in retrospect, from the parallelism in Joseph's wording of the interpretations: "The three branches are three days. . . . The three baskets are three days" rhymes with "The seven good cows are seven years, and the seven good ears are seven years."

In the context of Genesis, second, Egypt has so far been associated with "famine in the land" (12:10; 26:1), and the logic governing patriarchal history invites extension to Jacob's era as well. This expectancy has already gained point from the recurrence of another phrase: Abraham "went down to Egypt," Isaac was forbidden to "go down to Egypt," and recently Joseph "was taken down to Egypt" (39:1). Now it also gains imminence from the items composing the dream itself. Unlike the arbitrary signification of Moses' burning bush, for example, the Nile, reed grass, cows, and ears are all natural symbols of food,[24] and corpulence and leanness, of plenty and shortage. The relations imposed on these symbolic items, moreover, give their natural coherence the most ominous bearing. That the fat cows alone graze in the reed grass discourages loose interpretation by implying causal linkage between physical and agricultural condition. And why is it the cows that issue from the Nile rather than the ears of grain, which by natural association have a much stronger claim to such an origin? This incongruity, yoking cows and ears together by way of montage, undercuts their literal reading as self-contained entities and reinforces their symbolic value as synecdoches for food in general.

Third, the wider context also directs our integration of the symbolic parts into a whole by highlighting the forms of equivalence. All the dreams involving Joseph have thus far cohered as analogical pairs, whether matching (sheaves and heavenly bodies) or opposed (chief cupbearer vs. chief baker). And again, the new forecast's verbal composition articulates both modes of analogy to establish a unitary line of reading. Within each dream, the wording presses the apparitions into absolute contrast: "well-favored and fat-fleshed" as against "ill-favored and lean-fleshed" cows, or "fat and good" as against "lean and east-wind-blighted" ears. And within the pair of dreams as a whole, it hammers the correspondences (between cows and ears) into variation on a single theme. Not content with the general points of similarity—recurrent numbers, looks, happenings—the narrator sees to it that the linguistic features of the opening dream should reappear in its analogue. Grammatically, this manifests itself in the choice of natural symbols in the feminine gender—just as the branches and baskets in the noblemens' dreams are masculine—which also tightens the equivalence among the attendant verbs and adjectives. Constructionally, even a good translation will reflect the pains taken to carry over surface structures and operate with pairs of epithets. And semantically, continuity takes the form of a montage that produces on the level of language a discordance reminiscent of that already noted on the level of action (the emergence of the cows from the Nile). In the second round, we find the ears qualified by an adjective—"fat" (*beriot*)—that the Bible's normal semantics would reserve for the cows.[25] If elsewhere the language develops the pointing into a pinpointing of equivalence, here it moves even beyond pinpointing to conflation.

Not that the reader is supposed (as with Joseph's more transparent dreaming) to puzzle out the whole solution at this early phase. Rather, he has enough of the pieces in hand to know an acceptable interpretation when he hears one and at the same time to appreciate the difficulties besetting the characters—first the Egyptians, then Joseph—the more so since the characters have none of the benefit of the tale's compositional guidance. No wonder, therefore, that the two ensuing rounds of telescoped report— "Pharaoh told them his dream but there was none who could interpret them to Pharaoh"—should announce failure. The surprising thing is that this drastic summary manages to communicate that our advantage over the Egyptians is less than uniform.

Saddled with the inconsistency in grammatical number between "his dream" and "them"—edited out in some translations—we make the most of the loophole that "his dream" figures as grammatical object of the king's report ("he told") and "them" of the magicians' interpretive failure ("there was none who could interpret"). Accordingly, we make sense of the incongruity—as well as of the experts' very miss, at least in the client's eyes—in terms of a hidden disparity between Pharaoh's view (a single dream) and the magicians' (two dreams). By one of the Bible's rules of implication, behind a grammatical clash (between singular and plural, active and passive, well-formedness and ill-formedness) there may lurk a perspectival clash. Gratifyingly, that reading also dovetails with both the foregoing member and the sequel. With the foregoing member, due to the suggestive variation in the endings of the two parts, "Pharaoh awoke" as opposed to "Pharaoh awoke, *and behold, a dream!*" That the endings as well as their antecedents are otherwise correspondent encourages us to apply the single asymmetrical element to the pair as a whole; and that the biblical "and behold" (*ve'hinneh*) prefaces free indirect thought marks that closure as an insight into Pharaoh's own mind. Indeed, the direct quotation of Pharaoh's address to Joseph will soon cast both objects in the singular: "I have dreamed *a dream* and there is none who can interpret *it*" (verse 15). He thus seems aligned with the reader against the magicians.

But this hypothesis changes direction as Pharaoh goes on to narrate his dream to Joseph. Interestingly, his departures from the original account have been shrugged off not only by source critics and the party of facile harmonizers (like Radak, "We have already written that in repeating one omits or alters things, only taking care that the sense should remain the same") but even by exegetes notable for their close scrutiny of the text. Thus Abravanel: "Pharaoh told his dream to Joseph and altered a few things, whether by adding the word 'miserable' or varying from 'favour' to 'form.' . . . For the sense is alike and the text has said less in one place and more in another as it saw fit."

This unfortunate consensus only points afresh the moral of communication, especially in artful discourse. The weight of a variant is determined not per se but in relation to its mates, not by its formal but by its contextual semantics, including all the parameters (not least sound, grammar, and style) established as relevant by the underlying norms and functions. What distinguishes the narrator's telling from Pharaoh's retelling is not so much that the king interpolates subjective or emotive expressions ("I have never seen their likes for poorness," "no one would have known that they had consumed them") as that he unmakes the symmetry that the narrator has taken such care to make. Within each vision, Pharaoh blurs the contrast between the units; and within the pair of visions as a whole, he blurs the similarity. Consider the fortunes of the narrator's structural parallels in repetition. Pharaoh sometimes employs three consecutive adjectives ("miserable and very ill-formed and thin-fleshed"), sometimes two ("full and good"), sometimes only one ("lean"). At times he opposes to each series of positive adjectives a corresponding number of negatives ("lean" versus "good"), but usually he prefers numerical disproportion ("seven fat-fleshed and well-formed cows" versus "seven other cows, miserable and very ill-formed and thin-fleshed—I have never seen their likes"). Often he will not even maintain the equivalence in the modes of coordination ("full *and* good" versus "withered, lean, east-wind-blighted"). As with formal symmetry, so with interlinkage by lexis and semantics. Of the abundant adjectives, for example, not even one survives the passage from the first vision to the second; still less is there any trace of forced recurrence by way of metaphorical montage. As we began to see as early as the Wooing of Rebekah, however miscellaneous-looking the forms of divergence, they may all tend in the same communicative direction: for instance, the exposure of Pharaoh's misinterpretation.

The tightening of analogical bonds having been framed as a key to and a measure of comprehension, does their loosening mean that we are now supposed to abandon the hypothesis about the perspectival split between Pharaoh and his magicians? Not necessarily; we are only required to modify it. It indeed becomes difficult to sustain the reading that Pharaoh stands closer to the narrator and ourselves than do the magicians; but it is not easier to explain why, if the Egyptian viewpoint is in principle uniform, the text should have grammaticalized the "his dream . . . them" conflict. The way out of this double bind is indicated by the modes of subjective variation in repetition. These combine under a new hypothesis that will station the Egyptian figures at an equal distance from the tale's own view— the truth—and yet preserve the impression of a split given by the shift from the singular to the plural.

For the dream can be grasped as "one" in two distinct senses: unity of manifest dream-plot and/or unity of latent meaning. So far it has appeared that Pharaoh differs from his magicians in sensing (like ourselves) the unity of meaning: that is, that the two dream-plots form variations on a single theme, with the intermediate arousal ("Pharaoh awoke") breaking the continuity of the dream narrative only to foreground the correspondence in signification. But Pharaoh's loosening and fissuring of the meaning's analogical unity suggest that he believes in the unity of the manifest level itself; that to him the dream is also one in terms of plot coherence. There accordingly emerge not two but three different interpretations: (1) the reader's: two dreams but a single meaning; (2) the magicians': two dreams and two meanings; (3) Pharaoh's: a single dream and hence a single meaning.

If the full royal report conveys the reporter's position, no wonder that when Pharaoh told "his dream" in the foregoing scene, "there was none who could interpret them *to him*" and he was left dissatisfied. But this is precisely where Joseph demonstrates his superior skill and inspiration. How he came to assign the proper temporal values to the septets—only God knows, quite literally. He does at any rate carry the reader with him, as well as the dramatic audience. In part this is due to his record, to his confident tone, to the ease with which he decodes the natural symbols. But he mainly convinces us by his ability to surmount the obstacles and misdirections unwittingly interposed throughout Pharaoh's report. Unlike the reader, with his privileged clues, Joseph proceeds from the same starting line as the magicians. Unlike the magicians, however, he realizes that Pharaoh has simply misreported his dream; so he restores in interpretation what the dreamer himself disturbed in narration.

Of course, not having read the Bible, Joseph does not repeat the narrator's original wording. But he does repeat the narrator's method. The link he creates between the positive sides of the two visions is welded through the recourse to the same adjective: "The seven good cows . . . and the seven good ears." Then we find the link between their negative sides pinpointed even more strikingly: "The seven thin [*rakot*] cows . . . and the seven empty [*rekot*] ears." In the interests of wordplay, itself a form of montage, Joseph invents an adjective for the ears that has not appeared in any of the preceding versions, so as to give the equivalence in sense the firmest anchorage in sound. Pharaoh's dream is one.

Basic Axes and Natural Combinations

The analysis of Pharaoh's dream highlights some major issues in biblical semantics—such as the relations between language and discourse, form (phonic, lexical, grammatical) and meaning, or text and context—that we have encountered in previous chapters and will revert to in what follows. Now I want to start by generalizing its more specific implications for the art of retelling.

From the functional standpoint, this chain of repetition develops a multiple and shifting play of perspectives: among the omniscient narrator's, the reader's, Pharaoh's, the magicians', Joseph's, and, most covert but also most dominant, God's. As far as the bare plot exigencies are concerned—the need to devise a causal sequence that will reverse Joseph's fortune from imprisonment to Grand Viziership—some of the members could be omitted or at least thoroughly reduced. (And such ellipsis would bring relief to bored underreaders.) But what a naturalistic plot might allow, if not require, would mar the ideological plot that underlies the visible march of events and shapes the tale's theme and rhetoric. It is the intention to establish Joseph's stature as God's elect rather than Pharaoh's that accounts for the variety of the implied viewpoints, the nature of their discrepancies, and the order of their surfacing.

In contrast to Joseph's own dreaming, almost self-explanatory (if not equally reliable) to all concerned, Pharaoh's is so ambiguated in form and sense as to elicit a spectrum of interpretations. A neutral-looking account first challenges the reader to play interpreter as the enigma still plays itself out. While withholding the solution, however, the narrator affords enough light to put us in a position that best suits his designs. Intermediate between understanding and bafflement, that position will make for an informed check on Joseph's decoding and yet engender a firsthand appreciation of what he takes in his stride. (As with Solomon's Judgment, one might otherwise forget that the gaps would defeat any human not inspired by God.) This complex effect then arises anew from the ensuing rounds. With the summoning of the oneiromancers, the narrator switches to a perspective of total incomprehension, thus laying the ground for a climax that will show Joseph triumphing where "all the magicians of Egypt and all its wise men" have failed. The dreamer's own view and account then heighten the effect from a new direction. For the discordance between the narrator's telling and Pharaoh's retelling, the breakdown of the initial illusion that the king knows better than his magicians, and the emergence of still another line of decipherment—all reimpress on us the difficulty of the task. And the reader having been manipulated into the proper frame of mind, there follows a shift all the way to the opposite pole, embodied in the inspired ease and authority with which Joseph unfolds the solution. The whole structure is thus thoroughly typical in building a spectrum of positions into the movement of the plot. And the plot transforms as a result from a chronicle of externals suffering from redundancy and heterogeneity into a process of a different order: unified, motivated, nuanced, anchored in human psychology, and inculcating a divine frame of reference.

But this play of perspectives closely relates to another notable feature of our tale, namely, the meeting of several axes integral to the Bible's as to all sophisticated structures of repetition. One axis opposes *verbal and nonverbal objects* of presentation; the other, *deliberate and nondeliberate variation (or replication)*. In principle, the oppositions along these axes are independent of each other. The first concerns the (re)presented object's status within the world of the narrative: the object rendered in discourse may have been originally nonverbal (an event, a state of affairs) or verbal (monologue, dialogue, interior speech). To be sure, in the text itself everything assumes linguistic form—but does the text retain in transmission the form inherent in a piece of language or impose that form on a piece of reality? Whereas the second opposition concerns the repeater's awareness that his account of the object (whatever its original form) is precise or variant at such and such points.

However distinct the axes may be in principle, certain "natural" correlations yet appear to suggest themselves. With an originally nonverbal object, there arises a natural cause (warrant, expectancy) for deviance in repetition. Discrepancies between the representation of the object and the object itself, and also among the various representations, make sense in terms of each representer's character, competence, knowledgeability. Different people see and say things in different ways. Here, accordingly, it is verbatim repetition that becomes less than natural, if not downright incongruous, and therefore perceptible. To refer back to a previous example, it is surprising that Hagar's conduct in pregnancy receives the same formulation ("Since she saw that she had conceived, her mistress became contemptible in her eyes") from two such diverse observers as the narrator and the injured party, Sarah herself. This is why the reader infers from the equivalence in language an equivalence in vision where the character's involvement might otherwise cast doubt on her objectivity. Given the infinity of standpoints from which an event or person may be viewed, we rather expect contextual shifts to go with physical variation in repetition. Indeed, this option is artfully exploited to reflect and contrast different perspectives on the same piece of reality, whether the narrator's as against the characters' (as throughout Pharaoh's Dream) or one character's vis-à-vis another's:

> Israel loved Joseph more than all his sons, for he was the son of his old age; and he made him an ornamented (?) tunic. When his brothers saw that it was him their father loved more than all his brothers, they hated him and could not speak peaceably to him. (Gen 37:3-4)

This double account of the familial tangle—studded with the subjective verbs "loved," "saw," "hated,"—invites us to motivate the variations by appeal to two viewpoints: Jacob's versus the brothers'. To Jacob, the favorite is "Joseph," an intimate and specific figure opposed to the amorphous mass of "all his sons"; to the brothers, it is a nameless "him": not even once do they refer to him by name and their opprobrious circumlocutions ("this master of dreams") indeed bear out the statement that they "could not speak peaceably to him." To Jacob, favoritism means an exercise of patriarchal ("Israel") privilege in regard to his subordinates ("his sons"); to the brothers it means an intolerable superiority enjoyed by one of a dozen equals ("his brothers"). Again, Jacob has a reason ("the son of his old age") for his preference. Disregarding the cause, however, the brothers focus on the effect: the change in both selection (the motive omitted) and arrangement ("Israel loved him" reordered into the less normal "Him their father loved") suggests that the brothers take ill the very fact of preferential treatment and blame its recipient ("him") rather than its giver ("their father").[26] The two verses thus turn from two members of enactment (the narrator renders the world in his own name) into two members of report or of enactment centered in report (the narrator unfolds the world through different internal prisms). And this new sense resolves redundancies and discrepancies alike, so as to fill out the psychological contours of the tale.

A nonverbal object's repetition with variation, moreover, serves not only to oppose different perspectives at a single point in time but also to trace their development over a period of time:

(1) The Amalekites had made a raid on the Negeb and on Ziklag. They overcame Ziklag and they burnt it with fire, (2) and they took captive all the women in it, both small and great. They killed no one, but carried them off and went their way. (3) And David and his men came to the city, and behold, burnt with fire and their wives and sons and daughters taken captive. (4) Then David and the people who were with him raised their voices and wept, until they had no more strength to weep. (1 Sam 30:1–4)

(25) The Lord said to [Gideon], Take thy father's bull, the second bull seven years old, and pull down thy father's altar to Baal and cut down the Asherah beside it; (26) and build an altar to the Lord thy God on top of this stronghold here, and take the second bull and offer it as a burnt offering with the wood of the Asherah which thou wilt cut down. (27) And Gideon took ten men of his servants and did as the Lord had told him; and since he was too afraid of his father's family and of the men of the town to do it by day, he did it by night. (28) The men of the town rose early in the morning, and behold, the altar of Baal had been torn down and the Asherah on it cut down and the second bull offered on the built altar. (29) And they said to one another, Who has

> done this thing? And they searched and inquired, and said, Gideon the
> son of Joash has done this thing. (Judg 6:25–29)

In each instance, we find the repetition (verses 3 and 28, respectively) not
only less detailed than the original narrative but cast in the passive voice
as well: they burnt → burnt; they took captive → taken captive; pull down
→ torn down; cut down → [been] cut down; offer → offered. And as
indicated by the herald of biblical free indirect thought—"and behold"—
both the selectional and the transformational variations cohere in terms
of a shift in point of view. The vantage point of the omniscient narrator,
from which we receive a full account of the forecast and/or the performance, gives way to the limited vision of the characters, who register the
disaster without the least idea of its antecedents.

    The deviant registration of the attack on Ziklag even heightens this sense
of shock. For while Gideon's townsmen at once recover, David and his men
are so numbed with grief that for some time it does not occur to them
to ask "Who has done this thing?" But then follows a process of discovery—in
Samuel extensive, in Judges telescoped into "they searched and inquired"—
whereby the different perspectives move into synchronization. What is
more, perspectival and grammatical synchronization coincide, the one being
expressed by the other. For the investigation culminates in yet another
account, but this time in the active voice and with the logical subject articulated in its proper place: "The men of the town said to Joash, Bring out
thy son and let him die, for he tore down the altar of Baal and cut down
the Asherah" (Judg 6:30); "I am . . . a servant to an Amalekite. . . . We
burnt Ziklag with fire" (1 Sam 30:13–14).[27]

    In the foregoing cases, the variations in repetition served to evoke dis-
sonant viewpoints, either equally static (Jacob vs. his sons) or one static
(e.g., the narrator's) and the other dynamic (the townsmen's, David's).
Elsewhere, all the viewpoints confronted undergo some development. While
Ahima'az and the Cushite are taking their different routes to David with
news about the quelling of Absalom's rebellion,

> David was sitting between the two gates; and the watchman went up
> to the roof of the gate by the wall, and he lifted up his eyes and saw,
> and behold, a man running alone! And the watchmen called out and
> told the king; and the king said, If he is alone, there are tidings in his
> mouth. And he drew nearer and nearer. Then the watchman saw another
> man running, and the watchman called to the gate and said, Behold,
> a[nother] man running alone! And the king said, He also brings tidings.
> Then the watchman said, The running of the first looks to me like the
> running of Ahima'az the son of Zadok. And the king said, He is a good
> man and comes with good tidings. And Ahima'az cried out and said
> to the king, All is well. And he bowed to the king with his face to the

ground and said, Blessed be the Lord thy God, who has delivered up the men who raised their hands against my lord the king. (2 Sam 18:24–28)

At this tense juncture, when the characters within the walls are anxious to learn the outcome of the battle and the reader to observe David's reaction to the death of his favorite son, the narrator keeps everyone on tenterhooks. He interposes a retardatory scene with a view to prolonging suspense about essentials while dramatizing the gradual comprehension of an otherwise incidental plot link. The informational advantage conferred on the reader concerning the "what" focuses his attention on the multiphase "how" that results from the interplay of David's and the lookout's perspectives. Thanks to the chronological ordering, typical of the Bible's art of repetition, we of course know that what happens is "Ahima'az brings the tidings of victory." But the lookout, handicapped by his limited knowledge and (literally) vision, can at first report only what his eyes make out, without any commentary: "A man running alone!" Therefrom David draws an inference that brings him one step closer to the full reconstruction: "If he is alone, there are tidings in his mouth." (The same movement from factual to conjectural account later recurs, as retardation within retardation, on the appearance of the Cushite.) Next, as the runner draws nearer, the lookout can improve on his report at one point: he identifies the messenger by the style of his running. And David again tries to wring as much meaning as possible from the scanty evidence—this time, to deduce the tenor of the message from the character of the messenger. But while the lookout, who adheres to the visible facts, makes progress from one report to another, David's secret fears lead him into wishful thinking. His process of discovery, therefore, is marked by ups and downs, success and failure, or indeed objective success and subjective failure at once: "He is a good man and comes with good tidings." Ironically, the tidings prove "good" to everyone, except the king.

All the patterns discussed so far have a basic feature in common. There arises a natural link between the nonverbal character of the repeated object (one textual fact) and the variant character of the repetition (another fact) through the hypothesis that the different members originate in different sources of information. The area and extent of discrepancy in retelling make sense by reference to the discrepancy in perspective (insight, awareness, attitude) between the observers of the action or state of affairs. Such observers need not even be conscious of the variation among themselves, since it follows from the terms of the case. The very refraction of the object through diverse prisms naturally yields diverse subjectivities; and any change in position—in time, place, knowledge, perceptual context, relations between subject and object—may bring about changes even in renderings anchored in the same mind.

With a verbal object of presentation, on the other hand, the feasibility and probability of verbatim repetition greatly increase, since the retelling then operates on a replicable (within limits[28]) piece of discourse: an order, advice, prophecy, statement, characterization. Accurate repetition of the original words (or at least their spirit) poses no special problems, or else there would be little sense in employing messengers. Here, therefore, it is *deviant* repetition that frustrates our natural expectancies and its intelligibility in terms of deliberate garbling that comes to the fore.

Indeed, just as with a nonverbal object biblical narrative takes advantage of the "natural" option of variance, so with a verbal object does it often realize the "natural" option of verbatim echoing. And again, the naturalness of the latter means neither formulaic implementation on the narrator's part nor suspended alertness or inference on the reader's. Accurate repetition becomes as perceptible in the case of a verbal as of a nonverbal object, only for different reasons. With a nonverbal original, we recall, it gains perceptibility from its infringement of realism: from the odd identity in expression between independent observers. With a verbal object, such identity loses its oddity; but if it becomes "natural," this is only by realistic as opposed to artistic standards. The more realistically expected the precise rehearsal of the original member, the sharper the sense of informational redundancy. If a messenger is supposed to rattle off his message word for word, why should his delivery be quoted in full? And this abstract reasoning and questioning gains relevance from the narrative practice, which establishes anew the Bible's norm of economy. For such members of report are often subjected in transmission to various processes of abridgment, including perfunctory mention and the telescoping of direct discourse into "such and such." Accordingly, not only the sense of waste nor only the option of deviance but also the frequency of summary repetition—far more common than in Homer or Oriental literature and even more drastic than in most novels—impels us to explain those structures that requote the language or at least the drift of the original utterance.

Like the other forms of redundancy, such a pattern serves more than one end. Often the Bible will complicate realistic expectation by way of early suspense and/or of surprise after the event. Given the quoting speaker's character, dilemma, or relations with the prospective addressee, it is far from certain whether he will repeat the message accurately or at all:

> All the prophets prophesied so, and said, *Go up to Ramoth Gilead and succeed; the Lord will deliver it into the hand of the king* [Ahab]. And the messenger who had gone to call Micaiah spoke to him, saying, Behold, pray, the prophets have spoken favourably to the king with one voice; let thy word,

pray, be like the word of one of them and speak favourably. And Micaiah said, As the Lord lives, what the Lord says to me that shall I speak. Then he came to the king and the king said to him, Micaiah, shall we go to Ramoth Gilead to battle or shall we refrain? And he said to him, *Go up and succeed; the Lord will deliver it into the hand of the king.* (1 Kgs 22:12–15)

Those who encourage Ahab, and with one voice,[29] to make war on the Arameans must be false prophets. It is hard to believe that God will grant victory to Naboth's murderer, least of all over that enemy whose sparing in the previous campaign has brought down on Ahab the doom, "Thy life shall be forfeit for his life and thy people for his people" (1 Kgs 20:42). Hence our surprise when Micaiah—the loner thus far standing aloof from the mass of tame prophets and sworn to utter God's word alone—parrots the official version: "Go up and succeed; the Lord will deliver it into the hand of the king." In a reign that put true prophets to the sword, does Micaiah lie to save his skin? Is he, on the contrary, being sarcastic at the expense of the king and his parasites, as Ahab's angry reaction and plea for "truth in God's name" seem to imply? Or has God, after all, forgiven Ahab on account of his repentance after the Naboth affair? But not only the reversal of expectation and the dance of hypotheses justify the precise echoing. So does, in the immediate sequel, the contrast with Micaiah's true prophecy—its impact redoubled by the opposition between the initial "Go up and succeed" and the ultimate "go up and fall," with its oxymoronic twist. The second stage, then, manifests a further role of precise repetition: to enhance the cohesiveness of the recurrent member with a view to its effective shattering on the rebound. Verbatim repetition serves to foreground marked variation.

This effect of suspense or frustration arises from the recurrence of discourse in the teeth of a shift in context, not necessarily in speaker. It may come even where speech is followed by *self*-quotation. In Saul's war against the Philistines, his unconsidered oath, "As the Lord who delivers Israel lives, though it [the sin] be in Jonathan my son, he shall surely die"— sworn in complete ignorance of Jonathan's having tasted of the honey— sounds like an extravagant mode of showing determination. But the reader's ironic view of Saul ("Little does he know . . .") gives place to a sense of shock as soon as Jonathan admits his guilt. For the father now repeats his forecast in all seriousness: "God do so to me and more also, thou shalt surely die, Jonathan" (1 Sam 14:39, 44). The *artistic* point of the repetition again lies in the fact that the narrator has engineered a context where repetition is less than natural in terms of *realistic* probabilities. Its predictability once lowered, the act of (self-)quotation becomes disturbing and suggestive rather than automatic.

To be more precise, we must distinguish between the very existence of the member of report within the narrated world and the extent of its particularity (and especially of its replication) within the narrative text. In the instances just cited, the member's existence easily coheres by appeal to plot motivation—it forms, in rehearsal as well as in original utterance, part of the sequence of events. Whereas the redundancy incurred by the liberal space given it in the text receives a purely artistic, communicative motivation. That is, the desired effect of clash between expected and actual speech turns on precise echoing, and the drama would suffer were the tale to content itself with summaries or free variations, such as "Micaiah's word was like the word of one of them" or "The king said, Kill Jonathan." As usual in the Bible, the art of indirection takes over where the surface intelligibility of plot leaves off. Indeed, with the disappearance of the nominal motivation for reiterating a piece of language, our sense of redundancy sharpens apace:

> They took him [Naboth] outside the city and stoned him with stones and he died. And they sent to Jezebel, saying, Naboth has been stoned and he died. And when Jezebel heard that Naboth had been stoned and he died, Jezebel said to Ahab, Arise and take possession of the vineyard of Naboth the Jezreelite, which he refused to give thee for money; for Naboth is not alive, but dead. And when Ahab heard that Naboth was dead, Ahab arose to go down to the vineyard of Naboth the Jezreelite to take possession of it. (1 Kgs 21:13–16)

The opening duplication, "stoned him with stones and he died" followed by "Naboth has been stoned and he died," integrates with the causal movement from the performance to the reporting of the judicial murder. But what can justify the further repetition, "when Jezebel heard that Naboth had been stoned and he died?" Does not that "hearing" refer to the very same event as the previous "saying"? The explanation first seems to lie in the portrayal of Jezebel, who does not scruple to act at once on the news. But it soon turns out that Jezebel herself serves to illuminate the figure of Ahab, the next in line for the report. Having already done the dirty work on her husband's behalf, Jezebel continues to spare his tender conscience by watering down the brutal "Naboth had been stoned and he died" into the generalized "Naboth is not alive, but dead." Interested in results not details, Ahab swoops on the vineyard with the same alacrity as Jezebel displayed in inviting him to take possession of it:

> When Jezebel heard . . . Jezebel said
> When Ahab heard . . . Ahab arose

Considering the analogy in indecent haste, the difference in what they heard reflects no special credit on Ahab.

The repetition of the account thus combines with the variation from one addressee to another to produce a multiple effect along a sequence where (as with Micaiah) the ordering of echo and deviance plays a large role. The doubling of each report, with its shift from external message to internal reception, exposes the character of each reportee through his attitude to the information received. The disparity between the two doubled reports—the Jezebel-oriented being accurate and the Ahab-oriented censored—suggests a psychological contrast within the royal family. Whereas the formal similarity divests that contrast of normative import: the ruthless executioner and the squeamish beneficiary are, morally, birds of a feather.

From Natural to Functional Combinations

We have so far dwelt on the links between the object itself and its form in repetition: nonverbal object and unwitting variation on the one hand, verbal object and (near-)duplication on the other. These links, with the expectancies and effects attaching to them, have extremely significant implications for biblical poetics, especially against the background of corpora and styles often lumped together with it. Thus, they dispose of the sweeping claim that so-called primitive narrative fails to separate word from thing and hence to exploit their discontinuity. In *Gilgamesh* or *Enuma Elish,* for example, the differences between the objects of discourse (like those between the subjects, including narrator vs. agents and gods vs. humans) are leveled in the stylized homogeneity of precise repetition. No matter what the object and who the subject, their rendering comes out the same each time. The Bible's structure of repetition, however, not only allows for but also dramatizes the workings of human perception: it exploits the differences between percepts as well as perceivers to fashion one of the most context-sensitive arts of perspective in literary history.

Still, precisely because these two axes appear to fall into "logical" or "natural" correlations—words with echoing, things with variance—it must be emphasized that there is no kind of package deal, no automatic linkage in either direction. The bonds they form are reasonable and meaningful in context but not inevitable, prevalent but far from exclusive. Both the Bible's storytelling and world picture introduce further variables that widen the combinatory spectrum of repetition.

Consider first the powers and attitudes of the biblical narrator, who plays an active part in the structure of repetition as the communicator of at least one member. Unlike other sources and informants—his own dramatis personae, or modern tellers from Tristram Shandy to Humbert Humbert— this narrator exercises quasi-divine privileges: omniscience, reliability, control. As he thereby transcends the limitations that hamper and blind humans, the opposition of deliberateness vs. nondeliberateness does not apply to him at all. Whatever he does—in regard to a verbal or nonverbal object, to verbatim or variant reading—is presumed to be deliberate, artistically deliberate.

This has one general and several more specific implications. The general implication concerns the two frameworks by appeal to which we motivate (explain, justify, bring into pattern) the various aspects of repetition: the very fact of recurrence, the degree of correspondence between the recurrent members, the particularity of their treatment, etc. These two frameworks of motivation are omnipresent in literature, but their relation to the narrator (or in poetry, speaker) varies with his attributes.

Of the two, *quasi-mimetic motivation* establishes coherence in the text by appeal to the represented world: the psychology of the agents, their state of awareness, their predicament, constraints, motives, relations, and the like. Within this world-oriented logic, the opposition between "deliberately" and "nondeliberately" is always available, supplying two alternative explanations for the characters' behavior in general and their handling of repetition in particular. Thus, to say that a certain variation on the part of a certain reporting figure is deliberate or nondeliberate is to account for an objective fact—the variant report in its given shape—by assimilating it to the surrounding situation: the reporter's viewpoint and circumstances. Jezebel, we *infer*, produces the euphemism "Naboth is not alive but dead" to spare Ahab's feelings; whereas Pharaoh diverges from the truth of the dream for lack of understanding, and the second account of the raid on Ziklag varies from the first owing to its refraction through the limited perspective of David and his men. The same logic makes sense of verbatim repetition. Micaiah echoes the prophetic consensus because he wants to flatter (or mock) Ahab; Saul reiterates his oath because he is proud or stubborn; two speakers hit on the same formula due to natural coincidence or, as with Jonathan and the Philistines (1 Sam 14:9–12), to supernatural interference with their thought processes. In each case, then, the repetition and/or variation opens a gap concerning the reteller's state of mind. And the reader fills in the gap through a hypothesis that assigns to this retelling character some form of deliberateness or nondeliberateness in transmission, according to the factors and pointers available in context— including the nature of the retold object. Whatever its form and grounds, such a hypothesis follows the way of the world, the rules of quasi-mimetic (or for short, mimetic) motivation.

This framework, however, always coexists with and overlies another logic of motivation, which establishes *aesthetic or rhetorical* rather than lifelike coherence. Hence it explains the features of repetition not in terms of the narrated world but of the narrative art; not in terms of the relations between characters but between text or author and reader; not by reference to (conscious or unconscious) psychological motives or situational constraints or perceptual obstacles but to (invariably conscious) poetic goals and effects, like the rise and fall of expectation, indirect character-drawing, viewpoints exposed and juxtaposed, tacit commentary or the control of attitude. The very interpretive movement *repetition → gap → hypothesis about the repeater* that distinguishes mimetic motivation forms part of the work's aesthetic logic. For such a movement is blocked in literature governed by formulaic conventions of repetition. It also reflects a preference for suggesting over stating psychological processes, and it leads to further effects on the reader that wholly transcend the world of the characters and arise behind their backs. In fact, to allude to a theme that we have been pursuing all along, aesthetic motivation subsumes all those patterns (linkages, meanings, effects) reserved for the reader as opposed to his fellow interpreters within the drama.

The two logics that motivate the structure of repetition—as they do every other device—are therefore not mutually exclusive but complementary; each operates to make sense in its own domain, with the aesthetic-rhetorical motivation underlying or lurking behind the mimetic. Yet the explanations they produce remain distinct in both bearing and specifics. If Jezebel edits the report about Naboth to spare Ahab, the tale puts the variation in her mouth in order to condemn Ahab; Micaiah echoes the false prophecy out of (say) fear, while the narrator contrives the echo to spring a surprise on the reader and enhance the impact of the true prophecy. Each example thus shows the two faces of literary coherence, one turned to the discourse as representation, as a simulacrum of the world, and the other to the discourse as communication, as an artifice designed for a purpose. Further, the two motivational frameworks essentially differ in all that concerns the speaker's awareness of the accuracy or variance of his repetition. Within the quasi-mimetic sphere, the features of repetition can be explained (and the gap about the repeater closed) along both the "deliberate" and the "nondeliberate" line, according to contextual clues. Within the aesthetic or rhetorical sphere, however, the "deliberate" line of explanation enjoys a monopoly, because of the narrator's superhuman powers of knowledge and control. In what follows, therefore, the variable of deliberateness in repetition will apply (unless otherwise noted) to the characters alone.

Far from peculiar to the Bible, however, this twofold intelligibility is the rule of literary structure.[30] Every literary work can thus devise tensions in performance and intent between the lifelike handling of repetition by the characters inside their world and its artful handling by the narrator who pulls strings behind their backs. Ultimately, therefore, all the features of repetition (including not only the characters' versions but also the gaps opened and the closures implied in regard to them) go back to the storyteller as a primary manipulator, finding their coherence in his strategies vis-à-vis the reader. It is rather in the form imposed on this universal of art (or reading) that the Bible's structure of repetition manifests its distinctiveness.

Compare all those modern works that address us through the mediation of some unreliable narrator or speaker or center of consciousness—like Dowell in *The Good Soldier,* T. S. Eliot's Prufrock, Robbe-Grillet's Voyeur. Their strings of repetition certainly show the inevitable discrepancies in motivation between the logic of the text and the logic of the characters who repeat themselves or others for some lifelike reason. Within these discrepancies, however, the mediating teller or reflector is himself ranged on the side of the characters, equally subject to their fallibility and the text's ironies. So the ultimate aesthetic motivation for the handling of the discourse is attributed not to him but to the hidden author who manipulates him as a fictive voice, persona, middleman. In contrast, since the biblical narrator exists outside the enacted drama and exercises authorial power, this motivation directly relates to him and his own maneuvers. The distance between narrator and author once neutralized, each case of informational excess and variance also assumes special aesthetic perceptibility. For the procedures of an authoritative narrator such as the Bible's do not lend themselves to the mimetic explanation that would make sense of the activities of fallible counterparts: that the narrator is ignorant, confused, loquacious, absent-minded, or otherwise unreliable, and that the author has him perpetrate repetitions with a view to exposing these character traits. The inspired teller is rather the artificer than the victim of such exposures. (In principle, of course, one can always accuse the narrator of sloppy work, and biblical scholarship has indeed abused this resource. But even in responsible hands this entails a drastic shift of ground—from mimetic and aesthetic to genetic intelligibility, from the art of repetition to the origins of repetitiousness, from discourse to source—that lays the botch at the author's door as well. Whatever its cogency, therefore, such an explanatory line deals with the text's rather than the narrator's transmission, impugning his skill without at all affecting his status as prime manipulator *for better or worse.*)

Unlike many authorial as well as limited tellers, moreover, the biblical narrator is not content to quote the forecasts and reports uttered by the characters and manipulate them from behind the scenes. He himself steps forward to present at least one member of the repetition, and his involvement directly promotes the control over the reading and the combinatory options.

For one thing, this practice extends the range of information open to the reader and diversifies its sources and authority. Since the narrator freely brings his omniscience to bear on the world, the plot of repetition may include a variety of privileged material: solid clues or even exegesis, direct quotations from God's speech or thought, or, as with Jezebel and Ahab, members consisting in inside views of the agents. For another thing, the narrator's participation ensures the appearance of one member whose reliability is beyond doubt—an authorized reference-point to which we may safely appeal in order to sort out and motivate the versions originating in the other participants.

As far as the narrator (and the member offered in his name) is concerned, furthermore, the dividing line between verbal and nonverbal object of presentation vanishes along with that between deliberate and nondeliberate handling. This excludes any automatic linkage of the features of repetition to the nature of the repeated object. For whatever the object that the teller communicates, whether a speech or an event, his version figures as the tale's objective truth. Given his powers, there is no criterion of realistic naturalness by which we can explore his adherence to or deviation from alternative accounts. To account for his procedure, we can appeal neither to any dependence of his on the reports of others, nor to difficulties in penetrating the opacity of mind or situation, nor to psychological or dialogic constraints, nor to changes in perceptual conditions, personal interests, interpersonal affairs. So far as the concept of the "natural" applies to him, it must be dissociated from the mimetic (mental, situational, perspectival) coordinates that govern the characters' ways of repetition. Our "natural" expectancies of him, those which render fulfillment predictable and infringement meaningful, have a purely artistic or functional cast: they arise from his art of narrative (in terms of which redundancy, say, is less natural than ellipsis) or from the design of a particular story.

Consequently, any discrepancies within a series of members that apparently issue from the narrator himself reflect changes not in his powers and circumstances but in his choices and goals. We may then resolve the variations by inferring a movement from one perspective to another—from the narrator to the characters (as in the Ziklag raid) or among the characters themselves (as in the familial views of Joseph)—or from one state of affairs to another:

> The flood was forty days upon the earth, and the waters increased and bore up the ark and it rose above the earth. The waters prevailed and increased greatly upon the earth, and the ark floated on the surface of the waters. And the waters prevailed very greatly upon the earth, and all the high mountains under the whole heaven were covered. To the height of fifteen cubits did the waters prevail, and the mountains were covered. (Gen 7:17–20)

In parallel sequences of *figural* report, e.g., the scene of Ahima'az's running, we saw how the variations trace a development in perspective, whereby the observers gradually find out what happens. But here the observing perspective remains static—the narrator's and his alone, all humans being either dead or shut up in the ark—and what undergoes change is the observed world itself. The narrative follows the multiphase rage of the flood, using the recurrent elements to maintain continuity and the variants to outline development from the onset to the height of the flood. The sequence of members reflects a sequence of actions rather than perceptions.

This does not yet exhaust the motivations adducible for the narrator's doubling or departure from some previous account of his own. A fairly simple alternative is repetition with a view to retying a knot in plot time: to picking up a narrative thread that was earlier dropped to clear the stage for a parallel or digressive action.[31] Considering its mnemonic and resumptive role, no wonder that such harking back is summary and often miniaturized. Another possibility (which Cassuto occasionally invokes in disregard of his formulaic approach) is to resolve the discrepancy between equally authoritative versions in terms of a shift from the general to the particular. As early as the two opening chapters of Genesis, we thus note the passage from the emergence of man in the framework of Creation to the emergence of man in the context of the human drama.[32] Still another line of functional motivation may offer a more focused aid to understanding. Genesis 37 ends by telling that "the Midianites had sold Joseph into Egypt, to Potiphar, an officer of Pharaoh, the Chief Steward"; and chapter 39 starts by retelling that "Joseph had been taken down to Egypt and Potiphar, an officer of Pharaoh, the Chief Steward, an Egyptian, bought him from the Ishmaelites." This rehearsal evidently combines the first two functions. It harks back to the hero's fortunes after the extended digression of chapter 38 (the Judah and Tamar affair). It also moves from the general to the particular. (This involves a shift from the brothers and the Midianites to Joseph and Potiphar, encoded both grammatically, in the shift to the passive form "had been taken down," which demotes the agency, and semantically, in the shift from "sold him" to "bought him.") But this repetition with variation performs yet another compositional service. As I argued in the analysis of Pharaoh's Dream, the new occurrence of the verb "go down" in the Joseph context unifies patriarchal history and specifically influences the reading of the dream.

To sum up. Given the narrator's omnicompetence, we motivate the incongruities (from redundancy through modification to clash) between his versions by transferring the incongruous member or elements to a framework other and more hidden than that to which they nominally belong. While seeming to repeat or entangle himself, we infer, the artist has covertly moved from one state of affairs to another (so as to present two stages rather than two accounts of the plot); or from one viewpoint (usually his own) to another (centered in a character) and hence also to another type of member (report instead of enactment); or from one compositional pattern or function to another. Since the narrator himself does not change from telling to retelling, something else must: the object, angle, focus, or point of his narration. All these interpretive resources, then, essentially differ from corresponding motivations and frame-switches of members that overtly originate in the dramatis personae, since their logic rises above the limitations of awareness and control inherent in the human condition.

But the human condition need not, and in ancient literature does not, embrace even the whole narrated world. Indeed, the Bible's model of reality (as well as of storytelling) vetoes any automatic linkage of the axes of repetition. There is one major exception to all that has just been said about the qualitative differences in privilege between narrator and character: the figure of God (and to a lesser extent, his delegates). In a sense, of course, the narrator's control of his world—including God himself, his mind penetrated and his judgments pressed into service—overpasses that of the very deity whose name and might he sets out to exalt. Nor do they perform quite the same roles in the structure of repetition, which favors a division of labor whereby God voices the forecast and the narrator the enactment. But their equivalence suffices to mark God as a superagent, a law unto himself within the Bible's field of reality. The motivations for his behavior and discourse are as world-oriented ("quasi-mimetic") as the rest of the dramatis personae's; yet his powers bespeak an authority comparable to the narrator's. This unique status both enriches and further explains the combinatory play of repetition.

Like the narrator, God (or his emissary) may credibly provide the structure with inaccessibles like the hidden thoughts of others. Examples would be the charitably variant repetition in the scene of Sarah's inner laughter or the verbatim repetition following Cain's fit of jealousy. The incorporation of such members to harmonize with the narrator's is part of the rhetoric devised for glorifying God's lordship, especially his omniscience vis-à-vis the blindness and illusions of his creatures. Since this theme has figured as a leitmotiv throughout my argument, I will here emphasize only the crucial service rendered by the plots of repetition and then turn to a more specific point. Because of his omniscience, God is no more subject than the narrator to the distinctions that govern and motivate human (mis)reporting: "deliberateness vs. nondeliberateness" and "verbal vs. nonverbal object," with all their combinations within the state of fallibility. His rendering of events (Cain's fallen face) is every bit as controlled and authoritative as his rendering of speech (Sarah's laughter).

Just as God's omniscience validates his reports of past and present, establishing them as objective measures of the trustworthiness of other versions, so does his omnipotence invest his forecasts with supreme power that he alone can neutralize. The range of ends served by this divine privilege—variety, anticipation, narrative self-effacement together with God's foregrounding—explains the favorite division of labor in repetition to which I alluded earlier. Thus, God's control of the future promotes the narrator's control of tempo: a series of divinely predetermined repetition structures—like the Plagues of Egypt—can modulate its rhythm by eliding or telescoping members without detriment to the overall awesomeness and intelligibility. The same divine attribute also enables the narrator to foreshadow and retard the issue without having to choose between thrusting himself forward to anticipate matters and weakening the sense of an irreversible future: to delegate the foretelling to God is to promise the fulfillment of expectation in some retelling to come. At the same time, this act of delegation is even more an end in itself than a means to adopting the desired narrative stance. That the narrator's self-effacement is God's spotlighting inculcates anew the Bible's model of reality and history with each actualization of the divine scenario. Hence also a further move against the barrier separating verbal from nonverbal objects. We have seen the implications for omniscience of the harmony between narratorial and divine view. In the same way, the narrator often effects a minute correspondence between God's language of forecast ("Let there be light") and his own language of enactment ("and there was light") to maximize the sense of divine omnipotence: divine speech is a world-changing act.

So much for the wielding of verbatim and variant repetition to dramatize the tensions in the human context between forecast and enactment or enactment and report, to highlight the equivalences and smooth the transitions between them in the divine context, and to oppose the two contexts. This figures among the most powerful indirections at the service of the Bible's ideology (as well as its psychology, multiple viewing, artless-seeming artfulness). And its power largely derives from the adherence elsewhere to natural correlations of human restrictedness, all of which God transcends in a manner that would be unnatural were it not supernatural.

Considering its position in the Bible's world and storytelling, the God–narrator alliance definitely exerts its influence on all other participants and aspects of repetition. Still, outside the charmed circle of superhumans there remain some factors that allow combination further latitude.

Many literary traditions comply with the norm (and generate the expectancy) that each retelling of a nonverbal object should either vary, in form if not in meaning, from previous accounts or appear in summary shape. Such practice rests on a chain of assumptions: (1) From the *aesthetic* standpoint, the different members referring to the same object, especially if they are of the same type as well, must originate in different subjects—speakers, observers, minds—or else the text will incur tiresome redundancy. Hence (2): from the *realistic* standpoint, given the different sources of information, identity in retelling becomes improbable. And the larger the recurrent unit of discourse—that is, the number of choices available to each speaker—the more expected the variation and the more flagrant the duplication.

These premises operate as early as the epic tradition of the Middle Ages, where the German *Tristan and Isolde* or the Icelandic saga keep down recurrent members by drastic summary; and they rise to dominance in modern narrative, literary and cinematic, with its taste for perspectival variations à la *Rashomon*. Biblical narrative itself recognizes their claims, as I have shown, to a degree unrivaled in ancient art. In line with its horror of schematism, however, it will not allow them to exercise dictatorial powers. They figure as *a* not *the* norm.

The first assumption is denied absolute rule because for certain purposes the verbatim mode serves best, even or precisely where the source of information remains constant. In the epilogue to Judges, the narrator repeats no less than four times (twice with a follow-up) the statement "In those days there was no king in Israel": during the exposition of the Micah story (17:6), before the first reference to the Danite migration (18:1), at the head of the Rape of Gibeah scandal (19:1), and at its end (21:25), which also ends the whole book. Ostensibly superfluous beyond the need for temporal anchorage, this refrain yet performs yeoman service. In purely formal terms, oriented to the very fact of repetition and its placing along the sequence, it combines a segmentary with a unifying function. For the occurrences delimit the various episodes or stages while binding together what looks like a miscellany—not least the opening and closure of the series, for which the full variant, including "every man did what was right in his own eyes," is appropriately reserved. Even more notable are the semantic functions, which go on to exploit the meaning of the echo phrase by reference to the contexts that surround it. In the context of interepisodic relations, the phrase figures as a causal point of departure and as a theme for the various episodes to ring the changes on: anarchy ("no king") in the form of idolatry, daylight robbery, gang rape, murder, civil war, near-extermination of a whole tribe. In the context of the two framing episodes, it operates as datum and demonstrandum on its first appearance and as Q.E.D. on its last appearance. And in the larger biblical context, it ends Judges on a note that prepares for the rise of the monarchy in Samuel.

Nor does the second, "realistic" norm always prevail, and for reasons that go beyond the Bible's departure from empirical realism in postulating two superhuman informants. Their control of the world extends to structures of repetition where they rub shoulders with humanity. The forecast → enactment chain, we recall, may unfold a divine command with a human performance to match in order to demonstrate the performer's obedience, as with Noah's entry into the ark. In enactment → report sequence, the doubling confers reliability on the reporter when he might otherwise be misbelieved, as when Sarah attacks Hagar or Obadiah refuses to bear Elijah's message to Ahab. The narrator portrays Obadiah as a man who "feared the Lord greatly" and rescued a hundred prophets from Jezebel's sword; then, in his appeal to Elijah, Obadiah more or less reproduces this testimonial (1 Kgs 18:3-13). By validating the man's self-characterization in advance and to the last detail, the narrative gives us a measure of the religious terrorism of the times, which cowed even an Obadiah: the king "will kill me," he pleads, betraying to what an extent he has come to fear Ahab more than God. This in turn underscores Elijah's mettle and heightens suspense about the impending confrontation of prophet and king.

The same "unrealistic" equivalence in representation marks even series involving neither of the privileged informants, except behind the scenes. Before his exploit against the Philistines, Jonathan announces a double sign to his armor-bearer ("If they say to us, Wait until we come to you, then we will stand still in our place. . . . But if they say, Come up to us, then we will go up, for the Lord has delivered them into our hand"); and the enemy indeed echoes the second forecast: "Come up to us and we will show you a thing" (1 Sam 14:9-12). This brings to mind the scene in which Gilgamesh unwittingly echoes the old hunter's plan for trapping Enkidu, but with one typical difference. In *Gilgamesh,* the offense against realism makes no sense except as a symptom of conventionality that amounts to a failure (or refusal) to distinguish words from things and a string from a plot of repetition. That different speakers should independently express themselves in the same language is supposed to be no more incongruous than that they should refer to the same object. And, by formulaic fiat, the two coincidences go together. Whereas in the Bible such echoing becomes credible, if not strictly realistic, because it follows from the premises built into the model of a world regulated by an all-powerful God. It also becomes more functional, because it dramatizes in action the omnipotence of God, whose hand directs both forecast and fulfillment: a replicated sign is a God-given sign, so that Jonathan (like the Wooer of Rebekah before him) manifestly acts with God's blessing. This reveals afresh the Bible's flexibility—now appealing to artistic convention, now scrupulously exploring reality, and constantly interrelating the two—against the background of frozen styles often passing for its relatives.

Deliberate Variation: (Figural) Rhetoric within (Narratorial) Rhetoric

We now arrive at a fourth reason against freezing the linkage between the nature of the object and the nature of the repetition. All the earlier reasons derive from features marking the Bible's world and poetics, and serve to legitimate precise repetition even vis-à-vis a nonverbal object. This one concerns a feature common to all worlds, real or fictive, and "naturally" extends the possibilities of divergent repetition. I refer to *deliberate* variation on a character's part.

This is a key factor indeed. As well as being a distinctive constant of the narrator's practice, indispensable to the coherence of the narrative as artifact, deliberateness in variation is an option available to the whole dramatis personae as reporters. Of course, the narrator's motives will remain purer—aesthetic or communicative rather than worldly—and his control surer. In principle, however, a character intent on slanting or embroidering his report may (if caught) be punished after the fact, but no more prevented than one who misreports for lack of wit or knowledge. It follows that *every* structure of repetition is *throughout* a product not of two but three axes: the axis of the object ("verbal vs. nonverbal"), the axis of equivalence ("verbatim vs. variant") and the axis of motivation ("deliberate vs. nondeliberate").

There is a simple yet impressive measure of the extent to which this diversifies and entangles the combinatory choices. Where deliberate intent motivates the characters' misreporting—that is, closes the gap about why they deviate from antecedent members—the Bible levels verbal and nonverbal objects of report. The similarity does not lie only in the forms of variation (from incidentals to essentials, from retouching to monster falsehood, from ellipsis through substitution to change of order) to which the true facts are subjected in retelling. It extends to their functions as well, and for good reason. While unconscious variation mainly throws light on the character who falls into it—Pharaoh in speech, David and his men in thought—conscious variation presupposes the presence and influence of an addressee. No matter what the object presented, the effects of its misreporting center in the dramatic act of communication between the reporter and his audience.

At times, such a divergence spotlights—with an eye to judgment, character portrayal, or metonymic inside view—one of the interlocutors. This happens when Samuel, expected to act on Eli's coaching "If he calls to thee, thou shalt say, Speak, *Lord*, for thy servant hears," actually responds "Speak, for thy servant hears." The elision of the vocative betrays the novitiate's fear of uttering God's name (1 Sam 3:1-10). As with omission, so with substitution. Having been ordered to build an altar "to the God who appeared to thee when thou fleddest from thy brother Esau," Jacob changes the original time reference into a less unflattering generality: he will build an altar, he tells the family, "to the God who answered me in the day of my distress" (Gen 35:1-3). In either case, then, the motivation for the shift in wording turns on a shift in role undergone by a dialogist as the plot goes forward: from a (passive) addressee in one scene to an (active) speaker in another.

For a more intricate example of betraying motive by misquotation, consider the charge leveled by Gideon at the people of Succoth after his victory over Midian: "Behold Zebah and Zalmunah [the kings of Midian], concerning whom you taunted me, saying, Is the fist of Zebah and Zalmunah now in thy hand, that we should give bread to thy weary men?" (Judg 8:15). However villainous the quoted people of Succoth, they could hardly go so far as to load the dice against themselves by referring to the army they refuse to feed as "weary men." Indeed, checking the quotation against their actual words given earlier, we find that they did nothing so foolish. Gideon has simply effected a montage between his original appeal ("Give, pray, loaves of bread to the people that follow me, for they are weary") and their original response ("Is the fist of Zebah and Zalmunah now in thy hand, that we should give bread to thy army?"), so as to blacken the accused before destroying them. And the very same function borne by ellipsis (Samuel) or substitution (Jacob, Gideon, Joseph interpreting Pharaoh's dream) may attach to displacements of order as well. As if putting the Gideon technique to a new use, Saul thus sharpens the indictment of the Nob priests as David's accomplices. For he rearranges the charges listed by his spy ("He inquired of the Lord for him and gave him provisions and gave him the sword of Goliath") into an ascending order of treason: "Why have you conspired against me, thou and the son of Jesse, in that thou gavest him bread and a sword and hast inquired of the Lord for him?" (1 Sam 22:9, 13).

Elsewhere the variation throws light not on the speaker but on the addressee. When the elders of Israel address to Samuel the demand "Now make for us a king to judge us like all the nations," the prophet's response is cited as "the thing was evil in the eyes of Samuel when they said, Give us a king to judge us" (1 Sam 8:5-6). 'That is what he heard,' the truncated report suggests. What was the thing found "evil in the eyes of Samuel"? Not so much the wish to become "like all the nations" as that to replace the judging prophet by "a king to judge us." Where we might expect prophetic indignation, we encounter prophetic self-interest. In context, the hint at motives less than pure gains validation from its sandwiching between a chain of anticipatory echoes to the key verb ("Samuel judged Israel . . . and he judged Israel . . . and he made his sons judges over Israel . . . judges in Beersheba") and the blunt corrective provided in God's own response ("It is not thee that they have rejected, but me that they have rejected from being king over them"). In line with the principled discontinuity between form and function, however, the shortened retelling from the addressee's standpoint may equally do duty for a favorable inside view. The emphasis on the exact point at which Eli broke down while listening to the message of defeat supplies a telling contrast to Samuel's self-centeredness: "The bringer of the tidings answered and said, Israel has fled before the Philistines, and there has also been a great slaughter among the people, and thy two sons Hophni and Phineas are also dead, and the ark of God has been captured. And when he mentioned the ark of God, Eli fell over backward from his seat . . . and his neck was broken and he died" (1 Sam 4:17-18).

Most often, however, deliberate deviance exposes not so much the secret life of either party to the dialogue as their relations and the things left unsaid or implicit in the official record of the speech-event:

> Eli was very old, and he heard all that his sons were doing to all Israel and how they lay with the women who served at the entrance to the tent of meeting. And he said to them, Why do you do such things? For I hear of your evil doings from all the people. Nay, my sons, it is no good report that I hear. (1 Sam 2:22-24)

> Abraham and Sarah were old, advanced in years; it had ceased to be with Sarah after the manner of women. So Sarah laughed to herself, saying, After I have withered, shall I have pleasure—and my husband old? Then the Lord said to Abraham, Why did Sarah laugh, saying, Shall I indeed give birth, old as I am? (Gen 18:11-13)

He [Amnon] would not listen to her and overpowered her and forced her and lay with her. . . . Tamar put ashes on her head, and tore the ornamented (?) tunic which she wore, and laid her hand on her head and went away, crying aloud as she went. Then Absalom her brother said to her, Has Amnon thy brother been with thee? (2 Sam 13:14-20)

These doublings seem to have little in common. Apart from the nature of the reported object, they differ in the reporter's modes of variation from it: elision, telescoping, shift of grammatical person, and assorted forms of paraphrase. Yet they all perform the same communicative function, central to the biblical repetition-within-dialogue: the tactful mention of awkward subjects. The unpleasantness may be blurred, softened, skirted in transmission, and the tact itself may range from a mere fig leaf for the transmitter's cowardice to a sincere desire to spare the addressee.

Far from taxing his sons with the foregoing record of sacrilege, Eli does not even properly summarize it. He opts for such empty formulas— "these things," "no good report," at most "evil doings"—that no wonder God holds him responsible for their criminality. (As in Pharaoh's dream, the summary form proves no less functional than detailed repetition, verbatim or variant.) With Sarah's laughter, each of the two final members is a selective variant of the narrator's opening: "Abraham and Sarah were old" → "my husband old" → "old as I am." Each is therefore true as far as it goes; and the shift of person God effects in his report to Abraham is only, as the rabbis charmingly put it, in the interests of peace (*Bereshit Rabba* 48:21). Still more revealing is Absalom's allusion to the outrage against Tamar. Following the narrator's blunt language, this understatement made to a sister in agony displays Absalom at his most attractive and at the same time, by its almost superhuman self-control, lays the ground for the future revenge.

The deliberately variant retrospect often plays an even more active part in biblical dialogue, one that subsumes "tactful" reference as a gambit, softening-up flattery, or snare for the addressee. The speaker's deviations then make sense in terms of his endeavor to move, persuade or impose his will on his interlocutor by contriving an ad hominem version of an antecedent speech or event. Such a scene marks an intersection of two distinct rhetorics: the inset rhetoric, directly brought to bear by the reporting speaker on some other character, and the framing rhetoric by which the narrator manipulates his reader behind their backs. The intersection thus goes with a remarkable symmetry between inset and frame, since both speakers are rhetorically self-conscious—unlike the asymmetrical pattern of nondeliberate variation, where the narrator simply exploits the figure's blind spots for his own ends.

But even communicative symmetry by no means entails equivalence in intention and performance. On the contrary, given the fundamental disparity in addressee and privilege and motivation, this is precisely where one should expect to find a clash of interests. (With the equally predictable exception of God's discourse, as in the symmetrical *and* harmonious contexts of the omnipotence effect.) Thus, while the narrator's own version maneuvers (as usual) between the truth and the whole truth but draws the line at untruth, the dramatis personae show no such scruples in reporting. Since the name of their game is life and often survival rather than history writing, they play by far looser and rougher rules, not excluding the self-conferred license of free invention. Their mendacity may be as blatant as the lies David tells Achish about his raids on Israel. It may also produce subtler fictions, restrained in scope and impressive in technique. This is the case with the address to Rebekah's family, with the comedy of errors among David, Joab and the messenger in the Bathsheba affair, with the oratory whereby the Hivite leaders urge the alliance with Jacob's clan (pp. 464–66 below). For a meeting of these extremes, look at the art of poisonous repetition commanded by Potiphar's wife:

> (11) One day, he [Joseph] came into the house to do his work, and none of the men of the house was there in the house. (12) And she caught him by his garment, saying, Lie with me. And he left his garment in her hand and fled and got outside. (13) When she saw that he had left his garment in her hand and fled outside, (14) she called the men of her house and spoke to them, saying, Look, he has brought us a Hebrew man to play games with us; he came in to me to lie with me, and I cried out with a loud voice. (15) And when he heard that I raised my voice and cried, he left his garment by me and fled and got outside. (16) She kept his garment by her until his master came home. (17) Then she spoke to him according to these words, saying, There came in to me the Hebrew slave that thou hast brought us to play games with me. (18) And as I raised my voice and cried, he left his garment by me and fled outside. (19) When his master heard the words of his wife which she spoke to him, saying, Such and such things did thy slave do to me, his anger was kindled. (20) And Joseph's master took him and put him into the prison where the king's prisoners were confined. (Gen 39:11–20)

The seduction scene itself (verses 11–12) is followed by four reports (verses 13, 14–15, 17–18, 19), of which the first and the last seem wholly redundant and the rest overtreated. "The device," one critic complains, "is used in a shoddy fashion. . . . Must the author be so unimaginatively repetitive?"[33] As always, however, it is the reader who must be imaginative in going below the opaque surface of repetition. The plot itself will then look different. With the proper closure of the gaps, the fivefold series tightens into a well-formed causal chain where the secret life assumes such importance and its workings are explored with such delicacy as to raise the episode to a different order of art from the comparable Egyptian "Story of Two Brothers."

Joseph's flight not only enrages but also compromises his mistress. He may well report her for sexual assault, and even if he holds his tongue, others may prove less discreet. The otherwise excessive mention of the house as arena ("He came into the house . . . none of the men of the house was there in the house") suggests the nearness of the servants; hence the probability of their having observed that between entry and exit the young man lost his garment (and in the Samaritan version, "his garments"). Potiphar's wife at once senses this danger. Note the repetition "she saw that he had left his garment in her hand and fled outside"—ushered in by the subjective reporting verb "saw" and concluding with the spatial adverb "outside" that betrays less concern about Joseph's escape than about its direction. But if it first appears that self-preservation is her motive for summoning the household, then once she opens her mouth, it turns out that the same piece of repetition signaled offensive intent as well. It occurred to her that the two incriminating facts are mute witnesses—just like David's spoils (1 Samuel 27) or Brunhild's ring and girdle in the *Nibelungenlied*—and therefore amenable to an interpretive twist that will point an accusing finger at Joseph himself. "When she saw that he had left his garment in her hand and fled outside": (1) therefore his exit will draw attention. (The stress falls on "left his garment" and "fled outside." This also explains why she fails to echo the narrator's more accurate version "fled and got outside": the danger lies in his egress in undress, particularly if it looks like flight.) (2) Therefore he laid himself open to a circumstantial frame-up. (The emphasis falls on "in her hand," which still clutches the evidence. In this offensive context, the brevity of "fled outside" links up both with her sense of injury ["He ran away from me"], which cries out for revenge, and with the final impression ["He panicked and ran"] that she hopes to produce.)

Potiphar's wife thus decides on the spot to forestall all possible tale-bearing and at the same time to lay the ground for the tale she herself will spin for her husband. Hence the movement from the first to the second report. The vocal address ("said") to the servants is no more a digression or an interlude than the internal discourse ("saw") that went before it, but rather falls into place as another link in the woman's plot. For the achievement of either goal turns on the servants as the potential witnesses for good or for ill. Indeed, she launches the operation by making a supreme effort to enlist their sympathy and backing.

"When she saw . . . she called": losing no time, she raises the alarm to give color to her story. Then, shrewdly manipulating the evidence, she retouches as well as resets the basic facts (the garment has been left not "in my hand,"[34] naturally, but "by me"); waves the mute exhibit before their eyes ("Look"); and addresses herself to the ears, too, through the evocation of outraged sound—"I cried out in a loud voice . . . I raised my voice and cried"—designed to insinuate into the audience's mind a sequence of screaming that extends from the moment of attempted rape to their own arrival on the scene. Where the persuader concentrates her efforts, though, is on forging an alliance with the auditors by arguing her case ad hominem.

That argument works by a strategy of affective reference, combining the rhetoric of grammatical person with the rhetoric of descriptive terms. The mistress wins over her slaves by establishing a common, democratic frame of pronominal reference ("to us," "with us") and adducing the sexual assault on herself as an illustrative consequence of importing a Hebrew "to play games with us." With the social status of her audience in mind, she of course guards against referring to Joseph as a servant: he is a "man"—just like them, "the men of the house." Yet she finds other and more artful ways to clinch solidarity by playing on the inferior's antagonism to his superior. The fellowship of "we" is opposed to the partnership in domination and guilt of the pair cast in the third person singular, one being none other than the master who subjected them to the misrule of his trusty: to the unholy alliance, cemented in Hebrew by limpid word-play, between him who "brought [*hebi*] to us" and him who "came [*ba*] in to me." That the licensed game-player is "a Hebrew" crowns social insult with ethnic injury. It is no accident that these incitements crowd together in her exposition: they work up a frame of mind where the body of the report will be swallowed with howls of rage.

Having covered her back, the woman can freely operate on her husband. There is no longer any need for self-defense, like dwelling on one's screams beyond the point natural for any innocent victim. Gone is also the need for a scrupulous adherence, on pain of refutation, to observable facts. The men of (and about) the house received the true sequence of events, "He fled and got outside"; now she can afford to feed her husband the more blackening version "He fled outside." With the confidence born of having behind her a group of servants eager to testify that she screamed and he bolted, she now moves into the offensive, armed with a version furbished once again ad hominem.

The arousal of ethnic prejudice ("the Hebrew") again goes with social incitement, but in the reverse direction. With Potiphar now figuring as addressee, Joseph is no longer termed "man" but "slave," just as "us" shifts in reference (and solidarity) from the household to the master and mistress. To sting her husband into action, she again throws on him part of the blame, though, by another clever readjustment of psychological tactics, in a manner less shrill and more cautious. Now the report changes from

> *He has brought us a Hebrew man to play games with us. He came in to me to*
> *lie with me*
> into
> *There came in to me the Hebrew slave that thou hast brought us to play games*
> *with me.*

This offers a signal lesson in applied rhetoric. As part of the tactics of softening, she varies (1) the proportions between Potiphar's and Joseph's roles; (2) the order of "bringing" and "coming," with a similar effect; (3) the linkage between these acts, from a general–particular to a looser main clause–relative clause bond that turns the accusation implicit (as in Adam's apologetics to God, "the woman *whom* thou gavest to be with me, she gave me of the fruit of the tree and I ate"); and (4) the syntactic embedding of the purpose phrase "to play games with," from univocal to ambiguous subordination. In the address to the servants, the phrase was clearly subordinated to "he brought" and therefore leveled against Potiphar as instigator. But now the phrase falls either under "brought" and Potiphar,

> There came in to me the Hebrew slave (that thou hast brought us to
> play games with me)

or under "came" and Joseph:

> There came in to me the Hebrew slave (that thou hast brought us) to
> play games with me.

Within this syntactic equivocation, each alternative reading involves a different degree of blame. Nominally, the wife takes cover behind the second, minimal structure. Even so, she sees to it that the imputation should strike home. The four softening touches are counterbalanced by four sharpenings: (1) The causal link implicit in the common root of "brought" and "came" (cf. "give" in Adam's excuse above) now tightens owing to the increased continuity, textual and syntactic, between the two verbs. (2) The relative clause, with its flick at the bringer, gains perceptibility from its awkward embedding in the heart of the main clause. (3) "Came in to me" may be understood as either "approached" or, euphemistically, "lay with." This lexical ambiguity, unlike the syntactic one in (4) above, is indeed temporary but still deliberately prolonged. The woman holds the two meanings (and her spouse's hope and fear) suspended through a grammatical pattern of retardation, where the in-between relative clause is calculated to heighten Potiphar's sense of guilt while delaying the phrase that resolves the tension. (4) That phrase itself effects a provocative variation in the sense of the key verb: "to play games with me" (= to have sexual intercourse) in place of "to play games with us" (= to abuse), chosen earlier to encompass and win over "the *men* of the house."

So the conspiracy achieves its goal; but, ironically, more due to of the conspirator's wholesale lying than to her talent for pressing the right buttons. The fourth report of the event— "when his master heard the words of his wife which she spoke to him, saying, Such and such things did thy slave do to me, his anger was kindled"—looks extremely odd. It forms a repetition of the repetition just perpetrated by the wife. Further, it bears only the faintest resemblance to the account it supposedly echoes. And it shows the most heterogeneous composition: ostensibly a direct rehearsal of the woman's speech, it in fact consists of a bit of summary interpolated by the narrator ("Such and such things") and a bit of quotation that is anything but quotation-like ("did thy slave do to me"). All these incongruities make sense, however, as a multiple clue to a shift in perspective: they invite us to grasp "when his master heard" as a reporting phrase of consciousness that prefaces another subjective view, just like "When she saw" of verse 13. (The two even correspond in terms of plot, the one marking the germination and the other the fruition of the frame-up.) The quote following the verb thus reflects not the wife's (the speaker's) viewpoint but her husband's (the addressee's), as if to suggest 'This is what he heard her say,' 'Such is his evaluation of the affair.'

In this context, the referring term "thy slave" leaps to the eye, as the only element in the repetition that has escaped the flattening process of summary. Indeed, this term holds the key to "his anger was kindled." In its light, it is not the racial pressure that has done the trick (or else the text would read "thy Hebrew slave"); nor has the social agitation (for the text fails to repeat the woman's simple definite article, "*the* slave"); nor has the personal needling (as would be implied by "the slave whom thou hast brought to us"). What above all infuriated Potiphar is the thought that the offender is *his* special slave, who has betrayed the position of trust to which he has been raised. (Joseph's early appeal to his mistress underscores the enormity of such a betrayal: "He is not greater in this house than I am; nor has he kept anything back from me except thyself, because thou art his wife. How then can I do this great evil and sin against God?") It is no accident that toward the end of the tale the narrator twice reverts to the term "his master," which appeared at the outset and then disappeared as the relations between Potiphar and Joseph got closer. The enraged patron again turns master and throws his seemingly ungrateful slave into prison, from which he will rise to an even more brilliant career under Pharaoh himself. Nor is it fortuitous, perhaps, that no sooner has Joseph's new master invested him with authority over all Egypt than he provides him with a wife of his own. Just to be on the safe side.

Generic Transformation into Parable

The maneuvers executed by Potiphar's wife show how and why the rhetorical encounter within the world—like any other function of repetition, above all of the deliberately deviant type—may involve assorted forms of variation that cooperate ad hoc. It is the speaker's designs on his addressee within the inset act of communication and the narrator's on the reader in the frame that determine and explain the means. In terms of the operations of reading, our business is, as always, to establish relations between the means as the givens to be organized and the ends as the organizing hypotheses. We start by identifying the objective forms of variation, therefore, with a view to linking or motivating them in terms of the speaker's rhetoric (or, in unconscious deviance, state) on the one hand and the narrator's on the other. In successful interpretation, all these forms will find their place, though not the same place, within this twofold communicative process.

Still, there is one form of repetition-with-variation that operates in an exceptionally constant manner: the shift from standard narrative into the genre of parable. Unlike the corresponding "symbolic" transformation from or into dream, the parable as a member of the biblical structure of repetition is always (1) located toward the end of the sequence; (2) delegated to one of the agents within the drama; (3) manipulated even in the sphere of dramatic communication. None of these distinctive features appears in, say, Pharaoh's dream: neither the order of telling (the dream leads the way), nor the source of telling (which overtly includes the narrator himself), nor the "deliberate" motivation for the variant retelling (Pharaoh deviates from incomprehension).

This fixed configuration enables the narrator to enable his characters to put the generic shift to two uses, both assimilating the parable to the overall movement of the action. Even its more conventional use, as manifested in Jotham's parable in Judges 9, yields the parablist some gains in rhetoric. It provides him with a "natural" justification for recasting the facts of his case—however well-known to the addressee—into the terms that will best serve his purpose. (Jotham thus loads the dice against the enemy by speaking of the Shechemites as trees and of Abimelech as the bramble that they made king over them.) It also enables him to present the new version to his audience in an objective guise and to invest the moral with general validity.

Of course, these are the reasons that the parable—just like the joke in everyday discourse—has always enjoyed such popularity. But whether the parable appears as a self-contained genre or as a unit within another genre, this tactics suffers from two drawbacks. The audience may not be taken in by the parablist's pretense of departing from the facts only in inessentials and because of generic constraints: he may well meet with responses like "Comparisons are imperfect" or, more bluntly, "Argument by analogy is an old trick." As with the citizenry of Shechem harangued by Jotham, moreover, the parable will have little effect on interested parties. In either case, the audience remains unmoved.

In the parable as an independent genre directly addressed to the reader, these drawbacks often result indeed in artistic failure. Yet they may be turned to artistic account once parable is incorporated, as loaded repetition, into the drama—precisely thanks to the built-in disparity in viewpoint between dramatic speaker and manipulating narrator, dramatic addressee and implied reader. Like everything else set into the world, the parable then comes to lead a double existence. Jotham does not in the least move the partisan Shechemites. But his failure is the narrator's success, indeed the point and the making of the whole cycle. For it serves to articulate the theme under cover of indignant repetition, to dramatize the fitness of the parable in terms of its ineffectuality, and to propel the action toward the enactment of its moral: the mutual destruction of the townsmen and the usurper.

What is more, even where concerned to ensure the parablist's success, the narrator may retain all the advantages of the standard parable and yet eliminate from the structure of repetition its generic weak point: the addressee's awareness of being brainwashed by means of a symbolic analogy. How to preserve the symmetry in awareness between speaker and narrator while creating an asymmetry between auditor and reader? The Bible's solution is the *veiled parable,* a trap reserved for kings.

Consider the Poor Man's Ewe-Lamb (1 Samuel 12), the Tekoite woman's appeal for justice (2 Samuel 14), and the disguised prophet's complaint to Ahab (1 Kings 20). In each scene, the king labors under the illusion that he is listening to a teller not a reteller: that he is dealing with a genuine legal case, utterly divorced from his own affairs. Having engineered this ironic discrepancy, the parablist speaking as appellant is free from the endemic handicaps of the genre and can exploit its strengths to trick the judge into self-judgment. First, because veiled rhetoric is the most effective in "life" as in "art." Second, because the speaker may then remold the facts at will, not under the transparent artistic pretext "Such is the genre" but in the realistic guise of "Such is the case." Third, because the deviations, far from being registered as deviations, further distract the addressee's notice from the analogy with his own situation.[35] Fourth, because, once the pressures of self-interest are lifted, the auditor is easily led into passing the desired objective sentence—just as, having passed it, he will find it difficult to wriggle out of its application to himself. At the moment of truth, when the springing of "Thou art the man" reveals the whole scandalous tale as a variation by parable on royal conduct, it is too late to extricate oneself from the trap, certainly for a king sitting in judgment. Not even Ahab has the face to prevaricate. The difference in point of view thus explains why in the Bible's world all overt parables fall flat and all veiled ones come off as rhetorics of repetition.

Permutations and Some Complications

Table 1 on pages 432–35 recapitulates the play of five key variables discussed throughout. It will bring out something of the Bible's combinatory range (slashed deletion indicates nonviability within its discourse). If even the Bible leaves some permutations void, this is by reason of its narrative model. The narrator so merges into the implied author that his version, whatever the object it images and the equivalence-relations borne by the imaging, always makes artistic sense. In vain, therefore, shall we look here for the complications arising where the teller is himself a struggling human, his reports devoid of any privileged status over others and possibly even self-contradictory. Yet such a failure to exhaust the theoretical options carries no normative import—and not only because, historically, the unreliable narrator is a late arrival. Indispensable to biblical poetics as a whole, the narrator's authority is a cornerstone of the structure of repetition itself: it heartens the reader with a promise of none too remote control throughout his quest for coherence between the Scylla of redundancy and the Charybdis of disharmony, and arms him with an objective key to each puzzle. In literature as in language, abundance and shortage are measured by reference to the needs or goals to be fulfilled rather than to some a priori inventory of means. And the Bible sets a limit to its repertoire at what would become in context the point of diminishing returns.

On the other hand, note that the table does not cover all the factors I have discussed but focuses on the three axes whose interplay proved to control and ramify the entire technique. Even that interplay is not fully captured, in the absence of such variables as God's transcendent status or the applicability of the "deliberate–nondeliberate" opposition to the addressee as well. Nor does the table reflect the Bible's practice of "crossing" the basic factors themselves, so as to produce mixed objects, sources, or motivations.

The story of Samson's birth (Judges 13) thus presents a mixed object, combining a piece of reality with a piece of discourse. The appearance of "the angel of the Lord" to the mother-to-be (who demotes him in her report to her husband to "a man of God" with a countenance "like an angel of God, very terrible," so that the narrator's fact becomes a verbal figure in baffled transmission) goes together with the angel's message (which likewise suffers at the addressee's hands). A mixture of sources occurs whenever a single member of repetition combines the viewpoints of one personage with another's (as with Gideon misquoting the men of Succoth) or, more often, with the narrator's, as in Potiphar's response to his wife's concoction or in numerous instances of the free indirect style. The result is perspectival duality or montage.

Especially widespread are the complications in the reasons for verbatim and above all deviant retelling. Different members may thus oppose different motives, as when the serpent's cold-blooded garbling of God's ordinance ("Even though God said, You shall not eat of all the fruit of the garden") brings out the resentment lurking in the woman's unconscious divergence and her ripeness for seduction. Even a single member may suggest different motivations. If the prospective mother omits from her account of the angel's forecast that the son will "deliver Israel from the hand of the Philistines," the gap invites closure in terms of inattention or forgetfulness: her family concerns understandably crowd out the national issues that dominate the book.[36] But her omission of the angel's solemn exordium—"Behold, thou art barren and hast not given birth," which echoes the narrator's own exposition—is of course a matter of deliberate amnesia, a piece of self-tact, so to speak.

Further, a single variant may invite the same dual motivation as a whole report or series of reports. Take the sequence of explanations for Naboth's refusal to sell his vineyard to Ahab (1 Kgs 21:1-6). The reason given by Naboth himself was, "The Lord forbid that I should give the inheritance of my fathers to thee." Ahab then returns home "vexed and sullen because of the word which Naboth the Jezreelite had spoken to him, saying, I will not give thee the inheritance of my fathers." And when questioned by Jezebel, he quotes Naboth's response to his offer as "I will not give thee my vineyard."

The two retrospects mark a progressive decrease in the weight and civility of the original negative. In the privacy of his own mind, Ahab first replaces the horrified "God forbid that I should give" by the self-willed gruffness of "I will not give." Also, he both weakens and sharpens Naboth's explanation: "the inheritance of my fathers to thee," where the direct object with all its causal and emotive load precedes the indirect object, is misrecalled in an order that smuggles in a note of defiance. For "I will not give thee" changes the emphasis into 'You may be king, but I remain master of my property,' if not 'I might sell to others but not to you.' In the dialogue with his wife, Ahab then suppresses Naboth's grounds altogether: "I will not give thee my vineyard." As with Eve's switch of God's admonition against

Table 1. Basic Guide to the Structure of Repetition

combination No.	object of presentation	first source of presentation	source of retelling	mode of retelling
1	nonverbal	the narrator	the narrator	(near-) verbatim
2	"	"	"	"
3–4	"	"	a character	"
5-6	"	a character	the narrator	"
7	"	"	a character	"
8	"	"	"	"
9–10	"	the narrator	the narrator	variant
11-12	"	"	a character	"

motivation for mode of retelling	Examples and Comments
deliberately	"In those days there was no king in Israel" (Judges 17:6–21:25)
non~~delibe~~rately	presumption of control
deliberately/nondeliberately	A biblical character cannot hark back to the narrator's wording, which lies outside his ken, but can only describe the facts accessible to him and unwittingly coincide with the narrator, as Sarah does in her charge against Hagar.
deliberately/non~~delibe~~rately	Rare in the Bible's *report* → *enactment* sequence, because opposed to normal order. Common in *prospect* → *enactment* sequence: "God said, Let there be light" etc. Grounded in convention, these frequencies vary elsewhere.
~~deliberately~~	Impossible: if his account refers to another's, the object becomes verbal; and if not, how can the repetition be deliberate?
nondeliberately	Only by Gilgamesh-like stylization of reality
deliberately/non~~delibe~~rately	The swelling of the Flood
deliberately/nondeliberately	Cf. 3–4 above: owing to their different frames of existence, a biblical character can no more choose to diverge from than to rehearse the narrator's version. But the character may diverge, deliberately (Potiphar's wife) or nondeliberately (Pharaoh), from the facts objectified in the member of enactment.

Table 1. Basic Guide to the Structure of Repetition

combination No.	object of presentation	first source of presentation	source of retelling	mode of retelling
13–14	nonverbal	a character	the narrator	variant
15	"	"	a character	"
16	"	"	"	"
17–18	verbal	the narrator	the narrator	(near-) verbatim
19–20	"	"	a character	"
21–22	"	a character	the narrator	"
23	"	"	a character	"
24	"	"	"	"
25–26	"	the narrator	the narrator	variant
27–28	"	"	a character	"
29–30	"	a character	the narrator	"
31	"	"	a character	"
32	"	"	"	"

motivation for mode of retelling	Examples and Comments
deliberately/nondeliberately	Rare in the Bible's *report* → *enactment* sequence, because opposed to normal order (but see 2 Sam 16:3 → 19:25). Common in *forecast* → *enactment* sequence, notably where man proposes but God disposes (e.g., the Baal prophets' vain appeal in 1 Kgs 18:26).
deliberately	Micaiah's true prophecy
nondeliberately	Ahima'az's tidings
deliberately/nondeliberately	Not in the Bible: only in texts where the narrator quotes (as distinct from repeats) himself, after the fashion of Joseph's "It is as I have said to you, You are spies."
deliberately/nondeliberately	Cf. 3–4 above.
deliberately/nondeliberately	Cf. 5–6 above: the rebuilding of Jericho, Joseph's testament (Gen 50:25 → Exod 13:19)
deliberately	scrupulous messengers or God quoting overheard human discourse (Exod 32: 4, 8)
nondeliberately	Jonathan's sign
deliberately/nondeliberately	Cf. 17–18 above
deliberately/nondeliberately	Cf. 11–12 above
deliberately/nondeliberately	Samuel and the elders of Israel
deliberately	Gideon and the Succoth men
nondeliberately	Jonathan misquoting David (1 Sam 20:6, 28–30)

eating from "the tree of the knowledge of good and evil" into "the tree within the garden," the thing indicated remains constant but not the charged phrase indicating it. So the emotion of the original answer gives place to an equable tone, its logic of the heart to arbitrariness, and its apologetic detail to a curt negative.

This variation certainly proves deadly, in the most literal sense, but is it deliberate? Does Ahab misquote Naboth by one of those tricks memory plays on a mind reliving a humiliating scene, or with a view to stinging Jezebel into action? The clues to this central repetition gap point both ways. On the one hand, the devaluation of Naboth's refusal began as early as Ahab's mulling it over on his way home. On the other hand, he does not lift a finger to prevent the murder, and God explicitly lashes him with "Hast thou killed and also taken possession?" The ambiguity squares, moreover, with the wider context of the reign. Given the tendency of Kings to draw a distinction within villainy between Ahab and Jezebel, it is appropriate that it should introduce here a slight ambivalence in his favor by leaving the motivation for the garbling "mixed" while categorically denouncing the results.

Finally, we encounter diverse cross-couplings along the sequence of repetition. In Pharaoh's Dream, for example, Pharaoh unwittingly varies from the nonverbal reality unfolded in his dream, whereas Joseph makes a point of varying from Pharaoh's form of words in order to correct its variations and reconstruct the original object. Or the messenger deliberately varies from Joab's text, thereby misrepresenting the course of the battle that led to Uriah's elimination, only because he is ignorant of the king's death warrant and of what lies behind Joab's (deliberately deviant) performance and (deliberately faithful) report.

Repetition and Narrative Art: Some General Consequences

The structure of repetition exhibits a number of principles and alliances that have far-reaching implications for biblical poetics and for literary theory in general.

First, the argument throws some light on the intricate problem of the literary norm (convention, scheme, model): the difference between formal and functional regularity, the possibility of retaining the matrix of a convention or formula while divesting it of its inert and schematic features, or the links between models of composition and reality. The comparison with the ancient tradition that produced a *Gilgamesh* and on the other hand with modern literature turns out especially enlightening. In the very frequency of repetition and its objective control, biblical narrative is of its time and place. Yet in the flexibility of form and operation, it not only anticipates but often surpasses the achievements of modernism. Such is the range of variables endowed with distinctive force—the type of member, the nature of the object, the source of presentation, the degree of specificity and redundancy, the kind of correspondence effected, the order of serialization, or the motivational logic—as to do more than invalidate any formulaic approach. None of the possibilities of repetition—neither verbatim nor variant nor telescoped, for example—is allowed to assume control as the general norm against the background of which any departure gains its perceptibility and meaning. We have here not a single normative (let alone binding and mechanical) scheme but rather a set of equipollent options—large yet delimited—so that the choice of each stands out and calls for explanation against the background of the rejected alternatives.

This stamps the art of repetition with the hallmark of the Bible's narrative economy and locates it poles apart from the Near Eastern conventions under which Cassuto (and other overenthusiastic Orientalists) would have us subsume it. Avoiding the babble about the talkative Oriental and the nodding redactor, Cassuto places ancient Israelite literature in its proper tradition, but still in a misleading perspective. Of all the synchronic and diachronic features that go to make a tradition, the aspect of similarity receives exclusive notice—with the result that the foregrounding of geographical, cultural, and historical continuity comes at the price of overlooking the distance that separates the primitive from the sophisticated, the tradition-bound from the tradition-sensitive, the rule from the innovation that transforms everything except the shell or family resemblance. Within formulaic storytelling, after all, *Baal and Anath* or *Gilgamesh* cannot compare even with Homeric epic. "It goes against the grain with me to repeat a tale already plainly told," Odysseus tells the Phaeacians; and in this he certainly speaks for his creator. But Homer's repetition is still a far cry from the Bible's, which for historical reasons alone operates with a scheme where effects familiar from modern literature emerge in the guise of homogeneity between members, by way of slight and relatively hidden variations, rather under the banner of manifest heterogeneity and artifice. The old forms are revitalized and their constraints stretched to accommodate a new poetics.

Thus oriented but not assimilated to convention, biblical narrative also follows a universal of art and art history that I elsewhere called the Proteus Principle: the resistance to any automatic linkage of form and function. Given the appropriate contexts, the same means may serve different semantic and rhetorical ends, and different means (including precise and deviant repetition) the same end. Without as well as within repetition itself, due attention to this principle might wean biblical scholarship away from such habits as confusing the lack or scarcity of evaluative statements on the narrator's part ("objectivity" as nonintervention) with evaluative neutrality ("objectivity" as noninvolvement) and the lack of overt inside views with a lack of interest in psychology.[37]

To accomplish this protean functionality, third, the structure of repetition interacts with all other aspects and levels of biblical narrative. Its partners range from verbal art (phonic and lexical equivalence, syntactic form, semantic shift or ambiguity), through world picture (with its absence of modern technology or its omnipresent God) and dialogue and analogy, to ideological thematics and generic repertoire. But the closest interrelation is with the narrative modes, especially with the two areas about which the narrator is most reticent: the inner life of the agents and the ethical value of their acts. Repetition systematically illuminates those dark spots. The role of inside view is not necessarily fulfilled by a psychological statement nor that of judgment by a normative statement. Both are performed by a structural measure that could hardly appear less related to them.

In this regard, moreover, there emerge surprising bonds between repetition and gapping. Ostensibly, these mark polar principles: extreme redundancy on the one hand and extreme ellipsis on the other. Yet the incompatibles turn into complementaries, yoked together in the service of a unitary artistic logic. It is not only that both work by indirection, nor only that repetition draws notice to gaps and gaps to repetition. The repetition itself opens gaps of its own and closes gaps not of its own making as well. Each marking a pole of incoherence, juxtaposed opposition included, the two meet as routes to difficult coherence.

Fourth, the Bible's structure of repetition is so versatile that it offers a model for literary redundancy. Its many theoretical lessons are ultimately reducible to a set of motivating or interpretive rules. In terms of the operations of reading, the basic strategies of explaining and thus eliminating the redundancy assume the form of shifting it from its nominal (and inadequate) framework to one or more latent alternatives:

1. the framework of actional dynamics (i.e., as an index of a change in the state of affairs—say, the Flood—relative to the foregoing member);
2. the framework of presentational dynamics (i.e., as a twist given to the expectation—about Micaiah's prophecy, say—aroused in the foregoing member);
3. the perspectival framework (as a change in viewpoint from narrator to character, from character to character, from speaker to addressee, from single to multiple voice);

4. the framework of judgment (evaluating what has gone before, as with the rhetoric that shapes our attitude to God's powers or Noah's obedience or Ahab's wrongdoing);
5. the compositional framework (e.g., change in the focus of interest, movement from the general to the particular, or the resumption of a suspended narrative thread);
6. the generic framework (modulations into the key of poetry, parable, dream);
7. the poetic or aesthetic framework (notably by appeal to the Bible's tendency to dissimulate rather than bare artifice or to highlight variants against the background of constants—both preferences calling for a measure of equivalence between members, even at the price of a certain redundancy).

Singly or together, these establish meaning and coherence beyond the transparent plot intelligibility. So the shift from the nominal to the tacit framework of repetition coincides with the progress from minimal to maximal reading, from the truth to the whole truth.

More specifically, the strategies yield an impressive array of functions and effects. These include the double cohesion (in terms of both plot and parallelism) of the episode; the linkage of different points along the sequence; multiple views; variations in tempo, genre, sense; the manipulation of curiosity, suspense, and surprise; the filling out of internal processes; implicit commentary and thematic development; and, of course, the enhancement of reading activity. It is hard to think of a part that the structure of repetition cannot be made to play.

In view of certain misapplications of my theory, however, I want to end by reiterating my original caveat. As with other fundamentals of biblical art, one must not expect each instance of repetition to unlock the secrets of the tale. In a corpus of such diversity, the technique may at times cohere only in terms of more general services like variety, symmetry, emphasis, retardation, or control of tempo. Compared with the formulaic style, this does not often happen. But the possibility must be considered, as must also that of textual misadventure, however dissuasive its traditional abuse. By the law of reaction, the old and self-defeating extreme of exegetical and/or genetic atomism makes the opposite extreme of holism doubly attractive. But the gains of substituting "Everything makes sense" for "Nothing makes sense" turn on its operation as a working hypothesis to explore the text with, after the universal manner of pattern-making, rather than its enthronement as another tyrant. In particular, one could hardly do worse than succumb to the urge to impose a certain motivation only because it struck gold elsewhere and wring subtleties from the text at all costs. A potent antidote to this occupational temptation of interpreters lies in the example set by a distinguished member of the guild. Rabbi Simeon (or Nehemiah) the Amsonite was famous for his readings of the accusative particle *et* in Scripture, according to a rule of inclusion. By this rule, *et*'s appearance (supposedly optional and hence redundant) suggests the inclusion of something or someone left unmentioned in the direct object that follows. However, as the Talmud recounts more than once, when Rabbi Simeon came to the verse "Thou shalt fear [+ *et*] the Lord thy God," he fell silent: to apply the iron rule of *et* as elliptical inclusive would be to make the Deuteronomist enjoin the recognition of deities over and above God. "Then his disciples said to him: 'But, Rabbi, what is to become of all those *et*'s you have explained?' He said to them: 'Just as I have been rewarded for explaining, so will I be rewarded for abstaining.'"

·12·

THE ART OF PERSUASION[1]

To say the truth, in a court of justice drunkenness must not be an excuse, yet in a court of conscience it is greatly so.
Henry Fielding, *Tom Jones*

Persuading in the Court of Conscience

My epigraph comes from the scene where Tom Jones, in love with Sophia, yet lets Molly seduce him. No sooner has he fallen than Fielding rushes to the rescue with the explanation that the hero was drunk at the time and drink had taken away his wits. Alluding to his professional life as a judge, the storyteller then concludes his plea with a generalization that goes to the heart of literary rhetoric.

That literary judgment sits as a court of conscience will be familiar to everyone from his reading experience. It is not just that the rules and criteria by which we evaluate the products of art—character, action, society—are not strictly judicial. The normative codes involved and the views formed by no means overlap, and at times violently break, with their counterparts in ordinary life. Further, there is no telling in advance where and how the judgment passed in the court of conscience will diverge from the judicial or quotidian line. Sometimes we find ourselves condemning a character who would be found not guilty in law or nothing out of the common in life. At other times we find ourselves siding with a personage or a cause or an act that we would denounce in any other context.

Part of the readiness to frame or adopt such variant norms in the reading traces back to the features of literary discourse as an artwork. Kant's formula for the aesthetic experience, "purposiveness without purpose," applies here in a somewhat different sense from what he had in mind. The reader's response to the world of literature develops in relative immunity from narrow and egocentric considerations. Things, as it were, have no personal reference to him; his judgments have no practical implications one way or the other. With the pressures of expediency relaxed, if not lifted, the reader can afford what he normally cannot: to judge the case on its

441

own merits and regardless of consequences, appealing if necessary to an ideal value system. Where else can the dream of *fiat justitia ruat coelum* find its fulfillment? Hence the familiar but not quite self-explanatory experience of doing justice with no reflection on self. As readers, we often set our standards so high that we would never dream of applying them to ourselves—or even to our neighbors—and blame characters for faults and practices and omissions that we manage to live with on more or less comfortable terms.

The court of conscience may thus seem the court of hypocrisy. As Anthony Trollope comments at a juncture where his hero, Frank Greystock, would like to marry for love but must think of money and status:

> Frank Greystock, the writer fears, will not have recommended himself to those readers of his tale who think the part of lover to the heroine should always be filled by a young man with heroic attributes. And yet [Frank] was by no means deficient of fine qualities, and perhaps was quite as capable of heroism as the majority of barristers and members of parliament among whom he consorted, and who were to him the world. . . .
>
> It is only when we read of such men that we feel that truth to his sweetheart is the first duty of man. I am afraid that is not the advice which we give our sons. (*The Eustace Diamonds,* chapter 76)

Trollope no doubt points to the double standard of his Victorian readers: extreme idealism in literature as against extreme materialism in life. But the fact that he numbers himself among them ("we," "our") reflects his awareness that such duality is neither confined to a certain type of reader (or public) nor necessarily symptomatic of pecksniffery. Rather, the two sets of norms adhere to different conditions, institutions, frames of reference. Duplexity rhymes with complexity not duplicity.

The implications of the literary as aesthetic experience are reinforced by the combined effects of its enclosedness and particularity. Discourse that enjoys artistic license is the only context presumed to have access to all the facts relevant to judgment—including privileged information—and therefore to invite judgment by reference to the particular world delimited for the reader's eyes. We get to know all that we need to know about certain characters in certain situations, so that even gaps count as evaluative signals rather than (in the manner of everyday inaccessibles) as deterrents. Judgment becomes not so much easier as more warranted, flexible, attached to the distinctive coherence of the represented world.

All this can also be formulated from another standpoint. In the ethics of everyday life, norms are at once rigid and elastic, absolute yet relative. We are all supposed to know good from evil, along lines that have varied so little with time as to appear natural. But once special circumstances come in, the abstract value system must stretch to meet them and valuation turns relative to context. What is in principle a clear-cut imperative or veto—for example, regarding truthfulness or murder—may in application elicit judgments ranging from positive to negative, as when we speak of white lies or mercy killing. Now literature specializes in the special circumstance, rendering the concrete by privilege and choice. Hence the widely variant attitudes evoked by characters and situations that roughly fall under the same heading:

> Even something as universally deplored as cruelty to children can be molded to radically different effects. When Huck's father pursues him with the knife, or when the comic strip father beats his child because he's had a bad day at the office; when Jim in "Haircut" and Jason in *The Sound and the Fury* disappoint the children about a circus . . . ; when Medea kills her children; when Swift's Modest Proposer arranges to have the infants boiled and eaten . . . and finally, when the child is beaten to death in *The Brothers Karamazov,* our reactions against the perpetrators range from unconcerned amusement to absolute horror, from pitying forgiveness to hatred.[2]

The court of conscience, in a word, is also the court of the concrete universal.

All these features of literary discourse clear the ground for the working of the values and valuations peculiar to each text. Like nature, communication abhors a vacuum. The text always exploits the abeyance of external pressures to subject the reader all the more forcefully to its own, arising from the rhetoric devised to persuade (talk, seduce, manipulate) us into normative harmony with its world view. What varies is only the relation between the general features and licenses of literariness and the specific rhetorical strategy.

The more conventional the work's normative groundwork in terms of its period or culture, the less need there is for persuasive art. The author may count on a negative response to Goneril and Regan's persecution of their father in *King Lear* or to Pecksniff's hypocrisy in *Martin Chuzzlewit* or to the lynching of Joe Christmas in *Light in August;* just as he can count on a favorable reception of Ajax's courage in the *Iliad* or Milly's magnanimity in *The Wings of the Dove.* He may wish to intensify the condemnation or the sympathy, but he launches his operations from a secure base. On the other hand, the more novel or complex the light in which character and event appear, the greater the importance assumed by the rhetorical strategy. For the desired world view and particular views to be imposed on the reader, his stock responses must be undercut, reshaped, or even inverted. How else will he come to sympathize with a coward like Lord Jim and a murderer like Raskolnikov or to dissociate himself from a hero that he would normally regard as a paragon of virtue? It is either control and a prospect of consensus or laissez faire and certain failure.

The traditional neglect of the Bible's art of persuasion would seem to indicate—and this is sometimes even voiced in effect—that the Bible belongs to the first of these categories. But the narrative practice bears out neither of the underlying assumptions: that the Bible faces or envisages a homogeneous audience and that it swims with the current or at least with the one it envisages. We have already traced enough of the energy that the Bible invests in its rhetorical strategies, beginning with those of omniscience and omnipotence, to dismiss the idea that it implies a like-minded reader, whose attitudes can be safely presupposed or if necessary dictated. And the closer one looks, the more visible the signs of uphill work for consensus and, what is more, of work undertaken by free poetic choice as well as under doctrinal exigency.

In this regard, it is important to distinguish control strategies bearing on the relations between God and man from others oriented to interpersonal relations in the human sphere. Of course, the line between the properly ideological and the ethical must not be drawn too sharply, because God is in principle involved in all earthly affairs. As our analysis of the play of omnipotence and suspense has already shown, however, there is in practice a very real difference between direct or immediate and oblique involvement; and the difference, again, affects the narrator's poetic latitude.

Where concerned with God's ways to man, the narrator operates under the severest constraints, because he must justify God at any cost. How he minimizes the cost, how he preserves his integrity as artist, how he reconciles the ideological need for vindication with the rhetorical need for persuasion: these will be the subject of the next chapter. My present subject is the rhetoric of interpersonal relations, where the Bible comes closest to developing an ethical code governed by a vision of human conduct rather than divine order. The emphasis now shifts to the problematics of the self vis-à-vis society: to the psychology of fear and desire, to the conflict of will and virtue, to the triangle of honor, morality, and self-preservation. Here, then, the Bible also approaches the normal conditions of literary discourse as a court of conscience. Normative latitude combined with informational privilege equals something like a free hand in shaping drama and response.

Typically, however, the narrator forgoes the respite from ideological pressure. As if the exploration of man as a social being did not present enough of a challenge, the use he makes of his freedom is to steer into new trouble. It is not that he saddles himself with another inflexible value system but that he spurns the appeal to ready-made codes that would smooth the way of persuasion. He chooses to complicate his rhetorical task by entangling the moral issues and going counter to stock response.

The story of the Rape of Dinah (Genesis 34) offers a model for this rhetoric of interpersonal relations. The chapter focuses on two acts of violence—the rape of Dinah and the revenge taken by her brothers—seeking to bring the crime and the punishment into balance. The trouble is that mass slaughter will not balance against rape according to conventional normative scales. The narrator needs no telling that if he lets the facts "speak for themselves," it is the victims of the massacre that are likely to gain most of the sympathy: the reader could hardly help condemning Jacob's sons for the shocking disproportionateness of their retaliation. This, as any attentive reading of the finished work will establish, is beyond doubt. The generalization already cited that in stories of this kind we must expect only "themes that would appeal to rough humor and rouse the chuckles of the fairly low audience for whom they were designed, who doubled with merriment at the thought of 'the uncircumcised'"[3] reflects quite a few things, but the Bible's moral sense is not among them.

Of course, the narrator could lighten his task either by making monsters of the rapist and his people or by glossing over the revenge. But neither of these simplifications (which also involve rhetorical patterning) meets his artistic standards. In fact, he does the very opposite, of which the clearest measure is that he lingers over the reprisals more than over the rape. Like Shakespeare in *Macbeth*, he seems to welcome the challenge of achieving his goal—here, balanced response—in the face of self-imposed difficulties and constraints. In compositional terms, avoiding the line of least resistance means working *against* the normal force or effect of the materials: the replacement or remolding or even reversal of their intrinsic load by way of structural manipulation. It means, in short, staking everything on the art of relations. And if the rise to the challenge is typical, so is the virtuosity of the performance. The rhetorical measures brought to bear on material and reader—many of them old acquaintances by now—will be isolated and organized toward the end of the chapter. Let us first trace them in coordinated action.

Delicate Balance in the Rape of Dinah

As befits an art of sequence, the tale's ordering plays the dominant role in persuasion, since it controls even the effect of the intrinsically nonsequential forms and devices. In the Bible's reading as in its living, process is all. Here, the rhetorical strategy passes through three main stages:

1. verses 1–12: the *accumulation* of maximal sympathy for Jacob's sons;
2. verses 13–26: the *complication* of response, through a progressive balancing of the two sides;
3. verses 27–31: the *stabilization* of the balanced attitude, with Simeon and Levi turned protagonists.

The function of the opening phase is to reflect as much credit as possible on Jacob's sons. To achieve the ultimate balance, the narrator lays in a store of sympathy for them as long as their actions, and theirs alone, are unexceptional. That initial accumulation tips the scales of judgment so heavily on the brothers' side (as victims) that their following excesses (as victimizers) only produce emotional and moral equilibrium.

Since violent shifts in attitude are not just a matter of arithmetical proportion of merits and demerits—first impressions may collapse with a vengeance, as chapter 8 has illustrated—all this is easier said than done. Even the first stage achieves its purpose only because the narrator takes full advantage of the reader's ignorance. Due to the opacity of the future, the reader is unaware of the rhetorical manipulation to which he is being subjected in the present. The lowering of resistance heightens vulnerability to the softening-up process. It enables the narrator to lead the reader by degrees into a complete identification with the brothers at the expense of all the other characters: first Shechem in his role as rapist, then Jacob as indifferent parent, then Shechem and *his* father as suitors.

Much of this anticipatory sympathy derives from the unequivocal condemnation of the assault:

> (1) Dinah, the daughter of Leah whom she had borne to Jacob, went out to see the daughters of the land. (2) Shechem, the son of Hamor the Hivite, the chief of the land, saw her, and he took her and lay with her and abused her. (Gen 34:1–2)

The verbs selected to describe the crime project a sharp judgment on the highest authority. What for lack of an equivalent I translated as "lay with" is in fact a transitive verb (*va'yishkab otah,* i.e., "laid her") that reduces the victim to a mere object and thus exceeds the properly intransitive construction "lay with" (*va'yishkab ittah*);[4] "abused" speaks for itself. The threefold repetition, where a single verb might denote the occurrence, quashes the idea of seduction. It also dwells on the scene to imprint it on the reader's mind as the opening note. And its redundancy also calls for an integration of the verbs in some ascending order of violence, like that suggested by the rabbis: "'Lay with her'—in the normal way; 'and abused her'—in an abnormal way" (*Bereshit Rabba* 80:4).

Bent on accumulating sympathy for the future avengers, the tale yet draws the line at a black-and-white polarization of character. Instead, it qualifies response in the immediate sequel. The three verbs of forcing give way to three verbs of endearment:

> (3) And *his soul clung* to Dinah the daughter of Jacob, and *he loved* the maiden, and *he spoke tenderly* to the maiden. (4) And Shechem spoke to his father Hamor, saying, Get [literally, Take] me this girl for a wife.

Verse 3 does not quite counterpoise, still less cancel out, the impact of its predecessor. The evaluative implications of its series of verbs are more oblique, and its consequences far less in evidence. The correspondence between the orders of action and presentation likewise keeps down the softening effect. The narrator could intensify this effect by arranging either order along the lines of the Rape of Tamar. He could devise another order of occurrence—if only by indicating, proleptically, that Dinah was handsome—whereby Shechem fell in love with the girl before assaulting her. Or he could reverse the order of discourse alone, producing a temporary (and misleading) impression of such a causal chain. Yet the narrator both constructs and unfolds a sequence that will preclude this extenuating circumstance: he first shocks us by the suddenness of the rape and only then proceeds to its aftereffects on the rapist.

The surprising thing is not that the rhetorician stops short of balance here but that he moves toward it at all. First comes an inside view of Shechem—"his soul clung to Dinah . . . and he loved the maiden"—whose length and strength go beyond plot exigencies. The feeling moderates the impression of barbarity given by the act. Its high authority guarantees sincerity. Its doubling and specification—neither frequent in the biblical context—prolong reading time to match with the verbs of violence and suggest the replacement of violent behavior by violent emotion. The ensuing sweet talk ("and he spoke tenderly to the maiden") develops the same line through an outside view. Finally, the appeal to Hamor shows Shechem suiting the action to the word, with the irreversible "taking" by force opposed to the envisaged "taking" in marriage.

The scene now shifts to bring on the rest of the cast:

> (5) Jacob heard that he had defiled Dinah his daughter—his sons were with his livestock in the field—and Jacob kept still until they came. (6) And Hamor the father of Shechem went out to Jacob to speak to him. (7) And Jacob's sons came in from the field when they heard it. The men were grieved and very angry, because he had committed an outrage in Israel by lying with [*lishkab et*] Jacob's daughter, a thing not done.

This introduces the opposition between Jacob and his sons, which will by degrees occupy the normative (and even more covertly, the dramatic) center of the tale. The different generations of kinsmen exhibit different reactions, and the difference does not redound to the father's credit.

Jacob's response is conspicuous by its absence. He "kept still" (*hekherish*). In the Bible's usage, this verb often has the pejorative connotations of inertness or neglect (e.g., 2 Sam 19:11; Hab 1:13; Esth 4:14). But our context charges the verb with its maximal sense of a double omission: both to act and to speak. Jacob certainly stirred no finger before the arrival of his sons. The ordering of the verse implies that "his sons were with his livestock in the field" stands not merely in a geographical but in a causal relation to "Jacob kept still until they came." If so, the least one might expect is prompt communication. But the phrasing of verse 7 (with the agentless "when they heard") brings into doubt whether he even summoned them from the field for an emergency meeting.

Moreover, the narrator also leaves it uncertain whether verses 6 and 7— focusing on the Hivites and the sons respectively—project successive or simultaneous actions. The discourse leaves the relative order undetermined, the sons' arrival unsituated, and that of the Hivites wholly unmentioned. Together with the shift in repetition from verse 6 ("to speak to him") to verse 8 ("spoke to them"), this uncertainty might be taken as a symptom of the genetic misadventures for which this tale has become notorious in source criticism. As so often, however, behind the muddled appearance lies the difficult coherence of ambiguity. The variant hypotheses achieve maximal effect through minimal disclosure: mutually exclusive in terms of reality, they are mutually supporting in terms of rhetoric.

On the sequential reading of these events, Hamor and Shechem's departure preceded the sons' arrival. There accordingly emerges a plot link from the variation between the two accounts of the Hivite initiative: "Hamor the father of Shechem went out to Jacob to speak to *him*" versus "Hamor spoke to *them*." The pronominal shift in retelling arouses the suspicion that the Hivites first came to Jacob with their proposal, but since he chose to "keep still," they had to wait for the sons to (re)open negotiations. Whereas the simultaneous reading highlights Jacob's do-nothingness from another angle. This gap-filling produces an impression of busy activity on all sides, the Hivites leaving their home and the sons returning to theirs.[5] Only Jacob, on whom all eyes are fastened and all movements converge, holds his peace. By deforming the plot into ambiguity, then, the narrator exposes Jacob to attack from several directions at once.

Even stranger than Jacob's failure to act is his failure to react. Taking action, an apologist might somehow argue at this stage, is a matter to be deliberated by the whole family. ("Somehow," because an immediate summons would expedite such deliberation. "At this stage," because even the causal appearance of "Jacob kept still until they came" later turns out to be an ironic misdirection: he no more does or says anything after than before their homecoming.) But showing emotion—shock, grief, anger— requires no tactical coordination but just family feelings; and its absence bespeaks the worst. Incompatible with basic human norms, such a lack of response also jars against the biblical code of behavior. A comparison with David (hardly the most emotional of men) as he learns about the rape of Tamar gives a concrete measure of the distance separating the normal reaction of a father from Jacob's inertia: "King David heard all these things and he was very angry" (2 Sam 13:21), indeed like Dinah's brothers ("When they heard, the men were grieved and very angry"). Nor is Jacob a law unto himself among biblical fathers. When calamity befalls another child, Joseph, he barely survives the shock—rending his garments, putting on sackcloth, mourning endlessly, refusing all comfort except the thought of reunion in the grave (Gen 37:34–35). A suitable companion piece, this, for the lament over Absalom.

The convergence of the various norms—universal, biblical, personal— foregrounds Jacob's divergence. And not content to abstain from any mitigating explanation, the narrator radicalizes the incongruity with virtuoso skill. First, the lexis and syntax of verse 5 deepen the unfavorable impression given by its ending ("kept still"). The beginning, "Jacob heard that he had defiled Dinah his daughter," seizes our interest through the normative load of the object clause. That load stands out because the whole clause is informationally redundant and syntactically omissible. It also combines multiple affects. For the kinship term "his daughter" (super-redundant after "Dinah") sounds a familial and emotional note; while the introduction of "defilement" shows the crime in a new, ideological perspective. The narrator could have reiterated the flat "lay with" or even made do with the anaphoric filler that occupies the corresponding position in the Tamar story ("David heard *all these things*"). Yet he prefers to charge the report with the evaluative "defiled," which goes even beyond the emotive "abused" (the peak of the member of action) in implying moral and religious outrage as well.

The verse's forceful opening leads the reader to expect a proportionately energetic sequel. That expectation is at once heightened by retardation, the longish "his sons were with his livestock in the field" interposed between hearing and response. After the staircase-like progression, therefore, the do-nothing ending "and Jacob kept still until they came" lets us down with a vengeance; and who if not Jacob is to blame for the anticlimax? The discontinuity of cause ("daughter," "defiled") and effect ("kept still") thus tops off the sense of the patriarch's deviation from the norm established, among other ways, through the inside view originating in himself.

At the same time, the wider context shows up these omissions by consistently presenting him as the key to the whole affair. He figures as injured party, as social center of authority, as geographical focus, as cynosure. The Hivites hasten "to Jacob to speak to him"; so do the sons. And the terms chosen to point to the Israelite side, Dinah notably included, take their orientation from him (and him alone) throughout the opening. Whether made by the narrator or the dramatis personae, all these references assume the form not simply of relational but of familial terms, with Jacob as the fixed point of reference. The tale introduces Dinah as "the daughter of Leah, whom she had borne to Jacob." It goes on to recount that Shechem fell in love with "Dinah, the daughter of Jacob," though the noun phrase neither serves to identify the beloved nor to disclose her lover's state of mind. Then, the very verse devoted to the father's strange omissions casts the tidings in the words "that he had defiled Dinah his daughter." Later, where the brothers might be expected to rage at the assault on their *sister,* they instead feel "the outrage he had committed in Israel [Jacob's new name] by lying with Jacob's daughter." Even when Hamor addresses the entire family ("them"), he portrays Shechem as longing for "your daughter."

Since the analysis of the first anointment scenes, we have often observed the extent to which the Bible's poetics of indirection depends on the choice and linkage of referring terms. Whether in the form of names or descriptive phrases, they fulfill the most various roles: from implying subjective vision through shaping objective judgment to focusing interest. Indeed, the art of perspective would be inconceivable without them, since a whole modern scene may be packed into a biblical appellation or a change in viewpoint (from character to character, narrator to character, external to internal report) signaled by nothing but its variation. Rarely, however, do their versatility and contribution appear to greater advantage than in the Rape of Dinah. From beginning to end, with subtle shifts at key junctures, they reflect the dynamics of the plot and control the dynamics of our response.[6]

Like relational reference in general, the anchorage of the relation in the father is not the rule in biblical narrative, not even in the Jacob cycle. The familial point of reference varies with the narrator's goals and needs, sometimes within a single tale. From a certain stage in this very chapter we shall find Dinah related to the brothers with the same consistency as she previously was to Jacob. And the larger the unit considered, the more unmistakable the dynamics of reference. No later than chapter 37, the relational center thus switches from the father to the brothers, especially to Joseph. Where the Dinah story would call the younger generation "Jacob's sons," the next phase favors "Joseph's brothers." So chapter 37 alone contains about twenty fraternally-oriented references, in both narrative and dialogic discourse; and the brothers are less often attributed to Jacob (*sons of*) than he to them (*father of*), e.g., "He told it to his father and to his brothers."

In short, the narrator exploits the multiple possibilities of familial reference to highlight the centers of interest: Joseph and the bond of fraternity toward the end of Genesis or Jacob as paterfamilias here. In the absence of the expected response on his part, the device for focusing thematic attention turns into a rhetorical weapon for focusing condemnation. Is Jacob, we are led to wonder, a father (just as Samuel is a seer) only in name? And the less automatic the referring terms in the first place, the less informative they become in repetition, and the less congruous the paternal orientation of their language with the paternal detachment in reality—the greater their condemnatory force.

The more so since the implications of the language tie in with larger patterns, notably contrastive analogy with other characters. Thematically, Jacob stands in sharp opposition to his Hivite equivalent: the understanding, energetic, and selfless Hamor. Negotiations with aggrieved kinsmen, harsh conditions from political dependents, change of the status quo, mass conversion—not to mention bodily pain—nothing deters this exemplary father. To pinpoint the contrast, the bond between parent and child again assumes referential form, brought out by way of monopoly and superfluity: "Shechem the son of Hamor the Hivite . . . saw her"; "Shechem spoke to his father Hamor"; "Hamor the father of Shechem went to Jacob" (though Shechem accompanies him, Hamor alone is named in order to underline Jacob's recent "stillness" on hearing about the "defilement" of "his daughter"); "The soul of my son Shechem longs for your daughter" (note the link between the children); "Jacob's sons answered Shechem and his father with deceit"; "Their words pleased Hamor and Shechem the son of Hamor"; "Hamor and Shechem his son came to the gate of their city"; "All . . . listened to Hamor and his son Shechem"; "Hamor and Shechem his son they killed." Only this time the familial language of reference mirrors rather than mocks the familial reality; and their harmony is a contextual measure of how far Jacob falls below the norm.

Within the family itself, the brothers' reaction points the contrast anew:

> (7) Jacob's sons came in from the field when they heard it. The men were grieved and very angry, because he had committed an outrage in Israel by lying with Jacob's daughter, a thing not done.

What the rhetorical devices packed into this verse have in common is that they all commend the sons by oblique opposition to the father.

The rabbis have already numbered this among the "undecidable texts"

(*Bereshit Rabba* 80:5)—they might add, untranslatable—which lend themselves to more than one grammatical segmentation and analysis:

    a. Jacob's sons came in from the field when they heard it. The men were grieved and very angry;

    b. Jacob's sons came in from the field. When they heard it, the men were grieved and very angry.

The undecidability goes beyond syntactic form to plot sequence, a mode of ambiguation in which this tale specializes. Is the order of occurrence (a) news followed by homecoming or (b) homecoming followed by news? The two readings of the time-line are mutually exclusive; but, again, the multiple system, far from betraying loss of control, perfectly dovetails into the rhetorical strategy. Just as with the related gap, about whether verses 6 and 7 narrate successive or simultaneous events, the chronological duplicity sustains the many-sided attack on Jacob and thus indirectly heightens sympathy for his sons.

The first order nicely coheres with the *simultaneous* plotting of events in verses 6 and 7. It fixes Jacob's immobility by projecting a state of convergent movements launched by the rape. The Hivites depart "to speak to him," the sons abandon their work as soon as they "hear" to join him; he alone holds his peace. The second hypothesis about the order hits the same target with different ammunition. In reversing the sequence of events, it breaks the causal link between the sons' "hearing" and "coming in": Jacob not only failed to do anything himself, but even neglected to send a message. If the first plotting still gives him the benefit of doubt ("when they heard": from whom?), the second takes it all away.

This alternative, moreover, also exposes the father in concert with the *sequential* reading of verses 6 and 7. Hamor and Shechem, it connotes, first arrived at Jacob's tent "to speak to him"; but, since he neither responded nor summoned any other negotiator, they had to mark time until the sons returned from their day's work in order to speak "to them." The same reading, furthermore, maximizes the oddity of Jacob's dispassion. It gains support from the logic of analogy in that the joining of "when they heard" to the brothers' response yields a more symmetrical pattern: "Jacob heard . . . and Jacob kept still" versus "when they heard, the men were grieved and very angry." The symmetry makes for a sharper as well as firmer opposition, in which each act of hearing is followed by the absence or presence of feeling.[7]

Even for the Bible, to be sure, this doubling of double plots carries ambiguity to an extreme. Still, it does observe the strategic relations between the truth and the whole truth. However variant and ramified the gap-fillings, the value system remains constant. Since the competing interpretations of what happened join forces on the thematic level, even the reader who takes one direction at each fork of the plot cannot go seriously wrong. He will indeed miss most of the fun and much of the ethical clinching, both supplied by the pincer attack below the surface. But the thrust of the narrative is unmistakable: judgment by antithesis.

The oppositional effect is reinforced by the crafty wording and development of the brothers' emotions. Given the Bible's restraint and miniature scale, of course, the strength and very length of this inside view reflect on Jacob's character. But what proves most effective is the sentence's combinatory art, especially the manipulations of order and viewpoint.

In his so-called blessing, Jacob will reduce the vengeance taken by Simeon and Levi on the Hivites to an outbreak of blind fury: "In their rage they killed men and in their willfulness they hamstrung oxen. Cursed be their rage, for it is fierce; and their wrath, for it is cruel" (Gen 49:6–7). But, as often in repetition, the narrator tells a different story. As early as this point, he summons his omniscient authority to undermine the reliability of Jacob's late version. His inside view unfolds a more complex, and far more sympathetic, picture of the motives actuating the future revengers. The brothers' feelings are not limited to rage. In the authorized telling, grief over the rape of their sister leads the way and anger comes second. The order of presentation reflects an order of occurrence *and/or* a scale of importance in the subject's mind. It thus fulfills a rhetorical role in the response to as well as in the commission of the crime; but here it functions to soften our judgment rather than, as in Shechem's case, to harden it.

As with the ordering of the brothers' response, so with its warranting. While the value-laden clause "that he had defiled Dinah his daughter" heightens the incongruity of the paternal stillness, the even more laden explanation centered in the brothers heightens the plausibility of their feelings, anger and all: "because [*ki*] he had committed an outrage in Israel by lying with Jacob's daughter, a thing not done." As a guide to the contextual norms, this key sentence goes a long way toward aligning at this stage the viewpoints of the brothers, the narrator, and the reader—and, ultimately, toward producing the balanced attitude to the act of vengeance.

This blunt and unqualified explanation owes its power to four main factors. One is that the judgment it makes is wholly "covered" by the enormity of the deed. Another is the reiterated suggestion ("an outrage in Israel," "lying with Jacob's daughter") that the brothers think less of themselves than of their father, who represents the whole clan. Still another is that these sentiments do even more than the foregoing "defiled" to extend the proportions of the offense: it goes beyond the abuse of an innocent maiden ("the men grieved") or familial dishonor ("Jacob's daughter") to trample on national identity and religious taboo ("outrage," "in Israel," "a thing not done"). Finally, one must reckon with the narrator's skill in making the most of his scanty material, notably by provoking rival interpretations of the same piece of language and pressing them all into service. Here the resource of semantic thickening by controlled ambiguity manifests itself in yet another form, along the perspectival dimension. To whom does the judgment "because [*ki*] he had commited an outrage" belong? It can be attributed both to the brothers and to the narrator himself. Needless to say, it is the narrator who communicates this sentence. The question facing the reader, however, is one of origination (and hence validity) rather than (possibly uncommitted) transmission. Does the discourse reflect the painful feelings of the brothers ("They were grieved and very angry because *they felt that* he had committed an outrage" etc.)? Or does it interpolate an evaluative comment on the narrator's own part, designed to justify their feelings ("They were grieved and very angry, *and no wonder,* since he had committed an outrage" etc.)? We have here, in short, the kind of perspectival ambiguity traditionally thought to be peculiar to the age of the novel. Where does the inside view end, or where does the narrator's voice begin? What is the narrator's standing in and attitude to the explanatory statement? Its weight crucially depends on the answer.

The Bible's norms of narration in *ki*-sentences bring out the perspectival tangle here.[8] On the one hand, the clause contains some formulations that seem most appropriate to the narrator, who stands above the represented world, looks ahead as well as back, and generalizes with the voice of authority. The decided closure "a thing not done" thus shows a range of generality similar to many explanations voiced by the narrator himself, where the conjunction *ki* modulates from the direct causality of "because" into the backgrounding or expository sense of "for." E.g., "Samson made a feast there, for so the young men used to do (Judg 14:10), "He [Mordecai] went up to the entrance of the king's gate, for no one might enter the king's gate wearing sackcloth" (Esth 4:2). Though certainly aware of the customs of his time, Samson or Mordecai has other things to do at the moment than actively meditate upon them; it is we, not they, who require a reason. The opening "*ki* he had committed an outrage in Israel" would likewise appear to originate in the narrator, particularly since at the time "Israel" had not yet become a nation. The characters can hardly think and judge in terms of a category shrouded in the future, but no such limitation hampers the omniscient teller. Finally, if elsewhere the narrator ironizes the evaluation expressed in the causal clause—as when Goliath "saw David and disdained him, because he was a youth, ruddy and good-looking" (1 Sam 17:42)—here he goes out of his way to endorse it by his handling of the crime.

On the other hand, the text lends support to the reading of the clause as a notation of what takes place in the brothers' minds in the narrative present. Does the sequence extending from "the men were grieved" to "done" make (1) a two-part justification or (2) a single unit devoted to the brothers' feelings? The former hypothesis is the more complex. Accordingly, the reader tends to integrate the causal clause as a sequel to the initial inside view, whose strength of feeling is explained from within in terms of the strength of judgment: "They got very upset because in their view the crime was very serious." Indeed, the brothers later resort to similar normative phrasing, like "for that would be a disgrace to us."

As is usual with multiple systems, moreover, the arguments that favor the rival hypothesis prove less than decisive. Thus, broad generalizations are appropriate but not exclusive to the narrator. We encounter both in Tamar's plea to Amnon: "No, my brother, do not abuse me, for such a thing is not done in Israel; do not commit this outrage . . ." (2 Sam 13:12–13; cf. Gen 20:8; 29:26). Likewise, the reading of "outrage in Israel" as the narrator's anachronism is attractive but not mandatory. Instead of a synecdoche for the whole Israelite people, "Israel" may figure as a literal reference to Jacob, lately renamed by the angel (32:27–28) and already shown to employ the new designation in the verse that immediately precedes our chapter (33:20). The literal reading even enjoys contextual patronage. It makes sense that the brothers would consider Shechem's "outrage" an offense against Jacob, the familial point of reference in what has gone before *and* in verse 7 itself. For what is the outrage that Shechem committed in Israel?—"to lie with Jacob's daughter." (In fact, the Septuagint directly attributes this ending to them.)

The two possibilities thus remain equipollent. The reader could easily be spared the hesitation between them, by means of an introductory verb and/or vocal speech and/or direct report ("because *they said,* He committed . . ."). But for rhetorical reasons the narrator chooses to ambiguate where he could elucidate, since the undecidable perspective enables him to elicit maximum sympathy for his heroes. The reading of the language as a burst of emotion gives it tremendous psychological force and appeal: it heightens our present feeling for the brothers (and conditions our response to their ultimate violence) through an inside view of their manifold sense of outrage. Whereas the opposed attribution makes a normative contribution, investing an otherwise personal judgment with the authority reserved for the narrator. Subjectivity joins forces with objectivity to establish the most favorable climate of opinion for one of the tale's three parties.

So far we have traced the process whereby the first impressions are generated through the handling of the crime and the criminal, then intensified through a play of contrasts within the stricken family. The next scene furthers the anticipatory buildup by reverting to the Hivites:

(8) Hamor spoke to them, saying, The soul of my son Shechem longs for your daughter. Pray, give her to him for a wife. (9) And make marriages with us: give your daughters to us and take our daughters for yourselves. (10) You shall dwell with us and the land shall be open before you; dwell and trade in it and acquire holdings in it. (11) And Shechem said to her father and her brothers, Let me find favor in your eyes, and whatever you say to me I will give. (12) Ask of me ever so much dowry and gift, and I will give whatever you say to me; only give me the maiden for a wife.

These overtures sound conciliatory and appealing, nor can they be dismissed as insincere. Yet they betray some less agreeable features out of which the tale makes normative capital. Central among the indirections that shape our response to the Hivite proposal are a series of antagonizing omissions and excesses.

One is first struck by the brazen disregard of antecedents. The narrator has steadily built up a sense of all-round outrage: human, familial, national, religious. But Hamor and Shechem make no apology for or even allusion to the crime, speaking as if nothing has happened except that a young man has fallen in love and wants to negotiate a marriage according to custom. The effrontery of this pretense is brought out by another major feature of the tale's composition: the dynamics of recurrent verbs (notably "take," "give," and "go out"). Interspersed along the sequence in changing contexts, the verb accumulates a range of connotations, so that each new appearance looks back to all the different and/or analogous meanings packed into its mates. The narrator thus links together various situations or figures and implicitly confronts them, with thematic and rhetorical profit as well as the formal gain in unity.[9] This proves especially effective in a miniature narrative where, as in poetry, every word counts and every echo resounds. Here, the speaker's reiterated plea to be "given" Dinah jars against Shechem's initial "taking" of her, and even the generously offered "taking" of Hivite daughters by the Israelites brings to mind that brutal "taking" out of wedlock.

Worse, the soft-spoken Hivites negotiate from a strong position unfairly obtained. Another of the things left unsaid by the two is the crucial fact discovered by the reader only in retrospect, after the massacre, but obvious to the parties concerned: that they have detained Dinah in their house.[10] No explicit mention need ruffle the smoothness of their approach, since the leverage given by the possession of the bride is clear to all. The more so—and Hamor loses no chance to harp on *this* inequality—when the bargaining takes place between the lords of the land and their political dependents. So, for all their fine language, the Hivites leave their interlocutors no real choice: they again and again ask to be "given" in due form, but, in marriage negotiation as in rape, they start with a unilateral taking. Later, at a critical moment, the narrator will suddenly lay bare the iron fist hidden all along in their verbal glove, thus persuading the reader that Jacob's sons had good reason to counter by guile and violence.

Even their immediate response suggests, however, that the Hivites add insult to injury. Jacob continuing to hold his peace, it is the sons who reply:

> (13)The sons of Jacob answered Shechem and Hamor his father with deceit, and spoke *asher* [to him who / because he / and literally, who] had defiled Dinah their sister. (14) And they said to them, We cannot do this thing, to give our sister to one who is uncircumcised, for that would be a disgrace to us. (15) Only on this condition will we consent to you: if you become as we are, every male of you circumcised. (16) Then we will give our daughters to you and we will take your daughters for ourselves, and we will dwell with you, and we will become one people. (17) And if you will not listen to us and be circumcised, we will take our daughter and go.

The speech and counterspeech proceed along very different lines. The Hivites multiply financial and economic seducements, which the Israelite side entirely disregards in its insistence on matters of principle. Hamor and Shechem cast their proposal in terms of a business deal: conveniently forgetful of the original "taking," they draw a picture of reciprocal "giving." Jacob's family will deliver the prospective bride ("give her to him," "give me the maiden") in exchange for money ("gift") and trading rights; this will go with a matrimonial "give" and "take" on a national scale. To them, rape or no rape, the commodities are perfectly equivalent. Even Shechem's emotional appeal follows Hamor's sober periods in balancing "Ask of me ever so much dowry and *gift*" against "*give* me the maiden."

Time will show that this businesslike approach only aggravated matters in the eyes of the brothers. But their present answer already rejects the deal together with its underlying scheme of values. As befits characters who have so far appeared as the tale's paragons, in opposition to the Hivites on the one hand and Jacob on the other, they move to a higher ground. The financial temptations are passed over in silence, and even the only item taken up—the offer of integration—shifts in recurrence from a pragmatic to a national-religious framework.

Their three-part reply formulates a clear-cut stand. The exordium, going against the very logic of the Hivite language of exchange, rules out all possibility of a commercial transaction: "That would be a disgrace to us." A double-edged condition follows. First appears a counterproposal in the form of an ideological ultimatum ("Only . . . if you become as we are, every male of you circumcised"). This will pave the way for the only give-and-take deemed honorable, because informed by social rather than traderly equivalence ("we will give our daughters to you and we will take your daughters for ourselves"). Finally, translating their introductory statement into operational terms, they repeat that no other solution is conceivable: "we will take our daughter and go." If this laconic finale now sounds uncompromising, then in retrospect it will turn out to be nothing less than a defiance. Once the reader learns of Dinah's whereabouts pending the negotiations, this apodosis assumes for him, too, a threatening tone, sharpened by the techniques of verbal association. Unless the counterproposal is accepted, the brothers imply, what was "taken" by force will be "taken" back by force.[11]

The idealistic response elicits further sympathy for the kinsmen, this time at the expense of the Hivites. Indeed, we would fully identify with their viewpoint were it not for the fact that just here the narrator takes the first step to distance himself from them too—through the omniscient comment that they spoke "with deceit." This qualification launches the second phase of the overall rhetorical strategy.

Hence the importance of determining the weight of the phrase. Its negative force must not be underestimated, still less reversed, in the manner of some traditional commentators.[12] But nor must it be blown up into categorical opprobrium and dissociation on the narrator's part. Rather, it indicates a limited complication of judgment, made possible by the linguistics of biblical Hebrew and effected by the art of biblical narrative. Since the Bible's forte is the art of context, the evaluative direction given to the basic sense predictably results from contextual loading.

The "deceit," we observe, attaches to the brothers' words in the given situation, not to the credo itself. Were it established that they parade scruples hardly felt in reality, that their idealism is nothing but a camouflage for treachery, that their religious demands are fabricated only to give an impression of hard bargaining and to lull the Hivites into tranquillity—in this case, our attitude to the violators of the covenant (in more than one sense) would drastically change for the worse. But the text guards against anything of the sort. Instead of elucidating, it multiply ambiguates the bearing of the deceit (and its actual point indeed turns out entirely unexpected). Does the deceit cover the whole speech or a part only? And which part? What do the brothers really aim for in driving such a hard bargain: to enter into an alliance on their own terms or inoffensively ("with deceit") to scotch an offensive alliance with their powerful neighbors by setting the most exhorbitant conditions they can think of? Does the deceit confine itself to the specific proposal or extend to its rationale?

The last question is of course the most decisive, and as long as it continues unresolved, the reader must suspend judgment. It is to good effect, therefore, that the narrative keeps this gap open and the whole inner life opaque almost to the end, where the brothers finally emerge as prevaricators rather than hypocrites. They indeed consider themselves dishonored by the rape: some of them (at least) view the rapist's attempt to buy them off with "gifts" as the last straw; none would consider an exogamous marriage; and all feel that nothing short of rescue and reprisal can settle the score. But the reprisal they have in mind is not the mass circumcision but bloodshed on a much larger scale. In short, if we take the exordium as the key to their standpoint, then the "deceit" turns out to bear not on the framing generalization but on its parenthetical specification: "We cannot do this thing [nominally: to give our sister to one who is uncircumcised; actually: to give our sister away in such circumstances], for that would be a disgrace to us."

Apart from arranging this long-term counterweight, the narrator at once balances our response to "with deceit" by manipulating the syntactic pattern that encloses it. Note how incongruously the last part of verse 13 is left hanging. The biblical *asher* ushers in a relative clause; but, unlike the normal location of such a clause, this one does not immediately follow the noun phrase that it qualifies. The grammatical displacement serves a number of ends, all tending in the same rhetorical direction.

The very occurrence of the redundant-looking clause, just before the narrator quotes the piece of deception, brings back to mind the extenuating circumstances. And its softening force yet redoubles thanks to the positioning of the clause not just after the phrase it qualifies but even after "spoke," where one would expect the reporting formula to end and the report itself to begin. Hence it could not be more awkwardly placed. Just as in linguistic terms it plays havoc with the syntax, so in narrative terms it retards the flow of events. But the multiple offense against order and continuity makes good rhetorical sense. The anomalous location invests the mitigating clause with maximum perceptibility. It also leaves the last word, so to speak, to the genuine cause ("defiled Dinah their sister") rather than to the problematic effect ("with deceit"). So we approach the brothers' speech with these words ringing in our ears and conditioning our response: whatever ensues will be viewed in their favorable light.

To restrain our judgment of the brothers immediately before the citation of their double-dealing, moreover, the clause looks backward as well as forward. It effects a multiple retrospection by way of hidden glances at things already said or done, including the "deceit." Normally placed— after "Shechem" or between "his father" and "with deceit"—it would function only as a relative clause; but the delay to an anomalous position urges the reader to look round for grammatical intelligibility and to explore various possibilities of subordination. The unit then assumes three distinct roles and meanings:

1. Formally, of course, it operates as a relative clause (*asher* = who) that qualifies "Shechem" (or "Shechem and Hamor") as the defiler of Dinah.

2. Taking *asher* as an abbreviated form of *al asher* (because), we have a causal clause that goes back to both "with deceit" and "spoke" and supplies a motive or reason (i.e., some justification) for the brothers' double-talk. They spoke with deceit, and not without cause, for they were addressing the defiler of their sister.

3. Since both "answer" and "speak" are transitive verbs in the Bible, verse 13 may divide into two parallelistic sentences, each composed of a main clause and an object (clause):

The sons of Jacob answered	Shechem and Hamor his father with deceit
and they addressed ("spoke")	him who [*asher*] had defiled Dinah
	their sister.

Under this third mode of integration, the language gains a new pattern and the rhetoric a new target and point. For the parallelism not only harps afresh on the causal link between deceit and defilement. By equating "Shechem and Hamor" with "him who had defiled" it also suggests the complicity of father and son in the brothers' eyes and accordingly widens, for the first but not the last time, the bearing of their sense of injury. This combinatory implication ties in with an otherwise pointless selection of grammatical person: though the antecedent is plural ("Shechem and Hamor"), the verb that refers back to it comes in the singular ("him who had defiled").[13] So within the parallelism, the corresponding objects vary in number and the addressees shrink from two to one. Biblical (as opposed to modern) Hebrew allows such grammatical discordance; but this does not yet reduce the concordant and discordant options to mere stylistic variants.[14] Considering the verse's otherwise balanced structure and the tale's internal norms of judgment, the grammatical choice breaks the formal parallelism only to augment its rhetorical load. It first intimates what the sequel will bear out and Simeon and Levi express at the very end: that the brothers regard the offer of "gifts" as a harlot's pay ("Shall he treat our sister as a harlot?") and therefore lump Shechem and Hamor together as collaborators in Dinah's defilement.

All this surpasses even the syntactic ambiguity of verse 17 in the narrative about Joseph and Potiphar's wife. The triple reading of the subordinate clause brilliantly illustrates the correspondence (as well as the interaction) of verbal microcosm and narrative macrocosm within the Bible's art of sequence. That correspondence shows in both form and function. In form, because the normal (natural, logical, conventional, transparent) sequence suffers deformation at each level. The order of words here diverges from grammatical rule, just as the order of events does from chronological norm. But the similitude also extends to functionality, along three interrelated lines. In purely aesthetic terms, each form of disrupting sequential coherence makes for an active reading process, since it heightens the text's perceptibility as an artful design and generates a play of indeterminacy. This effect is equally produced by the two different temporal manipulations of verse 13, the one that leaves the scheme behind the brothers' deceit obscure and the one that leaves the clause that mentions the deceit suspended. Semantically, moreover, each discontinuity enriches meaning, for it impels the reader to repair the omission and explain its commission. To make sense of the text, he must himself resolve its ambiguities, fill out its implications, order what it disordered. And since the opaque text provides only indicators rather than explicit directives, it maneuvers him into framing multiple hypotheses—about causal or syntactic pattern—so as to achieve density where a coherent sequence would yield a lean intelligibility. From the standpoint of rhetoric, finally, to deform and ambiguate structure is to complicate response far beyond the limits of straightforward presentation. Whether operating on word or world, it enables the narrator to conceal as much as to reveal, to time his effects by distributing information, to mold attitude by concerted pressure at each point. In combination, therefore, each temporal (dis)arrangement may serve both to enhance and to balance the force of the other. In our verse, however, the two join forces. The gapping of the brothers' plot, inverting the natural logic of cause (motive) and effect (speech), reinforces the advocacy of the dislocated clause, and vice versa; whereas the dislocation of that clause into final note mitigates the deceitful speech that ensues. Word order and world order thus dovetail in the overall strategy of persuasion.

But so do language and composition in general. The pressures exerted on the reader by the manifold art of sequence fall into line with the phrasing of the *asher*-clause and its retrospective bearing. The recurrence of the loaded "defiled" clearly indicates how lexical choice heightens both the intensity and the validity of the brothers' motive for deception. But the narrator also chooses here, for the first time in the history of his references to the young woman, to substitute the fraternal for the paternal reference point: "defiled Dinah *their sister*." This marks a shift to a more subjective formulation than "Jacob's daughter," one that approximates to the terms in which the brothers themselves would think of the victim. As such, it tightens the causal link between feeling and proceeding, violent action and guileful counteraction. Moreover, the suggestiveness of this mode of familial reference is due not only to selectional measures, either the departure from the norm established so far or the redundancy of "their sister" after "Dinah";[15] it derives equally from combinatory patterns. The action now taken by the brothers against "him who had defiled Dinah their sister" makes a quiet but none the less telling contrast to the inaction of the father on hearing "that he had defiled Dinah his daughter." The subjective "his daughter" and the charged "defiled" have already served to alienate us from the father; but now the minute opposition exploits them anew to vindicate the brothers, who cannot and will not pass over the crime in (literal, among others) silence.

All the more so since that opposition provides a still deeper insight into the brothers' mind, explaining as well as justifying their behavior at the expense of the father. It confirms the suspicions aroused by the importunate gap about what lies behind Jacob's unnatural stillness. The opening has already insinuated that Jacob does little because he feels little. The expositional verse itself prepares us for such a closure of the gap: "Dinah, the daughter of Leah whom she had borne to Jacob, went out to see the daughters of the land." This style of identification leaps to the eye for more than one reason. The double familial reference, even to both parents, is rare enough in the Bible; but, considering the recent appearance of Dinah (Gen 30:21), this one looks overflowing. It also acquires extra palpability owing to the lack of realistic motivation. For the cumbersome reference does not emerge from a dialogue scene where a character's identity is specified in answer to an inquiry (as in 2 Samuel 11:3), but goes from a reticent narrator to a reader in the know. Since the label's informative value bears no relation to its detail and prominence, we hope to account for it along other lines, yet hidden. As soon as the plot comes to Jacob, therefore, it occurs to the reader that the twofold identification of the poor girl accounts for Jacob's attitude in terms of her being the daughter of his hated wife, whose suffering and strife for her husband's love loomed so large in the previous chapters. (No wonder, then, that Jacob reacts so differently to the catastrophe that befalls Rachel's child.) This suspicion gains in probability as the narrative throws into relief the oddity of his conduct: through the exclusive attribution of Dinah to him, his freezing as the point of convergence for the movements of others, the use of Hamor to set up a contextual norm of paternality, or, within the family, the contrast with the brothers. So the sharpening of this contrast in verse 13, pointed by the recurrence of "defiled" amid the switch from "his daughter" to "their sister" as soon as the brothers take over, now validates the hypothesis, with a further polarization of response. Apart from the opposition itself, these effects derive from what amounts to an internal view of the brothers' view of Jacob's view. If the modified kinship term reflects the workings of their minds, they would seem to share our suspicion; and their overreaction as present deceivers and future avengers may well have been caused by the father's indifference to "their sister" in defilement. The combinatory art of the clause thus includes perspectival as well as sequential and analogical rhetoric.

A final effect of perspective concerns a new variation on a device already encountered in "because he had committed an outrage in Israel" etc. On the one hand, the *asher*-clause is so patterned as to suggest an inside view of the brothers (who indeed refer to Dinah as "our sister" in the following verse). At the same time, its location after the *verbum dicendi* "spoke" charges it with objective as well as emotive force. It is as if the brothers are about to reply but the narrator would not let them do so at once. Instead, he arrests for a moment the flow of events to remind us, on his own authority and in the strongest language, of the human ("their sister") and religious ("defiled") norms that should govern our judgment of the deceit. Further, this objectifying of the clause into an in-between comment explains the recourse to yet another formula ("and they said to them") to close the parenthesis in verse 13 and herald the actual quotation in verse 14 (cf. 2 Sam 21:2–3). By constructively ambiguating the viewpoint between subjectivity and objectivity, the narrator has again maximized the persuasive impact of a minimal piece of discourse.

All these anticipatory measures, in conclusion, operate to influence and balance judgment at this early point. In retrospect, however, it also turns out that the choice to mention the deceit in advance is much the lesser of two evils. Though it introduces a note of censure, the timely warning manages to keep the brothers far more sympathetic than would any delayed disclosure. Did the narrator suppress this awkward fact and mislead us into implicit faith in the brothers' sincerity, then the abrupt surfacing of the treachery toward the end might irretrievably discredit them—precisely because its abruptness would shatter the image of righteousness cultivated thus far. We have seen enough of the revulsion produced by the breakdown of first impressions—by, say, the discovery that David's friendly words to Uriah are nothing but a camouflage for a fiendish plot—to appreciate the narrator's wisdom in devising the opposite treatment for conspirators who deserve a more favorable hearing.

As the brothers state their counterproposal, then, their guile does not make too heavy inroads on the sympathy accumulated throughout the opening phase. But this first complication of judgment at once modulates into another, centered in the Hivite acceptance of the ultimatum. Again, the narrator's progression is cautious and gradual, three steps forward and two backward.

On the one hand, he obliquely harps on the fraternal double-dealing in and through the account of the Hivite rise to the challenge:

(18) Their words pleased Hamor and Shechem the son of Hamor. (19) And the youth did not delay to do this thing, for he desired Jacob's daughter; and he was the most honored of all his family. (20) Hamor and Shechem his son came to the gate of their city and spoke to the men of their city, saying: (21) These men are friendly toward us. Let them dwell in the land and trade in it: the land, behold, is large enough for them. Let us take their daughters for wives and let us give them our daughters. (22) Only on this condition will the men accede to our wish for them to dwell with us, to become one people: that every male among us be circumcised, as they are circumcised. (23) Will not their cattle and their property and all their beasts be ours? Only let us accede to their wish, and they will dwell with us. (24) All those who went out at the gate of his city listened to Hamor and to his son Shechem; and every male was circumcised, all who went out of the gate of his city.

The suitors not only assent to the condition but hasten ("did not delay") to fulfill it; and in regard to Shechem—"the most honored of all his family," i.e., the most eligible man in the district—the motivation is explicitly noted as youthful ardor ("for he desired Jacob's daughter"). Given the opacity of the secret life, this prompt acceptance baffles all attempts to peep behind the intransigence of Jacob's sons. Would they consider an exogamous marriage on their own terms? Did they attach hard conditions only in the hope of discouraging the suit (which, we add in retrospect, would provide an excuse for demanding their sister's return or liberating her by force)? Did the Hivite assent catch them by surprise, set in motion a contingency plan, or play into their hands? The gap yawns to the end, prolonging moral ambivalence together with dramatic tension. It leaves the deceit suspended over the deceivers' heads while the antagonists carry out their part of the bargain.

On the other hand, the public address arouses wonder and suspicion about the other side as well. If the leaders' speech merely echoed the agreement reached with the Israelites, its full quotation would be at variance with the Bible's narrative economy and poetics of retelling. Indeed, as soon as faced with this member of report, the reader can think of two possible motivations for the narrator's indulging in redundancy where he could opt for summary. One is that, considering the trickiness of the commitment undertaken, its performance has a claim to representation. The second is that the Hivites have been less than straightforward in the negotiations and the narrator wishes to expose their hidden designs. Since the two explanations contrast—in both judgment and plot structure—which one fits the case? The truth can emerge only from the interstices of repetition.

Hence the attention commanded by the dramatized appeal, the rhetoric within rhetoric.

A comparison of the original proposal (embraced without demur by the "pleased" suitors) with its retelling brings out suggestive disparities in arrangement, proportions, and emphasis. Each speech falls into three parts. But with Jacob's sons, the possible accession ("We will give our daughters to you" etc.) is flanked by the double-barreled ideological condition; while here the condition is sandwiched between an opening and an ending concerned with the pragmatic gains that would accrue to the Hivite people from the alliance. The agreement's center of gravity thus shifts in transmission from principle to expediency.

The details, elaborating the practical consequences of the agreement, even widen the variation. Like all experienced persuaders, Shechem and Hamor know the importance of putting one's best foot forward. They do not begin with the Israelite stipulation but rather pave the way for its divulgence. Nor do they so much as allude to the private stake they have in the matter (with which Hamor prefaced his address to Jacob's clan, "The soul of my son Shechem longs for your daughter") but speak in the name of the public interest alone. These newcomers being friendly with us, why not let them settle and trade in the land? To forestall any possible objection, they hasten to remind their audience that there is little danger of overcrowding or competition: "The land, behold, is large enough for them." What is more, such a concession will benefit the Hivite people if the deal includes intermarriage, a built-in guarantee for peaceful coexistence and national growth. A splendid prospect all round, with only one little catch. To ensure our integration into one people, the foreigners stipulate that every male among us be circumcised; and this is no humiliating or arbitrary demand, for they do it themselves ("as they are circumcised").

The original ultimatum is thus diplomatically wrapped up: its negative ideological antecedent ("We cannot do this thing") replaced by a socio-economic positive; its harsh conditional phrasing ("if . . . and if not") softened; the antagonizing reference to the disgrace of an alliance with the uncircumcised wholly elided; and circumcision itself converted from the soul into the seal of the alliance. But what if the condition still proves too much for the assembly? Alive to this danger, the speakers make no attempt to avert it by quoting the obverse face of the Israelite position ("If you will not listen to us . . . we will take our daughter"). They do not wish to reveal their personal involvement, still less to put ideas into the audience's head by raising the possibility of noncompliance. After all, the assembly may reject the terms even if the consequences of rejection assume a national guise, for what would be to the leaders a domestic tragedy would be to the people a maintenance of the status quo.

Rather than playing fair, therefore, the speakers make light of the terms by a new weighting of the profits. And this time they go so far as to overstep the most liberal margins of salesmanship. They have already implied that the Hivites will dominate the future alliance: "Let us take their daughters for wives and let us give them our daughters." This twists round the assignment of active and passive roles made in their original offer ("Make marriages with us: give your daughters to us and take our daughters for yourselves") and sealed in the brothers' repetition ("We will give our daughters to you and take your daughters for ourselves"). But the opening switch in the identity of the takers-and-givers looks innocent beside the concluding temptation: "Will not their cattle and their property and all their beasts be ours?" In flagrant breach of the spirit of the agreement, this promises the Hivites (if they only ensure "accession" by "accession") such control over their future allies as extends to their very goods. And this pledge, formally given in assembly, may well reflect the hidden intentions of the speakers all along.

But if the breach of contract manages to tip the scales within the dramatized rhetoric, it has a balancing effect within the narrator's rhetoric. For the ominous peroration impresses on the reader that the Hivite side does not stop at "deceit" either, and with less excuse. They are as far from "friendly" in reporting the agreement as in making their proposal.

This local balance once achieved, verse 25 launches the crucial phase in the strategy of overall balance. In a segment more condemnatory of the brothers than all its antecedents together, the point of their guile suddenly comes to light. After the Hivites have scrupulously (note the thrice-repeated "all" in verse 24) gone through the ceremony:

> (25) On the third day, when they were in pain, two of the sons of Jacob, Simeon and Levi, Dinah's brothers, took each man his sword, and came upon the city in security, and killed all the males. (26) And Hamor and Shechem his son they killed with the edge of the sword, and took Dinah out of Shechem's house and went out. (27) The sons of Jacob came upon the slain, and plundered the city, for [*asher*] they had defiled their sister. (28) They took their flocks and their herds and their asses and whatever was in the city and whatever was in the field. (29) And all their wealth and all their little ones and their wives they captured and plundered; and all that was in the houses.

With the massacre and the looting in full view, we at last understand what drove the narrator to amass so much sympathy for his heroes. Some poetic justice does attach to the discovery that Shechem's punishment started exactly where his sexual crime did, and that the self-inflicted soreness made the rest easy. Still, the reprisal is out of all proportion to the crime. The facts speak for themselves: the entire city falls together with the culprit, against the natural justice that God himself respects ("Will one man sin and thou wilt be angry with the whole congregation?"). And the handling of those facts redoubles their condemnatory force, as when the specification of the pillage moves far beyond the heading ("they plundered the city") that could cover it for all informative purposes.

Indeed, the narrator disdains the line of least resistance. Just as in the account of the outrage he did not suppress Shechem's change of heart, so when he comes to the retribution he does not gloss over the brothers' excesses. From beginning to end, it appears as though he seeks out the dangers of complexity, if not evenhandedness, as both an artistic challenge and a rhetorical policy: the more difficult he makes the task of persuasion for himself, the more difficult will it become for us to withstand its guidance. Avoiding the crudities of polarization, he aspires to such mixed responses as leave him a narrow margin of safety and threaten him with failure if he for a moment loses control of his materials and his audience. If his aspiration is a matter of principle, then his performance is a measure of skill, especially of his foresight and his nice estimate of the requirements of the task he set himself.

With the same ends in view, for example, a more timorous or partisan rhetorician would play down the act of reprisal. A less accomplished rhetorician might brave it but, through failures in execution, irretrievably turn us against the protagonists. The biblical artist both takes the risk and gets away with it. By itself, of course, the present stage shows the killers and despoilers in a repellent light. But in sequential context it follows a history of credits that now operate as checks and balances. The narrator has need of every bit of sympathy that he has managed to accumulate in favor of the brothers. Nor does he rest content with past accumulations, but proceeds to replenish the stock at the very moment that draws most heavily on it. To ensure the delicate balance of the whole, despite the imbalance of this part, he now harks back to a variety of existing justifications and even brings up some new ones.

Note first how the forward-moving action illuminates and reshapes what has gone before. The reader suddenly learns what the dramatis personae have known all along: that Dinah has been detained at Shechem's house since the rape and, therefore, that the Hivite negotiation technique has included blackmail. The dislocation of chronology now yields an eye-opener. As with all surprise gaps, this one turns out to have been imperceptibly opened only when we find it closed: the disclosure is sprung before we realize that there is a disclosure to be made. Wisely, the narrator decided against playing this trump card as long as the reader sided with the brothers anyway. Instead, having kept it up his sleeve since verse 5, he now throws it on the scales of judgment at the critical moment.

The timing is perfect, since the retrospective effect of discovery compels us to revaluate character and reinterpret the whole sequence of events. Placed where it is, moreover, this flashback unmasks the Hivites amid their destruction and renews sympathy for the Israelites amid their violence: the victims have doubly victimized their executioners. They have largely brought down that violence on themselves by seeking to impose their will on Jacob's family. With Dinah in Shechem's hands, the option of polite declining is closed to her guardians. And once the brothers refused to submit to the Hivite version of a shotgun wedding, they were left no avenue to the retrieval of their sister except force. Hence also the need for "deceit." Considering the numerical superiority of the troops behind "the prince of the land" — "two of Jacob's sons" faced a whole city—no wonder the brothers resorted to trickery to make odds more even. And the order of presentation supports the reading of the slaughter as an act enforced and purposive rather than expressing blind fury. First comes the attack on the townsmen, next the killing of Hamor and Shechem, and only then the extrication of Dinah: to rescue their sister, this orderly movement implies, they had to deal with all possible resistance, let alone future retaliation. There is not even a hint that the mass slaughter came as a revenge, and even the disposal of Shechem and Hamor mixes business with, no doubt, pleasure.

Furthermore, the massacre is prefaced by the long and retardatory notice that the sword-wielders were "two of Jacob's sons, Simeon and Levi, Dinah's brothers." Like "when they were in pain" and "in security" of the same verse, which work in the opposite direction, this apparently factual statement performs an important affective role. Under the guise of a referring term, meant only to identify the agents, it directly relates them to Dinah just before the extreme action they take on her behalf. Nor can this linkage escape notice, thanks to both its arresting effect at a point of suspense and the redundancy of the familial attribution that encloses the names. Why resort to a threefold identification where a single one would do? The need to motivate this choice impresses on the reader, at a crucial juncture, another redeeming circumstance of great potency. Before exposing us to the slaughter scene, the text freezes movement to interpolate a reminder that the slayers are not only "Jacob's sons" but "Dinah's brothers." They also have the same mother, and (as Jacob's attitude to her daughter's misfortune has just testified anew) an unloved mother at that. Their very names encapsulate this marital history by way of etymology. Leah called the one S[h]imeon "because the Lord has heard [*shama*] that I am hated," and the second Levi in the hope that "this time my husband will be joined [*yilaveh*] to me" (Gen 29:33–34). The innocent-looking minutiae of identity thus bring to the surface the network of subterranean tensions within the family—jealousy, rivalry, sense of deprivation—grown out of the patriarch's favoritism. They also hint at the solidarity engendered from birth in the children of a wronged mother. All this makes psychological sense of a crux that the disclosure of the Hivite blackmail will soon resolve in terms of practical exigency as well: why Simeon and Levi will stop at nothing to do the right thing by Dinah. In the filling of this gap, then, emotion and tactics meet to give intelligibility to the causal sequence and a sympathetic turn to our response.

But the familial overspecification also associates the doings of "Jacob's sons, Simeon and Levi, Dinah's brothers" with the suffering of "Dinah, the daughter of Leah whom she had borne to Jacob." The parallel excess in reference falls into a larger pattern designed to evoke the original crime in and through the working of retribution. What is the attack "in security" on the Hivites if not a counterpart of Shechem's assault on the unsuspecting Dinah, with little risk and even less provocation? But the firmest linkage between the two episodes that duplicate the text's thematic structure—crime and punishment—consists in the recurrence of certain key words that first appeared in the rape scene. Such recurrence interrelates the spatial and the temporal dimensions of the narrative, since it establishes analogies that impose continuity on discontinuous stages in the plot. Consider the semantic fortunes of the verb "take." The context of the rape having charged it with one intimation of violence ("he took her"), this verb now bristles with others ("took each man his sword," "took Dinah out," and then comes a listing of the plunder that Jacob's sons "took"). It is as if one brutal "taking" led to the rest, and what followed Shechem's sexual "taking" was not the legal "taking" for which he came to yearn but "takings" more analogous to that with which he launched the chain of violence. This lexical wanderer finds a mate in the equally unobtrusive and echoing verb "go out," to which I shall return. It opens the account of the first crime ("Dinah . . . went out"), then opens the negotiation episode where the second crime of insult and extortion was perpetrated ("Hamor went out"), and finally closes the narration of the punishment ("and they went out"). In language as well as geography, the plot ends where it began.

Most surprising of all, the persuader divides (the characters) in order to conquer (the reader): the balance of sympathy and censure abruptly varies in regard to different participants in the counterattack. If Jacob's sons have so far figured as a collective character—all standing or falling together in terms of rhetoric as well as of plot and viewpoint—then from verse 25 onward they split into two groups. One consists of "two of Jacob's sons, Simeon and Levi," who did the killing; the second, of the rest of "Jacob's sons," who did the looting. The subgrouping assumes both dramatic and compositional form. Dramatically, it is Simeon and Levi alone that Jacob accuses of having endangered the whole clan: long before his deathbed blessing, he draws a sharp line between the takers of life and of loot. (And even if Jacob lashed out only at them because the others were still away, this would likewise establish that the two took no part in the plundering. Of all the brothers, they alone have carried out their assignment and returned home to face the music.) Compositionally, it is with the killing that the action comes full circle. The sequence that began with "Dinah went out" and "[Shechem] took her" now ends with those very verbs in reverse order, according to the logic of circular movement: "they took Dinah out of Shechem's house and went out." The chiastic symmetry between the crime verbs and the punishment verbs, the final-sounding ("and went out") closure of the circle, and the opening of the next verse ("Jacob's sons came upon the slain") with an insistent parallel to verse 25 ("two of Jacob's sons . . . came upon the city"), as if to announce a new stage: these interlocking clues suggest that "went out" drops the curtain on Simeon and Levi's involvement. Their sister left home for the Hivite town; they now leave the town with her to return home; and only on their departure did the plundering start.

Simeon and Levi thus part company with the rest of Jacob's sons. Were the episode torn out of context, they would seem to differ for the worse, since by conventional standards of morality looting pales beside slaughter. In context, however, the "court of conscience" overrules the attitude indicated by the "court of justice." Not that this attitude is ignored or even suspended by artistic fiat. Precisely because the narrator is aware that we bring our habitual norms and scales of value to the reading, his main concern has been to subject them to such pressure as will modify and transform, if not invert, automatic response. He has deployed his masterly rhetoric to shape the reader in his own image, to bring their viewpoints into alignment by appeal to the features and conditions that distinguish literary from everyday experience and interpersonal drama from imbroglios in which God himself is a side.

So far the control strategy operated to equalize rape and bloodshed. From now on, however, it also addresses itself to a resulting task of persuasion, one that bears not so much on interfamilial as on intrafamilial disparities, first between brother and brother (verses 25–29) and then between brother and father (verses 30–31). Having traced the conflict between the two parties to the bloody end, the narrator goes on to unveil and explore the rifts among the winning side. Most immediately, having re-scaled the offenses of the two camps, he now proceeds to do the same in regard to those perpetrated by the two groups of brothers: killing vs.

looting. This involves a notable shift in strategy. Simeon and Levi now benefit not only from past manipulations in favor of Jacob's offspring as a whole; nor only from the counterbalancing measures brought to bear on the mass slaughter. To round it all, they gain in stature and dignity from an unexpected source, namely, a process of favorable comparison with their own kinsmen.

The redirection of sympathy explains the remaining selectional and combinatory features of verses 25–29. This segment divides into two parts with analogous openings, each focused on another group of brothers. Considering the normal status of killing as against looting, the choice to allot the two acts the same amount of space (thirty-six versus thirty-seven words in the Hebrew) would become incongruous were it not of a piece with the contextual reassessment: the equivalence in length presses for an equivalence in valuation. And the effect of these representational ratios is carried even further by the particular design of selection. For all its dramaticness, the account of the slaughter limits itself to the bare essentials ("they killed all the males, and Hamor and Shechem his son they killed with the edge of the sword"), wrapped moreover by mitigating factors: the loaded reference on one side and the rescue of Dinah on the other. This throws into high relief the lingering over the despoilment, much in excess of plot requirements and biblical practice alike. As with quantity, so with ordering. While the act of violence proceeds in a straight line—from city through leaders to rescue—the plundering involves verbose and multiple repetition, notably of the general headings before, after, and amidst the particulars they subsume. This artful incoherence stretches the duration of the passage even beyond its actual length, giving the reader a sense of an orgy of looting.

Tempo and continuity link up with a number of more specific oppositions between the two groups. Thus, Simeon and Levi having taken all the risk ("came upon the city"), the second wave assumes a hyena-like appearance ("came upon the slain"). Normative sympathy, moreover, goes with emotional appeal. The brothers' "deceit" has been left so indeterminate—What does it portend? Is its idealistic rationale a credo or a façade?—that the reader has had to suspend judgment on it since verse 13. Only now is the gap closed; and its closure in terms of plot involves a cleavage in terms of ideology that vindicates the killers at the expense of the looters.

True, the poetic justice that adheres to the choice of circumcision as the instrument for punishing rape also extends to the spoliation of those who made an alliance under the slogan "Will not their cattle and their property and all their beasts be ours?" Still, the greed betrayed by the plunderers reduces them to the moral level of the Hivites, a demotion reinforced by analogical linkage to the "deceit" verse. The main justification for the deceit, we recall, lay in the final "*asher* had defiled Dinah their sister." This clause now recurs ("they plundered the city *asher* had defiled their sister"), again with apparent redundancy and in a strategic position, toward the end of a verse and at a point (between heading and catalogue) where it retards the flow of the narrative. But this time the clause does not operate to soften judgment. On the contrary, the echoing reference to the enormity of the rape produces an ironic clash between the brothers' fine words and their ugly deeds, between idealistic façade and materialistic reality, between deceit as sacred rage and as unholy calculation. The irony even sharpens owing to the perceptibility of the expression, the wealth of meaning packed into it, and the correspondence between its occurrences. The normative force of the clause is thus reversed in repetition. Within each scene, the retrospect on the defilement serves as a kind of affective anticipation, conditioning our response to what follows. But as it moves from verse 13 to 27, its effect modulates all the way from extenuation to damnation. The irony prejudges the looting even before the reader is exposed to its unsavory details.

As the details unroll, therefore, the long-suspended judgment comes down on the looters with a vengeance. By the same token, the debunking of the majority brings out the consistency of "two of Jacob's sons, Simeon and Levi, Dinah's brothers" (note how the last phrase links them, too, with "*asher* had defiled Dinah their sister") and the relevance of their proceeding. Simeon and Levi turn out to be the only ones who cling to the anti-materialistic norms ("it would be a disgrace to us") formulated in the Israelite reply to the Hivites. In their clean dissociation from the orgy of looting, they practice what the others only preach.[16] Their concern has been selfless and single-minded: to redress the wrong done to their sister and the whole family, which includes the prevention of an exogamous marriage, by hook or by crook.

Only toward the end, then, does the narrative reveal its true focus of interest. It started by giving the impression that this focus lay in the Shechem-Dinah affair, then it brought Jacob into the limelight, and later still foregrounded the relation between the two peoples. As its tortuous progression draws to a close, however, Simeon and Levi emerge as the real heroes. Unlike the cast of the Sisera narrative, where human interest branches out rather than focuses along the sequence, they earn the right to heroship. But nor do they play this role in the manner of, say, Raskolnikov in *Crime and Punishment* or Stephen Dedalus in *Portrait of the Artist,* who overshadow the other inhabitants of their world and figure as centers of consciousness as well as action. Our tale centers not in a psychological state or process but in a moral issue, and it is above all concerned to explore different approaches to that issue. Within these horizons of interest, it accords Simeon and Levi a closer and more distinctive treatment than their human environment: the Hivites, Jacob, or the rest of the brothers, who remain an anonymous and faceless collective. Those two gradually move from off stage to on stage to central position: their idealistic and uncompromising stance makes them the most intricate, colorful, and attractive characters in the story. And as soon as they break away from the amorphous mass of "Jacob's sons," it turns out that all the other characters, their own brothers included, largely serve to illuminate them.

This applies to the sequel as well as to the antecedents of the massacre. In fact, the action proper comes to an end with Simeon and Levi's exit from Shechem's house (it is not for nothing that this stage has received such an incisive closure). What remains is devoted to a final placing of their viewpoint and a final stabilization of the reader's complex attitude to them—in short, to the third phase of the rhetorical strategy. The looting thus functions to disclose an antithesis between them and their fellow attackers, with whom they suddenly part company. Whereas the final verses clinch our sympathy for them by renewing the opposition with the father. The disparity implied in the reactions to Shechem's crime escalates into an open clash after the punishment:

> (30) Jacob said to Simeon and Levi, You have brought trouble on me by putting me in bad odor with the inhabitants of the land, the Canaanites and the Perizzites; my numbers are small, and if they gather themselves against me and attack me, I shall be destroyed, I and my house. (31) And they said, Should he treat our sister like a harlot?

Jacob breaks his long silence only to reveal himself as the tale's least sympathetic character. The cowardice betrayed (not for the first time, but never so perceptibly as vis-à-vis the boldest of his sons) is less damning than the immorality. If Jacob reproached the pair for the massacre or the abuse of the rite of circumcision or even the breach of contract, he would gain a measure of understanding and support from the reader. But he does not even remotely protest against any of these offenses. A moral note appears only as late as his deathbed dissociation ("My soul will not enter their council") from the men of violence, whose rage he curses. But Jacob makes this diatribe many years later, in Egypt, when the dangers of the Hivite affair are long past and he can afford to play the moralist. That he adopts no such viewpoint at present—just as he never glances at the despicable but less risky business of looting—suggests that he finds the slaughter reprehensible only in its consequences. His approach, like the words of the Hivites and the deeds of his other sons, is informed by those pragmatic considerations against which the narrative has leveled so much of its rhetoric.

Of the various brands of pragmatism, moreover, his is the most incongruous, being divorced from any form of activity or commitment or even self-expression apart from keeping still until overtaken by events. It is also the most univocally condemned in terms of biblical history and world view. For his inaction amounts to an acquiescence in what a patriarch, whatever his paternal instincts, must fight tooth and nail: exogamous marriage. Dinah must be extricated even at a risk. But Jacob proves blind to tradition and destiny as well as to morality, and the insistent harping on the "I" throughout his outburst ("brought trouble upon me . . . putting me in bad odor . . . my numbers are small . . . gather themselves against me and attack me . . . I shall be destroyed, I and my house") slyly delimits the range of his vision.

Whatever its force elsewhere, therefore, Jacob's argument sounds shabby in the Bible's court of conscience. The ending rubs in the point by having his wordy and terror-driven onslaught countered by Simeon and Levi's proud and epigrammatic "Should he treat our sister like a harlot?" The voice of egocentricity and self-preservation finds itself opposed by the voice of idealism. Damn the consequences, they say, and their response vibrates with the sense of injury that drove them to seek redress in the sword. Shechem treated Dinah like a whore not only by his cavalier way with her virtue but also by his subsequent offer of "gifts" to her protectors. The idiom for harlot's pay (*etnan zona*) eloquently rhymes with that key verb (*ntn*) of the Hivite blandishments.

Addressed to Jacob, moreover, "our sister" trembles with passion against the father as well. The long-standing tensions created by favoritism and reflected in the polar attitudes to the rape have thus far smoldered in the dynamics of the kinship terms. As a result of the father's ultimate provocation, however, they burst into flame, because Simeon and Levi can no longer endure Jacob's indifference to the fate of Leah's daughter. In this connection, note that the last verse closes another circle opened in the first, making a chiasm no less suggestive than the "went out and took" already traced. The story ends ("our sister") just as it began ("Dinah, the daughter of Leah whom she had borne to Jacob"), with a kinship term referring to the same character. In view of the intervening developments in plot and rhetoric, however, it is no accident that the character thus indicated should take her reference from different kinsmen at the two extremities of the circle. Throughout the opening, it would no more occur to the brothers than to any other participant to refer to Dinah by any expression but "Jacob's daughter." Even at the turning point in verse 13 they only *think* of her in fraternal terms ("defiled Dinah their sister"), whereas their following *speech* still shifts between "our sister" and, as if in Jacob's voice, "our daughter." But now they in effect wrest her out of the father's guardianship: she may not be your daughter, but she certainly is "our sister" and no one will treat her like a whore.

Alternatively, however, their response is directed not at all to but against Jacob: "Will he [Jacob] treat our sister like a harlot?" This reading is allowed by the grammar and the logic of the immediate context;[17] it also makes sense in terms of the whole design. On this hypothesis, Simeon and Levi remain silent under attack and give vent to their feelings later, in private conversation. The tale's implicit criticism of Jacob from the outset, progressively sharpening but still never vocalized under the alternative resolution, is articulated at the end by those who have earned the right to protest. And the interplay of the two readings—one denouncing Shechem outright and Jacob indirectly, the other reversing the scale of explicitness—carries thematic and evaluative implications. He who twiddles his thumbs about the rape and deems the gifts fair compensation is as guilty of making a whore of Dinah as the rapist and giver himself.

The narrator no more pronounces judgment on this family quarrel than he did on the conflict with the Hivites. He seems to leave the issue open for the reader to decide. But he remains far from neutral. The dilemma raised by the story is so complex and each choice so problematic that he cannot fully identify with any of the positions taken. After all, whatever Jacob's callousness and selfishness, he does right to think of the safety of his house. Whereas the brothers do right to champion Dinah; but they pay the price in deceit and bloodshed, they increasingly act from personal motives rather than horror of exogamy and in disregard for consequences rather than out of trust in God's providence, which validates their proceeding (35:5) after the event. From the narrator's vantage point, therefore, none of the dramatized views rises above the level of stuff for plot and polyphony. Yet his rhetorical maneuvers throughout, the final set of oppositions, and, above all, his giving the last word—and what a last word!—to Simeon and Levi, leave no doubt where his sympathy lies.

The Rhetorical Repertoire

I want to conclude with a spectrum of fifteen rhetorical devices, ranging from the most explicit to the most covert, through which the Bible shapes our response to character and event. This repertoire also serves the Bible's other purposes, notably characterization or the rendering of inner life, and, in the light of my argument throughout the book, can be easily recast into their terms. By now, indeed, even its rhetorical dimension lends itself to brief summary:[18]

1. *Narratorial evaluation of an agent or an action through a series of epithets (or their equivalent).* Apart from its high authority, this is also the most perceptible form of judgment. Within the Bible's miniature scale, it corresponds to a whole novelistic portrait; and it specially stands out where its expression arrests the flow of events. Compare the preliminary "blameless and upright, one who feared God and eschewed evil" (Job 1:1) with the intercalated and thus retardatory "Now the man Moses was meek, more than all men who were on the face of the earth" (Num 12:3).

2. *Through a single epithet,* with the evaluation still solid but deprived of cumulative force and perceptibility. As in (1), moreover, this may bear on all normative axes: social, emotional, ethical, ideological. It also maintains the difference in absoluteness between the judgment of the agent and the action. A personal epithet (e.g., "base fellows") covers a facet of personality, while a behavioral equivalent ("answered with deceit") is relative to context and may shift to the point of opposition through a person's history. Hence the difference in absoluteness correlates with one in flexibility and valence.

3. *Through a choice of loaded language,* without at all interrupting the onward rush of the plot. Instead of superadding an evaluation, the narrator fuses it with the representation itself through normatively loaded phraseology, whether verbs ("abused," "defiled") or referential terms ("He said to the doer of the wrong, Why dost thou strike thy fellow?" [Exod 2:13]). Each piece of language here does double duty, as plot (predication, reference) and as judgment. Note also how the distinction between deed and doer still holds in the examples.

4. *Explicit judgment left ambiguous between narrator and characters,* by way of perspectival montage: for example, the play between the objective and the subjective readings of "He had committed an outrage in Israel."

5. *As in (1), (2), and (3), except that the judgment is delegated to characters.* Here we move not only from direction to indirection but from authoritativeness to fallibility, since the judging figures are themselves objects of judgment. And the narrator's view of their own attitude may range from full endorsement (most clearly, when he makes them repeat his own words) to total dissociation (as when Goliath disdains David because of his youth and good looks). Of course, only in authoritative narration like the Bible's (or Fielding's) do (1) to (4) outrank (5). Where a character doubles as narrator, the scale begins with (5): no evaluation assumes validity unless aligned with the norms of the implicit author.

6. *Judgment through a nonverbal objective correlative,* in the form of a drastic act that speaks for itself: the revenge taken by Jacob's sons, Moses' shattering of the tablets, or even an omission like the refusal of Saul's servants to massacre the Nob priests. Coming in response to other acts, the drastic act serves as a (or the) vehicle of judgment on them and their agents:

Shechem and his rape, Israel and their golden calf, Saul and his insane order. But like the verbal evaluation which it supports or replaces, the drastic act expresses a judgment subject to the narrator's own judgment and, therefore, potentially as warped and condemned as Jezebel's murder of Naboth. While (1) to (3) mark variations in overtness within reliability, the instances of (4) to (6) also diverge in reliability according to context.

7. *Charged dramatization, lingering over and thus foregrounding the plot elements designed for judgment.*

8. *Informational redundancy.*

Common to these two measures is their reference to the text's principles of selection (as opposed to the combinatory logic of analogy or temporal ordering). Because of the logical correlation between space and importance in discourse, the more specified or dramatized a piece of world, the more perceptible its evaluative aspects and grounds and requirements. The well scene between the servant and Rebekah extends an invitation to judgment both more peremptory and more suggestive than the corresponding glimpse offered of Moses with Jethro's daughters. And if the intrinsic loading of materials may do duty for specificity in inviting judgment—as does the elliptical reference to Reuben's incest with his father's wife compared with, say, Amnon's rape of Tamar—it does not always enable the reader to act on the invitation.

The quantitative indicator further grows in significance as detailed rendering crosses the line that separates particularity from redundancy, dramatization from repetition. In a highly selective and functional discourse, there is no room for excess; and therefore informational superfluity launches a search for coherence in other terms, evaluative for example. We have already seen this mechanism at work, most often in the analysis of repetition structure and most variously throughout the Rape of Dinah. Instances would be the variant repetitions of and within the familial terms pointing to Dinah, the punctuating reference to her "defilement," the over-treatment of the rape scene and then of the rapist's change of heart, the proposals in their different versions, or the disorderly movement between the general and the particular when it comes to the looting. Less direct than (3) to (6), these selectional manipulators of judgment are no less potent and certainly more authoritative because, like all the following indirections, they proceed from the narrator himself.

9. *Direct inside view of the characters* and

10. *The play of perspectives.*

There is little to support the oft-made claim that the Bible judges man by his deeds rather than by his thoughts. One must not confuse God's management of the plot with the narrator's management of our attitude to the plot. The Rape of Dinah shows every one of its characters from within, some more than once, and never without molding the reader's response to the subjects of consciousness, often to others as well and in opposed directions at that. Nor is this use of privileged information exceptional either in frequency or in rhetorical flexibility. The laying bare of internals may operate, for example, to increase sympathy by reliably establishing the sincerity of external conduct or to undercut or qualify it by exposing insincerity ("with deceit"). It serves to complicate judgment by exploring the complexity of feeling (e.g., mixed motives) or to harden it by foregrounding their baseness; it may counteract the impact of action past, present, and future (as when Shechem's love follows his assault) or simply render the agent intelligible even at his worst. As a rule, every inside view performs more than one of these rhetorical functions; and so, as with the handling of Jacob's silence, may the denial of an inside view where it might be expected or affective.

From another side, the inside view ties up with point of view in general, because its free manipulation presupposes an omniscient narrator and affords the reader access to secrets otherwise humanly known only to the party concerned. Therefore, the sharing or withholding of the inside view forms a special case of the three reading positions: the reader-elevated, the character-elevated, and the evenhanded. At this stage, I believe, this hint will suffice to bring to mind the links traced throughout between knowledge and judgment as axes of point of view and the rhetorical implications carried by the play of perspectives. For good measure, the next chapter will focus on a splendid example of the relations between viewpoint and persuasion, with the former split and ranked and dynamized to justify Saul's fall.

11. *Order of presentation,* its effects deriving from the structural flexibility of literature as a time art, where elements and patterns unfold in a sequence devised by the artist but imposed on the reader to form a determinate process of (mis)understanding. Unavailable in the sequences of life, each ordering choice assumes significance against the background of the rejected options. This holds true even for natural-looking organizations of time, as often in the order of suspense or in the Dinah story. Here the narrative mainly adheres to chronology, but only in order to open and end with episodes charged with rhetorical power. The rape followed by the father's stillness followed by the Hivite proposal can best accumulate the anticipatory store of sympathy for the brothers, especially since the irreversible linearity of the discourse prevents the reader from knowing where and why he is led. And the looting followed by paternal hysterics countered by a proud epigram can best generate the retrospective sympathy required for the delicate balance.

As with global, so with local ordering. The placement of verbs of forcing before verbs of loving or the brothers' grief before their anger, the incoherence of the looting series, the "last word" given to the avengers at the end not only of the whole tale but (as in the crucial verse 13) of parts too: these illustrate the cunning deployment of the microsequence by the persuader. Whatever the scale, the objective load of judgment attaching to the units either grows or diminishes under the pressure of time.

12. *Order of presentation involving the displacement of conventional patterns.* If natural sequence yields rhetorical gains, then its manipulation and discontinuity do so far more perceptibly. Indeed, this would give it priority along a range of overtness were it not for the fact that some of the biblical varieties of dechronologization still enjoy natural or rather supernatural motivation, notably divine forecasting. But, since it is the narrator who opts for the supernaturalized no less than the naturalized order of discourse, both require artistic motivation just like their openly denaturalized equivalents.

Again, the extent to which this motivation for gaps and multiple reading proceeds along rhetorical lines—temporal disordering pressed into the service of evaluative ordering—hardly needs any rehearsal now. But a few reminders from the latest case in point may not come amiss. Thus, compare the effect of the permanent gap concerning the causes of Jacob's stillness (or the plot sequence of the more dynamic strands or the addressee of the final outburst) with that of the temporary gap about his sons' real intentions. Compare the immediate play of ambiguity launched by either— in Jacob's disfavor and the brothers' favor—with the dynamics of the surprise gap concerning Dinah's whereabouts. Compare also the rhetoric of retrospection or recognition informing all these displacements of the past with the rhetoric of prospection anchored in the cryptic "with deceit." Finally, recall the correspondence between plot macrocosm and verbal microcosm, whereby the dislocation of the *asher*-sentence produces a typical foolproof design: syntactic ambiguity (or rather, triguity) with evaluative unity.

13. *Analogical patterning.* As analogy presupposes similarity, its nature turns on the relative weight of dissimilarity, which may be reduced to concretizing the analogues or heightened to the point of opposing them. The rhetorical impact varies accordingly. In the Bible, serialization offers the clearest instance of straight analogy, since its variety only brings out the dominant unity in the interests of, say, the omnipotence effect; whereas the plainest type of contrasted analogy emerges from the qualitative opposition of God to man in knowledge and power. In between these poles lie the truly interesting mixtures, which vary from revealing dissimilarity amid similarity to revealing similarity amid dissimilarity. In each case, the rhetorical force of the dominant equivalence-relation stems from its imposition on a subordinate that resists and complicates it. The analogy between David and Abimelech thus drags down the higher term to the level of the low. The

antithesis between Jacob and his sons goes counter to familial affinities and responsibilities shared by the agents and shaped by the composition. The pairing of Deborah and Jael in opposition to Barak and Sisera cuts across national and inverts sexual relations.

Another type of patterning relates to (11) and (12) above, for even the suprasequential form of analogy is not immune to the processing of sequence. Under the pressure of developments and disclosures, even an initially straight analogy may transform into a contrast, as with the splitting of the common front presented by the brothers into swordsmen and looters. Even more adventureful, Moses and Aaron begin as partners, then fall into opposition in the Golden Calf affair, and finally revert to brotherhood in a common fate. Since the reader does not possess all the analogical ingredients before the end, their emergence may be so fashioned as to maneuver him into the desired attitudes all along the route.

14. *Recurrence of key words along the sequence,* which forms a special case or analogy and miniaturizes its principles. Yet it deserves separate mention on account of its increased covertness. For the units analogized are (a) small, usually verbs and referring terms; (b) formally incorporated into the discourse under a linguistic rather than a compositional guise; (c) unobtrusive in themselves, since they give an impression of the most ordinary lexical items: "Dinah" or its familial equivalents, "take," "give," "go out." In fact, their recurrence along the sequence charges them with a rhetorical as well as a semantic load, which may be activated on each new occurrence. The raping "take" thus clashes with the matrimonial "take," the offered "giving" of money reflects and evaluates attitudes to the "giving" of the bride in exchange. This variously corresponds to the adventures of "see" in the anointment episodes, of "blessed" in the Wooing narrative, of old age and blindness in patriarchal or good looks in royal history. Even more notable, the linkage of the punishment to the crime through "take" and "go out" shapes response by implying a chain as well as a ratio of violence: like the tit-for-tat design in the Joseph story, it invests the spatial confrontation of the key verbs with a linear-causal force. On the whole, the Bible wields these simple-looking words to the same effect as modernism does clusters of figurative language.

15. *Neutral or pseudo-objective narration,* where incidental details seem to gain not just equality but even priority to essentials. Rare in biblical literature as it is elsewhere, this mode governs the David and Bathsheba tale. But the Rape of Dinah typically rules it out together with the opposite extreme. On the one hand, direct and authoritative judgment by way of epithet does not suit a strategy designed to produce an attitude complex, balanced, ambivalent, full of emotional and ethical tensions. More flexible, though no less reliable, control measures like (3), not to speak

of the indirections starting with (4), enable the narrator to endorse one act while condemning another by the same agent or even, as with the deceit, elicit both responses at once. On the other hand, the strategic goals equally rule out the pose of neutrality. The Bathsheba episode can afford to press this ironic mode to an extreme—to present horrors as if they were nothing out of the ordinary, to foreground the incidentals of plot and judgment at the expense of essentials, to play on the discontinuity between matter and manner—only because the normative groundwork and its application are so self-evident. The reader may be counted on to order the artfully disordered pattern of evaluation. Where the problem lies in the normative design and in guiding the reader's modification or even reversal of conventional views, as throughout the Dinah affair, such extremity would only confuse matters. Here the narrator must exercise his freedom of moving up and down the rhetorical scale to meet the exigencies of control. The Bible thus reconciles the demands of artistic and foolproof structure by establishing an inverse proportion between the overtness and the transparence of judgment.

The Bible is a reticent text, but its reticence varies in sphere and degree and function according to context. That is why even a single tale of about four hundred words brings to bear a range of persuasion that few literary works could emulate. Indeed, its maneuvering supplies almost all the principles that would compose a general outline of narrative rhetoric.

·13·

IDEOLOGY, RHETORIC, POETICS[1]

> The Scripture stories do not, like Homer's, court our favour, they
> do not flatter us that they may please us and enchant us—they seek
> to subject us, and if we refuse to be subjected we are rebels.
> Erich Auerbach, *Mimesis*

In the widest sense, "rhetoric" embraces the whole discourse in its communicative aspect, as a set of means chosen and organized with an eye to an audience rather than to self-expression or pure making. One may then speak, though I have rarely done so, of the rhetoric of narrative interest or character-drawing or repetition or ambiguity or any other pattern designed for effect. But the term "rhetoric" also has a stricter and more traditional sense, which narrows its range from communication as such to communication with persuasive intent. As persuader, the rhetorician seeks not just to affect but to affect with a view to establishing consensus in the face of possible demur and opposition. Success has only one meaning and one measure to him: bringing the audience's viewpoint into alignment with his own. In the Bible, this holds equally true for the rhetoric of interpersonal relations analysed in the last chapter and for the rhetoric of doctrinal relations, to which the omniscience and the omnipotence effects do not yet set the most demanding task.

Justifying the Ways of God to Man: Saul's Rejection

Like all speakers, from the humblest dialogists going about their daily business to the most highbrow artists in their ivory towers, the biblical storyteller is a persuader in that he wields discourse to shape response and manipulate attitude. Unlike most speakers, however, his persuasion is not only geared to an ideology but also designed to vindicate and inculcate it. Even among ideological persuaders, he has a special claim to notice, due less to the theology preached than to the rules and rhetoric of its preaching.

482

Of the various challenges facing the biblical narrator as ideological persuader, the most basic and formidable derives from the tension between two constraints. One is his commitment to the divine system of norms, absolute and demanding and in application often ruthless; the other, his awareness of the necessity and difficulty of impressing it on a human audience. The problem is always how to harmonize rhetoric and ideology: how to get man to adopt a world picture that both transcends and threatens man; how to win the audience over to the side of God rather than of their fellow mortals; how to accomplish the task of persuasion without dwarfing, betraying, or compromising the object of persuasion. This would make the narrator the servant of two masters, were it not for the fact that one of these he serves with a view to subjecting him all the more effectively to the other. Only a fool like Rehoboam, whose fate is indeed a lesson in rhetorical as well as political control, would disregard the advice of the wise old men about apparent service as the way to real domination.

Thus suspended between heaven and earth, the narrator must perform feats of tightrope walking in order to maintain his balance and achieve his dual goal. The trickiness of that performance has few equivalents in literature, religious or secular, ancient or modern. Obviously, nothing like it constrains Homer's narrative strategy in the *Iliad,* where the gods' squabbling provides comic relief from the intensity of the human tragedy, and their petty score-keeping, a contrastive background to the hero's absolute norms. The irreverent treatment of the gods in Homeric epic has its counterpart in the rough handling of the audience in prophetic discourse, for a Jeremiah can afford to lash out where the storyteller would entice and manipulate. In the absence of either license, the narrator must establish consensus while observing both the articles of faith and the decorums of communication.

On top of all this, as if to make things even more difficult for himself, the biblical narrator avoids the line of least resistance in presenting character, event, and the march of history. Unlike the didactic persuader, with whom he is so often confused, he will rarely stoop to the polarization of values and effects, with repulsive villains pitted against all-round paragons; nor to the wholesale evocation of stereotype and stock response; nor to homiletic address and lecturing. Didacticism is ideological writing, but not vice versa, and the dividing line is precisely where ethics and aesthetics meet to generate the *art* of persuasion.

Still, at times the Bible's task is relatively simple. Even the God of wrath, after all, does not always need much vindication. In the story of David and Bathsheba or Ahab and Naboth, for example, the king's sins are so odious that the human and the divine systems of norms converge and point the same way. But in many other instances, likewise based on a scheme of "crime and punishment," the narrator's rhetorical powers are stretched to the utmost, because the plain facts of the tale by no means suffice to ensure such harmony. Where God condemns, man may well condone.

These are accordingly the real test cases, and the story of Saul and Amalek (1 Samuel 15) illustrates the challenge they present. Does Saul's sparing of "Agag and the best of the sheep and the oxen" justify God's tearing the kingdom from him? Has not Saul followed the essential instructions in destroying Amalek "from Havilah as far as Shur," and doesn't this make his one aberration forgivable, if not negligible? Isn't there a glaring disproportion between achievement and reward, sin and penalty? These are the normative questions that the reader is sure to pose. And these are indeed the very questions that the narrator prepares to meet and resolve, by way of subtle persuasive art rather than blunt ideological fiat.[2]

Nothing else can account so well for the tale's selective and combinatory procedures, notably for the manifold repetition that governs its whole sequence. This striking feature seems here not merely to incur redundancy, as usual, but to carry it far in excess of normal biblical practice. While the biblical structure of repetition requires (and often makes do with) only two members, Saul's ordeal involves all the three possible types: (1) the member of forecast, defined in terms of expectation about the narrative future: God orders Saul to smite the Amalekites; (2) the member of enactment: Saul smites Amalek; (3) the member of report, defined in terms of retrospection on the past: Saul tells Samuel how he smote Amalek. Even more excessive, the first type of member repeats a long-standing prospection from Deuteronomy (25:17–19) and is in turn repeated to Saul after as well as before the smiting of Amalek; and the last type recurs again and again in Saul's apologetics. Finally, this extended series of repetitions alternates with another that centers in Samuel, once he arrives on the scene to confront the king. What might otherwise appear a hodgepodge of redundancies, however, makes perfect rhetorical sense in terms of an overall strategy that wields repetition as a battering ram against Saul and, indirectly, the possibly doubtful reader. As in the interpersonal rhetoric, the preference is again given to the arts of indirection.

In fact, the rhetorical strategy devised to justify the ways of God to man begins as early as the opening member of the repetition, in that it gives the divine command its shape and emphasis:

(1) Samuel said to Saul, It was me the Lord sent to anoint thee king over his people, over Israel; now therefore listen to the voice of the Lord. (2) Thus says the Lord of hosts, I remember what Amalek did to Israel, how he waylaid him when he came up from Egypt. (3) Now therefore go and smite Amalek and utterly destroy all that he has; and do not

> spare him, but kill both man and woman, both infant and suckling, both ox and sheep, both camel and ass. (1 Sam 15:1–3)

At this point, of course, the normative crux is still hidden from the reader's eyes—not just left unannounced but artfully camouflaged, in fact, since the opening focuses attention on Amalek's rather than Saul's crime and punishment. But the narrator looks ahead and, having misled the reader about his target and intentions, prepares the real line of attack. Seemingly concerned only to highlight the odium and justify the doom of the past offender, he actually lays the ground for producing the very same effects in regard to the future offender, who desecrates the workings of retribution. If Amalek's fate now appears to the reader well deserved, so will Saul's later: it is this logic that drives the hidden persuader to start by manipulating our response to future developments in a variety of ways, each turning on a "prospect + prospect" mode of repetition.

First, to anticipate and offset the ruthlessness of the extermination order, the text leads up to it by a specific exposition. As regards the sequence of discourse, it is not just that the member of prospect (or forecast) antecedes the action, as is the rule in the Bible. Within the member of prospect itself, a retrospect leads the way: the explanation comes before the command, the cause before the effect, the mention of the crime ("what Amalek did to Israel" etc.) before the demand for punishment ("Now therefore go and smite Amalek"). Thus, the expository movement from past to future, the wording of the retrospect, even the general–particular relation between its parts—all these bring to mind the original *memento mori* in Deuteronomy:

> Remember what Amalek did to thee on the way as you came out of Egypt. How he beset thee on the way and cut off at the rear all who straggled behind thee, when thou wert faint and weary; and he feared not God. Therefore, when the Lord thy God has given thee rest from all thy enemies round about, in the land which the Lord thy God gives thee for an inheritance to possess, thou shalt blot out the remembrance of Amalek from under heaven. Thou shalt not forget. (Deut 25:17–19; cf. Exod 17:8–16; Num 14:45)

To reinforce the parallels, by way of structural as well as thematic allusion, is to reinforce the present command by investing it with historical resonance and continuity.

Second, again as with the original command from the times of the desert, the explanation is cast in terms that are national no less than religious: "I remember what Amalek did to Israel." This is not a private quarrel, then, between God and Amalek. Nor is this just an ancestral grudge, an exceptional *casus belli* within an otherwise harmonious coexistence. The speech does not explicitly indicate that, apart from the first unforgivable act of aggression, Israel also has more recent scores to settle with Amalek, from the days of the Judges. Rather, these later contexts are now implicitly activated by way of pointed intertextual allusion. Note the verbal analogy devised between Israel's coming revenge and Amalek's periodic invasions in the Gideon era: the prospective "both ox and sheep, both camel and ass" rhymes with the retrospective "they left no sustenance to Israel, neither sheep nor ox nor ass . . . and their camels were without number" (Judg 6:3–5). The tit-for-tat patterning, so dear to the biblical rhetoric of retribution,[3] not only eliminates all traces of arbitrariness from the divine command but also evokes a long and eventful history of one-sided aggression.

Third, the intertextual analogy also serves to explain an otherwise obscure point. Why is the command addressed to Saul rather than to one of his predecessors or successors, and why at this particular moment? The answer lies in another artfully pinpointed link between past and present. The historical visions expressed in Deuteronomy to a landless people in the words "when the Lord thy God has given thee rest from all thy enemies round about [*misaviv*]" have now come true to the last detail: the end of the previous chapter describes Saul's victories against "all his enemies round [*saviv*], against Moab and against the Ammonites and against Edom and against the kings of Zobah and against the Philistines." Repatriation, settlement, national security *misaviv:* all the promises in the subordinate clause having now been kept, the main clause falls due. No wonder God picks up the thread ("I remember") just where he dropped it ("Thou shalt not forget"). The time for revenge has finally come, and it is Saul's duty and privilege to settle the outstanding account.[4]

Indeed, the fourth feature of the rhetorical preparations consists in making Saul (as well as the reader) aware of his personal responsibility for closing that account. The opening reference to Saul's having been anointed "king over [God's] people, over Israel" already implies his role in dealing with "what Amalek did to Israel." And that implication is soon made explicit in the grammatical person of the imperatives, which (with the one exception I have italicized) assumes the singular form: "Go and smite . . . and *utterly destroy* . . . and do not spare . . . but kill."[5] Again, the allusion to Deuteronomy sharpens and validates the effect. While in the early forecast the second person singular refers to the people, in the version repeated here its reference shifts to their king: God is "I," Saul "thou," and Israel "he." The shift in reference pinpoints a shift in responsibility, one that hints at the recent transformation of social structure with the rise of the monarchy and will later prove of crucial importance as soon as Saul tries to shift responsibility back to the people who delegated it to him.

Finally, as with the burden of responsibility, so with its object. It is not only that the charged language of the ban (*kherem*), reserved for holy war and fortified by the absolute "all," imposes the duty of total destruction. Its operational meaning is at once spelt out. Cast in blunt terms and symmetrical specifications, the decree leaves no room for misunderstanding and excuses, in regard to either enemy population or property: "both man and woman, both infant and suckling, both ox and sheep, both camel and ass."

At the stage of prospection, then, the preliminary rhetoric serves a complex of functions, apparently straightforward but in fact double-edged. It is designed (1) to base the command on the widest possible (and hence most widely acceptable) normative grounds; (2) to issue it to the most definite addressee and in the most definite terms; (3) to gain understanding and assent for its various conditions (timing, drasticness, reponsibility, and all); and thus (4) to maximize the reader's desire as well as expectations of a swift and meticulous performance on the king's part.

That performace indeed starts on an encouraging, though unexpected, note. Having summoned the people,

> (5) Saul came to the city of Amalek, and lay in wait in the valley. (6) And Saul said to the Kenites, Go, depart, come down from among the Amalekites, lest I put an end to thee with them; and thou showedst kindness to all the people of Israel when they came up from Egypt. And the Kenites departed from among Amalek.

It is precisely what looks like a divergence from the letter of the divine command that proves so encouraging, since it manifests a remarkable grasp of the spirit informing that command. God having sent him on his mission armed with a reason as well as a sword, Saul wisely infers that those who showed Israel kindness "when they came up from Egypt" must not perish with those who stabbed Israel in the back "when he came up from Egypt." If the terms of reference are the settling of historical debts, then gratitude counts no less than revenge: the execution of justice must work both ways.

At this point, then, the tale goes out of its way—even literally so, the Kenite episode being a digression from the main line of events—to give Saul credit for his energetic ("Go, depart, come down") initiative. Its very inclusion speaks for itself; the echoing reference to the time of the Exodus confirms the approval by way of analogy; and that nobody chides Saul for having thereby jeopardized the whole campaign suggests that the risk was well worth taking. But within the rhetorical strategy as a whole, the very normative insight displayed by Saul here is later to be turned against him, in more than one way. It enables the narrator to avoid black-and-white portraiture (an avoidance that forms not only an aesthetic feature of his storytelling but a shrewd weapon of persuasion as well: "Who wishes to blackguard the man? Whenever he deserves praise, he gets it"). An even more boomerang-like effect produced by Saul's insight is that it serves to reimpress on the reader's mind the historical rationale of the war, this time from the positive side, and concretize the distinction between justified and unjustified divergence. And in terms of the play of expectations about the future, it looks as good as a promise that Amalek, too, will get his just deserts from the scrupulous king. Given the pointed contrast in regard to the past, the logic of analogy would seem to leave no room for any other development.

That expectation is even further reinforced by the immediate sequel, especially since the member of action starts ("And Saul smote Amalek") by echoing the member of prospect ("go and smite Amalek"). So its frustration, just when everything seemed to be going so well, redoubles our surprise, disappointment, condemnation:

> (7) Saul smote Amalek, from Havilah as far as Shur, which is east of Egypt. (8) And he took Agag the king of Amalek alive, and all the people he utterly destroyed with the edge of the sword. (9) And Saul and the people spared Agag, and the best of the sheep and of the oxen and of the fatlings, and the lambs, and all that was good, and would not utterly destroy them; and all the despised and rejected property, this they utterly destroyed.

Actional and rhetorical surprise come together. For through the sudden unfolding of Saul's misconduct, the narrator also unfolds for the first time his own focus of interest and object of attack. Such drastic shifts and turns are far from rare, still less accidental. As argued in my analysis of the "dynamics of recognition" and later of the Dinah story, based on a double twist, they relate to the Bible's management of the narrative sequence and the narrator's control of our reponse throughout the reading process. The Bible's persuasive repertory thus includes the disappointment of both the reader's expectation (in terms of the structure of probabilities) and his preference or judgment (in terms of the structure of values). For each mode of frustration produces surprise, a retrospective repatterning of anterior elements, and hence a sharpening of impressions and attitudes. The effect of the newly revealed material then derives not only from the preparations made by the narrator but also from the unpreparedness of the reader, whose attention has been diverted elsewhere till the moment judged suitable for springing the surprise that will canalize it into the desired grooves.

Consider the present case of sequential shift in focus. Only when his hero falls into sin does the narrator show his hand. It is (we now discover) Saul's crime, not Amalek's, that forms the real theme, and his punishment that raises the moral-ideological question marks and thus calls for justification. But this does not at all mean that the narrator has so far been wasting his time on a mere effort to mislead us about his target and intentions. Nor is it just that lulling our suspicions about what lies ahead serves his purposes because it lowers any possible resistance on our part to his initial manipulations and then enables him to catch us unprepared at the transitional stage of disclosure. The point is that as soon as Saul emerges as the real center of interest and judgment, all that has gone before appears in a new light and acquires new significance in relation to him. The whole normative weight of the tale's opening, seemingly designed to crush the Amalekites or any pity their fate may evoke, now recoils upon Saul.

This is evidently the case with the member of forecast, now transformed all along the line from an explicit judgment on the original offenders into an implicit judgment on the appointed avenger of the their offense. But take the distinction just made between what deserves to be annihilated (Amalekites) and what spared (Kenites). Having so far served to vindicate the divine command, by emphasizing its ideological basis, it now serves to condemn the human performance, by emphasizing the mercenary basis of its distinctions, whether motivated by vanity (Agag) or greed (sheep, cattle, etc.). The contrastive effect extends even further. That divergence from the letter of God's order now opposes, and thus exposes, the violation of its very spirit. It is not simply that the holy war is desecrated by the looting, but that its whole point is rudely reversed by the principle of choice: the pride of Amalek should have been the first object of total destruction, not of selective "sparing."

Still, despite its boomerang-like effect at this point in the sequence, Saul's behavior to the Kenites at least reflected some credit on him at the time. In contrast, his handling of the Amalekites instantly bristles with condemnation and leaves him no leg to stand on in the future. The act itself is bad enough, of course, but its impact on the reader can largely be traced to the shape given to it by verse 9. A turning point in the action and the rhetorical strategy alike, this forms one of the most intricate pieces of persuasion in the Bible:

> Saul and the people spared Agag, and the best of the sheep and of the oxen and of the fatlings, and the lambs, and all that was good, and would not utterly destroy them; and all the despised and rejected property, this they utterly destroyed.

Since the performance of the command is a nonlinguistic object—a piece of action that the narrator could render in any number of ways—each of the choices involved in its representation assumes a special significance:

a. Of all the verbs and verbal forms available to the rendering of the offense, the narrator chooses that root ("spare") and that number (singular, though the subject is plural) which will most directly conflict with the language of God's order: "spared" (*va-yakhmol*) in the action as against "do not spare" (*lo takhmol*) in the prospection.

b. From the semantic and perspectival standpoint, moreover, "spare" (literally, "have pity") does not merely denote an action or omission. Unlike otherwise equivalent verbs like "took" or even "failed to destroy," it gives us an *inside view* of the agent, so that the subjective motive for the omission emerges together with its objective result. The same verb becomes even more conspicuous in retrospect, since (coupled with "would not destroy them," which validates and reinforces its import) it provides the only inside view of Saul throughout the narrative. And this monopoly over the inner life ensures its crushing effect in relation to later as well as foregoing members of the structure of repetition. The king's long series of prevarications in the coming members of report—from the version that it is the people who did the sparing to the version that it is his fear of the people that drove him into sin—will be exposed and denounced vis-à-vis the authoritative reference point established by the narrator in the member of the action.

c. Even within the present sentence itself, the combinatory features of the verb sharpen the rhetorical effect of its selection. Thus, in his rendering of the sin the narrator not only takes preventive action by dissociating the "sparing" from the natural (and hence emotionally problematic) objects of pity, like the infant and the suckling named in the command. He goes so far as to lay an ironic trap for the reader: "spared"—Whom? The weak? The helpless?—"Agag and the best of the sheep and of the oxen." (The surprise and irony are even finer in the original word order—literally, "And spared Saul and the people Agag and the best" etc.—since the interposition of the grammatical subject between the predicate and the objects gives the reader more time to entertain the illusive hypothesis.) So the miniature twist within the sentential sequence, like the coincident large-scale twist marking the whole tale's structure of expectations, impresses on our minds that there is no question here of any humanitarian motives whatsoever: sparing (*kh-m-l*) is nothing but an ironic euphemism for greed (*kh-m-d*).[6]

d. Order of presentation is also put to another artful use within the verbal microcosm. Given the flexibility and ambiguity of syntactic coordination, one cannot tell whether in the course of events itself the "sparing" really followed any order (e.g., whether it was initiated by Saul or perpetrated in concert with the people). But the narrator takes advantage of the fact that in language things cannot be simultaneously communicated to arrange the subjects of the sentence in the order most unfavorable to Saul: "Saul and the people spared." As initial subject, Saul appears to be the initiator of the action, since the sequence of words gives an impression of a corresponding sequence of events. And even if placed first on hierarchical rather than chronological grounds, the king must still shoulder most of the blame.[7]

e. As the sentence continues to unfold, one pattern of coordination gives place to another, more extended but on the face of it equally innocent. In fact, like that of the grammatical subjects, the series of objects is so ordered as to invite and deepen the reader's condemnation while pretending to supply him with factual information. Take the strongest and most perceptible points in any sequence, the beginning and the ending. Agag's appearance at the head of the list of the "spared" startles the reader and hardens his response in advance. And the closure of the list with the jarring phrase "all that was good"—referentially indeterminate (What does it indicate or include?), normatively incongruous (How can an abomination be "good"?), and perspectivally ambiguous (Who thinks in such terms? Surely not the narrator?)—operates to shock the reader anew into a retrospective hardening of judgment. Moreover, the fact that both the subjects and the objects of the "sparing" fall into two groups (Saul : people, Agag : livestock) places Saul in a serial position corresponding to Agag's and thus reinforces our sense of his personal responsibility for the survival of Amalek's very epitome.[8] "Reinforces," because the wording of verse 8 ("And he took Agag the king of Amalek alive") has already coupled the two kings in a similar form.

f. Finally, the selectional art of the sentence as a whole (What is said? What is not said? How much is said?) effectively dovetails with its combinatory pattern. There is not even a hint of the kind of extenuating circumstance later adduced by Saul: that the army was actuated by the desire to keep the best of the spoil for sacrifice. On the contrary, the narrative does its utmost to demolish any possible illusion about mistaken zeal and, instead, to bring home to us that their motives were pure only in the sense of being purely self-regarding. For Agag, who heads the list, is hardly a prospective sacrifice. The ensuing series of objects manifests, apart from sheer length, such stylistic inelegance and such odd shifts between the general and the particular (the general term "the best of the sheep and of the oxen" followed by the particular "the fatlings and the lambs" followed by the all-inclusive "all that was good") as to produce an impression of an orgy of looting. The progression from the human (Agag) through the animate (the livestock) to the miscellaneous (the "good") deepens this impression by suggesting the range and variety of the plunder. And the glaring contrast between the destroyed and the preserved, in both representational form (order vs. disorder) and proportions (phrase vs. catalogue), dispels any remaining doubt about motivation. Considering the member-of-action's role in hardening our heart against the offender, it is no accident that the negative first impression generated here about the looters is more intense and homogeneous than in any of the subsequent stages. There, the very location of Saul and his army in Gilgal implies a possible intention to share the pickings with God. But, however dubious its mitigating effect, even the geographical picture emerges only later; and when it does, the tale already has additional weapons to direct against Saul.

By the end of verse 9, then, the case for the prosecution becomes so formidable that it is hard to believe that the narrator has put it together without uttering so much as a single word of overt condemnation. Another look at the fifteen devices ranged along our rhetorical scale will establish that the first four have not been employed at all—nor will they be in the sequel—while all the rest have variously been put to work in the space of a few verses. Rather than directly operating against his target, the narrator prefers to shape and manipulate response through his favorite indirections, whose power derives from a sophisticated art of relations. His control strategy includes selective ratios and combinatory modes of presentation, intertextual and intratextual linkage, repetition and variation on all levels, devices of sequence and suprasequential patterns of analogy, the interplay of grammatical design and semantic context, and the mutual reinforcement of language and world. And no less notable than the repertoire of indirections is the skill with which they are coordinated into a single persuasive whole.

Accordingly, the clash between forecast and enactment maneuvers the reader into concluding that Saul has seriously abused, if not betrayed, his office. But does his sin justify a punishment so final and terrible as dismissal? After all, the prophet Samuel himself protests that it does not:

> (10) And the word of the Lord came to Samuel, saying, (11) I repent that I have made Saul king, for he has turned away from following me and has not performed my commandments. And Samuel was enraged and he cried to the Lord all night.

To persuade us that the sin nevertheless does justify such rejection, to narrow and bridge and smooth over any possible gap between divine and human judgment, ideally to the point of perfect accord: this is the narrator's main task, whose trickiness shows him operating at his rhetorical best.

Dancing in Chains

But before proceeding to trace the strategy by which the reader is manipulated into the desired judgment, we need to understand more precisely the nature of the task and the rules for its performance. By rules I mean a set of self-imposed limitations as well as self-authorized licenses, since the Bible does not consider that the end of serving two masters and bringing their viewpoints into harmony justifies all means. Thus, as a matter of artistic principle, the biblical narrator does not make things easy for himself by minimizing in advance the rhetorical problems to be overcome. Just as in the story of the rape of Dinah he does not present the Hivites as monsters, just as his historico-ideological commitment to Jacob does not preclude giving Esau a sympathetic hearing, just as none of his righteous men is perfect and few of the unrighteous wholly evil—so in our tale he avoids the line of least resistance. The narrator does not rob Saul of his impressive victory over Amalek, not even to the customary extent of adverting to some intervention on God's part. Nor does he turn Saul into a rebel against God. Nor does he burden Saul with such a heinous crime against his fellow men as will (like the murder of Naboth) immediately warrant the most extreme retaliation according to human as well as divine norms. It is precisely here that he rejects the ideological simplifications of didacticism and melodrama: his is the art of self-constraint, of meeting challenges, of dancing in chains. Even in ideological commitment and strait, he takes risks where lesser or more single-minded persuaders would take shortcuts.

On the other hand, it is equally typical of the biblical artist that, as a matter of rhetorical principle, he should avoid both the normative even-handedness open to uncommitted literature and the dogmatist's suicide missions of the "all or nothing" variety. Whatever the appeal of truth or balance or the *difficulté vaincue* or psychological complexity and realism, the persuader's main business is to carry his audience with him to the pre-determined terminus. Where this is at stake in the Bible, no wonder that any other ideal, aesthetic or historical, should bend to the pressures of ideology. The wonder is rather that the narrative should deny them anything like full control over its choices and procedures. It usually observes such constraints only in regard to doctrinal essentials; and even then it usually so implements their dictates as to leave room for other interests and to suit with the poetics of indirection. Not that the narrator is lacking in ideological zeal, but that he abounds in the artistic energy that impels and qualifies great literature to reconcile opposites without unduly sacrificing either. His zeal itself, moreover, is pragmatic rather than dogmatic:

this is a distinctive feature with enormous explanatory power, and the failure to appreciate it has led biblical studies into endless error and trouble. Being pragmatic means, as I shall soon argue, that when the exigencies of manipulating the audience do require some sacrifice, the doctrine as well as the art or the history may have to pay the price of indoctrination.

When things come to the crunch, therefore, we find the rhetoric determined indeed to produce the appropriate effect, but not by the easy, certainly not the easiest, way. It is not just that the narrator prefers winning the audience over to (what often proves the undoing of the dictatorial speaker, God and his prophets included) laying down the law to them. His own communication, that is, rests on nothing like the "either slaves or rebels" basis suggested in my epigraph. Nor is it just that the narrator favors the indirect approach, through the mediation of a represented world, where the preacher would go in for a frontal assault, direct address and all. Some of his favorite techniques as indirect persuader cannot be accounted for in terms of mere expediency. Thus, faced with a task of persuasion that bristles with difficulty, the biblical narrator would rather go to extra compositional trouble than simply load the dice for or against the problematic character or cause. A typical solution for him would be to distribute the difficulty over a number of episodes (as well as to elaborate the devices within each), with a view to overcoming our possible resistance by degrees. This is the case with many biblical doublets, usually explained in genetic terms. Take Hagar's flight from Abraham's house before she is forcibly driven out years later, or Esau's sale of his birthright to Jacob before being cheated out of his blessing. In each variation on the principle, the narrator so extends and divides his treatment as to lead up to a crucial scene that might otherwise prove too much for the reader: the first episode softens our response to the second by getting us used to the idea of the antagonist's deprivation or, more radically, splitting it into two gradated and differently motivated acts on the protagonist's part.

Where the art of sequential distribution will not reduce the problem to manageable size by itself, it may be buttressed or replaced by some biased tampering with plot or character. Whether invidious or apologetic or laudatory, however, such tampering is akin to, but not quite identical with, the notorious loading of the dice in doctrinal writing. For one thing, it shows a moderation that stops well short of dichotomizing the world into paragons and brutes, attractive protagonists and repulsive antagonists. Esau and Saul, even Abimelech and Ahab, have their sympathetic features; while Jacob and David, or even Elijah, are certainly not idealized. For another, it tends not so much to simplify as to shift or "deflect" the terms of the normative conflict, freely switching from one set of norms to another in order to produce the desired impression. The result is a foregone conclusion, but not the means to its achievement or vindication; the fight has indeed been fixed, but often athwart rather than along ideological boundaries.

Hence many a tricky clash, where merit opposes merit, is actually resolved by the Bible in terms of the persons rather (or no less) than the causes involved. Examples are the characterization of the Hivites as twisters in the Dinah story, or of Esau as a glutton indifferent to his primogeniture, both designed to complicate, if not to confuse, the moral issue in favor if the inevitable victor: Jacob and his line. Were the antagonist treated differently—the Hivites portrayed as scrupulously honest, Esau as self-controlled as well as loving—his cause would assume such weight as to meet the opposite cause on something like even terms, enforce a clear-cut choice between right and right or value and value, and thus endanger the protagonist's moral status. As it is, the point may have been made to some extent on the "wrong" (e.g., personal or emotional rather than doctrinal) grounds, but it has nevertheless been made.

In general, the biblical narrator neither loads the opposed terms of a conflict (or the responses they elicit) with the total partiality of the didacticist nor sharpens and balances them with the total impartiality open to the freethinking artist. Instead, he prefers to subject opposites to such (and so much) mixing, blunting, and even twisting operations as will have the most persuasive impact on his audience. Naturally, far from serving to project what a philosopher would regard as an integrated doctrine and a moralist as a clear lesson, such shifting or deflection of terms produces normative blurs, if not discontinuities and inconsistencies. But the narrator aims at effective rather than coherent theology, at pragmatic rather than dogmatic morality. As long as he can maintain (and drive home) his general frame of reference, the details worry him far less than they seem to worry so many of his critics, as unmindful of the exigencies of communication as of the arts and licenses of storytelling. This means, in short, that to gain his rhetorical ends he is ready to pay even in ideological coin.

It is this logic of persuasion that now explains two measures taken by the narrator in the Amalek story, viewed as an ideological drama where Saul plays antagonist to God's protagonist. One measure consists in an anticipatory softening-up of our moral resistance to God's decision, by way of a precedent located at an earlier stage of the same cycle. The Amalek affair operates not as an isolated exception but as an intensified reenactment of a foregoing drama of sin and punishment:

> Samuel said to Saul, Thou hast done foolishly; thou hast not kept the
> commandment of the Lord thy God, which he commanded thee; for

> now God would have established thy kingdom over Israel forever. But
> now thy kingdom shall not endure. (1 Sam 13:13–14)

Saul's first sin of disobedience, in the war against the Philistines, now combines with the second to give him the image of a habitual offender; and
its having already cost him the hope of founding a dynasty now leaves
his own position the only target for God's wrath. Thus, the narrator orders
and welds the double pattern into a two-phase process of retribution, which
enables him not just to proceed gradually but to "improve" the moral proportion (or moderate the disproportion) between cause and effect. On the
one hand, Saul having learned nothing from his previous aberration, the
sin now looms larger; on the other hand, the dynasty having already been
doomed, the punishment now looks milder.

This gradated and cumulative progression makes rhetorical sense not
only of an otherwise disturbing redundancy, predictably dismissed by
scholars in genetic terms, like multiple origin. It likewise integrates other
sequential features of the cycle. Note the curiously delayed introduction
of Saul's sons—above all, of the heir who will play such a decisive role
in the first war. That he is hardly mentioned before his father's clash with
the prophet, while richly drawn thereafter, forms a preventive measure
within the overall rhetoric of retribution. For even the dynastic doom must
appear a foregone conclusion before the reader can be allowed to encounter
its immediate victim: the lovable and brave and pious Jonathan, whose
trust in God presents such a contrast to his father's lack of faith. Jonathan
being endowed with the very moral attributes in which Saul is deficient,
his premature spotlighting would compromise God's first decree—far from
unworthy of succeeding, he would seem the natural choice—and thus
endanger the whole tactics of gradual deposition. Whereas, the punishment having fallen on more or less anonymous heads, Jonathan's emergence
after the fact minimizes the incongruity and even serves to expose Saul
anew by way of opposition. It is all a matter of persuasive timing, the order
of presentation being determined by ideological rather than chronological
exigencies.

If this anticipatory step forms a characteristic "rhetorical softening-up,"
then its complement within the tale itself forms a characteristic "rhetorical
deflection." The tale, that is, refrains from putting the opposition between
the divine and the human norms to the supreme test. Instead, it correlates
the two sets of norms, operating against Saul with a double or mixed standard, persuading on two fronts, so to speak. True, the prophet formulates
the relations between sin and punishment in the stark and lucid terms
of *lex talionis*, "Because thou hast rejected the word of the Lord, he has
rejected thee from being king." But the narrator himself will not balance

them on such a razor's edge. He could easily manage to stage a head-on collision between the will of God (as moral protagonist) and the disobedience of man (as moral antagonist): for instance, to depict Saul as a king perfect by all social as opposed to divine standards, and to risk everything on the attempt to persuade us that even such a Saul deserves to go the way of all offenders. Here as elsewhere, however, the narrator avoids this line of showdown (reserving it for Moses alone, the model leader denied entrance into the promised land for having struck instead of spoken to the rock). And its avoidance, as Moses' case indeed shows, hardly lends itself to explanation in the simplistic (if not circular) terms that such a polarity is inconceivable within his world picture. It is for reasons of rhetoric rather than doctrine that he chooses throughout to broaden as far as possible the basis and area of agreement between the reader and himself, by exposing Saul to a two-pronged attack.

The narrator, caught between the ideological rage for coherence and the rhetorical need for consensus, thus "deflects" the moral drama that the prophet, who faces no such task of persuasion, can afford to sharpen and radicalize. The persuader is willing to settle for less than the absolute measure for measure— "rejection" for "rejection"—as long as he can maintain the principle of the rightness and supremacy of God's judgment. Hence, far from operating on purely religious grounds, right from the start he presents the war against Amalek as a national affair and later he goes out of his way to demonstrate Saul's unfitness for kingship from the social as well as the divine viewpoint. It is not that this deflection makes the job of bringing the viewpoints into harmony easy to perform, but that it entails a doctrinal compromise, certainly a complication. The difference between "almost all or nothing" and "all or nothing" is equally vital for the understanding of the Bible's structure of norms and its art of narrative.

All this explains the variety of devices now marshaled against Saul (and, in a different sense, the reader). One is the allusion to historical precedents, both without and within the book of Samuel. Like that of forecast, the members of action and report derive much of their rhetorical power from implicit intertextual and interepisodic relations. The intertextual analogy-by-allusion is this time to Joshua 7, which follows the earliest instance of total destruction, with spoils put under the ban and all. The conquest of Jericho, we are made to recall, involved an analogous transgression ("Achan, the son of Carmi . . . took some of the banned things, and the anger of the Lord burned against the people of Israel"); and, again, the points of similarity between the two tales are specified far beyond this broad thematic correspondence. The similarity established is also linguistic (e.g., the recurrence of the charged term *kherem,* or the epigrammatic turn given to the judgment), geographical (both crimes have "Gilgal" for a setting), and, most remarkable, situational. For the Jericho narrative likewise dramatizes, in the same terms and even the same sequence, a normative distinction between justified and unjustified deviation from God's command: between going beyond its letter (and again, in favor of a benefactor of Israel, "only Rahab the harlot shall live") and going against its spirit (like Achan).

Of the two looters, the text now invites us to conclude, Saul deserves death even more than Achan, in view of the difference in status and enemy. And it is another impressive measure of the deliberateness of the whole intertextual coupling that, the allusion once perceived, not only Saul's death itself but its manner and concomitants become predictable. For the dynamics of this analogy involves its covert extension or propulsion from the phase of sin to that of punishment. The expectation generated as early as this stage, that Achan's end foreshadows Saul's, comes true later in the book. Like his historical mirror image, Saul dies a violent death, his sons fall with him, and, what is otherwise inexplicable in terms of Hebrew culture and has indeed always puzzled scholars, the corpses are set on fire (the phrase "burnt them" of Joshua 7:25 recurring in 1 Samuel 31:12).[9]

Moreover, by a kind of associative chain reaction, some features of Achan's story also bring to mind the war with the Philistines that immediately precedes the Amalek affair. In each case, God turns away from the embattled Israel due to a "breach of contract" on the part of some warrior—Achan's theft, Jonathan's tasting the honey—whose identity and offense finally come to light through the drawing of lots (Joshua 7:14–21, 1 Samuel 14:36–64). The assorted violations thus fall into a tripartite analogy, which directs against Saul a telling *argumentum ad hominem* (or more precisely, *argumentum ex concessis*): even the precedents and premises he himself set now rise to condemn him. If Saul wanted to execute ("thou shalt surely die, Jonathan") his victorious son ("who has wrought this great deliverance in Israel") for having unwittingly broken ("Jonathan had not heard") the king's impulsive and senseless oath ("Cursed be the man who eats any food until evening"), then what penalty does he himself deserve for violating God's reasoned command?

Furthermore, the two external analogies, established as early as the member of enactment, combine with two internal analogies that open and round off the sequence of reports. One is the contrast between the king and the prophet, who objects to the mission God lays on him ("Samuel was enraged and he cried to the Lord all night") and yet hastens to perform it ("Samuel rose early to meet Saul in the morning"). The other is the parallel that surprisingly bridges the distance between the two kings. For the prophet's arrival on the scene leads to an ironic peripety in the fates of both. Saul falls from the heights of victory ("behold, he set up a monument for himself") to the depths of rejection; Agag has a rude awakening from the illusion of survival ("Surely the bitterness of death is past") to the reality of death by the sword ("Samuel hewed Agag in pieces"). And the double peripety culminates in the figurative-literal relations between the "tearing" away of the one's kingdom and the "hewing" of the other's body. Apart from reinforcing the dramatic irony and extending the appearance-and-reality theme, this tripartite pattern carries the most unpleasant normative implications for Saul, due to the "unnaturalness" of the two pairings: on the one hand, the disparity revealed between king and prophet, whom we would expect to stand together, and on the other hand, the parity between king and king, whom we would expect to form diametric opposites all along the line. In fact, the two royal enemies are drawn so close together, as brothers in crime and self-delusion and sudden reversal of fortune, that their analogy looks like a realization of another old promise *cum* warning: the Lord "will give their kings into thy hand and thou shalt make their name perish from under heaven. . . . And thou shalt not bring an abomination into thy house, lest thou become an accursed thing [*kherem*] like it" (Deut 7:24–26).

But what proves most damaging to Saul's image is the final development of the repetition structure, effected between these internal analogies and occupying the whole middle of the tale (verses 13–31). Actually, we encounter here two interlaced structures of repetition—one consisting in the series of Saul's "reports" about his performance and the other in Samuel's "reports" about God's judgment. In dialogic combination, they assume the following form:

Samuel came to Saul,

and Saul said to him: "Blessed be thou to the Lord! I have performed the commandment of the Lord."

And Samuel said: "What then is this bleating of the sheep in my ears and this lowing of the oxen that I hear?"

And Saul said: "They have brought them from Amalek; for the people spared the best of the sheep and of the oxen, to sacrifice to the Lord thy God. And the rest we have utterly destroyed."

And Samuel said: "Stop, and I will tell thee what the Lord said to me this night. . . . Though thou art small in thy own eyes, art thou not the head of the tribes of Israel? The Lord anointed thee king over Israel and the Lord sent thee on a mission and said: 'Go and utterly destroy the sinners, the Amalekites, and fight against them until they are are consumed.' Why then didst thou not listen to the voice of the Lord, but didst swoop on the spoil and didst what was evil in the eyes of the Lord?"

And Saul said to Samuel: "I did listen to the voice of the Lord, and I have gone on the mission on which the Lord sent me, and I have brought Agag the king of Amalek, and I have utterly destroyed Amalek. And the people took of the spoil, sheep and oxen, the best of the things devoted to utter destruction, to sacrifice to the Lord thy God in Gilgal."

And Samuel said: "Is the Lord as pleased with burnt offerings and sacrifices as with listening to the voice of the Lord? Behold, listening is better than sacrifice, to hearken better than the fat of rams. For rebellion is the sin of divination, and stubbornness is iniquity and idolatry. Because thou hast rejected the word of the Lord, he has rejected thee from being king."

And Saul said to Samuel, "I have sinned, for I have transgressed the utterance of the Lord and thy commandments, because I feared the people and listened to their voice. Now, pray, forgive my sin and return with me, and I shall prostrate myself before the Lord."

And Samuel said to Saul: "I will not return with thee; for thou hast rejected the word of the Lord, and the Lord has rejected thee from being king over Israel."

>   And Samuel turned to go
>   and he laid hold of the skirt of his robe,
>   and it tore.

And Samuel said to him: "The Lord has torn the kingdom of Israel away from thee this day, and has given it to a neighbor of thine, who is better than thou. Also, the Strength of Israel will not lie and will not repent, for he is not a man that he should repent."

And he said: "I have sinned. Now honour me, pray, before the elders of my people and before Israel, and I shall prostrate myself before the Lord thy God."

>   Then Samuel returned with Saul,
>   and Saul prostrated himself before the Lord.

Vertically, we have in each column a sequence of reportive variations that gradually but inexorably moves toward a climax. Saul comes all the way from the exulting "I have performed the commandment of the Lord" to the about-facing "I have sinned"; and Samuel, from the mild query about the bleating of the sheep to a brutal statement of rejection. Horizontally, we have a sequence of exchanges whose speech-and-counterspeech logic dramatically motivates the nature, extent, and movement of the repetition and produces one of the Bible's most elaborate dialogues.

The development and interweaving of the two structures of repetition in terms of dialogic alternation indeed yields a coherent and striking pattern. But to appreciate its goals and achievements, one needs to understand the difficulty with which the formation of that natural-looking pattern confronted the narrator. The difficulty derives from the unequal status of the two series of "repetitive" speeches: the equality they show in the text, far from a natural feature, is the result of brilliant craftsmanship. As far as concerns the aims of the tale—indeed, of the whole book—the vital part of the dialogue centers in the speeches made by Saul, who is meant to condemn himself by his incessant shifts and turns. And this structure of repetition makes excellent sense in dramatic (psychological, situational) as well as rhetorical terms: Saul has every reason to conceal or whitewash his sin, and he retreats only step by step, version by defensive version. But what about Samuel's structure of repetition, each of whose members causally leads to a further retreat on Saul's part? How can it be likewise justified? How can it be made not only to avoid a monotonous reiteration of the same message, but to progress in terms of dramatic logic, notably including the give-and-take of dialogue?

This problem inspired a solution that turns the difficulty to rich compositional account. In the first place, the narrator leaves Samuel considerable freedom of action—certainly of speech—in that he refrains from specifying the prophet's terms of reference as envoy. In this respect, there emerges a suggestive contrast in the handling of his two missions to the king. The tenor of the first mission having been developed into a central fact, that of the second is now reduced to an informational gap. For if the Saul-centered structure of repetition opens with a quote of God's peremptory command, the Samuel-centered structure opens with a general statement by God ("I repent that I have made Saul king") and suppresses all the rest: not only Samuel's nightlong appeal but even God's final instructions. Whatever took place between them, we are kept in the dark about it; and for all dramatic and rhetorical purposes, therefore, Samuel is burdened with no categorical message to the king. That blurring and withholding of information makes it possible for the narrator to have the best of both worlds—to present Samuel as one who (unlike Saul) adheres to the spirit of God's orders and yet adjusts his conduct to the situational requirements—since we can never tell which of the messenger's five verbal shots derives from God's original message and which comes on his own initiative. This goes to show, again, the flexibility of the Bible's principle of repetition. Underrepetition (to the point of gapping) is no less feasible and functional than overrepetition (to the point of redundancy), and the two can even perfectly well dovetail to serve an overall strategy.

Second, the informational gap that results from the blurring of the member of forecast addressed to Samuel is exploited in another way for the same end. The part disclosed to the reader complements and reinforces the effect of the part suppressed. If the suppression makes a flexible Samuel acceptable, then the disclosure gives his flexibility an active causal legitimation: it suggests that God himself has not yet irrevocably committed himself to deposing Saul. For compared with normal expressions of divine wrath and with the prophet's own violence in the sequel, what we actually find in verse 11 is cast in relatively mild language. In fact, it emphasizes past misdeed ("he has turned back from following me") and present emotion ("I repent") more than the future scenario typical of a forecast. And the sense of an *open* future gains further support from the built-in reminder that God is quite capable of changing his mind with the change of circumstance. Having started by repenting, he may well finish by repenting this repentance.

That Samuel denies this possibility—the "Strength of Israel will not lie and will not repent, for he is not a man that he should repent"—rather highlights than precludes it. It is not only that Samuel speaks in anger and toward the end of the dialogue, when Saul has already convicted himself beyond redemption; that Samuel's moral and informational viewpoint has by then long been distinguished from God's; that God often forgives (or at least, as with Ahab in 1 Kings 21, reprieves) the penitent, to the despair of the Jonahs among his prophets. In flat opposition to Samuel's absolute denial, the narrator himself opens God's counteraction with "'I repent'" and ends it with "the Lord repented." Still, given the differences in speaker and context, nothing could be more gratuitous than the popular appeal to an interpolator to explain the "contradiction." Except to a reader bent on imposing harmony on the perspectives that the Bible takes such care to discriminate and play off against one another, the three statements are perfectly easy to accommodate in a single tale. Even if Samuel literally meant what he says—and his own conduct suggests that he knows better—then his claim would just expose his own unreliability. To guide our expectation, we look to the lord of history and the master of narrative, rather than to any creature of theirs, however eminent; and these two speak here with one voice.

Hence the impression that, whether or not Samuel has a formal mandate to suit the judgment to the results of the confrontation, there is still room for another "repentance" on God's part. Saul still has a chance, even after the fact, and everything now depends on his response to the charges made against him. Within the internal structure of time, the future is thus left opaque, indeterminate, contingent on moral choice; and to good effect. This effect forms a rhetorical end in itself, in that it "improves" God's image and the proportions between sin and punishment; and also a means to justify the repetitive series, in that it heightens our sense of the prophet's legitimate freedom of action.

Third, the narrator gives Samuel a good psychological reason to make use of that freedom: his sympathetic attitude to Saul, not much in evidence in their previous dealings but now established beyond doubt by the "anger" and "crying" of verse 11. The reader cannot help wondering why for two whole rounds the prophet does not simply tell his interlocutor about his dismissal but rather asks him questions: first one pretending ignorance of what happened ("What then is the bleating of the sheep . . . ?") and then a sharper follow-up ("Why then didst thou not listen to the voice of the Lord . . . ?"). The most probable explanation is that he wants to put Saul to the test, and only when convinced of his favorite's hopelessness does he pronounce sentence, with understandably escalating brutality.[10] This produces a striking correspondence between the character's psychological and the narrator's rhetorical motives for drawing out the interview: the gradated and dilatory ("repetitive") tactics employed by Samuel is also the best tactics for demonstrating to the reader that even one who starts by appealing against God's judgment must finally come to admit its justness. The prophet's very sympathy for Saul thus becomes a weapon for condemnation in the hands of the artful persuader.

As the crucial dialogue opens, then, the structure of point of view is characterized by informational and normative tensions between the various perspectives involved. On the axis of information, the omniscient narrator and God contrast with the benighted Saul, who has no knowledge of either past commotion or impending catastrophe. In between the poles, Samuel knows at least what he has been instructed to say the night before; while the reader's view of past and future has been sufficiently blurred (gapped, ambiguated) to generate the impression of a fluid state of affairs, where events wait on the moral character of the agents and Saul once again holds his fate in his own hands at the crossroads of history.

On the axis of judgment, another perspectival division shows itself here. The narrator and God stand together, as usual, their rejection of Saul equally absolute, though the one's is silent and the other's vocal. And again, this coalition is not only poles apart from Saul's own view of his behavior, but also faces a less extreme and yet more serious opposition, likewise composed of one silent and one vocal member. These are of course the reader, who still needs to be persuaded, and Samuel, torn between duty and feeling.

On the face of it, while the informational discrepancies effectively serve the tale's overall strategy, the normative variations appear self-defeating. For if the end of every rhetorical strategy is to resolve or at least minimize ideological tensions, so as to bring the audience's viewpoint into alignment with the text's—here obviously represented by the God–narrator alliance—then the multiplication of differences in judgment would seem to go counter that end. Above all, the prophet's midway position splits the divine front and threatens the whole rhetoric of retribution: if the Lord's own seer grieves and wavers, can the ordinary person (including the reader) be expected to do less?

However, what looks like a damaging oversight is actually a calculated risk and proves a source of strength throughout. In general, the difference between running and running away from such risks corresponds to nothing less than difference between two orders of rhetoric, largely exemplified by biblical narrative and poetry respectively. Naive rhetoric plays the ostrich in all that concerns attitudes (norms, responses, valuations, perspectives, world pictures) other than its own, whether by simply ignoring or dismissively caricaturing them, Jeremiah fashion. Whereas sophisticated rhetoric gives (or at least pretends to give) such divergent attitudes not just recognition and voice but something like a fair hearing, with a multiple end in view. Aesthetically, this goes to meet the poetic demands for tension and variety and complexity, for courting danger as a challenge and a source of interest. Thematically, rather than reducing issues to opposites, this makes (at least on the personal and interpersonal level) for a polyphonic treatment, richer in opportunities for nuancing character and viewpoint. Even on the rhetorical balance sheet itself, the dangers incurred are more than compensated for by the gains: the impression of open-mindedness, evenhandedness, awareness of alternatives and variations (etc.) strengthens the persuader's reliability and ultimately improves his chances of bringing the audience over to his side.

In short, if the final end of persuasion consists in aligning the addressee's viewpoint with the speaker's, the tactics employed along the route to that terminal may well include ideological understatement, complication, plurality, even disharmony and conflict. Hence a whole set of features typical of biblical narrative, especially when dealing with major cruxes and figures. Consider the avoidance of preaching and black-and-white portraits; the abstention from a fully explicit moral evaluation of the dramatis personae, sometimes leading to a judgment of the act rather than the agent; the establishment of normative gradations in preference to stark polar extremes; and what immediately concerns us, the (not always illusive) distribution of "authoritative" commentary between narrator, God, and prophet.

Accordingly, though the game that the narrator plays in splitting the forces against Saul is indeed dangerous, the rendering of the prophet as a character in conflict proves one of the story's most telling devices. Rhetorically, where strict orthodoxy on Samuel's part would just stamp and distance him as a mouthpiece for God's thunder, his surprising ambivalence draws him closer to us. It reflects the reader's (actual or possible) state of mind at this point along the sequence. Samuel's mixed feelings thus turn him at once into "our man" in the represented world and will invest his final judgment, precisely because it is wrung from him, with tremendous power and authority. Just as, in dramatic terms, they motivate the prolongation of his dialogue with Saul—impelling him to inquire and check and double check before delivering the final blow.

Dialogue as Pressure, Variations as Judgment

All this makes sense of the dialogue that gradually unfolds and consistently interweaves the two alternating structures of repetition. In fact, its progress has been rendered so natural and its implications so forceful that the narrator can dispense with all overt commentary. Carrying the dialogic principle to an extreme, he effaces himself more than ever. His presence manifests itself in little more than the neutral reporting verb "said," which punctuates the ping-pong movement of the dialogue. Despite the extraordinary length of the exchange, by biblical standards, he does not even provide any stage directions (regarding tone, gesture, setting) till he comes to the punch line. Despite the seriousness of the things revealed, he makes no normative comment except through the art of relations: the internal patterning of the scenic give-and-take, its linkage with the foregoing discourse, and the intertextual analogies. Despite the agitation and the playacting and the maneuvering of the two speakers—both deeply troubled, Samuel in conflict and increasing rage, Saul fighting for survival—no inside view of their minds is given. Instead of exposing Saul's inner life, the narrator lets Saul expose himself. And instead of formulating the pressures that lead to the prophet's ever-sharpening attacks and the king's series of retreats, he leaves the whole task to the reader: we are invited to fill in the gaps, to reconstruct motive and psychological process, to draw the normative conclusions for ourselves. "Let them play before us," the reportorial voice seems to be saying; but like every stage manager, he always remains in control by pulling the strings from behind the scenes.

Saul, little suspecting what awaits him and perhaps genuinely unaware of any wrongdoing ("behold, he set up a monument for himself"), greets Samuel with the elated "I have performed the commandment of the Lord." Still, the prophet does not come out with the crushing refutation ready to his hand—God's "he has not performed my commandments"—but prefers to counter with a question: "What then is this bleating of the sheep in my ears, and the lowing of the oxen which I hear?" Since Samuel already knows the truth, the reader has no doubt about the rhetorical nature of this question. At the same time, the very choice to open not with blunt denunciation but with oblique sarcasm immediately raises the possiblity that Samuel is first concerned to test Saul's response.[11]

Unlike the reader, however, Saul does not know that Samuel knows. He apparently thinks his visitor has come on his own initiative and, misled by the questioner's appeal to sense data ("in my ears," "hear") rather than to supernatural knowledge imparted by God, takes at face value the newcomer's show of innocence. He therefore treats the question not as a piece of irony but as a genuine call for information:

> They have brought them from Amalek; for the people spared the best of the sheep and of the oxen, to sacrifice to the Lord thy God; and the rest we have utterly destroyed.

This countershow of innocence launches a complex play of viewpoints and levels of awareness, with Saul as its ironic target. Although actually invited to make a moral response—a full confession of guilt being the only gesture that might save him—Saul delivers a factual report. Having misinterpreted the present state of affairs, Saul now misrepresents the past and thus leaves himself no future. And blind to his own informational disadvantage, he seeks to take advantage of his addressee's.

Saul, in other words, now realizes that his opening account cannot stand. But, clinging to the optimistic assumption of Samuel's ignorance, he still hopes to extricate himself from trouble by means of a revised version. And this version departs from the objective truth, as established by the narrator in verses 7–9, at quite a few material points. First, it makes no reference to the heaviest sin of all—the sparing of Agag—but confines itself to explaining the facts ("sheep" and "oxen") directly indicated by the question. If Samuel does not know, why volunteer information? Even in regard to what it must and does disclose, Saul's version ("the best of the sheep and of the oxen") is strikingly selective compared with the narrator's ("the best of the sheep and of the oxen and of the fatlings, and the lambs, and all that was good"). Strikingly, because the truncation of the original catalogue—the reported whole is only the enacted beginning—brings out the anxiety to play things down. Moreover, these factual omissions go together with an explanatory addition designed to whitewash the offense by assigning to it a pious motive: "to sacrifice to the Lord thy God." Since the dialogue does take place in the sacral Gilgal, the reader must thereupon review the effect produced by the member of action: that the looting was motivated by pure self-interest. But the reviewing does not lead to a definite revision for the better, because nothing in the text now shakes the first impression of orgiastic plunder. The alleged intention shows no sign of past or coming fulfillment. The new semantic twist given to the verb "spare"—in the direction of thrift rather than greed—looks doubly forced, therefore, its irony heightened both by the factual groundlessness of the claim and the textual resonance of the language. And so does the replacement of the narrator's distinction between what the army "would not utterly destroy" and what "they utterly destroyed" by a new ingenious distinction between what was reserved for sacrifice and what relegated to destruction. When joined to the telltale failure to mention Agag, these forms of incongruity combine to establish that Saul is lying. His version introduces the element of doubt only to expel it, with another boomerang effect, and to pave the way for Samuel's dismissal of the excuse on theological as well as factual grounds.

Finally, exploiting what I call the rhetoric of grammatical person, Saul tendentiously redistributes the credit (and correspondingly also the blame, which, however, barely surfaces at this stage). His tale falls into three parts, each with its grammatically distinct agent ("they," the collective "he" of the people, "we") and its morally distinct action ("brought," "spared," "destroyed"). Those parts are arranged in hierarchical rather than chronological sequence, so that the report progresses by correlating two movements: the tripartite shift in person goes with a tripartite shift in merit. First, some undefined "they" are made to bear the responsibility for the problematic act of looting, euphemized into "they have brought them from Amalek." The redeeming motive for the problematic act is them attributed to the people, likewise cast into the third person but differentiated (in Hebrew) by number: "for the people spared the best of the sheep and of the oxen to sacrifice to the Lord thy God." And only when he comes to the wholly unexceptionable item, the performance of the command itself, does Saul give himself a role and a share: "And the rest we have utterly destroyed." According to this ascending order of merit, then, everyone (except perhaps for the conveniently anonymous "they") has both meant well and done well, but none more so than the king.

Suppression, invention, manipulation: from the reader's vantage point of dramatic irony, this distorted account of what we know to have happened aggravates the effect of the happenings themselves. The evasion of the truth is as scandalous as it is futile; and so is the evasion of responsibility, manifested in the acrobatics of grammatical person. In this, the royal report diverges fron each of the preceding members within the structure of repetition. It diverges from the initial command, dominated by the second person singular that holds the king accountable for the performance. It also diverges from the narrator's representation, which laid most of the actual (and all of the "ministerial") blame on Saul, using the identical verb and person (*va-yakhmol*) that Saul now reserves (*khamal*) for the people. (Hence another reason for the narrator's choice in verse 9 to couple a verb in the singular with a plural subject: just as his "spared" maximized at the time the retrospective clash with God's "do not spare," so does it now prove to have anticipated Saul's own "spared"). And it even diverges from Saul's previous and exclusively first-person version: "I have performed the commandment of the Lord." Once the monopoly (*I*) over the "performance" turns out to be double-edged, the king is at most prepared to share with his subjects (*we*) the credit for "destroying" but none of the guilt (*they, he*) of "bringing" and "sparing."

This is how the narrator activates the twofold (human-divine or religio-social) frame of normative reference, whose establishment as early as the stage of forecast and importance for his rhetorical operations I have already discussed. From now on, he will consistently bring it to bear on his target, employing Samuel's responses in each dialogic round both as overt aids to judgment on Saul's versions and as situational pressures that elicit from Saul some further pieces of double self-incrimination. Of course, Samuel performs this service against his will. His judgments are oriented to God rather than society, and his pressures are meant to save Saul from himself rather than damn him in the eyes of others. But the narrator so stage manages the play of speech and counterspeech as not only to accommodate or neutralize but even to exploit such perspectival discrepancies. He lets the two speakers express themselves in their own terms and for their own ends—as if they were free agents and he merely an impartial recorder—while canalizing their discourse (the illusion of autonomy included) into his strategy of persuasion.

Thus, Samuel having been stationed at a point of observation analogous to the reader's, his response to the king's current tale is sufficiently familiar to confirm the socially based judgment, sufficiently prophetlike to echo God's voice and thus forward the theological line of attack, and yet sufficiently restrained to leave the door open. He will not take the trouble to dispute Saul's claims. By implication, he does wave away the pronominal sophistry not only as irrelevant and dishonorable ("thou art the head of the tribes of Israel") but also, mentioning for the first time his official status and divine sources of information ("Stop, and I will tell thee what the Lord said to me this night"), as lacking in fullness ("until they are consumed," i.e., you have forgotten Agag) and in truth ("thou didst swoop on the spoil"). But his main concern is to reestablish the proper frame of reference for the issue, namely, that consisting in the original decree which he himself relayed at the very start and now repeats. In its terms, the responsibility falls on the king alone. The second person singular, which in the member of prospect functioned to assign responsibility, thus becomes in second transmission a series of blows: "The Lord anointed thee . . . and sent thee . . . and said, Go and utterly destroy . . . and fight . . . Thou didst not obey . . . thou didst swoop . . . thou didst evil." Nevertheless, having clarified the issue, the prophet is in no hurry to close it by pronouncing sentence. Instead, he ends with another rhetorical question ("Why then didst thou not obey?"), overtly an expression of bitterness and disappointment, but covertly also an invitation to repentance that may still avert disaster.

But Saul receives none of these signals. Blind to the folly of rewriting history in the presence of God's envoy, to the implications of shirking responsibility, to the chance secretly offered him to retrieve his fortunes, he persists in denial. A concrete measure of the enormity as well as the futility of this proceeding is the contrast it forms with three analogical instances— past, present, and future. Achan after the Jericho battle ("Indeed I have sinned against the Lord God of Israel"), Jonathan ("Here I am, ready to die") in contemporary times, David in the next generation: each promptly confesses his sin once charged with it.

Even worse than the denial itself, if Saul's response now varies from that of the previous round, it is only in carrying prevarication to new lengths. The repetition with variation thus follows the pattern of causal balance that shapes the whole dialogue: Samuel having just sharpened his censure, Saul now recasts his protestations of innocence into a form that will, he hopes, withstand the attack. He starts by flatly denying God's general charge of disobedience ("Why didst thou not obey the voice of the Lord?" → "I have obeyed the voice of the Lord") and then goes on to contest its details, point by point and often phrase by phrase. To the wording of the divine command, as just requoted by Samuel, he selectively opposes formulations of his own that are meant to establish the impeccability of his performance. (Hence the echoing of "the Lord sent thee on a mission and said, Go" by "I have gone on the mission on which the Lord sent me," and of "utterly destroy the sinners, the Amalekites" by "I have utterly destroyed the Amalekites.") The taking of Agag alive, no longer omissible, gets interpolated in the middle of the denial, for reasons that the dialogic text leaves unspecified along with the rest of the inner life. Is it because Saul hopes to smuggle it in between "positive" neighbors? Because he wants to demonstrate that he did not "swoop on the spoil" in any gross material sense? Because he wishes to minimize the single aberration by contrasting it with the impressive sum total ("I have utterly destroyed the Amalekites")? Or, strange but perhaps most probable, because of a confused idea that the seizure of Agag may somehow redound to his credit? Clearly, in the absence of any inside view, each gap-filling hypothesis damns Saul on different grounds.

From the social viewpoint, what makes this new retrospect even more damning is that it involves still another, third distribution of positives and negatives. The pressure on Saul having increased, he counteracts it by a more drastic forging of the balance sheet. The three-point ascending scale of merit gives place to a descending order that unfolds something like an opposition between good and evil. This time Saul takes all the credit (probably including the capture of Agag) for himself: on the plus side of the balance sheet, the first person is no longer plural ("we have utterly destroyed") but uniformly singular ("I have obeyed . . . I have gone . . . I have brought . . . I have utterly destroyed").[12] For polarity, next, all the blame for the looting gets squarely thrown on the people (who "took of the spoil, sheep and oxen, the best of the things devoted to utter destruction"), with certain variations that on the whole tend to show them in a more negative light than before.

On the one hand, Saul indeed replaces the problematic verb "spare," directly conflicting with the original decree, by the neutral "take"; he still retains the extenuating motive ("to sacrifice to the Lord thy God") and even heightens its plausibility by indicating the geographical location ("in Gilgal," i.e., they have not taken the livestock straight home). On the other hand, the blackening far outweighs the whitewashing. For Saul now drops the anonymous scapegoat in the form of the third person singular and transfers its role directly to the people ("they have brought them" → "the people took"). He injects into the people's share of the report the charged phraseology ("spoil," *kherem*) that he took such care to avoid (e.g., by omitting "the sinners" from his echo of Samuel's words) when glorifying his own. And far from highlighting, as he has just done in regard to himself, he does not even glance at the creditable part of their activities, namely, the collective destruction of "all the despised and rejected property" or (in his own recent euphemism) "the rest."

Accordingly, if in his first version Saul monopolized the credit but suppressed the blame and if in the second he turned aside the blame but shared out the credit, now he radicalizes the opposition between himself (who did well) and the people (who only meant well). Whether these shifts are improvised in panic or in cold blood—the narrator, as usual, provides no inside view but lets the results speak for themselves—Saul's mendacity and unmanliness as well as his ungodliness are beyond doubt. What becomes increasingly doubtful is his fitness for kingship.

Indeed, this is precisely the conclusion that "our man" in the drama likewise reaches from his own viewpoint. Samuel not only continues to disdain Saul's wriggling but also despairs of getting him onto the right track. Modulating into formal discourse, he begins with a tongue-lashing about the duty of obedience as supreme value ("Is the Lord as pleased with burnt offerings and sacrifices as with listening to the voice of the Lord?" With his bitter experience in mind, he hastens to supply his own answer to the rhetorical question, "Behold, listening is better than sacrifice" etc.). And the ideological statement having paved the way for the application, the prophet ends by delivering the long-deferred sentence. Appropriately echoing the judgment pronounced by Joshua on Achan ("Why hast thou troubled us? The Lord shall trouble thee this day"), his sentence assumes a tit-for-tat form that matches crime with punishment and encapsulates the logic in the language of retribution: "Because thou hast rejected the word of the Lord, he has rejected thee from being king."[13]

Convergence with Belated Discovery: Rhetorical Overkill

The three opening rounds of dialogue thus unfold a pattern of causal symmetry: as one side gets increasingly entangled and demoralized, the other gets straightforward and resolute. Given the series of Saul's "repetitive" versions, the reader needs little other guidance to trace the erosion of self-confidence, of moral fiber, of royal dignity. The breakdown under pressure takes place before our eyes, gradual enough to compel belief, rapid enough to suggest organic weakness, thoroughgoing and many-sided enough to justify drastic counteraction. At the same time, within the chain of repetition formed by Samuel's speeches, the recurrent formal and semantic elements bring out the three-stage progression that has just reached a climax. We see him moving from a question so innocent-sounding that the addressee may (and does) interpret it as genuine, through a question whose factual antecedent underlines its rhetorical nature, to a question from which the inquirer himself draws the operative conclusion; from a colloquial tone through prophetic thundering to the solemn and measured accents of doom; from ironic criticism through formal reproof to utter rejection.

As for the dialogue's (and the whole tale's) correlated structure of repetition, it also progresses from speech to speech and from round to round, but in a more complex manner than either of its dramatic flanks. Here the reticent narrator does indeed (and will continue to) benefit from all the rhetorical advantages yielded to him by the expressive prophet: from the articulation of the judgments themselves, from their escalating sharpness, and from the weight they carry by virtue of being wrung fron a secret sympathizer. But he commits himself to none of their rhetorical disadvantages, notably the narrowness and abstractness of the ideological basis for judgment. While the prophet's tirades are geared to divine law, the narrator exploits Saul's string of responses to bring into play the social code as well. The conclusion reached and preached is the same, and so is the timing, but not the grounds or frames of reference. So the two perspectives meet rather than coincide, and the prophet's voice forms only one component within the orchestration that reflects the narrator's more inclusive viewpoint and implement his strategy. But since the frames of reference are compatible and the judgments oriented to them increasingly converge as the dialogue progresses, this stage also marks a climax of normative harmony: the dovetailing of the explicit and the implicit, of divine and human viewpoint, of the attitudes taken by the doctrinally committed and the reluctantly aligned and the artfully persuaded.

Hence this stage is also a landmark in the relations between what I called the informational and the normative axes of point of view. These relations (governed by the logic that contrasts Laban to the Wooer) manifest a notable shift along the sequence of the dialogue. At the starting point, Saul's is informationally the least privileged of the five relevant viewpoints, since he knows nothing about the threat hanging over his head; but he is still closer to the reader than to Samuel, let alone to God and the narrator. Normatively, Saul's is also the least reliable perspective, but, again, at that point it still has more in common with the ambivalent and undecided reader than with the polar extreme of divine wrath. As the dialogue moves forward, however, these perspectival positions change along both axes, in an equally gradual but otherwise almost diametrically opposed fashion. Saul, who discovers something about his plight with each round, draws closer and closer to the reader (as well as to the other participants and observers) till their viewpoints reach the stage of virtual synchronization. But the further Saul progresses toward the reader along the informational axis, the further does the reader (together with the prophet) retreat from him along the normative axis toward God and the narrator, till their viewpoints reach the stage of virtual polarization. Convergence in knowledge goes with divergence in judgment; as dramatic irony decreases, emotional and moral distance increases. And the two opposed movements are not only juxtaposed or correlated but causally related. For what may be excusable with an agent ignorant of his own offense and its implications ("I have performed the commandment of the Lord") becomes intolerable once that agent learns the true state of affairs. Even our pity for the floundering man is hardly a proper emotion for a king to elicit. Indeed, God is right: Saul must go.

The Q.E.D. secured, it may seem that the art of persuasion has done its work and it only remains to wind up the tale. But the narrator, resolved to make doubly sure, has a final surprise in store for us. Saul has not given up hope yet:

> I have sinned, for I have transgressed the utterance of the Lord and thy words, because I feared the people and listened to their voice. Now,

pray, forgive my sin and return with me and I will prostrate myself before
the Lord.

This is a weapon for rhetorical overkill, launched on both normative fronts
to deepen conviction and broaden consensus. If any reader has a lingering doubt about the justice of Saul's rejection, the newly fabricated account
will banish it for good. Saul indeed starts by confessing his sin, at long
last. But he immediately relapses and, blind to the implications of his argument, throws the blame on others. He thus disqualifies himself on all
possible grounds. In social terms, the blatancy of his lie ("I feared the
people") exceeds all previous limits; and even if this were the whole truth,
what better proof would one need of his unfitness for kingship? And in
religious terms, he in effect admits that he fears the people more than he
fears God. He also chooses the unhappiest (from the hidden persuader's
side, the happiest) phrase to express the results of his fear: "I listened to
their voice."[14] This loaded verb, whose sense extends from hearing to
obedience, resonates more than any other throughout the structure of repetition: as a command ("Now therefore *listen* to the voice of the Lord"); as
a call to battle ("Saul *summoned* the people"); as a sarcastic show of innocence
("What then is this bleating . . . which I *hear?*"); as a direct accusation ("Why
then didst thou not *listen* to the voice of the Lord?"); as a self-justifying
denial ("I *did listen* to the voice of the Lord"); and as a doctrinal priority
("Is the Lord as pleased with burnt offerings and sacrifice as with *listening*
to the voice of the Lord?"). So its new appearance, in the context of *vox
populi,* galvanizes in retrospect a whole chain of meaning: it infringes the
command, confirms the accusation, denies the denial, reverses the scale
of priorities. And that the voice of the army has been falsely invoked only
makes things worse, if possible, while sparing the persuader the awkward-
ness of enforcing an ideological choice between *vox populi* and *vox dei.*
   It is in this state of double betrayal—where he allegedly betrayed God
for fear of the people and actually betrays the people for fear of God—
that Saul still expects a happy ending. But that blindness only provokes
increasingly trenchant responses, so trenchant indeed as to arouse the suspicion that Samuel finds relief for his personal feelings in the cruelty of his
prophetic diatribes. First comes an answer that sharpens the foregoing,
religiously oriented version by hinting at Saul's disgraceful treatment of
his subjects ("the Lord has rejected thee from being king *over Israel*") and
crowns the verbal rebuff with the drastic act of refusing to appear with
the king in public ("I will not return with thee"). Then comes the symbolic interpretation given to the tearing of the coat as a visual figuration
of history, barbed by the reference to the unkinging as an accomplished

fact ("The Lord *has* torn the kingdom of Israel from thee"), the disclosure that a successor has already been chosen ("and given it to a neighbor of thine, who is better than thou"), and the emphasis on the finality of the sentence ("the Strength of Israel will not lie and will not repent, for he is not a man that he should repent").

Only this terrible crescendo of rejection manages to bring it home to Saul that what is done cannot be undone. He now competely inverts his first version ("I have performed" → "I have sinned") and resigns himself to the loss of God's favor ("I will prostrate myself before the Lord" modulates into "I will prostrate myself before the Lord thy God"). All he wishes is to save his face by turning the worship of God in the prophet's company into a public show of solidarity ("before the elders of my people and before Israel"). In typical disregard for the dynamics of repetition, this natural finale has been twisted into incongruity and explained away as the second of the tale's "two conclusions: (1) vv 24–29, in which Saul confesses his sin, asks Samuel to return to Gilgal with him to worship, and is sharply refused; and (2) vv 30–31, in which Saul confesses his sin, asks Samuel to return to Gilgal with him to worship, and is obliged."[15] In fact, the two units form structural rather than genetic variants. For the confessions are not identical but discrepant, not alternative but successive and gradated, moving from qualified to plain avowal of guilt. Rhetorically, of course, Saul must finally confess in proper form, too late to escape punishment but just in time to seal its vindication. Yet it also makes good psychological sense that he should thus confess, if not from his heart, then at least with a view to moving the prophet.

Samuel, his mixed feelings easily imaginable and soon to find a catharsis of sorts in the dismemberment of Agag, Saul's formal antagonist and veiled analogue, indeed yields to that new appeal—as if to illustrate his recent generalization that man may repent. But no later than the next chapter will he be burdened with a mission destined to undermine Saul's social prestige as well. Still mourning for one king, Samuel is dispatched to anoint another, whose conduct toward God and people, in adversity as well as in prosperity, will exhibit the sharpest contrast to his predecessor's. This is the king who, having committed his first offense and listened to the prophet's denunciation, at once responds by the simple words "I have sinned," which only a series of rounds can wring from Saul. This is also the king who, having committed his second (and last) sin and brought God's wrath down on the people, has only one request to make: "Behold, I have sinned and I have done wickedly; but these sheep, what have they done? Let thy hand, pray, be against me and my father's house" (2 Sam 24:17). While one of the persuader's eyes focuses on the individual episode unfolding in the narrative present, the second looks ahead to the future and the development of the book as a whole. With David, as with Saul, the two normative frames of reference inextricably fuse together. But the difference that emerges from their joint application motivates the different fates of the two leaders and is supposed to explain the course of history.

NOTES

Chapter 1 / Literary Text, Literary Approach: Getting the Questions Straight

1. "The King Through Ironic Eyes: The Narrator's Devices in the Story of David and Bathsheba and Two Excursuses on the Theory of the Narrative Text," *Hasifrut* 1 (1968) 262–91. Even Robert Alter, who embraces this and the following moves "towards the definition of a specific poetics of biblical narrative," then goes on to advocate a literary approach (*The Art of Biblical Narrative* [New York: Basic Books, 1981] pp. 17ff.). But in his case the difference is indeed less substantive than usual, and so, with one or two exceptions, is my criticism in what follows.

2. David Robertson, *The Old Testament and the Literary Critic* (Philadelphia: Fortress Press, 1977).

3. For the full list see Kenneth R. R. Gros Louis, "Some Methodological Considerations," in *Literary Interpretations of Biblical Narrative II,* ed. Kenneth R. R. Gros Louis with James S. Ackerman (Nashville: Abingdon, 1982) pp. 14–15.

4. Monroe C. Beardsley, "Intentions and Interpretations: A Fallacy Revived," in *The Aesthetic Point of View,* ed. Michael J. Wreen and Donald M. Callen (Ithaca and London: Cornell University Press, 1982) p. 188.

5. W. K. Wimsatt and Monroe C. Beardsley, "The Intentional Fallacy," in *The Verbal Icon* (New York: Noonday, 1958) p. 10.

6. For a vigorous critique see E. D. Hirsch, *The Aims of Interpretation* (Chicago: University of Chicago Press, 1976).

7. "The King Through Ironic Eyes," 292; for some of the repercussions of this statement see the references in chapter 6, n. 1 below.

8. The following example draws on a variety of detailed inquiries into the epistemology of biblical narrative: for example, the narrator's knowledge versus the reader's in "The King Through Ironic Eyes" and "Between the Truth and the Whole Truth in Biblical Narrative: The Rendering of Inner Life by Telescoped Inside View and Interior Monologue" (*Hasifrut* 29 [1979] 110–46); knowledge and judgment in "Delicate Balance in the Rape of Dinah: Biblical Narrative and the Rhetoric of the Narrative Text" (*Hasifrut* 4 [1973] 193–231); the rhetoric of divine omniscience and the opposition of God's to man's knowledge in "The Structure of Repetition in Biblical Narrative: Strategies of Informational Redundancy" (*Hasifrut* 25 [1977] esp. 124–28, 134–37).

9. This is one example of many. On the principle that I elsewhere described as "reconciling versions rhetorically, though not historically" (*Expositional Modes*

and Temporal Ordering in Fiction [Baltimore and London: Johns Hopkins University Press, 1978] pp. 2–3), this book will repeatedly show that what has been decomposed by geneticists makes a poetic and purposive composition. To keep the argument in focus, however, most of the references to the genetic view are kept below the surface. For welcome attempts at a revaluation of the Bible's "composite artistry" see also Joel Rosenberg ("Meanings, Morals, and Mysteries: Literary Approaches to Torah," *Response* 9 [1975] esp. 81–94) and Alter (*The Art of Biblical Narrative*, pp. 131ff.), which diverge to good effect from the usual practice of the literary approach.

10. Richard G. Moulton, *The Literary Study of the Bible* (New York: AMS Press, 1970; first published 1899) pp. VIII–IX. For a more sophisticated version see Robert Polzin, *Moses and the Deuteronomist* (New York: Seabury, 1980) pp. 5–7. His citations from literary theory indicate that the struggle for priority is not confined to the biblical arena.

11. On the relevance of modern to ancient textual prehistories see Matitiahu Tsevat's discussion in "Common Sense and Hypothesis in Old Testament Study," *The Meaning of the Book of Job and Other Biblical Studies* (Dallas: Ktav, 1980) pp. 189–203.

12. Leland Ryken, "Literary Criticism of the Bible: Some Fallacies," in *Literary Interpretations of Biblical Narratives,* ed. Kenneth R. R. Gros Louis, James S. Ackerman, and Thayer S. Warshaw (Nashville: Abingdon, 1974) p. 30.

13. Yair Zakovitch, "The State of the Art: A Survey of the Literary Criticism of the Bible in Israel," *Newsletter of the World Association of Jewish Studies* 20 (1982) 27.

14. Jonathan Culler, *Structuralist Poetics* (London: Routledge and Kegan Paul, 1975) p. 113.

15. Robert H. Pfeiffer, *Introduction to the Old Testament* (New York: Harper & Row, 1948) pp. 27–28.

16. Hermann Gunkel, *The Legends of Genesis,* trans. W. H. Carruth (New York: Schocken Books, 1964; first published 1901).

17. Herbert N. Schneidau, *Sacred Discontent: The Bible and Western Tradition* (Berkeley: University of California Press, 1977) p. 215. It is rather strange, as we shall see, that this largely rests on Erich Auerbach's argument to the contrary in *Mimesis,* trans. Willard Trask (Garden City, N.Y.: Anchor Books, 1957) pp. 11–17.

18. For a modern equivalent, concerning the status of hard fact within fiction, see my "Knight meets Dragon in the James Bond Saga: Realism and Reality Models," *Style* (1983) 142–80.

19. Henry James, *The Art of the Novel* (New York: Scribner, 1962) p. 46.

20. J. H. Hexter, *Doing History* (London: Allen and Unwin, 1971) pp. 167–68.

21. Arnaldo Momigliano, *Essays in Ancient and Modern Historiography* (Oxford: Blackwell, 1977) p. 195.

22. Herbert Butterfield, *The Origins of History* (New York: Basic Books, 1981) pp. 80–95.

23. See Tsevat's lucid argument in "Israelite History and the Historical Books of the Old Testament," *Meaning of Job,* pp. 182–87.

24. Among other things, this discloses the emptiness of the slogan that to reconstruct the original intention is to impoverish the text. It is because of rather than in spite of its unique premises of discourse, which modernism does not and cannot replicate for all its ingenuity, that Scripture emerges as the most interesting as well as the greatest work in the narrative tradition.

25. James L. Kugel, *The Idea of Biblical Poetry* (New Haven and London: Yale University Press, 1981) p. 303.

26. René Wellek and Austin Warren, *Theory of Literature* (Harmondsworth: Penguin, 1956) pp. 29–30.

27. Elder Olson, "William Empson, Contemporary Criticism, and Poetic Diction," in *Critics and Criticism,* ed. R. S. Crane (Chicago: University of Chicago Press, 1952) pp. 66–67, also pp. 588ff.

28. Roman Jakobson, "Linguistics and Poetics," in *Style in Language,* ed. T. A. Sebeok (Cambridge, Mass.: MIT Press, 1966) pp. 350–77.

29. M. H. Segal, *The Books of Samuel* (Jerusalem: Kiryat Sefer, 1971) p. 364.

30. Probably through a misunderstanding of some key terms—like "junction," "tension," "aesthetic"—Robert Alter objects to an earlier formulation of this structure and then proceeds to offer a similar view in more traditional and less precise language (*Art of Biblical Narrative,* pp. 18–19, and reference there).

31. Note that the mediation works through the feature of *time and process* common to all three, being necessarily present in story and history but exceptionally so in ideology. This junction will assume even greater importance in what follows, as the rationale of the Bible's dynamics of meaning along the narrative sequence.

32. This applies also to other devices that have been left unmentioned, such as repetition. For its bearing on knowledge divine and human see the reference to "The Structure of Repetition" in n. 8 above, incorporated here as chapter 11.

33. Frank Kermode, *The Genesis of Secrecy* (Cambridge, Mass. and London: Harvard University Press, 1980) p. XI.

34. T. S. Eliot, *The Use of Poetry and the Use of Criticism* (Cambridge, Mass.: Harvard University Press, 1933) p. 153.

35. Bruce Vawter, *On Genesis: A New Reading* (Garden City, N.Y.: Doubleday, 1977) p. 359.

36. For a detailed treatment of this and related modes see my "Between the Truth and the Whole Truth" (n. 8 above) and "Language, World and Perspective in Biblical Art," *Hasifrut* 32 (1983) 88–131.

Chapter 2 / Narrative Models

1. "Joshua wrote his own book. But is it not written, 'And Joshua son of Nun the servant of the Lord died'?—It was completed by Eleazar. But is it not also

written in it, 'And Eleazar the son of Aaron died'?—Phineas finished it. Samuel wrote his own book. But is it not written in it, 'Now Samuel was dead'?—It was completed by God the seer and Nathan the prophet." See also 1 Chronicles 29:29.

2. Translated from Segal's *The Books of Samuel* (Jerusalem: Kiryat Sefer, 1971) pp. 25–26. See also his *The Pentateuch and Other Biblical Studies* (Jerusalem: Magnes Press, 1967) pp. 185–86.

3. For a brief summary of the alternatives, to which Segal does less than justice, see Otto Eissfeldt, *The Old Testament: An Introduction,* trans. Peter R. Ackroyd (New York: Harper & Row, 1972) pp. 137–39; and John Gray, *I & II Kings* (Philadelphia: Westminster Press, 1963) pp. 24–25. Abiathar, first suggested by Bernard Duhm (1901) and identified by others with the Yahwist (J) himself, is now considered too involved to have been the court historian but sufficiently informed to have written about the adventures of David as an outlaw. Ahima'az, A. Klostermann's (1887) candidate, rose to power (hence knowledge) as high official and Solomon's son-in-law. Gray himself opts for Nathan, who combines the recommendations of courtier, accomplice, moralist, critic of the old and instructor of the young king. In this shadowboxing, the contenders are thus fairly evenly matched.

4. *Ancient Near Eastern Texts,* ed. James B. Pritchard (Princeton: Princeton University Press, 1969) pp. 431–32.

5. See W. G. Lambert, "Ancestors, Authors, and Canonicity," *Journal of Cuneiform Studies* 11 (1957) 1–14; and "A Catalogue of Texts and Authors," *Journal of Cuneiform Studies* 16 (1962) 59–81, which reconstructs and discusses the Ashurbanipal catalogue.

6. *Ancient Near Eastern Texts,* p. 601. "Apparently he means thereby to protest his religious and political innocence in face of the rather daring views expressed in his composition" (W. W. Hallo, "New Viewpoints on Cuneiform Literature," *Israel Exploration Journal* 12 [1962] 14).

7. *Ancient Near Eastern Texts,* p. 141. On ancient colophons see E. Leichty, "The Colophon," *Studies Presented to A. Leo Oppenheim* (Chicago: University of Chicago Press, 1964) pp. 147–54.

8. Stressing "the importance of categories of form" in ancient literature, W. F. Albright thus rightly warns "against using canons of style and vocabulary too rigidly in trying to determine authorship of passages in the Old Testament" (*From the Stone Age to Christianity* [Garden City, N.Y.: Anchor Books, 1957] p. 77).

9. Robert Scholes and Robert Kellogg, *The Nature of Narrative* (New York: Oxford University Press, 1966) p. 72.

10. See George R. Stewart, "The Two Moby-Dicks," *American Literature* 25 (1954) 414–48; Franz Stanzel, *Narrative Situations in the Novel,* trans. James P. Pusack (Bloomington: Indiana University Press, 1971) pp. 70ff.

11. See *The Notebooks for 'Crime and Punishment,'* ed. Edward Wasiolek (Chicago: University of Chicago Press, 1971); and Dorrit Cohn, "K. enters *The Castle:* On the Change of Person in Kafka's Manuscript," *Euphorion* 62 (1968) 28–45.

12. For the relevant passages see *Ancient Near Eastern Texts,* pp. 43–44 versus 93–95; and Samuel Noah Kramer, *History Begins at Sumer* (London: Thames and Hudson, 1961) pp. 266–67.

13. See my *Expositional Modes and Temporal Ordering in Fiction* (Baltimore and London: Johns Hopkins University Press, 1978) pp. 254ff.; and Tamar Yacobi, "Reliability as a Communicative Problem," *Poetics Today* 2 (1981) esp. 119–21.

14. Translation from *Hesiod and Theognis,* ed. Dorothea Wender (Harmondsworth: Penguin, 1973) pp. 23–26.

15. See *Ancient Near Eastern Texts,* pp. 418–19; and John Wilson, *The Burden of Egypt* (Chicago: University of Chicago Press, 1951) pp. 131, 267–68.

16. For a penetrating sociopoetic study of Plato's affair with literature see Eric A. Havelock, *Preface to Plato* (Cambridge, Mass.: Harvard University Press, 1963).

17. Lambert, "Ancestors," 6; "Catalogue," 72–73.

18. See, for instance, how this theme runs through the three volumes of *The Cambridge History of the Bible* (Cambridge: University Press, 1963).

19. See Scholes and Kellogg, *The Nature of Narrative,* pp. 259–62, and the references in n. 13 above.

Chapter 3 / Ideology of Narration and Narration of Ideology

1. T. H. Huxley, *Science and Hebrew Tradition* (London: Macmillan, 1893) p. 211.

2. For additional examples, see Yoseph Heinemann, *The Ways of the Aggadah* [*Darkhei Ha'aggadah*] (Jerusalem: Magnes Press, 1954) pp. 39–41, 130.

3. The phrasing is so vague, though, that it remains unclear what kind of empirical authority he actually claims. A clue to his evasiveness on this point is supplied by the Muratorian Fragment, which records that Luke "wrote in his own name from his own point of view," though he had never "seen the Lord in the flesh" (translation from Philip Carrington, *The Early Christian Church* [Cambridge: University Press, 1957] vol. II, p. 347).

4. Quoted in H. Frankfort et al., *The Intellectual Adventure of Ancient Man* (Chicago: University of Chicago Press, 1977) p. 76; see also "The Loyalist Instruction," in *The Literature of Ancient Egypt,* ed. William Kelly Simpson (New Haven and London: Yale University Press, 1973) p. 199.

5. Alexander Heidel, *The Gilgamesh Epic and Old Testament Parallels* (Chicago: University of Chicago Press, 1963) p. 16. That Gilgamesh does not prove all-knowing only betrays further how careless ancient literature was about this attribute.

6. Some, though, go beyond the immediate concerns of this book; see especially my "Between the Truth and the Whole Truth in Biblical Narrative: The Rendering of Inner Life by Telescoped Inside View and Interior Monologue," *Hasifrut* 29 (1979) 110–46.

7. No less luminously, the Story of Eden opposes that of Adapa, considered the first of the Akkadian seven sages, whose name is possibly even a cognate of Adam (*Ancient Near Eastern Texts,* pp. 101–3). Offered divine nourishment, Adapa had only to partake of it to gain immortality. But he refused it by the disingenuous advice of a god, whereupon the high god compensated him with the gift of sagacity. "To him he had given wisdom; eternal life he had not given him": Adapa was fobbed off, as it were, with a consolation prize.

8. As Hermann Gunkel still does in the fantastic comment that God learned of the murder from the crying of Abel's blood (*Genesis* [Göttingen: Vandenhoeck & Ruprecht, 1902] p. 39).

9. For conjectures about the real etymology see W. F. Albright, *From the Stone Age to Christianity* (Garden City, N.Y.: Anchor Books, 1957) p. 303.

10. To readers predisposed to identify the prophet's viewpoint with God's and the characters' voice with the narrator's, the irony will of course pass for a factual statement or even for glorification; see, for instance, J. Lindblom's account of the story in *Prophecy in Ancient Israel* (Philadelphia: Fortress Press, 1976) pp. 89–90.

11. Robert Alter likewise picks out the root "see" as the *Leitwort* here (*The Art of Biblical Narrative* [New York: Basic Books, 1981] p. 149).

12. Some of the differences have recently been explored and illustrated in Tamar Yacobi's doctoral dissertation "The Narrator's Reliability in Fiction" (Tel-Aviv University, 1981/2), especially chapters 2–5.

13. For good surveys, with bibliography, see Frankfort et al., *The Intellectual Adventure of Ancient Man;* and W. F. Albright, *Yahweh and the Gods of Canaan* (Garden City, N.Y.: Anchor Books, 1969).

14. A. E. Speiser, "The Biblical Idea of History and Its Common Near Eastern Setting," in *Oriental and Biblical Studies* (Philadelphia: University of Pennsylvania Press, 1967) p. 190.

15. Quoted in Benjamin Farrington's *Greek Science* (Harmondsworth: Penguin, 1953) p. 275.

16. Gerhard von Rad, *Old Testament Theology,* trans. D. M. G. Stalker (Edinburgh and London: Oliver and Boyd, 1962) vol. I, pp. 48ff.

17. *The Babylonian Genesis,* trans. Alexander Heidel (Chicago: University of Chicago Press, 1963) p. 37.

18. Recently, it has often been asserted that this feature is common to all deities in the ancient Orient (e.g., Frederick L. Moriarty, "Word as Power in the Ancient Near East," in *Light Unto My Path,* ed. Howard N. Bream et al. [Philadelphia: Temple University Press, 1974] pp. 345–62). I hope to show elsewhere that the claim is much exaggerated, as indeed are others that try too hard to provide the Bible with ancestors and relatives. The most interesting of these bears on the workings of history. Bertil Albrektson thus argues, with impressive documentation, against the long-held view of the Bible as the only world picture that links history to divinity: "The Old Testament idea of historical events as divine revelation must be counted among the similarities, not among the distinctive traits: it is part of the common theology of the ancient Near East" (*History and the Gods* [Lund: Gleerup,

1967] p. 114). But Albrektson himself notes in passing a number of radical dissimilarities, and he might well have added the rhetoric of historical omnipotence
that we are tracing here.

19. The basic texts are J. L. Austin, *How To Do Things with Words* (New York:
Oxford University Press, 1962); and John R. Searle, *Speech Acts* (Cambridge:
University Press, 1969).

20. On Homer's rhetoric, see my *Expositional Modes and Temporal Ordering in Fiction* (Baltimore and London: Johns Hopkins University Press, 1978) pp. 56ff.; on
Ian Fleming's, see my "Knight Meets Dragon in the James Bond Saga: Realism
and Reality Models," *Style* (1983) 142–80.

21. On these "paradigms" see the opening section of chapter 7 below.

22. Even apart from the doctrinal context, perception through the senses—
especially the visual—dominates the Bible's psychology of learning and credence.
"I did not believe the reports," the queen of Sheba confesses to Solomon, "until
I came and my own eyes saw this" (1 Kgs 10:6). The compositional implications,
for point of view and the argument from history, are evident. But this principle
also indicates the need to reconsider the sharp contrast drawn between vision-
oriented Greek and voice-oriented Hebrew culture (e.g., by Thorlief Boman, *Hebrew
Thought Compared with Greek* [Philadelphia: Westminster Press, 1960]).

23. Speaking of Deuteronomy, Robert Polzin describes Moses as alternating
"his point of view between one who presents himself as above his hearers in special
knowledge and one who emphasizes shared experiences with his fellow Israelites"
(*Moses and the Deuteronomist* [New York: Seabury, 1980] p. 45). This sharpens another
difference separating personal from impersonal narration: even Moses only alternates between the positions that the biblical narrator fuses throughout.

24. Jean Paul Sartre, *Literary and Philosophical Essays,* trans. Annette Michelson
(New York: Collier Books, 1967) pp. 15, 25. On the dogmas of Sartre and his
contemporaries see the excellent critique in Wayne C. Booth, *The Rhetoric of Fiction* (Chicago: University of Chicago Press, 1961).

25. See the detailed analysis in my *Expositional Modes,* pp. 23ff.

26. The story of this tradition has yet to be told. For its modern parts see Ingrid
Strohschneider-Kohrs, *Die romantische Ironie in Theorie und Gestaltung* (Tübingen:
Niemeyer, 1960); and Robert Alter, *Partial Magic* (Berkeley and Los Angeles:
University of California Press, 1975).

27. Denis Diderot, *Jacques the Fatalist and His Master,* trans. J. Robert Loy (New
York: Norton, 1959) p. 4.

28. For the versions see *Ancient Near Eastern Texts,* pp. 3– 10; and John A. Wilson,
The Burden of Egypt (Chicago: University of Chicago Press, 1951) pp. 58–60.

29. *Ancient Near East Texts,* pp. 125–26.

30. See, for example, Umberto Cassuto, *A Commentary on the Book of Genesis*
(Jerusalem: Magnes Press, 1961); and Nahum M. Sarna, *Understanding Genesis* (New
York: Schocken Books, 1972).

Chapter 4 / Viewpoints and Interpretations

1. See my *Expositional Modes and Temporal Ordering in Fiction* (Baltimore and London: Johns Hopkins University Press, 1978) pp. 260ff.

2. Benno Jacob, the acutest commentator on Genesis, reads the discourse backwards by inventing a peculiar context of utterance: the reporter is an old friend of Abraham's, who suggests "eine Frau für deinen Sohn, aus deinen nähesten Familie" and to this end goes into Rebekah's descent (*Das erste Buch der Torah: Genesis* [Berlin: Schocken, 1934] p. 504).

3. Some translations (e.g., A. E. Speiser's *Genesis* [Anchor Bible; Garden City, N.Y.: Doubleday, 1964] p. 167) spoil the effect of camouflage by ending the message to Abraham just before the reference to Rebekah: this draws undue notice to her as the point of transition to the narrator's own discourse.

4. On this and related names see the comments and bibliography in John Bright, *A History of Israel* (London: SCM Press, 1974) p. 77.

5. For some exceptions see Speiser, *Genesis,* p. 174; Umberto Cassuto, *A Commentary on the Book of Genesis* (Jerusalem: Magnes Press, 1961) pp. 187–88.

6. Bruce Vawter, *On Genesis: A New Reading* (Garden City, N.Y.: Doubleday, 1977) p. 266. For some good comments on the tale's repetition, following the lines of rabbinic exegesis, see Nehama Leibowitz, *Studies in the Book of Genesis* (Jerusalem: World Zionist Organization, 1972).

7. Predictably, genetic criticism has smoothed out the "awkward sequence" of verses 28–30 by "transposing v. 29b between v. 30a and 30b" (Gerhard von Rad, *Genesis,* trans. John H. Marks [London: SCM Press, 1970] p. 252).

Chapter 5 / The Play of Perspectives

1. See my "Between the Truth and the Whole Truth in Biblical Narrative: The Rendering of Inner Life by Telescoped Inside View and Interior Monologue," *Hasifrut* 29 (1979) esp. 137–46; and "Proteus in Quotation-Land: Mimesis and the Forms of Reported Discourse," *Poetics Today* 3 (1982) 123–24.

2. *Expositional Modes and Temporal Ordering in Fiction* (Baltimore and London: Johns Hopkins University Press, 1978) pp. 185–203, 258–73.

3. Henry James, *The Art of the Novel* (New York: Scribner, 1962) pp. 63–64.

4. Hermann Gunkel, *The Legends of Genesis,* trans. W. H. Carruth (New York: Schocken Books, 1964) p. 50.

5. Like the cow in the Egyptian "Story of Two Brothers" (*Ancient Near Eastern Texts,* ed. James B. Pritchard [Princeton: Princeton University Press, 1963] p. 24).

6. Henry James, *The Art of the Novel,* p. 257.

7. Steven J. Brams, *Biblical Games* (Cambridge, Mass.: MIT Press, 1980) pp. 4–5, 103, and passim.

8. Herbert N. Schneidau, *Sacred Discontent: The Bible and Western Tradition* (Berkeley: University of California Press, 1977) p. 211.

9. Ibid., pp. 213-14; A. E. Speiser, *Oriental and Biblical Studies* (Philadelphia: University of Pennsylvania Press, 1967) pp. 205-6.

10. Robert Polzin, *Moses and the Deuteronomist* (New York: Seabury, 1980) pp. 189-91; cf. 199-200.

11. Ibid., p. 191. This quotation also pinpoints the difference between Speiser's line and Polzin's, which usually illuminates the text by giving the storyteller proper credit for authority and only overreaches itself in propounding the paradox of *the authoritative local undermining of authority.*

Chapter 6 / Gaps, Ambiguity, and the Reading Process

1. The basis of this chapter is a programmatic essay written in collaboration with Menakhem Perry ("The King Through Ironic Eyes: The Narrator's Devices in the Story of David and Bathsheba and Two Excursuses on the Theory of the Narrative Text," *Hasifrut* 1 [1968] 262-91). The stir its appearance made can be inferred from the two earliest responses, Boaz Arpali's "Caution: A Biblical Story" (*Hasifrut* 2 [1970] 580-97) and Uriel Simon's "An Ironic Approach to a Bible Story" (*Hasifrut* 2 [1970] 598-607)—both rebutted in "Caution: A Literary Text! Problems in the Poetics and the Interpretation of Biblical Narrative" (*Hasifrut* 2 [1970] 608-63). Later repercussions, too numerous to trace here, reflect the developments that have been taking place in the field since the sixties.

The present version follows but does not always replicate the original essay. The analysis of the story has been touched up, the concepts brought into line with my later work on narrative theory and interpretation, and the argument adjusted to its role as a chapter in this book. Though seldom radical, all these changes are entirely my responsibility, and anyone interested in the original is referred to the publication cited above.

2. Nikolai Gogol, "The Nose," in *The Diary of a Madman and Other Stories,* trans. Andrew R. MacAndrew (New York: New American Library, 1960) pp. 54-55.

3. A nineteenth-century social novel contains the following passage: "For over an hour he told Madeleine about his travels. Suddenly, looking closely at her, he found her eyes shut and her face expressionless; he thought she was asleep." No doubt the reader feels pity for the poor girl who has fallen asleep through sheer exhaustion or boredom. This is a hypothesis that can be confirmed or undermined by further details supplied by the text. Now consider another passage, from a recent detective story: "For over an hour he told Madeleine about his travels. Suddenly, looking closely at her, he found her eyes shut and her face expressionless; he thought she was asleep." Surely the reader now expects the police to be called in to discover the mysterious murderer. The two passages employ the same verbal material, but they presuppose entirely different gap-fillings. For the different expectations set up by the two literary genres—social versus detective novel—activate meanings that diverge in their implications even where arising from the very same sentence. (Recall also the two conflicting interpretations of Nathan's Poor Man's Ewe-Lamb, as history and as parable, mentioned in my first chapter.)

4. As argued in the preceding chapters, the linkages or gap-fillings to which the world of literature invites the reader are bound to differ from those normally performed either in real life or within the simulacrum of real life inhabited by the characters. The question is only how, where, and to what end they differ.

5. This technique of presentation, sometimes called "the dramatic mode" (Norman Friedman, "Point of View in Fiction: The Development of a Critical Concept," *PMLA* 70 [1955] 1160–84), resembles that used by Henry James in *The Awkward Age* and by Hemingway in "The Killers." According to Friedman, this mode involves an extreme degree of "showing." But he typically (con)fuses two factors, each independently affecting the degree to which the narrator's presence is felt: (1) presentation or nonpresentation of the characters' thoughts; (2) mode of presentation of the incidents (by way of "telling" or "showing"). It is by no means necessary for the author to correlate these narrative aspects, and in the story under discussion they indeed part company. James and Hemingway, for example, present external events by way of drastic "showing"; the story of David and Bathsheba likewise restricts itself to externals, yet often resorts to the mode of summary or "telling" (e.g., in verses 1 and 4).

This again goes to show that the typology of narrative, for all its recent overhauling, is still in need of serious revision. Biblical narrative, precisely because it lies outside the novelistic tradition to which theorists usually address themselves, may operate as a touchstone and incentive to such revision.

6. Thus, R. Scholes and R. Kellogg go too far in citing the David and Bathsheba story to illustrate their generalization that the Bible, like all "primitive" literature, observes its characters only from the outside (*The Nature of Narrative* [New York: Oxford University Press] pp. 166-67). In fact, the biblical narrator uses this extreme method wherever it serves his purposes and abandons it wherever another suits them better. In view of the shift of narrative form according to contextual role, there is nothing of "primitive narration" about this reticence, deliberately prolonged and subtle in effect. For a systematic analysis of the rendering of inner life in the Bible, notably including free indirect discourse, see my "Between the Truth and the Whole Truth: The Rendering of Inner Life by Telescoped Inside View and Interior Monologue," *Hasifrut* 29 (1979) 110–46, and "Language, World and Perspective in Biblical Art," *Hasifrut* 32 (1983) 88–131—both incorporated in the forthcoming *Voices of the Bible*.

7. Even 1 Chronicles 20:1, which gives a parallel account focused on Joab's campaign, shortens the preliminaries: "At the time of the turn of the year, at the time when kings go forth to battle, Joab led out the power of the army and ravaged the land of the Ammonites and came and besieged Rabbah, and David stayed in Jerusalem."

8. Much of the beauty of the irony in this chapter lies in its covertness. The game of hide-and-seek played by the narrator behind the ambiguous *ve* is often lost in translation. Take the Authorized Version: "David sent Joab, *and* his servants with him, *and* all Israel; *and* they destroyed the children of Ammon, *and* besieged Rabbah. *But* David tarried still at Jerusalem" (italics added). Note how the *ve* ("and") turns univocal when replaced by "but," and the asymmetry is radicalized by the division of the verse into two sentences. With the irony overarticulated, this passage falls between translation and interpretation. How can one prevail on translators to leave the Bible's art of parataxis alone?

9. Passing in respectful silence over the whole Bathsheba affair, the Chronicler (1 Chr 20:1–5) treats the war not by ironic analogy to another action but as a context in its own right. For similar reasons, his version omits Joab's message to David to hurry up before the city falls. But the formulations of 2 Samuel, designed to serve an ironic purpose, are ill-suited for an ordinary chronicle. As a result, the reappearance of the ending in Chronicles makes an incoherent story: it is not clear how David, left behind in Jerusalem, appropriates the crown of the king of Rabbah, smites all the Ammonite cities, and returns with all the people to Jerusalem. Worse, this confused version inadvertently exposes its darling to the sharpest irony by crediting Joab with the whole victory and proportionately discrediting David's swooping on the loot.

10. The sparsity of detail also involves omissions that cannot be supplied for lack of clues. For example, it is impossible to determine Bathsheba's attitude, though one would not imagine that she showed much resistance. The Bible does not portray her as a very clever woman (see 1 Kings 2). The rabbis, ideologically committed to David and his line, argued that it was she who had seduced the king—why else should she have bathed naked on the roof? (see *Ginzei Schechter: Midrashim* [New York, 1928] vol. 1, p. 166).

11. Such formulations are for convenience only. More precisely, the absence of explicit value judgments and incriminating facts (e.g., motives) is a textual feature; this, together with several others, produces the impression of the narrator's "objectivity." But once such an image of the narrator is established, it can be used to explain further details, which concurrently validate the explanatory principle itself.

12. Even the fact that Bathsheba is a married woman is something the narrator does not straightforwardly report in his own name, lest such a disclosure should jar against the objective-"naive" tone. The information gets in not by way of nar-ratorial "telling" but through scenic means; and even in the dialogue the fact is submerged, appearing as one item in a sentence whose declared purpose is to reveal Bathsheba's identity ("the daughter of Eliam, the wife of Uriah"). A markedly different impression would have ensued had the sentence read: "That is Bathsheba, the wife of Uriah."

13. One of the great medieval commentators seriously takes this to be the point: "To inform us that he did not lie with her while she was unclean, for she had already been purified from her uncleanness" (Radak, ad loc). So does the Authorized Version, which explicitly renders the coordinator *ve* as *for:* "and he lay with her; for she was purified from her uncleanness." Again, the violated parataxis will have its revenge.

14. Since the point of this bit of information remains problematic (at this stage at least), the reader looks round for other explanations; and while considering "and he lay with her, and she was purifying herself from her uncleanness," he must be struck by the incongruity of a woman just purified from uncleanness falling into an even greater uncleanness.

15. To explain Uriah's recalcitrance, modern scholars often invoke the prohibition of sexual intercourse laid on the Israelite soldier in wartime. (Carried *ad absurdum,* this yields the argument that David's original offense was against the sacral taboo, and only a later generation transferred the offense to the moral sphere

of adultery; see Eric Voegelin, *Order and History* [Baton Rouge: Louisiana State University Press, 1956] vol. I, pp. 259ff.). Such a taboo is a figment of the scholarly imagination, nowhere listed or dramatized in the Bible among the laws of purity devolving on soldiers (Deut 23:10–15). If anything, our narrative itself establishes its nonexistence. If it existed: (1) How could David propose to Uriah to go home and expect him to violate the taboo? (2) Why, instead of preaching solidarity, does not Uriah simply mention in response the duty of celibacy? (3) Why does he bracket "eating" and "drinking" with "sleeping," as if the three acts were equally reprehensible? (4) What actually deterred Uriah from having a meal or a wash at home, without sleeping with his wife? Even stranger, if possible, is the insistence of pro-tabooists on reading the *derekh* in David's remonstrance as "campaign" (rather than "journey"): "Hast thou not come from a [campaign]? Why didst thou not go down to thy house?" Such a reading would surely prove the very opposite, for David then appeals to Uriah's having been on active duty as the strongest argument *for* relaxing at home.

16. This opposition of the stay-at-home king to the warriors roughing it in the field does not fully exploit the presence of "the Ark." But the David and Bathsheba story is part of a long (and well-constructed) cycle, in which the Holy Ark points another ironic link—this time, by retrospection. In chapter 7, David himself appears disturbed by the incongruous fact that he dwells in a "house of cedar" while the Ark "dwells within curtains" in a tent. True, God lets David know that he is not worthy of building a house for the Ark, but this need not prevent David (if he feels so ill at ease) from leaving his house of cedar. Uriah's precept and practice thus activate an irony in this broader context, and a person's attitude to the Ark becomes an index of character.

17. Not for nothing did the rabbis call Uriah "a rebel against the kingdom" (*Shabbat* 56a). Cf. "It is not done to acknowledge the authority of others in the presence of the king" (Rashi, ad loc.).

18. Even if Uriah is innocent of any such intentions and a mere puppet in the hands of the narrator, the irony is still there in the situation itself. For in this case Uriah does not realize the stinging effect of his own words or how well they suit the occasion, these being the words he would have used had he been aware of the king's machinations.

19. These facts, too, can of course be given alternative explanations that would tie in better with the rival hypothesis.

20. A man who sees through the king's plot and hatches a counterplot will on no account "go down to his house," even after a day or two. But a prolonged stay in such close proximity to wife and home may wear down the resistance of one actuated by abstract "ideals." If David assumes (at least at this stage, before the three days have passed) that Uriah does not know, then it is quite sensible of him to keep Uriah in Jerusalem.

21. In principle there is, of course, a third possibility: that on his arrival in Jerusalem Uriah was completely in the dark—and his behavior on the first night therefore quite innocent—but that during his stay in the city, among the king's servants, he got wind of the affair. It is even possible, among other variations, that when the king first sent him home, he actually intended to go, but learnt of the affair as he was leaving the palace. Thus the two hypotheses we have been

considering are really only master hypotheses. All other hypotheses will not so much give new insights into the features of the text as reorganize the existing insights in different patterns.

22. There is only a partial correspondence between the factors that may lead David and the factors that may lead the reader to endorse (or reject) a certain hypothesis. As in the Wooing of Rebekah—where discrepancies in perspective separate even the most like-minded interpreters—this is largely due to the different nature of gap-filling in reality and in literature. Even where all other things are equal, the reader's expectations are directed also by the text's poetics and rhetoric, by effects produced and lessons learned earlier in the reading, by the tendency to opt for the hypothesis that presents textual details in the most interesting light or characters as more complex or rounded, and so on: all of them factors that can hardly influence David, who has to deal with the gaps in "real life." On the other hand, David is possessed of data unavailable to the reader, such as previous knowledge of Uriah's personality, inferences from Uriah's facial expression, etc.

23. As integral to this play of ambiguity, a detail that emphatically supports one hypothesis may yet be accounted for in terms of the other.

24. If, so far, the rumors have been little more than idle gossip, then the act of bringing Bathsheba to the palace will surely lend them substance.

25. It is still possible that, contrary to the king's suppositions, Uriah knows nothing and dies for nothing. At this stage, then, the two hypotheses about David generate four alternative plots: (1) Uriah does not know, and David believes that Uriah does not know; (2) Uriah knows, and David believes that Uriah does not know; (3) Uriah does not know, and David believes that Uriah knows; (4) Uriah knows, and David believes that Uriah knows.

26. Some readers, a minority I believe, would not acknowledge them even after the publication of the original analysis (see n. 1 above). Ultimately, as I shall argue in chapter 11, such attitudes have their roots in time-honored misconceptions of the Bible's strategy of repetition.

27. We encountered a similar technique (of implying a meritorious feature that is soon quashed in an ironic reversal) in the construction "and she was purifying herself from her uncleanness."

28. Joab's trap resembles that laid for David by the prophet Nathan in chapter 12. Both unfold a story that David does not relate to the Uriah affair; and only after David has made a spontaneous response, based on abstract norms, do they disclose his personal involvement: "Thou art the man!"

29. This would have been an open analogy had the text read: "And if the king's wrath arises and he says to thee: Who smote Abimelech the son of Jerubbesheth? Did not a woman cast a piece of millstone upon him from the wall, so that he died in Tebez?"

30. Though the interpretation has focused on a single link of the David cycle, it gains support from the structure and progress of the text as a whole. Note the location of chapter 11. On the one hand, it is preceded by a consistently favorable presentation of David as a God-fearing, successful, and victorious king. On the other hand, it is followed by a long chain of mishaps and disasters: the aftermath

of the Bathsheba affair, Tamar's rape and Amnon's murder, Absalom's usurpation of the throne, the Sheba ben Bichri rebellion, the three-year famine, and the
census followed by the plague. Within the composition of the book, therefore, ours
is a central chapter in that it pinpoints the where and why of David's change of
fortune. See also the final section of chapter 10 below.

31. All these differ, then, from the obscurity surrounding matters of no special
importance: such omissions are unfillable because the work does not see fit to provide the reader with the narrative data required for the operations of closure.
Nor—and this is equally relevant to the Bible—does the concept of ambiguity
apply to the products of negligence or sheer muddling in the composition of the
work.

32. For classic articles on the subject see G. Willen's anthology *A Casebook on
Henry James's "The Turn of the Screw"* (New York: Thomas Y. Crowell, 1960). Of the
articles, Edna Kenton's (1924) was the first to raise the possibility that the tale
was not a ghost story. This hypothesis, actually suggested even before Kenton,
became far more widely known ten years later, with Edmund Wilson's "The
Ambiguity of Henry James" (also in the Willen anthology). A fairly complete
bibliography can be found in T. M. Cranfill and R. L. Clark, Jr., *The Anatomy
of "The Turn of the Screw"* (Austin: University of Texas Press, 1965). The authors
classify the approaches to the work and, in their introduction, outline the phases
of the controversy. Four important items are worth noting among those not listed
in this bibliography: three were overlooked by Cranfill and Clark, and one appeared
after their book was published. See Monroe C. Beardsley on the problem of elucidation in this tale (*Aesthetics* [New York: Harcourt, Brace, and World, 1958]
pp. 243-44); Wayne C. Booth's comments in *The Rhetoric of Fiction* [Chicago:
University of Chicago Press, 1961] pp. 311-16; and E. Solomon, "The Return of
the Screw," *University Review* 30 (Spring 1964) 205-11 (reprinted in the Norton critical
edition of *The Turn of the Screw*, ed. R. Kimbrough [1966] pp. 237-45). This brilliant
article fixes on Mrs. Grose, the "prosaic" housekeeper, as the wily and malicious
villain of the piece and accuses her of murder. A similar view of Mrs. Grose has
been taken by an American psychiatrist, C. K. Aldrich ("Another Twist to *The
Turn of the Screw*," *Modern Fiction Studies* 13 [1967] 167-77).

Postscript 1981. Since 1968, when this discussion originally appeared, the screw
has been turned so many times and ways, that the foregoing note can hardly be
brought up to date here. It is sufficient to say that in recent years the argument
for deliberate and functional ambiguity has gained more acceptance among
theorists as well as biblicists than its authors could reasonably expect when first
presenting it. In Shlomith Rimmon's *The Concept of Ambiguity: The Example of James*
(Chicago: University of Chicago Press, 1977)—to mention one instance—much
of the conceptual framework of gaps and multiple systems of gap-filling has been
adopted and also applied to Jamesian narratives other than *The Turn of the Screw*.

33. Quoted in Willen, *Casebook*, pp. 115, 175.

34. Beardsley (*Aesthetics*, pp. 243-44) seems unaware that his approach and
findings in regard to the tale's "elucidation" are inconsistent with his semantic definition of literature (as discourse marked by various kinds of implicitness and hence
density of meaning). And the reason for this inconsistency is fairly typical. Multiple
meanings at the verbal level are not always mutually exclusive. Even when such
conflicts arise in a lyric poem, it is often possible to give them a realistic grounding

in the lyric "I" (e.g., "the phrase is ambiguous and thereby expresses the speaker's 'ambivalence' or 'his sarcasm and his irony'" etc.). It is quite another matter when it comes to the reconstruction of events in a story: here we cannot "really" have two opposite things taking place at one and the same time. It is the impossibility of devising a realistic motivation for the multiple, alternative systems of plot that has apparently deterred critics and theorists from legitimating them.

35. C. K. Aldrich, "Another Twist," 167.

36. Elements that sustain one hypothesis and block another can, of course, be explained a posteriori, though at times not easily or elegantly, within the framework of the second hypothesis. This is the case with the David and Bathsheba story. Many features that seem "strong" and salient when we favor or consider one hypothesis, naturally turn "weak" with the shift to another. Other elements sustain or weaken one hypothesis without much affecting its rival(s) one way or other.

Moreover, one has to distinguish between general arguments, for or against hypotheses, and elements in the text that indicate this or that hypothesis. In the short (five-hundred-word) story of David and Bathsheba, for example, the rival hypotheses conflict more in terms of arguments bearing on the same material than of specific textual elements ranging themselves on one side or the other. Whereas in James's long story each hypothesis gains support from a complex system of details—casting its peculiar light upon those elements that sustain it, those it manages to explain, and even upon "neutral" bystanders. In stories with such elaborate multiple systems, one cannot rule out the possibility of finding elements that directly contradict one or another hypothesis, provided that they are not too central or conspicuous.

37. For example, Vladimir Nabokov, *Nikolai Gogol* (New York: New Directions, 1944) p. 148; Leo Stilman, "Gogol's 'Overcoat'—Thematic Pattern and Origins," *The American Slavic and East European Review* (1952) 142ff. Even these critics have not stressed the support that the text lends to the realistic reading. They mention the possibility without noting the "dynamite" it contains and the remarkable interplay of elements it sets in motion.

38. Yosef Haefrati pointed out a similar kind of tension between realism and fantasy in a poem by H. N. Bialik ("Bialik's 'The Dead of the Desert': A Descriptive Poema," *Hasifrut* 1 (1967) 101–29.

39. Agnon remarried them in his novel *A Lodging for the Night,* but that is a piece of external evidence to which the earlier tale has no commitment.

40. A comparison of the tale's different versions suggests that Agnon deliberately complicated matters by elaborating the narrative mechanism designed to preclude resolution and univocality. The first version (*Davar,* December 1933) lent massive support to the hypothesis that Tony dislikes her ex-husband, but later revisions made this closure less and its rival more probable. James's method of revising *The Turn of the Screw* for the New York edition also makes for balance. The biblical genesis is, as usual, irrecoverable.

41. In *The Rhetoric of Fiction,* Booth sharply criticizes the modern techniques of limited narration for failing to provide readers with sufficient guidance to enable them to make actional and normative sense of the text. His attack manifests again the widespread rage for univocality in all that concerns the level of the fictive world.

Whether one likes it or not, the interest offered by such narratives lies in a skillful manipulation of an "internal" viewpoint, resulting in multiple readings.

Chapter 7 / Between the Truth and the Whole Truth

1. For an even more entangled case of irresolvable chronology—a doubling of double plots—see my analysis of verses 5-9 in the Rape of Dinah (reprinted in chapter 12 below). A similar view of the David gap has recently been taken by Robert Alter (*The Art of Biblical Narrative* [New York: Basic Books, 1981] pp. 147ff.). His expressive phrase for this technique, "binocular vision," does not of course set it apart in form or effect from the rule of multiple gap-filling. But his account of the writer's juxtaposition of conflicting versions supports the poetic principle and may even correspond to the genetic process.

2. *Expositional Modes and Temporal Ordering in Fiction* (Baltimore and London: Johns Hopkins University Press, 1978) esp. pp. 56-128.

3. For the underlying theory see *Expositional Modes,* pp. 50ff. and further references there. Note especially the distinctions (e.g., p. 50 n. 29, p. 322 n. 15) between this approach and Wolfgang Iser's, which I find inadequate in conception as well as in terminology.

4. Henry James, *The Art of the Novel* (New York: Scribner, 1962) pp. 252-53.

Chapter 8 / Temporal Discontinuity, Narrative Interest, and the Emergence of Meaning

1. Lucian, *Satirical Sketches,* trans. Paul Turner (Harmondsworth: Penguin, 1961) p. 224.

2. Erich Auerbach, *Mimesis,* trans. Willard Trask (Garden City, N.Y.: Anchor Books, 1957) pp. 2-20; see also my discussion of Homer in *Expositional Modes and Temporal Ordering in Fiction* (Baltimore and London: Johns Hopkins University Press, 1978) esp. pp. 84-85.

3. The best treatment of this scheme is by my doctoral student Yaira Amit in her dissertation "The Composition of Judges" (Tel-Aviv University, 1984).

4. In "Faulkner's Light in August and the Poetics of the Modern Novel" (*Hasifrut* 2 [1970] esp. 501-5), I traced a similar zigzag and distribution of the leading role in Faulkner's work. The likeness even extends to the purpose served by this tortuous focus-shifting: the demotion of the human cast in favor of a more abstract agency (social pressure rather than God).

5. The narrative, some say, refers to two different places called Kedesh: Barak's Kedesh Naphtali in southeastern Galilee and Kedesh near the Kenite encampment in the north (see, e.g., Robert G. Boling, *Judges* [Anchor Bible; Garden City, N.Y.: Doubleday, 1957] p. 97). Such a distinction hardly finds any support in the text. Not even a marathon runner in top form could cover the distance between the battlefield at the Kishon river and northern Kedesh. In terms of composition, moreover, why would the narrator spoil the ironies of having the glory snatched

from Barak on his own home ground and leaving him where he came from? On the verbal level, of course, the link holds on either reading of the topography.

6. See Luis Alonso-Schökel, "Erzählkunst im Buche der Richter," *Biblica* 42 (1961) 161.

7. The level of discussion seems to be steadily rising. For some close readings see Eric I. Lowenthal, *The Joseph Narrative in Genesis* (New York: Ktav, 1973); Robert Alter, *The Art of Biblical Narrative* (New York: Basic Books, 1981) pp. 159–76 (particularly suggestive on the question of knowledge); and, most recent and best, James S. Ackerman, "Joseph, Judah, and Jacob," in *Literary Interpretations of Biblical Narratives, II,* ed. Kenneth R. R. Gros Louis with James S. Ackerman (Nashville: Abingdon, 1982) pp. 85–113.

8. For the Bible's classic formulation of how guilt breeds hate, see the volte-face Amnon makes after raping Tamar, especially 2 Samuel 13:15. The analogy in our own tale is even more specific and eloquent, since Potiphar's wife's *revulsion* of feeling involved the same *reversal* of roles now performed by Joseph.

9. According to Israelite law, these would-be killers finally exchanged one form of murder for another in selling Joseph into slavery: their actual crime still carries the death penalty. For a comparative study of the Bible's ruling to this effect, see Moshe Greenberg, "Some Postulates of Biblical Criminal Law," in *The Jewish Expression,* ed. Judah Goldin (New Haven: Yale University Press, 1976) pp. 24–29.

10. See now Ackerman's references to "plot doubling," subsumed under a different motive and in turn covering more traditional ground ("Joseph, Judah, and Jacob," pp. 93–94).

Chapter 9 / Proleptic Portraits

1. *Expositional Modes and Temporal Ordering in Fiction* (Baltimore and London: Johns Hopkins University Press, 1978) p. 197.

2. *Njal's Saga,* trans. Magnus Magnusson and Hermann Palson (Harmondsworth: Penguin, 1967) p. 73.

3. Luis Alonso-Schökel, "Erzählkunst im Buche der Richter," *Biblica* 42 (1961) p. 148.

4. Speaking of obscenity, I find no trace of the sexual innuendoes ascribed to the story (by Robert Alter, *Art of Biblical Narrative,* p. 39); and considering the stigma they must put on the most admirable of the judges, I would be extremely surprised to find any. Scatology is a laughing matter only because it makes *natural* humor.

Chapter 10 / Going from Surface to Depth

1. For further discussion see my "Ordering the Unordered: Time, Space, and Descriptive Coherence," *Yale French Studies* 61 (1981) esp. 62ff.

2. Erich Auerbach, *Mimesis,* trans. Willard Trask (Garden City, N.Y.: Anchor Books, 1957) pp. 14–15.

3. "There they buried Abraham and Sarah his wife; there they buried Isaac and Rebekah his wife; and there I buried Leah" (Gen 49:31).

4. Compare the threefold series of epithets leading from one queen to another in the book of Esther: (1) Vashti is "good-looking" (1:11); (2) Ahasuerus deposes Vashti in the hope of finding a queen "better than she" (1:19); (3) Esther is "beautiful and good-looking" (2:7).

Chapter 11 / The Structure of Repetition: Strategies of Informational Redundancy

1. This chapter originally appeared as "The Structure of Repetition in Biblical Narrative: Strategies of Informational Redundancy," *Hasifrut* 25 (1977) 109-50. The only objections raised against it, in Yair Hoffman's "Between Conventionality and Strategy: On Repetition in Biblical Narrative" (*Hasifrut* 28 [1979] 89-99), did not show enough appreciation of the problems involved (and formulated in my argument) to justify a reply. See Robert Alter's brief but apt comment in *The Art of Biblical Narrative* (New York: Basic Books, 1981) pp. 102-3, and n. 37 below.

2. I have further discussed the Bible's analogical patterning in "Caution: A Literary Text! Problems in the Poetics and Interpretation of Biblical Narrative" [with Menakhem Perry], *Hasifrut* 2 (1970) esp. pp. 633-36; "Delicate Balance in the Story of the Rape of Dinah: Biblical Narrative and the Rhetoric of the Narrative Text," *Hasifrut* 4 (1973) esp. pp. 228- 30; and "Patterns of Similarity: Part and Whole in Biblical Composition" (The Eighth World Congress of Jewish Studies, August 1981). For some other discussions, see James Muilenburg, "A Study in Hebrew Rhetoric: Repetition and Style," *Vetus Testamentum Supplement* 1 (Leiden: Brill, 1953) pp. 97-111; L. Alonso-Schökel, "Erzählkunst im Buche der Richter," *Biblica* 42 (1961) 143-72; and Robert Alter, "Biblical Narrative," *Commentary* (1976) 61-67. They treat under "repetition" a complex of techniques that I distinguish (see this section and the next) into similarity patterns, redundancy, and repetition. This still characterizes Alter's recently expanded version (*Art of Biblical Narrative,* pp. 88-113), which widens the scope of his account and rightly indicates some parallels to mine.

3. On the whole, even modernism preserves this distinction.

4. The best introduction to the field, with an excellent bibliography, is still Colin Cherry's *On Human Communication* (Cambridge, Mass.: M.I.T. Press, 1966).

5. For some examples of these types of redundancy see my "Bound and Productive Forms in Language and Literary Language," *Hasifrut* 22 (1976) 107, 118-22.

6. Translated from Umberto Cassuto's *Biblical Literature and Canaanite Literature* (Jerusalem: Magnes Press, 1972) vol. I, pp. 31-32.

7. In the biblical context, this is the position taken in Theodor H. Gaster, *Myth, Legend, and Custom in the Old Testament* (London: Duckworth, 1969) pp. XLVII-XLVIII.

8. See Patrick W. Skehan, "Exodus in the Samaritan Recension," *Journal of Biblical Literature* 74 (1955) 182-87, and "The Biblical Scrolls from Qumran and the Text of the Old Testament," *Biblical Archaeologist* 28 (1965) 87-100.

9. See, for instance, the reference to von Rad in chapter 4, n. 7 above.

10. Sean E. McEvenue, *The Narrative Style of the Priestly Writer* (Rome: Biblical Institute Press, 1971) pp. 12–18.

11. For example, Radak on Genesis 3:1–5; 7:4; 12:1; 21:12; 27:7.

12. Umberto Cassuto, *A Commentary on the Book of Genesis* (Jerusalem: Magnes Press, 1961).

13. The text appears in Samuel Noah Kramer, *The Sumerians* (Chicago: University of Chicago Press, 1963) pp. 244–46.

14. Technological advances have played a role in the history of repetition structures. The facilities for direct communication, by telephone or even writing, have on the whole made a change for the worse, but not all along the line. As indicated by the shift from David's letter to Joab's message in the Bathsheba story, the availability of writing thus widened the range of the Bible's tactical options compared with oral literature. The ancient Sumerian epic "Enmerkar and the Lord of Aratta," by the way, tells that Enmerkar invented the system of writing on clay tablets because his herald was "heavy of mouth" and could not repeat a long message. (For the poem see Samuel Noah Kramer, *History Begins at Sumer* [London: Thames and Hudson, 1961] pp. 58ff.).

15. Umberto Cassuto, *A Commentary on the Book of Exodus* (Jerusalem: Magnes Press, 1967) p. 164.

16. The miniature proportions of the biblical scene render the episode the smallest quasi-independent unit.

17. This again exemplifies the implications that a poetics of the Bible may have for subjects as far removed from it as textual criticism. The art of a *Gilgamesh Epic* legitimates the scholarly filling-in of lacunae by inference from adjoining members, since its structure of repetition aims for correspondence among the members all along the line, including representational proportions. Whereas the Bible's opposed tendency negates the widespread belief that the Septuagint preserves the Samson tale's original version, which got shortened by haplography in the Masoretic Text.

18. For an analysis of this and related modes of intrusion ("departicularization") into direct discourse, see my "Between the Truth and the Whole Truth in Biblical Narrative: The Rendering of Inner Life by Telescoped Inside View and Interior Monologue," *Hasifrut* 29 (1979) esp. 134–35, and "Point of View and the Indirections of Direct Speech," *Language and Style* (1982) 67–117, esp. 93–100.

19. As he could do, significantly, with parallelism in biblical poetry, e.g., "Sheol cannot thank thee, death praise thee" (Isa 38:18).

20. In *Gilgamesh*, where all types of repetition still form primitive devices, internal recurrence indeed bears this function alone. Narrator and characters alike repeat themselves at moments of stress or excitement: for example, during the struggle of Gilgamesh and Enkidu (p. 33 in the Heidel edition), the goddess Ishtar's announcement of having provided for the seven years of famine (p. 53) or the lamentation of Gilgamesh over his comrade (p. 63).

21. Marvin Mudrick, *Jane Austen: Irony as Defense and Discovery* (Princeton: Princeton University Press, 1952) p. 102.

22. "Bound and Productive Forms," (see above n. 5).

23. On the dream in antiquity see Freud's survey in *The Interpretation of Dreams*, and A. Leo Oppenheim, *The Interpretation of Dreams in the Ancient Near East* (Philadelphia: American Philosophical Society, 1956).

24. The Israelites thus look back in synecdochic nostalgia on the days when they "sat by the fleshpot and ate bread to the full" (Exod 16:3).

25. This is the only case where the Bible extends the epithet "fat" (*bari*) from the animate (human and nonhuman) sphere to the inanimate. And the deliberate-ness of this extension is also suggested by the adjective's shifts along the sequence. The adjective first appears in the full form "fat-fleshed" but thereafter contracts, thrice, into "fat." Since "flesh" can hardly apply to "ears," it is eliminated as early as possible in the bovine context in order to maximize the correspondence to the following context of grain.

26. Two further combinations enhance the sense of subjective viewing. One is the implicit causal-oppositional link between "him loved" and "hated him." The other is that the new sequential permutation deepens the ambiguity of *mi'kol* ("more than all" or "of or among all"?) and with it the impression of Joseph's monopoly on the father's love.

27. In *Oliver Twist*, Dickens likewise renders a character's process of discovery through a movement from divergence to synchronization. As long as Fagin is too stunned to register the judge's words, Dickens does not convey them except by metonymic allusion: "The judge assumed the black cap. . . . The address was solemn and impressive." Only when Fagin's mind recovers do the words cohere into the well-known form of the British death sentence: "He began to remember a few disjointed fragments. . . . These gradually fell into their proper places, so that in a little time he had the whole. . . . To be hanged by the neck, till he was dead—that was the end. To be hanged by the neck till he was dead" (chapter 52).

28. For those limits see my "Proteus in Quotation-Land: Mimesis and the Forms of Represented Discourse," *Poetics Today* 3 (1982) 107–56, and the references in n. 18 above.

29. Given the Bible's realistic norms of speech, there may be some ground for the rabbinic claim that Jehoshaphat, king of Judah, distrusted those prophets and insisted on calling in an outsider, exactly because they all spoke with one voice (*Sanhedrin* 89a).

30. For reasons I discussed in "Mimesis and Motivation: The Two Faces of Fictional Coherence," in *Literary Criticism and Philosophy*, ed. Joseph P. Strelka (University Park: Pennsylvania State University Press, 1983).

31. Cf. L. Kuhl, "Die 'Wiederaufnahme'—ein literaturkritisches Prinzip," *Zeitschrift für die alttestamentliche Wissenschaft* 64 (1952) 1–11.

32. This transition was already encoded by the rabbis as one of the rules for interpreting Scripture, and Cassuto often uses it to good effect (e.g., *Commentary on Genesis*, pp. 90–92).

33. Donald B. Redford, *A Study of the Biblical Story of Joseph* (Leiden: Brill, 1970) pp. 77–78. Josephus apparently thought the same, for his version (*Jewish Antiquities*

2.4.3-2.5.1 §§ 45-60) elaborates the seduction scene while minimizing or omitting altogether all the reports except that to Potiphar.

34. As the Samaritan text reads, by a mechanical repetition that would make the woman throw suspicion on herself.

35. Hence the groundlessness of the frequent complaint that the meaning insufficiently resembles its surface structure and of the genetic speculation to which this distance gives rise. No more justified is the opposite extremism—ultimately deriving from the same atomistic approach and current among traditional exegetes, such as Abravanel—that invents similarities between the two. For a more balanced view see Uriel Simon, "The Poor Man's Ewe-Lamb: An Example of a Juridical Parable," *Biblica* 48 (1967) 207-42. Recall also the opposition drawn in my first chapter between the transparence of the Bible's parables and the opacity of the New Testament's.

36. Abravanel argues, not very convincingly, for a deliberate elision on her part.

37. But old habits die hard. In the face of my argument about the Bible's stand against package-dealing form and function, Hoffman (see n. 1) complains in effect that its acceptance would dissociate form and function. For the Bible and its analysis to make sense to him, then, they would have to substitute one formulaic scheme for another. However understandable this yearning for the security of immutable order, the surrender to it makes nonsense not only of art and its criticism but even of the most ordinary communication. As speakers and addressees, we could not long survive unless we operated with regularities rather than fixities of discourse; and literature specializes in turning this universal flexibility to account.

Chapter 12 / The Art of Persuasion

1. This chapter is based on an essay entitled "Delicate Balance in the Story of the Rape of Dinah: Biblical Narrative and the Rhetoric of the Narrative Text," *Hasifrut* 4 (1973) 193-231. Among the critiques it evoked are the following: Haviva Nissim, "On Analyzing the Biblical Story," *Hasifrut* 24 (1977) 136-43; Nissan Ararat, "Reading According to the 'Seder' in Biblical Narrative: To Balance the Reading of the Dinah Episode," *Hasifrut* 27 (1978) 15-34; Yair Zakovitz, "A Survey of the Literary Study of the Bible in Israel," *Newsletter of the World Association for Jewish Studies* 20 (1982) 19-38. The first two responses attempt, with little success, to whitewash Jacob's figure. The last two would do away with the rape, the one turning it into a seduction and the other into an accretion.

2. Wayne C. Booth, *The Rhetoric of Fiction* (Chicago: University of Chicago Press, 1961) pp. 112-13.

3. Bruce Vawter, *On Genesis: A New Reading* (Garden City, N.Y.: Doubleday, 1977) p. 359.

4. In biblical Hebrew, the semantic distinction between the two forms is not automatic but still ever-available. Of special interest is the passive transformation of the transitive "lie" (e.g., Isa 13:16; Zech 14:2), and the contrast drawn in the analogical tale of Amnon and Tamar. Amnon first tries to seduce Tamar, "Come,

lie with me [*immi*], my sister"; but when she refuses him, he "overpowered her and abused her and lay with her [*otah*]" (2 Sam 13:11, 14).

5. Maya Fruchtman rightly observes that the pluperfect-like form of "came" [*bau*] may indicate a shift in space rather than time. This makes it hard to see why she objects to my equivocal reading of the sequence ("A Few Notes on the Study of Biblical Narrative," *Hasifrut* 22 [1976] 64–65).

6. For additional discussions of the interplay between reference and viewpoint see my "Between the Truth and the Whole Truth in Biblical Narrative: The Rendering of Inner Life by Telescoped Inside View and Interior Monologue," *Hasifrut* 29 (1979) 110–46; "Language, World and Perspective in Biblical Art," *Hasifrut* 32 (1983) 88–131; and "Deictic Sequence: World, Language and Convention," in *Essays on Deixis,* ed. Gisa Rauh (Tübingen: Gunter Narr, 1983) pp. 277–316. Among other things, these more recent studies indicate the need for flexibility in applying a principle that has proved so attractive since the original appearance of the Dinah analysis.

7. This reading also has another effect. Even the alternative hypothesis tends to exclude Jacob from the "men" who were "grieved and very angry": in order to experience such feelings, if he had them, he would hardly wait for the family reunion. But the second hypothesis settles any remaining doubt by way of contrast.

8. For some further analysis of point of view in this construction see "Delicate Balance in the Rape of Dinah," 202–3, and "Between the Truth and the Whole Truth," 131–32.

9. In this tale, the occurrences of the key verbs are usually far between. But sometimes their linkage is immediate, as in the ironic opposition between "Dinah . . . went out to see the daughters of the land" and "Shechem . . . saw her."

10. Like Bathsheba and unlike Deborah, Dinah plays no role in the tale beyond the generation of crisis. Her plot function once fulfilled, therefore, the reader assumes that she returned home (and informed Jacob of her misfortune). All this follows the dynamics of the surprise gap.

11. The Aramaic rendition of Jonathan ben Uziel detected this menacing note. Because of its tendency to overarticulation and its disregard for the management of sequence, however, it makes the threat explicit as early as this stage: "If you do not listen to us and be circumcised, we shall take our daughter by force [*betokfa*) and go."

12. Onkelos goes too far in translating "with deceit" as the laudatory "wisely." Not that the Bible attaches to "with deceit" (and its semantic cognates) any fixed pejorative load. True, it often employs such adverbs to condemn the character or act qualified by them. Isaac, trembling with shock and distressed by the "exceedingly great and bitter cry" of his favorite, says: "Thy brother has come with deceit [*bemirmah* again] and taken away thy blessing" (Gen 27:33–35). Here, Onkelos's apologetic rendering as "wisely" makes nonsense both of the speaker's psychology and the narrator's problematic treatment. But such a reversal of the normative charge does take place in other contexts of deceit, as when Jehu summons all the Baal prophets and worshippers under the pretext of having "a great sacrifice to offer to Baal" (2 Kgs 10:18–28). In view of his real (and laudable) intention, the elucidatory comment "Jehu did it with cunning [*beokba*]," interpolated

before the mass slaughter, reads as a pat on the back for the clever trick devised to wipe out God's enemies at one blow. Nor do the changed connotations derive from the changed term: Esau uses the very same root (*akb*) to fashion a new and derogatory etymology (*ya'akob*, "he will deceive") for his dishonest brother. The third synonym, *beorma*, exhibits the same flexibility. Applied to the disguised Gibeonites who "acted with guile" (Josh 9:4) to fool Israel—or worse, to the willful murderer that kills "with guile" and is therefore to be led away to death even from God's altar (Exod 21:14)—*beorma* assumes condemnatory force; yet in Proverbs the verb *arm* and its derivatives signify wisdom (e.g., 1:4; 8:5; 22:3). All this indicates a distinction between lexical sense (as constant) and normative charge (as variable). Since the lexicon of biblical Hebrew does not encode the opposition between justified and unjustified deception—by reserving special items for each—the primary (or intertextual) meaning of such adverbs relates to fact rather than judgment. It simply denotes ruses, pretense, untruth. Whereas the evaluative orientation and power of the adverbs depend on contextual frameworks, sometimes as intricate as here.

13. The Samaritan Bible makes the point in a different way—smoother but less subtle—by casting the verb in the plural form *time'u* ("them who had defiled").

14. See the discussion of 1 Samuel 15:9 in the next chapter.

15. Here is a more obvious example of how a redundant familial attribution implies motive: "When Jacob saw Rachel the daughter of Laban *his mother's brother* and the sheep of Laban *his mother's brother*, Jacob went up and rolled the stone from the well's mouth and watered the flock of Laban *his mother's brother*" (Gen 29:10).

16. Jacob's words in his blessing, "In their rage they killed men and in their willfulness they hamstrung oxen," may even suggest that Simeon and Levi went so far as to destroy the loot taken by their brothers.

17. The sentence has two notable features. First, its subject ("Should he") remains indeterminate, because Shechem has not been mentioned in the dialogue before. Second, this is the only place where the tale fails to specify the addressee ("said" to whom?). Elsewhere he is identified by a direct or indirect object that immediately follows the reporting verb—even when his identity (as in verses 13- 14) could be safely presupposed. These two anomalies amount to an evasion of transparent reference.

18. Much briefer than the outline presented in the original version of this chapter, parts of which have been otherwise incorporated in this book ("Delicate Balance in the Rape of Dinah," pp. 216-31; and see also the earlier analysis by Menakhem Perry and myself in "Caution! A Literary Text: Problems in the Poetics and Interpretation of Biblical Narrative," *Hasifrut* 2 [1970] esp. 618-26). Compare also the outline of Homer's repertoire of control measures in *Expositional Modes and Temporal Ordering in Fiction* (Baltimore and London: Johns Hopkins University Press, 1978) pp. 105-6.

Chapter 13 / Ideology, Rhetoric, Poetics

1. This chapter is based on an essay entitled "The Bible's Art of Persuasion: Ideology, Rhetoric, and Poetics in Saul's Fall," *Hebrew Union College Annual* (1983) 45-82.

2. Of the kind imposed by the Chronicler, who lays down the law without going to any trouble to make it intelligible, let alone palatable: "Saul died for his unfaithfulness to the Lord, on account of the commandment of the Lord that he did not keep" (1 Chr 10:13).

3. In the Joseph story and especially throughout the Rape of Dinah, we encountered the use of verbal echoes to imply or pinpoint causal links between action and counteraction (see [14] in the list of rhetorical devices in chapter 12).

4. The very same structure recurs later in the book (2 Sam 7:1-3 alluding to Deut 12:10-11), so as to suggest the contrast between David and Saul as keepers of ancestral obligations. Far from needing a reminder to build a temple "when the Lord had given him rest from all his enemies round about," David takes the initiative at the earliest possible moment.

5. Even that single plural disappears in the Targum and Septuagint versions, perhaps by analogy to verse 18.

6. This ironic wordplay gains support from the analogous misdeed in Joshua 7:21, where Achan himself admits that he "coveted" the spoils.

7. Again, this device is still more effective in the original. Since the Hebrew text both preposes the verb and casts it in singular form, the reader integrates predicate and kingly subject into a well-formed whole ("spared Saul") before discovering that another, coordinate subject ("and the people") lies ahead. For a theoretical analysis, with implications for the ordering of parallel units in biblical prose and poetry, see my "Ordering the Unordered: Time, Space, and Descriptive Coherence," *Yale French Studies* 61 (1981) 60–88. The argument shows how a series of formal parallels may draw on hidden links to assume a tighter and more meaningful organization: hierarchical, perspectival, chronological, or even properly narrative, to the point of tracing a miniature plot.

8. Not for nothing does Josephus claim that Saul "took prisoner the enemy king, Agag, out of admiration for his beauty and his status," while the people "spared the beasts and the cattle . . . and all the chattels and riches" (*Jewish Antiquities* 6.7.2 §§ 137–39).

9. The Chronicler, who omits the Amalek episode, omits also the unusual detail of burning from the parallel account of the exploit performed by the Jabesh-gileadites (1 Chr 10:10-11).

10. The alternative explanation—that Samuel starts with questions because he is ignorant of the facts behind God's displeasure—would make no sense. It plays havoc with the relations between God and prophet, and is flatly contradicted by the reference to "what the Lord said to me this night." The informational gap about the member of forecast is the reader's, not the prophet's.

11. The Septuagint, favored by some modern scholars, prefaces the dialogue with the stage direction that Samuel found Saul "offering as holocausts to the Lord the best of the spoils he had brought from Amalek." This addition (together with the corollary that the Masoretic Text has lost the passage as a result of scribal haplography) makes even less sense than usual, because it goes against both the situational logic of the tale and the structural logic of biblical repetition in general. Situationally, if Samuel discovered Saul at sacrifice, he would cast his opening

question not in terms of hearing ("in my ears . . . hear") but of sight (e.g., "in my eyes . . . see"). Nor does such sacrifice cohere with Samuel's later accusation of "swooping on the spoils" or Saul's own admission of having "feared" the people: to reduce the point at issue to a difference between summary and more ceremonial destruction is to deprive the king's plea, not to mention God's judgment, of all color of reason. In fact, structurally speaking, this is a typical instance of the Septuagint's misdirected rage for harmony in repetition. True to its policy of squaring the early (verse 13) with the late (verses 15–21), regardless of contextual and informational variations, it produces here a montage of the member of "enactment" with that of "report" and thus identifies the narrator's objective with Saul's unreliable version (see also n. 12 below and the chapter on repetition). This goes to show, again, the need for considering—and often deciding between—textual variants in the light of textual poetics.

12. Predictably, the Septuagint (again with a following among modern scholars) already reads "*I* have utterly destroyed" in the previous report to Samuel. In its eagerness to smooth away apparent inconsistencies by way of retrospective adjustments, it again misses and skews the effect designed by the structure of repetition— this time not the disharmony between the narrator's and Saul's versions but that between Saul's shifting versions themselves.

13. While the epigrammatic balance is common to both instances, though, its force is significantly heightened here. The whole rhetorical strategy being devised to maximize our sense of proportionateness, the narrator does not rest content with verbally pinpointing, Joshua fashion, the relations between crime and punishment. To preclude any impression of arbitrariness, the key term that does the pinpointing by appearing on both sides of the equation must follow from the represented developments. That is why we find it drawn from the account of the crime itself, so as to link the verb "reject" and the adjective "reject(able)" into suggestive wordplay: "Whoever devoted the reject to God, sealed his own rejection."

14. Compare now Robert Alter's passing comment on the verb in *The Art of Biblical Narrative* (New York: Basic Books, 1981) p. 93.

15. P. Kyle McCarter, Jr., *I Samuel* (Anchor Bible; Garden City, N.Y.: Doubleday, 1980) p. 268.

INDEXES

Index of Persons and Subjects

Abravanel, Don Isaac, 368, 398, 536 n. 35, n. 36

Ackerman, James S., 516 n. 3, 532 n. 7, n. 10

"Adapa," 521 n. 7

Agnon, S. Y., 227, 530 n. 40

Albrektson, Bertil, 521 n. 18

Albright, W. F., 519 n. 8, 521 n. 9, n. 13

Aldrich, C. K., 224, 529 n. 32, 530 n. 35

Alonso-Schökel, Luis, 532 n. 6, n. 3, 533 n. 2

Alter, Robert, 24–30 passim, 516 n. 1, 517 n. 9, 518 n. 30, 521 n. 11, 522 n. 26, 531 n. 1, 532 n. 7, 532 n. 4, 533 n. 1, n. 2, 540 n. 14

Ambiguity: between addressees, 474–75 (*see also* Dialogue, ambiguity in); biblical vs. modern, 51–56, 222–35, 380–82; of character, 139–40, 201–13, 231–33, 253–55, 285–308, 321–64 passim; in curiosity, *see* Curiosity; defined in relation to gaps, 235–36 (*see also* Gap; Gap-filling); and deformed chronology, 235–364; of divine forecast, 278–83, 318–20, 395–400, 501–3; as dynamic process, *see* Dynamics; in foolproof composition, 46–56, 194, 230–35, 272, 380–82, 448, 451–53, 479, 480–81 (*see also* Foolproof composition); functions of, 46–56, 98–99, 139–40, 208–9, 212–13, 227–28, 257–364, 436, 451–75, 479, 501–2; of future, 264–83 (*see also* Suspense); in genre, 222–26; grammatical, 426–27, 451–52, 459–61, 479, 535 n. 26; and ideological vs. didactic writing,

36–38, 156–57, 340–41; between inner and outer world, 51–53, 217, 243, 256, 263, 398, 453–55, 463, 476, 491, 523 n. 3; and literary structure, 43, 156–57, 202, 222–30; in "lucid" commentary, 122, 217, 280, 321–64, 458–61, 476; in modern criticism, 222–27; mutually exclusive vs. complementary, 186–364 passim, 445–75 passim (*see also* relations between hypotheses, below); as narrative interest, 258–364 (*see also* Interest, narrative); between narrator and character, *see* between inner and outer world, above; object of, 232–34, 285, 314, 322–25, 355; of past, 283–320 (*see also* Curiosity; Surprise); in quotation, *see* Quotation, ambiguity in; for reader vs. character, *see* Point of view, reader-character relation in; of reference, *see* Referring term, ambiguity of; relation between hypotheses in, 48–56, 201–35, 245, 309–14, 348–64, 479 (*see also* Foolproof composition; Reading, levels of); of representation vs. evaluation, 54, 194, 233–35, 238–39, 448, 451–53, 458–59, 464, 471–72, 480–81, 512–13; in repetition, *see* Repetition, and gaps; between spatial and temporal sense, 277, 280–81; between speech and thought, 97, 381, 409, 420–21, 427, 430; between successive and simultaneous action, 231, 232, 448, 451–53, 479, 523 n. 7, 531 n. 1; in surprise, *see* Surprise; in suspense, *see* Suspense; temporary vs.

541

Derrida, Jacques, 36

Description: vs. action, 120, 198 (*see also* Characterization; Exposition); as implied action, 331–64 (*see also* Exposition, forward-looking)

Deuteronomist, 16, 182, 184

Dialogue: ambiguity in, 54, 203–9, 215–22, 238–39, 287–94, 297–99, 300-1, 303–8, 381, 474–75; and artistic originality, 12; chains of, 154, 288–308; double-framed, 215–16, 219–22, 307, 317, 379 (*see also* Rhetoric, figural within narratorial); discordance in, 243–44, 246; echoing interrogative in, 240–41, 243, 247, 248, 249, 252, 258, 313, 317, 389; elision in, 319–20, 372–73, 420; expressiveness of, 16, 155, 157–58, 160, 219, 246, 256–57, 304, 312, 388, 399; gambit in, 181, 250, 300, 422, 505–6; with God, 77, 96–98, 112–13, 163, 501–3; inaudible, 97–98; irony and levels of awareness in, 91–98, 145–52, 159–72, 199-222, 273–320 passim, 351–54, 395–401, 404–5, 407–9, 419–30, 455–75, passim, 499–15 (*see also* Irony; Point of view, reader-character relation in); last word in, 474–75; and monologue, xii, 39, 72, 86, 246, 257, 385, 431, 436; and omniscience, 32, 34, 41, 62–63, 84, 86, 87, 91–98 (*see also* irony and levels of awareness, above); Platonic, 78; in poetry, 72; and politeness, 139, 140, 142, 200, 204–5, 421–22, 431, 436, 465; redundancy in, 168, 368; reference to place in, 134–35, 147, 168, 424, 492; and repetition, 147–52, 162–63, 168, 214–22, 242–47, 276, 297–98, 305–8, 355, 368–440 passim, 464–66, 499–515; rhetoric within rhetoric in, *see* Rhetoric, figural within narratorial; and role-shifting, 408-9, 420–21; and self-revelation, *see* irony and levels of awareness in,

above; sequence in, 142; silence in, 98, 138, 206-7, 238–39, 252, 287, 297, 300, 305, 318, 320, 456, 457, 473, 475, 478; snatches of, 164; stage directions and other commentary in, 18, 91, 95, 120, 505, 523 n. 2, 539 n. 11; and nonverbal response, 137, 151. *See also* Monologue; Point of view; Quotation

Dickens, Charles, 27, 329, 443, 535 n. 27

Didactic writing: defined, 37, 156; foreign to Bible, 38, 156; and formal structure, 39; vs. ideological literature, 36–38, 42, 44, 156–57, 177–78, 283, 340–41, 483, 493, 494–95. *See also* Ideology

Diderot, Denis, 124–25 Difficulty, as artistic challenge, 42, 43, 47, 179, 444–45, 467, 483, 493

Digression, 133, 301, 366, 418, 424, 487–88. *See also* Coherence; Redundancy; Representational proportions

Discourse-oriented inquiry: defined by its object, 14–15, 19–21; into fiction vs. history, 23–35; questions posed by, 15; relations with source-oriented line, 14–35; variety of means to, 20–21. *See also* Source-oriented inquiry, and individual discourse features

Discovery, plot of: 53, 91–118 passim, 135, 140–42, 151–52, 172–73, 176–79, 232, 234, 254, 256, 286–308, 324, 404–5, 414, 503–15. *See also* Plot; Point of view; Surprise

Donne, John, 36

Dostoevsky, Fyodor, 25, 36, 74, 76, 77, 261–62, 329, 382, 443, 444, 472, 519 n. 11

Dryden, John, 1

Duhm, Bernard, 519 n. 3

Dynamics: of action vs. presentation, 235–36, 237–40, 252, 264–65, 266-67, 278, 302, 313, 319–20, 322, 324, 331–64, 375–77, 378–80, 408, 413–15,

Index of Biblical Characters

Index of Biblical Passages